EXPLORING DELINQUENCY

CAUSES AND CONTROL

Dean G. Rojek
University of Georgia

Gary F. Jensen
Vanderbilt University

Roxbury Publishing Company

Library of Congress Cataloging-in-Publication Data

Exploring delinquency: causes and control: an anthology/[compiled by] Dean G. Rojek, Gary F. Jensen.
    p. cm.
    Includes bibliographical references.
    ISBN 0-935732-71-3
    1. Juvenile delinquency—Research—United States. 2. Juvenile delinquency—Law and legislation—United States. 3. Juvenile delinquency—United States—Prevention. 4. Juvenile justice, Administration of—United States. 5. Juvenile corrections—United States. I. Rojek, Dean G. II. Jensen, Gary F.
    HV9104.E99 1996
    364.3'6'0973—dc20   95-9650
                                                                                                     CIP

EXPLORING DELINQUENCY: CAUSES AND CONTROL

Copyright © 1996 Roxbury Publishing Company. All rights reserved under International and Pan-American Copyright Conventions. No part of this publication may be reproduced, stored in a retrieval system, or transmitted in any form or by any means, electronic, mechanical, photocopying, recording, or otherwise without prior written permission of the publisher.

Publisher and Editor: Claude Teweles
Developmental Editor: Sacha Howells
Production Editor: Dawn VanDercreek
Production Assistants: Anton Diether and Joyce Rappaport
Cover Design: Marnie Deacon
Typography: Synergistic Data Systems

Printed on acid-free paper in the United States of America. This book meets the standards for recycling of the Environmental Protection Agency.

ISBN 0-935732-71-3

ROXBURY PUBLISHING COMPANY
P.O. Box 491044
Los Angeles, California 90049-9044
(213) 653-1068 • Fax (213) 653-4140
E-mail: roxbury@crl.com

Table of Contents

General Introduction — x
Acknowledgements — xi
About the Authors — xiv

Section I
Delinquency and Juvenile Justice

Introduction — 1

1. What Stays the Same in History? — 3
   Thomas J. Bernard
   Bernard identifies perennial beliefs about juvenile crime that are reflected in cyclical shifts between harsh and lenient juvenile justice policies.

2. A. Delinquency Cases in Juvenile Court, 1992 — 9
   Jeffrey A. Butts

   B. How Juveniles Get to Criminal Court — 10
   Melissa Sickmund

   C. The Juvenile Court's Response to Violent Crime — 11
   Verne L. Speirs
   Excerpts from government reports illustrate the processing of delinquency cases, the mechanisms for trying juveniles as adults, and the outcome of adult versus juvenile processing of similar cases.

3. Public Attitudes Toward Juvenile Crime and Juvenile Justice: Implications for Public Policy — 13
   Ira M. Schwartz, Shenyang Guo, and John Johnson Kerbs
   A Center for Youth Policy opinion poll shows considerable public support for the treatment and rehabilitation goals of the juvenile court but also shows that the public wants the most serious juvenile offenders tried in adult court.

Section II
Legal Issues

Introduction — 19

4. *In re Gault et al.* — 22
   This is one of the most significant cases on juvenile court proceedings. The Supreme Court ruled on certain issues relating to due process of law.

5. *New Jersey v. T.L.O.*   29

    This case dealt with the issue of school searches for drugs. The Supreme Court extended authority of teachers to maintain order on school grounds.

6. *Elizabeth Qutb et al. v. Annette Strauss et al. v. Steve Bartlett et al.*   34

    The question arose regarding the legality of cities imposing curfews. The court ruled that municipalities have the right to restrict the right of juveniles in public places.

7. *In re Gault* Revisited: A Cross-State Comparison of the Right to Counsel in Juvenile Court   39
    Barry C. Feld

    Feld looks at the implementation of the Gault case and finds half of the states not to be in compliance.

Section III
Measuring Delinquency

Introduction   53

8. Juvenile Offenders and Victims: A National Report   57
    Howard N. Snyder and Melissa Sickmund

    The Office of Juvenile Justice and Delinquency Prevention summarizes information on recent trends in juvenile violence, including weapons violence and victimization.

9. National Survey Results on Drug Use From Monitoring the Future Study, 1975-1993   62
    Lloyd D. Johnston, Patrick O'Malley, and Jerald Bachman

    University of Michigan surveys carried out each year since 1975 show that most forms of drug use peaked in the early to mid-1980s, declining until quite recently when signs of an upsurge have appeared.

10. Culture, Gender, and Delinquency: A Study of Youths in the United States and India   69
    Clayton A. Hartjen and Sesharajani Kethineni

    The gender gap in arrest rates and self-reports of delinquent behavior for girls and boys in the United States and India are examined and possible sources of cultural variation discussed.

11. Serious Violent Offenders: Onset, Developmental Course, and Termination   80
    Delbert S. Elliott

    In his Presidential address to the American Society of Criminology, Delbert Elliott discusses criticisms of the use of self-report methods to study delinquency and shows that patterns by gender, race, and age are consistent with others ways of measuring delinquency.

12. Minorities and the Juvenile Justice System:
   A Research Summary   91
   Carl Pope and William Feyerherm
   This report to the Office of Juvenile Justice and Delinquency Prevention examines research on racial biases in juvenile justice processing and specifies the direction such research must take in addressing the problem.

Section IV
Theories of Delinquency

Introduction   99

13. Biological Perspectives in Criminology   102
    Diana H. Fishbein
    Modern-day biological research suggests that there may be a relationship between delinquency and biology.

14. Biological Positivism   109
    Michael R. Gottfredson and Travis Hirschi
    Gottfredson and Hirschi emphatically reject any notion that biological research plays a role in the study of delinquency.

15. Social Learning and Deviant Behavior:
    A Specific Test of a General Theory   120
    Ronald L. Akers, Marvin D. Krohn,
    Lonn Lanza-Kaduce, and Marcia Radosevich
    Adolescent drinking and drug behavior are examined from the perspective of social learning theory. The authors conclude that social learning theory is strongly supported.

16. Age, Peers, and Delinquency   128
    E. Mark Warr
    Warr argues that the age-delinquency relationship can be explained by Sutherland's concept of differential association. Peer influence is a critical variable in understanding delinquency.

Section V
Social and Cultural Causation

Introduction   137

17. Poverty, Income Inequality, and Community Crime Rates   142
    E. Britt Patterson
    The types of community characteristics, emphasized by early social disorganization theorists as undermining informal community controls and neighborhood social bonds, are found to be particularly important for understanding rates of victimization.

18. Foundation for a General Strain Theory of
    Crime and Delinquency   150
    Robert Agnew

    Agnew outlines several different ways in which frustration can be generated among youth and result in delinquent behavior as a means of solving or escaping such problems.

19. Parents and Drugs: Specifying the
    Consequences of Attachment   168
    Gary F. Jensen and David Brownfield

    Jensen and Brownfield test distinct hypotheses about the impact of bonds to "straight" and drug-using parents suggested by social learning theory and some brands of social control theory.

20. Structural Position and Violence:
    Developing a Cultural Explanation   176
    David F. Luckenbill and Daniel P. Doyle

    Luckenbill and Doyle propose an explanation for high rates of murder and assault in terms of a "culture of violence" in which public threats to honor require a violent response.

Section VI
The Family, Schools, and Peer Groups

Introduction   187

21. Family Life, Delinquency, and Crime:
    A Policymaker's Guide   192
    Kevin N. Wright and Karen E. Wright

    A review of the research on family life and how it relates to delinquent behavior.

22. School Bonding, Race, and Delinquency   210
    Stephen A. Cernkovich and Peggy C. Giordano

    The relationship of school to delinquency and how this relates to the issue of race.

23. The Influence of Delinquent Peers:
    What They Think or What They Do?   219
    E. Mark Warr and Mark Stafford

    An examination of the influence of the behavior of friends versus the attitudes of friends in the study of delinquency.

24. Gangs, Drugs, and Delinquency in a Survey of Urban Youth   228
    Finn-Aage Esbensen and David Huizinga

    Do gangs increase delinquent behavior or do delinquents gravitate toward gang membership?

Section VII
Media and Religion

Introduction — 243

25. Television and Aggression: Results of a Panel Study — 246
    J. Ronald Milavsky, Ronald Kessler, Horst Stipp, and William S. Rubens

    Children and teenagers are followed over time (i.e., a panel study) to assess whether television violence is a significant correlate of subsequent aggression, violence, or delinquency.

26. Movies and Juvenile Delinquency: An Overview — 256
    Scott Snyder

    Snyder reviews the theories and evidence relevant to the link between movies and delinquency.

27. Religiosity and Delinquency: A Contextual Analysis — 264
    Kirk W. Elifson, David M. Petersen, and C. Kirk Hadaway

    Research on the relevance of religion to delinquency suggests that religiosity is related to delinquency through its connection with family and peer relationships.

28. Crime and Delinquency in the Roaring Twenties — 275
    Rodney Stark, William Sims Bainbridge, Robert D. Crutchfield, Daniel P. Doyle, and Roger Finke

    Stark and his colleagues examine the relevance of religious, moral, and social intergration to crime and delinquency in the early twentieth century.

Section VIII
Deterrence and Labeling

Introduction — 285

29. Court Processing Versus Diversion of Status Offenders: A Test of Deterrence and Labeling Theories — 288
    Sharla Rausch

    Rausch examines whether variations in intervention in the lives of status offenders lead to escalating careers, as labeling theory suggests, or inhibits further offending, as deterrent theory predicts.

30. The Preventive Effects of the Perceived Risk of Arrest: Testing an Expanded Conception of Deterrence — 297
    Daniel S. Nagin and Raymond Paternoster

    Using questionnaire data from a panel of high school students, Nagin and Paternoster find that the perceived threat of legal sanctions, as well as the perceived costs of getting caught, have crime-inhibiting effects.

31. Felony Murder and Capital Punishment:
An Examination of the Deterrence Question 308
Ruth D. Peterson and William C. Bailey

The authors add a new piece of evidence to the long history of research on the general deterrent effect of capital punishment by studying the impact of television coverage of executions on felony murder.

Section IX
Imprisonment and Alternatives
Introduction 323

32. Juveniles Taken into Custody: Fiscal Year 1991 327
Barry Krisberg and Robert DeComo

This report lists the number of juveniles being admitted to public and private institutions for specific offenses and the length of stay in institutions.

33. Conditions of Confinement: Juvenile Detention and Corrections Facilities 345
ABT Associates, Inc.

This study examines the conditions at public and private juvenile facilities in terms of space, health care, and procedural standards.

34. Comprehensive Strategy for Serious, Violent, and Chronic Juvenile Offenders 354
John J. Wilson and James C. Howell

There is an increasing need to focus on the high-risk juvenile offender and to develop a comprehensive strategy, utilizing community-based sanctions and community prevention.

Section X
Diversion, Restitution, and Shock Treatment
Introduction 365

35. Juvenile Diversion and the Potential of Inappropriate Treatment for Offenders 370
Dean G. Rojek

The proliferation of juvenile diversion programs introduces the possibility of inappropriate treatment. It is suggested that such services may not only be wasteful but also produce negative effects.

36. Restitution and Juvenile Recidivism 382
Jeffrey A. Butts and Howard N. Snyder

Restitution offers the possibility of providing some compensation for victims of crime as well as lowering the recidivism rates of offenders.

37. Restitution as a Sanction in Juvenile Court   388
    William G. Staples

    Staples suggests that restitution may not be appropriate for use in the juvenile court because of high unemployment rates for teenagers.

38. Juvenile Intensive Supervision: The Impact on Felony Offenders Diverted From Institutional Placement   393
    Richard G. Wiebush

    Wiebush examines the pros and cons of intensive supervision as an alternative to institutionalization. His analysis reveals significant costs associated with intensive supervision.

39. The Impact of Shock Incarceration Programs on Prison Crowding   407
    Doris Layton MacKenzie and Alex Piquero

    Boot camps may have no impact on prison populations if boot camps are used as an alternative to probation.

40. A Critical Look at the Idea of Boot Camp as a Correctional Reform   422
    Merry Morash and Lila Rucker

    Morash and Rucker suggest that boot camps may be dehumanizing and question the efficacy of boot camps in enhancing prosocial behavior.

Section XI
The Future of the Juvenile Justice System

Introduction   433

41. History Overtakes the Juvenile Justice System   437
    Theodore N. Ferdinand

    Ferdinand argues that the state has not provided adequate support to the juvenile court. He feels that more attention needs to be given to treatment strategies.

42. Juvenile (In)Justice and the Criminal Court Alternative   448
    Barry C. Feld

    Feld contends that the distinction between the juvenile and adult court has become increasingly blurred. He argues that the juvenile court needs to find its philosophical roots or risk being abolished.

43. Rethinking the Juvenile Justice System   459
    Travis Hirschi and Michael R. Gottfredson

    Hirschi and Gottfredson question the very existence of the juvenile court. They see no justification for having a separate system for juveniles and for adults.

Introduction

We are bombarded daily with news, television specials, and political speeches about the epidemic of juvenile violence, teenage drug use, and other forms of juvenile delinquency. A common response to such revelations is a call for a "war" on the problem, attributing blame to enterprises that allegedly set bad examples for juveniles (for example, the entertainment industry) or the leniency of the juvenile justice system charged with protecting their interests. Other sources of the problem cited in popular discourse include the "breakdown of the family" or vaguely described social conditions such as "a decline in moral values." The typical response is a cry for some form of legislation to increase penalties, reform the juvenile court, regulate the media, or eliminate the "causes" of decline.

Few people and even fewer politicians want to hear about the complexities of these problems or consider them in a historical perspective. The readings in this book provide an opportunity to delve deeper into the sources of these problems. Readers may be surprised to discover that scholars have been compiling data on crime for over 150 years. There are literally thousands of studies of juvenile delinquency, with the amount of literature growing exponentially each year.

Many authors of this literature use sophisticated statistical analysis to test their theories. Some of the theories and the research supporting them will ring true to people with conservative political leanings, while others will appeal to people with liberal inclinations. It may be personally difficult to think of favored ideas as "theories," but this approach will greatly facilitate class discussion and critical thinking. We hope you will share a willingness to contemplate the pros and cons of different positions, to discuss the strengths and weaknesses of different ways of looking at a problem, and to avoid simplistic divisions of ideas into "good" and "bad" based on ideological preferences.

This anthology offers a broad sample of contemporary literature which explores dimensions of delinquency. **Section I** begins the exploration with an historical perspective on delinquency, including details on the operation of juvenile justice and an overview of representative public opinion on what the juvenile justice system ought to be doing. Most contemporary beliefs about delinquency, as well as proposals for reform, have historical precedents, and some scholars argue that we are caught in an endless vacillation between harsh and lenient philosophies of juvenile justice—both equally ineffective. The juvenile justice system is expected to do a little bit of everything—to make sure that justice is done and youth are properly punished, but also to treat and rehabilitate them.

These conflicting expectations and cross-pressures are paralleled by vacillating and conflicting views of the rights of juveniles and their relations to government authority. **Section II** provides detail on key court decisions as the court has moved from a "hands off" position to juvenile rights, decisions that reaffirm a distinctly subordinate status for juveniles. Of course, court decisions are not necessarily reflected in the operating realities of the system; therefore, research documenting the extension of rights of due process is included as well.

Section III includes readings about the types of data that are used to discern patterns over time and space among categories of people, as well as ways in which theories are tested and the effects of policies and programs are measured. While the "facts" about delinquency may vary with different types of data, there are nevertheless areas of agreement. One source of disagreement between "official" (i.e., police and court) statistics and survey data on delinquency is bias in the processing of juveniles with differing social characteristics. The possibility of bias in processing by race is currently a topic of national concern, and it may exaggerate the variation in delinquency among youths of racial categories.

Section IV offers an introduction to the debate over the role of biological characteristics in the explanation of crime and delinquency. Research suggesting that biological factors affect the probability of delinquency has grown increasingly sophisticated, both theoretically and methodologically, but it is still subject to considerable criticism by many sociologists. These theorists argue that the learning mechanisms of delinquency can be differentiated, observed, and measured, and that the most salient mechanisms involve interaction with other people. Even variations by age that can be interpreted as biologically driven can be shown to reflect variations in social relationships.

Sections V through VIII present readings that illustrate the major sociological theories of delinquency and include examples of research affecting them. Three approaches are covered in **Section V**: social disorganization/social bond theories, strain-frustration theories, and cultural deviance theories. **Section VI** deals with social institutions and the forces presumed by sociologists to be most relevant in shaping the behavior of youth—family, school, and peers. **Section VII** addresses the relationship of media and religion to delinquency. Research on the effect of television on delinquency suggests that it is less responsible for delinquency than personal relationships with parents, peers, and others. In contrast, research on religion and delinquency suggests that religiosity correlates with the types of friends and family that a youth develops.

Section VIII is the first of three sections on the consequences of organized responses to early signs of delinquency. Two perspectives underlie much of this literature: labeling theory and deterrence theory. From a labeling perspective, efforts to control delinquency by labeling, detaining, and imprisoning youth can have boomerang effects, resulting in youths who are progressively alienated, bitter, and drawn to criminal lifestyles. By contrast, the theory underlying most justice systems is that legal sanctions should deter would-be offenders (general deterrence) and make those punished think twice about committing another offense (specific deterrence). While there is some support for this theory, it has not been established that variations in the severity of legal intervention make much difference in recidivism (offenses committed after a sanction has been imposed).

Sections IX and **X** deal with imprisonment, alternatives to imprisonment, shock incarceration, boot camps, and restitution. The current political climate calls for increased use of imprisonment for juvenile and adult offenders and greater attention to justice for victims. However, with the expense of imprisonment comparable to the cost of sending a youth to college, less expensive alternatives are being actively explored. For example, while boot camps have not proved any more successful than other alternatives at reducing recidivism, they are less expensive to build and maintain than additional training schools. Justice for victims is one rationale for restitution programs in which juveniles are required to work to repay victims or the community. Restitution programs also appeal to justice criminologists concerned about rehabilitation because they lead offenders to see that their actions result in injury to real people.

Section XI includes three articles on the future of juvenile justice. Numerous critics of the system argue that neither the interests of juveniles nor of society are served by a separate juvenile court for dealing with criminal activities. We are approaching the 100th anniversary of the inception of the juvenile court and are still debating its worth. It is supposed to protect and punish, to rehabilitate and enforce justice, to incapacitate serious offenders without ruining their chances for reform. At the same time, it deals with problems of abuse, family breakdown, and children who have been rejected by every other social institution in society. The odds are that it will continue as part of the justice system but with increasingly limited jurisdiction over the most serious offenders.

Acknowledgements

Several people deserve acknowledgement for their advice on this anthology. We would like to thank reviewers of the various drafts and earlier proposals: Ronald

Akers (University of Florida), Finn-Aage Esbensen (University of Nebraska at Omaha), Lin Huff-Corzine (Kansas State University), Donald J. Shoemaker (Virginia State University), and Richard A. Wright (University of Scranton). We are particularly grateful to the publisher-editor of Roxbury Publishing Company, Claude Teweles, for his careful, personal attention to detail as well as his patience and understanding. Finally, we would like to thank our respective universities, the University of Georgia and Vanderbilt University, for their enduring support of our scholarship.

*To Our Remarkable Wives,
Kathy and Sheila*

About the Authors

The authors of the articles in this anthology are listed below, along with the institutions where they are affiliated.

Robert Agnew
Department of Sociology
Emory University

Ronald L. Akers
Department of Sociology
University of Florida

Jerald Bachman
Institute for Social Research
University of Michigan

William C. Bailey
Graduate College
Cleveland State University

William Sims Bainbridge
National Science Foundation
Washington, D.C.

Thomas Bernard
Department of Sociology
Pennsylvania State University

David Brownfield
Department of Sociology
University of Toronto

Jeffrey A. Butts
Office of Juvenile Justice and Delinquency Prevention
Washington, D.C.

Stephen A. Cernkovich
Department of Sociology
Bowling Green State University

Robert D. Crutchfield
Department of Sociology
University of Washington

Robert DeComo
National Council on Crime and Delinquency
San Francisco, California

Daniel P. Doyle
Department of Sociology
University of Montana

Peggy C. Giordano
Department of Sociology
Bowling Green State University

Kirk W. Elifson
Department of Sociology
Georgia State University

Delbert S. Elliott
Department of Sociology
University of Colorado

Finn-Aage Esbensen
Department of Criminal Justice
University of Nebraska-Omaha

Barry C. Feld
College of Law
University of Minnesota

Theodore N. Ferdinand
Administration of Justice
Southern Illinois University

William Feyerherm
Regional Research Institute
Portland State University

Roger Finke
Department of Sociology and Anthropology
Purdue University

Diana H. Fishbein
Department of Criminal Justice
University of Baltimore

Michael R. Gottfredson
Management and Policy
University of Arizona

Shenyang Guo
School of Social Work
University of Michigan

C. Kirk Hadaway
Center for Urban Church Studies
Nashville, Tennessee

Clayton Hartjen
Department of Sociology, Anthropology and Criminal Justice
Rutgers University

Travis Hirschi
Deparment of Sociology
University of Arizona

David H. Huizinga
Institute of Behavioral Science
University of Colorado

Gary F. Jensen
Department of Sociology
Vanderbilt University

Lloyd D. Johnston
Institute for Social Research
University of Michigan

John Johnson Kerbs
School of Social Work
University of Michigan

Ronald Kessler
Department of Sociology
University of Michigan

Sesharajani Kethineni
Criminal Justice Sciences
Illinois State University

Barry Krisberg
National Council on Crime and Delinquency
San Francisco, California

Marvin D. Krohn
Department of Sociology
SUNY-Albany

Lonn Lanza-Kaduce
Department of Sociology
University of Florida

David F. Luckenbill
Department of Sociology
Northern Illinois University

Doris L. MacKenzie
Department of Criminal Justice and Criminology
University of Maryland

J. Ronald Milavsky
Department of Social Research
National Broadcasting Company

Merry Morash
School of Criminal Justice
Michigan State University

Daniel S. Nagin
School of Urban and Public Affairs
Carnegie-Mellon University

Patrick O'Malley
Institute for Social Research
University of Michigan

Dale G. Parent
Office of Juvenile Justice and Delinquency Prevention
U.S. Department of Justice

Raymond Paternoster
Department of Criminal Justice and Criminology
University of Maryland

E. Britt Patterson
Department of Criminal Justice
Shippensburg University

Alexis R. Piquero
Department of Criminology
University of Maryland

David M. Petersen
Department of Sociology
Georgia State University

Ruth D. Petersen
Department of Sociology
Ohio State University

Carl Pope
Criminal Justice Program
University of Wisconsin-Milwaukee

Sharla Rausch
Research Division
National Institute of Corrections

Dean G. Rojek
Department of Sociology
University of Georgia

William S. Rubens
Department of Social Research
National Broadcasting Company

Lila Rucker
Criminal Justice Studies
University of South Dakota

Rodney Stark
Department of Sociology
University of Washington

Ira M. Schwartz
School of Social Work
University of Pennsylvania

Melissa Sickmund
National Center for Juvenile Justice
Pittsburgh, Pennsylvania

Howard N. Snyder
Systems Research
National Center for Juvenile Justice

Scott Snyder
Adolescent Psychiatric Program
Charter Winds Hospital
Athens, Georgia

Vernon L. Speirs
Office of Juvenile Justice and Delinquency Prevention
Washington, D.C.

Mark Stafford
Department of Sociology
University of Texas-Austin

William G. Staples
Department of Sociology
University of Kansas

Horst Stipp
Department of Social Research
National Broadcasting Company

E. Mark Warr
Department of Sociology
University of Texas-Austin

Richard G. Wiebush
National Council on Crime and Delinquency
San Francisco, California

Karen E. Wright
Planned Parenthood Association of Delaware and Otsego Counties
Oneonta, New York

Kevin N. Wright
School of Education & Human Development
SUNY-Binghamton

Section I
Delinquency and Juvenile Justice

'The New Mutant Juvenile'

People have always accused kids of getting away with murder. Now that is all too literally true. Across the U.S., a pattern of crime has emerged that is both perplexing and appalling. Many youngsters appear to be robbing and raping, maiming and murdering, as casually as they go to a movie or join a pickup-baseball game. A new, remorseless, mutant juvenile seems to have been born, and there is no more terrifying figure in America today.

This statement from *Time* magazine summarizes the outrage reflected in numerous public, political, and media depictions of teenage crime in America. Teenage crime is a plague—an epidemic involving a new enemy in our midst, the mutant teenager. Although such claims capture the image of juvenile crime in the mid-1990s, the quotation comes from an article in the July 11, 1977, issue of *Time*, entitled "The Youth Crime Plague" (p. 18).

The "new, remorseless, mutant juvenile" has been born and reborn so many times that the label has begun to lose its meaning. Juveniles have accounted for a disproportionate share of crime for as long as national statistics have been compiled and, during some spans of time, they have accounted for a growing share of violence. With the drama surrounding juvenile crime, it is easy to overlook the fact that adults, people 18 years of age or older, accounted for 84 percent of the 150,000 robberies cleared by an arrest in 1992, 91 percent of the 20,000 murders cleared by arrest, and 88 percent of 33,000 rapes cleared (See Snyder and Sickmund, Section III). Ninety-six percent of arrests for offenses against family and children and 99 percent of arrests for driving under the influence of alcohol were adults. Moreover, the savings and loan scandal of the late 1980s and early 1990s cost the American public more than all juvenile property crimes during that same span of time (Jensen and Rojek 1992). Juveniles are a perennial part of the crime problem, but the problem cannot simply be reduced to the rise of a new remorseless breed of juveniles.

The first selection in this book provides a historical perspective on reactions to juvenile delinquency as a social problem. Thomas Bernard identifies the public belief that delinquency and youth crime are increasing as one of the constants in the history of juvenile justice. That belief is a reflection of a broad tendency to believe that the current state of society is worse than it was previously, and that each generation of teenagers is more degenerate than the last.

Not only do people always believe that the world is in worse shape than it has ever been, but the proposed solutions always fall within a limited and repetitive range. Since the situation is always a crisis, the response is to make quick, immediate changes which do not solve the deep-rooted causes of the problem. Thomas Bernard argues that we vacillate between two poles and continually reinvent the same solutions. We are currently in a "get tough" phase, and have been for the past decade or so. A key target for attack in this swing of the pendulum is the juvenile court. The *Time* article labeled the court a "kiddies court" because of alleged leniency and deemed it to be "a big part of the problem."

The public is understandably alarmed when the juvenile justice system holds hearings to determine whether to deal with cases of violent juvenile offenders as a juvenile court matter or to "remand" the cases to adult criminal court. The possibility that young murderers might be back in the community in a few years alarms people. However, it is important to recognize that such cases constitute a tiny fraction of those dealt with by the juvenile court. Just as the crime problem tends to be "compartmentalized" as a problem of mutant juveniles, so do attacks on the juvenile court "compartmentalize" the problems with justice machinery in our society. The third article combines three reports on the processing of juvenile offenders. With all of the emphasis on juvenile violence, it is easy to ignore the fact that property crimes are most overrepresented, and that the juvenile court spends most of its time dealing with offenses such as shoplifting, vandalism, and various forms of theft. Moreover, alarmist responses to the juvenile court are based on a belief that adult criminal justice is much tougher than juvenile justice. This selection ends with a comparison of the juvenile court's response to violent crime with the adult criminal court's response to similar crimes. There are differences, but they do not justify wholesale indictments of the juvenile justice system when compared to decisions of the adult court in similar cases. The Office of Juvenile Justice and Delinquency Prevention (OJJDP) study concludes that "the juvenile court intervened in the lives of a greater proportion of violent offenders than did criminal courts." This comparison does not mean that everyone will believe justice is being done or that they are being adequately protected from repeat offenders, but it does mean that simply moving problems from one system to another will not guarantee our safety.

Finally, the last selection reports the results of a survey of Americans by Ira Schwartz, Shenyang Guo, and John Kerbs at the Center for the Study of Youth Policy. The overall public response calls for tighter controls on the processing of certain serious offenders but, overall, suggests that the public expects the court to do what it was created to do. Most people believe that the main purpose of the juvenile court should be to treat and rehabilitate rather than to punish. However, most people also believe that juveniles charged with selling large amounts of drugs or violent crime should be tried as adults. The juvenile court is expected to treat, rehabilitate, punish, protect, and step in where other institutions have failed.

As will be highlighted in later sections of this anthology, it is time to consider the possibility that we have failed to solve our crime problem because we always react in the same alarmist fashion, hit upon easy political solutions that have no effect, identify simplistically conceived targets to blame, and, for whatever reasons, avoid truly innovative alternatives. The last section of this reader will include studies relevant to future alternatives.

References

Jensen, Gary F. and Dean G. Rojek. 1992. *Delinquency and Youth Crime*. Prospect Heights, Illinois: Waveland Pres, Inc.

Snyder, Howard N. and Melissa Sickmund. 1995. *Juvenile Offenders and Victims: A Focus on Violence*. National Center for Juvenile Justice.

Time Magazine. 1977. "The Youth Crime Plague." *Time* (July 11): 18-28. ✦

1
What Stays the Same in History?

Thomas J. Bernard

Views of Adults about the Behavior of Youth

According to Donovan, "every generation since the dawn of time has denounced the rising generation as being inferior in terms of manners and morals, ethics, and honesty." The view that adults have of juveniles is separate from how juveniles actually behave. This view goes as far back as history records, so it probably will remain the same into the future.

Many adults today complain about how rotten kids are, but this was true in Colonial America as well. Harvey Green says:

> One of the most consistent and common themes in the history of relations between American parents and their children is criticism of the younger generation. From almost the moment the settlers of Jamestown and Plymouth stepped off their boats in the early seventeenth century, there arose the cry that children were disobeying their parents as never before.

This phenomenon is not confined to America. Over two thousand years before the Pilgrims, Socrates had his own complaints about youth:

> Children now love luxury. They have bad manners, contempt for authority, they show disrespect for elders and love chatter in place of exercise. They no longer rise when their elders enter the room. They contradict their parents, chatter before company, gobble up dainties at the table, and tyrannize over their teachers.

From *The Cycle of Juvenile Justice*, pp. 31-39. Copyright © 1991 by Oxford University Press, Inc. Reprinted by permissison.

We can go back even further than that. Fourteen hundred years before Socrates, a Summarian father wrote to his son:

> Because my heart had been sated with weariness of you, I kept away from you and heeded not your fears and grumblings. Because of your clamorings, I was angry with you. Because you do not look to humanity, my heart was carried off as if by an evil wind. Your grumblings have put an end to me; you have brought me to the point of death.... Others like you support their parents by working.... They multiply barley for their father, maintain him in barley, oil, and wool. You're a man when it comes to perverseness, but compared to them you are not a man at all. You certainly don't labor like them—they are the sons of fathers who make their sons labor, but me, I didn't make you work like them.

Juveniles as Serious Criminals

Most of the above quotes apply to what we now call status offenses. Perhaps kids today are engaged in serious, horrifying crimes, terrible offenses. Today, you might argue, many kids are the worst kind of criminals. There may have been a lot of minor delinquencies in the past, but the serious, hard-core juvenile crime of today is new.

For example, in 1989, *Time* magazine described "the beast that has broken loose in some of America's young people." The following series of quotations gives a sense of the article while omitting numerous examples presented to illustrate each point:

> More and more teenagers, acting individually or in gangs, are running amuck.... To be sure, teenagers have never been angels. Adolescence is often a troubled time of rebellion and rage.... But juvenile crime appears to be more widespread and vicious than ever before.... Adolescents have always been violence prone, but there are horrendous crimes being committed by even younger children.... The teen crime wave flows across all races, classes, and life-styles. The offenders are overwhelmingly male, but girls too are capable of vicious crimes.... What is chilling about many of the young criminals is that they show no remorse or conscience, at least in-

itially. Youths brag about their exploits and shrug off victims' pain.

The author suggested that this recent "upsurge in the most violent types of crimes by teens" began in 1983. However, five years before this juvenile crime wave apparently began, *Time* magazine seemed to be just as alarmed about the juvenile crime problem:

> Across the U.S., a pattern of crime has emerged that is both perplexing and appalling. Many youngsters appear to be robbing and raping, maiming and murdering as casually as they go to a movie or join a pickup baseball game. A new, remorseless, mutant juvenile seems to have been born, and there is no more terrifying figure in America today.

The author of the 1989 article must have neglected to read this 1977 article. How could the wave of juvenile violence start in 1983 if *Time* had already carried an article about it in 1977?

Views of Adults in Earlier Times

These quotations from *Time* magazine occur during a time in which juvenile crime, including serious violent and property crime, declined by about one-third. Similar quotations can be found during times when juvenile crime is rising. For example, in 1964, the long-time head of the FBI J. Edgar Hoover was similarly convinced that things had changed:

> In the Twenties and Thirties, juvenile delinquency, in general, meant such things as truancy, minor vandalism and petty theft. Today, the term includes armed robbery, assault and even murder.... We should not permit actual crimes to be thought of in terms of the delinquencies of a past era. I am not speaking of the relatively minor misdemeanors usually associated with the process of growing up. It is the killings, the rapes and robberies of innocent people by youthful criminals that concern me.

Ten years earlier, in 1954, a New York City judge made a similar statement in *Newsweek*, except that he described the low juvenile crime as being in the 1900s and 1910s, rather than in the 1920s and 1930s:

> Back before the first world war, it was a rare day when you saw a man under 25 up for a felony. Today it's the rule. And today when one of these kids robs a bank he doesn't rush for a businesslike getaway. He stays around and shoots up a couple of clerks. Not long ago I asked such a boy why, and he said: "I get a kick out of it when I see blood running."

The article was entitled: "Our Vicious Young Hoodlums: Is There Any Hope?"

That same year, *Time* magazine ran an article about the "teenage reign of terror [that] has transformed New York City's public school system into a vast incubator of crime in which wayward and delinquent youngsters receive years of 'protection' while developing into toughened and experienced criminals." It said that in some schools, half the pupils carried switchblades or zipguns, others carried homemade flame throwers or plastic water pistols filled with blinding chemical solutions, and other students threatened or beat up teachers who gave them poor grades. It suggested that this behavior had begun "in the past few years."

Views of Adults as an Aspect That Stays the Same

Similar alarms were raised in the 1940s, 1930s and 1920s. At those times, people believed (as they do today) that the country was being overwhelmed in a rising tide of juvenile delinquency and crime, and that it had not been a serious problem only forty or fifty years ago. Juvenile crime itself seems to go up and down, but the quotations about how terrible juveniles are seem to stay the same. Whether juvenile crime is high or low, many people believe that it is worse today than ever before.

Belief That Juvenile Justice Policy Increases Crime

A[n] ... aspect of juvenile delinquency and juvenile justice that has stayed the same for at least two hundred years is a belief that the system for processing juvenile offenders increases juvenile crime. This belief seems to be widely held at all times and all places, whether a lot of delinquency or only a little occurs, and whether juveniles are harshly punished or leniently treated.

Presently, widespread concern exists that lenient treatment increases juvenile crime. But that concern tends to alternate in history with the opposite concern: that harsh punishment increases juvenile crime. Let us look at these two concerns historically.

Concern That Leniency Increases Juvenile Crime

People have always been concerned that lenient treatment increases crime among juveniles. This was a major point in the 1978 *Time* magazine article quoted above:

> When [a juvenile offender] is caught, the courts usually spew him out again. If he is under a certain age, 16 to 18 depending on the state, he is almost always taken to juvenile court, where he is treated as if he were still the child he is supposed to be. Even if he has murdered someone, he may be put away for only a few months. He is either sent home well before his term expires or he escapes, which, as the kids say, is "no big deal." Small wonder that hardened juveniles laugh, scratch, yawn, mug and even fall asleep while their crimes are revealed in court.

Several years earlier, Ted Morgan argued a similar point in an article entitled "They Think, 'I Can Kill Because I'm 14.'" Ten years before that, J. Edgar Hoover similarly warned against the "misguided policies which encourage criminal activity, resulting in the arrogant attitude: 'You can't touch me. I'm a juvenile!'"

Concern about Leniency in Earlier Times

Today, many people believe that leniency causes juvenile crime and blame the juvenile justice system for this leniency. They suggest that if juveniles were tried in adult courts and sent to adult institutions, the problem would be solved. But the juvenile justice system was originally established because the adult court were believed to be too lenient on juveniles. This suggests that sending juveniles to the adult system will not necessarily result in harsher treatment.

... Before the establishment of the first juvenile institution in New York City in 1825, only adult prisons were available for punishing juveniles. These were viewed as very harsh places that would increase the likelihood that juveniles would commit more crime. Prosecutors, judges, and juries in the criminal courts all naturally tried to avoid sending juvenile offenders to these institutions, with the result that many were freed with no punishment at all.

The chief judge in New York was concerned that freeing these juveniles without any punishment encouraged them to commit further crime. He helped establish the first juvenile institution to receive these youngsters who otherwise would get off scot-free. One year after the establishment of the institution, the New York City District Attorney stated that the new institution had solved the problem.

Around that same time, a "Report of the Committee for Investigating the Causes of the Alarming Increase of Juvenile Delinquency in the Metropolis" was issued in London that expressed similar concerns. The problem, as it existed in both London and New York, was that only harsh punishments were available in the adult system, but that the natural tendency to provide more lenient treatments to juveniles resulted in many of them being let off without any punishment whatsoever. The juvenile justice system was originally invented to correct this problem: its goal was to provide some punishments for those who were receiving no punishments at all from the adult system.

Concern about Harshness Increasing Crime

Just as there have been concerns for a long time that leniency increases juvenile crime, there also have been concerns that harsh punishments increase juvenile crime. For example, many law-abiding adults committed at least some crimes when they were juveniles for which they might have been sent to an institution. Most of them were not caught or, if caught, received lenient treatment. Most of them then quit committing crimes, since their behavior was part of growing up.

Now suppose instead of this lenient treatment, they had been sent to an institution. Such harsh punishment might have increased the likelihood that they would continue to commit crimes in the future, rather than simply growing out of it. This is the purpose of leniency—to allow juveniles to "get out while the getting is good."

Concern about Harshness in Earlier Times

This has not just been a concern in recent times. For example, the judge in New York City in the early 1820s was quoted above as being concerned that letting juveniles off scot-free would encourage them to commit crime. That same judge was also concerned that sending juveniles to the prisons and jails would be "a fruitful source of pauperism, a nursery of new vices and crimes, a college for the perfection of adepts in guilt." That is, this judge had to choose between providing harsh punishments or doing nothing at all, and he believed that both choices increased crime among juveniles.

A similar concern about harshness later provided the motivation for establishing the first juvenile court in Chicago in 1899.... Because of an Illinois Supreme Court decision in 1870, lenient handling of juvenile offenders was severely restricted. This meant that juvenile justice officials faced the same dilemma as the earlier officials in New York City: they either had to provide harsh punishments to juvenile offenders or they could do nothing at all. Like the New York City judge, they believed that both choices increased crime among juveniles. The juvenile court was invented partly to provide lenient treatments for juveniles who were being harshly punished in Chicago's jails and poorhouses, and partly to provide lenient treatments for juveniles for whom nothing was being done at all in the adult courts.

Concern about Juvenile Justice Policy Stays the Same

If you think about the problem faced by officials in New York and London in the early 1800s and in Chicago in the late 1800s, then it becomes apparent that the concern that leniency causes juvenile crime and that harshness causes juvenile crime are really two sides of the same coin. Their relation is described by what Walker calls the "law of criminal justice thermodynamics":

> An increase in the severity of the penalty will result in less frequent application of the penalty.

The "law" explains the basic problem faced by these officials. Only harsh punishments were available to respond to juvenile crime. Some juveniles received those punishments, but others were let off because the punishments seemed inappropriate and counterproductive. In terms of the above "law," the penalties were so severe that they were infrequently applied.

Another way to phrase it is to say that *certainty and severity are enemies*. If you increase the severity of a penalty, you usually decrease the certainty with which it is applied. If you want to increase the certainty with which a penalty is applied, usually you must reduce its severity. This is exactly what criminal justice officials in London, New York, and Chicago did: they reduced the severity of penalties for juveniles in order to increase the certainty of applying them. That is, they established a "lenient" juvenile justice system.

The continual concern about the effectiveness of juvenile justice policies arises from this relationship between certainty and severity. If juvenile justice policies provide harsh punishments, then some juveniles will receive those punishments but others will receive no punishment at all because the punishments seem inappropriate and counterproductive. Concern about the effectiveness of these policies arises because both of these two choices are thought to increase crime.

But if the policies provide lenient treatments, then many juveniles receive the treatments but some laugh and feel free to commit serious crime with impunity. Concern about the effectiveness of these policies arises because people believe that if we had only "gotten tough" with these juveniles earlier, then the serious crimes would never have occurred.

The Cycle of Juvenile Justice

Juvenile offenders always are treated more leniently than adults who commit the same offenses, and juveniles who initially commit minor offenses are treated very leniently by the justice system. At least some of these juveniles go on to commit serious crimes. Many people conclude that these serious crimes would not have occurred if the juvenile had been punished severely for the earlier offenses. They argue that leniency encourages juveniles to laugh at the system, to believe they will not be punished no matter what they do, and to feel free to commit more frequent and serious crimes.

In response to these views, justice officials begin to "toughen up" their responses to juvenile offenders, and the "lenient" responses become less available. Some minor offenses receive the harsh punishments, but others are released because the harsh punishments seem ineffective and counterproductive.

Despite "getting tough," juvenile crime rates remain high (as they always do). Some minor offenders who received harsh punishments go on to commit serious crimes, along with some for those who were let off. This generates increased efforts to provide even harsher punishments. But as the penalties become more severe, they are less frequently applied: even more minor offenders are released with no punishment at all. The juvenile crime rate still remains high.

Throughout all of this, many people remain convinced that the "juvenile crime wave" began only recently, that it did not exist back in the "good old days," and that it can be ended through proper justice policies. Eventually, enough time passes so that the "good old days" was before the whole "get tough" movement began, when juvenile offenders were treated leniently.

Since they are now convinced that there was no problem of serious juvenile crime back then, they conclude that harsh punishment actually increases juvenile crime. Like the reformers in New York and London in the early 1800s and in Chicago in the late 1800s, they argue that these punishments embitter the juveniles, cut off their legitimate options, and teach them the ways of crime. They also argue that harsh punishments indirectly increases juvenile crime because so many juveniles are let off scot-free when only harsh punishments are available.

The juvenile system then is reformed to take account of this argument, and juvenile offenders once again receive lenient punishments. But while juvenile crime rates remain high, adults remain convinced that the problem is recent and that it did not exist in the "good old days," and that it can be solved through proper justice policies. Eventually, enough time passes so that the "good old days" are back when officials "got tough" with juvenile offenders. Because people are now convinced that there was no problem with serious juvenile crime back then, they naturally conclude that the problem lies in the leniency with which juvenile offenders are now treated. A new reform movement then reintroduces harsh punishments.

The "cycle of juvenile justice" arises from the fact that juvenile crime rates remain high, regardless of justice policies that are in effect at the time. But many people are always convinced that these high rates only occurred recently, that back in the "good old days" juvenile crime was low, and that juvenile crime would be low again if only we had the proper justice policies in effect. These people then generate continual pressure to abandon whatever justice policies are in effect at the time and replace them with new policies. Because only a limited numbers of policies are possible to begin with, the result is that the juvenile justice system tends to cycle back and forth between harshness and leniency.

This cycle cannot be broken by any particular justice policy since every conceivable policy confronts the same dilemma: after it is implemented, many people will continue to be convinced that juvenile crime is exceptionally high, that it was not a serious problem in the "good old days," and that it would not be a serious problem today if we only had the proper justice policies in effect.

This dilemma confronts not only our current juvenile system but also any conceivable organizational arrangements for processing juvenile offenders. Earlier organizational arrangements for processing juvenile offenders grappled with (and were discarded because of) the same dilemma. New and different organizational arrangements that might be created in the future to process offenders would soon confront the same dilemma. ✦

2
A. Delinquency Cases in Juvenile Court, 1992

Jeffrey A. Butts

Courts and Trends

Juvenile courts in the United States processed an estimated 1,471,200 delinquency cases in 1992. Delinquency cases involve juveniles charged with criminal law violations. The number of delinquency cases handled by juvenile courts increased 26% between 1988 and 1992. Since 1988, cases involving offenses against persons increased 56% while property offense cases increased 23%. During this 5-year period, cases involving charges of robbery and aggravated assault grew 52% and 80%, respectively. Although the number of drug law violation cases was down 12% compared with 1988, the number of drug cases increased 15% between 1991 and 1992.

These national estimates of the cases handled by juvenile courts in 1992 are based on data from more than 1,500 courts that had jurisdiction over 57% of the U.S. juvenile population in 1992. The unit of count . . . is a case disposed during the calendar year by a court with juvenile jurisdiction. Each case represents one youth processed by a juvenile court on a new referral, regardless of the number of individual offenses contained in that referral. An individual youth can be involved in more than one case during the calendar year . . . .

Detention

One of the first decisions made in processing juvenile delinquency cases is whether or not the juvenile should be detained in a secure facility to await the next court appearance. Juveniles are sometimes detained to protect the community from their behavior, sometimes to protect the juveniles themselves, or to ensure their appearance at court hearings. Juveniles were securely detained in 20% of the delinquency cases processed in 1992. Detention was used in 35% of drug law violations, 24% of person offense cases, and 17% of property offenses handled by juvenile courts, 47% of cases involving detention in 1992 were property offense cases.

Intake Decision

After reviewing the details of a case, a decision is made either to dismiss it, handle it informally, or formally process the case by taking the matter before a judge. More than one-fifth (23%) of 1992 delinquency cases were dismissed at intake, often for lack of legal sufficiency. Another 26% were processed informally, with the juvenile agreeing to a voluntary disposition (e.g. probation). Half (51%) of the delinquency cases handled in 1992 were processed formally, and involved either an adjudicatory hearing or a hearing to consider transferring jurisdiction to the adult court.

Adjudication and Disposition

Adjudicatory hearings are used to establish the facts in a delinquency case (analogous to determining guilt or innocence) and to decide whether to place the juvenile under the supervision of the court. In 1992 juveniles were adjudicated in more than half (57%) of the 743,700 cases brought before a judge. Once adjudicated, the majority of cases (57%) were placed on formal probation, while in 28% the juvenile was placed out of the home in a residential facility, and 11% resulted in other dispositions (referral to an outside agency, community service, restitution, etc.). In most delinquency cases where the juvenile was not adjudicated, the case was dismissed by the court.

Between 1988 and 1992, the number of cases in which an adjudicated delinquent was ordered by the court to be placed in a residential facility increased 19%, while the

---

Jeffrey A. Butts, from *Justice and Delinquency Cases in Juvenile Court Fact Sheet #18*, July 1994. U.S. Department of Justice: Office of Juvenile Justice and Delinquency Prevention.

number of formal probation increased 24%. In 1992, 57% of probation cases involved property offenses and 20% involved person offenses. Out-of-home placement cases, on the other hand, were slightly more likely to involve person offenses (23%) and slightly less likely to involve property offenses(48%).

Gender

In 1992, four out of five delinquency cases involved a male juvenile (81%). This was the same proportion found in 1988. Males accounted for 79% of person offense cases, 81% of property cases, and 88% of drug law violation cases.

Age

Compared with 1988, the delinquency cases handled by juvenile courts in 1992 involved slightly younger youth. Sixty percent of the juvenile delinquency cases processed in 1992 involved a juvenile under 16 years of age, compared with 57% in 1988. In 1992, juveniles younger than age 16 were responsible for 62% of all person offense cases, 64% of all property offenses cases, and 39% of drug law violation cases.

Race

In 1992, 80% of the juvenile population was white and 15% was black. White juveniles, however, were involved in 65% of the delinquency cases handled by juvenile courts. Black juveniles were involved in 31% of delinquency cases—27% of property offense cases and 40% of person offense cases. . . .

B. How Juveniles Get to Criminal Court

Melissa Sickmund

All States allow juveniles to be tried as adults in criminal court under certain circumstances. A juvenile's case can be transferred to criminal court for trial in one of three ways—judicial waiver, prosecutorial discretion, or statutory exclusion from juvenile court jurisdiction. In any State, one, two, or all three transfer mechanisms may be in place.

Judicial Waiver

As of year end 1992, in all States except Nebraska and New York, juvenile court judges may waive jurisdiction over a case and transfer it to criminal court. . . . Such action is usually in response to a request by the prosecutor. However, in several States, juveniles or their parents may request a transfer. In many States, statutes limit judicial waiver by age, offense, or offense history. Frequently, statutory criteria such as the juvenile's amenability to treatment must also be considered.

An estimated 11,700 juvenile delinquency cases were transferred to criminal court by judicial waiver in 1992. Waivers increased 68% from 1988 to 1992. Over this 5-year period, the number of waivers doubled or nearly doubled for all offense categories except property offenses.

Judicially waived cases accounted for fewer than 2% of the cases formally processed in juvenile courts in 1992. . . . Drug and person offense cases were more likely to be judicially waived than cases involving property or public order offenses.

The offense profile of waived cases changed somewhat from 1988 to 1992. . . . Person offense cases accounted for a greater proportion and property cases for a smaller proportion of waived cases in 1992 than in 1988.

Prosecutorial Discretion

In some States, prosecutors are given the authority to file certain juvenile cases in either juvenile or criminal court under concurrent jurisdiction statues. Thus, original jurisdiction is shared by both criminal and juvenile courts.

Melissa Sickmund, from *Juvenile Justice Bulletin*, October 1994. U.S. Department of Justice: Office of Juvenile Justice and Delinquency Prevention.

Prosecutorial discretion is typically limited by age and offense criteria. . . . Often concurrent jurisdiction is limited to charges of serious, violent, or repeat crimes. Juvenile and criminal courts frequently share jurisdiction over minor offenses such as traffic, watercraft, or local ordinance violations, as well.

There are no national data at the present time on the number of juvenile cases tried in criminal court under concurrent jurisdiction provisions. There is, however, some indication that they may outnumber judicial waivers in States allowing such transfers. In one State with both judicial waiver and concurrent jurisdiction provisions, there were two cases filed directly in criminal court for every one judicially waived in 1981. By 1992 there were more than six direct filings for every case judicially waived.

Statutory Exclusion

Legislatures transfer large numbers of young offender to criminal court by statutory excluding them from juvenile court jurisdiction. . . . Although not typically thought of as transfers, large numbers of youth under age 18 are tried as adults in the 11 States were the upper age of juvenile court jurisdiction is lower than 18. Nationwide, an estimated 176,000 cases involving youth under age 18 were tried in criminal court in 1991 because they were considered adults under State law.

Many States exclude certain serious offenses from juvenile court jurisdiction—some also exclude juvenile who have been previously waived or convicted in criminal court. . . . State laws typically also set age limits for excluded offenses. The serious offenses most often excluded are murder (and other capital crimes) and other offenses against persons. Several States exclude juveniles charged with felonies if they have prior felony adjudications or convictions. Minor offenses such as traffic, watercraft, or fish or game violations are often excluded from juvenile court jurisdiction as well. There are no national data on the number of juvenile cases tried in criminal court as a result of theses types of statutory exclusions.

In many States, juveniles tried in criminal court may receive dispositions involving either criminal or juvenile court sanctions. Several States also have provisions for transferring "excluded" or "direct-filed" cases from criminal court under certain circumstances. This is sometimes referred to as "reverse" waiver or transfer. . . .

C. The Juvenile Court's Response to Violent Crime

Verne L. Speirs

Juvenile and Adult Court Processing Compared

Many assume that for similar offenses adults receive more severe dispositions in criminal court than juveniles do in juvenile court; researchers compared the handling of similar cases in both courts to evaluate this notion. Since crimes by juveniles are likely to be less serious than those by adults—even though the crimes may be identically classified—researchers, using data collected by the Offender-Based Tracking System, compared the processing of adults in criminal court with the processing of older youth, 16 and 17 years old in juvenile court.

Juvenile courts petitioned violent offense referrals at the same rate that adult courts prosecuted such cases—81 percent compared to 82 percent. . . . In both courts robbery cases were prosecuted at a higher rate than aggravated assaulted cases. Adult courts were more likely to incarcerate violent offenders than were juvenile courts. The probability that a juvenile charged with a violent offense would be either transferred

---

Verne L. Speirs, from *Juvenile Justice Bulletin*, January 1989, pp. 4-5. U. S. Department of Justice: Office of Juvenile Justice and Delinquency Prevention.

to adult court or placed in a residential facility was nearly equally to the likelihood that an adult charged with the same offense would be incarcerated. In addition, a much larger percentage of juvenile than adult violent offenders was placed on probation.

One approach to comparing the two courts is to determine the proportion of cases that result in a substantial disposition—one in which a court restricts or monitors the behavior of the offender beyond the point of disposition. In the adult system, this includes the dispositions of incarceration and probation; in the juvenile system, this includes transfer to adult court, placement in a residential facility, and probation.

Using this criterion juvenile courts intervened in the lives of a greater proportion of violent offenders than did criminal courts. In all, 59 percent of 16- and 17-year-olds charged with violent acts were transferred to criminal court or placed in residential facilities or on formal probation, while only 46 percent of adults charged with a violent crime were incarcerated or placed on probation. ✦

3
Public Attitudes Toward Juvenile Crime and Juvenile Justice: Implications for Public Policy

Ira M. Schwartz
Shenyang Guo
John Johnson Kerbs[1]

Introduction

As a society, we have ambivalent views toward children and when they should be considered responsible for their own behavior and treated as adults. In no area is this ambivalence more apparent than in juvenile justice. For example, there are significant differences between the states with respect to the maximum age of juvenile court jurisdiction.[2] States differ in their policies regarding the circumstances under which juveniles can be tried in adult courts.[3,4] Juvenile court delinquency proceedings are open to the public in some states and closed in others.[5] Also, despite being rooted in the *parens patriae* philosophy, juvenile courts are becoming more punishment-oriented with juvenile court proceedings resembling those of adult criminal courts.[6]

Elected public officials and juvenile justice professionals often claim crime control policies directed toward juveniles reflect public wishes and demands. In reality, juvenile justice policies are not typically based on systematic samplings of public opinion.

This paper presents and discusses major findings from the first comprehensive national opinion survey on public attitudes toward juvenile crime and juvenile justice. The survey findings illuminate the thinking of citizens on a variety of issues that should prove helpful in making future juvenile justice policy. In particular, this paper focuses on public attitudes regarding due process for juveniles and whether juveniles who commit serious crimes should be tried in the adult courts and punished as adults.

Data and Methodology

The Center for the Study of Youth Policy commissioned the Survey Research Center of the Institute for Social Research at the

Figure 1
Percived Changes in Juvenile Crime for Respondents' State and Neighborhood (From Schwartz et al. 1992)

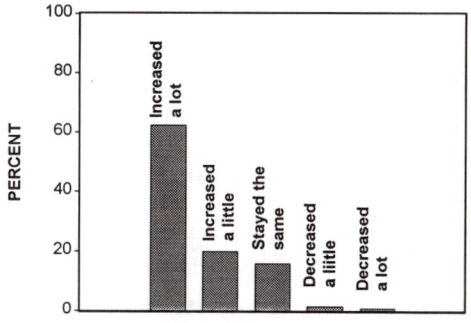

In the last three years, there has been a change in the amount of serious crime committed in my state by 10 to 17 year olds

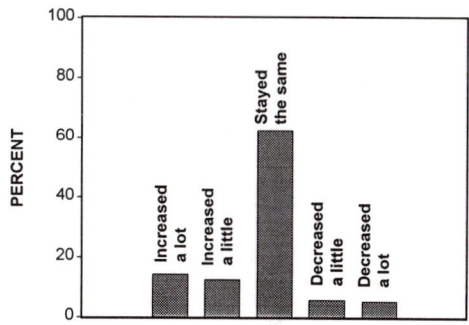

In the last three years, there has been a change in the amount of serious crime committed in my neighborhood by 10 to 17 year olds

---

From an edited version of draft manuscript with graphics added by Gary Jensen. Reprinted by permission of Ira M. Schwarz.

University of Michigan (Ann Arbor) to administer a national survey of public attitudes towards juvenile crime and juvenile justice. The survey was completed in 1991 using a dual-frame design telephone sample.[7] The study examined respondent opinions regarding due process, trying juveniles who commit serious crimes in adult courts, sentencing juveniles to adult prisons, and youth correctional intervention options.

General Findings

Public Perceptions About Juvenile Crime

The overwhelming majority of survey respondents (82%) believed the amount of serious juvenile crime increased in their respective states during the last three years (See Figure 1). Sixty-two percent believed it increased substantially, with 20% feeling it increased a little. In contrast, only 27% believed the amount of serious juvenile crime increased in their neighborhoods during that period. Sixty-three percent thought the volume had remained constant, while 11% thought it declined.

Attitudes Toward Juvenile Court and Funding of Correctional Interventions

Because of the controversies surrounding the juvenile court, questions were included about the court and the legal processing of delinquents. Almost 83% of the respondents thought juveniles should have the same due process protections accorded adults (See Figure 2). Seventy-eight percent thought the primary purpose of juvenile court should be treatment and rehabilitation while only 12% thought the main purpose should be punishment. Ten percent felt the court should emphasize both equally (Figure 2).

In addition to supporting a treatment-oriented juvenile court, the public also supported funding community-based correctional programs. Table 1 reflects respondent references for spending state juvenile crime control funds. The percentages represent the proportion of respondents who indicated that it was "very important" to spend money on a particular correctional intervention.

There was comparatively little support for spending money on training schools and other residential services. This may have stemmed from the fact that only 56% of the national survey respondents believed juveniles who served time in training schools would be less likely recidivate. Also, only about 50% believed sending juveniles to training schools would deter other youths from committing crimes.

Attitudes Toward Trying Juveniles in Adult Courts and Sentencing Juveniles to Adult Prisons

While there was still strong support for a treatment-oriented juvenile court, a sub-

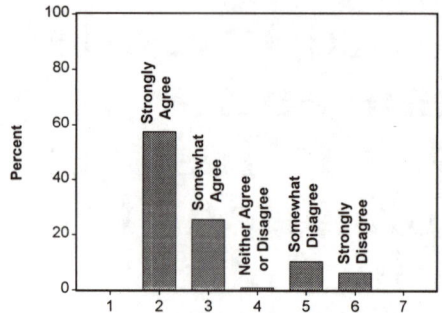

Figure 2
Due Process and Purpose of the Juvenile Court (From Schwartz et al., 1992)

A juvenile accused of a crime should receive the same due process as an adult.

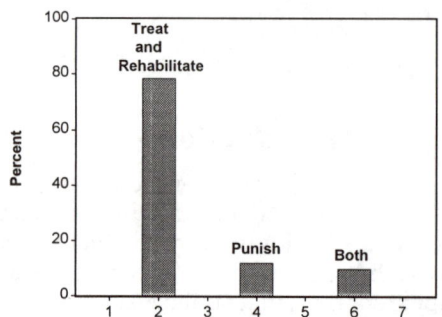

The main purpose of the juvenile court system should be to treat and rehabilitate young offenders or to punish them?

Table 1
How State Juvenile Crime Control Funds Should Be Spent

FUNDING OPTION	VERY IMPORTANT TO FUND
Restitution programs	81%
Job training and employment opportunities	70%
Community-based programs emphasizing education	69%
Community-based counseling	57%
Very close supervision at home or in the community	47%
Special foster homes in small group homes	36%
Building more training schools	36%

SOURCE: National Juvenile Crime Study Data and Documentation (October 15, 1991) (unpublished document, on file with the Center for the Study of Youth Policy).

stantial proportion of the respondents wanted to see juveniles accused of serious crimes tried in adult criminal courts. Approximately 50% of the respondents thought juveniles charged with a serious property crime should be tried in adult courts. Sixty-two percent thought juveniles charged with selling large amounts of drugs should be tried in adult courts, and 68% thought juveniles charged with serious violent crimes should be tried as adults (See Figure 3).

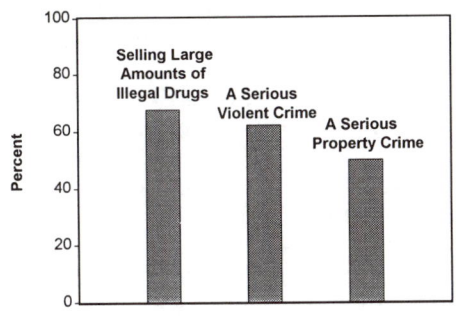

Figure 3
Response to Juvenile vs. Adult Offender

A juvenile charged with _____ should be tried as an adult.

Although many respondents favored trying juveniles who committed serious offenses in adult courts, they did not think juveniles should receive the same sentences as adults, nor be sentenced to adult prisons. For example, 62% of the respondents did not think juveniles should receive the same sentences as adults (See Figure 4). Eighty-

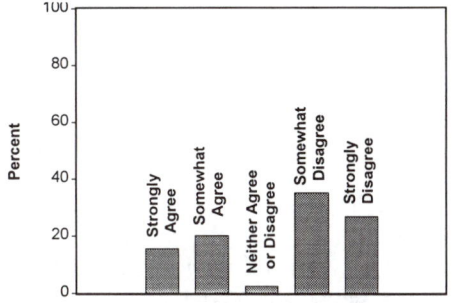

Figure 4
Response to Juvenile vs. Adult Offenders

A juvenile convicted of a crime should receive the same sentence as an adult, no matter what the crime?

three percent did not want juveniles sent to adult prisons for serious property crimes, and 68% did not support imprisoning juveniles for selling large amounts of drugs. Fifty-five percent did not favor sentencing juveniles to adult prisons for serious violent crimes. Interestingly, as the seriousness of the offense increased, so did the proportion of respondents who favored trying juveniles in adult courts and sentencing them to adult prisons (See Figure 5).

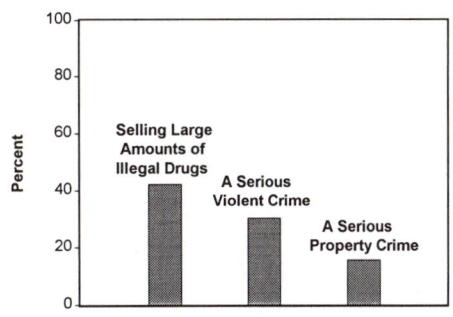

Figure 5
Response to Juvenile vs. Adult Offenders

Juveniles should be sent to adult prisons for _____.

Policy Implications

The public supports the juvenile court and its traditional emphasis on treatment and rehabilitation. The public also prefers that tax dollars be spent on community-based programs as compared to training schools and other costly residential services. This suggests that policymakers and juvenile justice professionals—particularly those in states experiencing financial difficulties—might find it productive to explore how existing juvenile crime fighting dollars could be used differently and, perhaps, more efficiently. For example, policymakers and juvenile justice officials in a number of states (e.g., Kentucky, Massachusetts, Missouri, Texas, Utah) have demonstrated they can administer youth correction systems that largely rely on the use of community-based programs without compromising public safety.[8,9]

There is also broad support for giving juveniles the same due process protections accorded adults. However, the public would like to see juveniles charged with felonies (i.e., serious property crimes, and selling large amounts of drugs) tried in adult court. Moreover, the more serious the crime the more likely people are to want juveniles prosecuted as adults. These findings are very interesting and will undoubtedly add fuel to the growing debate about the future of the juvenile court in the United States.

There are many possible explanations for the public wanting juvenile felony cases tried in adult courts. This study found that fear of being a victim of violent crime leads to increased support for trying juveniles in adult courts. In addition, such fears lead to increased support for incarcerating juveniles in adult prisons for serious violent crime. Beyond fear of victimization, the public may feel the juvenile court is simply not the appropriate place for processing juvenile felons. Because delinquency proceedings are confidential in most jurisdictions, the public may not have confidence in juvenile courts because they do not know what is going on there. Also, the public may simply want harsher treatment for juveniles charged with felonies. There appears to be some evidence to support this contention in this survey as well as in one completed by Yankelovich et al.[10] The Yankelovich survey indicated that 79% of the respondents favored tougher criminal penalties for juvenile offenders as a strategy for trying to curb teenage violence.[11]

Trying juveniles accused of felonies in adult criminal courts raises the question of whether a separate juvenile court can be justified. If juvenile felonies were handled in adult criminal courts, only misdemeanors and status offense cases would be left. One can hardly justify maintaining a separate court for those cases.

Abolishing juvenile courts would have significant and far reaching implications. It might eliminate the idiosyncratic and patchwork network of juvenile waiver policies that exist in the states. It would also probably result in ensuring that young people receive the same due process protections accorded adults.[12,13] Juvenile court critics have long opposed the lack of due process protections for juveniles.[14,15] They have also been critical of juvenile court as an institution and will probably be heartened by the public's view on trying juvenile felony cases in adult courts. However, it must be pointed out that the public's support for moving juvenile felony cases to the adult criminal justice system may be motivated by their desire to treat juveniles more harshly. Moreover, they seem to be particularly motivated to do so if they are quite fearful about being the victim of a violent crime.

The abolition of juvenile court may also have significant adverse implications. If juveniles are considered mature enough to be tried as adults, they may be seen as mature enough to be sentenced as adults. Also, prosecuting juveniles in adult court may lead to the pre-trial incarceration of them in adult jails. This would roll back years of progress in removing juveniles from those institutions.

Great care needs to be taken in debating the future of juvenile court. Unless the public's fear of being victims of violent crime is addressed and abated, it is conceivable that juvenile court and the youth corrections system could be abolished. If such fear continues to spread, one day a majority of the public might support using adult prisons for juveniles. Because policymakers look to their constituents and not to legal scholars, academics, or juvenile justice professionals for advice, public sentiment on this issue could lead to exclusive use of adult criminal courts and correctional systems for a large proportion of (if not all) juveniles offenders.

In any event, the findings from this survey indicate the time has come for legal scholars, researchers, juvenile justice and child welfare professionals, and elected public officials to begin thinking about alternatives to juvenile court. Public views about the legal processing of juveniles accused of serious crimes are inconsistent with the *parens patriae* model. They want juveniles to receive the same due process protections accorded adults, to be tried in an open court setting and, if found guilty, to be held accountable for their actions. However, the public does not want to abandon the juvenile model for youth detention and correction.

Conclusion

Public policy should not be developed simply by assessing public views on an issue at any particular point. The public may not be well informed on the issue to be decided. They may need to be educated on the topic before they can participate meaningfully in the policymaking process. Nevertheless, public views are important and need to be considered when critical policy issues are being debated.

This paper reports selected findings from the first comprehensive survey on public attitudes toward juvenile crime and juvenile justice. The findings indicate the public is deeply concerned about these issues and has much to contribute to policy discussions.

One major juvenile justice policy issue that is beginning to be debated nationally is the future of the juvenile court. The findings from this survey should contribute significantly to that dialogue. The findings should also be of interest to policymakers and juvenile justice officials who may be interested in restructuring their youth correction systems.

In addition, the findings indicate that fear of being the victim of a violent crime is a significant predicator of punitive attitudes toward juvenile offenders. This is another example of the impact of violence in our society and underscores the need for elected public officials and professionals to move this issue to the top of the public policy agenda.

Notes

1. The authors would like to thank Martha Smith, Danielle Hogston, Cindy Guillean for their editorial assistance.
2. See generally Ira M. Schwartz, *(In)Justice for Juveniles: Rethinking the Best Interests of the Child* (1989).
3. See generally Barry Krisberg, et al., "The watershed of juvenile justice reform," *Crime and Delinquency* 32:5-38 (1986).
4. See generally Dean J. Champion & G. Larry Mays, *Transferring Juveniles to Criminal Courts: Trends and Implications for Criminal Justice* (1991).
5. Schwartz, *supra* note 1.
6. See generally Barry C. Feld, "Juvenile court meets the principle of offense: Punishment, treatment, and the difference it makes," *Boston University Law Review* 68: 821-915 (1988).
7. All telephone interviews were conducted between August and September of 1991. Approximately half the sample was taken from a national frame (excluding Alaska and Hawaii) of 1,200 listed household telephone numbers which was purchased from Survey Sampling Incorporated (a survey research firm located in Fairfield, Connecticut). Although the Survey Sampling frame was continually updated using a 1-in-6 sample of all listed household numbers, it did not provide perfect coverage of all listings due to: (1) new listings created after the frame was generated; and (2) other causes. This frame did not encompass all listed numbers at any one time. The lack of perfect coverage (which affected the probability of selection) was taken into consideration when sample weights were computed. All numbers not caught by this sampling frame were considered "unlisted" for purposes of weighing.

The other sample half was generated using a random digit dialing (RDD) procedure. An equal probability sample of random numbers was generated using a version of the "PPS-to-listed counts" two-stage RDD design which James Lepkowski of the Survey Research Center has been researching. This design has several advantages over the traditional two-stage RDD design which involves primary number screening: (1) The cost of primary number screening is eliminated; and (2) the procedure for handling RDD cases in the telephone facility is simplified. No replacement procedure for non-working numbers is needed. The RDD cases can be handled in the same way as list cases. There is one disadvantage of this design compared to the design which uses primary numbers. In the "PPS-to-listed counts" design, unlisted numbers in a hundred series which had no listed numbers do not have a chance of selection. This type of occurrence is probably unusual and a very minor coverage problem.

8. See generally James Austin et al., *Unlocking Juvenile Corrections: Evaluating the Massachusetts Department of Youth Services* (National Council on Crime and Delinquency) (1991).
9. See generally James Austin et al., "The impact of juvenile court sanctions: A court that works," *National Council on Crime and Delinquency Focus* (March 1990).
10. Bureau of Justice Statistics, Department of Justice, *Sourcebook of Criminal Justice Statistics* 157 (1990).
11. *Id.*
12. See generally Katherine Hunt Federle, "The abolition of the juvenile court: A proposal for the preservation of children's legal rights," *Journal of Contemporary Law* 16:23-51 (1990).
13. Feld, *supra* note 5.
14. Federle, *supra* note 55.
15. Feld, *supra* note 5. ✦

Section II
Legal Issues

Unlike the adult criminal justice system, which dates back some eight centuries, the juvenile justice system is a relative infant. The first juvenile court was established on July 1, 1899, in Cook County, Illinois and by 1925 all but two states had this new court system. This new court was not to be encumbered with all of the legal technicalities of the adult system but was to function like a concerned and caring parent. As such, the juvenile court was to be a civil, not a criminal, court (Davis, 1995). The legal trappings of due process of law, the adversarial nature of court hearings, and even the notion of being innocent until proven guilty were not central to the juvenile court. The primary focus of the court was treatment and rehabilitation. Children were to bypass the harshness of the criminal court, avoid the stigma of a criminal trial, and thereby be helped by a kindly "parent," called a juvenile court judge.

While the juvenile court was created with the best of intentions, it obscured or perhaps even obliterated the rights of children. The juvenile court was given virtually unlimited power and children who had "problems," ranging from typical adolescent problems like skipping school or smoking cigarettes to serious criminal infractions, were brought before this court. The court itself seemed to walk a tightrope, never giving a clear signal whether it was actually a court of law or a social work agency. The Supreme Court maintained a strict hands-off policy for the first 60 years of the juvenile court's existence. However, in 1966 the Supreme Court finally agreed to hear a case dealing with the juvenile court (*Kent v. United States*) and for the first time the United States Supreme Court extended some element of procedural and due-process rights to children in juvenile court (Musick, 1995). The Kent case opened the door in 1967 for the landmark juvenile case *In re Gault*.

The first reading in this section contains excerpts from the Supreme Court's ruling on the matter of 16-year-old Jerry Gault. The Court stated unambiguously that juveniles have a right to due process of law. Justice Fortas, who wrote the opinion, delivered a blistering indictment of the juvenile court when he stated, "Under our Constitution, the condition of being a boy does not justify a kangaroo court." Reading this case makes it clear that many basic rights that are taken for granted in the adult court were not granted to juveniles. The significance of this case was astounding, but it did not abolish the juvenile court, *nor did it grant full protection of due-process-of-law guarantees to juveniles*. It is also important to note that Justices Harlan and Stewart did not agree with the other members of the Court. Justice Harlan stated that "the Court has gone too far," and Justice Stewart argued that "the Court's decision is wholly unsound as a matter of constitutional law, and sadly unwise as a matter of judicial policy." However, the Gault case is, in a sense, the starting point for discussing the juvenile court's problems, and leads to many other legal questions.

Additional juvenile court cases were brought to the Supreme Court in the 1970s and 1980s. In some cases due-process-of-law rights for juveniles were strengthened, but in other cases the Court acknowledged that the juvenile court is different from the adult court and the standards of due process are not applicable. The second Court case, entitled *New Jersey v. T.L.O.*, shows the Court struggling over the issue of Fourth Amendment rights for juveniles. The Court concluded that certain categories of individuals, in this case public school children, are afforded less than full protection under the Fourth Amendment. Public school officials do not need search warrants or probable cause to search or seize evidence from students. The Court argued that a reduced standard was justified because of the "substantial" government interest in maintaining a proper learning environment in which to educate children. In this case and in several other related cases, the courts have affirmed that children in school do not have a "legitimate expectation of privacy." *New Jersey v. T.L.O.* has a decidedly different tone from *In re Gault* and it reaffirms the principle that the rights of juveniles are distinctly different from those of adults.

The third case, entitled *Qutb v. Strauss*, deals with the constitutionality of curfew ordinances. Can a local government decree that juveniles cannot be on the streets at certain times? A U.S. District Court in Texas ruled that the curfew ordinance enacted by the city of Dallas was overly broad and too restrictive. However, a U.S. Court of Appeals disagreed and stated that local governments have a "compelling interest" to reduce juvenile crime and to promote the well-being of juveniles. Such a decree aimed at adults would be unconstitutional, but a different set of legal standards is in force for juveniles. Again, the general tenor of the Qutb case is decidedly different from the arguments presented in *Gault*.

The final reading in this section examines the presence of legal counsel in juvenile court and the impact of legal representation. While the Supreme Court spoke very clearly in the Gault case that juveniles are entitled to a lawyer, this does not automatically mean that lawyers are present in juvenile court. Similarly, the Court ruled in 1954 that segregated schools were in violation of the U.S. Constitution but school segregation did not end in 1954. Barry Feld discovered wide variability in the use of lawyers in the states he examined and found that when lawyers are present, they are usually court-appointed lawyers or public defenders. What is most puzzling is the fact that the presence of legal counsel might make matters worse rather than better. Clearly, Feld struggles to explain this puzzling finding. This reading suggests that *Gault* is routinely ignored, at least in the area of legal counsel, but when it is followed juveniles are punished for asserting their rights.

The four readings in this section are presented to show that many areas relating to the rights of juveniles are unclear, and when the Court issues a landmark decree it is not necessarily followed. Juveniles have been granted some rights, but the Court is reluctant to grant them the full protection of the U.S. Constitution. Similarly, it is difficult to predict how the Court will react to legal issues related to the juvenile court. The 1967 Gault case was quite progressive, but the 1985 T.L.O and 1993 Qutb cases can be seen as excluding juveniles from the phrase, "We, the people of the United States."

It is ironic that we may have come full circle in the past hundred years in our thinking about the need for a separate juvenile court. In the 1890s the cry was to divert juveniles from the adult system, and now in the 1990s the cry is to divert juvenile offenders from the juvenile court into something akin to an adult court. Many states are beginning to redefine the jurisdictional age limits of the juvenile court. For example, in Illinois a child 15 years of age or older who is charged with armed robbery is automatically transferred to the adult court. In Connecticut a waiver would be mandatory for a 14-year-old felony offender who had previously been an adjudicated delinquent in juvenile court. Albanese (1993) argues that the Supreme Court in the 1960s and 1970s was concerned with due-process-of-law protections in the juvenile court but in the 1980s and 1990s the Court "consistently advocated punishment, detention, and censorship of juveniles" (1993: 122). Similarly, society is becoming disillusioned with the very concept of a juvenile court and seems to endorse a "get tough" approach to juvenile delinquency.

References

Albanese, Jay S. *Dealing with Delinquency: The Future of Juvenile Justice.* Chicago: Nelson-Hall, 1993.

Davis, Samuel D. *Rights of Juveniles: The Juvenile Justice System.* Deerfield, Il.: Clark Boardman Callaghan, 1995.

Musick, David. *An Introduction to the Sociology of Juvenile Delinquency.* Albany, NY: State University of New York Press, 1995. ✦

4
In re Gault et al.
Supreme Court of the United States

Argued December 6, 1966—Decided May 15, 1967

On Monday, June 8, 1964 at about 10 a.m., Gerald Francis Gault and a friend, Ronald Lewis, were taken into custody by the Sheriff of Gila County. Gerald was then still subject to a six months' probation order which had been entered on February 25, 1964, as a result of his having been in the company of another boy who had stolen a wallet from a lady's purse. The police action on June 8 was taken as the result of a verbal complaint by a neighbor of the boys, Mrs. Cook, about a telephone call made to her in which the caller or callers made lewd or indecent remarks. It will suffice for purposes of this opinion to say that the remarks or questions put to her were of the irritatingly offensive, adolescent, sex variety.

At the time Gerald was picked up, his mother and father were both at work. No notice that Gerald was being taken into custody was left at the home. No other steps were taken to advise them that their son had, in effect, been arrested. Gerald was taken to the Children's Detention Home. When his mother arrived home at about 6 o'clock, Gerald was not there. Gerald's older brother was sent to look for him at the trailer home of the Lewis family. He apparently learned then that Gerald was in custody. He so informed his mother. The two of them went to the Detention Home. The deputy probation officer, Flagg, who was also superintendent of the Detention Home, told Mrs. Gault "why Jerry was there" and said that a hearing would be held in Juvenile Court at 3 o'clock the following day, June 9.

From 387 U.S. 1, 78-81 (1967).

Officer Flagg filed a petition with the court on the hearing day, June 9, 1964. It was not served on the Gaults. Indeed, none of them saw this petition until the habeas corpus hearing on August 17, 1964. The petition was entirely formal. It made no reference to any factual basis for the judicial action which it initiated. It recited only that "said minor is under the age of eighteen years, and is in need of the protection of this Honorable Court; [and that] said minor is a delinquent minor." It prayed for a hearing and an order regarding "the care and custody of said minor." Officer Flagg executed a formal affidavit in support of the petition.

On June 9, Gerald, his mother, his older brother, and Probation Officers Flagg and Henderson appeared before the Juvenile Judge in chambers. Gerald's father was not there. He was at work out of the city. Mrs. Cook, the complainant, was not there. No one was sworn at this hearing. No transcript or recording was made. No memorandum or record of the substance of the proceedings was prepared. Our information about the proceedings and the subsequent hearing on June 15 derives entirely from the testimony of the Juvenile Court Judge, Mr. and Mrs. Gault and Officer Flagg at the habeas corpus proceeding conducted two months later. From this, it appears that at the June 9 hearing Gerald was questioned by the judge about the telephone call. There was conflict as to what he said. His mother recalled that Gerald said he only dialed Mrs. Cook's number and handed the telephone to his friend, Ronald. Officer Flagg recalled that Gerald had admitted making the lewd remarks. Judge McGhee testified that Gerald "admitted making one of these [lewd] statements." At the conclusion of the hearing, the judge said he would "think about it." Gerald was taken back to the Detention Home. He was not sent to his own home with his parents. On June 11 or 12, after having been detained since June 8, Gerald was released and driven home. There is no explanation in the record as to why he was kept in the Detention Home or why he was released. At 5 p.m. on the day of Gerald's release, Mrs. Gault received a note signed by Officer Flagg. It was on plain paper, not letterhead. Its entire text was as follows:

"Mrs. Gault:

"Judge McGHEE has set Monday June 15, 1964 at 11:00 A. M. as the date and time for further Hearings on Gerald's delinquency.

"/s/Flagg"

At the appointed time on Monday, June 15, Gerald, his father and mother, Ronald Lewis and his father, and Officers Flagg and Henderson were present before Judge McGhee. Witnesses at the habeas corpus proceeding differed in their recollections of Gerald's testimony at the June 15 hearing. Mr. and Mrs. Gault recalled that Gerald again testified that he had only dialed the number and that the other boy had made the remarks. Officer Flagg agreed that at this hearing Gerald did not admit making the lewd remarks. But Judge McGhee recalled that "there was some admission again of some of the lewd statements. He—he didn't admit any of the more serious lewd statements." Again, the complainant, Mrs. Cook, was not present. Mrs. Gault asked that Mrs. Cook be present "so she could see which boy that done the talking, the dirty talking over the phone." The Juvenile Judge said "she didn't have to be present at that hearing." The judge did not speak to Mrs. Cook or communicate with her at any time. Probation Officer Flagg had talked to her once—over the telephone on June 9.

At this June 15 hearing a "referral report" made by the probation officers was filed with the court, although not disclosed to Gerald or his parents. This listed the charge as "Lewd Phone Calls." At the conclusion of the hearing, the judge committed Gerald as a juvenile delinquent to the State Industrial School "for the period of his minority [that is, until 21], unless sooner discharged by due process of law." An order to that effect was entered. It recites that "after a full hearing and due deliberation the Court finds that said minor is a delinquent child, and that said minor is of the age of 15 years."

No appeal is permitted by Arizona law in juvenile cases. On August 3, 1964, a petition for a writ of habeas corpus was filed with the Supreme Court of Arizona and referred by it to the Superior Court for hearing.

At the habeas corpus hearing on August 17, Judge McGhee was vigorously cross-examined as to the basis for his actions. He testified that he had taken into account the fact that Gerald was on probation. He was asked "under what section of . . . the code you found the boy delinquent?"

His answer is set forth in the margin. In substance, he concluded that Gerald came within ARS Sec. 8-201-6(a) which specifies that a "delinquent child" includes one "who has violated a law of the state or an ordinance or regulation of a political subdivision thereof." The law which Gerald was found to have violated is ARC Sec. 13-377. This section of the Arizona Criminal Code provides that a person who "in the presence or hearing of any woman or child . . . uses vulgar, abusive, or obscene language, is guilty of a misdemeanor. . . ." The penalty specified in the Criminal Code, which would apply to an adult, is $5 to $50, or imprisonment for not more than two months.

Asked about the basis for his conclusion that Gerald was "habitually involved in immoral matters," the judge testified, somewhat vaguely, that two years earlier, on July 2, 1962, a "referral" was made concerning Gerald, "where the boy had stolen a baseball glove from another boy and lied to the Police Department about it." The judge said there was "no hearing," and "no accusation" relating to this incident, "because of lack of material foundation." But it seems to have remained in his mind as a relevant factor. The judge also testified that Gerald had admitted making other nuisance phone calls in the past which, as the judge recalled the boy's testimony, were "silly calls, or funny calls, or something like that."

The Superior Court dismissed the writ, and appellants sought review in the Arizona Supreme Court. That court stated that it considered appellants' assignments of error as urging (1) that the Juvenile Code, ARS Sec. 8-201 to Sec. 8-239, is unconstitutional because it does not require that parents and children be apprised of the specific charges, does not require proper notice of a hearing, and does not provide for an appeal; and (2) that the proceedings and order relating to Gerald constituted a denial of due process of law because of the absence of adequate notice of the charge and the hearing; failure to notify appellants of certain constitutional rights including the rights to counsel and to confrontation, and the privilege against self-incrimination; the use of unsworn hearsay testimony; and the failure to make a record of the proceedings. Appellants further asserted that it was an error for the Juvenile Court to remove Gerald from the custody of his parents without a showing and finding of their unsuitability, and alleged a miscellany of other errors under state law.

The Supreme Court handed down an elaborate and wide-ranging opinion affirming dismissal of the writ and stating the court's conclusions as to the issues raised by appellants and other aspects of the juvenile process. In their jurisdictional statement and brief in this Court, appellants do not urge upon us all of the points passed upon by the Supreme Court of Arizona. They urge that we hold the Juvenile Code of Arizona invalid on its face or as applied in this case because, contrary to the Due Process Clause of the Fourteenth Amendment, the juvenile is taken from the custody of his parents and committed to a state institution pursuant to proceedings in which the Juvenile Court has virtually unlimited discretion, and in which the following basic rights are denied:

1. Notice of the charges;
2. Right to counsel;
3. Right to confrontation and cross-examination;
4. Privilege against self-incrimination;
5. Right to a transcript of the proceedings; and
6. Right to appellate review.

We shall not consider other issues which were passed upon by the Supreme Court of Arizona. We emphasize that we indicate no opinion as to whether the decision of that court with respect to such other issues does or does not conflict with requirements of the Federal Constitution.

Opinion of the Court

A boy is charged with misconduct. The boy is committed to an institution where he may be restrained of liberty for years. It is of no constitutional consequence—and of limited practical meaning—that the institution to which he is committed is called an Industrial School. The fact of the matter is that, however euphemistic the title, a "receiving home" or an "industrial school" for juveniles is an institution of confinement in which the child is incarcerated for a greater or lesser time. His world becomes "a building with whitewashed walls, regimented routine and institutional hours...." Instead of mother and father and sisters and brothers and friends and classmates, his world is peopled by guards, custodians, state employees, and "delinquents" confined with him for anything from waywardness to rape and homicide.

In view of this, it would be extraordinary if our Constitution did not require the procedural regularity and the exercise of care implied in the phrase "due process." Under our Constitution, the condition of being a boy does not justify a kangaroo court. The traditional ideas of Juvenile Court procedure, indeed, contemplated that time would be available and care would be used to establish precisely what the juvenile did and why he did it—was it a prank of adolescence or a brutal act threatening serious consequences to himself or society unless corrected? Under traditional notions, one would assume that in a case like that of Gerald Gault, where the juvenile appears to have a home, a working mother and father, and an older brother, the Juvenile Judge would have made a careful inquiry and judgment as to the possibility that the boy could be disciplined and dealt with at home, despite his previous transgressions. Indeed, so far as appears in the record before us, except for some conversation with Gerald about his school work and his "wanting to go to ... Grand Canyon with his father," the points to which the judge directed his attention were little different from those that would be involved in determining any charge of violation of a penal statute. The essential difference between Gerald's case and a normal criminal case is that safeguards available to adults were discarded in Gerald's case. The summary procedure as well as the long commitment was possible because Gerald was 15 years of age instead of over 18.

If Gerald had been over 18, he would not have been subject to Juvenile Court proceedings. For the particular offense immediately involved, the maximum punishment would have been a fine of $5 to $50, or imprisonment in jail for not more than two months. Instead, he was committed to custody for a maximum of six years. If he had been over 18 and had committed an offense to which such a sentence might apply, he would have been entitled to substantial rights under the Constitution of the United States as well as under Arizona's laws and constitution. The United States Constitution would guarantee him rights and protections with respect to arrest, search and seizure, and pretrial interrogation. It would assure him of specific notice of the charges and adequate time to decide his course of action and to prepare his defense. He would be entitled to clear advice that he could be represented by counsel, and, at least if a felony were involved, the State would be required to provide counsel if his parents were unable to afford it. If the court acted on the basis of his confession, careful procedures would be required to assure its voluntariness. If the case went to trial, confrontation and opportunity for cross-examination would be guaranteed. So wide a gulf between the State's treatment of the adult and of the child requires a bridge sturdier than mere verbiage, and reasons more persuasive than cliche can provide. As Wheeler and Cottrell have put it, "The rhetoric of the juvenile court movement has developed without any necessarily close correspondence to the realities of court and institutional routines."

Notice of Charges

Appellants allege that the Arizona Juvenile Code is unconstitutional or alternatively that the proceedings before the Juvenile Court were constitutionally defective because of failure to provide adequate notice of the hearings. No notice was given to Gerald's parents when he was taken into custody on Monday, June 8. On that night, when Mrs. Gault went to the Detention Home, she was orally informed that there would be a hearing the next afternoon and was told the reason why Gerald was in custody. The only written notice Gerald's parents received at any time was a note on plain paper from Officer Flagg delivered on Thursday or Friday, June 11 or 12, to the effect that the judge had set Monday, June 15, "for further hearings on Gerald's delinquency."

A "petition" was filed with the court on June 9 by Officer Flagg, reciting only that he was informed and believed that "said minor is a delinquent minor and that it is necessary that some order be made by the Honorable Court for said minor's welfare." The applicable Arizona statute provides for a petition to be filed in Juvenile Court, alleging in general terms that the child is "neglected, dependent or delinquent." The statute explicitly states that such a general allegation is sufficient, "without alleging the facts." There is no requirement that the petition be served and it was not served upon, given to, or shown to Gerald or his parents.

The Supreme Court of Arizona rejected appellants' claim that due process was denied because of inadequate notice. It stated that "Mrs. Gault knew the exact nature of the charge against Gerald from the day he was taken to the detention home." The court also pointed out that the Gaults appeared at the two hearings "without objection." The court held that because "the policy of the juvenile law is to hide youthful errors from the full gaze of the public and bury them in the graveyard of the forgotten past," advance notice of the specific charges or basis for taking the juvenile into custody and for the hearing is not necessary. It held that the appropriate rule is that "the infant and his parent or guardian will receive a petition only reciting a conclusion of delinquency. But no later than the initial hearing by the judge, they must be advised of the facts involved in the case. If the charges are denied, they must be given a reasonable period of time to prepare."

We cannot agree with the court's conclusion that adequate notice was given in this case. Notice, to comply with due process requirements, must be given sufficiently in advance of scheduled court proceedings so that reasonable opportunity to prepare will be afforded, and it must "set forth the alleged misconduct with particularity." It is obvious, as we have discussed above, that no purpose of shielding the child from the public stigma of knowledge of his having been taken into custody and scheduled for hearing is served by the procedure approved by the court below. The "initial hearing" in the present case was a hearing on the merits. Notice at that time is not timely; and even if there were a conceivable purpose served by the deferral proposed by the court below, it would have to yield to the requirements that the child and his parents or guardian be notified, in writing, of the specific charge or factual allegations to be considered at the hearing, and that such written notice be given at the earliest practicable time, and in any event sufficiently in advance of the hearing to permit preparation. Due process of law requires notice of the sort we have described—that is, notice which would be deemed constitutionally adequate in a civil or criminal proceeding. It does not allow a hearing to be held in which a youth's freedom and his parents' right to his custody are at stake without giving them timely notice, in advance of the hearing, of the specific issues that they must meet. Nor, in the circumstances of this case, can it reasonably be said that the requirement of notice was waived.

Right to Counsel

Appellants charge that the Juvenile Court proceedings were fatally defective because the court did not advise Gerald or his parents of their right to counsel, and proceeded with the hearing, the adjudication of delinquency and the order of commitment in the absence of counsel for the child and his parents or an express waiver of the right thereto. The Supreme Court of Arizona pointed out that "[t]here is disagreement [among the various jurisdictions] as to whether the court must advise the infant that he has a right to counsel."

The court argued that "the parent and the probation officer may be relied upon to protect the infant's interests." Accordingly it rejected the proposition that "due process requires that an infant have a right to counsel." We do not agree. Probation officers, in the Arizona scheme, are also arresting offers. The initiate proceedings and file petitions which they verify, as here, alleging the delinquency of the child; and they testify, as here, against the child. And here the probation officer was also superintendent of the Detention Home. The probation officer cannot act as counsel for the child. His role in the adjudicatory hearing, by statute and in fact, is as arresting officer and witness against the child. Nor can the judge represent the child. There is no material difference in this respect between adult and juvenile proceedings of the sort here involved. In adult proceedings, this contention has been foreclosed by decisions of this Court. A proceeding where the issue is whether the child will be found to be "delinquent" and subjected to the loss of his liberty for years is comparable in seriousness to a felony prosecution. The juvenile needs the assistance of counsel to cope with problems of law, to make skilled inquiry into the facts, to insist upon regularity of the proceedings, and to ascertain whether he has a defense and to prepare and submit it. The child "requires the guiding hand of counsel at every step in the proceedings against him."

Confrontation, Self-incrimination, Cross-examination

Appellants urge that the writ of habeas corpus should have been granted because of the denial of the rights of confrontation and cross-examination in the Juvenile Court hearings, and because the privilege against self-incrimination was not observed. The Juvenile Court Judge testified at the habeas corpus hearing that he had proceeded on the basis of Gerald's admissions at the two hearings. Appellants attack this on the ground that the admissions were obtained in disregard of the privilege against self-incrimination. If the confession is disregarded, appellants argue that the delinquency conclusion, since it was fundamentally based on a finding that Gerald had made lewd remarks during the phone call to Mrs. Cook, is fatally defective for failure to accord the rights of confrontation and cross-examination which the Due Process Clause of the Fourteenth Amendment of the Federal Constitution guarantees in state proceedings generally.

We conclude that the constitutional privilege against self-incrimination is applicable in the case of juveniles as it is with respect to adults. We appreciate that special problems may arise with respect to waiver of the privilege by or on behalf of children, and that there may well be some differences in technique—but not in principle—depending upon the age of the child and the presence and competence of parents. The participation of counsel will, of course, assist the police, Juvenile Courts and appellate tribunals in administering the privilege. If counsel was not present for some permissible reason when an admission was obtained, the greatest care must be taken to assure that the admission was voluntary, in the sense not only that it was not coerced or suggested, but also that it was not the product of ignorance of rights or of adolescent fantasy, fright or despair.

The "confession" of Gerald Gault was first obtained by Officer Flagg, out of the presence of Gerald's parents, without counsel and without advising him of his right to silence, as far as it appears. The judgment of the Juvenile Court was stated by the judge to be based on Gerald's admissions in court. Neither "admission" was reduced to writing, and, to say the least, the process by which the "admissions" were obtained and received must be characterized as lacking the certainty and order which are required of proceedings of such formidable consequences. Apart from the "admissions," there was nothing upon which a judgment or finding might be based. There was no sworn testimony. Mrs. Cook, the complainant, was not present. The Arizona Supreme Court held that "sworn testimony must be required of all witnesses including police officers, probation officers and others who are part of or officially related to the juvenile court structure." We hold that this is not enough. No reason is suggested or appears for a different rule in respect of sworn testimony in juvenile courts than in adult tribunals. Absent a valid confession adequate to support the determination of the Juvenile Court, confrontation and sworn testimony by witnesses available for cross-examination were essential for a finding of "delinquency" and an order committing Gerald to a state institution for a maximum of six years.

Appellate Review and Transcript of Proceedings

Appellants urge that the Arizona statute is unconstitutional under the Due Process Clause because, as construed by its Supreme Court, "there is no right of appeal from a juvenile court order. . . ." The court held that there is no right to a transcript because there is no right to appeal and because the proceedings are confidential and any record must be destroyed after a prescribed period of time. Whether a transcript or other recording is made, it held, is a matter for the discretion of the juvenile court.

The Court has not held that a State is required by the Federal Constitution "to provide appellate courts or a right to appellate review at all." In view of the fact that we must reverse the Supreme Court of Arizona's affirmance of the dismissal of the writ of habeas corpus for other reasons, we need not rule on this question in the present case or upon the failure to provide a transcript or recording of the hearings.

Mr. Justice Black, Concurring

The juvenile court planners envisaged a system that would practically immunize juveniles from "punishment" for "crimes" in an effort to save them from youthful indiscretions and stigmas due to criminal charges or convictions. I agree with the Court, however, that this exalted ideal has failed of achievement since the beginning of the system. Indeed, the state laws from the first one on contained provisions, written in emphatic terms, for arresting and charging juveniles with violations of state criminal laws, as well as for taking juveniles by force of law away from their parents and turning them over to different individuals or groups or for confinement within some state school or institution for a number of years. The latter occurred in this case. Young Gault was arrested and detained on a charge of violating an Arizona penal law by using vile and offensive language to a lady on the telephone. If an adult, he could only have been fined or imprisoned for two months for his conduct. As a juvenile, however, he was put through a more or less secret, informal hearing by the court, after which he was ordered, or, more realistically, "sentenced," to confinement in Arizona's Industrial School until he reaches 21 years of age. Thus, in a juvenile system designed to lighten or avoid punishment for criminality, he was ordered by the State to six years' confinement in what is in all but name a penitentiary or jail.

Where a person, infant or adult, can be seized by the State, charged, and convicted for violating a state criminal law, and then ordered by the State to be confined for six years, I think the Constitution requires that he be tried in accordance with the guarantees of all the provisions of the Bill of Rights made applicable to the States by the Fourteenth Amendment.

Mr. Justice Stewart, Dissenting

Juvenile proceedings are not criminal trials. They are not civil trials. They are simply not adversary proceedings. Whether treating with a delinquent child, a neglected child, a defective child, or a dependent child, a juvenile proceedings' whole purpose and mission is the very opposite of the mission and purpose of a prosecution in a criminal court. The object of the one is corrections of a condition. The object of the other is conviction and punishment for a criminal act.

In the last 70 years many dedicated men and women have devoted their professional lives to the enlightened task of bringing us out of the dark world of Charles Dickens in meeting our responsibilities to the child in our society. The result has been the creation in this century of a system of juvenile and family courts in each of the 50 States. There can by no denying that in many areas the performance of these agencies has fallen disappointingly short of the hopes and dreams of the courageous pioneers who first conceived them. For a variety of reasons, the reality has sometimes not even approached the ideal, and much remains to be accomplished in the administration of public juvenile and family agencies—in personnel, in planning, in financing, perhaps in the formulation of wholly new approaches.

I possess neither the specialized experience nor the expert knowledge to predict with any certainty where may lie the brightest hope for progress in dealing with the serious problems of juvenile delinquency. But I am certain that the answer does not lie in the Court's opinion in this case, which serves to convert a juvenile proceeding into a criminal prosecution. ✦

5
New Jersey v. T.L.O.

Supreme Court of the United States

Argued March 28, 1984, Reargued Oct. 2, 1984—Decided Jan. 15, 1985

On March 7, 1980, a teacher at Piscataway High School in Middlesex County, N.J., discovered two girls smoking in a lavatory. One of the two girls was the respondent T.L.O., who at that time was a 14-year-old high school freshman. Because smoking in the lavatory was a violation of a school rule, the teacher took the two girls to the Principal's office, where they met with Assistant Vice Principal Theodore Choplick. In response to questioning by Mr. Choplick, T.L.O.'s companion admitted that she had violated the rule. T.L.O., however, denied that she had been smoking in the lavatory and claimed that she did not smoke at all.

Mr. Choplick asked T.L.O. to come into his private office and demanded to see her purse. Opening the purse, he found a pack of cigarettes, which he removed from the purse and held before T.L.O. as he accused her of having lied to him. As he reached into the purse for the cigarettes, Mr. Choplick also noticed a package of cigarette rolling papers. In his experience, possession of rolling papers by high school students was closely associated with the use of marihuana. Suspecting that a closer examination of the purse might yield further evidence of drug use, Mr. Choplick proceeded to search the purse thoroughly. The search revealed a small amount of marihuana, a pipe, a number of empty plastic bags, a substantial quantity of money in one-dollar bills, an index card that appeared to be a list of students who owed T.L.O. money, and two letters that implicated T.L.O. in marihuana dealing.

Mr. Choplick notified T.L.O.'s mother and the police, and turned the evidence of drug dealing over to the police. At the request of the police, T.L.O.'s mother took her daughter to police headquarters, where T.L.O. confessed that she had been selling marihuana at the high school. On the basis of the confession and the evidence seized by Mr. Choplick, the State brought delinquency charges against T.L.O. in the Juvenile and Domestic Relations Court of Middlesex County. Contending that Mr. Choplick's search of her purse violated the Fourth Amendment, T.L.O. moved to suppress the evidence found in her purse as well as her confession, which, she argued, was tainted by the allegedly unlawful search. The Juvenile Court denied the motion to suppress (*State ex rel. T.L.O.*, 178 N.J.Super. 329, 428 A.2d 1327, [1980]). Although the court concluded that the Fourth Amendment did apply to searches carried out by school officials, it held that

> a school official may properly conduct a search of a student's person if the official has a reasonable suspicion that a crime has been or is in the process of being committed, *or* reasonable cause to believe that the search is necessary to maintain school discipline or enforce school policies.

(*Id.*, 178 N.J.Super., at 341, 428 A.2d, at 1333 [emphasis in original])

Applying this standard, the court concluded that the search conducted by Mr. Choplick was a reasonable one. The initial decision to open the purse was justified by Mr. Choplick's well-founded suspicion that T.L.O. had violated the rule forbidding smoking in the lavatory. Once the purse was open, evidence of marihuana violations was in plain view, and Mr. Choplick was entitled to conduct a thorough search to determine the nature and extent of T.L.O.'s drug-related activities (*Id.*, 178 N.J. Super., at 343, 428 A.2d, at 1334). Having denied the motion to suppress, the court on March 23, 1981, found T.L.O. to be a delinquent and on January 8, 1982, sentenced her to a year's probation.

From 105 S. Ct. 733 (1985).

On appeal from the final judgment of the Juvenile Court, a divided Appellate Division affirmed the trial court's finding that there had been no Fourth Amendment violation, but vacated the adjudication of delinquency and remanded for a determination whether T.L.O. had knowingly and voluntarily waived her Fifth Amendment rights before confessing (*State ex rel. T.L.O.*, 185 N.J. Super. 279, 448 A.2d 493 [1982]). T.L.O. appealed the Fourth Amendment ruling, and the Supreme Court of New Jersey reversed the judgment of the Appellate Division and ordered the suppression of the evidence found in T.L.O.'s purse (*State ex rel. T.L.O.*, 94 N.J. 331, 463 A.2d 934 [1983]).

The New Jersey Supreme Court agreed with the lower courts that the Fourth Amendment applies to searches conducted by school officials. The court also rejected the State of New Jersey's argument that the exclusionary rule should not be employed to prevent the use in juvenile proceedings of evidence unlawfully seized by school officials. Declining to consider whether applying the rule to the fruits of searches by school officials would have any deterrent value, the court held simply that the precedents of this Court establish that "if an official search violates constitutional rights, the evidence is not admissible in criminal proceedings" (*Id.*, 94 N.J., at 341, 463 A.2d, at 939 [footnote omitted]).

With respect to the question of the legality of the search before it, the court agreed with the Juvenile Court that a warrantless search by a school official does not violate the Fourth Amendment so long as the official "has reasonable grounds to believe that a student possesses evidence of illegal activity or activity that would interfere with school discipline and order" (*Id.*, 94 N.J., at 346, 463 A.2d, at 941-942). However, the court, with two justices dissenting, sharply disagreed with the Juvenile Court's conclusion that the search of the purse was reasonable. According to the majority, the contents of T.L.O.'s purse had no bearing on the accusation against T.L.O., for possession of cigarettes (as opposed to smoking them in the lavatory) did not violate school rules, and a mere desire for evidence that would impeach T.L.O.'s claim that she did not smoke cigarettes could not justify the search. Moreover, even if a reasonable suspicion that T.L.O. had cigarettes in her purse would justify a search, Mr. Choplick had no such suspicion, as no one had furnished him with any specific information that there were cigarettes in the purse. Finally, leaving aside the question whether Mr. Choplick was justified in opening the purse, the court held that the evidence of drug use that he saw inside did not justify the extensive "rummaging" through T.L.O.'s papers and effects that followed (*Id.*, 94 N.J., at 347, 463 A.2d, at 942-943).

We granted the State of New Jersey's petition for certiorari (464 U.S. 991, 104 S.Ct. 480, 78 L.Ed.2d 678 [1983]). Although the State had argued in the Supreme Court of New Jersey that the search of T.L.O.'s purse did not violate the Fourth Amendment the petition for certiorari raised only the question whether the exclusionary rule should operate to bar consideration in juvenile delinquency proceedings of evidence unlawfully seized by a school official without the involvement of law enforcement officers. When this case was first argued last Term, the State conceded for the purpose of argument that the standard devised by the New Jersey Supreme Court for determining the legality of school searches was appropriate and that the court had correctly applied that standard; the State contended only that the remedial purposes of the exclusionary rule were not well served by applying it to searches conducted by public authorities not primarily engaged in law enforcement.

Although we originally granted certiorari to decide the issue of the appropriate remedy in juvenile court proceedings for unlawful school searches, our doubts regarding the wisdom of deciding that question in isolation from the broader question of what limits, if any, the Fourth Amendment places on the activities of school authorities prompted us to order reargument on that question. Having heard argument on the legality of the search of T.L.O.'s purse, we are satisfied that the search did not violate the Fourth Amendment.

II.

[1] In determining whether the search at issue in this case violated the Fourth Amendment, we are faced initially with the question whether that Amendment's prohibition on unreasonable searches and seizures applies to searches conducted by public school officials. We hold that it does.

[2] It is now beyond dispute that "the Federal Constitution, by virtue of the Fourteenth Amendment, prohibits unreasonable searches and seizures by state officers." Equally indisputable is the proposition that the Fourteenth Amendment protects the rights of students against encroachment by public school officials:

> The Fourteenth Amendment, as now applied to the States, protects the citizen against the State itself and all of its creatures—Boards of Education not excepted. These have, of course, important, delicate, and highly discretionary functions, but none that they may not perform within the limits of the Bill of Rights. That they are educating the young for citizenship is reason for scrupulous protection of Constitutional freedoms of the individual, if we are not to strangle the free mind at its source and teach youth to discount important principles of our government as mere platitudes.

(*West Virginia State Bd. of Ed. v. Barnette*, 319 U.S. 624, 637, 63 S.Ct. 1178, 1185, 87 L.Ed. 1628 [1943])

These two proposition—that the Fourth Amendment applies to the States through the Fourteenth Amendment, and that the actions of public school officials are subject to the limits placed on state action by the Fourteenth Amendment—might appear sufficient to answer the suggestion that the Fourth Amendment does not proscribe unreasonable searches by school officials. On reargument, however, the State of New Jersey has argued that the history of the Fourth Amendment indicates that the Amendment was intended to regulate only searches and seizures carried out by law enforcement officers; accordingly, although public school officials are concededly state agents for purposes of the Fourteenth Amendment, the Fourth Amendment creates no rights enforceable against them.

Against the child's interest in privacy must be set the substantial interest of teachers and administrators in maintaining discipline in the classroom and on school grounds. Maintaining order in the classroom has never been easy, but in recent years, school disorder has often taken particularly ugly forms: drug use and violent crime in the schools have become major social problems (See generally 1 NIE, U.S. Dept. of Health, Education and Welfare, Violent Schools—Safe Schools: The Safe School Study Report to the Congress [1978]). Even in schools that have been spared the most severe disciplinary problems, the preservation of order and a proper educational environment requires close supervision of schoolchildren, as well as the enforcement of rules against conduct that would be perfectly permissible if undertaken by an adult. "Events calling for discipline are frequent occurrences and sometimes require immediate, effective action" (*Goss v. Lopez*, 419 U.S., at 580, 95 S.Ct., at 739). Accordingly, we have recognized that maintaining security and order in the schools requires a certain degree of flexibility in school disciplinary procedures, and we have respected the value of preserving the informality of the student-teacher relationship (See *id.*, at 582-583, 95 S.Ct., at 740; *Ingraham v. Wright*, 430 U.S., at 680-682, 97 S.Ct., at 1417-1418).

How, then, should we strike the balance between the schoolchild's legitimate expectations of privacy and the school's equally legitimate need to maintain an environment in which learning can take place? It is evident that the school setting requires some easing of the restrictions to which searches by public authorities are ordinarily subject. The warrant requirement, in particular, is unsuited to the school environment; requiring a teacher to obtain a warrant before searching a child suspected of an infraction of school rules (or of the criminal law) would unduly interfere with the maintenance of the swift and informal disciplinary procedures needed in the schools. Just as we have in other cases dispensed with the warrant requirement when "the burden of obtaining a warrant is likely to frustrate the governmental purpose behind the search" (*Camara v. Municipal Court*, 387 U.S., at 532-533, 87 S.Ct., at 1733), we hold today that school officials need not obtain a warrant before searching a student who is under their authority.

[9] There remains the question of the legality of the search in this case. We recognize that the "reasonable grounds" standard applied by the New Jersey Supreme Court in its consideration of this question is not substantially different from the standard that we have adopted today. Nonetheless, we believe that the New Jersey court's application of that standard to strike down the search of T.L.O.'s purse reflects a somewhat crabbed notion of reasonableness. Our review of the facts surrounding the search leads us to conclude that the search was in no sense unreasonable for Fourth Amendment purposes.

The incident that gave rise to this case actually involved two separate searches, with the first—the search for cigarettes—providing the suspicion that gave rise to the second—the search for marihuana. Although it is the fruits of the second search that are at issue here, the validity of the search for marihuana must depend on the reasonableness of the initial search for cigarettes, as there would have been no reason to suspect that T.L.O. possessed marihuana had the first search not taken place. Accordingly, it is to the search for cigarettes that we first turn our attention.

The New Jersey Supreme Court pointed to two grounds for its holding that the search for cigarettes was unreasonable. First, the court observed that possession of cigarettes was not in itself illegal or a violation of school rules. Because the contents of T.L.O.'s purse would therefore have "no direct bearing on the infraction" of which she was accused (smoking in a lavatory where smoking was prohibited), there was no reason to search her purse. Second, even assuming that a search of T.L.O.'s purse might under some circumstances be reasonable in light of the accusation made against T.L.O., the New Jersey court concluded that Mr. Choplick in this particular case had no reasonable grounds to suspect that T.L.O. had cigarettes in her purse. At best, according to the court, Mr. Choplick has "a good hunch" (94 N.J., at 347, 463 A.2d, at 942).

[10] Both these conclusions are implausible. T.L.O. had been accused of smoking, and had denied the accusation in the strongest possible terms when she stated that she did not smoke at all. Surely it cannot be said that under these circumstances, T.L.O.'s possession of cigarettes would be irrelevant to the charges against her or to her response to those charges. T.L.O.'s possession of cigarettes, once it was discovered, would both corroborate the report that she had been smoking and undermine the credibility of her defense to the charge of smoking. To be sure, the discovery of the cigarettes would not prove that T.L.O. had been smoking in the lavatory; nor would it, strictly speaking, necessarily be inconsistent with her claim that she did not smoke at all. But it is universally recognized that evidence, to be relevant to an inquiry, need not conclusively prove the ultimate fact in issue, but only have "any tendency to make the existence of any fact that is of consequence to the determination of the action more probable or less probable than it would be without the evidence" (Fed. Rule Evid. 401). The relevance of T.L.O.'s possession of cigarettes to the question whether she had been smoking and to the credibility of her denial that she smoked supplied the necessary "nexus" between the item searched for and the infraction under investigation (See *Warden v. Hayden*, 387 U.S. 294, 306-307, 87 S.Ct. 1642, 1649-1650, 18 L.Ed.2d 782 [1967]). Thus, if Mr. Choplick in fact had a reasonable suspicion that T.L.O. had cigarettes in her purse, the search was justified despite the fact that the cigarettes, if found, would constitute "mere evidence" of a violation (*Ibid.*).

[12] Our conclusion that Mr. Choplick's decision to open T.L.O.'s purse was reasonable brings us to the question of the further search for marihuana once the pack of cigarettes was located. The suspicion upon which the search for marihuana was founded was provided when Mr. Choplick observed

a package of rolling papers in the purse as he removed the pack of cigarettes. Although T.L.O. does not dispute the reasonableness of Mr. Choplick's belief that the rolling papers indicated the presence of marihuana, she does contend that the scope of the search Mr. Choplick conducted exceeded permissible bounds when he seized and read certain letters that implicated T.L.O. in drug dealing. This argument, too, is unpersuasive. The discovery of the rolling papers concededly gave rise to a reasonable suspicion that T.L.O. was carrying marihuana as well as cigarettes in her purse. This suspicion justified further exploration of T.L.O.'s purse, which turned up more evidence of drug-related activities: a pipe, a number of plastic bags of the type commonly used to store marihuana, a small quantity of marihuana, and a fairly substantial amount of money. Under these circumstances, it was not unreasonable to extend the search to a separate zippered compartment of the purse; and when a search of that compartment revealed an index card containing a list of "people who owe me money" as well as two letters, the inference that T.L.O. was involved in marihuana trafficking was substantial enough to justify Mr. Choplick in examining the letters to determine whether they contained any further evidence. In short, we cannot conclude that the search for marihuana was unreasonable in any respect.

Because the search resulting in the discovery of the evidence of marihuana dealing by T.L.O. was reasonable, the New Jersey Supreme Court's decision to exclude that evidence from T.L.O.'s juvenile delinquency proceedings on Fourth Amendment grounds was erroneous. Accordingly, the judgment of the Supreme Court of New Jersey is *Reversed.* ✦

6
Elizabeth Qutb et al. v. Annette Strauss et al. v. Steve Bartlett et al.

United States Court of Appeals, Fifth Circuit

November 19, 1993

I.

On June 12, 1991, in response to citizens' demands for protection of the city's youth, the Dallas City Council enacted a juvenile curfew ordinance. This ordinance prohibits persons under seventeen years of age from remaining in a public place or establishment from 11 p.m. until 6 a.m. on week nights, and from 12 midnight until 6 a.m. on weekends. As defined by the ordinance, a "public place" is any place to which the public or a substantial group of the public has access, and includes streets, highways, and the common areas of schools, hospitals, apartment houses, office buildings, transport facilities, and shops. "Establishment" is defined as "any privately-owned place of business operated for a profit to which the public is invited, including but not limited to any place of amusement or entertainment."

Although the ordinance restricts the hours when minors are allowed in public areas, the ordinance also contains a number of exceptions, or defenses. A person under the age of seventeen in a public place during curfew hours does not violate the ordinance if he or she is accompanied by a parent or guardian, or is on an errand for a parent or guardian. Likewise, minors would be allowed in public places if they are in a motor vehicle traveling to or from a place of employment, or if they are involved in employment related activities. Affected minors could attend school, religious, or civic organizational functions—or generally exercise their First Amendment speech and associational rights—without violating the ordinance. Nor is it a violation to engage in interstate travel, or remain on a sidewalk in front of the minor's home, or the home of a neighbor. And finally, the ordinance places no restrictions on a minor's ability to move about during curfew hours in the case of an emergency.

A minor violates the curfew if he or she remains in any public place or on the premises of any establishment during curfew hours, and if the minors' activities are not exempted from coverage. If a minor is apparently violating the ordinance, the ordinance requires police officers to ask the age of the apparent offender, and to inquire into the reasons for being in a public place during curfew hours before taking any enforcement action. An officer may issue a citation or arrest the apparent offender only if the officer reasonable believes that the person has violated the ordinance and that no defenses apply. If convicted, an offending party is subject to a fine not to exceed $500.00 for each separate offense.

Like minors who have violated the offense, a parent of a minor, or an owner, operator, or employee of a business establishment is also subject to a fine not to exceed $500 for each separate offense. A parent or guardian of a minor violates the ordinance if he or she knowingly permits, or by insufficient control allows, a minor child to remain in any public place or on the premises of any establishment during curfew hours. An owner, operator, or employee of a business establishment commits an offense by knowingly allowing a minor to remain upon the premises of the establishment during curfew hours.

II.

On July 3, 1991, two weeks after the ordinance was enacted, Elizabeth Qutb and three other parents filed suit—both indi-

---

From 11 F.3d 488 (5th Cir. 1993).

vidually and as next friends of their teenage children—seeking a temporary restraining order and a permanent injunction against the enforcement of the juvenile curfew ordinance on the basis that the ordinance is unconstitutional. The district court certified the plaintiffs as a class that consisted of two subclasses: persons under the age of seventeen, and parents of persons under the age of seventeen. One week later, the court advanced the trial on the merits, and consolidated the trial with the hearing on the plaintiffs' request for temporary and permanent injunctions. The case was tried on July 22-23, and the district court denied the plaintiffs' request for a temporary injunction. The city, however, voluntarily delayed enforcement of the curfew pending the district court's decision on the merits.

On June 12, 1992, before the district court issued its final order on the merits of the case, the city voluntarily amended the curfew ordinance. the amended ordinance deleted or altered some of the provisions of which the plaintiffs complained, while expanding some of the defenses available to affected minors. In response to the revised ordinance, the plaintiffs filed an amended complaint and an amended motion for a permanent injunction against enforcement of the curfew. The district court held a second evidentiary hearing, where both parties presented additional evidence and arguments concerning validity of the revised ordinance under the United States and Texas constitutions. On August 10, 1992, the district court held that the curfew impermissibly restricted minors' First Amendment right to associate, and that it created classifications that could not withstand constitutional scrutiny. Accordingly, the district court permanently enjoined enforcement of the curfew, and the city now appeals.

III.

A.

[1,2] We review *de novo* the district court's conclusions of constitutional law (*Peyote Way Church of God, Inc. v. Thornburgh*, 922 F.2d 1210, 1213 [5th Cir. 1991]; *Shillingford v. Holmes*, 634 F.2d 263, 266 [5th Cir.1981]). The minor plaintiffs argue, *inter alia*, that the curfew ordinance violates the Equal Protection Clause of the Fourteenth Amendment. The Equal Protection Clause "is essentially a direction that all persons similarly situated should be treated alike" (*City of Cleburne v. Cleburne Living Ctr., Inc.*, 473 U.S. 432, 439, 105 S.Ct. 3249, 3254, 87 L.Ed.2d 313 [1985]). Only if the challenged government action classifies or distinguishes between two or more relevant groups must we conduct an equal protection inquiry (*Brennan v. Stewart*, 834 F.2d 1248, 1257 [5th Cir.1988]). Here, it is clear that the curfew ordinance distinguishes between classes of individuals on the basis on age, treating those persons under the age of seventeen differently from those persons age seventeen and older. Because the curfew ordinance distinguishes between two groups, we must analyze the curfew ordinance under the Equal Protection Clause.

[3,4] Under the Equal Protection analysis, we apply different standards of review depending upon the right or classification involved. If a classification disadvantages a "suspect class" or impinges upon a "fundamental right," the ordinance is subject to strict scrutiny. Under the strict scrutiny standard, we accord the classification no presumption of constitutionality (*Town of Ball v. Rapides Parish Police Jury*, 746 F.2d 1049, 1059 [5th Cir. 1984]). Instead, we ask whether the classification promotes a compelling governmental interest and, if so, whether the ordinance is narrowly tailored such that there are no less restrictive means available to effectuate the desired end (*Pugh v. Rainwater*, 557 F.2d 1189, 1195 [5th Cir.1977], *vacated on other grounds*, 572 F.2d 1053 [5th Cir. 1978]).

In this case, no one has argued, and correctly so, that a classification based on age is a suspect classification (*See Gregory v. Ashcroft*, ___U.S. ___, ___, 111 S.Ct. 2395, 2406, 115 L.Ed.2d 410 [1991] [holding that age is not a suspect class]). the minor plaintiffs, however, have argued that the curfew ordinance impinges upon their "fundamental right" to move about freely in public. For purposes of our analysis, we assume without deciding that the right to move about freely is a fundamental right. We are mindful, however, that this ordinance is directed solely at the activities of juveniles and, under certain circumstances, minors may be treated differently from adults.

B.

[5] Because we assume that the curfew impinges upon a fundamental right, we will now subject the ordinance to strict scrutiny review. As stated earlier, to survive strict scrutiny, a classification created by the ordinance must promote a compelling governmental interest, and it must be narrowly tailored to achieve this interest (*Plyler v. Doe*, 457 U.S. at 216-17, 102 S.Ct. at 2394-95). The city's stated interest in enacting the ordinance is to reduce juvenile crime and victimization, while promoting juvenile safety and well-being. The Supreme Court has recognized that the state "has a strong and legitimate interest in the welfare of its young citizens, whose immaturity, inexperience, and lack of judgment may sometimes impair their ability to exercise their rights wisely" (*Hodgson v. Minnesota*, 497 U.S. 417, 444, 110 S.Ct. 2926, 2942, 111 L.Ed.2d 344 [1990]). In this case, the plaintiffs concede and the district court held that the state's interest in this case is compelling. Given the fact that the state's interest is elevated by the minority status of the affected persons, we have no difficulty agreeing with the parties and with the district court.

In the light of the state's compelling interest in increasing juvenile safety and decreasing juvenile crime, we must now determine whether the curfew ordinance is narrowly tailored to achieve that interest. The district court held that the city "totally failed to establish that the ordinance's classification between minors and non-minors is narrowly tailored to achieve the stated goals of the curfew." We disagree.

The articulated purpose of the curfew ordinance enacted by the city of Dallas is to protect juveniles from harm, and to reduce juvenile crime and violence occurring in the city. The ordinance's distinction based upon age furthers these objectives. Before the district court, the city presented the following statistical information:

1. Juvenile crime increases proportionally with age between ten years old and sixteen years old.
2. In 1989, Dallas recorded 5,160 juvenile arrests, while in 1990 there were 5,425 juvenile arrests. In 1990 there were forty murders, ninety-one sex offenses, 233 robberies, and 230 aggravated assaults committed by juveniles. From January 1991 through April 1991, juveniles were arrested for twenty-one murders, thirty sex offenses, 128 robberies, 107 aggravated assaults, and 1,042 crimes against property.
3. Murders are most likely to occur between 10:00 p.m. and 1:00 a.m. and most likely to occur in apartments and apartment parking lots and streets and highways.
4. Aggravated assaults are most likely to occur between 11:00 p.m. and 1:00 a.m.
5. Rapes are most likely to occur between 1:00 a.m. and 3:00 a.m. and sixteen percent of rapes occur on public streets and highways.
6. Thirty-one percent of robberies occur on streets and highways.

Although the city was unable to provide precise data concerning the number of juveniles who commit crimes during the curfew hours, or the number of juvenile victims of crimes committed during the curfew, the city nonetheless provided sufficient data to demonstrate that the classification created by the ordinance "fits" the state's compelling interest.

Furthermore, we are convinced that this curfew ordinance also employs the least restrictive means of accomplishing its goals. The ordinance contains various "defenses" that allow affected minors to remain in public areas during curfew hours. Although the district court concluded that "[i]t is what the Ordinance restricts . . . and not what it exempts that matters the most," it is clear to us that neither the restrictions of the curfew ordinance nor its defenses can be viewed in isolation from each other; the ordinance can be examined fairly only when the defenses are considered as a part of the whole. To be sure, the defenses are the most important consideration in determining whether this ordinance is narrowly tailored.

In the past, curfew ordinances have been held unconstitutional because of their broad general applications. (In *Johnson v. City of Opelousas*, 658 F.2d 1065, 1074 [5th Cir. 1981]). Furthermore, we stated that "[w]e express no opinion on validity of curfew ordinances narrowly drawn to accomplish property social objectives" (*Id.* at 1072). In declaring the *Johnson* ordinance to be an undue burden on the rights of minors, we noted that:

> [U]nder this curfew ordinance minors are prohibited from attending associational activities such as religious or school meetings, organized dances, and theater and sporting events, when reasonable and direct travel to or from these activities has to be made during the curfew period. The same inhibition prohibits parents from urging and consenting to such protected associational activity by their minor children. The curfew ordinance also prohibits a minor during the curfew period from, for example, being on the sidewalk in front of his house, engaging in legitimate employment, or traveling through [the city] even on an interstate trip. These implicit prohibitions of the curfew ordinance overtly and manifestly infringe upon the constitutional rights of minors in [the city]. (*Id.*)

We therefore concluded that the "curfew ordinance, *however valid might be a narrowly drawn curfew to protect society's valid interests*, [swept] within its ambit a number of innocent activities which are constitutionally protected" (*Id.* at 1074 [emphasis added]). In *Johnson*, we further stated that

> [r]egardless of the legitimacy of [the city's] stated purposes of protecting youths, reducing nocturnal juvenile crime, and promoting parental control over their children, less drastic means are available for achieving these goals. *Since the absence of exceptions in the curfew ordinance precludes a narrowing construction,* we are compelled to rule that the ordinance is constitutionally overbroad. (*Id.* [emphasis added])

With the ordinance before us today, the city of Dallas has created a nocturnal juvenile curfew that satisfies strict scrutiny. By including the defenses to a violation of the ordinance, the city has enacted a narrowly drawn ordinance that allows the city to meet its stated goals while respecting the rights of the affected minors. As the city points out, a juvenile may move about freely in Dallas if accompanied by a parent or a guardian, or a person at least eighteen years of age who is authorized by a parent or guardian to have custody of the minor. If the juvenile is traveling interstate, returning from a school-sponsored function, a civic organization-sponsored function, or a religious function, or going home after work, the ordinance does not apply. If the juvenile is on an errand for his or her parent or guardian, the ordinance does not apply. If the juvenile is involved in an emergency, the ordinance does not apply. If the juvenile is on a sidewalk in front of his or her home *or* the home of a neighbor, the ordinance does not apply. Most notably, if the juvenile is exercising his or her First Amendment rights, the curfew ordinance does not apply.

[7,8] In addition to the claims presented by the minor plaintiffs, the parental plaintiffs argue that the curfew ordinance violates their fundamental right of privacy because it dictates the manner in which their children must be raised. Although we recognize that a parent's right to rear their children without undue governmental interference is a fundamental component of due process (see, e.g., *Ginsberg v. New York*, 390 U.S. at 639, 88 S.Ct. at 1279), we are convinced that this ordinance presents only a minimal intrusion into the parents' rights. In fact, the only aspect of parenting that this ordinance bears upon is the parents' right to allow the minor to remain in public places, unaccompanied by a parent or guardian or other authorized person, during the hours restricted by the curfew ordinance. Because of the broad exemptions included in the curfew ordinance, the parent retains the right to make decisions regarding his or her child in all other areas: the parent may allow the minor to remain in public so long as the minor is accompa-

nied by a parent or guardian, or a person at least eighteen years of age who is authorized by a parent or guardian to have custody of the minor. The parent may allow the minor to attend all activities organized by groups such as church groups, civic organizations, schools, or the city of Dallas. The parent may still allow the child to hold a job, to perform an errand for the parent, and to seek help in emergency situations.

IV.

In conclusion, we find that the state has demonstrated that the curfew ordinance furthers a compelling state interest, *i.e.*, protecting juveniles from crime on the streets. We further conclude that the ordinance is narrowly tailored to achieve this compelling state interest. Accordingly, we hold that the nocturnal juvenile curfew ordinance enacted by the city of Dallas is constitutional. The judgment of the district court is therefore *Reversed*. ✦

7
In re Gault Revisited: A Cross-State Comparison of the Right to Counsel in Juvenile Court

Barry C. Feld

More than twenty years ago in *In re Gault*, the U.S. Supreme Court held that juvenile offenders were constitutionally entitled to the assistance of counsel in juvenile delinquency proceedings. The *Gault* Court mandated the right to counsel because "a proceeding where the issue is whether the child will be found to be "delinquent" and subjected to the loss of his liberty for years is comparable in seriousness to a felony prosecution" (*Gault*, 1967, p. 36). Gault also decided that juveniles were entitled to the privilege against self-incrimination and the right to confront and cross-examine their accusers at a hearing. Without the assistance of counsel, these other rights could be negated. "The juvenile needs the assistance of counsel to cope with problems of law, to make skilled inquiry into the facts, [and] to insist upon regularity of the proceedings. . . . The child 'requires the guiding hand of counsel at every step in the proceedings against him'" (*Gault*, 1967, p. 36). In subsequent opinions, the Supreme Court has reiterated the crucial role of counsel in the juvenile justice process. In *Fare v. Michael C.*, the Court noted that "the lawyer occupies a critical position in our legal system. . . . Whether it is a minor or an adult who stands accused, the lawyer is the one person to whom society as a whole looks as the protector of the legal rights of that person in his dealings with the police and the courts" (*Fare*, 1979, p. 719).

In the two decades since *Gault*, the promise of counsel remains unrealized. Although there is a scarcity of data, in many states less than 50% of juveniles adjudicated delinquent receive the assistance of counsel to which they are constitutionally entitled (Feld, 1984, pp. 187-190). Although national statistics are not available, surveys of representation by counsel in several jurisdictions suggest that "there is reason to think that lawyers still appear much less often than might have been expected" (Horowitz, 1977, p. 185).

In the immediate aftermath of *Gault*, Lefstein, Stapleton, and Teitelbaum (1969) examined institutional compliance with the decision and found that juveniles were neither adequately advised of their right to counsel nor had counsel appointed for them. In a more recent evaluation of legal representation in North Carolina, Clarke and Koch (1980, p.297) found that the juvenile defender project represented only 22.3% of juveniles in Winston-Salem, NC, and only 45.8% in Charlotte, NC. Aday (1986) found rates of representation of 26.2% and 38.7% in the jurisdictions he studied. Bortner's (1982, p. 139) evaluation of a large, midwestern county's juvenile court showed that "over half (58.2%) [the juveniles] were not represented by an attorney." Evaluations of rates of representation in Minnesota also indicated that a majority of youths are unrepresented (Feld, 1984, p. 189; Fine, 1983, p. 48). Feld (1984, p. 190) reported enormous county-by-county variations within the state in the rates of representation, ranging from a high of over 90% to a low of less than 10%. A substantial minority of youths removed from their homes or confined in state juvenile correctional institutions lacked representation at the time of their adjudication and disposition (Feld, 1984, p. 189).

There are a variety of possible explanations for why so many youths appear to be unrepresented: parental reluctance to re-

From *Crime and Delinquency*, Volume 34, Number 4 (October 1988), pp. 393-424. Copyright © 1988 by Sage Publications, Inc. Reprinted by permission.

tain an attorney; inadequate public defender legal services in nonurban areas; a judicial encouragement of and readiness to find waivers of the right to counsel in order to ease administrative burdens on the courts; a continuing judicial hostility to an advocacy role in a traditional, treatment-oriented court; or a judicial predetermination of dispositions with nonappointment of counsel where probation is the anticipated outcome (Feld, 1984, p. 190; Bortner, 1982, pp. 136-147; Lefstein, Stapleton, and Teitelbaum, 1969; Stapleton and Teitelbaum, 1972). Whatever the reason and despite *Gault's* promise of counsel, many juveniles facing potentially coercive state action never see a lawyer, waive their right to counsel without consulting with an attorney or appreciating the legal consequences of relinquishing counsel, and face the prosecutorial power of the state alone and unaided.

Even when juveniles are represented, attorneys may not be capable of or committed to representing their juvenile clients in an effective adversarial manner. Organizational pressures to cooperate, judicial hostility toward adversarial litigants, role ambiguity created by the dual goals of rehabilitation and punishment, reluctance to help juveniles "beat a case," or an internalization of a court's treatment philosophy may compromise the role of counsel in juvenile court (Stapleton and Teitelbaum, 1972; Lefstein, Stapleton, and Teitelbaum, 1969; Fox, 1970; Platt and Friedman, 1968; Ferster, Courtless, and Snethen, 1971; McMillian and McMurtry, 1970; Kay and Segal, 1973; Bortner, 1982; Clarke and Koch, 1980; Blumberg, 1967). Institutional pressures to maintain stable, cooperative working relations with other personnel in the system may be inconsistent with effective adversarial advocacy (Lefstein, Stapleton, and Teitelbaum, 1969; Stapleton and Teitelbaum, 1972; Bortner, 1982; Blumberg, 1967).

Several studies have questioned whether lawyers can actually perform as advocates in a system rooted in *parens patriae* and benevolent rehabilitation (Stapleton and Teitelbaum, 1972; Fox, 1970). Indeed, there are some indications that lawyers representing juveniles in more traditional "therapeutic" juvenile courts may actually disadvantage their clients in adjudications or dispositions (Stapleton and Teitelbaum, 1972, pp. 63-96; Clarke and Koch, 1980, pp. 304-306; Bortner, 1982). Duffee and Siegel (1971, pp. 548-553), Clarke and Koch (1980, pp. 304-306), Stapleton and Teitelbaum (1972), Hayeslip (1979), and Bortner (1982) all reported that juveniles with counsel are more likely to be incarcerated than juveniles without counsel. Bortner (1982, pp. 139-140), for example, found that "when the possibility of receiving the most severe dispositions (placement outside the home in either group homes or institutions) is examined, those juveniles who were represented by attorneys were more likely to receive these dispositions than were juveniles not represented (35.8% compared to 9.6%). Further statistical analysis reveals that, *regardless of the types of offenses with which they were charged*, juveniles represented by attorneys receive more severe dispositions."

The Present Study

The present study provides the first opportunity to analyze systematically variations in rates of representation and the impact of counsel in more than one juvenile court or even one jurisdiction. It analyzes variations in the implementation of the right to counsel in six states—California, Minnesota, New York, Nebraska, North Dakota, and Pennsylvania, as well as Philadelphia. These statistical analyses provide the first comparative examination of the circumstances under which lawyers are appointed to represent juveniles, the case characteristics associated with rates of representation, and the effects of representation on case processing and dispositions.

This study uses data collected by the National Juvenile Court Data Archive (NJCDA) to analyze the availability of and effects of counsel in delinquency and status offense cases disposed of in 1984. While 30 states now contribute their annual juvenile court data tapes to the NJCDA, the six states included in this study were selected solely because their data files included information on representation by counsel.

Because of the many hazards and pitfalls in using juvenile court data, an overview of the juvenile justice process and a description of the individual state's data precedes the cross-state comparisons. The NJCDA's unit of count is "cases disposed" of by a juvenile court. Typically, juvenile delinquency cases begin with a referral to a county's juvenile court or a juvenile probation or intake department. Many of these referrals are closed at intake with some type of *informal* disposition: dismissal, counseling, warning, referral to another agency, or probation. These referrals, whether disposed of informally or petitioned to the juvenile court, also generate county record-keeping activities that are reported to the state agency responsible for compiling juvenile justice data.

The sample in this study consists exclusively of *petitioned* delinquency and status offense cases. It excludes all juvenile court referrals for abuse, dependency, or neglect, as well as routine traffic violations. Only formally *petitioned* delinquency and status cases are analyzed because the right to counsel announced in *Gault* attaches only after the formal initiation of delinquency proceedings.

The filing of a petition—the formal initiation of the juvenile process—is comparable legally to the filing of a complaint, information, or indictment in the adult criminal process (Feld, 1984, p. 217). Since different county intake or probation units within a state, as well as the various states, use different criteria to decide whether or not to file a formal delinquency petition, the cross-state comparisons reported here involve very different samples of delinquent populations. The common denominator of all these cases is that they were formally processed in their respective jurisdictions. As indicated in Table 1, the proportion of referred cases to petitioned cases differs markedly, from a high of 62.8% in Nebraska to a low of 10.7% in North Dakota.

In most jurisdictions, a juvenile offender will be arraigned on the petition. Since the constitutional right to counsel attaches in juvenile court only after the filing of the petition, it is typically at this stage, if at all, that counsel will be appointed to represent a juvenile (Feld, 1984). At the arraignment, the juvenile admits or denies the allegations in the petition. In many cases, juveniles may admit the allegations of the petition at their arraignment and have their case disposed of without the presence of an attorney.

The types of underlying offenses represented in the formally filed delinquency petitions differ substantially; the large urban jurisdictions confront very different and more serious delinquency than do the more rural, midwestern states (Nimick et al., 1985). In this study, the offenses reported by the states are regrouped into six analytical categories. The "felony/minor" offense distinction provides both an indicator of seriousness and is legally relevant for the right to counsel (*Gideon v. Wainwright*, 1963; *Scott v. Illinois*, 1979). Offenses are also classified as person, property, other delinquency, and status. Combining person and property with the felony and minor distinctions produces a six-item offense scale for cross-state comparisons. When a petition alleges more than one offense, the youth is classified on the basis of the most serious charge. This study also uses two indicators of the severity of dispositions: out-of-home placement and secure confinement. The data were originally collected by the California Bureau of Criminal Statistics and Special Services, the Minnesota Supreme Court Judicial Information System, the Nebraska Commission on Law Enforcement and Criminal Justice, the New York Office of Court Administration, the North Dakota Office of State Court Administrator, and the Pennsylvania Juvenile Court Judges' Commission.

Data and Analysis

Part of these analyses treat the availability and role of counsel as a dependent variable using case characteristics and court processing factors as independent variables. Other parts treat counsel as an independent variable, assessing its relative impact on juvenile court case processing and dispositions. These analyses attempt to answer the interrelated questions regarding when lawyers are appointed to represent juveniles, why they are appointed, and what difference does it make whether or not a youth is represented?

Petitions and Offenses

Initially, the appearance of counsel must be placed in the larger context of juvenile justice administration in the respective states. Table 1 introduces the six states' juvenile justice systems, reports the total number of referrals where available, the total number of petitions, the percentage of referrals to petitions, and the types of offenses for which petitions were filed.

The juvenile courts in the various states confront very different delinquent populations. In part, these differences reflect the nature of the prepetition screening. While California, Nebraska, and Pennsylvania courts formally petition approximately half of their juvenile court referrals, North Dakota juvenile courts only charge about 10.7% of their referrals. The numbers of petitions involved also differ substantially. The large, urban states handle far more cases than the rural midwestern states. Indeed, Philadelphia alone processes more delinquency petitions than Nebraska and North Dakota together.

The nature of the offenses petitioned also differs substantially among the states. Felony offenses against the person—homicide, rape, aggravated assault, and robbery—are much more prevalent in the large, urban states. In Philadelphia, for example, 38.1% of the juvenile court's caseload involves violent offenses against the person, primarily robbery. By contrast, a substantial portion of the mid-western states' caseloads consists of minor property offenses such as theft and shoplifting.

The states also differ markedly in their treatment of status offenders. Pennsylvania/Philadelphia juvenile courts do not have jurisdiction over status offenders. Similarly, status offenders in California appear to be referred to juvenile courts only as a last resort. By contrast, in the midwestern states, status offenses are the second most common type of delinquency cases han-

Table 1
Petitions and Petitioned Officers

	California	Minnesota	Nebraska	New York	North Dakota	Pennsylvania	Philadelphia
Number of Referrals	147422	—	6091	—	7741	18926	—
Number of Petitions	68227	15304	3830	21383	831	10168	6812
% Referrals/Petitions	46.3%	—	62.8%	—	10.7%	53.7%	—
Felony Offense Against % Person N	8.7 (5946)	2.2 (338)	1.0 (39)	8.2 (1764)	.2 (2)	13.0 (1320)	38.1 (2592)
Felony Offense Against Property	27.2 (18571)	14.3 (2196)	11.1 (427)	14.9 (3192)	15.8 (131)	25.9 (2653)	19.7 (1339)
Minor Offense Against Person	6.1 (4166)	5.0 (766)	3.7 (143)	6.6 (1414)	2.8 (23)	12.5 (1275)	3.7 (255)
Minor Offense Against Property	17.1 (11700)	29.9 (4574)	43.9 (1680)	18.8 (4019)	29.8 (248)	24.9 (2632)	24.9 (1694)

dled. The maximum age of juvenile court jurisdiction in New York is 16 years of age, rather than 18 as in the other states. The New York juvenile justice system deals with a significantly younger population, which includes a substantially larger proportion of status offenders.

Rates of Representation

Table 2 shows the overall rates of representation by counsel in the respective states, the percentages of private attorneys and public attorneys—court appointed or public defender—and the rates of representation by type of offense. Although *Gault* held that *every* juvenile was constitutionally entitled to "the guiding hand of counsel at every step of the process," *Gault's* promise remains unrealized in half of these jurisdictions.

The large, urban states are far more successful in assuring that juveniles receive the assistance of counsel than are the midwestern states. Overall, between 85%-95% of the juveniles in the large, urban states receive the assistance of counsel as contrasted with between 37.5% and 52.7% of the juveniles in the midwestern states. Indeed, these data may actually understate the urban state/rural state disparities. The California Bureau of Criminal Statistics and Special Services cautions that a coding error may be responsible for some of the juveniles who were reported to be unrepresented.

The first rows of Table 2 report the percentages of private attorneys and public attorneys (court appointed or public

Table 2
Representation by Counsel (Private, Public Defender/Court Appointed)

	California	Minnesota	Nebraska	New York	North Dakota	Pennsylvania	Philadelphia
% Counsel	84.9[1]	47.7	52.7	95.9	37.5	86.4	95.2
Private	7.6	6.4[2,3]	13.3	5.1	10.5	14.6	22.0
CA/PD[a]	77.3		39.4	90.8	27.1	71.9	73.2
Felony Offense Against Person	88.7	66.1	58.8	98.5	100.0	91.4	96.3
Private	11.2	9.9	14.7	4.3	—	22.0	29.9
CA/PD	77.5	66.3	44.1	94.2	100.0	69.4	66.4
Felony Offense Against Property	86.8	60.6	59.9	98.1	38.9	87.1	95.0
Private	9.0	6.2	14.4	8.3	12.2	15.1	20.5
CA/PD	77.8	54.4	45.5	89.7	26.7	72.0	74.5
Minor Offense Against Person	86.7	73.5	41.3	99.0	47.8	89.3	96.1
Private	8.6	7.3	14.9	9.5	17.4	16.4	22.4
CA/PD	78.1	66.1	26.4	89.5	30.4	72.9	73.7
Minor Offense Against Property	83.8	46.8	49.6	96.2	38.3	85.6	94.7
Private	6.1	5.3	14.1	6.6	12.5	11.9	16.1
CA/PD	77.7	41.4	35.5	89.7	25.8	73.6	78.7
Other Delinquency	83.4	55.5	48.9	96.8	33.1	82.1	93.2
Private	6.4	5.9	16.0	8.0	10.8	10.8	12.3
CA/PD	77.0	49.6	32.8	88.7	22.3	71.4	80.9
Status Offense	74.1	30.7	66.1	93.8	37.2	N/A	N/A
Private	3.3	3.9	10.3	2.3	7.3		
CA/PD	70.8	26.9	46.3	91.6	29.9		

a. Court Appointed, Public Defender

1. The California Bureau of Criminal Statistics and Special Services cautions that this rate may understate the actual rate of representation, that is, that an even larger percentage of California's juveniles are represented....

defenders) reflected in the overall rates of representation. In every jurisdiction and regardless of the overall rate of representation, public attorneys handle the vast bulk of delinquency petitions by ratios of between 3:1 and 10:1.

Table 2 clearly shows that it is possible to provide very high levels of defense representation to juveniles adjudicated delinquent. More than 95% of the juveniles in Philadelphia and New York state, and 85% or more in Pennsylvania and California were represented. Since the large urban states process a greater volume of delinquency cases, their success in delivering legal services is all the more impressive. While it may be more difficult to deliver legal services easily in all parts of the rural midwestern states, county by county analysis in Minnesota shows substantial disparities within the state; even the largest county in the state with a well-developed public defender system provides representation to less than half the juveniles (Feld, 1984, pp. 189-190). These variations suggest that rates of representation reflect deliberate policy decisions.

Table 2 also shows the rates of representation by type of offense. One pattern that emerges in all of the states is a direct relationship between the seriousness of the offense and the rates of representation. Juveniles charged with felonies—offenses against person or property—and those with offenses against the person generally have higher rates of representation than the state's overall rate. These differences in representation by offense are typically greater in the states with lower rates of representation than in those with higher rates because of the latter's smaller overall variation. In Minnesota, for example, while only 47.7% of all juveniles are represented, 66.1% of those charged with felony offenses against the person, 73.5% of those charged with minor offenses against the person, and 60.6% of those charged with felony offenses against property are represented.

A second and similar pattern is the appearance of larger proportions of private attorneys on behalf of juveniles charged with felony offenses—person and property—and offenses against the person than appear in the other offense categories. Perhaps the greater seriousness of those offenses and their potential consequences encourage juveniles or their families to seek the assistance of private counsel. Conversely, private attorneys are least likely to be retained by parents to represent the status offenders with whom the parents are often in conflict.

Offense and Disposition

There is extensive research on the determinants of juvenile court dispositions (Fagan, Slaughter, and Hartsone, 1987; McCarthy and Smith, 1986; Dannefer and Schutt, 1982; Thomas and Cage, 1977). However, "even a superficial review of the relevant literature leaves one with the rather uncomfortable feeling that the only consistent finding of prior research is that there are no consistencies in the determinants of the decision-making process" (Thomas and Sieverdes, 1975, p. 416). In general, the seriousness of the present offense and the length of the prior record—the so-called "legal variables"—explain most of the variance that can be accounted for in juvenile sentencing, with some additional influence of race (Fagan, Slaughter, and Hartsone, 1987; McCarthy and Smith, 1986). However, in most of these studies, the legal variables account for only about 25% to 30% of the variance in dispositions (Thomas and Cage, 1977; Clarke and Koch, 1980; McCarthy and Smith, 1986; Horwitz and Wasserman, 1980).

Although this cross-state comparison cannot identify fully the determinants of dispositions, the data lend themselves to an exploration of the relationships among offenses, dispositions, and representation by an attorney. Table 3 uses two measures of juvenile court dispositions: (1) out-of-home placements, and (2) secure confinement. These categories provide clear-cut delineations that lend themselves to cross-state comparisons. They also have legal significance for the appointment of counsel, since the Supreme Court has held, at least for adults, that all persons charged with felonies must be afforded the right to counsel (*Gideon v. Wainwright*, 1963), and that no person convicted of a misdemeanor may be incarcerated unless he or she was afforded the assistance of counsel (*Scott v. Illinois*, 1979).

Table 3 shows both the overall rates of out-of-home placements and secure confinement in the respective states as well as by categories of offenses. The states differ markedly in their overall use of out-of-home placements and secure confinement, ranging from a high of 30.8%/14.5% in California to a low of 10.3%/1.1% in Philadelphia. The ratio of out-of-home placement to secure confinement also varies from 17:1 in Pennsylvania to about 2:1 in California.

As expected, the seriousness of the present offense substantially alters a youth's risk of removal and confinement. In every state, felony offenses against the person garner both the highest rates of out-of-home placement and secure confinement, typically followed either by minor offenses against the person or felony offenses against property, for example, burglary. Conversely, minor property offenses—primarily petty theft, shoplifting—and status offenses have the lowest rates of removal or confinement.

Offense and Disposition by Counsel

Table 4 adds the counsel variable to the information contained in Table 3. Within each offense category of youths who receive out-of-home or secure dispositions, Table 4 shows the disposition rates for those youths who had counsel and those who did not. Thus Table 3 shows that when juveniles commit felonies against the person in California, 39.5%/20.4% receive out-of-home placement and secure confinement disposi-

Table 3
Present Offense Disposition: Out-of-Home Placement/Secure Confinement

	California	Minnesota	Nebraska	New York	North Dakota	Pennsylvania	Philadelphia
Overall:							
Home %	30.8	17.2	15.2	16.1	28.0	22.1	10.3
N =	(21048)	(2631)	(584)	(3255)	(233)	(2213)	(628)
Secure %	14.5	3.3	5.2	7.1	9.6	1.3	1.1
N =	(9902)	(504)	(199)	(1423)	(80)	(132)	(76)
Felony Offense Against Person:							
Home	39.6	30.2	28.2	22.3	50.0	28.7	12.6
Secure	20.4	9.5	15.4	19.2	50.0	2.5	1.7
Felony Offense Against Property:							
Home	31.2	27.4	18.5	18.6	35.1	21.3	11.3
Secure	15.7	9.2	12.2	12.0	17.6	.9	.8
Minor Offense Against Person:							
Home	25.8	21.5	21.7	12.7	39.1	13.5	5.7
Secure	11.5	3.3	9.1	9.6	13.0	.2	.4
Minor Offense Against Property:							
Home	24.3	14.6	8.5	14.1	28.6	18.8	6.9
Secure	11.5	3.5	9.1	9.6	8.1	.6	.6
Other Delinquency:							
Home	32.5	20.2	15.9	16.1	27.3	27.5	11.4
Secure	15.2	1.9	8.8	10.6	14.4	2.4	1.0
Status Offense:							
Home	27.9	10.7	22.3	15.6	23.6	N/A	N/A
Secure	1.0	0.5	1.8	1.3	4.5	—	—

tions. The same cell in Table 4 shows that youths *with counsel* were somewhat more likely to receive severe dispositions than those *without counsel*—40% versus 35.5% out of home and 21.0% versus 15.4% secure confinement.

Except for North Dakota, with its very small numbers and low rates of representation, a comparison of the two columns in each state and at each offense level reveals that youths with lawyers receive more severe dispositions than do those without lawyers. With twelve possible comparisons in each state—six offense categories times two dispositions—represented youths received more severe dispositions that unrepresented youth in every category in Minnesota, New York, and Pennsylvania, in all but one in California and Philadelphia, and in all but two in Nebraska. Even in the highest representation jurisdictions—New York and Philadelphia—this pattern prevails; there was virtually no secure confinement of unrepresented juveniles in these locales.

While the relationship between representation and more severe disposition is consistent in the different jurisdictions, the explanation of this relationship is not readily apparent. It may be that presence of lawyers antagonizes traditional juvenile court judges and subtly influences the eventual disposition imposed (Clarke and Koch, 1980). However, the pattern also prevails in the jurisdictions with very high rates of representation where the presence of counsel is not unusual. Perhaps judges discern the eventual disposition early in the proceedings and appoint counsel more frequently when an out-of-home placement or secure confinement is anticipated. Conversely, judges may exhibit more leniency if a youth

Table 4
Representation by Counsel and Disposition (Home/Secure)

	California		Minnesota		Nebraska		New York		North Dakota		Pennsylvania		Philadelphia	
Counsel →	Yes	No	Yes	No	Yes	No	Yes	No	Yes	No	Yes	No	Yes	No
Felony Offense Against Person:														
Home	40.0	35.5	32.8	21.4	25.0	28.6	22.6	0.0	50.0	—	31.0	16.8	12.9	4.9
Secure	21.0	15.4	9.5	4.9	15.0	21.4	19.5	0.0	50.0	—	2.8	.9	1.7	2.1
Felony Offense Against Property:														
Home	32.0	26.1	31.6	19.1	24.9	11.1	19.0	0.0	47.1	27.5	24.9	8.2	11.7	4.8
Secure	16.5	10.6	10.4	5.0	16.2	7.8	12.2	0.0	11.8	21.3	1.1	0.0	0.9	0.0
Minor Offense Against Person:														
Home	26.8	19.2	22.3	14.9	20.0	28.2	12.7	7.1	45.5	33.3	22.0	7.8	5.5	10.0
Secure	12.3	6.1	3.5	1.1	12.0	9.9	9.7	0.0	9.1	16.7	0.4	0.0	0.4	0.0
Minor Offense Against Property:														
Home	25.5	17.9	18.8	9.6	12.5	5.7	14.6	0.0	38.9	22.2	24.9	4.8	6.9	6.3
Secure	10.8	6.4	4.2	2.0	7.3	2.4	9.1	0.0	8.4	7.8	0.8	0.0	0.7	0.0
Other Delinquency:														
Home	34.4	22.8	28.1	9.8	24.2	9.0	16.7	0.0	32.6	24.7	37.6	17.4	11.4	44.1
Secure	16.5	9.1	2.2	.8	13.5	2.2	11.0	0.0	13.0	15.1	3.5	0.9	0.6	6.3
Status Offense:														
Home	30.4	20.8	16.5	7.6	34.1	14.2	16.6	1.0	32.7	18.2	N/A		N/A	
Secure	6.3	7.1	.9	.4	2.1	1.4	1.4	0.0	1.9	6.7				

is not represented. Or, still another possibility is that other variables besides the present offense may influence both the appointment of counsel and the eventual disposition.

Detention by Offense

Table 5 shows the overall percentage of juveniles against whom petitions were filed who were detained, as well as the rates of pretrial detention by offense category. *Detention,* as used here, refers to a juvenile's custody status following referral but prior to court action. It is important to note, however, that detention is coded differently in various jurisdictions. In California, for example, which appears to have a very high rate of pretrial detention, any juvenile brought to a detention facility is logged-in and counted as detained, even if he or she is held only for a short while until a parent arrives. By contrast, Minnesota, which appears to have a very low rate of pretrial detention, uses a very conservative definition of detention. Juveniles in Minnesota are coded as detained only if a detention hearing is held, which normally occurs 36 hours—about two court days—after apprehension (Feld, 1984). Thus the data in Table 5, while suggestive, are not directly comparable. Unfortunately, Philadelphia does not provide information on a juvenile's pretrial detention status.

Regardless of the jurisdictional definition of detention, its use follows similar patterns. Juveniles committing felonies against the person are the most likely to be detained, followed either by those committing minor offenses against the person or felony offenses against property. Since the evidentiary distinctions between a felony and a minor offense against the person, for example, the degree of injury to the victim, may not be apparent at the time of detention, these patterns are not surprising. . . .

Detention and Dispositions

Several studies have examined the determinants of detention and the relationship between a child's pretrial detention status and subsequent disposition (Krisberg and Schwartz, 1983; Frazier and Bishop, 1985; Clarke and Koch, 1980; McCarthy, 1987). These studies report that while several of the same variables affect both rates of detention and subsequent disposition, after appropriate controls, detention per se exhibits an independent effect on dispositions.

While this study cannot control for all variables simultaneously, Table 6 shows the relationship among a youth's offense, detention status, and eventual disposition. Table 6 reports the percentages of youths within each offense category who were detained and who were not detained who received

Table 5
Present Offense and Pretrial Detention Status

	California	Minnesota	Nebraska	New York	North Dakota	Pennsylvania
% Detained	54.0	9.4	12.6	18.0	14.7	29.0
Overall N =	(36100)	(1443)	(483)	(3841)	(122)	(2946)
Felony Offense Against Person	68.1	24.6	46.2	22.3	50.0	43.6
Felony Offense Against Property	56.6	15.0	20.1	17.5	16.3	30.6
Minor Offense Against Person	62.0	16.1	25.2	15.2	21.7	22.0
Minor Offense Against Property	45.5	7.1	9.8	16.1	11.3	27.4
Other Delinquency	54.7	10.6	13.7	20.2	20.1	24.7

out-of-home placement and secure confinement. Again, the results are remarkably consistent; in five of the six jurisdictions and at every offense level, youths who were detained received more severe dispositions than those who were not. Even in North Dakota with its small numbers, the relationship between detention and secure confinement appears in most offense categories.

What Table 6 shows, then, is that the same factors that determine the initial detention decision appear to influence the ultimate disposition as well. However, when one compares the zero-order relationship between offense and disposition (Table 3) with the relationship between offense/detention and disposition (Table 6), it is apparent that detained youths are significantly more at risk for out-of-home placement and secure confinement than are nondetained youths. Generally, pretrial detention more than doubles a youth's probability of receiving more severe dispositions.

Counsel, Detention, and Disposition

Table 5 reported the percentages of youths who were detained at each offense level. Table 6 examined the relationship between detention status and representation and reported that detention increased the likelihood of a youth receiving more severe dispositions.

Table 7 reports the relationship between detention and disposition when youth are represented by counsel to see whether the presence or absence of counsel affects their dispositions. Table 7 indicates that a detained youth who is represented by counsel is more likely to receive a severe disposition than a detained youth who is not represented. In New York, California, and Pennsylvania, which had very high rates of

Table 6
Impact of Pretrial Detention on Disposition (Home/Secure)

	California		Minnesota		Nebraska		New York		North Dakota		Pennsylvania	
Detention →	Yes	No	Yes	No	Yes	No	Yes	No	Yes	No	Yes	No
Felony Offense Against Person:												
Home	51.3	14.9	53.0	22.7	55.6	4.8	57.6	11.9	0.0	100.0	50.3	11.9
Secure	26.3	8.0	20.6	5.9	33.3	0.0	50.3	10.1	0.0	100.0	5.2	.4
Felony Offense Against Property:												
Home	42.2	17.1	46.5	24.0	51.2	10.3	49.6	11.7	30.0	36.0	47.0	10.0
Secure	19.6	11.0	22.5	6.9	36.0	6.2	32.0	7.5	30.0	15.3	2.2	0.3
Minor Offense Against Person:												
Home	38.9	11.6	46.3	16.8	41.7	16.0	45.4	6.8	60.0	33.3	40.4	5.9
Secure	16.6	6.3	6.5	2.6	22.2	4.7	39.0	4.3	60.0	5.6	0.7	0.1
Minor Offense Against Property:												
Home	37.1	13.7	40.2	12.7	35.8	5.5	45.4	7.9	28.6	28.6	48.5	7.5
Secure	12.8	8.2	15.3	2.6	22.4	2.5	31.5	4.3	7.1	8.2	2.0	0.1
Other Delinquency:												
Home	44.3	18.6	43.9	17.4	50.0	10.5	44.2	8.9	28.6	27.0	55.4	18.3
Secure	17.9	12.5	7.5	1.3	24.0	6.4	31.1	5.4	17.9	13.5	5.8	1.3
Status Offense:												
Home	31.6	26.4	37.2	9.1	59.4	17.7	40.2	10.2	17.5	24.6	N/A	
Secure	8.6	6.1	4.0	0.3	7.8	1.0	2.8	1.0	5.0	4.4		

representation, the represented/detained youths consistently received more severe dispositions than the small group of unrepresented/detained juveniles, as was also the case in Nebraska. Only in Minnesota and North Dakota was the presence of counsel not an "aggravating" factor at the sentencing of detained youth. Again, this may simply be the result of dwindling numbers, or perhaps the factors that influenced the initial detention decision took precedence over the presence of counsel in those states.

The data in Table 7 in New York and Pennsylvania further reinforce the findings reported in Table 4; there was virtually no removal from the home or incarceration of unrepresented youths. By contrast, substantial numbers and proportions of youths in the midwestern states were being detained and/or removed from their homes and placed in secure confinement without the assistance of counsel. . . .

Discussion and Conclusion

Nearly twenty years after Gault held that juveniles are constitutionally entitled to the assistance of counsel, half of the jurisdictions in this study are still not in compliance. In Nebraska, Minnesota, and North Dakota, nearly half or more of delinquent and status offenders do not have lawyers (Table 2). Moreover, many juveniles who receive out-of-home placement and even secure confinement were adjudicated delinquent and sentenced without the assistance of counsel (Table 4). One may speculate whether the midwestern states are more representative of most juvenile courts in other parts of the country than are the large urban states. In light of the findings from other jurisdictions (Clarke and Koch, 1980; Bortner, 1982; Aday, 1986), it is apparent that many juveniles are unrepresented.

Clearly, it is possible to provide counsel for the vast majority of young offenders.

Table 7
Representation by Attorney for Detained Juveniles and Disposition (Home/Secure)

	California		Minnesota		Nebraska		New York		North Dakota		Pennsylvania	
Attorney →	Yes	No	Yes	No	Yes	No	Yes	No	Yes	No	Yes	No
Felony Offense Against Person:												
Home	51.3	51.5	52.1	62.5	57.1	50.0	57.7	0.0	—	—	50.6	42.9
Secure	27.0	19.9	18.8	12.5	42.9	37.5	50.4	0.0			5.2	4.8
Felony Offense Against Property:												
Home	42.9	36.1	47.2	42.4	60.8	40.7	49.6	0.0	16.7	35.7	47.7	35.4
Secure	20.9	8.3	18.8	22.7	37.3	37.0	32.0	0.0	16.7	35.7	2.4	0.0
Minor Offense Against Person:												
Home	39.5	34.0	44.0	50.0	41.2	42.1	45.6	0.0	50.0	100.0	41.4	21.4
Secure	17.5	8.8	5.3	12.5	29.4	15.8	39.2	0.0	25.0	100.0	0.7	0.0
Minor Offense Against Property:												
Home	38.5	26.8	37.6	35.6	40.4	23.4	45.8	0.0	40.0	22.2	49.4	29.0
Secure	14.0	4.1	11.0	11.9	25.0	14.9	31.8	0.0	0.0	11.1	2.1	0.0
Other Delinquency:												
Home	45.4	35.3	44.3	37.9	68.1	33.3	44.5	0.0	60.0	21.7	57.9	25.0
Secure	19.2	7.0	3.8	8.6	29.0	8.3	31.3	0.0	40.0	13.0	6.0	2.3
Status Offense:												
Home	32.0	28.2	36.5	34.8	61.9	41.7	40.2	44.4	30.8	11.1	N/A	
Secure	9.4	2.6	3.2	8.1	3.8	33.3	2.9	0.0	0.0	7.4		

California, Pennsylvania and Philadelphia, and New York do so routinely. What is especially impressive in those jurisdictions is the very low numbers of uncounseled juveniles who receive out-of-home placement or secure confinement dispositions (Tables 4 and 7). While this study shows substantial differences in rates of representation among the different states, it cannot account for the greater availability of counsel in some of the jurisdictions than in others.

There are direct legislative policy implications of the findings reported here. In those states in which juveniles are routinely unrepresented, legislation mandating the automatic and nonwaivable appointment of counsel at the earliest stage in delinquency proceeding is necessary (Feld, 1984, pp. 184-190). As long as it is possible for a juvenile to waive the right to counsel, juvenile court judges will find such waivers. Short of mandatory and nonwaivable counsel, a prohibition on waivers of counsel without prior consultation with and the concurrence of counsel would assure that any eventual waiver was truly "knowing, intelligent, and voluntary" (Feld, 1984, pp. 186-187). Moreover, a requirement of consultation with counsel prior to waiver would assure the development of legal services delivery systems that would then facilitate the more routine representation of juveniles. At the very least, legislation should prohibit the removal from home or incarceration of any juvenile who was not provided with counsel. Such a limitation on dispositions is already the law for adult criminal defendants (*Gideon v. Wainwright*, 1963; *Scott v. Illinois*, 1979), for juveniles in some jurisdictions (Feld, 1984, p. 187) and apparently the informal practice in New York and Pennsylvania where virtually no unrepresented juveniles were removed or confined.

Apart from simply documenting variations in rates of representation, this research also examined the determinants of representation. It examined the relationship between "legal variables"—seriousness of offense, detention status, prior referrals—and the appointment of counsel. In each analysis, it showed the zero-order relationship among the legal variables and dispositions, the legal variables and the appointment of counsel, and the effect of representation on dispositions.

There is obviously multicollinearity between the factors producing more severe dispositions and the factors influencing the appointment of counsel. Each legal variable that is associated with a more severe disposition is also associated with greater rates of representation. And yet, within the limitations of this research design, it appears that in virtually every jurisdiction, representation by counsel is an aggravating factor in a juvenile's disposition. When controlling for the seriousness of the present offense, unrepresented juveniles seem to fare better than those with lawyers (Tables 3 and 4). When controlling for offense and detention status, unrepresented juveniles again fare better than those with representation (Tables 6 and 7) When controlling for the seriousness of the present offense and prior referrals, the presence of counsel produces more severe dispositions. In short, while the legal variables enhance the probabilities of representation, the fact of representation appears to exert an independent effect on the severity of dispositions.

Although this phenomenon has been alluded to in other studies (Bortner, 1982; Clarke and Koch, 1980), this research provides the strongest evidence yet that representation by counsel redounds to the disadvantage of a juvenile. Why? One possible explanation is that attorneys in juvenile court are simply incompetent and prejudice their clients' cases (Stapleton and Teitelbaum, 1972; Lefstein, Stapleton, and Teitelbaum, 1969; Fox, 1970; Platt and Friedman, 1968; Ferster, Courtless, and Snethen, 1971; McMillian and McMurtry, 1970; Kay and Segal, 1973; Bortner, 1982; Clarke and Koch, 1980). While systematic evaluations of the actual performance of counsel in juvenile court are lacking, the available evidence suggests that even in jurisdictions where counsel are routinely appointed, there are grounds for concern about their effectiveness. Public defender offices in many jurisdictions assign their least capable lawyers or newest staff attorneys to juvenile courts to get trial experience, and these neophytes may receive less adequate supervision than their prosecutorial counterparts. Similarly, court appointed counsel may be beholden to the judges who select them and more concerned with maintaining an ongoing relationship with the court than vigorously protecting the interests of their clients. Moreover, measuring defense attorney performance by dispositional outcomes raises questions about the meaning of effective assistance of counsel. What does it take to be an effective attorney in juvenile court? Why do fewer defense attorneys appear at dispositions than at adjudications? How might attorneys for juveniles become more familiar with dispositional alternatives?

Perhaps, however, the relationship between the presence of counsel and the increased severity of dispositions is spurious. Obviously, this study cannot control simultaneously for all of the variables that influence dispositional decision making. It may be that early in a proceeding, a juvenile court judge's greater familiarity with a case may alert him or her to the eventual disposition that will be imposed and counsel may be appointed in anticipation of more severe consequences (Aday, 1986). In many jurisdictions, the same judge who presides at a youth's arraignment and detention hearing will later decide the case on the merits and then impose a sentence. Perhaps, the initial decision to appoint counsel is based upon the same evidence developed at those earlier stages that also influences later dispositions.

Another possible explanation is that juvenile court judges may treat more formally and severely juveniles who appear with counsel than those without. Within statutory limits, judges may feel less constrained when sentencing a youth who is represented. Such may be the price of formal procedures. While not necessarily punishing juveniles who are represented, judges may incline toward leniency toward those youths who appear unaided and "throw themselves on the mercy of the court." At the very least, further research, including qualitative studies of the processes of initial appointment of counsel in several jurisdictions, will be required to untangle this complex web.

References

Aday, David P., Jr. 1986. "Court Structure, Defense Attorney Use and Juvenile Court Decisions." *Sociological Quarterly* 27:107-119.

Blumberg, Abraham. 1967. "The Practice of Law as a Confidence Game: Organizational Cooptation of a Profession." *Law and Society Review* 1:15-30.

Bortner, M.A. 1982. *Inside a Juvenile Court: The Tarnished Ideal of Individualized Justice.* New York: New York University Press.

Cicourel, Aaron V. 1968. *The Social Organization of Juvenile Justice.* New York: John Wiley.

Clarke, Stevens H. and Gary G. Koch. 1980. "Juvenile Court: Therapy or Crime Control, and Do Lawyers Make a Difference?" *Law and Society Review* 14:263-308.

Dannefer, Dale and Russell Schutt. 1982. "Race and Juvenile Justice Processing in Court and Police Agencies." *American Journal of Sociology* 87:1113-1132.

Duffee, David and Larry Siegel. 1971. "The Organization Man: Legal Counsel in the Juvenile Court." *Criminal Law Bulletin* 7:544-553.

Emerson, Robert M. 1969. *Judging Delinquents: Context and Process in Juvenile Court*, Chicago: Aldine.

Fagan, Jeffrey, Ellen Slaughter, and Eliot Hartstone. 1987. "Blind Justice? The Impact of Race on the Juvenile Justice Process." *Crime and Delinquency* 33:224-258.

Feld, Barry C. 1984. "Criminalizing Juvenile Justice: Rules of Procedure for Juvenile Court." *Minnesota Law Review* 69:141-276.

Ferster, Elyce Zenoff, Thomas F. Courtless, and Edith Nash Snethen. 1971. "The Juvenile Justice System: In Search of the Role of Counsel." *Fordham Law Review* 39:375-391.

Fine, Kerry. 1983. *Out of Home Placement of Children in Minnesota: A Research Report.* St. Paul: Minnesota House of Representatives.

Fox, Sanford J. 1970. "Juvenile Justice Reform: An Historical Perspective." *Stanford Law Review* pp. 1187-1239.

Frazier, Charles and Donna Bishop. 1985. "The Pretrial Detention of Juveniles and Its Impact on Case Dispositions." *Journal of Criminal Law and Criminology* 76:1132-1152.

Hayeslip, David. 1979. "The Impact of Defense Attorney Presence on Juvenile Court Dispositions." *Juvenile and Family Court Journal* 30:9-15.

Henretta, John C., Charles E. Frazier, and Donna M. Bishop. 1986. "The Effects of Prior Case

Outcomes on Juvenile Justice Decision-Making." *Social Forces* 65:554-562.

Horowitz, David. 1977. *The Courts and Social Policy*. New York.

Horwitz, Allan and Michael Wasserman. 1980. "Some Misleading Conceptions in Sentencing Research." *Criminology* 18:411-424.

Kay, Richard and Daniel Segal. 1973. "The Role of the Attorney in Juvenile Court Proceedings: A Non-Polar Approach." *Georgetown Law Journal* 61:1401-1424.

Krisberg, Barry and Ira Schwartz. 1983. "Rethinking Juvenile Justice." *Crime and Delinquency* 29:333-364.

Lefstein, Norman, Vaughan Stapleton, and Lee Teitelbaum. 1969. "In Search of Juvenile Justice: *Gault* and Its Implementation." *Law and Society Review* 3:491-562.

Matza, David. 1964. *Delinquency and Drift*. New York: John Wiley.

McCarthy, Belinda R. 1987. "Preventive Detention and Pretrial Custody in the Juvenile Court." *Journal of Criminal Justice* 15:185-200.

—— and Brent L. Smith. 1986. "The Conceptualization of Discrimination in the Juvenile Justice Process: The Impact of Administration Factors and Screening Decisions on Juvenile Court Dispositions." *Criminology* 24:41-64.

McMillian, Theodore and Dorothy Lear McMurtry. 1970. "The Role of the Defense Lawyer in the Juvenile Court—Advocate or Social Worker?" *St. Louis University Law Journal* 14:561-603.

National Juvenile Court Data Archive. 1986a. *California Juvenile Court Case Records 1980-1985: User's Guide*. Pittsburgh, PA: Author.

——. 1986b. *Nebraska Juvenile Court Case Records 1975-1985: User's Guide*. Pittsburgh, PA: Author.

——. 1986c. *New York Juvenile Court Case Records 1977-1985: User's Guide*. Pittsburgh, PA: Author.

Nimick, Ellen H., Howard N. Snyder, Dennis P. Sullivan, and Nancy J. Tierney. 1985. *Juvenile Court Statistics 1983*. Washington, DC: Office of Juvenile Justice and Delinquency Prevention.

Platt, Anthony and Ruth Friedman. 1968. "The Limits of Advocacy: Occupational Hazards in Juvenile Court." *University of Pennsylvania Law Review* 116:1156-1184.

Stapleton, W. Vaughan, and Lee E. Teitelbaum. 1972. *In Defense of Youth: A Study of the Role of Counsel in American Juvenile Court*. New York: Russell Sage.

Thomas, Charles W. and Robin Cage. 1977. "The Effects of Social Characteristics on Juvenile Court Dispositions." *Sociological Quarterly* 18:237-252.

Thomas, Charles W. and Christopher M. Sieverdes. 1975. "Juvenile Court Intake: An Analysis of Discretionary Decision-Making." *Criminology* 12:413-433. ✦

Section III
Measuring Delinquency

The survey by the Center for the Study of Youth Policy in Section I (Reading 3) revealed an interesting paradox about public perceptions of juvenile crime. The majority of respondents believe that crime by 10- to 17-year-old youths has "increased a lot" in their *state* but believe it has "stayed the same" in their own *neighborhoods*. This disparity likely reflects the influence of media coverage of juvenile crime on public perception. We are inundated with coverage of crimes across the nation, stories of gang violence, and politically motivated dramatizations of the problem of juvenile crime. The perception is that the problem of juvenile crime must be worse "out there" even if it has stayed the same in our neighborhoods.

How can we decide whether the problem is getting better or worse? How can we decide whether it is more common among some categories of citizens and in certain specific social conditions than others? Valid answers to such questions require reliable and valid measures of crime. Criminologists and social scientists have used three basic types of data in their search for answers to these and other questions about crime in general as well as about juvenile crime and delinquency: (1) the records compiled by police and courts, (2) interview and questionnaire surveys asking young people about their own behavior, and (3) interviews and surveys asking victims of crime about their experiences.

The two types of data most relevant to the measurement of delinquency are police and self-reported survey data. Figures 1 through 7 below summarize the percentage of high-school seniors who indicated that they were involved in violence and theft when asked about their activities during the twelve months preceding the survey. These data are gathered each year from thousands of students as part of the "Monitoring the Future" study, conducted by researchers at the University of Michigan (e.g., see Johnston, Bachman, and O'Malley 1992). Those data indicate upward trends in self-reports of most forms of violence with some indication of increases in the prevalence of theft of items worth more than fifty dollars. Violence using some form of weapon has increased quite recently for males. The most common forms of theft have been relatively stable.

The first article in this section summarizes patterns of juvenile offending and victimization based on police and victimization data. While the report highlights bits and pieces of data that are con-

Figure 1: Prevalence of Self-Reported Serious Fights by Gender (High School Seniors)

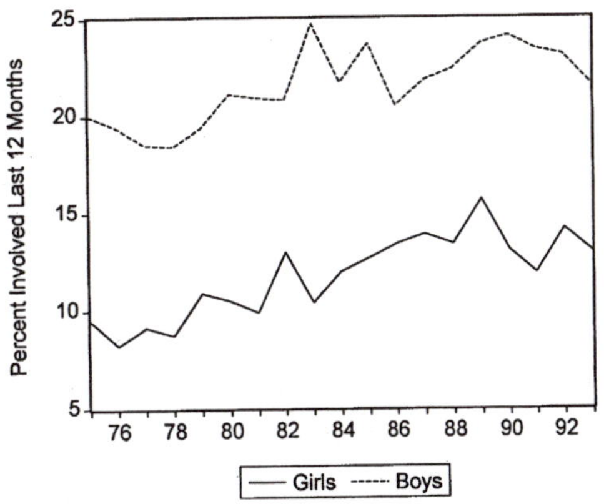

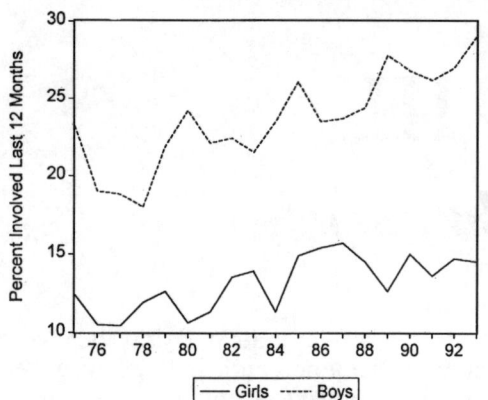

Figure 2: Prevalence of Self-Reported Group Fights by Gender (High School Seniors)

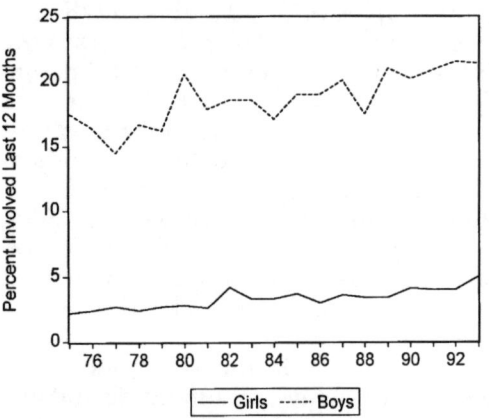

Figure 3: Prevalence of Self-Reported Serious Harm by Gender (High School Seniors)

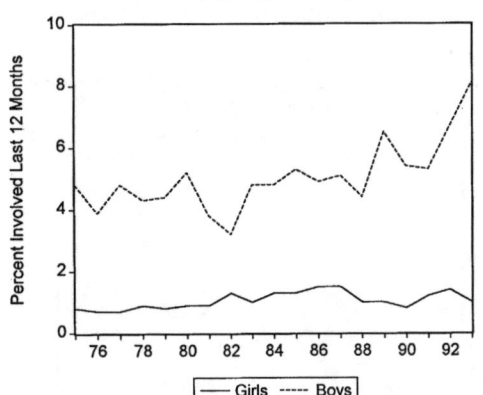

Figure 4: Prevalence of Self-Reported Weapon Offense by Gender (High School Seniors)

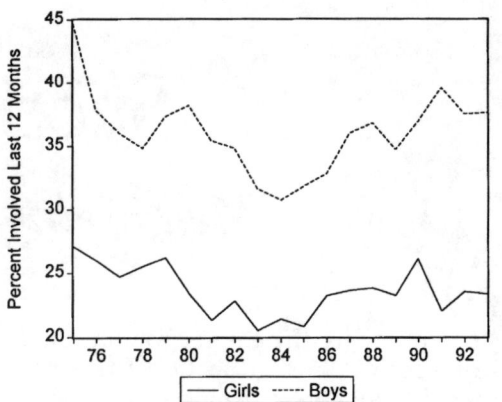

Figure 5: Prevalence of Self-Reported Shoplifting by Gender (High School Seniors)

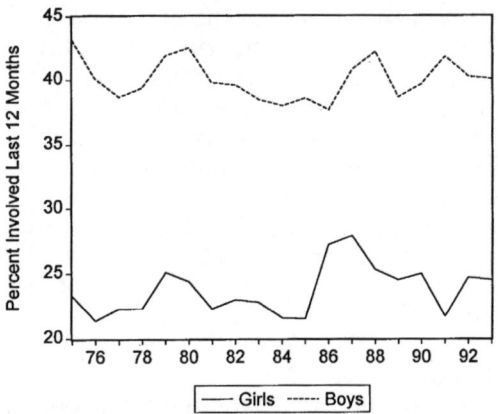

Figure 6: Prevalence of Self-Reported Theft <$50 by Gender (High School Seniors)

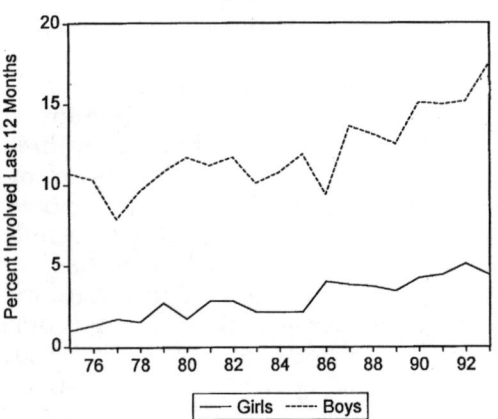

Figure 7: Prevalence of Self-Reported Theft >$50 by Gender (High School Seniors)

sistent with the growing national concern over violent juvenile crime, the data should lead to more precise views about the problem. Following the upward trend of the 1960s, arrests of juveniles for violent crimes were stable for much of the 1970s and 1980s, and then began an upward trend again in the late 1980s. There has been a recent surge in juvenile homicide involving firearms, with black males overrepresented as both offenders and victims. While the survey data we discussed above are based only on high-school seniors, they yield some similar conclusions. There has been a recent increase in weapons use, especially for boys, and most forms of violence have been increasing.

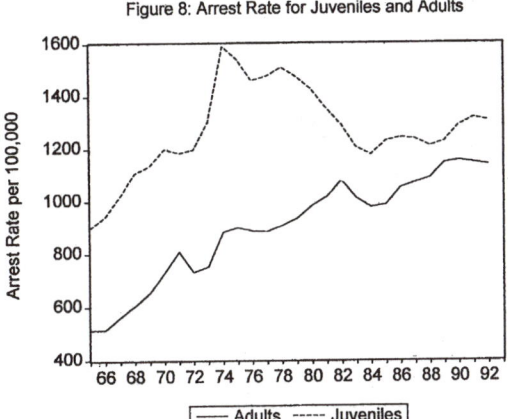

Figure 8: Arrest Rate for Juveniles and Adults

As depicted in Figure 8, the overall arrest rate for juveniles peaked in the mid-1970s and has been stable or declining since that time, while the adult arrest rate has followed a far more distinct upward trend. An overall decline in juveniles' participation in the most common forms of property crime helps to account for the decline in juvenile arrest rates (based on issues of Flanagan and Maguire, *Sourcebook of Criminal Justice Statistics*). These data are compatible with high-school seniors' self-reports of theft. The arrest data suggest a new upward turn since the mid-1980s, approximately the time that self-reported theft by high-school seniors increased as well.

The second article in this section summarizes the results of the University of Michigan surveys carried out every year since the mid-1970s to study illicit drug use among juveniles and young adults. Most Americans are likely to believe that the drug problem has been increasing for quite a long time, reaching epidemic proportions in recent years. If arrest rates for such offenses were the only data on the problem, this perception would be justified; however, there are several complications. Figure 9 summarizes arrest rates for drug abuse violations since 1965 for black and white adults and juveniles. There has been a rather dramatic increase in arrests of black adults, reaching a peak in 1989. The rates of arrest have increased several times for white adults and black juveniles as well. Arrest rates increased for white juveniles through the mid-1970s but have decreased since then.

The data gathered by the University of Michigan have suggested a different picture of the drug problem over time. Many forms of drug use peaked in the early and mid-1980s and declined until quite recently. Moreover, the type of racial differences suggested by arrest data have not been supported by self-reports of drug use. There are several possible explanations for such disparities, including biases in law enforcement, variations in willingness to admit to such activities, and the possibility that high-risk groups are missed by the surveys.

Of all basic background characteristics that have been examined in relation to delinquency and crime, whether using police, court, or survey data, a person's gender is the single best predictor. The gender difference among high-school seniors is illustrated in Figures 1–7. The third article in this section, by Clayton Hartjen and Sesharajani Kethineni, extends the study of gender differences to India—a society where girls are very closely supervised and controlled by their families. As in the United States, boys are much more delinquent than girls, but the gender gap is much larger in India. However, while U.S. boys and girls have higher arrest rates than their Indian counterparts, there is not much difference for boys when self-report data are used. Such findings suggest that arrest statistics may greatly exaggerate cultural differences among males.

As Hartjen and his colleague note, there has been an ongoing controversy about self-report surveys as a technique for discerning patterns of serious juvenile delinquency and youth crime. Using data from the National Survey of Youth, Delbert Elliott demonstrates that such limitations have been exaggerated and that numerous patterns discerned using police and court data can be found with a proper analysis of survey data. His analysis provides detail on the distribution of serious violence by race, gender, and age.

Since the disparities in patterns revealed by different types of data can reflect biases in law enforcement, research on such bias is important for assessing the meaning of police and court statistics. The last reading in this section is an overview of the results of research on racial bias in the juvenile justice system by the Office of Juvenile Justice and Delinquency Prevention. That report concludes that there is no universal conclusion about bias in juvenile justice processing that can be applied to all jurisdictions and times. Many studies offer evidence of bias at one stage or another; however, there are numerous research issues that need to be addressed before more definitive conclusions can be reached.

References

Flanagan, T.J. and K. Maguire (Editors). 1993. *Sourcebook of Criminal Justice Statistics*. U.S. Department of Justice: Bureau of Justice Statistics.

Johnston, L.D., J.G., Bachman, and P.M. O'Malley. 1992. *Monitoring the Future*. Ann Arbor: Institute for Survey Research—University of Michigan. ✦

8
Juvenile Offenders and Victims: A National Report

Howard N. Snyder
Melissa Sickmund

How Much of the Crime in the U.S. is Caused by Juveniles?

One of two continuous sources of information on the proportion of crime committed by juveniles is the National Crime Victimization Survey (NCVS). NCVS captures information on crimes committed against persons age 12 or older. Crimes committed against children below age 12 are not counted. As a result, significant numbers of crimes committed by juveniles and adults are not reported.

In 1991 NCVS found that victims age 12 and older reported that the offender was a juvenile (under age 18) in approximately 28% of personal crimes (i.e., rape, personal robbery, aggravated and simple assault, and theft from a person). These victims also reported that 88% of juvenile crimes were committed by male offenders and 10% by female offenders, with the remaining committed by both males and females. Adult offenders in 1991 had a similar sex profile....

In 1991 juveniles were responsible for 19% of all violent crimes (i.e., rape, personal robbery, and aggravated and simple assault) reported to NCVS in which there was a single offender. Persons most likely to be victimized by juveniles were individuals between ages 12 and 19 (remembering that crimes against children below age 12 are not a part of NCVS). The offender was a juvenile in nearly half of the violent crimes. In contrast, juveniles were seldom the offender in crimes against older victims. For example, 7% of robberies of persons ages 20-34 were committed by juveniles, and victims above age 50 rarely reported that they were robbed by juveniles.

Seventeen percent of all serious violent crimes in 1991 were committed by juveniles only, either alone (11%) or in juvenile groups (6%). Another 8% of serious violent crimes were committed by a group of offenders that included at least one juvenile and one adult. In all, 25% of all serious violent crime involved a juvenile offender; and of these crimes, more than one-half involved a group of offenders. Adults were less likely to commit crimes in groups; about one-third of serious violent crimes committed by adults involved a group of offenders.

Juvenile victims were more likely than adult victims to be victimized by a group of juvenile offenders. That is, 14% of all juveniles who were victims of a serious violent crime reported that they were victimized by two or more juvenile offenders, compared with 3% of adult victims. . . .

How Much of the Crime Problem is Caused by Juveniles?

Arrest proportions accurately characterize the ages of individuals entering the justice system. The fact that juveniles were 15% of all persons arrested for murder in 1992 implies that 15% of all persons entering the justice system on a murder charge were juveniles, not that the juveniles committed 15% of all murders.

Because juveniles are more likely than adults to commit crime in groups, arrest percentages are likely to exaggerate the juvenile contribution to the crime problem. The FBI clearance data provide a better assessment of the juvenile contribution to crime.

The juvenile contribution to the crime problem in the U.S. in 1992 varied considerably with the nature of the offense. Based on 1992 clearance data, juveniles were responsible for:

- 9% of murders.

From *Juvenile Offenders and Victims: A National Report*, by Howard N. Snyder and Melissa Sickmund, 1995, Washington, DC: Office of Juvenile Justice and Delinquency Prevention. Reprinted with the permission of the National Center for Juvenile Justice.

- 12% of aggravated assaults.
- 14% of forcible rapes.
- 16% of robberies.
- 20% of burglaries.
- 23% of larceny-thefts.
- 24% of motor vehicle thefts.
- 42% of arsons

Crimes with greater discrepancies between the arrest and clearance proportions may be those in which group behavior is more common. For example, while the discrepancy is small for forcible rape, it is relatively large for motor vehicle theft, burglary, murder, and robbery.

After More Than a Decade of Relative Stability, the Juvenile Violent Crime Arrest Rate Soared Between 1988 and 1992

During the period from 1973 through 1988 the number of juvenile arrests for a Violent Crime Index offense (murder and nonnegligent manslaughter, forcible rape, robbery, and aggravated assault) varied with the changing size of the juvenile population. However, in 1989, the juvenile violent crime arrest rate broke out of this historic range.

The years between 1988 and 1991 saw a 38% increase in the rate of juvenile arrests for violent crimes. The rate of increase then diminished, with the juvenile arrest rate increasing little between 1991 and 1992. This rapid growth over a relatively short period moved the juvenile arrest rate for violent crime in 1992 far above any year since the mid-1960s the earliest time period for which comparable statistics are available.

In 1983 the violent crime arrest rate for black youth was nearly 7 times the white rate. Between 1983 and 1992 the white arrest rate increased more than the rate for blacks (83% versus 43%). As a result, the white and black rates have moved closer together, but there is still a wide gap. In 1992 the rate of violent crime arrests for black youth was about 5 times the white rate.

The Increase in Violent Crime Arrest Rates Is Disproportionate for Juveniles and Young Adults

Over the 10-year period from 1983 through 1992, the violent crime arrest rate for youth of other races increased 42%, nearly equal to the increase in the black rate.

Over the 10-year period from 1983 to 1992, arrest rates for Violent Crime Index offenses increased substantially for juveniles as well as adults. Juveniles had the largest increases (averaging nearly 60%), but even the rates for persons ages 35 to 39 increased 47%.

The Violent Crime Index treats each of its four offenses equally—an arrest for aggravated assault is counted the same as an arrest for murder. While this may be reasonable statistically, these four crimes raise different concerns and should be understood separately.

In 1992 arrests for aggravated assault were 68% of all Violent Crime Index arrests. Thus, changes in violent crime arrest rates primarily reflected changes in aggravated assaults. As with violent crime overall, aggravated assault arrest rates increased substantially between 1983 and 1992 in all age groups, with juvenile rates up about 100% and the rates for persons in their twenties up about 60%.

In contrast to the overall violent crime and aggravated assault patterns, forcible rape arrest rates for juveniles grew between 1983 and 1992 by a relatively small 20%, while actually declining for persons in their twenties.

Robbery arrest rates increased in all age groups from 1983 to 1992. However, the growth was less than half of violent crime overall. The age groups with the smallest increases were those in their early twenties, with the juvenile increases similar to those of persons above age 25.

In 1992 persons above age 25 were arrested for murder at substantially lower rates than they were in 1983. For example, the murder arrest rate for persons ages 35-45 declined nearly 25% over the 10-year period. In stark contrast, murder arrest rates for juveniles and young adults soared, with increases far greater than in any other violent crime category. The average increase for juveniles was double the average increase for young adults.

The fact that murder arrests for all adults increased just 9% between 1983 and 1992 masks two very different trends within the adult age group. The substantial declines in murder arrest rates for adults above their mid-twenties almost offset the very large increases in murder arrests of young adults.

As in all violent crimes, 18-year-olds had the highest arrest rate for murder in 1992. However, the pattern of age-related growth in murder arrest rates was not mirrored in any other violent offense, but was paralleled in weapons arrests.

Although Adults Were Responsible for Most of the Recent Violent Crime Increases, Juveniles Contributed More than Their Fair Share

Violent crime is increasing and, based on their representation in the general population, juveniles are responsible for a disproportionate share of this increase. But is it accurate to say that juveniles are driving the violent crime trends?

The number of violent crimes reported to law enforcement agencies increased 23% between 1988 and 1992. Knowing that over this same period, juvenile arrests for violent crime grew 47%, while adult arrests for violent crimes increased 19%, it is easy to conclude that juveniles were responsible for most of the increase in violent crime. However, even though the percentage increase in juvenile arrests was more than double the adult increase, the growth in violent crime cannot be attributed primarily to juveniles.

An example shows how this apparent contradiction can occur. Of the 100 violent crimes committed in 1988 in a small town, assume that juveniles were responsible for 10, and adults for 90. If the number of juvenile crimes increased 50%, juveniles would be committing 15 (or 5 more) violent crimes in 1992. A 20% increase in adult violent crimes would mean that adults were committing 108 (or 18 more) violent crimes in 1992. If each crime resulted in an arrest, the percentage increase in juvenile arrests would be more than double the adult increase (50% versus 20%). However, nearly 80% of the increase in violent crime (18 of the 23 additional violent crimes) would have been committed by adults.

Large percentage increases can yield relatively small overall changes. Juvenile arrests represent a relatively small fraction of the total; consequently a large percentage increase in juvenile arrests does not necessarily translate into a large contribution to overall crime growth.

In 1988 the FBI reported juveniles were arrested in 9% of the violent crimes for which someone was arrested; this juvenile clearance percentage was 13% in 1992. If it is assumed that juveniles were responsible for similar percentages of the *unsolved* violent crimes in these years, then it is possible to estimate the number of crimes committed by juveniles and by adults in 1988 and 1992.

From FBI reported crime and clearance statistics, it was estimated that juveniles committed 108,000 more Violent Crime Index offenses in 1992 than in 1988, while adults committed an additional 258,000. Therefore, juveniles were responsible for 30% of the growth in violent crime between 1988 and 1992. Between 1988 and 1992 juveniles were responsible for 26% of the increase in murders, 41% of the increase in forcible rapes, 39% of the increase in robberies, and 27% of the increase in aggravated assaults. Juveniles contributed less to the increase in murder than to the increases in other violent crimes.

Recent Large Increases in the Homicide Rates of Black and Older Juveniles Are the Result of Increases in Firearms Homicides

According to the National Center for Health Statistics, injury was the leading cause of death for youth below age 20 in 1991. Homicide was second only to motor vehicle accidents as the leading cause of fatal injuries. Two in five injury deaths of these youth in 1991 were the result of motor vehicle collisions. More than 1 in 5 injury deaths resulted from homicide. Between 1986 and 1991, while the number of youth dying in motor vehicle accidents declined 20%, homicide deaths rose substantially. . . .

The growth in juvenile homicide has been most pronounced in larger cities, those more than one-quarter million in population. Although the rate of juvenile homicides has increased in the U.S. in recent years, growth has been smallest in the South.

Sixty-five percent of juvenile homicide victims between 1976 and 1991 were male. The risk of being murdered has increased since the mid-1980s for both boys and girls. However, the increase has been greater for males. As a result, the male proportion of juvenile homicide victims has increased. In 1985, 64% of juvenile homicide victims were males; in 1991 this proportion had increased to 72%.

Slightly more than half of the juveniles killed between 1976 and 1991 were white. In terms of rate per 100,000 persons, however, black juveniles were 4 times more likely than white juveniles to be homicide victims. As a result, young black males have the highest homicide victimization rate of any race/sex group. The rate for black males was twice that of black females, 5 times that of white males, and 8 times that of white females.

Race and sex differences in homicide victimization rates were even more pronounced among older juveniles. Among juveniles ages 14 to 17, blacks were 5 times more likely to be murdered than whites. Similarly, older boys were 3 times more likely to be killed than older girls.

These race and sex differences in homicide victimization rates have increased in recent years, especially among older juveniles. In 1984 among juveniles ages 14 to 17, the homicide victimization rate for black males was 3 times that of black females, 5 times that of white males, and 9 times that of white females. By 1991 among these older juveniles, the homicide victimization rate for black males was 7 times that of black females, 8 times that of white males, and 29 times that of white females.

In 22% of homicides involving a juvenile victim between 1976 and 1991, information about the offender is unknown because the case is unsolved. For cases in which the offender was known, 24% of juvenile victims were murdered by other juveniles. Most juveniles (76%) were killed by adults; 52% were killed by persons ages 18 to 29.

Most juvenile homicides involved victims and offenders of the same race. Ninety-two percent of the black juvenile victims were killed by blacks, and 93% of the white juvenile victims were killed by whites.

Forty percent of juvenile homicide victims were killed by family members, most of them by parents. Of these parent-killing-child cases, slightly more than half of the boys (53%) were killed by their fathers, and slightly more than half of the girls (51%) were murdered by their mothers.

Forty-five percent of juvenile homicide victims were murdered by friends, neighbors, or acquaintances. These incidents generally involved boys being killed by males (66%).

Fourteen percent of juvenile homicide victims were killed by strangers. In murders by strangers, one-third occurred during the commission of another felony, such as rape or robbery.

Children were more likely than were older juveniles to be killed by their parents. Fifty-nine percent of homicide victims under age 10 were killed by parents (more often the father). Fists or feet were the most common weapons in such killings (45%). Eighteen percent of these younger children were killed with a firearm. These younger homicide victims were slightly more likely to be male (54%).

A Bureau of Justice Statistics study of murder cases disposed in 1988 found that 4 in 5 children under age 12 murdered by their parents had been previously abused by the parent who killed them.

Homicide victims age 10 to 17 were more often killed by a friend or other acquaintance (61%) rather than by a family member (16%). More than 70% of these homicide victims were shot to death. The large majority of juvenile homicide victims in this age range were male (73%).

In 1991 approximately 57% of all juvenile homicide victims were killed with a firearm, 8% were killed with a cutting or stabbing instrument, and 17% were killed with personal weapons such as fists or feet. Overall, homicide victims under age 18 were less likely than were adult homicide victims to be killed with a firearm and more likely than were adult victims to be killed with personal weapons. Older teens (ages 15 to 19) were more likely than was any other age group to be killed with a gun, while the murderers of young children rarely used a gun.

The firearm homicide death rate for teens ages 15 to 19 increased 61% between 1979 and 1989, from 6.9 to 11.1 deaths per 100,000. During the same period, the nonfirearm homicide rate decreased 29%, from 3.4 to 2.4. Thus, the observed increase in the homicide rate for older teenagers was driven solely by the increase in firearm homicides.

Homicides involving firearms have been the leading cause of death for black males ages 15 to 19 since 1969. In 1979 there were fewer than 40 such deaths per 100,000 black males that age in the population—by 1989 the figure had increased to more than 85. In 1989 the firearm homicide death rate among black males ages 15 to 19 in metropolitan counties was 6.5 times the rate in nonmetropolitan counties.

Reference

Juvenile Offenders and Victims: A Focus on Violence. Statistics Summary. National Center for Juvenile Justice. May 1995: 24-26, 47, 101, 104, 110, 112-113. ✦

9
National Survey Results on Drug Use From Monitoring the Future Study, 1975-1993

Lloyd D. Johnston
Patrick O'Malley
Jerald Bachman

Trends in Illicit Drug Use

... 1993 was a year in which a turnaround in the long decline occurred for a number of drugs among the nation's secondary school students.

Marijuana use rose sharply in all three grade levels. In the case of eighth graders, this was the second year of increase. Among college students and all young adults, however, marijuana use leveled, following an earlier rise in use. One in forty high school seniors is a daily marijuana user (2.4%, up from 1.9% in 1992). This is still far below the peak rate of 10.7% daily use reached in 1978.

Among seniors, the proportions using *any illicit drug other than marijuana* in the past year rose from 14.9% to 17.1%, a rate which is still substantially below the 34% peak rate in 1981. There was little change for college students or young adults, 13% of whom report such use.

In the last couple of years we noted an increase in the use of *LSD*—a drug of the late 1960s and early 1970s—among college students and young adults. In 1992, all five populations showed an increase in annual prevalence of LSD use though the one-year increase was statistically significant only among eighth graders (from 1.7% to 2.1%). In 1993, the eighth, tenth, and twelfth graders showed an increase, and this time only the twelfth grade change was significant. The 1989-1992 increase for college students (from 3.4% to 5.7%), and for young adults (from 2.7% to 4.3%) ended in 1993.

Just prior to the significant increase in use among seniors, there was a significant 4.3% decline in 1992 and a nonsignificant, but continued decline in 1993 in the proportion seeing great risk associated with trying LSD. In 1992 there was also a two percentage point decline (nonsignificant) in the proportion disapproving it and this trend continued in 1993. Since LSD was one of the earliest drugs popularly used in the overall American drug epidemic, there is a distinct possibility that young people—particularly the youngest cohorts, like the eighth graders—are not as concerned about the risks of use. They have had less opportunity to learn vicariously about the consequences of use by observing others around them, or to learn from intense media coverage of the issue. This type of "generational forgetting" could set the stage for a whole new epidemic of use.

Prescription-controlled *stimulants*—one of the most widely used classes of drugs taken illicitly (i.e., outside of medical regimen)—also showed evidence of a turnaround in 1993, with annual and 30-day prevalence rates increasing among four of the five populations. (Young adults were the exception.) Annual prevalence had fallen from 20% in 1982 to 7% in 1992 among seniors and from 21% to 4% among college students. This increase in use among seniors in 1993 followed a sharp drop in perceived risk a year earlier. In 1993, perceived risk continued to decline and disapproval of amphetamine use began to decline as well. This pattern is consistent with our theoretical position that perceived risk can drive both use and disapproval.

The *inhalants* constitute another class of abusable substance where we observe a troublesome increase in 1993. This class of drugs is defined by the form of the substance and its mode of administration—fumes or gases which are inhaled to get high. It includes common household substances such as glues, aerosols, butane, solvents, and so on. One class of inhalants, *amyl* and *butyl nitrites*, became somewhat popular in the late 1970s, but their use has almost been eliminated. For example, annual prevalence among twelfth grade students was 6.5% in 1979 but 0.9% in 1993.

When the nitrites are removed from consideration it appears that all other inhalants taken together have had an upward trend in use, from 3.0% among seniors in 1976 to 7.0% in 1993. It appears from the retrospective usage data supplied by twelfth grade students that the increase in inhalant use (unadjusted to include the nitrites) also increased at lower grade levels, where inhalant use is more common, during the late 1980s. In 1993 all five populations showed some modest increase in inhalant use, though only the increases in eighth and tenth grade (both of which increased last year as well) reached statistical significance. Some 11% of the 1993 eighth graders and 8% of the tenth graders indicated use in the prior 12 months, making inhalants the most widely used class of illicitly used drugs for eighth graders and the third most widely used (after marijuana and stimulants) for the tenth graders. The inhalants can and do cause death, and tragically, this often occurs among youngsters in their early teens.

The overall prevalence of *crack* cocaine levelled in 1987 at relatively low prevalence rates, at least within these populations. (This occurred despite the fact that the crack phenomenon continued a process of diffusion to new communities that year.) Then it declined until 1993, when annual prevalence held steady at 1.5% for seniors (down from 3.5% in 1987). Among young adults one to ten years past high school, annual prevalence was 1.3%, but only 0.6% among college students—both relatively unchanged since 1991. In high school, annual crack prevalence among the college-bound is lower than among those not bound for college (1.2% vs. 2.7%). There is now rather little regional variation in crack use.

We believe that the particularly intense media coverage of the hazards of crack cocaine, which took place quite early in what could have been a considerably more serious epidemic, likely had the effect of "capping" that epidemic early by deterring many would-be users and by motivating many experimenters to desist use. While 2.6% of seniors report ever having tried crack, only 0.7% report use in the past month, indicating noncontinuation by 74% of those who try it. The longer-term downward trend can be explained both in terms of lower initiation rates among students and higher noncontinuation rates.

Unfortunately, while use did not rise in 1993, perceived risk and disapproval dropped in all three grade levels, which could presage an increase in use in 1994.

Cocaine in general began to decline a year earlier than crack; between 1986 and 1987 the annual prevalence rate dropped dramatically by roughly four-tenths in all three populations studied. As we had predicted earlier, the decline occurred when young people began to see experimental and occasional use—the type of use they are most likely to engage in—as more dangerous; and this happened by 1987, probably partly because the hazards of cocaine use received extensive media coverage in the preceding year, but almost surely in part because of the cocaine-related deaths in 1986 of sports stars Len Bias and Don Rogers.

In 1992, this broad decline continued, with annual prevalence falling by nonstatisically significant amounts in all populations *except* eighth graders, who actually showed a statistically significant increase in use. Annual prevalence of cocaine use fell by about two-thirds among the three populations for which long-term data are available. In 1993 cocaine use remained stable in all five populations except the young adults, where use continued to decline. Again, the story regarding attitudes and beliefs is more troubling.

Having risen substantially since 1986, the perceived risk of using cocaine in general showed no further change in 1991 among seniors and actually showed some (nonsignificant) decline in 1992. In 1993, perceived risk for cocaine other than crack fell sharply in all grades and disapproval began to decline in all grades, though not as sharply as perceived risk. As with crack, these changes in attitudes and beliefs do not auger well for usage rates next year.

Through 1989, there was no decline in perceived availability of cocaine; in fact, it rose steadily after 1984 suggesting that availability played no role in bringing about the substantial downturn in use. After 1989, however, perceived availability has fallen some among seniors; the decline may be explained by the greatly reduced proportions of seniors who say they have any friends who use, because friendship circles are an important part of the supply system. Eighth and tenth graders reported a significant increase in the availability of crack and other cocaine in 1992, but there was no significant change in 1993.

As with all the illicit drugs, lifetime cocaine prevalence climbs with age, exceeding 30% by age 28. Unlike all of the other illicit drugs, active use—i.e., annual prevalence or monthly prevalence—also climbs after high school.

PCP use fell sharply, from an annual prevalence of 7.0% in 1979 to 2.2% in 1982 among high school seniors. It reached a low point of 1.2% in 1988, increased a bit to 2.4% in 1989, and then fell back to 1.4% by 1991, where it has remained through 1993. For the young adults, the annual prevalence rate is now only 0.2%.

The annual prevalence of *heroin* use has been very steady since 1979 among seniors at 0.4% to 0.6%. (It had fallen from 1.0% in 1975.) It stands at 0.5% in 1993. The heroin statistics for young adults and college students have also remained quite stable in recent years at low rates (about 0.1% to 0.2%). Eighth and tenth graders have an annual prevalence about the same as, or slightly higher than twelfth graders (0.7%) which is probably due to the fact that the eventual dropouts are captured in the lower grades but not in twelfth grade. Their rates remained unchanged in 1993.

The use of *opiates other than heroin* had been fairly level over most of the life of the study. Seniors had an annual prevalence rate of 3% to 6% since 1975. In 1991, however, the first recent significant decline (from 4.5% to 3.5%) was observed, though no further changes occurred in 1992 or 1993. Young adults in their twenties have generally shown a very gradual decline from 3.1% in 1986 to 2.2% in 1993; college students have likewise shown a slow decrease, from 3.8% in 1982-1984 to 2.5% in 1993. Data are not reported for younger grade levels because we believe the students are not accurately discriminating among the drugs which should be included or excluded from this class.

A long and substantial decline, which began in 1977, occurred for *tranquilizer* use among high school seniors. By 1992 annual prevalence reached 2.8% compared to 11% in 1977, but there was a significant increase in 1993 to 3.5% For the young adult sample, annual prevalence has now declined to 3.1% and for the college student sample to 2.4%.

The long-term gradual decline in *barbiturate* use, which began at least as early as 1975, when the study began, halted in 1988; the annual prevalence among seniors fell to 3.2%, compared to 10.7% in 1975. (It stands at 3.4% in 1993). Annual prevalence of this class of sedative drugs is even lower among the young adult sample (1.9%), and lower still among college students specifically (1.5%). For these groups there has been little further change since 1988. As with the opiates other than heroin, we do not include data here for lower grades because we believe the younger students have more problems with the proper classification of relevant drugs.

Methaqualone, another sedative drug, has shown quite a different trend pattern than barbiturates. Its use rose steadily among seniors from 1975 to 1981, when annual prevalence reached 8%. It then fell rather sharply to 0.5% by 1991 and stands at 0.2% in 1993. Use also fell among all young adults and among college students, which had annual prevalence rates of only 0.3% and 0.2%, respectively in 1989—the last year in which they were asked about this drug. In recent years, shrinking availability may well have played a role in this drop, as legal manufacture and distribution of the drug ceased. Because of its very low usage rates, only the seniors are now asked about their use of this drug.

In sum, five classes of illicitly used drugs which have had an impact on appreciable proportions of young Americans in their late teens and twenties are *marijuana, cocaine, stimulants, LSD,* and *inhalants.* In 1993, high school seniors showed annual prevalence rates of 26%, 3%, 8%, 7%, and 7%, respectively. Among college students in 1993, the comparable annual prevalence rates are 28%, 3%, 4%, 5%, and 4%; and for all high school graduates one to ten years past high school (young adults) the rates are 25%, 5%, 4%, 4%, and 2%. It is worth noting that LSD has climbed in the rankings because it either has not declined, or in some cases has increased, during a period in which cocaine, amphetamines, and other drugs have declined appreciably. The *inhalants* have become relatively more important for similar reasons. Clearly, cocaine is relatively more important in the older age group and inhalants are relatively more important in the younger ones. In fact, inhalants are the most widely used of the illicit drugs in eighth grade.

* * * * * *

The annual prevalence among seniors of over-the-counter *stay-awake pills,* which usually contain caffeine as their active ingredient, nearly doubled between 1982 and 1990, increasing from 12% to 23%. Since 1990 this statistic has fallen back some to 19% in 1993. Increases also occurred among the college-age young adult population (ages 19-22), where annual prevalence had been as high as 26% in 1989, but is now down to 19% in 1993.

The other two classes of nonprescription stimulants—the *look-alikes* and the over-the-counter *diet pills* have also shown some fall-off among both seniors and young adults in recent years. Still, among seniors some 23% of the females have tried diet pills by the end of senior year, 12% have used them in the past year, and 5% in just the past month....

Trends in Alcohol Use

Regarding *alcohol* use in these age groups, several findings are noteworthy. First, despite the fact that it is illegal for virtually all high school students and most college students to purchase alcoholic beverages, experience with alcohol is almost universal among them (67% of eighth graders have tried it, 81% of tenth graders, 87% of twelfth graders, and 91% of college students) and active use is widespread. Most important, perhaps, is the widespread occurrence of occasions of heavy drinking—measured by the percent reporting five or more drinks in a row at least once in the prior two-week period. Among eighth graders this statistic stands at 14%, among tenth graders at 23%, among twelfth graders at 28%, and among college students at 40%. After the early twenties this behavior recedes somewhat, reflected by the 34% found in the entire young adult sample.

Regarding trends in alcohol use, during the period of recent decline in the use of marijuana and other illicit drugs there appears not to have been any "displacement effect" in terms of any increase in alcohol use among seniors. (It was not uncommon to hear such a displacement hypothesis asserted.) If anything, the opposite seems to be true. Since 1980, the monthly prevalence of alcohol use among seniors has gradually declined, from 72% in 1980 to 51% in 1993. *Daily use* declined from a peak of 6.9% in 1979 to 2.5% in 1993; and the prevalence of drinking *five or more drinks in a row* (binge drinking) during the prior two-week interval fell from 41% in 1983 to 28% in 1993—nearly a one-third decline.

In 1993 there were no statistically significant changes in any of the populations in the prevalence of drinking in the prior 30-days, i.e., "current prevalence." There was a significant increase in the binge drinking rate for the tenth grade population. Eighth graders showed increases on both measures, though they were not statically significant....

Drug Use in Eighth Grade

It may be useful to focus specifically on the youngest age group in the study—the eighth graders—who are about 13 to 14 years old, because the exceptional level of use that they already have attained helps illustrate the urgent need this country has to continue to address the problems of substance abuse among its young.

By eighth grade 67% of youngsters report having tried *alcohol* and more than a quarter (26%) say they have already been drunk at least once.

Cigarettes have been tried by nearly half of eighth graders (45%) and 17%, or one in seven, say they have smoked in the prior month. Only 52% say they think there is great risk associated with being a pack-a-day smoker.

Smokeless tobacco has been tried by 30% of the male eighth graders, is used currently by 11% of them, and is used daily by 2.9%. Rates are far lower among the female eighth graders.

Among eighth graders, almost one in five (19%) have used *inhalants* and 5% say they have used in the past month. This is the only class of drugs for which use is substantially higher in eighth grade than in tenth or twelfth grade.

Marijuana has been tried by one in every eight eighth graders (13%), and has been used in the prior month by 5.1%.

A surprisingly large number say they have tried prescription-type *stimulants* (12%); 3.6% say they have used them in the prior 30 days.

Relatively few eighth graders say they have tried most of the other illicit drugs yet. (This is consistent with the retrospective reports from seniors, which have been included in this series in the previous years.)

But the proportions having at least some experience with them still is not inconsequential: *tranquilizers* (4.4%), *LSD* (3.5%), *other hallucinogens* (1.7%), *crack* (1.7%), *other cocaine* (2.4%), *heroin* (1.4%), and *steroids* (1.6% overall, and 2.5% among males.)

The very large numbers who have already begun use of the so-called "gateway drugs" (tobacco, alcohol, inhalants, and marijuana) suggests that a substantial number of eighth grade students are already at risk of proceeding further to such drugs as LSD, cocaine, amphetamines, and heroin.

Summary and Conclusions

To summarize the findings on trends, over the last decade or so there have been appreciable declines in the use of a number of the *illicit drugs* among seniors, and even larger declines in their use among American college students and young adults. However, as we have previously warned, the stall in these favorable trends in all three populations in 1985, as well as an increase in active *cocaine* use that year, should serve as a reminder that these improvements are not inevitable and cannot be taken for granted. (Further, during the eighties, the use of *inhalants* other than nitrites continued to rise.)

While the general decline resumed in 1986 and, most importantly, was joined by the start of a decline in *cocaine* use in 1987 and *crack* use in 1988, in 1992 we heard a number of alarm bells sounding. While the seniors continued to show improvement on a number of measures in 1992, the college students and young adults did not. Further the attitudes and beliefs of seniors regarding drug use began to soften. Perhaps of greatest importance, the eighth graders exhibited a significant increase in *marijuana*, *cocaine*, *LSD*, and *hallucinogens other than LSD*, as well as a not-quite significant increase in *inhalant* use. (In fact, all five populations showed some increase on *LSD*, continuing a longer term trend for college students and young adults.)

In 1993 still more alarms went off. The eighth graders continued to show an increase in their use of a number of drugs and (as their prior shifts in attitudes and beliefs foretold) the tenth graders and twelfth graders joined them. Rises are seen in a number of the so-called "gateway drugs"—in this case *marijuana*, *cigarettes*, and *inhalants*— which may bode ill for the use of later drugs in the usual sequence of involvement. The softening of attitudes about *crack* and other forms of *cocaine* also is a basis for concern.

As this study has demonstrated over the years, changes in perceived risk and disapproval have been important causes of the downturns which have occurred in the use of a number of drugs. These beliefs and attitudes surely are in turn influenced by the amount and nature of the public attention being paid to the drug issue. The fact that this attention has declined so substantially in the past few years may help to explain why the increases in perceived risk and disapproval among students ceased, and some clear backsliding has begun.

Of particular concern here is not only the possibility that there may be an increase in the use of particular drugs like LSD and inhalants, but that we may be seeing the beginning of a turnaround in the drug abuse situation more generally among our youngest cohorts—perhaps because they have not had the same opportunities for vicarious learning from the adverse drug experiences of people around them and people they learn about through the media. Clearly there is a danger that, as the drug epidemic has subsided considerably, newer cohorts have far less opportunity to learn through informal means about the dangers of drugs. This may mean that the nation must redouble its efforts to be sure that they learn these lessons through more formal means—from schools, parents, and focused messages in the media, for example—and that this more formalized prevention effort become institutionalized so that it will endure for the long term.

The following facts help to put into perspective the magnitude and variety of substance use problems which remain among American young people:

By the end of eighth grade, one-third (32%) of American secondary school students have tried an *illicit drug* (if inhalants are included as an illicit drug). Almost two-fifths of tenth graders have done so (39%), and nearly one-half of twelfth graders (47%).

By their late twenties, over 75% of America's young adults today have tried an *illicit drug*, including over 50% who have tried some *illicit drug other than marijuana*. These figures do not include inhalants.

By age 28, about one-third of young Americans have tried *cocaine*; and as early as the senior year of high school 6% have done so. Roughly one in every forty seniors (2.6%) have tried the particularly dangerous form of cocaine called *crack*: in the young adult sample one in twenty-five (4.3%) have tried it.

One in forty (2.4%) of high school seniors in 1993 smoke *marijuana daily*, as is true among young adults aged 19 to 28 (2.4%). Among seniors in 1993, 9.6% had been daily marijuana smokers at some time for at least a month, and among young adults the comparable figure is 12.8%.

Some 28% of seniors have had *five or more drinks in a row* at least once in the prior two weeks, and such behavior tends to increase among young adults one to four years past high school. The prevalence of such behavior among male college students reaches 49%.

Some 30% of seniors are current *cigarette* smokers and 19% already are current daily smokers, and these numbers are *rising*. In addition, many of the lighter smokers will convert to heavy smoking after high school.

Thus, despite the improvements in recent years, it is still true that this nation's secondary school students and young adults show a level of involvement with illicit drugs which is greater than has been documented in any other industrialized nation in the world. Even by longer-term historical standards in this country, these rates remain extremely high. Heavy drinking also remains widespread and troublesome; and certainly the continuing initiation of a large and growing proportion of young people to cigarette smoking is a matter of the greatest public health concern.

Finally, we note the seemingly unending capacity of pharmacological experts and amateurs to discover new substances with abuse potential that can be used to alter mood and consciousness, as well the potential for our young people to "discover" the abuse potential of existing products, like RobitussinTM, and to "rediscover" older drugs, such as LSD. While as a society we have made significant progress on a number of fronts in the fight against drug abuse, we must continually be preparing for, and remaining vigilant against, the opening of new fronts, as well as the re-emergence of trouble on older ones.

The drug problem is not an enemy which can be vanquished, as in a war. It is more a recurring and relapsing problem which must be contained to the extent possible on a long term, ongoing basis.

Reference

Johnston, Lloyd D., Patrcia M. O'Malley, & Jerald G. Bachman. 1994. *National Survey Results on Drug Use*. Vol. 1. Rockville, Maryland: National Institutes of Health. Pp. 9-18, 22-25. ✦

10
Culture, Gender, and Delinquency: A Study of Youths in the United States and India

Clayton A. Hartjen
Sesharajani Kethineni

One of the persistent findings from epidemiological research in criminology carried out in the United States is the distinctive difference in offense rates between males and females. These rates suggest that males are substantially more criminal/delinquent overall compared to females, and especially so when it comes to violent and assaultive types of conduct. The gender-gap problem is highlighted by a number of self-report delinquency surveys conducted in the United States. This research also hints that male/female differences in offense behavior probably do exist. However, virtually all these inquiries suggest that the extent of the difference is considerably less than that revealed by official rates (Berger (1989); Chesney-Lind (1987); Chesney-Lind and Shelden (1992:7-28)). To what extent, if at all, this is true of gender-groups in other countries is simply not known.

A small number of international and comparative inquiries also suggest that the gender-gap phenomenon may be universal. Generally this research indicates that the extent of the differences in male/female offense behavior may be even greater in developing countries compared to the United States and various industrial Western-European nations (Adler (1984); Bowker (1981); Hartjen (1986); Pulkkeinen and Saastamoineu (1986); UN Social Defense (1984)). However, except for the self-report research on juveniles in the Western countries, virtually all this research has relied on official statistics—usually arrest or disposition data—which, at best, make any generalizations about differences in male/female offense behavior highly speculative and any cross-national assessment of gender-related involvement in crime/delinquency nearly impossible....

This paper is an exploratory inquiry in cross-culture criminological analysis. In it we analyze the official and self-reported delinquency rates of juveniles in the United States and India. In so doing, we hope to add to the general body of comparative inquiry and to offer some theoretically relevant speculations that may help to account for the variations in the rates we observe.

Theoretical Considerations

A number of arguments have been offered that purport to account for differences in the offense rates of males and females. Most promising among these are several that reflect major themes contained in general etiological theory. These include Morris' (1964, 1965) learning theory argument regarding differences in socialization, the notions of strain and opportunity as expressed in Adler's (1975) and Simon's (1975) liberation hypotheses, and more recently the social control implications provided by Hagan et al. (1985, 1987) power-control theory. Taken together, these arguments suggest a set of ideas that present a plausible nucleus for gender-related epidemiological theory (see Chesney-Lind and Shelden (1992:54-79)). Specifically, these arguments suggest that delinquency rates for girls and boys are likely to differ to the extent that they (1) experience different degrees or forms of inducements (e.g., strain, as per Agnew (1992)) to engage in delinquent acts; (2) are more or less subject to conventional social controls (e.g., social bonds); and/or, (3) are provided more or fewer opportunities to learn pro-delinquent sentiments and/or behavior (i.e., differential association/reinforcement).¹

The differences in crime/delinquency rates revealed by cross-cultural research also suggest that different societies (due to cultural, economic, and/or structural characteristics) are likely to exhibit variations in the factors that produce disparities in the relative involvement of males and females in crime and delinquency (Adler and Simon (1979); Adler (1984); Hartnagel (1982)). For example, a slight modification of the argument presented by Hoffman-Bustamante (1973), would suggest that societies vary in the extent to which they produce pressures or inducements to deviate among their inhabitants, or among portions of their populations (e.g., males vs. females). Similarly, the extent to which some members of different societies are subject to conventional social control is not likely to be identical across cultures. Finally, societies are also likely to differ in the extent to which their members are in positions to be differentially exposed to delinquent (or delinquency reinforcing) others. In terms of any or all of these factors, variations in rates of delinquent behavior, and/or rates of delinquent behavior of various types, are likely to occur across societies or among groups (such as gender groups) within societies (Cheung and Ng (1988); Defleur (1967); Sandhu (1987); Sarkar (1987); Shew (1988); Shim (1987); Singh and Agarwal (1986); Skinner (1986); UN Social Defense (1984); Wani (1984)).

If such notions as strain, learning, and social control do reflect universal causal factors in delinquent behavior, variations in rates of this behavior by gender and/or country reflect differences in sociocultural forces related to the operation of these forces, both within and across societies. Given this possibility, three variations in delinquency rates across sex-groups and countries can occur. Specifically, differences in delinquency rates could exist (1) between the youths of two different societies (regardless of gender); (2) between gender groups across societies (regardless of culture); or (3) among both boys and girls across various societies. . . .

Data

Four primary sources of data are drawn upon in this analysis: official arrest rates for India (Bureau of Police Research and Development (1988)) and the United States (Federal Bureau of Investigation (1984)), a self-reported delinquency survey of Indian boys and girls, and a comparison subsample of American high-school youths extracted from the National Youth Survey, 1978 (Elliott et al. (1983)).

Official Statistics

India and the United States both publish official crime reports presenting information on crimes known to the police as well as arrest statistics broken down by age and gender. Differences in laws, offense categories, and reporting methods make direct comparisons of these data tenuous at best. However, some sense of the similarities and differences in male/female delinquency within India and comparisons of India/U.S. patterns can be made from official reports (Hartjen (1986)).

Since India and most jurisdictions in the United States use age 18 as the dividing line between juvenile and adult status, age 18 is used as the upper limit for comparison purposes in this report. However, since the two reports use different offense categories to report arrests, rather than comparing individual crimes, offenses were grouped into broad types generally familiar to criminologists—i.e., personal, property, public disorder, and substance abuse offenses. . . .²

Self-Reported Delinquency Surveys

A self-reported delinquency survey was carried out by one of the authors among Indian youths during the fall of 1987. The findings from this survey augment the information on Indian delinquency obtainable from arrest statistics and allow us to make direct behavioral comparisons with findings obtained from the 1978 version of the National Youth Survey.

Indian Survey

The Indian survey sought to replicate and expand an earlier investigation completed in 1978 by Hartjen and Priyadarsini (1984), and the sampling strategy was largely dictated by that consideration. In the present survey samples of respondents were investigated in the cities of Madras and New Delhi. These cities were selected because of their distinctive economic, ethnic, and cultural differences, thereby providing samples of Indian juveniles reminiscent of India's extreme sociocultural diversity. Respondents were selected from a variety of high schools as well as correctional institutions for juveniles in and around the two cities resulting in a total sample of 2600 respondents. Since, in the present inquiry, no "correctional institution" population is identifiable in the National Youth Survey, this analysis is limited to the 2077 respondents sampled from the various high schools surveyed, producing usable questionnaires from 1013 boys and 1040 girls. . . .

The survey instrument was modeled after the one used in the 1978 National Youth Survey, although modified for the purposes of the study.[3] The questionnaire was first constructed in English and translated into colloquial Tamil (Madras) and Hindi (New Delhi) by persons fluent in English and the local language. The instruments were informally pretested using several high school-aged volunteers or first year college students. The questionnaire was administered to each class en masse by the researcher and Indian graduate-student assistants and coded by the assistants under the researcher's direction.

National Youth Survey

To provide a comparative assessment of the Indian self-report data, a subsample of the 1978 National Youth Survey (NYS) was extracted and recoded to match the codings and offense-item categories used in the Indian survey.[4] This sample consisted of NYS high-school respondents within the age range (approximately 13-18 years) sampled in the Indian survey. Since the design of this survey has been detailed by Elliott et al. (1983) and its results extensively reported in the literature, it would be redundant to review this material here. . . .

Analysis

Arrests

The data presented in Table 1 suggest several things about the probable involvement of American and Indian boys and girls in various forms of illegal behavior. What is clear from these data is that a considerably greater number (both absolute and relative) of American than Indian juveniles are apprehended by authorities. Indeed, the total number of Indian juveniles arrested is less than 3% of those apprehended in the United States. This is especially true of Indian girls since they equal only 1.25% of the American girls arrested, while the proportion of Indian boys arrested equals about 3.4% of the number of boys arrested in the United States. Moreover, juveniles make up about 17% of all those arrested in the United States. In India persons below age 18 account for only 1.4% of total arrests. In short, compared to the United States, juveniles, and especially juvenile girls, make up a minuscule portion of the persons accused of illegal conduct by authorities in India.

The total number of all arrests each year in India is equal to about one-half the number of arrests in the United States (5,238,543 compared to 10,275,047 for 1983). Given that the Indian population is about four times larger than the United States, the actual differences in arrest rates are considerable (approximately 616 versus 5119 per 100,000 population respectively). Even more dramatic are the differences in juvenile arrests since juveniles at risk (between ages 4 and 18) equal about 15% of the

Table 1
Arrests of United States and Indian Boys and Girls, 1983

OFFENSE CATEGORY	U.S. BOYS	U.S. GIRLS	RATIO B:G	INDIA BOYS	INDIA GIRLS	RATIO B:G
PERSONAL	128,169	25,000	5:1	1,162	93	13:1
PROPERTY	509,433	124,783	4:1	9,479	383	25:1
PUBLIC ORDER	303,134	111,077	3:1	8,767	1,107	8:1
SUBSTANCE ABUSE	192,304	48,372	4:1	4,869	468	10:1
OTHER	226,047	57,427	4:1	22,520	2,544	11:1
TOTAL ARRESTS	1,359,087	366,659	4:1	46,797	4,595	10:1

Source: Computed from Bureau of Research and Development (1988) and Federal Bureau of Investigation (1984)

United States population but are almost 30% of the Indian population. Thus, relative either to total population or the juvenile portion, the differences in arrest rates for juveniles between the United States and India are substantial. If we assume that arrests reflect actual involvement in illegality, it would appear that Indian youth are considerably less delinquent than their American counterparts.

Table 1 also suggests the possibility that rather substantial differences exist in the relative delinquency of male and female juveniles in the two countries. Overall, American boys are arrested about four times more often than are American girls. Comparatively, Indian boys are arrested about ten times more frequently than are Indian girls. These differences exist for every offense category, although the ratios for property crimes are even more disparate.

When the proportions (not shown) of each offense category to total arrests are compared, only slight variations are found for American boys and girls, while somewhat greater variability exists among the Indian juveniles arrested. Thus, although arrest frequencies differ by gender and across countries, no dramatic differences exist between boys and girls in either country as to the offense types for which they are more or least likely to be arrested. . . .

Self-Report Findings

Table 2 shows prevalence rates for individual offense items investigated in the self-report surveys. Although for many offenses these rates are quite low, at least some of the boys and girls in both the U.S. and India samples admit committing almost all of the offenses on at least one occasion. On the average about 17% of the American boys admit some involvement in each act, followed by Indian boys (13%), American girls (11%) and lastly, Indian girls (6%).

In order to assess differences or similarities in patterns of involvement, Spearman Rank Order coefficients (RHO) were computed for the various sample groups. These coefficients show that, although prevalence proportions may vary, gender groups within countries have remarkably similar offense patterns because when boys are compared to girls in both countries RHO's of .90 (U.S.) and .91 (India) are found. That is, boys and girls in either country are more or less frequently engaged in the same offense behaviors such that one group, for example, is not committing numerous property crimes while the other is heavily involved in personal assaults. Comparing the offense patterns of United States and Indian respondents coefficients remain strong and significant (boys = .66, girls = .50). However, the smaller size of the coefficients suggests that the relationship between gender and delinquency is culturally variable such that boys or girls in India compared to the U.S. are less similar than are boys and girls within either country. The low coefficient (.46) for American boys compared to Indian girls and the surprisingly high coefficient (.85) for Indian boys compared to American girls similarly highlights the impact cul-

Table 2
Percentage of United States and Indian Boys and Girls Admitting Offense on One

OFFENSE	PERCENT ADMITTING*			
	U.S.		INDIA	
	BOYS	GIRLS	BOYS	GIRLS
ASSAULT	6	2	11	2
GANG FIGHT	11	5	7	3
HIT PARENT	5	5	2	2
CONCEALED WEAPON	10	1	9	3
STEAL US/RS 50+	4	1	8	3
STEAL US/RS 5-50	7	3	3	1
STEAL US/RS < 50	20	10	10	3
STRONGARM OTHERS	4	1	8	4
BREAK AND ENTER	4	0	10	5
VEHICLE THEFT	2	0	1	1
JOY RIDE	6	3	13	2
STEAL FROM FAMILY	12	8	22	10
STEAL FROM SCHOOL	6	3	15	7
POSSESS STOLEN PROP.	14	2	10	2
AVOID PAYMENT	22	8	33	10
VANDALISM	35	16	27	11
THROW OBJECTS	48	29	19	6
DISORDERLY CONDUCT	33	25	16	5
DRUNK IN PUBLIC	25	16	2	1
BEG FOR MONEY	3	1	3	2
RUNAWAY	6	5	7	2
TRUANCY	43	33	38	21
LIE ABOUT SELF	31	30	34	21
CHEAT ON TEST	48	47	54	40
SOLD SOFT DRUGS	13	4	0	0
SOLD HARD DRUGS	2	1	0	0
USED SOFT DRUGS	33	28	2	1
USED HARD DRUGS	6	1	1	1
DRANK ALCOHOL	30	24	19	6
MEAN % PER OFFENSE	17	11	13	6
SAMPLE N	663	584	1013	1040

*Percentages rounded to nearest whole number

tural factors may have on the gender/delinquency relationship.

Although differences or similarities in patterns of behavior are revealing, the gender-gap issue primarily centers on the relative proportions of boys and girls engaged in delinquent behavior. PHI coefficients allow us to measure the strength of the gender/delinquency relationship within and across countries. Coefficients for individual offense items, by sample groups, are presented in Table 3.

Cross-Gender Comparisons

American boys register significantly higher prevalence rates compared to girls for all but four offenses. But in most instances PHI coefficients are extremely small, suggesting that profoundly different rates of involvement in most forms of delinquency do not exist between American boys and girls. Moderate coefficients were found for five of the 29 offense items (concealed weapon, possess stolen property, avoid payment, vandalism, and throw objects).

A similar observation can be made when Indian boys and girls are compared. In contrast to the American sample, somewhat stronger coefficients were found for some offenses, but no significant differences exist for four offenses and extremely small differences resulted for most other offenses. PHI coefficients in the .20-.30 range suggest that Indian boys were substantially more delinquent than Indian girls for a variety of offenses (i.e., avoid payment, vandalism, and throw objects in addition to joy riding and drinking alcohol).

Overall, the self-report findings suggest that in both India and the United States, while boys are somewhat more delinquent than girls, both with regard to types of behavior and relative proportions involved, the extreme differences found in arrest rates may not necessarily reflect extreme differences in actual behavior.

Cross-Cultural Comparisons

The comparative lack of offense-pattern similarity indicated by RHO between American and Indian boys also is seen in the PHI coefficients when offense-item preva-

Table 3
PHI Coefficients for Individual Offense-Item Prevalence Rates by Sample Group

OFFENSE	U.S. BOYS/ GIRLS	INDIA BOYS/ GIRLS	BOYS U.S./ INDIA	GIRLS U.S./ INDIA	INDIA BOYS/ U.S. GIRLS	U.S. BOYS/ INDIA GIRLS
ASSAULT	.10	.18	-.18	NS	.16	.10
GANG FIGHT	.11	.09	.09	05*	NS	.16
HIT PARENT	NS	NS	.08	.09	-.01	.08
CONCEALED WEAPON	.19	.13	NS	-.06	.16	.15
STEAL US/RS 50+	.09	.11	-.08	-.06	.15	NS
STEAL US/RS 5-50	.09	.07*	.09	.08	NS	.16
STEAL US/RS < 5	.14	.14	.14	.15	NS	.28
STRONGARM OTHERS	.09	.08	-.08	-.09	.15	NS
BREAK AND ENTER	.14	.09	-.11	-.14	.20	NS
VEHICLE THEFT	.10	NS	NS	-.06	NS	NS
JOY RIDE	.07	.21	-.11	NS	.16	.10
STEAL FROM FAMILY	.07*	.16	-.13	NS	.18	NS
STEAL FROM SCHOOL	.07	.13	-.14	-.08	.19	NS
POSSESS STOLEN PROP.	.22	.16	.08	NS	.15	.23
AVOID PAYMENT	.19	.28	-.12	NS	.28	.17
VANDALISM	.22	.21	.08	.07	.13	.29
THROW OBJECTS	.19	.20	.31	.36	-.11	.49
DISORDERLY CONDUCT	.09	.18	.20	.29	-.11	.36
DRUNK IN PUBLIC	.11	.02*	.36	.29	-.26	.39
BEG FOR MONEY	.07	NS	NS	NS	.01	NS
RUNAWAY	NS	.12	NS	.08	NS	.10
TRUANCY	.10	.19	.05*	.13	.01	.23
LIE ABOUT SELF	.06*	.15	-.09	.10	NS	.11
CHEAT ON TEST	NS	.14	-.06	.07	.01	.08
SOLD SOFT DRUGS	.16	**	.29	.16	-.16	.29
SOLD HARD DRUGS	NS	**	.11	.08	-.01	.11
USED SOFT DRUGS	.05	.06	.42	.42	-.40	.46
USED HARD DRUGS	.13	NS	.15	NS	NS	.15
DRANK ALCOHOL	.07*	.20	.13	.26	NS	.33

NS = NOT SIGNIFICANT, * = SIGNIFICANT < .05, ** = UNABLE TO COMPUTE, ALL OTHER COEFFICIENTS SIGNIFICANT < .01

lence rates are compared. For 10 of the 29 offenses, Indian boys exhibit higher prevalence rates compared to American boys. Although statistically significant, none of the coefficients are particularly large. Generally these differences involve property and status offense behavior. In contrast, for 15 offenses American rates exceed those of Indian boys. While also generally small, for some offenses the differences are fairly large. These typically involve public disorder forms of misconduct and drug/alcohol-related behavior.

The prevalence rates of Indian compared to American girls are significantly greater (although weakly so) for six offenses, almost all involving property crimes. No statistically significant differences were found, however, for another four of these offenses. Like American boys, American girls registered higher prevalence rates for about one-half the offenses. Of these the largest involved public order and drug/alcohol-related activity.

Generally speaking, while Americans do appear to be somewhat more delinquent than Indian youths, as far as prevalence is concerned, these differences primarily center on public disorder and substance-abuse activities. Somewhat greater proportions of the Indian respondents were involved in some property offenses, but status and personal offense behavior is quite similar across the two countries.

Gender/Culture Comparisons

When Indian boys are compared to American girls, no significant differences emerge for almost a third of the offenses. Indian boys have higher prevalence rates for about one-half the offenses, most regarding property offenses. American girls, however, had substantially higher prevalence rates for throw objects, disorderly conduct, drunk in public, using hard drugs, and selling hard drugs. Since the proportions admitting any of the substance-related offenses are very small for the Indian boys caution is warranted when interpreting the size of PHI coefficients. Surprisingly no significant differences were found in prevalence rates between American boys and Indian girls for seven offenses, almost all involving property crimes. Otherwise, greater proportions of American boys admitted involvement in all other offenses, and frequently the coefficients were moderate to large. Again, strong differences were particularly found for various public disorder offenses and substance-related behavior. . . .

Explaining the Delinquency Gender/Culture Gap

The foregoing analysis suggests that within India and the United States boys and girls engage in roughly similar types and patterns of offense behavior. With few exceptions, boys are also consistently more delinquent than girls (especially insofar as direct-predatory types of crimes are concerned); although the extent of this difference varies from country to country. In this regard, along with other cross-cultural research, this study suggests that a certain universality exists in delinquency to the extent that such conduct is found in societies with profoundly different social, cultural, and economic characteristics.

However, even though a goodly amount of commonality can be found in the delinquency involvement of youths throughout the world, significant differences also exist. . . .

Cultural Differences

In contrast to the pronounced involvement of American youths in the kinds of public and substance abuse behavior that is likely to get them into trouble with authorities, such conduct on the part of Indian youth is extremely rare. In part, this may reflect India's Hindu and Muslim cultural heritage. For example, in contrast to the United States and Western European countries, India is not a drinking society. Nor does it provide the kind of environment wherein an illicit drug culture is likely to flourish. Both alcohol and drugs are, of course, consumed in India. But the kind of social atmosphere that promotes such activity in the United States is decidedly absent in India (Mandelbaum (1972)). Thus, advertisements for alcoholic beverages are practically nonexistent in India. Tightly controlled and regulated outlets for alcohol do exist, but bars are inconspicuously located and public drinking rare. Except perhaps in some affluent, "Westernized" households, at-home drinking by parents and others is infrequent and typically a ceremonial rather than routine activity. National prohibition is periodically espoused by one group or another, and several states have enacted prohibition laws at various times since Independence. In short, little by way of sociocultural inducements or reinforcements for substance-abuse activity confront Indian youths. In this respect, opportunities to use, learn about, or be reinforced in the use of drugs and alcohol are comparatively limited for Indian compared to American youths.

In addition, unlike the United States, an adolescent "leisure class" of any consequence has simply not emerged in India

(Greenberg (1978)). Thus, unlike the rampant "consumerism" characteristic of most American youth, Indian youth are an economically dependent group. Indeed, the concept of an "allowance" or one's own earnings from part-time jobs are practically unheard of in India. Many Indian youths may steal because they are poor or get into legal trouble because they are exploited as beggars, prostitutes, sneak thieves, etc., by adults. But the economic ability, much less the physical opportunity, to "hang out" in adolescent enclaves out of sight or control of parents or other adults simply does not exist. In a poverty culture most Indian teenagers do not have cars of their own, nor do they have ready access to any they could drive on their own. All the potential delinquency the freedom of a car thus offers is nipped in the bud. In addition, adolescent parties (especially unsupervised ones) are exceptional. And even in large cities one is unlikely to ever come across a group (gang) of adolescents wandering the streets at night. Thus, much of the misconduct that a "hanging out" environment can inspire is unlikely to take place in India.

Western nuclear-type families are becoming more numerous in India. But, the most common family form is still the extended or joint family arrangement (Karve (1986); Mandelbaum (1972)). Along with this, Indian youth (indeed Indians generally) associate and interact primarily with family and kin. The center of one's existence is the home and family. School-peers may be identified as "friends." But outside the school setting, social activities primarily center around the household and related others. As such, Indian children are almost constantly under the direct supervision of an "interested" adult. Indeed a private room is a luxury few Indian families can afford, and sequestering oneself in one's room with peers out of view of adults would be an occasion for severe rebuke. Having one's own space or even privacy is something few Indians ever contemplate. Consequently opportunities to deviate, especially outside the family setting, are comparatively less for Indian than for American youths (Singh and Agarwal (1986)).

Equally important is the fact that one's family (and, more widely, "community") is the center of one's attention and personal identification. Indeed, as Mandelbaum (1968) observed, the "individual" simply cannot survive socially, and probably economically, in India, for the family and jati (sub-cast) remain the source of social life, economic reward, marriage prospects, and self identity. In this regard, a kind of "reintegrative shaming" (Braithwaite (1989)) is pervasive in Indian society. To shame oneself by delinquency is to equally shame one's family, and, as such, damage one's essential realm of existence in Indian society. Consequently, while one may play with school peers, it is the values of elders, not those of peers, that are most important and constantly transmitted to children and adolescents. To the extent that these values promote sobriety, respect for authority, obedience, and a sense of collective identity inconceivable to the individualistic orientation of Americans, Indian youth generally are both less able and less inclined to engage in serious (or stigmatizing) delinquent forms of behavior. This is especially true for those types of misconduct associated with public displays of rebellion, self-assertion, and self-indulgence that are seemingly a cultural feature of many young people in contemporary American society (Farnsworth (1984); Johnson (1986); Wells and Rankin (1988)). And as suggested by the comparatively high "family" and low "public" delinquency self-report rates for Indian respondents, when a youth "offends" in India the conduct is more likely to occur in, or be directed against, one's family. Thus, misconduct generally is less likely to be brought to the attention of authorities or result in official action.

Gender Differences

Of the rates explored in this paper, the extremely low rates for Indian females require special commentary. Gender-gap theories would lead us to predict that low rates of delinquency are likely to be found among girls, compared to boys, because (1) they are socialized in ways that orient them away from, rather than toward, delinquent activity; (2) they are much more subjected to social control and parental supervision than boys, thereby impeding opportunities to deviate or to acquire delinquent orientations; and, (3) their role expectations and limitations make it less likely that they will be in positions to have access to many forms of misconduct. If such arguments, do indeed, have explanatory relevance, the extremely low rates of delinquency among Indian girls are readily understandable (compare Caplan (1985); Desai and Krishnaraj (1987); Jain (1975) with Datesman et al. (1975); Henggeler et al. (1987); Morash (1986)).

If in the terminology of power-control theory, America represents an egalitarian society, India can be characterized as an extreme version of a patriarchal society (Hagan et al. (1987)). Females, especially unmarried ones, are at the bottom of the Indian social structure. Infant mortality rates for females are several times higher than those of males (both through female infanticide as well as wanton neglect). The birth of a girl is met with resignation if not sorrow, while an infant boy is heralded into the world with considerable ceremony. Often earlier than legally permissible, girls are "married off" to take up residence as the lowest-level servant in the family household of their husband. Out-of-home labor may be an economic necessity for many women and an object of choice for upper-middle-class, educated (Westernized) women. But it is still often expected that one's paycheck will be turned over to father or husband. And child rearing and all the chores of the household still remain the working-woman's realm of responsibility (Krishnaraj and Chanana (1989); Lebra et al. (1984); Murkhopadhyay (1984); Somjee (1989)).

For the vast majority of Indian females childhood socialization and supervision is almost exclusively directed to preparing them for marriage and their eventual departure from the household. Being a good wife, mother, and homemaker becomes their central purpose in life. Usually with the consent of the bride, marriages are arranged by the family, not something the individual is to pursue alone. Dating is practically unheard of, and the rare "love" marriage is an occasion for scandal (and in some reputed cases even murder). After adolescence, girls are almost constantly chaperoned by relatives or some responsible adult (e.g., teachers). Thus, "hanging out" with other girls, much less a mixed-sex group of (especially non-related) youths is not only unthinkable but also nearly impossible for the Indian female. The "bad name" it would bring would insure that prospective grooms would not materialize, leaving the girl to be an economic burden and disgrace to the entire family. Striking out on one's own to make one's way in the world is beyond imagination for most Indian females.

From a Westerner's point of view, this situation could produce strain and resentment among Indian females motivating them to deviate. This is a possibility. But, even then, Indian females, especially adolescents, are rarely in a position to do much about it outside the home environment. Indeed, the strong fatalistic orientation of Indians expressed in the belief in "karma" and a cyclical view of life helps to suppress resentment and efforts to alter their fate on the part of females and oppressed groups generally (Moffatt (1979)). For the Indian, "This is my fate in this life. I will do my 'dharma' (duty) so that it will be better in the next" is the prevailing ideology (Ashby (1974); Hobkins (1971)).

Both the cultural orientation toward women and the structural arrangements of Indian society make delinquent behavior (at least peer-inspired behavior) unlikely to be attempted by Indian girls and even less likely to be successfully accomplished. The ironic twist is that what Westerners are likely to view as the social oppression and control of Indian girls is itself probably largely responsible for their comparatively low rates of involvement in practically any form of delinquency....

Notes

1. Theories regarding the etiology of delinquent behavior have been severely criticized for failing to include the criminality of females within their explanatory focus and have been condemned, therefore, as being inadequate

to explain crime and delinquency on the part of females (Leonard (1982)). Although a clear sexist bent in causal theory does exist, the inability of these theories (or reformulated versions of them) to equally explain the delinquent behavior of boys and girls remains an empirical question (Jensen & Eve (1976); Pollock-Byrne (1990:8-35)). But, even then, theories directed to explaining the etiology of delinquent behavior are inappropriate for understanding variations in rates of this behavior, whether these rates are gender related or not (Daly & Chesney-Lind (1988); Gibbons (1971)).

2. We realize that these categorizations are somewhat arbitrary and may include offenses that are not strictly identical for both countries. However, cross-cultural research using available data cannot adjust for differences in the recording practices of officials in the countries studied. Thus, interpretation of these data should be made with caution, although we are confident that broad differences and similarities in the respective rates are correctly discernible from the categories used.

3. How representative school attendees are of the Indian juvenile population is not known. However, discussions with officials suggest that most youths do go to school even in to higher-secondary levels. "Drop outs" are largely poor youths forced by poverty to work at an early age to help support the family. We have no reason to believe that these youths are any more or less involved in delinquency than are those attending schools.

4. Generally the questionnaire was simplified and shortened for mass-administration purposes. Sexual misconduct items (e.g., sexual assault, intercourse, etc.) were excluded because of opposition by Indian authorities. Also after consulting with various Indian collaborators it was decided to collapse the extensive list of drug-abuse items found in the NYS into two categories ("hard"—heroin, cocaine and "soft"—marijuana, ganja) since neither Tamil or Hindi contain words into which various types of drugs could be translated.

References

Adler, Freda. 1975. *Sisters in Crime*. NY: McGraw-Hill.

———. 1984. *The Incidence of Female Criminality in the Contemporary World*. NY: NYU Press.

Adler, Freda and Rita James Simon, (Editors). 1979. *The Criminality of Deviant Women*. Boston: Houghton Mifflin.

Agnew, Robert. 1992. "Foundation For a General Strain Theory of Crime and Delinquency." *Criminology* 30:47-87.

Ashby, Philip H. 1974. *Modern Trends in Hinduism*. NY: Columbia University Press.

Bayley, David H. 1969. *The Police and Political Development in India*. Princeton, NJ: Princeton University Press.

Berger, Ronald J. 1989. "Female Delinquency in the Emancipation Era: A Review of the Literature." *Sex Roles* 21:375-399.

Black, Donald. 1980. *The Manners and Customs of the Police*. NY: Academic Press.

Bowker, Lee H. 1981. "The Institutional Determinants of International Female Crime." *International Journal of Comparative and Applied Criminal Justice* 5:41-50.

Braithwaite, John. 1989. *Crime, Shame and Reintegration*. Cambridge: Cambridge University Press.

Bureau of Police Research and Development. 1988. *Crime in India—1983*. New Delhi: Ministry of Home Affairs, Government of India.

Caplan, Patricia. 1985. *Class and Gender in India*. London: Tavistock.

Cernkovich, Stephen A. and Peggy C. Giordano. 1979. "A Comparative Analysis of Male and Female Delinquency." *The Sociological Quarterly* 20:131-145.

Cernkovich, Stephen A., Peggy Giordano, and Meredith D. Pugh. 1985. "Chronic Offenders: The Missing Cases in Self-Report Delinquency Research." *Journal of Criminal Law and Criminology* 76:705-732.

Chesney-Lind, Meda. 1987. "Girls and Violence: An Exploration of the Gender Gap in Serious Delinquent Behavior." In Crowell, David H., Ian M. Evans and Clifford R. O'Donnell, (eds.), *Childhood Aggression and Violence: Sources of Influence, Prevention, and Control*. NY: Plenum Press, pp. 207-229.

———. 1988. "Girls and Status Offenses: Is Juvenile Justice Still Sexist?" *Criminal Justice Abstracts* March: 145-165.

Chesney-Lind, Meda and Randall G. Shelden. 1992. *Girls, Delinquency, and Juvenile Justice*. Pacific Grove, CA: Brooks/Cole.

Cheung, Y.W. and A.M.C. Ng. 1988. "Social Factors in Adolescent Deviant Behavior in Hong Kong: An Integrated Theoretical Approach." *International Journal of Comparative and Applied Criminal Justice* 12:27-45.

Daly, Kathleen and Meda Chesney-Lind. 1988. "Feminism and Criminology." *Justice Quarterly* 5:497-538.

Datesman, Susan K., Frank R. Scarpitti and Richard M. Stephenson. 1975. "Female Delinquency: An Application of Self and Opportunity Theories." *Journal of Research in Crime and Delinquency* 12:107-123.

DeFleur, Lois B. 1967. "A Cross-Cultural Comparison of Juvenile Offenders and Offenses:

Cordoba, Argentina, and the United States." *Social Problems* 14:484-492.

Desai, Nura and Maithreyi Krishnaraj. 1987. "Women and Society in India." Delhi: Ajanta.

Elliott, Delbert S., Suzanne S. Ageton, David Huizinga, Brian A. Knowles, and Rachell J. Canter. 1983. *The Prevalence and Incidence of Delinquent Behavior: 1976-1980*. Boulder, CO: Behavior Research Institute.

Elliott, D.S., D. Huizinga and S. Menard. 1989. *Multiple Problem Youths: Delinquency, Substance Use, and Mental Health Problems*. NY: Springer-Verlag.

Empey, LaMar T. and Mark C. Stafford. 1991. *American Delinquency: Its Meaning and Construction*. Belmont, CA: Wadsworth.

Farnsworth, Margaret. 1984. "Family Structure, Family Attributes, and Delinquency in a Sample of Low-Income Minority Males and Females." *Journal of Youth and Adolescence* 13:349-364.

Federal Bureau of Investigation. 1984. *Crime in the United States 1983*. Washington, DC: U.S. Government Printing Office.

Gibbons, Don C. 1971. "Observations on the Study of Crime Causation." *American Journal of Sociology* 77:262-278.

Greenberg, David. 1978. "Delinquency and the Age Structure of Society." In Peter Wickman & Phillip Whitten (ed.) *Readings in Criminology*. Lexington, MA: D.C. Heath. Pp. 36-52.

Grove, Walter R., Michael Hughs, and Michael Gurken. 1985. "Are Uniform Crime Reports a Valid Indicator of the Index Crimes? An Affirmative Answer With Minor Qualifications." *Criminology* 3:451-501.

Hagan, John, A.R. Gillis, and John Simpson. 1985. "The Class Structure of Gender and Delinquency: Toward a Power-Control Theory of Common Delinquent Behavior." *American Journal of Sociology* 90:1151-1178.

Hagan, John, John Simpson, and A.R. Gillis. 1987. "Class in the Household: A Power-Control Theory of Gender and Delinquency." *American Journal of Sociology* 92:788-816.

Hartjen, Clayton A. and S. Priyadarsini. 1984. *Delinquency in India: A Comparative Analysis*. New Brunswick: Rutgers University Press.

Hartjen, Clayton A. 1986. "Crime and Development: Some Observations on Women and Children in India." *International Annals of Criminology* 24:39-57.

Hartnagel, Timothy F. 1982. "Modernization, Female Social Roles, and Female Crime: A Cross-National Investigation." *The Sociological Quarterly* 23:477-490.

Henggeler, Scott W., James Edwards, and Charles M. Borduin. 1987. "The Family Relations of Female Juvenile Delinquents." *Journal of Abnormal Child Psychology* 15:199-209.

Hill, Gary D. and Elizabeth M. Crawford. 1990. "Women, Race & Crime." *Criminology*. 28:601-626.

Hindelang, Michael J., Travis Hirschi, and Joseph G. Weis. 1979. "Correlates of Delinquency: The Illusion of Discrepancy Between Self-Report and Official Measures." *American Sociological Review* 44:995-1014.

Hindelang, Michael J., Travis Hirschi, and Joseph G. Weis. 1981. *Measuring Delinquency*. Beverly Hills, CA: Sage.

Hoffman-Bustamante, D. 1973. "The Nature of Female-Criminality," *Issues in Criminology* 8:117-123.

Hobkins, Thomas J. 1971. *The Hindu Religious Tradition*. Encino, CA: Dickenson.

Jain, Devaki (Editor). 1975. *Indian Women*. New Delhi: Ministry of Information & Broadcasting.

Jensen, Gary F. and Raymond Eve. 1976. "Sex Differences in Delinquency: An Examination of Popular Sociological Explanations." *Criminology* 12:427-448.

Johnson, Richard E. 1986. "Family Structure and Delinquency: General Patterns and Gender Differences." *Criminology* 24: 65-81.

Karve, Irawati. 1986. *Kinship Organization in India*. NY: Asia.

Krishnaraj, Maithreyi and Karuna Chanana (Editors). 1989. *Gender and the Household Domain: Social and Cultural Dimensions*. New Delhi: Sage.

Krohn, Marvin, Gordon P. Waldo and Theodore G. Chiricos. 1975. "Self-Reported Delinquency: A Comparison of Structured Interviews and Self-Administered Checklists." *The Journal of Criminal Law & Criminology*. 65:545-553.

Lebra, Joyce, Jay Paulson and Jance Everett (Editors). 1984. *Women and Work in India: Continuity and Change*. New Delhi: Promilla and Company.

Leonard, Eileen B. 1982. *Women, Crime, and Society: A Critique of Criminological Theory*. NY: Longman.

Mandelbaum, David Goodman. 1972. *Society in India*. Bombay: Popular Press.

———. 1968. "Family, Jati, Village." In Milton Singer and Bernard S. Cohn (eds.), *Structure and Change in Indian Society*. NY: Wenner-Gren Foundation.

Moffatt, Michael. 1979. *An Untouchable Community in South India: Structure and Consensus*. Princeton, NJ: Princeton University Press.

Morash, Merry. 1986. "Gender, Peer Group Experiences, and Seriousness of Delinquency." *Journal of Research in Crime and Delinquency* 23:43-67.

Morris, Ruth. 1964. "Female Delinquency and Relational Problems." *Social Forces* 43:82-89.

———. 1965. "Attitudes Toward Delinquency by Delinquents, Nondelinquents and Their

Friends." *British Journal of Criminology* 5:249-265.

Murkhopadhyay, Maitrayee. 1984. *Silver Hackles: Women & Development in India* Oxford: Oxfam.

Pollock-Byrne, Joycelyn M. 1990. *Women, Prison & Crime*. Pacific Grove, CA: Brooks/Cole.

Pulkkeinen, Lea and Marketta Saastamoineu. 1986. "Cross-Cultural Perspectives on Youth Violence." In Steven J. Apter and Arnold P. Goldstein (eds.), *Youth Violence: Programs and Prospects*. Elmsford, NY: Pergamon Press. Pp. 262-281.

Sampson, Robert J. 1985. "Sex Differences in Self-Reported Delinquency and Official Records: A Multiple-Group Structural Modeling Approach." *Journal of Quantitative Criminology* 1:345-367.

Sandu, Harjit. 1987. "Low Rates of Delinquency and Crime in India." *Indian Journal of Criminology* 15:9-16.

Sarkar, Chandan. 1987. *Juvenile Delinquency in India: An Etiological Analysis*. New Delhi: Daya Publishing House.

Shane, Paul G. 1980. *Police and People: A Comparison of Five Countries*. St. Louis: C.V. Mosby Co.

Shew, Chuen-Jim. 1988. "Juvenile Delinquency in the Republic of China: A Chinese Empirical Study of Social Control Theory." *International Journal of Comparative and Applied Criminal Justice* 12:73-80.

Shim, Young-Hee. 1987. "'Hidden Delinquency' in Korea." *Crime and Delinquency* 33:425-432.

Short, James F. 1990. *Delinquency and Society*. Englewood Cliffs, NJ: Prentice Hall.

Simon, Rita J. 1975. *Women and Crime*. Lexington, MA: Lexington Books.

Simpson, Sally S. 1991. "Caste, Class, and Violent Crime: Explaining Differences in Female Offending." *Criminology* 29:115-135.

Singh, Prakash and Padma Agarwal. 1986. "Family Environment & Delinquency." *Indian Journal of Criminology* 14:144-151.

Skinner, William F. 1986. "Delinquency, Crime and Development: A Case Study of Iceland." *Journal of Research in Crime and Delinquency* 23:268-294.

Somjee, Geeta. 1989. *Narrowing the Gender Gap*. NY:St. Martins.

Steffensmeier, Darrell and Cathy Streifel. 1992. "Time-Series Analysis of the Female Percentage of Arrests for Property Crimes, 1960-1985: A Test of Alternative Explanations." *Justice Quarterly* 9:77-103.

United Nations Social Defense Research Institute. 1984. *Juvenile Social Maladjustment and Human Rights in the Context of Urban Development*. Rome, Italy: Fratelli Palombi Edition.

Vatuk, Sylvia J. 1972. *Kinship and Urbanization: White-Collar Migrants in North India*. Berkeley, CA: University of California Press.

Wani, Abdul Latif. 1984. "Juvenile Delinquency in India." *Social Defense* 20:5-17.

Wells, Edward L and Joseph H. Rankin. 1988. "Direct Parental Controls and Delinquency." *Criminology* 26:263-285.

Wiebe, Paul D. 1975. *Social Life in an Indian Slum*. New Delhi: Vikas. ✦

11
Serious Violent Offenders: Onset, Developmental Course, and Termination—The American Society of Criminology 1993 Presidential Address

Delbert S. Elliott

The theme of this year's annual meeting is "Violence and Its Victims." The events of the past year underscore both the timeliness of our focusing on violence and the urgent need for building an adequate theoretical and empirical knowledge base to support the policy and intervention strategies that certainly will emerge over the next several years, as society searches for solutions to the "violence crisis." Adolescent homicide rates have reached the highest levels in history, the Surgeon General has declared violence a national health problem, states are rushing to pass new gun control laws, the President is pushing a new national crime bill, the First Lady says violence will be the top concern on her agenda after health care legislation is passed, and adolescent violence is a major campaign issue in this year's elections.

What role will the American Society of Criminology play in the search for solutions to the violence problem? Do we have an adequate theory and research base to inform prevention, control, and policy decisions? If we do, will this knowledge actually be used to inform policy and practice?

Members of the Society have contributed to three major reports on violence published in 1993: *Violence and Youth* (APA, 1993), the report by the American Psychological Association's Commission on Violence and Youth; *Losing Generations* (NRC, 1993), the report of the National Research Council's Panel on High-Risk Youth; and *Understanding and Preventing Violence* (Reiss and Roth, 1993), the report of the NRC's Panel on the Understanding and Control of Violent Behavior. We are highlighting the last of these reports at this meeting because members of the ASC played a central role in the preparation of this report. Of the two reports focusing most directly on violence, I believe that *Understanding and Preventing Violence* is more comprehensive in the sweep and balance of biological, psychological, sociological, and economic factors considered. It is an important statement, one that deserves our careful attention, and one that will make a substantive contribution to the national debate on the prevention and control of violence.

In part, my remarks are a response to what I believe is a significant limitation in the section of this report concerned with the development of violent careers.[1] The authors claim that self-report studies with general population samples are generally unsuitable for the study of violent careers. They cite three reasons in support of this claim: (1) the base rate of "unambiguously violent crimes" is too low for generating reliable estimates, given typical sample sizes; (2) truly violent persons are not included (or retained) in these samples; and (3) information about the ordering of different types of offenses is not (for practical reasons) collected.

I believe that all three assertions are incorrect. Moreover, general population studies employing self-reported measures of violent behavior, particularly projected longitudinal studies covering significant periods of the lifespan, have much to contribute to our understanding of the causes and the

From *Criminology*, Volume 32, Number 1 (1994), pp. 1-21. Copyright © 1994 by the American Society of Criminology. Reprinted by permission.

developmental course of violent careers. Both official record and self-reported measures of violence have their particular strengths and weaknesses. To abandon one in favor of the other is rather shortsighted; to systematically ignore the findings of either is dangerous, particularly when the two measures provide apparently contradictory findings on critical questions. Conceptually they are measures of different phenomena; a full understanding of the etiology of violent behavior and its development over the lifespan is enhanced by using and integrating both types of violence measures.

In light of the above claims about the unsuitability of self-report studies of violence and the general underutilization of these studies in the report by the violence panel, my aim in this address is to illustrate the value of general population studies employing projected longitudinal designs and self-reported measures of violence for understanding the causes and the developmental course of violent careers. In particular, I would call attention to several areas where studies based on official records and studies based on self-reports produce different findings about the parameters of violent careers, and I argue for caution in these areas until these discrepancies are understood. We should resist the tendency to rely too heavily on one measure or the other in these instances.

A Self-Reported Analysis of Serious Violent Careers

Five general questions about criminal careers are explored by using data from the National Youth Survey (Elliott et al., 1989). First, what is the prevalence of serious violent offending in the adolescent and young adult population, and how does it change over the life course? Second, when does involvement in serious violent offending begin? Third, how does the behavioral repertoire of a serious violent offender develop over time? Fourth, what proportion of those who initiate serious violent offending in adolescence continue their serious violent offending into adulthood? Fifth, can we predict the onset of serious violent offending? Each of these questions is central to our understanding of violent careers. In some instances, official record studies provide answers to these questions, and we can compare these findings. In others, we have no information from official record studies about these parameters of violent careers.

The National Youth Survey (NYS)

The NYS is a projected longitudinal study of a national probability sample of 1,725 youths age 11–17 in 1976. Nine waves of data are available on this youth panel, which was age 27–33 when last interviewed in 1993. Both self-reported and official record data are available for all respondents, and official record data are available for their parents or primary caretakers. Although an analysis integrating both types of measures is in progress, the present analysis uses only self-reported data from Waves 1 through 8 (1976–1989).

Self-Reported Measures of Violent Behavior

The Violence Panel Report is not alone in claiming that general population studies fail to capture "unambiguously violent" behavior or that truly serious violent offenders (like those in arrested or incarcerated samples) are not included in general population samples (e.g., see Cernkovich et al., 1985). Thus it seems appropriate to briefly discuss the validity of the NYS measure of serious violence.

The items employed in the measure of serious violent offenses (SVOs) include those designed to reflect aggravated assault, robbery, and rape.[2] Beginning with the fourth survey, a series of standard probes was used to follow up reported offense behaviors. For the above-mentioned violent behaviors, these probes asked about (1) whether the event involved an actual assault or a threat only, (2) how the assault was carried out, (3) whether the victim was hurt, (4) the level of injury, (5) whether a weapon was used or present, (6) offender's relationship to the victim, (7) the involvement of co-offenders, and (8) the use of drugs or alcohol immediately before the event.

An analysis of these follow-up probes for SVOs revealed that in 50% of these events, a weapon was used. Two-thirds of these weapon events involved a gun or a knife. In 67% of reported events, some medical treatment was required.[3] Two deaths were reported. Injury levels were particularly high for aggravated assaults (85%). Although only 35% of robberies involved some injury, weapons were much more likely to be involved in these events.

These indicators of the seriousness of these reported offenses are comparable to weapon and injury levels in samples of persons arrested for aggravated assault, robbery, and rape. In fact, the levels of both weapon use and injury are higher than reported in victimization studies; these levels are as high as, or higher than, those reported in samples of offenders arrested for these offenses (BJS, 1991; Cernkovich, et al., 1985; Hamparian et al., 1978; Skogan, 1978; Strausberg, 1984; Wolfgang et al., 1972). A substantial portion of those arrested for these offenses did not actually assault the victim, and their threats may or may not have involved a weapon. The fact is that *neither* official record nor self-report measures of serious violent offenses involve "unambiguously violent" offenses; the levels of injury and weapon use in self-reported SVOs are comparable to those found in victimization and arrest records.

The SVO measure employed in this analysis is restricted to those reported aggravated assaults, robberies, and rapes that involved some injury or a weapon.[4] This restriction resulted in excluding 36% of reported events, primarily because they involved only threats of violence (without a weapon) or because the assault was not completed for some reason. Thus the SVOs in this analysis are likely to be even more unambiguously violent than would be expected in a study of persons arrested for these offenses.

The Prevalence of Serious Violent Offending

Age-specific prevalence rates by gender and race are presented in Figures 1 and 2.

These estimates are based on longitudinal data from Waves 1–8 and reflect the experience of multiple birth cohorts passing through each of these ages. The most dramatic finding is the absolute magnitude of involvement in serious violent offending: at the peak age (17), 36% of African-American (black) males and 25% of non-Hispanic white (white) males report one or more SVOs. At the peak ages for females (15–16), nearly one black female in five and one white female in ten report involvement in serious violent offending, The age distribution of SVO prevalence also shows that involvement in serious violent behavior is primarily an adolescent-early adult phenomenon. For females, the rates after age 20 are less than those at age 12; for males after age 24 they are one-half those at the peak ages, and less than those at age 12.

We find three significant gender differences in the prevalence age curve (1) the peak age in prevalence is earlier for females; (2) the decline (maturation effect) is steeper for females; and (3) the gender differential becomes greater over time. At age 12, the

Figure 1
Prevalence of Serious Violence, NYS, Males

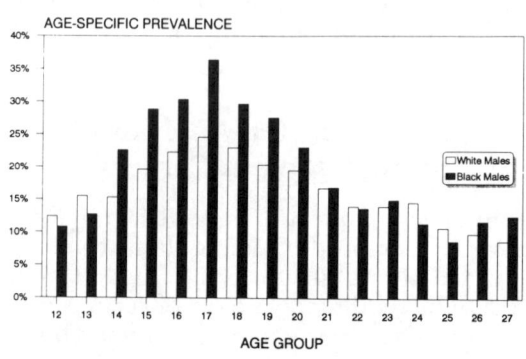

male-to-female differential is 2 to 1; by 18 it has increased to 3 to 1; by age 21, it is 4 to 1.

Differences in age- and gender-specific prevalence rates for blacks and for whites are statistically significant (in most cases) but relatively modest during the adolescent

Figure 2
Prevalence of Serious Violence, NYS, Females

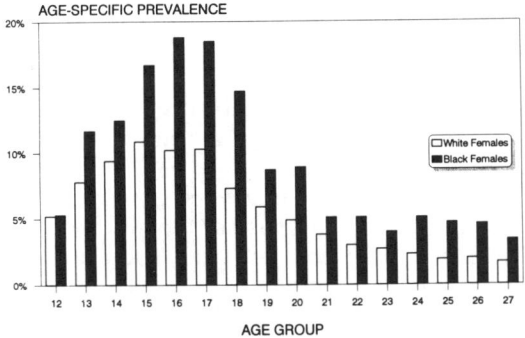

years: the maximum black-to-white differential is 2 to 1 for females and 3 to 2 for males. From ages 19 to 25 (23 for females) the race differential declines, but for both genders it increases thereafter to age 27. After the mid-twenties, age-specific prevalence rates for black males reverse direction and begin to increase again; by age 27, the male black-to-white differential is again 3 to 2. For females it is nearly 3 to 1. Over the entire age span, the race differential is greater among female than males.

Among lower-class whites and blacks, the prevalence rates are only slightly higher, and the race differentials for both males and females are smaller than those displayed in Figures 1 and 2. Relatively few age-specific race differentials among lower class youth are statistically significant.

This description of age-specific prevalence rates over the adolescent years and into adulthood for a set of seven birth cohorts (1959–1965) presents a different picture from that obtained or inferred from official record studies. First, although we expected higher rates, these prevalence rates are substantially higher than those obtained in official record cohort studies (see reviews of official record estimates in Blumstein et al., 1986 and Weiner, 1989; also see Shannon, 1988). Although comparative data from other national self-report studies are limited, the prevalence rates for 17-year-olds are in the same range as those reported for high school seniors in the Monitoring the Future (MtF) study (Osgood et al., 1989). Second, the peak ages of involvement are earlier than suggested by arrest studies, and the decline in involvement after age 15 (females) and 17 (males) is not reflected in arrest rates; these rates remain high between ages 18 and 25 (UCR, 1992).[5] This finding might be explained by increases in individual offending rates between ages 18 and 25, by age differences in arrest probabilities for these offenses, or by a number of other age-related factors. In any event, this is a measure-related difference that should be explored.

Of particular concern are the differences between official record and self-report estimates of gender and race differentials; differentials are substantially higher in official record studies. The few studies providing estimates of gender differences in arrest prevalence suggest differentials as high as 6 to 1 (e.g., Hamparian et al., 1978). UCR arrest differentials for serious violent offenses by gender are more than 8 to 1. Official record studies report male race differentials of 4 to 1 during the adolescent years (e.g., Hamparian et al., 1978; Wolfgang et al., 1972), but these differentials are 3 to 2 or less in the NYS. Until we have a clearer understanding of these discrepancies, some caution should be exercised in describing race and gender differences in the prevalence of serious violent behavior[6]. . . .

The Onset of a Serious Violent Career

I will examine the age of onset by calculating the hazard rate for any SVO through age 27 and by plotting the cumulative onset of serious violent offending through age 27. The hazard rates for black and for white males are depicted in Figure 3; the cumulative onset for black and for white males is shown in Figure 4.

In the total sample, the hazard rate is very low (< 0.5%) through age 11. Beginning with age 12, it increases sharply to 5.1% at age 16 and then declines sharply to 1.0% or less for ages 21–27. The rate doubles be-

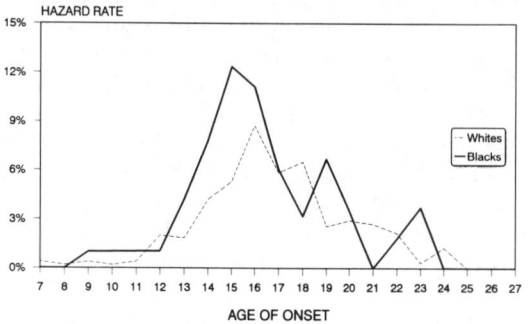

Figure 3
Hazard Rates, Onset of Serious Violent Offending, Males by Age and Race

tween ages 13 and 14 and is halved between ages 16 and 18; over half of all violent offenders initiate their violence between ages 14 and 17. Serious violent offending begins essentially between ages 12 and 20. The risk of initiation is close to 0 after age 20 (at least through age 27).

The hazard rates for males generally and for black males specifically are substantially higher than for females, but follow the same age pattern.[7] As illustrated in Figure 3, the highest risk of onset is found at age 15 for blacks and age 16 for whites: 12.4% of previously uninvolved blacks and 8.7% of previously uninvolved whites initiate a serious violent offense at these ages. The hazard rate for blacks is substantially higher than for whites between ages 13 and 16; this difference in risk of onset at these ages accounts for the higher ever-prevalence rates for black males.

The cumulative ever-prevalence (to age 27) of SVOs in the NYS sample is 30%: 42% for males and 16% for females. By age 18, nearly 40% of black males have become involved in serious violent offending, compared with 30% of white males; at age 27 these rates are 48% and 38% respectively. More than half of all black males who would become involved in serious violent behavior by age 24 had initiated their involvement by age 15; half of whites had initiated by age 16. When these ever-prevalence rates are compared with the age-specific rates presented earlier, it appears that over 60% of all males who will ever be involved (by age 27) in serious violent offending are actively involved at age 17.

An important finding is the fact that the male black-to-white ratio in ever-prevalence is approximately 5 to 4. This difference is statistically significant but substantively small. The difference between lower-class black and white males is even smaller, approximately 7 to 6. If this ever-prevalence rate is considered a crude indicator of some predisposition to violence, we find little difference in predisposition by race....

Progression of Offenses in the Behavioral Repertoire

Figure 5 represents the most typical temporal sequence of types of delinquent behavior and substance use for youths in the NYS sample. The proportions cited on the behavior transition paths in Figure 5 indicate the probability that one given type of behavior will be initiated *before or in the absence of* another.[8]

... There is no question, however, that minor forms of delinquent behavior and alcohol use are added to the behavioral repertoire before serious forms of criminal theft and violence. Also, minor delinquency seems clearly to precede all forms of illicit drug use. Thus the claim that self-reported studies cannot determine the onset sequence of behaviors is partially correct. In this analysis there is no way to order specific behaviors within the minor offense category with any confidence....

On the other hand, it is possible to establish the sequence of the three types of serious violent behavior used in this analysis. Aggravated assault precedes robbery in 85% of cases and rape in 92%. Robbery precedes rape in 72% of cases. Thus the typical sequence is from aggravated assault to robbery to rape.

The overlap in these behaviors within a serious violent career is quite high. Three-quarters of those with a rape or a robbery also have an aggravated assault in their repertoire. Only 30% of those with an aggravated assault, however, also have a rape or

Figure 4
Cumulative Onset of Serious Violent Offending, Males, by Age and Race

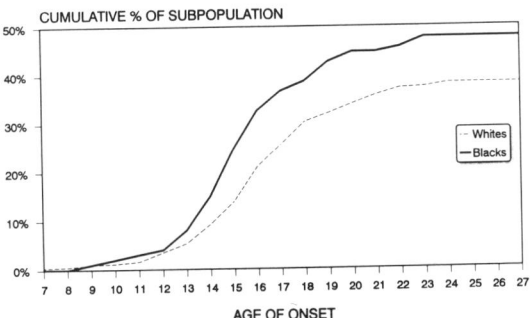

a robbery. The most frequent form of serious violent behavior is an aggravated assault; 88% of all serious violent offenders report this offense. About one-third have a robbery in their repertoire and 15% a rape.

The sequences established here suggest a clear escalation in the seriousness of criminal behavior over time in a criminal career. Official record studies on escalation report mixed findings (see Cohen, 1986; Hamparian et al., 1978; Rojek and Erickson, 1982; Shannon, 1988; Smith and Smith, 1984; Wolfgang et al., 1972, 1987). These self-report data contain much stronger evidence for escalation.

Offending Rates and Patterns

Self-reported individual offending rates for a wide range of behaviors are presented for those who were serious violent offenders in 1980 (see Table 1). At this point, the NYS sample was age 15–21, and the annual prevalence of serious violent offending had declined from its peak rate (11%) in 1976. The rates displayed in Table 1 represent serious violent offenders who reported a minimum of three serious violent offenses (without adjustment based on follow-up questions) in 1980, a different definition than used elsewhere in this address.[9]

Several generalizations can be made from this cross-section of a serious violent career. First, the annual prevalence rates show that these serious violent offenders are very versatile in their offending patterns: more than 50% are involved in *each type of offense* considered, other than robbery and rape. Second, their average annual individual offending rates are very high: they report an average of 11 index offenses and 116 total offenses each during 1980. Third, only 4% of their total offenses were serious violent offenses: over the eight waves of the NYS, 4% to 7% of serious violent offenders' offenses each year were SVOs. Finally, this group of serious violent offenders constituted less than 5% of the NYS sample in that year, but accounted for 83% of index offenses and half of all offenses reported.

A longitudinal analysis of individual careers, tracing offending rates and patterns (variety) of offenses over a three-year period before and after the onset of a SVO, revealed several additional findings. First, the variety of minor offenses tended to increase in the year before the onset of a SVO, but annual variety scores remained relatively constant after onset. Individual variety scores for felony thefts, on the other hand, tended to increase slightly over the three-year period after onset. The annual variety of SVOs after onset remained essentially unchanged.

Second, the frequency of minor offending increased threefold over the three-year period before the onset of a SVO; this trend continued after the SVO onset, although the increase was less dramatic. We also found

Figure 5
Developmental Progression by Type of Offense, NYS, Total Sample

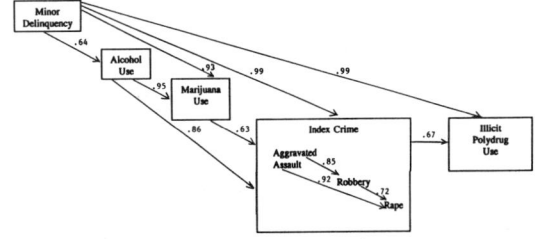

increases in the average individual offending rates for both felony thefts and serious violent offenses in the three-year period after onset.

These analyses show that the addition of a SVO to the behavioral repertoire was accompanied by an increase in offending rates for all types of offenses in the individual's repertoire. The range of offenses in the repertoire also tended to increase modestly when a SVO was initiated. Thus the behavioral progression through the career for serious violent offenders is characterized by an add-on pattern, not a substitution pattern; the general trend is toward diversification in offending, not specialization, and toward adding more serious offenses to the behavioral repertoire.

Official record studies also demonstrate the tendency toward diversification (Weiner, 1989), but fail to show the other patterns noted above. In this type of analysis, official record studies are limited by the number of offenses in the average career, particularly for studying the progression in serious violent offenses, because the great majority of offenders have only a single SVO in their career (Hamparian, 1978; Shannon, 1988; Weiner, 1988; Wolfgang et al., 1972).

The offending rates and offense patterns described in Table 1 are similar to those reported by the "intensive" subgroup of habitual violent offenders studied by Petersilia et al. (1977). They are also comparable to those reported by Peterson et al. (1981) in their survey of jail and prison inmates. This comparison provides additional confirmation that general population surveys include serious violent offenders, whose offending patterns are as frequent, as diverse, and as serious as those in arrested or incarcerated populations.

Continuity Into the Adult Years

I focus here on the transition into the adult years and on the continuity or discontinuity in serious violent offending over this transition. Figure 6 presents the proportion of those initiating a SVO before age 18 who continued their involvement in SVOs after age 20. Continuity rates are presented by race, gender, and social class.

The only significant differences in rates of continuity were those associated with the violent offender's race: nearly twice as many blacks as whites continue their violent careers into their twenties. The failure to find a significant gender difference in continuity was a surprise: far fewer serious violent offenders are females, but the proportion continuing into their twenties is close to that for males (18% and 22% respectively). Thus it appears that blacks have longer violent careers than whites. Further, blacks' violent careers are more likely to extend into the early adult years (twenties), when the risk of incarceration, if one is apprehended, is substantially higher than for the same offense before age 18.

An analysis of the relationship between age of SVO onset and continuity into the adult years confirmed the finding from official record studies: juveniles with an early onset are most likely to continue their violence into the adult years. Nearly half (45%) of those initiating a SVO before age 11 continued their violent careers into their twenties. Approximately one-fourth of those initiating at ages 11–12 continued into adulthood. The probability was lower and relatively constant for those who initiated at ages 13–17.

Several analyses currently are under way to explicate the race difference in juvenile-adult continuity rates. No differences in

Table 1
NYS Serious Violent Offenders' Offense Patterns, 1980[a]

Offense	Prevalence	Offending Rate/100	% Total
Felony Assault	80.6	501	77
Felony Theft	65.7	770	79
Robbery	25.4	206	89
Index	100.0	1140	83
Minor Assault	73.1	1513	57
Minor Theft	68.7	1069	44
Illegal Services	56.7	6640	66
Public Disorder	80.6	5942	26
Vandalism	71.2	571	40
Total Delinquency	100.0	16142	50
Alcohol Use	94.0	12075	12
Marijuana Use	85.1	14001	20
Polydrug Use	55.2	4352	36
Problem Drug Use	54.5	—	—
Mental Health Problems	21.2	—	—

[a] Represents 4.5% of total NYS sample for 1980 (N=67).

continuity rates exist for blacks and whites employed between ages 18 and 20, although such differences persist for unemployed persons (Elliott, 1993). For those living with a spouse or a partner, no significant differences are found between blacks' and whites' continuity rates, but this difference continues for those living by themselves or in other arrangements.

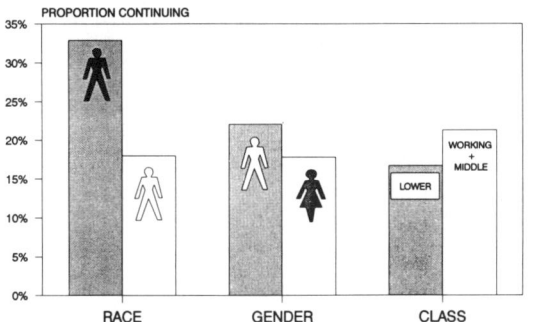

Figure 6
Continuity Rates for Serious Violent Offending, After Age 21

These data seem to support the maturational reform hypothesis that the transition into responsible adult roles leads to desistance from crime and violent behavior (Sampson and Laub, 1993). But why do we find the continued race difference for the unemployed and the unmarried or noncohabiting? Two possible explanations are currently being explored: (1) that whites are more likely than blacks to be living with their parents (i.e., in more conventional and more supportive environments), and (2) that blacks are more likely than whites to be involved in the illicit economy, particularly in the drug distribution networks in their neighborhoods. Should either of these explanations be valid, it would suggest that *where* one is living or working may be as important as *whether* one is working or is living with a partner. . . .

Discussion

I believe that the above analysis demonstrates the utility of self-report studies of serious violent offending in general population samples. By restricting reports of serious violent acts to those involving some injury and/or a weapon, we identified a more homogeneous class of serious violent offenders. The individual offending rates and offense patterns in this group compare quite favorably with those for incarcerated or arrested samples of violent offenders. Self-reported SVOs appear to be as unambiguously violent as violent events that are captured by arrests, and truly serious violent offenders are included and retained in longitudinal general population studies. In fact, persons with arrest histories and incarceration experience are among the most easily tracked, and seldom are lost in longitudinal studies.

Further, base rates for serious violent acts are not exceptionally low in general population studies; they are substantially lower in a single cross-section than in a longitudinal panel design, in which offenders cumulate over time. In the NYS, the highest prevalence rate in a single data collection wave was 11% (Wave 1); the cumulative ever-prevalence to age 27 was 30%; and for selected subpopulations, the cumulative ever-prevalence was nearly 50%.

The picture of serious violent careers that emerges from this analysis of self-reported violence differs in several respects from that derived from official record studies. The prevalence of SVOs is substantially higher; onset occurs much earlier; the demographic correlates are substantially weaker; evidence for escalation in frequency, seriousness, and variety of offenses over the career is much stronger; evidence for the sequencing of serious forms of violent behavior is stronger; and the continuity of serious violent offending from the juvenile into the adult years is similar for males and for females.

The findings also reveal similarities. The general pattern of progression involves diversification of offenses rather than specialization; the proportion of SVOs in the total set of criminal acts committed in any year is small; a small subset of serious violent offenders accounts for the majority of all SVOs; and the earlier the age of onset, the greater the probability of continuity into adulthood.

In addition, self-report findings may provide some insight into findings of official record studies. For example, in view of the self-reported evidence for increasing diversity, frequency, and seriousness over the violent career, it is not at all surprising that we see no consistent pattern of seriousness in arrest sequences, although we find an escalation in the seriousness of offenses in the behavioral repertoire. Because of the escalation in the rate of nonserious offenses that accompanies the addition of serious offenses, the probability of arrest for a nonserious offense is certainly as high as for a serious offense at any point in the career.

We must give particular attention to the differences in self-reported and official record findings regarding the race differentials in serious violent behavior. The self-reported ever-prevalence rates (to age 24) were very similar for blacks and for whites, and the hazard rates for both were essentially 0 from age 24 to 27. Together these findings indicate little or no substantive race difference in the propensity for violence. During the adolescent years we found small differences in age-specific prevalence rates but no substantive differences in individual offending rates among white and black SVO offenders (Elliott et al., 1989). These self-reported differences are not sufficient to explain 5-to-1 differences in arrest rates for violent offenses over the adolescent years (UCR, 1992). By the late twenties, however, race differences in the prevalence of self-reported serious violent offending were very similar to arrest differentials. The analysis of self-reported violent careers revealed race differences in the length of violent careers: blacks were more likely than whites to continue their violence into their adult years. Thus it appears that the difference in career-length and in spacing of the career over the lifespan accounts for the dramatic change in the race differential in the prevalence of violence by the late twenties.

I believe that this is an important insight into the high arrest rates and incarceration rates for young adult black males. The differences are small, at best, in the propensity for male violence by race, social class, and place of residence. Yet, once involved in a lifestyle that includes serious forms of violence, theft, and substance use, persons from disadvantaged families and neighborhoods find it very difficult to escape. They have fewer opportunities for conventional adult roles, and they are more deeply embedded in and dependent upon the gangs and the illicit economy that flourish in their neighborhoods. In a sense, they are denied adult status in our society; they are trapped in a perpetual adolescence, and in those forms of behavior which are characteristic of adolescence. Poverty is related less to the onset of violence than to the continuity of violence, once initiated. The evidence suggests that those who are successful in making the transition into conventional work and family roles give up their involvement in violence. We must target our interventions to facilitate a successful transition into conventional adult roles for all youths.

The possibility that 25% of all males at age 17 are involved in some form of serious violent offending is alarming—even more so if these youths now have access to, and are carrying, guns. Youths in the National Youth Survey were age 15 to 21 in 1980, well before the recent escalation in adolescent homicide rates. There is no reason to believe that serious violent offending is any less prevalent today. The need for theoretically and empirically grounded policy and prevention strategies is urgent. It is my hope that the American Society of Criminology will play a central role in providing this knowledge and in finding solutions to the problem of violence.

Notes

1. See Reiss and Roth (1993), Appendix A: "The Development of an Individual Potential for Violence," especially the section "Violent Crimes in Criminal Careers" (p. 373–378). This position on self-report general population studies appears to be unique to this section of the report. It is at odds with statements in the main body of the report and with the discussion of measurement issues in Appendix B.

2. The item for aggravated assault was ["Have] you attacked someone with the idea of seriously hurting or killing that person?"; for robbery, ". . . used force or strong-arm methods to get money or things from people?"; and for rape, ". . . had or tried to have sexual relations with someone against their will?"
3. A reported level of injury in which the victim was cut or bleeding, had broken bones/jaw/nose, was unconscious, was taken to a hospital, or died was classified as requiring medical treatment.
4. This measure also included offenses reported in response to the gang fight item that involved the use of a weapon or injury requiring medical treatment because they appeared to be aggravated assaults. Because follow-up data were not collected in the first three waves, this restriction could not be applied to SVO reports for these three years (1976–1978). Since nearly 40% of reported SVOs were judged to be trivial, prevalence was defined as two or more reported SVOs for Waves 1–3.
5. UCR arrest rates are not prevalence rates. Yet because the great majority of persons arrested for a serious violent offense have only one such offense in their career (Blumstein et al., 1989; Hamparian et al., 1978; Reiss and Roth, 1993), particularly in any single year of their career, annual UCR arrest rates may provide fairly close estimates of an arrest prevalence rate.
6. Hindelang et al. (1981) argued that there is a race difference in the validity of self-reported delinquency measures, which results in a serious underestimation of black males' prevalence and frequency rates. Elsewhere I have challenged this interpretation of the evidence on validity (Elliott, 1982; Huizinga and Elliott, 1986), but this issue remains controversial and is a possible explanation for the difference in official and self-reported race differentials. The observation that these two measures may produce similar race differentials in the adult years raises new questions about the differential validity hypothesis.
7. The hazard rates for females are lower at every age than those for males. The highest risk is at age 14, two years before the highest risk age for males.
8. A more highly detailed description of this analysis is presented in Elliott et al. (1989). Also given there are probabilities for cases in which both behaviors are initiated.
9. These data are taken from Table 3.1 in Elliott et al. (1989). The definition of serious violent offenders in this book was different from that employed elsewhere in this analysis and involved persons who reported three or more SVOs. No adjustments or corrections were made to the reports on the basis of follow-up data. Overall the minimum of three SVOs appears to be a more restrictive definition; the annual prevalence rate for 1980 is lower than that based on the definition of SVO employed elsewhere in this paper.

References

American Psychological Association (APA). 1993. *Violence and Youth*. Washington, D.C.: American Psychological Association.

Blumstein, Alfred, Jacqueline Cohen, Jeffrey A. Roth, and Christy A. Visher. 1989. *Criminal Careers and "Career Criminals."* Vol. 1. Washington, D.C.: National Academy Press.

Bureau of Justice Statistics (BJS). 1991. *Teenage Victims*. Washington, D.C.: U.S. Department of Justice.

Cernkovich, Stephen, Peggy Giordano, and Meredith Pugh. 1985. Chronic offenders: The missing cases in self-report delinquency research. *Journal of Criminal Law and Criminology* 76:705–732.

Cohen, Jacqueline. 1986. Research on criminal careers. In Alfred Blumstein, Jacqueline Cohen, and Christy A. Visher (eds.), *Criminal Careers and "Career Criminals,"* Vol. 1. Washington, D.C.: National Academy Press.

Elliott, Delbert S. 1982. Measuring delinquency (a review essay). *Criminology* 20:527–538.

———. 1993. Longitudinal research in criminology: Promise and practice. In Elmar G.M. Weitekamp and Hans-Jurgen Kerner (eds.), *Cross-National Longitudinal Research on Human Development and Criminal Behavior*. Dordrecht: Kleuwer.

Elliott, Delbert S., David Huizinga, and Suzanne S. Ageton. 1985. *Explaining Delinquency and Drug Use*. Newbury Park, Calif.: Sage.

Elliott, Delbert S., David Huizinga, and Scott Menard. 1989. *Multiple Problem Youth: Delinquency, Substance Use and Mental Health Problems*. New York: Springer-Verlag.

Hamparian, Donna M., Richard Schuster, Simon Dinitz, and John Conrad. 1978. *The Violent Few*. Lexington, Mass.: D.C. Heath.

Hindelang, Michael, Travis Hirschi, and Joseph G. Weis. 1981. *Measuring Delinquency*. Beverly Hills, Calif.: Sage.

Huizinga, David and Delbert S. Elliott. 1986. Reassessing the reliability and validity of self-report delinquency measures. *Journal of Quantitative Criminology* 2:293–327.

National Research Council (NRC). 1993. *Losing Generations: Adolescents in High Risk Settings*. Washington, D.C.: National Academy Press.

Osgood, D. Wayne, Patrick M. O'Malley, Jerald G. Bachman, and Lloyd D. Johnston. 1989. Time trends and age trends in arrests and self-reported illegal behavior. *Criminology* 27:389–417.

Petersilia, Joan, Peter W. Greenwood, and M. Levin. 1977. *Criminal Careers of Habitual Felons*. Washington, D.C.: U.S. Government Printing Office.

Peterson, M.A., H.B. Braiker, and S.M. Polich. 1981. *Who Commits Crimes: A Survey of Prison Inmates*. Cambridge, Mass.: Oelgeschlager, Gunn and Hain.

Reiss, Albert J., Jr. and Jeffrey A. Roth (eds.). 1993. *Understanding and Preventing Violence*. Washington, D.C.: National Academy Press.

Rojek, Dean and Maynard L. Erickson. 1982. Delinquent careers: A test of the career escalation model. *Criminology* 25:5-28.

Sampson, Robert J. and John H. Laub. 1993. *Crime in the Making: Pathways and Turning Points through Life*. Cambridge: Harvard University Press.

Shannon, Lyle W. 1988. *Criminal Career Continuity: Its Social Context*. New York: Human Sciences Press.

Skogan, Wesley. 1978. Weapons use in robbery. In James A. Inciardi and Anne E. Pettieger (eds.), *Violent Crime*. Beverly Hills, Calif.: Sage.

Smith, D.R. and W.R. Smith. 1984. Patterns of delinquent careers: An assessment of three perspectives. *Social Science Research* 13:129–158.

Strausberg, Paul. 1978. *Violent Delinquents*. New York: Monarch.

Uniform Crime Reports (UCR). 1992. *Crime in the United States 1991*. Washington, D.C.: U.S. Government Printing Office.

Weiner, Neil Alan. 1989. Violent criminal careers and "violent career criminals:" An overview of the research literature. In Neil Alan Weiner and Marvin E. Wolfgang (eds.), *Violent Crime, Violent Criminals*. Newbury Park, Calif.: Sage.

Wolfgang, Marvin E., Robert M. Figlio, and Thorsten Sellin. 1972. *Delinquency in a Birth Cohort*. Chicago: University of Chicago Press. ✦

12
Minorities and the Juvenile Justice System: A Research Summary

Carl Pope
William Feyerherm

Introduction

This report concludes a 15-month research project examining the role that minority status (African American, Hispanic, Asian/Pacific Islander, Native American) plays in the processing of youth by the juvenile justice system.

The research encompassed three major tasks. The first included a review and summary of existing research examining minority status and juvenile processing. The second task required developing a strategy for identifying existing programs and policies that may have dealt with differential processing of minority youth. Finally, a number of preexisting data bases were examined in order to identify methodological problems associated with previous work in this area and to aid in understanding the dynamics of juvenile processing. Based on the results of these tasks, we developed policy and program recommendations to address the issue of disproportionate involvement of minorities in the juvenile justice system, and we proposed an agenda for future research.

This report focuses on the official processing of minority youth and does not deal with the conditions that can lead minority youth into contact with the juvenile justice system. Disproportionate representation may be accounted for by some combination of selection bias on the part of the juvenile justice system and the nature and volume of offenses committed by minority youth. In the latter case, structural and economic factors associated with the urban underclass may result in an increase in the type and number of minorities coming into contact with the juvenile justice system. However, differential involvement in crime is a different issue from what happens to youthful offenders once they enter the juvenile justice system.

Literature Analysis

In the last three decades, a body of literature has accumulated which focuses on the problem of selection bias in juvenile justice systems. Much of this literature suggests that processing decisions in many State and local juvenile justice systems are not racially neutral: Minority youth are more likely than majority youth to become involved in the system. The effects of race may be felt at various decision points, they may be direct or indirect, and they may accumulate as youth continue through the system (Pope 1984; Pope and Feyerherm 1991).

Thus, the research literature raises concern regarding the juvenile system processing of minority youth and presents a number of issues that need to be addressed. It is critically important to examine this body of research so that strengths and weaknesses can be determined and gaps in our knowledge base be identified. Although racial effects on the adult criminal justice system have undergone thorough review no one has yet applied rigorous methodology to inquiring just what effect minority status has on juvenile justice.

Efforts to identify research literature on the processing of minority youth in the juvenile justice system centered on publications since 1969, and four data base searches of criminal justice abstracts, sociological abstracts, the social science citation index, and the legal resource index yielded more than 1,000 citations. Relevant

---

From edited version of *Minorities and the Juvenile Justice System: A Research Summary*. U.S. Department of Justice: Office of Juvenile Justice and Delinquency Prevention.

major journals included *The Journal of Research in Crime and Delinquency, Criminology, Crime and Delinquency,* and *Journal of Criminal Justice.* Professional society records identified more than 90 scholars who had written on race and crime, and letters to each of them inquired about unpublished or ongoing research in this area.

This process identified about 250 potentially relevant articles. In many of them, however, minority status was not a major focus of the analysis or specific juvenile justice decision were not included. The research staff selected 46 articles as most relevant,[1] and these constitute the core of the research. These were among the most salient findings.[2]

- Most of the literature suggests both direct and indirect race effects or a mixed pattern—racial effects are some stages and not at others. Roughly a third of the studies found no evidence of disparity. The remaining studies found evidence that minorities were treated disproportionately even after statistical controls were introduced. These, however, divided about evenly between those that found an overall pattern of disparity and those we call "mixed." The mixed label can apply when a study examines several decision points (such as intake decisions, detention, and judicial sentence) and finds disparities at only apparent for certain types of offenders or offenses (such as first offenses or personal offenses).

- The studies that found evidence of selection bias are generally no less sophisticated methodology than those that found no such evidence. Their data are of no less quality. There appears to be no relationship between the rigor of the studies and the findings of disparity. Studies using sophisticated analytic techniques such as log-linear analysis were no more or less likely to find disparities. Recent analysis has become much more sophisticated in its use of complex analytical techniques. Advanced techniques allow an examination of direct as well as indirect race effects that show how minority status may be linked to other case characteristics. For example, most of the studies that use a multivariate design also examine the effects of interaction between minority status and other case characteristics. The use of random samples as opposed to total populations or the use of large aggregations of jurisdictions (such as statewide) did not appear to explain the differences in findings.

- When bias does exist, it can occur at any stage of juvenile processing. We found studies in which disproportional treatment occurred at each of the major decision process of the police than that of any other major decisionmakers, and those studies tended to examine police decisions made *after* the decision to do *something*. A typical study examined the decision of police to transport a juvenile to a detention facility as opposed to issuing an order to appear at a later date.

- In some instances, small racial differences accumulate and become more pronounced as minority youth proceed further into the juvenile justice system. In particular, our own analysis of statewide data from both California and Florida illustrated this accumulation of disadvantages. Differences between minority and majority offenders increased as youth moved across various decision points.

- Many studies that found no evidence disparity or only mixed results reached that finding by using control variables in a multivariate analysis. One frequently used variable reflects the theme of family composition or stability. Controlling for such variables appears typically to reduce the difference in treatment received by majority and minority youth. However, in a logical sense what these studies identified was the mechanism by which majority and minority youth are distinguished. Thus, "family situation" may in fact mean "race." Even such "legally relevant" variables as prior arrests may not be racially neutral. If, for example, police were initially more likely to pick up and process African-American youth than white, it enhances race differences within the system. The system needs to address whether these types of variables ought to be used in juvenile justice system decision making and whether they ought to produce the degree of difference between majority and minority youth that they appear to produce. Finding a statistical method of reducing the difference between majority and minority youth is not enough. Instead we must address the propriety of using these variables at all.

Examining these studies together with our own previous research (Pope and Feyerherm 1990) suggests substantial support for stating that both direct and indirect race effects operate within certain juvenile justice systems. Perhaps the most interesting finding is the *number* of studies that report a race effect or a mixed pattern. Literature reviews of the adult criminal justice system often report that race effects are not common, but clearly this is not the case in the juvenile justice system. Here, the evidence suggests that race effects (or at least a mixed pattern) are more pronounced.

The Research and Policy Agenda

Research Guidelines

A number of issues can be identified to guide future research on minorities in the juvenile justice system. We write "guide" rather than "direct" because perfect research designs do not exists and probably never will. In addition, the way juvenile justice agencies compile information dose not lend itself completely to social science-based research. Critical pieces of information are sometimes missing, variables not specified in detail, information not consistently reported. Given these "real world" drawbacks, competent research is still possible while recognizing its limitations. The issues identified below should help future researchers.

The Problem of Aggregation and Disaggregation

Future research on minorities and juvenile processing must pay more attention to the fact that race effects may be masked when information is combined on a statewide or county basis.

The more our reporting systems aggregate (combine) data, from place to city to county to state, the more likely that evidence of racial disparity will be lost or hidden. Future research needs to pay attention to masking effects when dealing with aggregated data of any sort. Researchers should examine the data as finely as possible to determine the extent to which race effects are present. If this is not possible, researchers should recognize the limitations of the findings due to possible masking effects.

Multiple Decision Points

Research efforts should focus on the juvenile justice system in its entirety by examining multiple processing stages.

Research that does not examine multiple decision points in juvenile processing may be suspect. At the very least, the findings have to be considered incomplete. Again, race effects at any one stage of processing may be canceled out or enhanced at later stages. Only by examining multiple decision points can we gain a more complete picture of how minority status does or does not influence outcome decisions.

Quantitative vs. Qualitative Approaches

While not ignoring quantitative or statistical approaches, research should also incorporate sound qualitative strategies (field and observational studies) into its designs.

More qualitative approaches are needed in examining minority status and juvenile justice processing. Researchers should go beyond a quantitative analysis of case records and incorporate a qualitative approach. Ideally, a triangulated research design will use a variety of quantitative and qualitative approaches. Funding agencies should recognize the importance of this strategy and encourage researcher to pursue it.

Police and Correctional Processing

While research focusing on juvenile court processing should continue to be encouraged, more research should target police-juvenile encounters and correctional processing.

Without downplaying the continued importance of research of focusing on minority status and court processing, attention should also be given to the earlier and later stages in the system. Police are the gatekeepers controlling who is funneled into the juvenile courts. If such decisions are in any way racially biased, minority youth may be more at risk later during the correctional processing stages. Similarly, differences int he correctional experiences of white and nonwhite youth may have important implications. Thus, research designs focusing on the police encounter and juvenile corrections should be stressed.

Multivariate Models and Indirect Effects

Research examining data on minority youth and the juvenile process should employ techniques that are capable of detecting direct, as well as more subtle and indirect, race effects.

Research that fails to take into account proper control variables will remain suspect. Fortunately, most current research focusing on minorities and juvenile processing does employ multivariate models that accomplish this task. Researches seem to be aware of the necessity to do so. Similarly, more research is examining both direct and indirect race effects and acknowledging the fact that race may interact with other case characteristics to the disadvantage of minority youth. In sum, as a methodological strategy, multivariate models should be encouraged, especially those that are sensitive to indirect effects.

Organizational Characteristics

Research should be attentive to the organizational structure within which juvenile justice decisions are reached, as well as environmental influences in the communities of which they are a part.

While the importance of both internal and external environmental pressures have been recognized, they have not been adequately researched. As our examination of the research literature revealed, few studies have taken these factors into account. Part of the problem lies in the difficulty of coding and measuring organization characteristics. Still, it is important that future research address such factors if we are to increase our understanding of how decisions are made, especially those pertaining to race.

Identification of Minority Groups

Research should attempt to focus on minorities other than African Americans.

By far, the majority of the research literature has targeted African-American youth while virtually ignoring Hispanics, Asian/Pacific Islanders, and Native American populations. While there are reasons for this, future research on juvenile processing should include these additional groups. Also, researchers should specify the operational definitions that lead to the identification of the youth being studied.

Family Background

Research should attempt to include information on the family characteristics of those minority youth processed through the system.

When possible, information should be obtained on the family situation of those minority and majority youth who are being processed through the juvenile justice system. At a minimum, this should include whether the home is intact and with whom the youth resides. Information should also be collected on whether parents or guardians are willing or have the resources to provide support. A body of research indicates that youth from single-parent homes, especially if female-based, often face more severe dispositions than those from intact homes. These homes may have fewer resources to provide needed support. Since African-American youth are proportionately more likely to reside in single-parent homes, they may be more at risk than white youth. In other words, family situation may be one mechanism through which race indirectly affects outcome decisions.

Jurisdictional Differences

Research should focus on rural and suburban jurisdictions as well as on major metropolitan areas.

The bulk of research to date has examined race and juvenile processing in major metropolitan areas. Although certain minority groups such as African Americans are more likely to be found among urban populations, this is not necessarily true for Hispanics, Native Americans, or African Americans living in the South. Thus future research should give some attention to the way in which race may affect decisionmaking in rural and suburban settings.

Sample Selection Bias

Research should take into account changes in sample size as cases are processed through the system.

Within the juvenile justice system, sample sizes change as youth are screened and filtered out at various processing stages. Thus probabilities change at different decision points. Most previous research has not taken into account sample-attrition bias. One way of doing this is by computing a hazard rate, the probability that each case is eliminated at various stages. Another possibility would be to draw supplementary samples at later stages in the system. Future research designs should take this into account, if possible, in order to avoid misspecification.

Policy Guidelines

The first steps in developing program initiatives to address differential processing would be to educate local communities and juvenile justice agencies (including police, courts, corrections, and other agencies) so that they understand the nature of the problem, to develop a review and monitoring procedure, and to conduct training exercises to reduce the potential for disparate treatment. The following recommendations are offered for consideration:

1. As long as the juvenile justice system is fragmented and administered on a local level, programs and policy cannot be applied across the board but must be adapted to local communities. Therefore, states and local communities must conduct a self-assessment to determine if there is a problem with racially disproportionate representation and, if so, the exact nature of the problem. The means to accomplish these tasks would include the following steps:

- A systematic monitoring procedure should be developed to determine, at regular intervals, the percentage of minority and majority youth being processed at each stage of the juvenile justice system. As the literature review suggests, disproportionate representation may be evident at some stages but not at others. Therefore, it is important to target the decision points at which major disparities occur.

- A critical examination should be made of the local stages with the widest gaps between minority and majority youth. This would include a detailed evaluation of the criteria used in reaching those decision points in order to determine the role that minority status plays, by itself or in conjunction with other factors.

- A research program should be implemented to test the race-bias hypothesis. This model could be implemented at both the state and local levels.

2. If race bias is found to be a factor within any jurisdiction's juvenile justice system, programs should be implemented to eliminate it. Examples may include the following program recommendations:

- Consideration should be given to providing staff training to develop sensitivity to the issues of race within the system. In addition, efforts should be made to increase the representativeness of minority staff.
- Workshops modeled after sentencing institutes in the adult system should be held for juvenile court personnel (probation officers, judges, etc.). Such workshops would promote discussion and evaluation of decisionmaking with regard to minority youth.
- Where disparities appear to exist with regard to individual decisionmakers (such as those typically found in intake and detention), it may be feasible to restructure the decisionmaking process to include multiple decisionmakers. Thus, decisionmaking would not be the sole responsibility of one person, but rather a "check and balance" system. It may then be possible to establish a procedure for routine audit and review of these decisions to ensure fairness.
- Each jurisdiction should carefully evaluate the criteria used in reaching decisions at any given stage. This is particularly important given the fact that decisionmaking is much less constrained within the juvenile than the adult criminal justice system. Consideration should be given to developing guidelines to help decisionmakers reach outcome decisions. This is particularly important with regard to detention decisions, because previous research consistently demonstrates the importance of early detention on subsequent outcomes and that within many jurisdictions these decisions are relatively unconstrained. Development of a guideline-based approach to decisionmaking should be geared toward keeping youth from further penetration into the system. In other words, guidelines should state that youth may be detained only if they meet very specific criteria.

Postscript

While a draft of this report was completed in October 1989, comments and suggestions from outside reviewers, as requested by OJJDP, were received in February 1991. We then began making the final revisions for this report. Because of time pressures for publication and numerous requests for the final document, OJJDP and the principal investigators decided not to update the research and analyses or make any major substantive changes. We are aware, however, of additional research since this report was made final. On review, we believe this new research does not change the earlier findings and recommendations in any substantive manner. Moreover, we believe that the most recent research demonstrates that minority status does make a difference in outcome decisions and documents that need for more attention to this critical issue. In future publications we will address this additional body of literature. The following is a discussion of policy issues and research findings regarding minority overrepresentation in the juvenile justice system.

Policy Background

The Juvenile Justice and Delinquency Prevention Act of 1974, as amended in 1988, directed States that sought juvenile justice formula grants to address the overrepresentation of minority youth incarcerated within the juvenile justice system.[3] Regulations for complying with that requirement provided for two phases. Under Phase I, States must demonstrate whether minority youth were overrepresented in secure facilities with regard to their population base. In event of such overrepresentation, a State must take steps to account for it. Under Phase II, this typically took the form of examining additional stages in the juvenile process (that is, intake, detention, adjudication, and disposition), which often involved additional data collection.

To date, three States (Florida, Georgia, and Missouri) have completed research projects, thus complying with Phase Ii requirements. Together these projects lend further support to the argument that minority status does make a difference within the juvenile justice system.

Current Research

Bishop and Frazier (1990) used statewide data over a 3-year period to examine case processing through Florida's juvenile justice system. Their analysis revealed that race (if nonwhite) did make a difference with regard to outcome decisions. According to Bishop and Frazier (1990, 3):

> Nonwhite juveniles processed for delinquency offenses in 1987 received more severe (i.e., more formal and/or more restrictive) dispositions than their white counterparts at several stages of juvenile processing. Specifically, we found that when juvenile offenders were alike in terms of age, gender, seriousness of the offense which prompted the current referral, and seriousness of their prior records, the probability of receiving the harshest disposition available at each of several processing stages was higher for nonwhite than for white youth.

These disparities were found to exist for petition, secure detention, commitment to an institution, and transfers to adult court.

A second stage of this study included a telephone survey with a random sample of juvenile justice decisionmakers (e.g., intake workers, judges and the like). Interestingly, most respondents thought that race did make a difference within Florida's juvenile justice system. Responses indicated that race differences were tied to the lack of social and economic resources as well as prejudicial, attitudes within the system (Bishop and Frazier 1990, 5). Among the policy recommendations of this projects, the need was cited to establish clearer criteria to guide decisionmaking and to provide cultural diversity training. One of the more controversial recommendations centered on the lack of resources available to minority youth. In essence, the recommendation was the economic and family situation (e.g., whether the family is able or willing to provide support) should not have a negative impact on nonwhite youth.

Lockhart et al. (1990) examined racial disparity within Georgia's juvenile justice system. With 1988 as the base year, this study analyzed juvenile case records across Georgia's 159 counties. In addition, survey data were obtained through mailed questionnaires sent to court workers and juvenile court judges. Analysis of the case records revealed that a major determinant of outcomes was the severity of the current charge and the extent of prior contact with the juvenile justice system. Compared to white youth, African-American youth tended to have more prior contact an to be arrested for more severe offenses.

As the authors note:

> Thus, gross racial disparities do exist in Georgia's juvenile justice system. The fact that law enforcement officials have considerable discretion in the determination of how many and what types of charges to place against an alleged offender complicates the interpretation of such disparities. Black youth either are committing more serious crimes at younger ages than are white youth, or they are being charged with more serious crimes at younger ages than are white youth. In the former instance, we have understandable disparity. The second scenario constitutes racial discrimination. (Lockhart et al. 1990, 10)

These results point to the possibility that offense and prior record are not legally neutral actors. If bias influences these decisions, then race differences will be accentuated throughout the system.

Finally, Kempf, Decker, and Bing (1990) examined the processing of minority youth throughout the Missouri juvenile justice system. This study examined processing differences between African-American and white youth across eight juvenile circuit courts with varying degrees of urbanization. Results in the urban courts demonstrated that, all else being equal, African-American youth were more likely than their white counterparts to be held in detention ad were also more likely to be referred for felony offenses. Parental influences were also found to effect outcome decisions such as parental willingness to provide support and whether the youth resided in an intact home. For rural courts, however, African Americans received more severe outcomes at the disposition stage in that they were more likely than white youth to be placed out of the home. As Kempf, Decker, and Bing note (1990, 18):

> As shown in this study, race and gender biases do exist within juvenile justice processing in Missouri. They are less obvious than the glaring rural and urban differences, but they are no less important. Evidence exists that decision processes are systematically disadvantaging youths who are either Black, female, or both. They receive harsher treatment at detention, have more petitions filed "on their behalf," and are more often removed from their family and friends at disposition.

Perhaps one of the major findings of the Missouri study is the difference between the urban and rural courts. In essence, two different types of juvenile courts operate in Missouri—a legalistic court in urban areas and a traditional pre-Gault model in rural areas—each of which provides differential treatment that places African-American youth at greater risk.

Thus, recent research findings from Missouri, Georgia, and Florida again demonstrate that there are problems with the juvenile justice system and the manner in which it processes minority youth. Currently, a number of other states (Michigan, Ohio, California, Pennsylvania, and Iowa) are in various stages of research in addressing issues pertaining to minorities and the juvenile justice system, and these reports will be forthcoming.

Notes

1. In order to remain as objective as possible, the authors of this report excluded their own work from the sample.
2. The extracts that follow have been lightly edited from those appearing at the end of the "Literature Analysis" chapter of the full report.
3. JJDP Act 223(a)(23).

References

Bishop, D.M., and C.E. Frazier, 1990. *A study of race and juvenile processing in Florida.* A report submitted to the Florida Supreme Court Racial and Ethnic Bias Study Commission.

Kempf, K.L., S.H. Decker, and R.L. Bing, 1990. *An analysis of apparent disparities in the handling of black youth within Missouri's juvenile justice system.* Department of Administration of Justice, University of Missouri St. Louis.

Lockhart, L.L., P.D. Kurtz, R. Stutphen, and K. Gauger, 1990. *Georgia's juvenile justice system: A retrospective investigation of racial disparity.* Research report to the Georgia Juvenile Justice Coordination Council: Part I of the Racial Disparity Investigation. School of Social Work, University of Georgia.

Pope, C.E., and W. Feyerherm, 1990. "Minority status and juvenile justice processing." *Criminal Justice Abstracts*, 22(2), 327-336 (part I); 22(3), 527-542 (part II).

Pope, C.E., 1984. "Blacks and juvenile crime : A review." In D.E. Georges Abeyie (ed.). *The criminal justice system and blacks.* Clark Boardman. ✦

Section IV
Theories of Delinquency

Inherited Behavior Versus Learned Behavior

In Section III, the discussion focused on trends, patterns, and relationships that emerged from the study of juvenile delinquency. It is important to note that delinquent behavior is not simply a random event but one that evolves around a common set of characteristics. For example, there are glaring differences between males and females, significant differences by age, and differences in types of offenses committed by juveniles and adults. Furthermore, the overall trends can vary over time. Examining the data on delinquency helps us to get a better understanding of the nature and form of adolescent deviance, but the real task is to move beyond mere description to *predicting* delinquency. Facts and figures are meaningless in themselves unless an attempt is made to organize them into some sort of framework that allows us to get beneath the surface where we can begin to understand the dynamics of delinquency. This calls for the development of theories of delinquency that can highlight critical elements of adolescent misbehavior and, more importantly, organize these elements into a causal ordering that attempts to predict delinquent behavior.

Theory building is a search for causes (Gibbs, 1972). The scientific approach to delinquency calls for the acquisition of facts and then for an ordering of these facts in such a manner that they can predict human behavior. A social scientist develops a theory and then derives hypotheses that can be tested empirically. In the process of testing these hypotheses, a theory is accepted or rejected. In the process of replicating initial findings, the social scientist may revise his or her theory so that theory construction is a never-ending process of self-correction. Similarly, a theory is not a law that operates with absolute precision but a statement that seeks out critical and recurrent factors in human relationships. Social scientists strive to develop theories of human behavior that have a certain degree of truth to them. Predicting human behavior is extremely hazardous, and while social theories do not approach 100 percent accuracy, there may be some comfort in knowing that a particular behavior can be predicted one out of four times. Unlike the law of gravity, which can be measured with scientific rigor, human behavior is clouded in a web of complex social relationships that produces blurred images and endless measurement errors. Prediction is a much more modest enterprise in the realm of the social sciences than in the "hard" sciences where the researcher can dissect, purify, manipulate, and control a sample in a laboratory setting.

Because human behavior is so varied and complex, the student of delinquency will find not one but many theories of delinquency. Humans are affected by so many different social forces that there may be multiple causes of delinquent behavior. These causes may include poverty, inadequate socialization, peer pressure, racial or ethnic discrimination, sexism, alienation, low self-esteem, or dysfunctional families, to name but a few. The theories that will be discussed in this section tend to focus on the individual. The theories that will be discussed in Section V focus on society as the causal agent. Each theoretical approach that will be discussed in the next two sections can marshal sufficient evidence to lend credence to its position. The wide array of theories does not mean that absolute chaos or complete ignorance reigns in the field of delinquency, but that adolescent behavior is multifaceted and exceedingly complicated.

In this section, two theoretical perspectives are examined: that delinquency is the product of biological forces, and the opposing view that delinquency is not inherited but learned behavior. The article by Fishbein is a broad overview of some key propositions set forth by the biological school as well as a review of some of the central findings from recent work in the that school. The starting point of the biological school is with Lombroso, an Italian physician who published a book in 1876 entitled *The Criminal Man*. In this book, Lombroso argued that the criminal was a biological degenerate, a "throwback" in terms of human evolution. He called this degeneracy *atavism* that manifested itself in certain physical characteristics referred to by Lombroso as *stigmata*. Lombroso began cataloging what he thought were critical stigmata that would be useful in identifying "born criminals": large ears, protruding lips, greater strength in the left limbs, and insensitivity to pain, to name but a few. Lombroso's research has been severely criticized, but because of his obsession with gathering data he has become known as the father of the positivist (scientific) school of criminology. Fishbein's discussion looks at modern-day biological research as it relates to crime and delinquency and shows that the behavioral sciences such as endocrinology, psychopharmacology, and physiological psychology have produced some intriguing findings. While there is some evidence that biological perspectives may add to our understanding, Fishbein is careful to point out that many of these findings are still tentative. However, there is the strong suggestion that the incorporation of biological variables into the study of delinquency may enhance our ability to understand and predict human behavior.

The second reading, by Gottfredson and Hirschi, is far more critical of the biological perspective. They briefly review the findings of early biological positivism but focus most intently on contemporary findings. Gottfredson and Hirschi point out the methodological weaknesses in many of these studies. They are critical of slippery terms like "criminal record" or "registered criminality," differing sample sizes, and the questionable use of statistics. Gottfredson and Hirschi conclude that results from adoption studies offer very little evidence that heredity plays a role in understanding delinquency. The suggestion by Fishbein that biological research may have a role in the study of delinquency is emphatically rejected by Gottfredson and Hirschi.

The next two readings argue that delinquency is a product of the social environment. Delinquency is learned, not inherited. In 1939, Edwin Sutherland introduced his theory of *differential association*, which was critical of the biological and psychiatric theories that were popular at that time. Sutherland's central thesis is that delinquency is learned in the same way other behavior is learned: through interpersonal social interaction and communication in intimate groups. This is a processual theory that argues, "A person becomes delinquent because of an excess of definitions favorable to violation of law over definitions unfavorable to violation of law." One of the major criticisms of Sutherland's theory is that it is untestable: how do you specifically measure "an excess of definitions favorable to law violation?"

The third reading, by Akers, Krohn, Lanza-Kaduce, and Radosevich, discusses social learning theory, which grows out of differential association theory. The learning of delinquent behavior that Sutherland introduced is broadened in social learning theory to include B. F. Skinner's concept of operant conditioning. Unlike classical conditioning where a behavioral response is elicited by a prior stimulus, operant conditioning is behavior learned or conditioned because of the effects or outcomes generated by the behavior. In other words, behavior is influenced by feedback that can be a reward or a punishment. Differential reinforcement predicated on rewards and punishment becomes the key element in social learning theory. The critical test of social learning theory is whether differential reinforcement can be measured. Akers et al. examine adolescent drinking and drug-use and conclude that the theory is strongly supported. While there is evidence that social learning theory can explain less serious forms of adolescent misbehavior, questions still arise as to the utility of this theory in explaining serious criminal offending.

The final reading in this section, by Warr, is another test of Sutherland's theory couched in terms of the age distribution of delinquency. As Warr shows, delinquency increases rapidly with age, peaking around the ages of 17 or 18, and then declines. How do we explain this rapid increase in delinquency? Warr argues that the driving force in this age–delinquency relationship is essentially Sutherland's concept of differential association. Peer influence—when measured in terms of differential exposure to delinquent peers, time spent with peers, the importance of friends, and commitments or loyalty to friends—becomes of prime importance. While Warr finds support for differential association theory, he acknowledges that his test covers only a limited range of minor offenses. The question remains as to the applicability of this theory to more serious delinquent offenses. However, a theory that "works" even for a limited range of delinquent acts is a significant contribution to the study of delinquency.

References

Gibbs, Jack. 1972. *Sociological Theory Construction*. Hinsdale, IL: The Dryden Press.

Lombroso, Cesare. 1876. *The Criminal Man*. Milan: Hoepli.

Sutherland, Edwin H. 1939. *Principles of Criminology*. Third Edition. Philadelphia: J.B. Lippincott. ✦

13
Biological Perspectives in Criminology

Diana H. Fishbein

Wilson and Herrnstein (1985) recently published a massive evaluation of the implications of biological data for topics of interest to criminologists. Their message is that insufficient consideration has been given to biological and social interactions in criminological studies. Consistent observations that a small percentage of offenders are responsible for a preponderance of serious crime (Hamparin et al., 1978; Moffitt et al., 1989; Wolfgang, 1972) suggest that particular forces produce antisocial behavior in particular individuals. Further, much research shows that violent criminals have an early history of crime and aggression (Loeber and Dishion, 1983; Moffitt et al., 1989). The possibility that biological conditions may play a role in the development of antisocial and criminal behavior is accentuated by these reports and has spurred a search for biological markers in "vulnerable" subgroups (Mednick et al., 1987).

In the past, theories of the biological aspects of criminal behavior were marked by a general lack of knowledge regarding the human brain and by serious methodological shortcomings (see, e.g., Glueck and Glueck, 1956; Goddard, 1921; Hooten, 1939; Jacobs et al., 1965; Lombroso, 1918; Sheldon, 1949). Indeed, "biological criminology" was eventually discredited because its findings were largely unscientific, simplistic, and unicausal. Biological factors were globally rejected due to the inability of theorists to posit a rational explanation for the development of criminal behavior.

From *Criminology*, Volume 28, Number 1 (1990), pp. 27-57. Copyright © 1990 by the American Society of Criminology. Reprinted by permission.

More recently, biological aspects of criminal behavior have been investigated by numerous behavioral scientists employing a multidisciplinary approach that promises to enhance substantially the rigor of the findings. Scientists in such fields as genetics, biochemistry, endocrinology, neuroscience, immunology, and psychophysiology have been intensively studying aspects of human behavior that are relevant of the criminologist and the criminal justice practitioner. Due to the highly technical and field-specific language of much of this research, findings generated from these works are not usually included in the literature reviews of criminologists. The relative lack of interdisciplinary communication has resulted in a lack of awareness of data pertinent to the study of crime and criminal behavior. This paper is a small step toward filling that gap.

The primary purpose of this paper is to present an overview of biological perspectives on the study of crime. Once acquainted with the parameters and findings of biological research, criminologists may begin to incorporate reliable biological aspects of criminal behavior into their theoretical and applied frameworks. Specific findings in biology are presented for criminologists to consider. Although the paper provides only an initial, condensed introduction to the vast amount of work accomplished in the behavioral sciences, it may help develop a sound, scientific, and pragmatic framework for future criminological research with a multidisciplinary orientation....

Nature or Nurture?

The first issue that must be addressed before the parameters of biological research in criminology can be established is the age-old question of whether human behavior is a product of nature or nurture. Theoreticians of the past generally espoused one or the other viewpoint. Those who claim that nature contributes predominantly to an individual's behavior have been affiliated in the past with conservative political ideologies and were known as "hereditarians." In this circle, behavior was primarily attributed to inherited predispositions, and genetic influences were considered responsible for most of the variance in complex human behaviors.

The argument that nurture is the impetus for behavior was advocated by the "environmentalists," who were generally associated with a liberal ideology. Watson's (1925) interpretation of John Locke's *tabula rasa* (blank slate), for example, maintained that humans are born without predispositions to behave in any predetermined or predictable manner. Environmental inputs were considered primarily responsible for the final behavioral product, and manipulations of external inputs were thought to modify behavior.

These opposing views are reflected in past political and social movements, such as *radical behaviorism* and *social Darwinism*, many of which have had devastating social and scientific consequences. The concept of *predatory ethics*, couched in the possibility of the state's punitive sanctioning of "unacceptable" or merely predicted future behaviors, eventually contributed to a complete rejection of biological perspectives by many scientists and their sponsors. The threat of "control and oppression by science" was realized and feared.

Few behavioral scientists today adhere to either of these extreme views. A consensus has been emerging over the past 10 to 15 years that the "truth" lies somewhere in between—a "nature plus nurture" perspective (see Plomin, 1989). Although the nurture perspective has dominated fields such as criminology for the past few decades, substantial biological findings can no longer be ignored. Several studies on alcoholism, temperament, criminality, depression, and mental illness have established a solid role for genetic and biological influences (selected recent examples are detailed below). Even though behavioral scientists have yet to determine precisely the separate, relative contributions of biology and social learning to behavior, their findings are particularly relevant to the criminologist, who should play an instrumental role in their evaluation given the potential impact on policy.

Evidence for an interaction between nature and nurture comes from both animal and clinical studies, which demonstrates the strength and importance of the dynamic link between biological and acquired traits. One example of this interaction is that aggressive behavior in monkeys can be elicited by stimulating certain areas of the brain with implanted intracerebral electrodes (see Carlson, 1977:442-449). The final behavioral result depends on the hierarchical structure of the monkey colony. Dominant monkeys will exhibit aggressive behavior with electrical stimulation of the brain in the presence of a submissive monkey. The same monkeys will suppress aggressive behavior, on the other hand, if another dominant monkey is present. An example of this interaction in humans is illustrated by recent reports that gender differences in cognitive ability are decreasing (see Geary, 1989). Cognition, however, is fundamentally influenced by neural processes that operate during an individual's development (ontogeny). In an effort to explain changing trends in a seemingly immutable biological process, researchers are discovering that cultural and experiential conditions directly influence the developing pattern of cognitive abilities. For example, activity patterns (e.g., frequency of rough and tumble play) may alter cognitive ability (e.g., spatial skills) by modifying processes of brain development.

These illustrations remind us that as evidence for a substantial genetic influence grows we must be cautious not to replace environmental explanations with biological deterministic views. Instead, a more accommodating, balanced approach will carry more empirical weight.

Free Will or Determinism?

The acceptance of biological explanations for human behavior has been thought by many to preclude the possibility of free will. This fundamental fear has resulted in a pervasive rejection of biological contributions to behavior. Although some behavioral scientists are deterministic in their views, attributing behavior to everything from socioeconomic conditions to neurochemical events, most individuals prefer to credit their own free will for their behavior. A compromise reflecting a more accurate position on the forces behind human behavior is widely accepted, however—the theory of "conditional free will" (see Denno, 1988, for discussion of "degree determinism," a related view).

In probabilistic or stochastic theories, numerous causes or alternatives are presented to explain an effect. Each cause has a certain probability of resulting in that outcome, in some cases a measurable probability. Because it is rarely the case that an effect can be associated with only one cause, some dynamic interaction of causes, working in concert, is frequently responsible for the final result. In the assessment of human behavior, a most complex phenomenon, it is particularly difficult to separate those causes to assess their relative contributions.

In accordance with probability theory, social human behavior is contingent on a countless number of possible decisions from among which the individual may choose. Not all of those decisions are feasible, however, nor are the resources available that are required to act on them. Choosing a course of action, therefore, is limited by present boundaries, which narrows the range of possibilities substantially. Decision-limiting factors include current circumstances and opportunities, learning experiences, physiological abilities, and genetic predispositions. Each one of these conditions collaborates internally (physically) and externally (environmentally) to produce a final action. The behavioral result is thus restricted to options available within these guidelines, yet it is "indeterminable" and cannot be precisely predicted. Stable individuals generally behave with some degree of expectability, however. In other words, certain patterns of behavior are a common individual characteristic, and some patterns are more probable than others in a given situation in a given individual.

The principle of conditional free will does not demand a deterministic view of human behavior. Rather, it postulates that individuals choose a course of action within a preset, yet to some degree changeable, range of possibilities and that, assuming the conditions are suitable for rational thought, we are accountable for our actions. Given "rational" thought processes, calculation of risks versus the benefits, and the ability to judge the realities that exist, the result is likely to be an adaptive response, that is, the behavior will be beneficial for the individual and the surrounding environment.

This theory of conditional free will predicts that if one or more conditions to which the individual is exposed are disturbed or irregular, the individual is more likely to choose a disturbed or irregular course of action. Thus, the risk of such a response increases as a function of the number of deleterious conditions. For example, a child with a learning disability may function well in society. With the addition of family instability, lack of appropriate educational programs, and a delinquent peer group, however, the learning-disabled child may be more prone to maladaptive behavior, which may, in turn, result in actions society has defined as criminal. The child's range of possible decisions has, in other words, been altered. . . .

Conceptual Framework

. . . Individuals are not inherently criminal, nor do they suddenly become homicidal maniacs (except under unusual circumstances). Antisocial behavior has many precursors. Manifestations of a problem are frequently observed in childhood when innate tendencies toward antisocial behavior or other risk factors are compounded by suboptimal environmental and social conditions (Denno, 1988; Lewis et al., 1979, 1985; Mednick et al., 1984). These early seeds of maladaptive behavior are commonly ignored, inappropriately treated, or not recognized as complications that warrant intervention. In such cases, the severity of the condition and resultant behaviors are well advanced by adolescence and adulthood. According to this "developmental course" model of human behavior, criminal behavior is virtually always secondary to an underlying problem(s)....

Although low IQ or a learning disability is not inherently criminogenic, in the absence of proper intervention the child may become frustrated attempting to pursue mainstream goals without the skills to achieve them. Kandel et al. (1988) demonstrated that juveniles with high IQ who were otherwise at high risk for criminal involvement due to their family environments resisted serious antisocial behavior. The researchers stated that their results could be interpreted according to Hirschi's (1969) social control theory. Specifically, students with a high IQ find school more rewarding and, consequently, bond more strongly to the conventional social order. Parents and school systems that are ill equipped to deal with a child suffering from a learning disability, on the other hand, may indirectly contribute to delinquency by removing the child from the classroom, thereby alienating him or her from friends and inculcating the belief that the child is "different," possibly even inadequate. Self-esteem is likely to decline dramatically, and the child may learn that there are rewards to be gained from interacting with others who experience similar frustrations. Thus, the child's behavior elicits a negative response from his or her environment, which leads to further reactions from the child (see Patterson et al., 1989). Consequently, the cycle of negatively interacting forces continues and the risk of becoming delinquent and eventually criminal is heightened.

Once the individual attracts the attention of the criminal justice system, the problem is already significantly compounded and difficult to treat, and the costs to society are exorbitant. Evidence for the existence of a developmental phenomenon in antisocial behavior highlights the dire need for early detection and intervention. The earlier the intervention, the more favorable the outcome (Kadzin, 1987)....

Humans are equipped with the innate biological capacity to learn as a product of their genetic blueprint, which is physically expressed in the structure of the brain. When an individual is exposed to a stimulus from the internal (biological) or external (social) environment, permanent changes occur in the neural structure and biochemical function of the brain. This process is referred to as "memory," experiences coded and stored for retrieval in the form of chemical transformations.

Bodily functions involved in memory are multifaceted. Sensation and perception are activities of stimuli reception. Attention and arousal prepare the individual to receive stimuli and react to them selectively. Motivational processes operate so that the individual attends to and later retrieves information. And motor systems permit a response to a memory or experience. When stimuli are received and remembered, all future behaviors are modified, and perception will be subsequently altered. Thus, humans interrelate current experiences with information previously learned, and the future response to an equivalent stimulus may be different. The integrity of each of the above activities determines whether the learning experience will result in accurately encoded memories to produce an appropriate behavioral response.

The learning process of comparing new information with memories to produce a response frequently results in "behavioral conditioning." There is an innate foundation for learning in our biological structure that sets contingencies for behavioral conditioning in an individual, consistent with the premise of conditional free will. Consequently, behavioral sequences are neither programmed nor innate; they are acquired. The two forms of behavioral conditioning, classical and instrumental, both directly involve biological mechanisms. Classical conditioning refers to the response elicited by a neutral stimulus that has been associated with the acquisition of a reward or the avoidance of harm; for example, a white laboratory coat is associated with food and elicits salivation or viewing drug paraphernalia elicits craving for a drug.

Certain behaviors are reinforced when the following conditions exist: (1) the behavior and the stimulus occur together in time and space (continuity), (2) repetition of the association strengthens the conditions response, (3) the result either evokes pleasure or relieves pain, and (4) there is no interference, as in the form of new experiences, to weaken or extinguish the response. The concept of deterrence is founded on these principles.

In general, the criminal justice system relies on the association made between specific, in this case illegal, behaviors and the application of a painful or punitive sanction, which generally involves the removal of certain freedoms and exposure to unpleasant living conditions. The painful stimulus must be temporally associated with the behavior, consistently applied, and intense enough to prevent further such behaviors. According to the fourth condition listed above, the individual must not learn that the intrinsic reward properties of the behavior are greater or more consistent than the punishment. And finally, opportunities for preferred modes of behavior must be available. Due to the prevalence of low clearance rates, trial delays, inconsistently applied dispositions, legal loopholes, the learning of improper reward and punishment contingencies, and a lack of available legitimate opportunities, the criminal justice system and society at large have been unable to meet the criteria set above for deterrence and prevention.

The experience of a painful consequence being associated with a behavior is encoded into memory, and when we calculate the consequences of performing that behavior in the future we are deterred by the possible negative response. The impetus for such behavioral change resides in our nervous system. We feel anxiety when the threat of a negative repercussion exists because of the learned association between the behavior and its likely consequence. Subjective feelings of anxiety are a result of automatic nervous system responses (a portion of the nervous system that regulates functions not under our conscious control), such as increased heart rate, blood pressure, and hormone release. Thus, the brain initiates a release of hormones that stimulates a subjective feeling of stress whenever we contemplate a behavior that we have been effectively conditioned to avoid. Individuals with a properly functioning nervous system are quite effectively conditioned to avoid stressful situations given the learned contingencies discussed above. Most of us, for example, would experience psychological and physical discomfort at the thought of picking a pocket or burglarizing a convenience store. Thus, we make a rational choice based on a calculation of costs and benefits and, in this case, deterrence is most likely achieved....

Rewards and punishments influence behavior directly through brain mechanisms. Centers responsible for pain and pleasure are located in a section of the brain known as the limbic system. Not surprisingly, memories are encoded, stored, and retrieved in this same system. Direct electrical stimulation of certain areas within the limbic system (electrical stimulation of the brain, ESB) is inherently reinforcing, even in the absence of a biological or social drive (Olds and Milner, 1954). An animal quickly learns to perform for ESB due to its drive-inducing and intensely pleasurable effect. In humans, these areas are naturally stimulated when a behavior results in increases in specific neurotransmitters and peptides responsible for either pleasure (i.e., dopamine) or the reduction of pain (i.e., serotonin or beta-endorphins). In large part, which chemicals are released and in which areas depend on both biological and social learning contingencies.

This pain and pleasure mechanism is simply illustrated by the use of cocaine, which directly stimulates the release of dopamine in structures of the limbic system responsible for pleasure (Wise, 1984:15-33). The user quickly learns that cocaine is biologically rewarding, and, along with other reinforcing social circumstances associated with its use, he or she will be more likely to crave and reuse the drug. This is an example of both classical and instrumental conditioning. Other, more complicated, processes involving social learning or conditioning are also involved in the activation of pain and pleasure centers in the limbic system.

Imbalances of the limbic system may alter the proper stimulation of pain and pleasure centers. In schizophrenia, for example, the individual has disturbances in the ability to associate behaviors with a pleasurable outcome and behavior seemingly lacks purpose. It is believed that damage to neural reward structures has occurred (Stein and Wise, 1973). There is also evidence that some psychopaths experience intense pleasure from thrill-seeking or risk-taking activities and have a high pain threshold (Blackburn, 1978). Behaviors that involve an element of danger are not only exciting to these individuals, but they may be addictive in the conventional sense; they produce feelings of euphoria, and the participant may experience discomfort when unable to engage in such activities (Quay, 1965). The possibility that psychopaths have a disturbance in pain and pleasure centers is consistent with studies presented above showing that they have low levels of anxiety and are relatively "unconditionable." There is a large literature on the proneness of these individuals to become involved in delinquent and criminal activities (see Wilson and Herrnstein, 1985), again due to biological traits that are reinforced through social learning.

In sum, social behavior is learned through the principles of conditioning, which are founded on biological and genetic dictates in accord with stimulus-response relationships. Social rewards remain secondary to biological rewards; our desire for money is social, but it is secondary to being a means for obtaining food and shelter. Thus, social behavior satisfies biological needs and drives by providing adaptive mechanisms for reproduction, mating, rearing, defense, and numerous other biological functions. Even though these strategies are fundamentally biological, how we behave to satisfy them relies heavily on learning. . . .

References

Blackburn, R. 1978. Psychopathy, arousal, and the need for stimulation. In R.D. Hare and D. Schalling (eds.), *Psychopathic Behaviour: Approaches to Research*. Chichester, England: John Wiley & Sons.

Carlson, N.R. 1977. *Physiology of Behavior*. Boston: Allyn and Bacon.

Denno, D.W. 1988. *Human biology and criminal responsibility: Free will or free ride?* University of Pennsylvania Law Review 137(2):615-671.

Geary, D.C. 1989. A model for representing gender differences in the pattern of cognitive abilities. *American Psychologist* 44:1155-1156.

Glueck, S. and E.T. Glueck. 1956. *Physique and Delinquency*. New York: Harper & Row.

Goddard, H.H. 1921. *Juvenile Delinquency*. New York: Dodd, Mead.

Hamparin, D.M., R. Schuster, S. Dinitz, and J.P. Conrad. 1978. *The Violent Few: A Study of Dangerous Juvenile Offenders*. Lexington, Mass.: Lexington Books.

Hirschi, T. 1969. *Causes of Delinquency*. Berkeley: University of California Press.

Hooten, E.A. 1939. *The American Criminal: An Anthropological Study*. Cambridge, Mass.: Harvard University Press.

Jacobs, P.A., M. Brunton, M.M. Melville, R.P. Brittain, and W. McClemont. 1965. Aggressive behaviour, mental sub-normality, and the XYY male. *Nature* 108:1351-1352.

Kadzin, A.E. 1987. Treatment of antisocial behavior in children: Current status and future directions. *Psychological Bulletin* 102:187-203.

Kandel, E. and S.A. Mednick. 1988. IQ as a protective factor for subjects at high risk for antisocial behavior. *Journal of Consulting and Clinical Psychology* 56:224-226.

Lewis, D.O., S.S. Shanok, and D.A. Balla. 1979. Perinatal difficulties, head and face trauma, and child abuse in the medical histories of serious youthful offenders. *American Journal of Psychiatry* 136:419-423.

Loeber, R. and T. Dishion. 1983. Early predictors of male delinquency: A review. *Psychological Bulletin* 94:68-99.

Lombroso, C. 1918. *Crime, Its Causes and Remedies*. Boston: Little, Brown.

Mednick, S.A., W.F. Gabrielli, Jr., and B. Hutchings. 1984. Genetic influences in criminal convictions: Evidence from an adoption cohort. *Science* 224:891-894.

Mednick, S.A., T.E. Moffitt, and S.A. Stack. 1987. *The Causes of Crime: New Biological Approaches*. New York: Cambridge University Press.

Moffitt, T.E., S.A. Mednick, and W.F. Gabrielli, Jr. 1989. Predicting careers of criminal violence: Descriptive data and predispositional factors. In D.A. Brizer and M. Crowner (eds.), *Current Approaches to the Prediction of Violence*. Washington, D.C.: American Psychiatric Press.

Olds, J. and P. Milner. 1954. Positive reinforcement produced by electrical stimulation of septal area and other regions of rat brain. *Journal of Comparative and Physiological Psychology* 47:419-427.

Patterson, G.R., B.D. DeBaryshe, and E. Ramsey. 1989. A developmental perspective on antisocial behavior. *American Psychologist* 44:329-335.

Plomin, R. 1989. Environment and Genes: Determinants of Behavior. *American Psychologist* 44:105-111.

Quay, H.C. 1965. Psychopathic personality as pathological stimulation seeking. *American Journal of Psychiatry* 122:180-183.

Sheldon, W.H. 1949. *Varieties of Delinquent Youth*. New York: Harper & Row.

Stein, L. and C.D. Wise. 1973. Amphetamine and noradrenergic reward pathways. In E. Usdin and S.H. Snyder (eds.), *Frontiers in Catecholamine Research*. New York: Pergamon.

Watson, J.B. 1925. *Behaviorism*. New York: W.W. Norton.

Wilson, J.Q. and R.J. Herrnstein. 1985. *Crime and Human Nature*. New York: Simon & Schuster. ✦

14
Biological Positivism

Michael R. Gottfredson
Travis Hirschi

The classical conception of human behavior, with its emphasis on choice in the service of self-interest, eventually gave way to a positivist conception of human behavior, with an emphasis on difference and determinism. The positivist revolution was greeted with great optimism and enthusiasm, and its methods were soon applied to almost everything, including crime. This chapter traces the positivist revolution from its origins in biology to the current state of biological criminology. Along the way, we attempt to identify some of the problems that stem from strict application of positivistic conceptions to the study of crime and criminality.

The Origins of Biological Positivism

Charles Darwin's *The Origin of Species*, published in 1859, and his *The Descent of Man*, first published in 1871, are widely held to mark the end of "prescientific" (classical) thinking about the causes of human behavior.... Prior to Darwin, so the story goes, humans were assumed to be a species distinct from the rest of the animal kingdom. They were assumed to have free will, to be able to choose a course of action depending on their assessment of the pleasures and pains that various alternatives were likely to provide. With the advent of Darwin's theory of evolution, such views were seen by many as no longer tenable. According to evolutionary biology, humans are animals subject to laws of nature like all other animals. Human behavior, like any animal

From *A General Theory of Crime*, pp. 47-63. Copyright © 1990 by Stanford University Press. Reprinted by permission.

trait, must therefore be governed by the laws of nature rather than by free will and choice. It remained for scientists interested in behavior to isolate or identify those causal forces producing the criminal behavior of humans. It is not surprising that the first place they looked for such forces was in the biology of the offender.

The origins of scientific criminology are usually traced to the work of Cesare Lombroso (1835-1909), a physician employed in the Italian penal system. Lombroso saw himself as a scientist in tune with the biology of his day. He tells us that the science of criminology actually began with his discovery of an anomaly in a robber's skull, but the connection between Lombroso's theory of crime (i.e., criminals are throwbacks to an earlier stage of evolution) and Darwin's theory of evolution is so direct we must conclude that Lombroso's theory was at first deductive rather than inductive—that it was derived from general *substantive* principles and preceded observation rather than vice versa.[1]

As a positivist, however, Lombroso could not long restrict his attention to the differences between criminals and noncriminals that might be derived from the theory of evolution. On the contrary, as a positivist, he had to seek all of the correlates of crime and to try somehow to make sense of them. The statistics of Lombroso's day did not allow conclusions about the relative importance of the many potential differences between criminals and noncriminals, and Lombroso did not have a general theory of crime that would organize them in a meaningful way. He therefore sorted the correlates of crime into clusters or groups based on traditional divisions of the physical and social world. These clusters or groups of variables are strangely akin to modern "disciplines." In fact, the table of contents of later editions of Lombroso's major work (1918 [1899]) looks much like a university catalog, with sections on meteorological, geological, anthropological, demographic, educational, economic, religious, genetic, and political causes of crime.

The importance and generality of this fact should not escape notice: in its search for meaning in nature, positivism clusters independent variables and thereby creates disciplines. But positivism has no device for ranking "disciplinary" clusters of independent variables according to their relevance to a given problem (dependent variable). It must, therefore, put each problem up for grabs and hope that its various disciplines can resolve their competing claims and in the process somehow discover meaningful solutions to the problem at issue.

Put another way, the methods of positivism automatically produce multiple-factor conclusions whatever the "disciplinary" orientation of the particular positivist using them. These methods therefore lead automatically to disciplinary disputes that they cannot themselves settle. The result is a "science" much concerned with allocating "findings" to its constituent disciplines and not so concerned with understanding nature. In this regard, Lombroso's fate is instructive. Although he began with a biological theory of crime, he soon included variables from other disciplines and came eventually to see his own theory as accounting for a minority of criminals. That he is today regarded as the father of biological positivism and ignored by sociologists and psychologists attests to the tendency of modern disciplinarians to confuse positivism as a method with positivism as a theory of human behavior. In any event, Lombroso is as much the father of sociological or psychological as of biological positivism.

The biological positivists did not have a conception of crime derived from a general theory of behavior. They were therefore forced to accept the criminals provided them by the state: "A criminal is a man who violates laws decreed by the State to regulate the relations between its citizens" (Ferraro 1972 [1911]:3). Crimes were then merely acts in violation of the law. The biological positivist's problem seemed simple enough. All one had to do was locate the differences among people that produce differences in their tendencies to commit acts in violation of the law. Starting with the assumption that offenders differ from nonoffenders, positivism soon discovered that offenders also appeared to differ among themselves. It was obvious that offenders committed different kinds of crimes. Moreover, offenders committing the same kind of crime were not homogeneous on important characteristics.

Lombroso thus started with a theory of crime, a theory in which physical anomalies with hereditary origins distinguish those with a propensity to commit crime from those without such a propensity. Almost immediately he encountered cases that did not fit the theory—that is, offenders were not all alike nor did they differ in the same ways from nonoffenders. The solution to this problem adopted by Lombroso (at the urging of his student Enrico Ferri) was to subdivide the criminal population into types, each of which was meant to be internally homogeneous with respect to the causes of crime and different from other types on the same dimensions. As Ferri wrote:

> The work of Lombroso set out with two original faults: the mistake of having given undue importance, at any rate apparently, to the data of craniology and anthropometry, rather than to those of psychology; and, secondly, that of having mixed up in the first two editions, all criminals in a single class. In later editions these defects were eliminated, Lombroso having adopted the observation which I made in the first instance, as to the various anthropological categories of criminals. [1897:11, referring to Lombroso's *L'Uomo delinquente* (1876)]

Thus to Lombroso's born criminal Ferri added occasional criminals (those "who do not exhibit, or who exhibit in slighter degrees, the anatomical, physiological, and psychological characteristics which constitute the type described by Lombroso as the 'criminal man'"), pseudo-criminals ("normal human beings who commit involuntary offenses, or offenses which do not spring from perversity, and do not hurt society, though they are punishable by law"), political criminals, epileptic criminals, criminals by passion, incorrigible criminals, and homosexual offenders, to name only some.

Absent a conception of crime, the positivist has no choice but to elaborate types of offenders. These typologies may be based on the frequency of offending, the seriousness of the offense, the object of the offense, the characteristics of the offender, or the nature of prior and subsequent offenses, but whatever their dimensions, they lead to complication rather than simplicity, to confusion rather than clarity. Apparently little or no progress has been made on this point. Modern typologies—such as those based on sociological (Clinard and Quinney 1973) or psychological (Megargee and Bohn 1979) constructs, or on empirical clustering of criminal careers (Blumstein et al. 1986; Farrington, Ohlin, and Wilson 1986), or on the number of offenses committed (National Institute of Mental Health 1982)—all derive from the positivist problem that itself stems from the absence of an idea of crime, and none seems to solve the problem of internal diversity. Absent a conception of crime, the positivistic method leads ineluctably to typologizing without end.

Lombroso's criminal anthropology quickly became the subject of considerable controversy. The first tests of his theory naturally focused on its claims about the peculiar physiognomy of the offender. As early as 1913, these claims were vigorously disputed by Charles Goring. Goring's conclusions are widely misstated by criminologists, many of whom perhaps attend more to the tone of his remarks about Lombroso than to the actual results of his research. The famous statistician Karl Pearson (who assisted Goring in much of his work) summarizes that portion of Goring's findings dealing with Lombroso's view that the offender has a peculiar physiognomy:

> It is not too much to say that in the early chapters of Goring's work he clears out of the way for ever the tangled and exuberant growths of the Lombrosian School. He then turns to the constructive side of his work, and using precisely the same methods of investigation, tells us of the English criminal as he really is, not absolutely differentiated by numerous anomalies from the general population, but relatively differentiated from the mean or population type, because on the average he is selected from the physically poorer and mentally feebler portion of the general population. The criminal is not a *random* sample of the general population, either physically or mentally. He is, rather, a sample of the less fit moiety of it. [Pearson, in Goring 1913:xii]

It would be easy to conclude that Goring actually found substantial empirical support for the central contention of Lombroso's biological positivism—that the criminal is differentiated from the noncriminal in terms of biological or genetic characteristics. Whatever the details of their disagreement about the biological traits associated with crime, this disagreement is clearly within a context of fundamental agreement on the idea that crime is the product of biological deficiency. Where Lombroso saw physical anomalies as central, Goring disagreed: "No evidence has emerged confirming the existence of a physical criminal type, such as Lombroso and his disciples have described.... In fact, both with regard to measurements and the presence of physical anomalies in criminals, our statistics present a startling conformity with similar statistics of the law-abiding classes" (Goring 1919:96-97). But with respect to physical stature and physique, Goring reported differences:

> All English criminals, with the exception of those technically convicted of fraud, are markedly differentiated from the general population in stature and body-weight; in addition, offenders convicted of violence to the person are characterized by an average degree of strength and of constitutional soundness considerably above the average of other criminals and of the law-abiding community; finally, thieves and burglars (who constitute, it must be borne in mind, 90 per cent of all criminals) and also incendiaries, as well as being inferior in stature and weight, are also, relatively to other criminals and the population at large, puny in their general bodily habit. [1919:121]

Goring also found differences between the criminal and noncriminal populations with respect to "alcoholism, epilepsy, and sexual profligacy," but he concluded "that the one vital mental constitutional factor in the etiology of crime is defective intelligence" (ibid.:184).

So, in the end, Goring and Lombroso disagreed on the important biological differences between criminals and noncriminals, not on the idea that such differences were present. Working with inferior samples, measures, and statistical techniques, Lombroso was able only to speculate about differences, and naturally he focused on potential sources of differences that could be readily observed. Working with highly sophisticated statistics, Goring's findings naturally diverged in detail from those of Lombroso. They did not, however, dispute the general thrust of Lombroso's argument or the tenets of biological positivism (as is so widely assumed). Instead, the findings offered support for the expectation of important biological differences between offenders and nonoffenders, support for the multiple-factor approach, for rigorous empirical research, and for further differentiation of the offender population as required by causal analysis.

Goring examined the relations among the causes of crime he uncovered, and he asked himself what they might have in common:

> To resume: defective physique, extreme forms of alcoholism, epilepsy, insanity, sexual profligacy, and weak-mindedness—these are the constitutional conditions, and the only ones, which so far have emerged as significantly associated with the committing of crime in this country. An interesting question that arises is to what extent are these conditions several manifestations of one and the same thing? The correlation with criminality of alcoholism is .39, of epilepsy is .26, of sexual profligacy is .31, and of mental deficiency is .64. From the high value of the last coefficient we would presume that, if reducible to one condition, it is mental defectiveness which would most likely prove to be the common antecedent of the alcoholism, epilepsy, insanity, and sexual profligacy. [1919:183]

Goring's logic is revealing. He began by asking what the various correlates of crime may have in common, suggesting a search for a concept of criminality. But the search for commonality was limited to the causes of crime, and the question quickly focused on the possibility that one of the putative independent variables causes the others. Absent a conception of the dependent variable, Goring had nothing to guide his conceptualization of the independent variables, and he ended up treating all but one of them as conceptually equivalent to crime. That is, everything may be a consequence of the variable with the largest correlation with crime, mental deficiency.

Goring's reliance on an ill-defined empirical solution to his conceptual problem illustrates another characteristic of criminological positivism that survives to the present day. Modern criminologists often note intercorrelations among "crime types" as a platform for asking which causes which. It remains rare, however, for modern criminologists to suspect that various types of behavior—some criminal, some noncriminal—may have enough in common to justify treating them as the same thing. Goring glimpsed this solution to his conceptual problem, but the instinct of positivism to seek homogeneity through differentiation rather than abstraction was too strong to allow him to adopt it.

With the publication of Goring's work, biological positivism reached its natural limits. Without a concept of crime or of criminality, biological positivism is reduced to endless examination of lists of possible physiological, anatomical, and constitutional variables that may or may not be correlated with behavior defined as crime by contemporary political sanctions (see, e.g., Herrnstein 1983). Advances in the field must await improvements in sampling, measurement, or statistical procedures. Without a concept of crime, biological positivism, like any branch of positivism, has no way of ascribing importance to its independent variables, no way of understanding the relations among them, and, ultimately, no way of assessing the importance of its own findings. Furthermore, the separation of independent and dependent variables becomes problematic, resulting in frequent confusion of the two.

Contemporary Biological Positivism

These assertions are easily illustrated by contemporary biological positivism, the principle achievements of which have been to improve research design by the use of twin and adoption studies and to use measurement procedures more sophisticated than those previously available, such as measures of skin conductance and chromosomal abnormalities.

One of the most celebrated findings of modern biological positivism is that reported by Sarnoff Mednick and his colleagues from a large-scale study of a Danish adoption cohort, a study said to be confirmed by work in Sweden and Iowa. As Mednick summarizes the situation, these studies "irrefutably support the influence of heritable factors in the etiology of some forms of antisocial acts. Because we can only inherit biological predispositions, the genetic evidence conclusively admits biological factors among the important agents influencing some forms of criminal behavior" (1987:6). The conclusiveness of adoption studies apparently derives from the persuasiveness of their design: "Of all non-experimental designs, properly executed adoption studies constitute an extremely powerful design for isolating significant amounts of the influence of genetic factors from all conceivable environmental factors. . . . The reason for their power is that they actually approach a controlled experiment" (Ellis 1982:52). In a pilot study, Barry Hutchings and Sarnoff Mednick (1977) used a Copenhagen sample to examine the effects on the criminality of adopted boys of criminality in their biological and adoptive fathers. The results of this initial study are reproduced in Table 1.

Hutchings and Mednick note that the differences in Table 1 do not reach statistical significance, "but the direction of the difference favors the strength of the biological father's criminality" over that of the adoptive father's criminality (1977:137). The clear implication is that, were a larger sample of cases available, these impressive percentage point differences would reach conventional levels of statistical significance. With statistical significance, such differences would provide evidence for a strong genetic influence on crime as defined by the state of Denmark.

Table 1
Percentage of Adopted Sons Who Are Registered Criminals, by Background of Biological and Adoptive Fathers

		Is biological father criminal?	
		Yes	No
Is adoptive father criminal?	Yes	36.2% (of 58)	11.5% (of 52)
	No	22% (of 219)	10.5% (of 333)

Source: Hutchings and Mednick 1977:137.
Note: Tables 1-4 are to be read as follows: 36.2 percent of the 58 adopted sons whose biological and adoptive fathers both had a criminal record were also registered criminals themselves.

In pursuit of such evidence, Mednick and his colleagues expanded their study to encompass all nonfamilial adoptions in Denmark between 1924 and 1947. The results of this study are presented in Table 2.

Table 2
Percentage of Adopted Sons Who Have Been Convicted of Criminal Law Offenses, by Background of Biological and Adoptive Parents

		Are biological parents criminal?	
		Yes	No
Are adoptive parents criminal?	Yes	25.5% (of 143)	14.7% (of 204)
	No	20.0% (of 1,226)	13.5% (of 2,492)

Source: Wilson and Herrnstein 1985:96. See also Mednick, Gabrielli, and Hutchings 1984:892, 1987:79.

This table appears to confirm the results of Table 1 on a much larger sample. According to Mednick, Gabrielli, and Hutchings:

> In summary, in a population of adoptions a relation was found between biological parent criminal convictions and criminal convictions in their adoptee children. . . . A number of potentially confounding variables were considered; none proved sufficient to explain the genetic relation. We conclude that some factor transmitted by criminal parents increases the likelihood

that their children will engage in criminal behavior. [1984:893]

Table 2 differs from Table 1 in several respects, each of which would seem to bear on the interpretation of the results. First, the measure of criminality among adoptees appears to have shifted from "registered criminality" to "court convictions." Second, the criminality of biological and adoptive *fathers*, the independent variable in the pilot study, has changed to criminality of the biological and adoptive *parents* in the final study. Third, the numbers in the final study are much larger than in the pilot study, representing 4,065 adoptees in the final study as compared to 662 in the pilot study. Fourth, the final study is based on the population of "a small northern European nation" (Mednick, Gabrielli, and Hutchings 1984:891), whereas the pilot study was restricted to "the city and county of Copenhagen" (Hutchings and Mednick 1977:128). Fifth, the crime rate for the adoptee sample as a whole has declined from 16.6 percent in the pilot study to 15.9 percent in the final study. Finally, the differences in criminality between adoptees whose biological parents were criminal and those whose biological parents were not criminal are smaller in the final study than in the pilot study. In the final study, the differences are 9.8 percentage points when adoptive parents are criminal and 6.5 percentage points when adoptive parents are noncriminal. In the pilot study, these percentage differences were 24.7 and 11.5, respectively. In other words, in the final study the crucial differences for the biological effect hypothesis have declined to 40 percent and 56 percent of their original value.

As noted, the original (1977) adoptee study was defined as a pilot study. The subsequent study (reported in *Science* in 1984) would normally be defined as a replication study, an attempt to determine whether the results of the pilot study could be confirmed. Traditionally, such replications are independent—that is, they follow the same procedure on a different sample of cases from the same population. Independence of samples is essential to the interpretation of replication research.

Is the final 1984 sample independent of the initial or pilot study, or are the cases in the original study included in the final sample? The conclusions one draws about a genetic effect on crime are utterly dependent on the answer to this question.[2]

Table 3 is created under the assumption that the cases in the pilot study were included in the final study and that other differences between the two studies can be safely ignored. Under this assumption, we subtract the cases in Table 1 from the cases in Table 2 and compute the percentage of adoptees who are criminal in each of the cells of the replication sample.

Table 3
The Joint Effects of Biological Parents' and Adoptive Parents' Criminality on the Criminality of Adopted Sons, Denmark Other Than Copenhagen, 1924-47

		Are biological parents criminal?	
		Yes	No
Are adoptive parents criminal?	Yes	16.5% (85)	15.8% (152)
	No	19.6% (1,007)	15.3% (2,159)

Clearly, Table 3 shows no effect of the criminality of the biological parents on the criminality of their adopted sons. The differences are in the direction suggested by the genetic hypothesis, but they are at best insubstantial. On the basis of Table 3 we would be forced to reject the genetic hypothesis, to conclude that we are dealing here with a failure to replicate the findings reported in the first or pilot study. In order to reach this conclusion, however, we must consider in a systematic way the several differences between the two studies noted earlier.

First, could change in the criterion of criminality negate our conclusion? In the report of the second study in *Science*, Mednick and his colleagues do not directly compare the results of their two studies. However, the second study emphasizes the fact that the criterion of crime is a "court conviction" (see also Wilson and Herrnstein 1985), whereas the pilot study uses the terms "criminal record" and "registered criminality." These latter terms are defined as follows: "A separate criminal record (*Personalia Blad*) is kept on all persons who have at any time been convicted of offenses treated as *statsadvokatsager*. These correspond very closely to indictable offenses in British justice and can be contrasted with *politisager* (summary offenses). ... The distinction corresponds very roughly to the difference between felonies and misdemeanors in the United States" (Hutchings and Mednick 1977:129). Apparently, therefore, the criterion of conviction is used in both the pilot and the final study. (If the measure of the dependent variable actually changed from one study to the next, it would still be necessary to exclude the pilot study cases from the replication analysis. Otherwise, the differences in the final study could still be entirely due to differences in the pilot study, differences not in question.)

Second, Mednick and his colleagues shift from criminality of the *father* to criminality of the *parents* as the measure of the independent variable. They report that "in all our analyses, the relation between biological mother conviction and adoptee conviction is significantly stronger than that between biological father and adoptee convictions" (1984:893). In other words, changing the measure of the independent variable by adding mothers strengthened the apparent genetic effect over that shown in the pilot study (making the failure to replicate all the more dramatic). It did so by adding cases to those cells with small numbers and by adding "criminals" to the ranks of adoptees with criminal biological parents. (We estimate that mothers added about 200 cases to the criminal biological parent category in the final sample. Mednick et al. do not indicate whether this adjustment was applied to the pilot study cases and, if so, what effect it had on the conclusions for that sample.)

Recall that the major problem with the pilot study was that it lacked sufficient cases (in the criminal biological father category) to allow confident conclusions. Although the "replication" study was able to find 3,403 additional cases, the increase in the number of cases in the crucial category was from 58 to 85, and this increase included the children of criminal biological *mothers*. Given the virtual absence of a relation between parent criminality and the criminality of the son in the replication study, however, its numbers are sufficient to reduce rather than increase our confidence in the findings of the pilot study.

The shift in the sample from the city and county of Copenhagen to the entire country of Denmark could be interpreted as a critical difference between the replication and the pilot study. One possibility is that the record-keeping on convictions differs between Copenhagen and the rest of Denmark such that the genetic effect is obscured by poor record-keeping in the country or enhanced by poor record-keeping in the city. In this situation, combining the samples from the two locations is ill advised. A second possibility is that the genetic effect differs between the city and county of Copenhagen and the balance of Denmark. Neither of these hypotheses, in our judgment, has any merit.

In our view, the shift in the overall crime rate from the pilot to the final sample (from 16.6 to 15.9 percent) is evidence that the decline in the genetic effect between the two studies cannot be accounted for by the shift in the criterion. The small decline observed is consistent with what would be expected were an urban sample combined with a sample drawn from nonurban areas, areas with a typically lower crime rate.

In our judgment, then, the proper interpretation of the Mednick et al. "cross-fostering" research is that their second, larger study failed to replicate the finding of a genetic effect from their pilot study. Such failure to replicate is common in behavioral research, particularly when the initial findings suggest effects out of line with those normally encountered in the research area. We would not be surprised to learn that the true genetic effect on the likelihood of criminal behavior is *somewhere between zero and the results finally reported by Mednick, Gabrielli, and Hutchings*. That is, we suspect that the magnitude of this effect is minimal.

Table 4
Cross-Fostering in a Swedish Study of Male Adoptees: Percentage Committing "Petty Crimes" by Biological Predisposition

		Congenital predisposition	
		Low	High
Postnatal predisposition	Low	2.9% (666)	12.1% (66)
	High	6.7% (120)	40.0% (10)

Source: Cloninger and Gottesman 1987: 105.

The Mednick et al. results are often reported to be consistent with other research. According to Wilson and Herrnstein (1985:99), "a large Swedish study has confirmed and extended much of these Danish findings." The cross-fostering data for males from the Swedish study are therefore reproduced in Table 4.

The cases in this table were assembled by Robert Cloninger and Irving Gottesman (1987) from a Stockholm adoption study. According to the authors, in this analysis "congenital" refers to variables about biological parents, whereas "postnatal" refers to variables about adoptive placements. Several aspects of Table 4 merit comment. First, the total number of subjects with records for petty crimes was relatively small (39). The research project began with 108 convicted offenders. Second, note the greater likelihood of postnatal as opposed to congenital predisposition, a "finding" out of line with usual cross-fostering data (see Tables 1-3, above). The data suggest that Swedish procedures place 15 percent of adoptees in environments of "high" predisposition to petty crime, whereas the genetic makeup of the same adoptees puts only 9 percent of them at such risk. Third, the cell of most interest in this "large Swedish study" contains ten cases, four of which are classified as "petty criminals." Fourth, consider the classification "predisposition to petty crime." According to Cloninger and Gottesman, this classification "depends on whether the background variables are more like the average characteristics of adoptees with petty crime only (classified as high) than like those of adoptees with no crime and/or alcohol abuse (classified as low) (1987: 105).

In other words, Cloninger and Gottesman devised a "cross-fostering" table based on variables known to predict petty criminality in their own sample and said by them to reflect the environmental conditions of the biological parents (congenital) and of the adoptive parents (postnatal). Consequently, this aspect of their study has no bearing on the heritability question. Even if it were possible to overlook the constructed nature of the results, it would not be possible to overlook their ex post facto nature. How these results could be construed as supportive of the Danish research finding is entirely unclear. In fact, these results seem to support our reinterpretation of the Danish cross-fostering analysis. Also consistent with our view is this statement by Cloninger and Gottesman: "In the same Swedish population, Bohman [1972] found no excess of delinquency before the age of 12 years in adopted-away children from criminal biological parents" (1987:104).

The third study cited in support of the Danish adoption research is based on 52 adoptees born during a 31-year period in Iowa (Crowe 1975). Raymond Crowe identified female offenders in prison whose children had been adopted. (Some of these mothers contributed more than one child to the sample.) These adoptees were matched with a second set of adoptees on age, sex, and race. Comparison of subsequent records of criminality revealed seven arrests among the 37 children of prisoners and two arrests among the 37 adoptees in the control group for whom records were available. This difference is reported by Crowe to be significant at the .076 level (1975:98).

There is no need to quibble about this confidence level. The Crowe study is so far from minimal standards of scientific adequacy that it deserves only minimal comment. For one thing, no information was collected concerning the biological parents of the control group. They may have been less, equally, or more criminal that the biological parents of the prison adoptees. For another, no information is supplied about the arrest records of other relevant comparison groups. The Crowe study, best characterized as a "one-shot case study" (the control group is for all intents and purposes hypothetical), therefore provides no basis for the conclusion that crime is inherited in Iowa.

We began this section with a statement from Lee Ellis (1982) to the effect that adoption studies provide the strongest basis for inference concerning the heritability of criminal behavior. There is little disagreement about the strength of the adoption design: "The most convincing evidence for genetic influence on antisocial behavior comes from studies of adopted children who were separated at birth from their criminal biological parents" (Rowe and Osgood 1984:535). We agree that these studies are convincing. They provide strong evidence that the inheritance of criminality is *minimal*. We must therefore disagree with Wilson and Herrnstein, who conclude on the basis of this same body of empirical data: "All told, this small sample, like the much larger Danish and Swedish ones, suggests a strong biological resemblance between a parent and a child given up for adoption in some trait or traits that predispose people toward trouble with the law" (1985:100). On the contrary, we conclude that the magnitude of the "genetic effect," as determined by adoption studies, is near zero.

This result should not be surprising, and it should not be interpreted as showing that biology has nothing to do with crime. In our view, the best guess about the magnitude of a genetic effect would be derived as follows:

Take the correlation between the father's biology (i.e., genetic makeup) and his own criminal behavior, and multiply it by the correlation between his biology and his child's biology. Multiply the result by the correlation between his child's biology and his child's criminal behavior. (This path diagram is shown in Figure 1.)

To put the case for heritability in its strongest possible terms, assume an observed correlation of .25 between biology and crime in both generations, and a correlation of .5 between the biology of the father and the biology of his sons. These correlations would yield a correlation between father's and son's crimes of .031, a correlation that would require very large samples to reach statistical significance, and a correlation that if statistically significant would be substantively trivial.[3]

Conclusions

Biological positivism accepted the state's definition of crime as a violation of law and of the criminal as someone arrested, convicted, and sentenced for a crime. This decision allowed comparison of "criminals" and "noncriminals," subdivision of the "criminal" population by type of offense (e.g., property), and discussion of the possibility of a heritable "predisposition" to crime. The idea of predisposition suggests a theory or explanation of crime. It stems directly from the positivistic view that crime is caused by factors beyond the control of the criminal. Thus the idea of causation, meant to embody the neutrality of science, in fact brought with it a substantive theory of crime, a theory according to which people committing criminal acts are required or forced to do so by constellations of antecedent factors.

Acceptance of the state's definition of crime, science's presumed view of causation, and the substantive variables assigned to it by the disciplinary division of labor did not lead biological positivism to an idea of crime. On the contrary, they led it to search

Figure 1
Correlations necessary to Produce an Observed Correlation of .03 Between the Criminal Behavior of Fathers and Sons

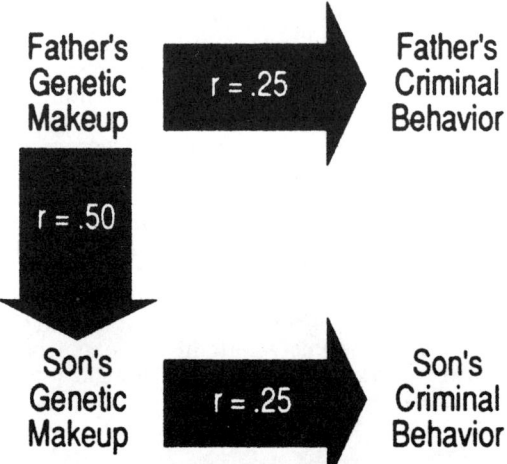

for the biological causes of state-defined crime, an ostensibly empirical enterprise that was actually massively constrained by a priori principles. As a result, biological positivism has produced little in the way of meaningful or interpretable research. Instead, as we have seen, it has produced a series of "findings" (e.g., physiognomy, feeblemindedness, XYY, inheritance of criminality) that survived only so long as was necessary to subject them to replication or to straightforward critical analysis.

Apparently, improvements in statistics, measurement, and sampling by themselves cannot overcome problems inherent in biological positivism. More than 100 years after Lombroso initiated this line of inquiry, the major contribution of biological research would appear to be data suggesting that biological variables may be correlated with crime. Unfortunately, this evidence is often so suspect that scholars friendly to the idea of biological causation are left wondering why this discipline has so much trouble contributing "acceptable" facts to the field of criminology.

The reasons for the absence of influence from biology are, in our view, not hard to find. The discipline proceeds without a concept of crime and without a concept of criminality. As a result, the Mednick et al. research is not unique in terms of its contribution to criminology. We discuss it at length because it illustrates the general problems of biological positivism. The history of XYY chromosome research tells a similar story: extraordinary effort expended to document the possible existence of a small effect, the significance of which is unclear even to those pursuing it (Witkin et al. 1977).

There is another tendency in this research with even greater implications for the ultimate contribution of biological positivism. Researchers in this tradition adopt in near serial fashion one dependent variable after another, suggesting that each is individually important in its own right (see the Mednick et al. shift from "registered criminality" to "court convictions") and paying no attention to the possible conceptual overlap among them. Thus the sample used by Mednick and his colleagues to study "crime" was originally collected to allow study of the genetic transmission of mental illness. The sample has also been used to study the genetic transmission of alcoholism, and it could be (if it has not been) used to study the genetic transmission of many other forms of behavior (such as smoking, obesity, truancy, or accidents). What escapes the notice of biological positivists is that such samples could also document the "genetic transmission" of illegitimate parenthood, unstable job performance, broken marriages, poor child-rearing practices, and being late for school. If these behaviors seem disconnected, it is because the behavioral sciences share with biological positivism the view that the study of concrete acts or items of behavior is scientific while study of abstract concepts is not. Recall that a major tenet of positivism is the view that acts have causes. All too frequently, the idea that acts have causes is translated via the research literature into the idea that specific acts have specific causes. For biological positivism, this leads to the search for a genetic component to account for variation in specific acts. (And leads, not surprisingly, to focus on "important" or "serious" acts—as though they can be explained independently of "trivial" acts in the same domain.) As we will see, these problems are not unique to the biological branch of positivism.

Notes

1. This is not meant to take anything away from Lombroso. In our view, he has been unjustly maligned by contemporary social scientists, most of whom appear to have read little of his work. Although it may be true that he is the father of biological determinism in criminology, his more important contribution perhaps comes from his advocacy of positivism and the principle of multiple causation. The first words in his famous *Crime: Its Causes and Remedies* address these issues: "Every crime has its origin in a multiplicity of causes, often intertwined and confused, each of which we must, in obedience to the necessities of thought and speech, investigate singly. This multiplicity is generally the rule with human phenomena, to which one can almost never assign a single cause unrelated to the others" (1918:1). In fact,

the 1918 version of his book includes twelve chapters on causation, and it anticipates virtually every concern of contemporary criminology, from white-collar crime to sex offenses, from differential association to poverty theory.

2. Mednick and his colleagues clearly do not share our concern with this issue. Apparently, they see the initial or pilot study as a "subsample of [the] adoption cohort" (Mednick, Gabrielli, and Hutchings 1983:21) or as "a large subsample of this population" (Mednick et al. 1987:89) and the final study as an "extension" of the original study. Although they occasionally note similarities in the results of the two studies (see Mednick et al. 1983:21; Mednick et al. 1984:893), so far as we have been able to determine they nowhere address the differences in results between them.

3. These correlation coefficients translate into a "heritability coefficient" of .177, which may be described as the theoretical upper limit of the correlation between father's criminality and son's criminality given our assumptions. We would not argue that this result proves the irrelevance of biology to crime. We would argue, however, that it shows the need for greater attention to conceptual matters by those interested in the connection between biology and crime.

References

Blumstein, Alfred, Jacqueline Cohen, Jeffrey Roth, and Christy Visher. 1986. *Criminal Careers and "Career Criminals."* Washington, D.C.: National Academy Press.

Bohman, M. 1972. "A Study of Adopted Children, Their Background, Environment, and Adjustment." *Acta Pediatrica Scandinavia*, 61:90-97.

Clinard, Marshall and Richard Quinney. 1973. *Criminal Behavior Systems: A Typology*. New York: Holt, Rinehart, and Winston.

Cloninger, Robert and Irving Gottesman. 1987. "Genetic and Environmental Factors in Antisocial Behavior Disorders." In *The Causes of Crime: New Biological Approaches*, edited by S. Mednick, T. Moffitt, and S. Stack (pp. 92-109). Cambridge, Engl.: Cambridge University Press.

Crowe, Raymond. 1975. "An Adoptive Study of Psychopathy: Preliminary Results from Arrest Records and Psychiatric Hospital Records." In *Genetic Research in Psychiatry*, edited by R. Fieve, D. Rosenthal, and H. Brill (pp. 95-105). Baltimore: Johns Hopkins University Press.

Ellis, Lee. 1982. "Genetics and Criminal Behavior." *Criminology*, 20:43-66.

Farrington, David, Lloyd Ohlin, and James Q. Wilson. 1986. *Understanding and Controlling Crime*. New York: Springer-Verlag.

Ferraro, Gina Lombroso. 1972 [1911]. *Criminal Man*. Montclair, N.J.: Patterson Smith.

Ferri, Enrico. 1897. *Criminal Sociology*. New York: D. Appleton and Company.

Goring, Charles. 1913. *The English Convict*. Montclair, N.J.: Patterson Smith.

———. 1919. *The English Convict*. Rev. ed. London: His Majesty's Stationery Office.

Herrnstein, Richard. 1983. "Some Criminogenic Traits of Offenders." In *Crime and Public Policy*, edited by J. Q. Wilson (pp. 31-52). San Francisco: Institute for Contemporary Studies.

Hutchings, Barry and Sarnoff Mednick. 1977. "Criminality in Adoptees and Their Adoptive and Biological Parents: A Pilot Study." In *Biological Bases of Criminal Behavior*, edited by S. Mednick and K. O. Christiansen (pp. 127-142). New York: Gardner.

Lombroso, Cesare. 1918 [1899]. *Crime: Its Causes and Remedies*. Rev. ed. Boston: Little, Brown.

Mednick, Sarnoff. 1987. "Introduction." In *The Causes of Crime: New Biological Approaches*, edited by S. A. Mednick, T. E. Moffitt, and S. A. Stack (pp. 1-6). Cambridge, Engl.: Cambridge University Press.

Mednick, Sarnoff, William Gabrielli, and Barry Hutchings. 1983. "Genetic Influences in Criminal Behavior: Some Evidence from an Adoption Cohort." Paper presented at the annual meetings of the American Society of Criminology, Denver, Colorado.

———. 1984. "Genetic Influences in Criminal Convictions: Evidence from an Adoption Cohort." *Science*, 224-891-894.

———. 1987. "Genetic Factors in the Etiology of Criminal Behavior." In *The Causes of Crime: New Biological Approaches*, edited by S. A. Mednick, T. E. Moffitt, and S. A. Stack (pp. 74-91). Cambridge, Engl.: Cambridge University Press.

Megargee, Edwin and M. Bohn. 1979. *Classifying Criminals*. Beverly Hills, Calif.: Sage.

National Institute of Mental Health. 1982. *Research Highlights 1982*. Vol. 1. Washington, D.C.: U.S. Department of Health and Human Services.

Rowe, David and D. Wayne Osgood. 1984. "Heredity and Sociological Theories of Delinquency: A Reconsideration." *American Sociological Review*, 49:526-40.

Wilson, James Q. and Richard Herrnstein. 1985. *Crime and Human Nature*. New York: Simon and Schuster.

Witkin, Herman, Sarnoff Mednick, Fini Schulsinger, Eskild Bakkestrom, Karl Christiansen, Donald Goodenough, Kurt Hirschorn, Claes Lundsteen, David Owen, John Philip, Donald Rubin, and Martha Stocking. 1977. "Criminality, Aggression, and Intelligence among XYY and XXY Men." In *Biosocial Bases of Criminal Behavior*, edited by S. Mednick and K. O. Christiansen (pp. 165-87). New York: Gardner. ✦

15
Social Learning and Deviant Behavior: A Specific Test of a General Theory

Ronald L. Akers
Marvin D. Krohn
Lonn Lanza-Kaduce
Marcia Radosevich

Introduction

In the last decade we have seen a dramatic shift away from sociological explanations of deviant behavior toward developing theoretical perspectives on societal reactions to and definitions of deviance and crime. Labelling and conflict formulations have become major foci of sociological theorizing as well as the sounding boards for most of the controversy and discourse in the field of deviance. This shift in focus was deemed necessary to redress the previous imbalance of attention to the deviant behavior itself (Akers, 1968), and it clearly has had that effect. Unfortunately, it also has led to the neglect of theoretical developments in the etiology of deviant behavior. Neither labelling nor conflict perspectives has offered a general explanation of deviant behavior, although some conflict theorists have offered preliminary but incomplete efforts in that direction (Taylor, et al., 1973; Spitzer, 1975). There have been other efforts directed toward explaining deviant behavior, but these have been fairly narrow in scope; they have usually been limited either to a specific type of deviant behavior or to a restricted range of substantive variables. For example,

From *American Sociological Review*, Volume 44 (August 1979), pp. 636-655. Copyright © 1979 by the American Sociological Association. Reprinted by permission.

a good deal of attention has been paid to the modern resurrection of deterrence theory (Gibbs, 1975; 1977; Waldo and Chiricos, 1972; Tittle, 1975; Silberman, 1976; Erickson et al., 1977; Meier and Johnson, 1977; Geerken and Gove, 1977). The scope of deterrence theory has been changed little, however, since its statement by the classical criminologists two centuries ago and is limited to the actual or perceived certainty, severity, and celerity of formally administered legal sanctions for violations of the criminal law. Another example is Travis Hirschi's (1969) control (social bonding) theory which is a more general explanation of deviance than deterrence theory, but which is, in turn, primarily restricted to informal social control which comes from individuals being bonded to groups and institutions.

The most notable exception to the diminished attention to general explanation of deviant behavior is a form of social learning theory developed first by Robert L. Burgess and Ronald L. Akers as differential association-reinforcement theory (Burgess and Akers, 1966; Akers et al., 1968) and elaborated on later by Akers (1973; 1977). As the name which Burgess and Akers originally chose to apply to this theoretical perspective makes clear, it was constructed as a revision of Edwin H. Sutherland's differential association theory (Sutherland, 1947; Sutherland and Cressey, 1974) in terms of general behavioral reinforcement theory (Skinner, 1953; 1959; Bandura and Walters, 1963; Bandura, 1969; 1977; Staats, 1975). Social learning theory as a general perspective in deviance is part of a larger move toward incorporation of modern behaviorism into sociological theory (Homans, 1961; Burgess and Bushell, 1969; Kunkel, 1975; Hamblin et al., 1971; Emerson, 1969; 1972; Kunkel and Nagasawa, 1973; Burgess and Nielsen, 1974; Chadwick-Jones, 1976; for reviews of the relevance of behavioral theory for sociology see Friedrichs, 1974; Tarter, 1973). As such it is a theoretical perspective which is compatible with the more specific forays into the explanation of deviant behavior. Indeed, the major features of such theories as deterrence and control theories (Hirschi, 1969) can be subsumed under the principles of social learning theory (Akers, 1977; Conger, 1976; 1977; Feldman, 1977). However, all too often the relevance for social learning theory of some of the deviance research has been ignored or unrecognized even when the authors employ central learning concepts such as reinforcement (Harris, 1975; 1977; Eaton, 1974; Meier and Johnson, 1977; Hirschi and Hindelang, 1977). This inattention is regrettable for, while other theories delineate the structural variables (class, race, anomic conditions, breakdown in social control, etc.) that yield differential rates of deviance, social learning stresses the behavioral mechanisms by which these variables produce the behavior comprising the rates. As such, social learning is complementary to other sociological theories and could be used to integrate extant formulations to achieve more comprehensive explanations of deviance (in this regard see Akers, 1977:63-8).

The basic learning principles on which this theory is based have received empirical support under laboratory and applied experimental conditions (see Skinner, 1953; Honig, 1966; Ullmann and Krasner, 1969; Bandura, 1969; 1977; McLaughlin, 1971; Staats, 1975). Also, prior research has been supportive of differential association theory (J. Ball, 1957; Short, 1957; Voss, 1964; R. Ball, 1968; Krohn, 1974; Jensen, 1972; Burkett and Jensen, 1975). However, there has been little direct research on learning principles as applied to deviant behavior in natural settings. Akers (1977) has organized a large body of existing research and theory on a wide range of deviant behavior supportive of or consistent with social learning, but his effort is a post hoc application of theoretical principles for he does not present research designed explicitly to test propositions from the theory (in this regard see also Feldman, 1977). The results of other studies are consistent with Akers's social learning approach (Jessor and Jessor, 1975; Thomas et al., 1975), and a couple of studies explicitly testing social learning using secondary data analysis have found support for it (Anderson, 1973; Conger, 1976). However, more crucial and conclusive tests await collecting the relevant primary data in the community. The present study does that. Our purpose here is to report a specific test of social learning theory using standard sociological techniques of data collection and data analysis.

Statement of Social Learning Theory

The social learning theory tested here is summarized from Akers (1977:39-68). The primary learning mechanism in social behavior is operant (instrumental) conditioning in which behavior is shaped by the stimuli which follow, or are consequences of the behavior. Social behavior is acquired both through direct conditioning and through *imitation* or modelling of others' behavior. Behavior is strengthened through reward (positive reinforcement) and avoidance of punishment (negative reinforcement) or weakened by aversive stimuli (positive punishment) and loss of reward (negative punishment). Whether deviant or conforming behavior is acquired and persists depends on past and present rewards or punishments for the behavior and the rewards and punishments attached to alternative behavior—*differential reinforcement*. In addition, people learn in interaction with significant groups in their lives evaluative *definitions* (norms, attitudes, orientations) of the behavior as good or bad. These definitions are themselves verbal and cognitive behavior which can be directly reinforced and also act as cue (discriminative) stimuli for other behavior. The more individuals define the behavior as good (positive definition) or at least justified (neutralizing definition) rather than as undesirable (negative definition), the more likely they are to engage in it.

The reinforcers can be nonsocial (as in the direct physiological effects of drugs) as well as social, but the theory posits that the principal behavioral effects come from interaction in or under the influence of those *groups which control individuals' major sources of reinforcement and punishment and expose them to behavioral models and normative definitions*. The most important of these groups with which one is in *differ-*

ential association are the *peer-friendship* groups and the *family* but they also include schools, churches, and other groups. Behavior (whether deviant or conforming) results from greater reinforcement, on balance, over punishing contingencies for the same behavior and the reinforcing-punishing contingencies on alternative behavior. The definitions are conducive to deviant behavior when, on balance, the positive and neutralizing definitions of the behavior offset negative definitions of it. Therefore, deviant behavior can be expected to the extent that it has been differentially reinforced over alternative behavior (conforming or other deviant behavior) and is defined as desirable or justified. Progression into more frequent or sustained use and into abuse is also determined by the extent to which a given pattern is sustained by the combination of the reinforcing effects of the substance with social reinforcement, exposure to models, definitions through association with using peers, and by the degree to which it is not deterred through bad effects of the substance and/or the negative sanctions from peers, parents, and the law.

The social learning theory proposes a process which orders and specifies the interrelationships among these variables. Differential association, which refers to interaction and identity with different groups, occurs first. These groups provide the social environments in which exposure to definitions, imitation of models, and social reinforcement for use of or abstinence from any particular substance take place. The definitions are learned through imitation, and social reinforcement of them by members of the groups with whom one is associated, and once learned, these definitions serve as discriminative stimuli for use or abstinence. The definitions in interaction with imitation of using or abstinent models and the anticipated balance of reinforcement produces the initial use or continued abstinence. After the initial use, imitation becomes less important while the effects of definitions should continue (themselves affected by the experience of use). It is at this point in the process that the actual consequences (social and nonsocial reinforcers and punishers) of the specific behavior come into play to determine the probability that use will be continued and at what level. These consequences include the actual effects of the substance at first and subsequent use (the perception of which may, of course, be modified by what effects the person has previously learned to expect) and the actual reactions of others present at the time or who find out about it later, as well as the anticipated reactions of others not present or knowing about the use.

From this depiction of them as aspects of the same learning process, we expect the independent variables to be positively interrelated, and we examine the zero-order relationships among them. Nonetheless, the major variables are conceptually distinct and our measures are empirically distinct enough that we do not expect their interrelationships to preclude separate independent effects. Thus, we also empirically order the independent variables in terms of how much variance is explained in the dependent variables. We test the general hypothesis from the theory that adolescent marijuana and alcohol use and abuse are related to each of the major sets of variables and to all of them combined.

Specifically, we expect that for both alcohol and drugs, the probability of abstinence decreases and the frequency of use increases when there is greater exposure to using rather than to abstinent models, when there is more association with using than with abstinent peers and adults, when use is differentially reinforced (more rewards, fewer punishers) over abstinence, and when there are more positive or neutralizing than negative definitions of use. Similarly, among users the probability of abuse increases with more exposure to abusing rather than moderate or abstinent models, more association with high frequency users or abusers, greater differential reinforcement for abuse over more moderate use, and with more positive and neutralizing rather than negative definitions of use....

Methodology

Sample and Procedure

Data were collected by administering a self-report questionnaire to 3,065 male and female adolescents attending grades 7 through 12 in seven communities in three midwestern states. A two-stage sample design was followed. First, we selected schools from within each participating school district which were representative in terms of school size and location within the district. In smaller districts this meant selecting all or most of the junior and senior high schools in the district. Secondly, we sampled two to three classrooms (depending on school and average class size) per grade level from among the required or general enrollment classes. Thus, although classrooms were sampled, each student has an approximately equal chance of being included in the sample. The questionnaire (which was pretested in a district not included in the final sample) was administered to all students in attendance in the selected classes on the day of the survey who had obtained written parental permission. The attrition from this parental permission procedure combined with absenteeism on the day of the survey was not great and 67% of the total number of students enrolled (95% of those with parental permission) in the sampled classes completed the questionnaire. . . .

Measurement of Variables

Dependent variables. Abstinence-use of alcohol and marijuana is measured by a six-point frequency-of-use scale ranging from nearly every day to never. A quantity frequency (Q-F) scale was also computed but since there is a near perfect correlation between the Q-F scale and the frequency-of-use scale, the analysis here includes only the latter measures. Abuse among users is measured by combining responses to the frequency questions with responses to a question asking the respondents to check whether or not they had experienced on more than one occasion any of a list of problems while or soon after using alcohol or marijuana. This combination produced a four-point abuse scale ranging from heavy abuse to no abuse.

Independent variables. From the summary of social learning theory presented above it can be seen that the main concepts to be measured are *imitation, differential association, definitions,* and *differential reinforcement.* For the present analysis, we distinguish between differential reinforcement comprised of social reinforcement combined with non-social reinforcement (experienced or anticipated drug or alcohol effects) and that comprised only of social reinforcement. Each of the resulting five concepts are operationalized by a set of items measuring different aspects of each concept. . . .

Findings

. . . The results of the regression analyses show strong support for the social learning theory of adolescent alcohol and drug behavior. When all the independent variables are incorporated into the full regression equation, the model explains 55% of the variance in drinking behavior (abstinence-frequency of use . . . and 68% of the variance in marijuana behavior (abstinence-frequency of use). . . .

. . . [T]he analyses also plainly show that some subsets of variables specified by the theory are more important than others. They are ranked in terms of relative effectiveness in explaining variance in alcohol and marijuana use as follows: (1) differential association, (2) definitions, (3) combined social/nonsocial differential reinforcement, (4) differential social reinforcement, and (5) imitation. Not only does the differential association subset explain the highest proportion of variance, but the differential peer association variable is the most important single variable. The definitions subset accounts for the second highest proportion of variance, and one's positive/negative definitions of the substances is the second most predicitve single variable, while one's law-abiding/violating definitions rank third among the single variables. The differential reinforcement variables are next, followed by imitation variables which explain the least amount of variance in the dependent variables.

The fact of peer group influence on substance use comes as no surprise; it is documented by several previous studies. But, previous studies have not shown what the mechanisms are by which peer influence is exerted, and why, therefore, peer group association is so important. Our data show, as predicted by social learning theory, what these mechanisms are—friends provide social reinforcement or punishment for abstinence or use, provide normative definitions of use and abstinence. and, to a lesser extent, serve as admired models to imitate. This is indicated by the fact that these other variables, on their own, explain a substantial amount of the variance in marijuana and alcohol behavior when the effect of the differential peer association variable is removed....

It is evident that social learning theory has been shown to be a powerful explanation of whether youngsters abstain from or are users of alcohol and marijuana. As predicted by the theory, the adolescents in our sample use drugs or alcohol to the extent that the behavior has been differentially reinforced through association in primary groups and defined as more desirable than, or at least as justified as, refraining from use....

The variable of parental reaction appears to be related to abuse in the direction opposite to that found in the analysis of use. For the latter a lower probability of use is found for those reporting the strongest or harshest parental punishment while for the former a lower probability of abuse is found for those reporting lesser punishment or no parental response.... [H]igher frequency of use and abuse is found with parental response (actual or anticipated) at both the most lenient (encourage or do nothing) and the harshest end of the scale (take some drastic action such as kick the youngsters out of the house or turn them over to the police). The highest probability of abstinence and the lowest levels of use and abuse are found among adolescents who report that their parents have responded or would respond to their use with a moderate negative reaction such as a scolding. Our post hoc interpretation of these relationships is that anticipated parental punishment is a deterrent to use and sustains abstinence. Even after use has begun a reasonable amount of parental punishment holds down the chances of increasing frequency of use or moving into abuse. However, once adolescents have gotten into heavy use or abuse, parental reaction has lost its effect and the increasing abuse of the substances by their children may produce ever harsher reactions by parents in increasingly desperate attempts to do something about it....

Summary and Conclusions

... All of the dependent variables are strongly related to the social learning variables of differential association, definitions, differential reinforcement, and imitation. The most powerful of these independent variables is differential association. The other variables stand on their own, however, and explain substantial portions of variance even without the differential association measures....

The strength of empirical support for the theory suggests that the theory will have utility in explaining the use and abuse of other substances by adolescents. These findings also indicate that social learning theory will do well when tested with other forms of deviant behavior in future research....

References

Abelson, H. I., R. Cohen, D. Shrayer, and M. Rappeport. 1973. "Drug experience, attitudes and related behavior among adolescents and adults." Pp. 488-867 in *Drug use in America: Problem in Perspective*, Vol. 1. Report prepared by the National Commission on Marijuana and Drug Abuse.

Akers, Ronald L. 1968. "Problems in the sociology of deviance: social definitions and behavior." *Social Forces* 46:455-65.

———. 1973. *Deviant Behavior: A Social Learning Approach*. Belmont: Wadsworth.

———. 1977. *Deviant Behavior: A Social Learning Approach*. 2nd ed. Belmont: Wadsworth.

Akers, Ronald L., Robert L. Burgess and Weldon Johnson. 1968. "Opiate use, addiction, and relapse." *Social Problems* 15:459-69.

Anderson, Linda S. 1973. "The impact of formal and informal sanctions on marijuana use: a test of social learning and deterrence." Master's thesis: Florida State University.

Ball, John C. 1957. "Delinquent and non-delinquent attitudes toward the prevalence of

stealing." *Journal of Criminal Law, Criminology and Police Science* 48:259-57.
Ball, Richard A. 1968. "An empirical exploration of neutralization theory." Pp. 255-65 in Mark Lefton, James K. Sipper and Charles H. McCaghy (eds.), *Approach to Deviance*. New York: Appleton-Century-Crofts.
Bandura, Albert. 1969. *Principles of Behavior Modification*. New York: Holt, Rinehart and Winston.
———. 1977. *Social Learning Theory*. Englewood Cliffs: Prentice-Hall.
Bandura, Albert and Richard H. Walters. 1963. *Social Learning and Personality Development*. New York: Holt, Rinehart and Winston.
Block, J. R., N. Goodman, F. Ambellan and J. Revenson. 1974. "A self-administered high school study of drugs." Hempstead: Institute for Research and Evaluation.
Burgess, Robert L. and Ronald L. Akers. 1966. "A differential association-reinforcement theory of criminal behavior." *Social Problems* 14:128-47.
Burgess, Robert L. and Don Bushell (eds.). 1969. *Behavioral Sociology* New York: Columbia University Press.
Burgess, Robert L. and Joyce McCarl Nielsen. 1974. "An experimental analysis of some structural determinants of equitable and inequitable exchange relations." *American Sociological Review* 39:427-43.
Burkett, Steven and Eric L. Jensen. 1975. "Conventional ties, peer influence, and the fear of apprehension: a study of adolescent marijuana use." *Sociological Quarterly* 16:522-33.
Calhoun, J. F. 1974. "Attitudes toward the sale and use of drugs: a cross-sectional analysis of those who use drugs." *Journal of Youth and Adolescence* 3:31-47.
Chadwick-Jones, J. K. 1976. *Social Exchange Theory: Its Structure and Influence in Social Psychology*. New York: Academic Press.
Conger, Rand D. 1976. "Social control and social learning models of delinquent behavior—a synthesis." *Criminology* 14:17-40.
———. 1977. Rejoinder. *Criminology* 15:117-26.
Drug Abuse Council, Inc. 1975. *A Report of the Drug Abuse Council* (by Yankelovich, Skelly, and White, Inc.) Washington, D. C.: Drug Abuse Council.
Eaton, William W. 1974. "Mental hospitalization as a reinforcement process." *American Sociological Review* 39:252-60.
Emerson, Richard M. 1969. "Operant psychology and exchange theory." Pp. 379-405 in Robert L. Burgess and Don Bushell, Jr. (eds.), *Behavioral Sociology*. New York: Columbia University Press.
———. 1972. "Exchange theory." Pp. 38-87 in Joseph Berger, Morris Zelditch, Jr. and Bo Anderson (eds.), *Sociological Theories in Progress*, Vol. 2. Boston: Houghton-Mifflin.

Erickson, Maynard L., Jack P. Gibbs and Gary F. Jensen. 1977. "The deterrence doctrine and the perceived certainty of legal punishment." *American Sociological Review* 42:305-17.
Fejer, Dianne and Reginald G. Smart. 1973. "The knowledge about drugs, attitudes toward them and drug use rates of high school students." *Journal of Drug Education* 3:377-88.
Feldman, M. P. 1977. *Criminal Behavior: A Psychological Analysis*. London: Wiley.
Friedrichs, Robert W. 1974. "The potential impact of B. F. Skinner upon American sociology." *The American Sociologist* 9:3-8.
Geerken, Michael and Walter R. Gove. 1977. "Deterrence, overload, and incapacitation: an empirical evaluation." *Social Forces* 56:424-47.
Gibbs, Jack P. 1975. *Crime, Punishment and Deterrence*. New York: Elsevier.
———. 1977. "Social control, deterrence, and perspectives on social order." *Social Forces* 56:408-23.
Groves, W. Eugene. 1974. "Patterns of college student use and lifestyles." Pp. 241-75 in Eric Josephson and Eleanor E. Carrol (eds.), *Drug Use: Epidemiological and Sociological Approaches*. New York: Wiley.
Hamblin, Robert L. David Buckholdt, Daniel Ferritor, Martin Kozloff and Lois Blackwell. 1971. *The Humanization Process: A Social Behavioral Analysis of Children's Problems*. New York: Wiley.
Hardt, Robert H. and Sandra Peterson-Hardt. 1977. "On determining the quality of the delinquency self-report method." *Journal of Research in Crime and Delinquency* 14:247-61.
Harris, Anthony R. 1975. "Imprisonment and the expected value of criminal choice: a specification and test of aspects of the labeling perspective." *American Sociological Review* 40:71-87.
———. 1977. "Sex and theories of deviance: toward a functional theory of deviant typescripts." *American Sociological Review* 42:3-16.
Hirschi, Travis. 1969. *Causes of Delinquency*. Berkeley and Los Angeles: University of California Press.
Hirschi, Travis and Michael J. Hindelang. 1977. "Intelligence and delinquency; a revisionist review." *American Sociological Review* 42:571-87.
Homans, George C. 1961. *Social Behavior: Its Elementary Forms*. New York: Harcourt Brace Jovanovich.
Honig, Werner. 1966. *Operant Behavior: Areas of Research and Application*. New York: Appleton-Century-Crofts.
Jensen, Gary F. 1972. "Parents, peers and delinquent action: a test of the differential association perspective." *American Journal of Sociology* 78:63-72.

Jessor, Richard. 1976. "Predicting time of onset of marijuana use: a developmental study of high school youth." *Journal of Consulting and Clinical Psychology* 44:125-34.

Jessor, R., M. I. Collins and S. L. Jessor. 1972. "On becoming a drinker: social-psychological aspects of an adolescent transition." *Annals of the New York Academy of Science* 197:199-213.

Jessor, R., T. D. Graves, R. C. Hanson and S. L. Jessor. 1968. *Society, Personality and Deviant Behavior: A Study of a Tri-Ethnic Community*. New York: Holt, Rinehart and Winston.

Jessor, R. and S. L. Jessor. 1975. "Adolescent development and the onset of drinking: a longitudinal study." *Journal of Studies on Alcohol* 36:27-51.

——. 1977. *Problem Behavior and Psychosocial Development: A Longitudinal Study of Youth*. New York: Academic Press.

Jessor, Richard, Shirley L. Jessor and John Finney. 1973. "A social psychology of marijuana use: longitudinal studies of high school and college youth." *Journal of Personality and Social Psychology* 26:1-15.

Jessor, R., H. B. Young, E. B. Young and G. Tesi. 1970. "Perceived opportunity, alienation, and drinking behavior among Italian and American youth." *Journal of Personality and Social Psychology* 15:215-22.

Johnston, L. 1973. *Drugs and American Youth*. Ann Arbor: institute for Social Research.

Kandel, Denise. 1973. "Adolescent marijuana use: role of parents and peers." *Science* 181:1067-70.

——. 1974. "Interpersonal influences on adolescent illegal drug use." Pp. 207-40 in Eric Josephson and Eleanor E. Carrol (eds.), *Drug Use: Epidemiological and Sociological Approaches*. New York: Wiley.

——. 1978. *Longitudinal Research on Drug Use*. Ed. by D. Kandel. New York: Halsted.

Kendall, Richard Fenwick. 1976. *The Context and Implications of Drinking and Drug Use among High School and College Students*. Ph.D. dissertation, Department of Psychology, New York University.

Kim, Jae-On. 1975. "Multivariate analysis of ordinal variables." *American Journal of Sociology* 81:261-98.

Krohn, Marvin D. 1974. "An investigation of the effect of parental and peer associations on marijuana use: an empirical test of differential association theory." Pp. 75-89 in Marc Reidel and Terrence P. Thornberry (eds.), *Crime and Delinquency: Dimensions of Deviance*. New York: Praeger.

Kunkel, John H. and Richard H. Nagasawa. 1973. "A behavioral model of man: propositions and implications." *American Sociological Review* 38:530-43.

Kunkel, John R. 1975. *Behavior, Social Problems, and Change: A Social Learning Approach*. Englewood Cliffs: Prentice-Hall.

Labovitz, Sanford. 1970. "The assignment of numbers to rank order categories." *American Sociological Review* 35:515-24.

——. 1971. "In defense of assigning numbers to ranks." *American Sociological Review* 36:521-22.

Lawrence, T. S. and J. O. Velleman. 1974. "Correlates of student drug use in a suburban high school." *Psychiatry* 37:129-36.

McLaughlin, Barry. 1971. *Learning and Social Behavior*. New York: Free Press.

Meier, Robert F. and Weldon T. Johnson. 1977. "Deterrence as social control: the legal and extralegal production of conformity." *American Sociological Review* 42:292-304.

National Commission on Marijuana and Drug Abuse. 1972. *Marijuana: A Signal of Misunderstanding*. New York: New American Library.

O'Donnell, John, Harwin L. Voss, Richard R. Clayton, and Robin G. W. Room. 1976. *Young Men and Drugs—A Nationwide Survey*. Rockville: National Institute on Drug Abuse.

Pearce, J. and D. H. Garrett. 1970. "A comparison of the drinking behavior of delinquent youth versus non-delinquent youth in the states of Idaho and Utah." *Journal of School Health* 40:131-5.

Rachal, J. V., J. R. Williams, M. L. Brehm, B. Cavanaugh, R. P. Moore, and W. C. Eckerman. 1975. *Adolescent Drinking Behavior, Attitudes and Correlates*. National Institute on Alcohol Abuse and Alcoholism: U. S. Department of Health, Education and Welfare, Contract No. HSM 42-73-80 (NIA).

Radosevich, Marcia, Lonn Lanza-Kaduce, Ronald L. Akers and Marvin D. Krohn. Forthcoming. "The sociology of adolescent drug and drinking behavior: a review of the state of the field: part 1, 2." *Deviant Behavior: An Interdisciplinary Journal*.

Rotter, Julian. 1954. *Social Learning and Clinical Psychology*. Englewood Cliffs: Prentice-Hall.

Short, James F. 1957. "Differential association and delinquency." *Social Problems* 4:233-9.

Silberman, Matthew. 1976. "Toward a theory of criminal deterrence." *American Sociological Review* 41:442-61.

Single, Eric, Denise Kandel and Bruce D. Johnson. 1975. "The reliability and validity of drug use responses in a large scale longitudinal survey." *Journal of Drug Issues* 5:426-43.

Skinner, B. F. 1953. *Science and Human Behavior*. New York: Macmillan.

——. 1959. *Cumulative Record*. New York: Appleton-Century-Crofts.

Spritzer, Steven. 1975. "Toward a Marxian theory of deviance." *Social Problems* 22:638-51.

Staats, Arthur. 1975. *Social Behaviorism*. Homewood: Dorsey Press.

Sutherland, Edwin H. 1947. *Principles of Criminology* 4th ed. Philadelphia: Lippincott.

Sutherland, Edwin H. and Donald R. Cressey. 1974. *Criminology*. 9th ed. Philadelphia: Lippincott.

Tarter, Donald E. 1973. "Heeding Skinner's call: toward the development of a social technology." *The American Sociologist* 8:153-8.

Taylor, Ian, Paul Walton and Jack Young. 1973. *The New Criminology: For a Social Theory of Deviance*. New York: Harper and Row.

Tec, Nechama. 1974a. *Grass is Green in Suburbia: A Sociological Study of Adolescent Usage of Illicit Drugs*. Roslyn Heights: Libra.

———. 1974b. "Parent-child drug abuse: generational continuity of adolescent deviancy?" *Adolescence* 9:351-64.

Thomas, Charles W., David M. Petersen and Matthew T. Zingraff. 1975. "Student drug use: a re-examination of the hang-loose ethic hypothesis." *Journal of Health and Social Behavior* 16:63-73/

Tittle, Charles R. 1975. "Deterrents or labeling?" *Social Forces* 53:399-410.

Ullmann, Leonard P. and Leonard Krasner. 1969. *A Psychological Approach to Abnormal Behavior* Englewood Cliffs: Prentice-Hall.

Voss, Harwin. 1964. "Differential association and reported delinquent behavior: a replication." *Social Problems* 12:78-85.

Waldo, Gordon P. and Theodore Chiricos. 1972. "Perceived penal sanction and self-reported criminality: a neglected approach to deterrence research." *Social Problems* 19:522-40.

Wechsler, Henry and Denise Thum. 1973. "Teenage drinking, drug use, and social correlates." *Quarterly Journal of Studies on Alcohol* 34:1220-7.

Whitehead, P. C. and R. G. Smart. 1972. "Validity and reliability of self-reported drug use." *Canadian Journal of Criminology and Corrections* 14:1-8. ✦

16
Age, Peers, and Delinquency

E. Mark Warr

A decade ago, Hirschi and Gottfredson's (1983) seminal paper entitled "Age and the Explanation of Crime" launched an era of research on the age-crime relation. The authors advanced strong and controversial ideas, most notably the assertion that the age distribution of crime is historically, culturally, and demographically invariant. That claim has not gone unchallenged (see especially Blumstein et al., 1988; Greenberg, 1985; Steffensmeier et al., 1989), but the authors have continued to maintain their position (Gottfredson and Hirschi, 1988, 1990).

Another equally strong assertion was Hirschi and Gottfredson's (1983:554) claim that "the age distribution of crime cannot be accounted for by any variable or combination of variables currently available to criminology. In their more recent reiteration of this position, Gottfredson and Hirschi (1990:124) point their finger more directly at sociological explanations: "With the failure of sociological theories to explain the variables they were initially designed to explain, their utility as explanations of the large correlates of crime—age, gender, and race—[is] no longer plausible."

The difficulties that arise in explaining the association between age and crime are indeed daunting. Chief among them is the fact that any explanation must account for seemingly contrary phenomena, that is, the rapid onset *and rapid desistance* from crime that, for most offenses, is centered in the middle to late teens. "Just at the point where the criminal group has been created, it begins to decline in size" (Gottfredson and Hirschi, 1990:131). In addition, the age gradient of crime is so steep that it requires from any explanation rather profound age-related changes in the explanatory variables.

Notwithstanding these difficulties, Gottfredson and Hirschi appear too willing to dismiss sociological explanations of the age-crime relation, and their arguments are at times less than convincing. For example, they reject Sutherland and Cressey's claim that differential association can account for the age distribution of crime, arguing that the claim is contradicted by research. The sole piece of research they cite, however, is an early study by Rowe and Tittle (1977). That investigation employed only four crude age categories (15-24, 25-44, 45-64, 65+), whereas most of the significant variation in criminal behavior occurs *within* the first category. In addition, peer influence was measured by asking respondents to recollect their associations with delinquents while they were growing up. Apart from questions of recall (older respondents had to reach back decades in time), the study seems to assume that association with delinquent peers during adolescence must produce a lifelong effect on behavior under the theory of differential association. But there is nothing in the theory that requires that assumption.

If Gottfredson and Hirschi are too quick to dismiss sociological explanations of the age-crime relation, it is nonetheless true that sociologists have done an inadequate job of providing affirmative evidence for their arguments. This paper examines a quintessentially sociological theory of delinquency—Sutherland's theory of differential association—and evaluates its ability to explain the age distribution of crime. The analysis is fitting, because Sutherland's theory was among the first major sociological theories of crime, and it helped to anchor criminology within the discipline of sociology (Matsueda, 1988).

Differential Association

Sutherland's theory of differential association locates the source of crime and delinquency in the intimate social networks of individuals. Emphasizing that criminal behavior is learned behavior, Sutherland argued that persons who are selectively or differentially exposed to delinquent associates are likely to acquire that trait as well. The primary mechanism by which this occurs is attitude transference, meaning that individuals acquire attitudes or "definitions" consistent with delinquency from significant others. In Sutherland's (1947:6) words, "A person becomes delinquent because of an excess of definitions favorable to violation of law over definitions unfavorable to violation of law." Although Sutherland did not limit his theory to peer influence, tests of the theory have conventionally examined the correlation between self-reported delinquency and the number of delinquent friends reported by adolescents. That association has proven to be among the strongest in delinquency research, and it is one of the most consistently reported findings in the delinquency literature (e.g., Akers et al., 1979; Elliott et al., 1985; Erickson and Empey, 1965: Hepburn, 1977; Jensen, 1972; Johnson, 1979; Matsueda and Heimer, 1987; Reiss and Rhodes, 1964; Short, 1957; Tittle et al., 1986; Voss, 1964; Warr and Stafford, 1991). Tests of the theory also consistently indicate, however, that attitude transference is not the sole or even primary mechanism of transmission (see Warr and Stafford, 1991), lending support to the behaviorist or social learning reformulation of the theory developed by Burgess and Akers (1966; see also Akers, 1985).

In his short statement of his theory, Sutherland stipulated certain features of social relations that he believed to be most relevant to differential association, that is, the frequency, duration, priority, and intensity of associations. Most tests of Sutherland's theory have ignored these variables, and part of the reason may be that Sutherland did not clearly define all of these dimensions and offered no help as to how they were to be measured or operationalized. I return later to these elements of differential association, but for now let us consider several aspects of peer relations that are consistent with Sutherland's general intentions as well as our immediate interest in age. These include (1) differential *exposure* to delinquent peers, meaning the number of delinquent peers reported by respondents at different ages, (2) *time* spent in the company of peers, (3) the *importance of friends* to respondents, and (4) respondents' *commitment or loyalty* to their own particular set of friends. After first describing the age distributions of these variables, the discussion turns to their capacity to explain the age distribution of crime. Some additional questions concerning age-related aspects of differential association are then entertained.

Data and Methods

The data for this study come from the National Youth Survey (NYS). The NYS is a longitudinal study of a national probability sample of 1,726 persons aged 11-17 in 1976 (see Elliott et al., 1985). The sample was obtained through a multistage, cluster sampling of households in the continental United States in 1976. Five consecutive annual waves of the survey were conducted from 1976 through 1980, and these five are used in this analysis.

The NYS is especially well suited for this analysis because it contains a unique set of carefully constructed questions about delinquent peers. Unlike most conventional questions about peers, the NYS questions refer to specific, concrete persons rather than some ill-defined set of friends. That is, respondents were asked to name individually the friends they "ran around with," and they were specifically instructed to think of those persons in subsequent questions. . . .

Findings

Age and Exposure to Delinquent Peers

The first portion of the analysis examines age-related changes in respondents' relation with and attitudes toward their peers. If peer influences account in any way for the age distribution of crime, then we must expect to observe substantial and rapid changes in peer variables across age groups.

Figure 1
Percentage of Respondents with No Delinquent Friends, by Age and Offense

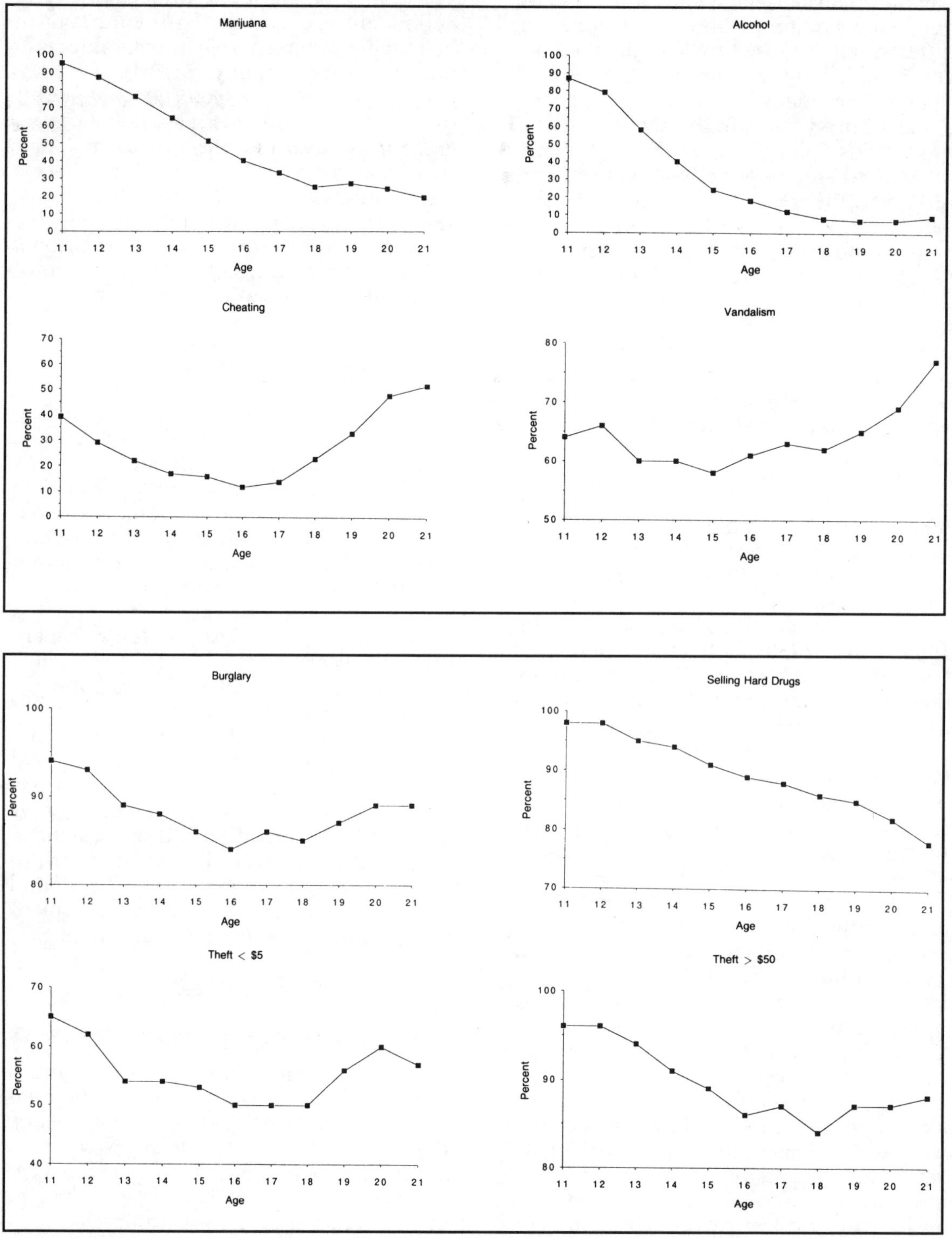

Consider, first, exposure to delinquent peers, that is, the number of delinquents within the respondent's immediate circle of friends. In the NYS, respondents were asked this question: "Think of the people you listed as close friends. During the last year how many of them have [act]?" (1 = none of them, 2 = very few of them, 3 = some of them, 4 = most of them, 5 = all of them). Following the question was a series of acts, including vandalism ("purposely damaged or destroyed property that did not belong to them"), cheating ("cheated on school tests"), marijuana use ("used marijuana or hashish"), petty theft ("stolen something worth less than $5"), alcohol use ("used alcohol"), burglary ("broken into a vehicle or building to steal something"), selling hard drugs ("sold hard drugs such as heroin, cocaine, and LSD"), and grand theft ("stolen something worth more than $50").

Figure 1 displays the relation between age and exposure to delinquent peers by showing the percentage of respondents by age and offense who report that none of their friends have committed the act during the prior year. The first plot pertains to marijuana use, and it paints a startling picture. At age 11, fully 95% of respondents report that none of their friends have smoked marijuana. Five years later, at age 16, that number has dropped to 40%, and at age 18 it hovers at only 25%. The decline from one age group to the next thus averaged about 10% per year.

The next plot shows even more dramatic figures for alcohol use. At age 11, approximately 9 out of 10 respondents (87%) report that none of their friends have used alcohol during the past year. Five years later, at age 16, the figure is merely 18%, falling yet further to 8% at age 18. The decline across age groups in the percentage of unexposed adolescents is so great as to be exponential.

The plots for alcohol and marijuana use are distinctive not only for the magnitude of change they exhibit, but also for their general shape. For both offenses (and for selling hard drugs as well), there is no significant decrease in the number of delinquent peers as respondents approach age 21, meaning that the peak age of peer involvement lies somewhere above that age. This pattern is consistent with self-report studies of the age distribution of alcohol and drug use (Akers, 1992; Bachman et al., 1984; Kandel and Yamaguchi, 1987). Of the remaining plots, however, all show a different pattern, with peer involvement peaking in the middle-to-late teens and declining thereafter. These plots, too, are consistent with self-report data on the age distribution of most nondrug delinquent offenses (Farrington, 1986; Steffensmeier et al., 1989).

The plots in Figure 1 also show that the absolute level of exposure to delinquent peers is heavily contingent on the seriousness of the act. Whereas a majority of respondents reported that at least some of their friends used alcohol, cheated, committed vandalism or other comparatively petty acts, no more than 20% report that any of their friends have committed burglary or serious thefts or sold hard drugs, even at the peak ages of peer involvement.

The evidence displayed in Figure 1, then, points to an initial conclusion. During their early life, individuals frequently undergo rapid and enormous changes in exposure to delinquent peers, from a period of relative innocence in the immediate preteen years to a period of heavy exposure in the middle-to-late teens. This intense exposure to delinquent peers begins to decline, however, for many, but not all offenses as individuals leave their teens and enter young adulthood.

Figure 2
Percentage of Respondents Reporting That They Averaged Three or More Nights Per Week Going "On Dates, To Parties, or to Other Social Activities," by Age

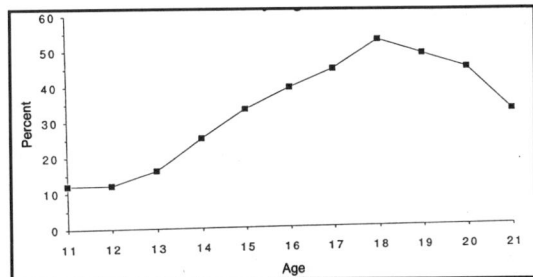

Other Elements of Peer Relations

Now consider the other elements of peer relations introduced earlier, beginning with the amount of time spent with peers. In each wave of the NYS, respondents were asked "How many evenings in an average week, including weekends, have you gone on dates, to parties, or to other social activities?" Figure 2 shows the percentage of respondents, by age, who reported that they averaged three or more days per week in such activities. The plot reveals a rapid increase with age in the amount of time spent with peers, from a low of 12% among 11-year-olds to a peak of 52% among 18-year-olds. After that age, time spent with peers drops rapidly, reaching 32% by age 21. Other questions in the NYS pertaining to time spent with peers show much the same pattern for weekends and evenings, but it is noteworthy that the number of afternoons spent with peers after school is roughly constant across the age groups, perhaps because of the daily journey from school.

Another element of peer relations is the importance that respondents place on activities with peers. In the NYS, respondents were asked "How important has it been to you to have dates and go to parties and other social activities?" (1 = not important at all, 2 = not too important, 3 = somewhat important, 4 = pretty important, 5 = very important). Figure 3 shows the percentage of respondents, by age, who reported that these activities were pretty important or

Figure 3
Percentage of Respondents Who Said That It Is "Very Important" or "Pretty Important" to "Have Dates and Go to Parties and Other Social Activities," by Age

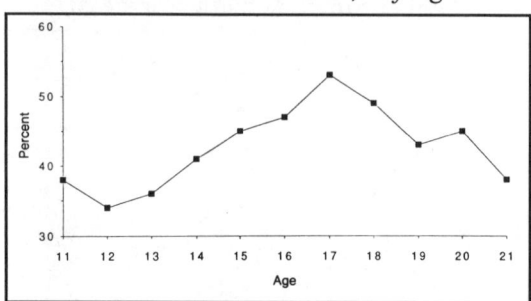

very important. The range in this percentage (19%) is not as great as in the preceding plot, but the shape of the plot is quite similar. The importance of peer relations peaks at age 17, and shows a rather steep descent thereafter. Without making too much of the point, it seems that friends begin to lose their central importance to many adolescents before they actually begin to disassociate themselves from them.

The importance that individuals place on peer activities can be analytically distinguished from the commitment or loyalty they feel toward their own particular friends. The NYS asked respondents several questions about their loyalty to their own

Figure 4
Percentage of Respondents Who Said That They Would Lie to Protect Their Friends if They Got into Trouble with the Police, by Age

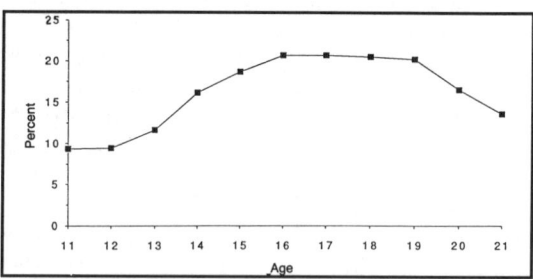

friends, specifically, how the respondent would react if their friends were "leading them into trouble." The most well-behaved item, and the most relevant for present purposes, questioned respondents about how they would react to illegal behavior on the part of their friends: "If your friends got into trouble with the police, would you be willing to lie to protect them?" (1 = no; 2 = yes). Figure 4 shows that respondents aged 16-19 are about twice as likely as their younger or older counterparts to respond yes to this question, meaning that their loyalty to friends extends even to covering illegal behavior.

The evidence considered thus far points to several conclusions. The relevance of peers in the lives of young persons reaches its zenith in the middle-to-late teens. Age-related changes in the importance of peers, the amount of time spent in their company, and loyalty to peers are substantial enough that they can reasonably be expected to exert strong, even profound, effects on the behavior of adolescents. And like the age distribution of crime itself, the role of peers is transitory, rising and falling quickly during a relatively brief period of life. . . .

Discussion and Conclusion

The results of this analysis have implications for both Sutherland's theory of differential association and Hirschi and Gottfredson's position on the age distribution of crime. Taking the former first, the results provide mixed support for Sutherland's arguments about priority and duration. Although the duration of delinquent friendships operates as Sutherland suggested, the priority of delinquent friendships acts in precisely the opposite fashion: recent rather than early friends have the greatest effect on delinquency. This finding may surprise some, but it is surely more consistent with modern social learning theory, with its emphasis on reinforcement, extinction, and modeling or imitation (e.g., Akers, 1985). As Vold and Bernard (1986:225) have observed, "Sutherland . . . was not a learning theorist and was not particularly familiar with the major theory and research on human learning that was going on at the time." Sutherland himself offered the concept of priority only tentatively, observing that the importance of priority "has not been adequately demonstrated" (1947:7).

Aside from priority and duration, the findings concerning "sticky friends" should be of general interest to criminologists. Labeling theorists will surely urge one interpretation of the phenomenon: Adolescents who acquire delinquent friends thereby lock themselves out of future friendships with "straight" kids through the stigma of delinquency. Subcultural theorists, too, will perceive evidence for their perspective in these data. The sticky-friends phenomenon, however, may reflect nothing more than the normal process of homophily (see below), heightened perhaps by the special camaraderie that comes from sharing illicit adventures. It is premature at this point to attach any definite interpretation to the phenomenon, especially when the domain to which it applies (i.e., offenses and persons) is not well established. But the matter clearly deserves further scrutiny.

Now recall the major issue of this paper. Hirschi and Gottfredson contend that the age distribution of crime cannot be explained by any variables known to criminology. The analysis presented herein shows that when measures of peer influence are held constant, the association between age and crime is substantially weakened and, for some offenses, disappears entirely. Instead of an impenetrable conundrum, the age-crime relation appears to be at least partially explicable by variables from Sutherland's theory of differential association.

This conclusion is likely to be challenged on several grounds, and some of those objections deserve mention. The analysis covers a relatively small number of offenses, and none of the offenses is a violent offense. In addition, the explanatory variables largely fail to explain age variation in one of those offenses—cheating on school tests. There are several possible explanations for this anomaly, however, and they raise some interesting theoretical questions. Although the analysis concentrated exclusively on peer influence, the relevant reference group when it comes to academic performance may well be *parents* rather than peers. That is, it seems much more likely that students cheat in order to win the approval of their parents rather than their peers. Another potential explanation comes from strain theory. Students with high aspirations and expectations for college would be expected under the theory to be the least delinquent and the least susceptible to delinquent peers. But those same students also have the greatest motivation to cheat in school in order to realize their goals. Hence, delinquent peers may have less relevance for cheaters than for other types of offenders. Still another possibility is that cheaters, like Cressey's (1953) embezzlers, have an unshareable problem—poor academic aptitude or performance—that they do not readily confide to their friends. Whatever the explanation, the point is that differential association cannot explain the age distribution of all offenses.

Another possible objection is a conventional criticism of differential association theory (or tests thereof), that is, the issue of causal order. Rather than reflecting the influence of peers, it is argued, the association between delinquent peers and self-reported delinquency may simply express the tendency of delinquents to select persons like themselves as friends. Gottfredson and Hirschi (1990:156) employ this argument in rejecting differential association:

> How much easier it would be to assume that the "delinquent peer group" is a creation of faulty measurement and the tendency of people to seek the company of others like themselves.

A growing body of longitudinal studies of differential association (for reviews, see Agnew, 1991; Elliott et al., 1985; Empey and Stafford, 1991), however, generally corroborates the causal order stipulated by differential association theory, but points to a more complex sequential, reciprocal process: Adolescents are commonly introduced to delinquency by their friends and subsequently become more selective in their choices of friends. The "feathering" and "flocking" interpretations, as Elliott et al. (1985) have noted, are therefore not mutually exclusive and may instead be part of a unified process. This position is consistent with the sticky-friends phenomenon reported earlier, although it is not the only explanation for it. Still, even if the causal order assumed in this analysis is incorrect, it nonetheless remains true that the introduction of peer variables largely obviates the effects of age in the models examined. If differential selection of peers accounts for the age distribution of crime, so be it.

Still another possible objection centers on the measurement of delinquent peers. In another line of argument, Gottfredson and Hirschi (1990:157) contend that measures of peer delinquency are in fact nothing more than "another measure of self-reported delinquency." That is, when asked to report their peers' delinquent behavior, adolescents report their own behavior:

> One might reasonably ask the basis of the respondent's answers to questions about the delinquency of his friends. Several possibilities come to mind: (1) the respondent may have been at the scene, himself engaging in the activity; (2) the respondent may impute his own qualities to his friends; (3) the respondent may impute friendship to people like himself; (4) the respondent's friends may have told him about delinquencies he did not himself witness; or (5) the respondent may have heard about his friend's delinquencies from people who witnessed or heard about them. If "delinquency of peers" is really "delinquency of respondent" (see points 1, 2, and 3), the causal-order question is hardly resolved by this research. If "delinquency of peers" is really hearsay or rumor (points 4 and 5), the value of the measure is obviously suspect (and is again contaminated by the characteristics of the respondent).

A careful examination casts doubt on the validity of these arguments, especially as they pertain to the NYS. First, it may well be true that respondents are frequently witnesses to or participants in the delinquent acts of their friends. But how does this undermine the accuracy of respondents' reports? If the contention is true, it would seem to substantiate rather than undermine the validity of peer measures. Then, too, it is difficult to understand why respondents in the NYS would feel a need to impute their own behavior to their peers, especially when respondents are asked about their own behavior at a point in the interview *well after* they have been questioned about their peers. Moreover, it seems unlikely that respondents would give frivolous or cavalier responses to the peer questions; recall that the NYS asks questions about specific persons that the respondent has already identified by name. And it is difficult to argue that adolescents do not know about the behavior of their closest friends; whose behavior would they know better? Finally, it is not clear why respondents' reports about their peers should be any less reliable than their reports about their teachers or parents, information that is routinely utilized by control theorists.

A final possible criticism of the findings is that they reflect nothing more than a spurious association. That is, peer delinquency explains the age distribution of delinquency because respondent's delinquency and friends' delinquency share a common association with age. That conclusion, however, is contradicted by the analysis. Recall that when age and peer behavior are introduced into the same equation, it is age—not peer behavior—that is rendered insignificant. Consequently, it is difficult to avoid the conclusion that it is *age* that is spuriously associated with delinquency.

If differential association does at least partially explain the age distribution of crime, it still does not resolve all questions. For example, if adolescents learn delinquent attitudes or behaviors from their friends, where do those attitudes or behaviors ultimately originate? Greenberg (1979:122) argues that participation in adolescent society requires resources to purchase "clothes, cosmetics, alcoholic beverages, narcotics, phonograph records, transistor radios, gasoline," and other requisites of membership:

> When parents are unable or unwilling to subsidize their children's social life at the level required by local convention, when children want to prevent their parents from learning of their expenditures, or when they are reluctant to incur the obligations created by taking money from their parents, alternative sources of funds must be sought. (1979:123)

Others (cf., Campbell, 1969; Hagan, 1991) characterize adolescent society (or segments thereof) as a "party" culture in which adolescents flirt with illegal behavior in their collective search for fun. However, the very "groupiness" of adolescent behavior may be intrinsically criminogenic if one assumes that individuals are more susceptible to situational inducements to break the law when they are in groups than when they are alone (Turner and Killian, 1987).

At the very least, this analysis suggests that it is premature to reject differential association as an explanation for the age distribution of crime. Rejecting a correct theory is no less serious than affirming a false one, and the evidence against differential association is simply insufficient at this time to justify rejection. The social character of crime, after all, is as persistent a feature as the age distribution of crime, and the two phenomena may be more closely related than criminologists have previously realized.

References

Agnew, Robert. 1991. Strain and subcultural crime theories. In Joseph Sheley (ed.), *Criminology: A Contemporary Handbook*. Belmont, Calif.: Wadsworth.

Akers, Ronald. 1985. *Deviant Behavior: A Social Learning Approach*. Belmont, Calif.: Wadsworth.

———. 1992. *Drugs, Alcohol, and Society*. Belmont, Calif.: Wadsworth.

Akers, Ronald, Marvin Krohn, Lonn Lanza-Kaduce, and Marcia Radosevich. 1979. Social learning and deviant behavior: A specific test of a general theory. *American Sociological Review* 44:636-645.

Bachman, Jerald, Patrick O'Malley, and Lloyd Johnston. 1984. Drug use among young adults: The impacts of role status and social environment. *Journal of Personality and Social Psychology* 47:629-645.

Blumstein, Alfred, Jacqueline Cohen, and David Farrington. 1988. Criminal career research: Its value for criminology. *Criminology* 26:1-35.

Burgess, Robert and Ronald Akers. 1966. A differential association-reinforcement theory of criminal behavior. *Social Problems* 14:128-147.

Campbell, Ernest. 1969. Adolescent socialization. In D. Goslin (ed.), *Handbook of Socialization Theory and Research*. Chicago: Rand McNally.

Cressey, Donald. 1953. *Other People's Money*. New York: Free Press.

Elliott, Delbert, David Huizinga, and Suzanne Ageton. 1985. *Explaining Delinquency and Drug Use*. Beverly Hills, Calif.: Sage.

Empey, LaMar and Mark Stafford. 1991. *American Delinquency: Its Meaning and Construction*. Belmont, Calif.: Wadsworth.

Erickson, Maynard and LaMar Empey. 1965. Class position, peers, and delinquency. *Sociology and Social Research* 49:268-282.

Farrington, David. 1986. Age and Crime. In Michael Tonry and Norval Morris (eds.), *Crime and Justice: An Annual Review of Research*. Chicago: University of Chicago Press.

Gottfredson, Michael and Travis Hirschi. 1988. *Science, public policy, and the career paradigm.* Criminology 26:37-55.

———. 1990. *A General Theory of Crime.* Stanford, Calif.: Stanford University Press.

Greenberg, David. 1985. *Age, crime, and social explanation.* American Journal of Sociology 91:1-21.

———. 1979. Delinquency and the age structure of society. In David Greenberg (ed.), *Crime and Capitalism: Readings in Marxist Criminology.* Palo Alto, Calif.: Mayfield.

Hagan, John. Destiny and drift: *Subcultural preferences, status attainments, and the risks and rewards of youth.* American Sociological Review 56:567-582.

Hepburn, John. 1977. *Testing alternative models of delinquency causation.* Journal of Criminal Law and Criminology 67:450-460.

Hirschi, Travis and Michael Gottfredson. 1983. *Age and the explanation of crime.* American Journal of Sociology 89:553-584.

Jensen, Gary. 1972. *Parents, peers, and delinquent action: A test of the differential association perspective.* American Journal of Sociology 78:562-575.

Johnson, Richard. 1979. *Juvenile Delinquency and Its Origins.* New York: Cambridge University Press.

Kandel, Denise and Kazuo Yamaguchi. 1987. *Job mobility and drug use: An event history analysis.* American Journal of Sociology 92:836-878.

Matsueda, Ross. 1988. *The current state of differential association theory.* Crime and Delinquency 34:277-306.

Matsueda, Ross and Karen Heimer. 1987. *Race, family structure, and delinquency: A test of differential association and social control theories.* American Sociological Review 52:826-840.

Reiss, Albert J., Jr., and Albert Rhodes. 1964. *An empirical test of differential association theory.* Journal of Research in Crime and Delinquency 1:5-18.

Rowe, Alan R. and Charles R. Tittle. 1977. *Life cycle changes and criminal propensity.* Sociological Quarterly 18:223-236.

Short, James. 1957. *Differential association and delinquency.* Social Problems 4:233-239.

Steffensmeier, Darrell, Emilie Allan, Miles Harer, and Cathy Streifel. 1989. *Age and the distribution of crime.* American Journal of Sociology 94:803-831.

Sutherland, Edwin. 1947. *Criminology.* 4th ed. Philadelphia: Lippincott.

Tittle, Charles R., Mary Jean Burke, and Elton Jackson. 1986. *Modeling Sutherland's theory of differential association: Toward an empirical clarification.* Social Forces 65:405-432.

Turner, Ralph and Lewis Killian. 1987. *Collective Behavior.* Englewood Cliffs, N.J.: Prentice-Hall.

Vold, George and Thomas Bernard. 1986. *Theoretical Criminology.* New York: Oxford University Press.

Voss, Harwin. 1984. *Differential association and reported delinquency behavior: A replication.* Social Problems 12:78-85.

Warr, Mark and Mark Stafford. 1991. *The influence of delinquent peers: What they think or what they do?* Criminology 29:851-866. ✦

Section V
Social and Cultural Causation

Among all of the academic disciplines, sociology has played the most central role in the development of theories of crime and delinquency. Sociological theories focus on the characteristics of times, social settings, and people that affect involvement in criminal and delinquent conduct. The major characteristics emphasized have varied among theories and over time with "strain-deprivation" theorists according priority to economic forces and frustrations, "cultural deviance" theorists according priority to subcultural beliefs and styles of interpersonal interaction, and "disorganization-control" theorists according priority to the breakdown or ineffectiveness of conventional social institutions such as the family. While advocates of distinct perspectives differ on what aspect is most important, the theories are all sociological in the sense that opportunities, human relationships, and cultural lifestyles are viewed as the likely sources of variation in either law-breaking or law-abiding conduct. One of the first systematic statements of a sociological theory of crime and delinquency was elaborated by Willem Bonger in *Criminality and Economic Conditions* (1916). Bonger argued that economic organization is fundamental to the explanation of crime and criminality. Patterns of crime over time and social space could be explained in terms of the distribution of poverty, inequality, and fluctuations in the economy. Individual criminality could be attributed to the money-driven "egoism" engendered in Western capitalist society. He argued that self-centered egoism facilitated juvenile criminality, but inhibiting forces such as adult supervision could overcome such pressures.

In the United States, delinquency became a major focus for the application of general sociological ideas among sociology faculty, students, and graduates of the University of Chicago—located in Cook County, Illinois, birthplace of the first juvenile court. Scholars in that department—W. I. Thomas, Florian Znaniecki, Robert Park, and E. W. Burgess—encouraged the development of general sociological notions that were applied to delinquency. From a sociological perspective, criminal and delinquent behavior were affected by the nature of relationships in neighborhoods and groups. The processes involved in learning such behavior were similar to those leading to law-abiding behavior. These basic tenets of a sociological approach were verified in research by Chicago students Frederick Thrasher and Clifford Shaw. Observing hundreds of youth, Thrasher (1927) established the peer group nature of delinquency as the common activity of individuals interacting with one another. Using data on the distribution of delinquency in areas of Chicago, Clifford Shaw published *Delinquency Areas* (1929), emphasizing the social conditions of those areas as the source of variation in delinquency rates. The shared problems of people living under socially disorganized conditions and not their racial or ethnic traits explained high delinquency rates. Their attempts to explain ecological variations emphasized the breakdown or absence of familial and communal ties and the development of alternative criminogenic traditions.

Based on his training at the University of Chicago, Edwin Sutherland expanded and systematized a sociological explanation of crime and criminality in editions of his *Principles of Criminology*, first published in 1924. By the 1939 version, he had developed a clear set of propositions. He proposed an explanation that emphasized (1) conflicting definitions of appropriate and inappropriate conduct as key to the distribution of crime among social settings and (2) differential association with conflicting definitions as a key to the explanation of individual criminality. Definitions were the symbolic messages communicated in everyday interaction with significant others such as parents, peers, and teachers. Sutherland's systematic elaboration of a theory of both crime and criminality in a set of nine fundamental propositions earned him honors as the most influential theoretical criminologist of the twentieth century. Applied to delinquency, the central proposition of differential association was simply that "a person becomes delinquent because of an excess of definitions favorable to violation of law over definitions unfavorable to violation of law." Sutherland's perspective was defended and applied to a variety of types of crime by his student, Donald Cressey.

By the 1940s, the notion that certain areas of cities were criminogenic because they were "disorganized" had been replaced by the notion that such areas were "differentially" organized. Areas with high crime rates had different traditions or competing and conflicting subcultural traditions. With his work titled *Culture, Conflict and Crime* (1938), the University of Pennsylvania criminologist Thorsten Sellin played a major role in reinforcing the shift away from social disorganization and toward conflicting subcultural norms in the explanation of crime. Solomon Kobrin, who did some of his graduate work at Chicago and worked at Shaw and McKay's Institute for Juvenile Research, added to this shift by stressing the duality of conduct norms in the urban child's neighborhood. Similar ideas about the subcultural origins of gang delinquency were elaborated in later years by Walter Miller, a cultural anthropologist. In the 1960s, Marvin Wolfgang and Franco Ferracuti proposed an explanation of regional, racial, and demographic variations in violence in terms of subcultural norms and traditions as well.

A distinct theoretical tradition emphasizing a specific type of social-cultural disorganization as a source of criminality was elaborated by the Columbia sociologist, Robert K. Merton, in 1938. Merton expanded on the notion of anomie, which had been introduced by the French social theorist Emile Durkheim in the explanation of suicide. Durkheim had argued that economic crises and fluctuations could drive people to suicide as rules regulating behavior become unstable and ambitions get out of step with reality. Applying a similar logic, Merton argued that high rates of deviance are generated in anomic social systems where there is a strong cultural emphasis on economic success coupled with inequality in opportunity to realize such success legitimately. The pursuit of success by illegal, "innovative" means was one adaptation to strain. Illegal innovation in pursuit of commonly shared success goals is viewed as a common lower-class response to frustrated ambitions, but there are other ways to adapt as well. Some people might adapt to strain by giving up pursuit of success goals and retreating into drug use, suicide, or mental illness. Still others might rebel and attempt to change the system.

The logic of Merton's theory, with its emphasis on widely shared goals coupled with unequal opportunity, is the basis for designating it as a "strain" theory. Other theorists have followed the same logic, introducing other forms of discrepancy between goals and means as a source of frustrated ambitions. In 1955, Albert Cohen took issue with Merton's rather instrumental view of lower-class crime and delinquency and introduced emotion and anger into strain theory. He sought to explain male gang delinquency and what he believed to be the hostile, negativistic content of a gang counterculture. The source of anger and hostility was status frustration. Such frustration was generated by the widely shared desire for the good opinion of teachers coupled with limited possession of the social and cultural attributes necessary to achieve such respect. Just as Merton's innovators could overcome limited opportunity through criminal and delinquent activity, Cohen's youth could solve status problems collectively by reversing conventional standards of evaluation. Cohen argued that a delinquent counterculture was a collective solution to lower-class status frustration.

Another elaboration of strain theory logic was proposed by Richard Cloward and Lloyd Ohlin in *Delinquency and Opportunity* (1960). They proposed that the outcome of strain varied depending on the nature of illegitimate opportunities available to youth. If adult criminal enterprises were available, the outcome would be a criminal subculture of delinquent youth. In settings where organized illegitimate opportunities were not available, delinquent gangs would exhibit the characteristics of a violence-prone, conflict subculture. Youth who were unable to join or succeed in conflict or criminal subcultures were double failures and candidates for retreatist subcultures. Their theory was a theoretical integration of elements of Merton's strain theory and Sutherland's theory emphasizing illegal associations and opportunities.

The most popular causal theories of juvenile delinquency and adult criminality in the 1970s and 1980s were Travis Hirschi's social control theory (1969) and Ronald Akers' social learning theory (1977). In contrast to earlier American theories, neither social control theory nor social learning theory focused specifically on variations among classes or demographic categories. Both proposed more immediate variables that affect criminality, regardless of their distribution in the social system. Hirschi's social control theory shared many of the characteristics of earlier social disorganization theories and similar theories proposed by Scott Briar and Irving Piliavin, F. Ivan Nye, Walter Reckless, Albert Reiss, Gresham Sykes and David Matza, and Jackson Toby. When applied to delinquency, the theory posited that the odds of delinquent behavior were low when youth were emotionally bonded to others (attachment), committed to conventional goals (commitment), accepted laws as morally binding (belief), and were occupied in conventional activities (involvement). While most of these variables had been proposed in earlier theories, Hirschi's elaboration drew considerable attention because he identified crucial differences between this perspective and both strain and cultural deviance theory.

An article on social learning theory was included in Section IV because it bridges sociology and psychology in the explanation of delinquency. It focuses on learning mechanisms through which social and cultural variations in crime and delinquency are produced and sustained and has roots in earlier sociological traditions. As a theory of criminality, social learning theory emerged from a combination of principles derived from behaviorist operant learning theory (most closely identified with the psychologist B. F. Skinner) and other psychological theories stressing vicarious learning and imitation (Albert Bandura and Richard Walters). Robert Burgess and Ronald Akers reformulated differential association theory in terms of operant learning theory in 1966, and Akers elaborated a more general social learning theory in later works. According to social learning theory, the balance of criminal or delinquent conduct versus conforming behavior is a function of (a) differential reinforcement of those behaviors, (b) differential learning of norms or rules that govern behavior at other times, and (c) the observed behavior and its consequences for primary sources of reinforcement such as parents and friends. In contrast to the exclusive emphasis of social control theory on barriers, social learning theory added learned motivational forces. Moreover, although it was originally proposed as a reformulation of Sutherland's theory, the inclusion of nondefinitional and nonsocial learning processes distinguishes it from that perspective.

The most recent lines of theoretical development in the explanation of criminality have been (1) a revival of the tenets of the social disorganization theory, (2) attempts at theoretical integration, and (3) modified versions of control and strain theory. Tenets of the social disorganization approach have been revitalized by Rodney Stark and others (1980) in the form of a social integration theory. While social disorganization was defined in terms of the breakdown or absence of ties or bonds among people, social integration refers to the presence of such bonds. A positive term has been substituted for a negative one, but the underlying concept is the same.

Theoretical integration has taken two forms. One form is the attempt to combine elements of strain, cultural deviance, and control theory into an integrated theory. Delbert Elliott, David Huizinga, and Suzanne Ageton (1985) have proposed an integrated theory of delinquency in which high levels of status frustration (a strain theory variable), and weak conventional bonds (a control theory variable) lead youth to seek out and imitate delinquent peers (a differential association-social learning variable) with delinquent peers as the major intervening mechanism leading to delinquency. This form of integration focuses on proximate causal mechanisms in each theory and ignores conflicting assumptions at the macro-level concerning such issues as delinquent subcultures, countercultures, and the structural origins of motivational forces.

Another form of integration combines biological, psychological, and sociological variables. James Q. Wilson and Richard J. Herrnstein (1985) propose an integrated theory emphasizing criminality as a choice that is affected by variables at the bio-psychological level such as conditionability and psychopathology as well as proximate mechanisms stressed by control, strain, and cultural deviance theorists. While proposed as a theory, there is no clear specification of the range of variables to be included. All the theory demands is the inclusion of some variables from each category.

Modified versions of control and strain theory have been proposed recently as well. John Hagan, A. R. Gillis, and John Simpson (1985) combine the neo-Marxist emphasis on power relationships as the most crucial dimension of stratification with some elements of social control theory to predict a positive relation between class and delinquency. Michael Gottfredson and Travis Hirschi (1989) have proposed a modified version of control theory emphasizing "self-control" as the key mechanism for understanding criminality and other forms of reckless, fraudulent, or dangerous behavior. Opportunity to commit offenses is included as a variable as well, a notion borrowed from another recent theory called "routine activities theory." Lawrence Cohen and Marcus Felson (1979) propose to explain crime and victimization rates in terms of the availability and vulnerability of people and property, variables that affect the opportunity for crime. While not proposed as a theory of individual criminality, the opportunity to commit crimes can affect the degree to which other causal factors actually result in criminal or delinquent behavior. Finally, Robert Agnew (1992) proposes a version of strain theory called a "general strain" theory, arguing that criminality is affected by (a) actual or anticipated failure to achieve virtually any positive goal, (b) actual or anticipated removal of positively valued stimuli, and (c) actual or anticipated presentation of negatively valued stimuli. It is a "revised" strain theory in the sense that a much broader range of possible discrepancies between needs or desires and the world that juveniles confront is introduced as possible motivational forces behind delinquent behavior.

It is not possible in a book of readings covering the full range of issues involved in the study of delinquency and juvenile justice to include examples of all of the sociological theories and research relevant to those theories. The four included in this section should offer examples of the emphases characterizing relatively recent extensions or applications of major traditions. The summary of theoretical perspectives presented above should provide a sense of the sociological heritage of contemporary theory and research as well as accord credit to key scholars in the development of those traditions.

The first selection to follow represents a contemporary exploration of the characteristics of communities or areas that help to explain variation in criminal victimization. E. Britt Patterson examines the type of economic characteristics that are thought to affect crime but also examines the effect of communal bonds or social integration. Variables affecting communal bonds are found to be particularly crucial and may explain why other characteristics of communities appear to be related to crime as well.

The second reading is Robert Agnew's presentation of a "general strain theory" of crime and delinquency. He proposes three possible sources of strain that provide the motivational force leading to delinquency. One of the most theoretically unique forms of strain proposed is "adverse relations" with others. Agnew argues that his general strain theory "is the only major theory to focus explicitly on negative relations with others and to argue that delinquency results from the negative affect caused by such relations" (1992: 76).

The third article compares some of the predictions derived from Travis Hirschi's social control perspective with social learning theory. Control theory emphasizes attachment to parents as a barrier to delinquency and, in its most extreme version, posits that attachment to parents inhibits delinquency regardless of the behavior of parents. In contrast, social learning theory posits that attachment inhibits delinquency primarily when parents are "straight" themselves. The results suggest that attachment to parents inhibits juvenile drug use most effectively when parents are straight.

The fourth reading proposes a "cultural explanation" of violence. Social disorganization-social control theories focus on the failure of communities and conventional institutions to control and socialize children. Strain theory focuses on status deprivations, frustration, and anger as motivations generated out of situations where society has failed to live up to its promises. In contrast to both of these, cultural explanations focus on values, norms, and beliefs that make criminal and delinquent conduct acceptable, if not required, forms of behavior in certain situations. David Luckenbill and Daniel Doyle hypothesize that "young adults, males, blacks and lower income persons, and urban and southern residents are more likely than their respective counterparts to be disputatious and aggressive when a negative outcome bears on a personal attribute, stems from a harmdoer who shares the victim's status, and occurs in public than when it does not" (1989: 428). A violent response is "normative" in certain settings and groups when honor is at stake.

References

Agnew, R. "Foundation for a General Strain Theory of Crime and Delinquency." *Criminology* 10 (1992):47–87.

Akers, R. L. *Deviant Behavior*. Belmont, CA: Wadsworth, 1977.

Bonger, W. *Criminality and Economic Conditions*. Boston: Little Brown, 1916.

Burgess, R. L., and R. L. Akers. "A Differential Association Reinforcement Theory of Criminal Behavior." *Social Problems* 14 (1966):128–47.

Cloward, R. A., and L. E. Ohlin. *Delinquency and Opportunity*. New York: Free Press, 1960.

Cohen, A. K. *Delinquent Boys*. New York: Free Press, 1955.

Cohen, L., and M. Felson. "Social Changes and Crime Rate Trends: A Routine Activity Approach." *American Sociological Review* 46 (1979):505–24.

Elliott, D. S., D. Huizinga, and S. S. Ageton. *Explaining Delinquency and Drug Use*. Beverly Hills, CA: Sage, 1985.

Hagan, J., A. R. Gillis, and J. Simpson. "The Class Structure of Gender and Delinquency: Toward a Power-Control Theory of Common Delinquent Behavior." *American Journal of Sociology* 90 (1985):1151–1178.

Hirschi, T. *Causes of Delinquency*. Berkeley: University of California Press, 1969.

Merton, R. K. "Social Structure and Anomie." *American Sociological Review* 3 (1938):672–82.

Miller, W. "Lower Class Culture as a Generating Milieu of Gang Delinquency." *Journal of Social Issues* 14 (1958): 5–19.

Sellin, T. *Culture, Conflict and Crime*. New York: Research Council, 1938.

Shaw, Clifford. *Delinquency Areas*. Chicago: University of Chicago Press, 1929.

Stark, R., W. S. Bainbridge, R. D. Crutchfield, D. P. Doyle, and R. Finke. "Crime and Delinquency in the Roaring Twenties." *Journal of Research in Crime and Delinquency* 20 (1983): 4–23

Sutherland, E. H. *Principles of Criminology*. Philadelphia: J.B. Lippincott, 1939.

Thrasher, F. M. *The Gang*. Chicago: University of Chicago, 1927.

Wilson, J. Q., and R. J. Herrnstein. *Crime and Human Nature*. New York: Simon and Schuster, 1985.

Wolfgang, M., and F. Ferracuti. *The Subculture of Violence*. London: Tavistock, 1967. ✦

17
Poverty, Income Inequality, and Community Crime Rates

E. Britt Patterson

What is the relationship between crime rates and the economic conditions of social areas? After more than a century and a half of empirical and theoretical investigations (beginning with Guerry, 1833, and Quetelet, 1835), this question remains controversial. Recent research on the social ecology of criminal activity has renewed attention to this question and contributed to the controversy (e.g., Blau and Blau, 1982; Messner, 1982; O'Brien, 1983; Sampson, 1985; Williams, 1984). This paper identifies some issues in the debate and empirically examines the association between crime rates and economic conditions in 57 small residential areas.

Crime Rates and Economic Conditions

Poverty and Crime

The relationship between economic environment and crime has been considered in conflict theories (Bonger, 1916; Taylor et al., 1973), subcultural theories (Cloward and Ohlin, 1960; Wolfgang and Ferracuti, 1967), strain theory (Merton, 1949), opportunity theories (Cantor and Land, 1985; Cohen et al., 1980), and social disorganization theory (Kornhauser, 1978; Shaw and McKay, 1942). Common to many of these perspectives is the position that variation in the spatial distribution of crime are associated with the degree of poverty characterizing an area. In summarizing this orientation, Vold and Bernard (1986:138) pointed out that it is "the lack of some fixed level of material goods necessary for survival and minimum well-being" that causes criminal activity (personal as well as property) to flourish in an area.

... [R]esearch reveals contradictory support for the poverty/crime thesis.[1] For example, some studies show that poorer areas have higher levels of certain types of violent offending, such as homicide (Bailey, 1984; Loftin and Parker, 1985; Messner, 1983; Smith and Parker, 1980) or assault (Crutchfield et al., 1982; Harries, 1976). Others claim that such relationships are spurious and that once other characteristics of social areas are taken into account, poverty has little if any relationship with homicide, forcible rape, or aggravated assault rates (Blau and Blau, 1982). Still other studies, such as Messner (1983), report that standard metropolitan statistical areas (SMSAs) with high poverty levels have lower homicide rates. Such contradictory evidence also emerges in studies using victimization-based measures of violent crime rates. For example, Sampson and Castellano (1982) and Sampson (1986) report that personal victimizations are significantly higher in poverty-stricken areas, but Decker (1980) found poverty to be negatively related to violent victimizations when robbery was excluded from a violent victimization index.

Fewer studies have examined the relationship between poverty and property crime rates, but the evidence shows a more consistent pattern. Both Mladenka and Hill (1976) and Crutchfield et al. (1982) report that official rates of burglary are positively associated with the percentage of the population living below the poverty level, and research using aggregated victimization data supports this relationship (Sampson, 1986). However, these studies as a rule have examined the relationship between areal crime rates and poverty while controlling for only a few other characteristics of social areas.

Economic Inequality and Crime

Complicating the picture of how economic conditions are related to areal crime

From *Criminology*, Volume 29, Number 4 (1991), pp. 775-776. Copyright © 1991 by the American Society of Criminology. Reprinted by permission.

rates is a debate regarding the most appropriate way to measure poverty. Some argue that poverty is a subjective concept: "Poverty is always in part a subjective condition, relative to what others have, rather than any simple objective fact of the presence or absence of a certain amount of property or other measure of wealth" (Vold and Bernard, 1986:138). Similarly, the Social Science Council (1968:227-228) concluded that "people are 'poor' because they are deprived of opportunities, comforts, and self-respect regarded *as normal in the community* to which they belong" (italics added). Consequently, some argue that "relative" poverty (or economic inequality), not absolute poverty, is a more relevant variable for explaining areal variation in criminal activity. From this perspective, the percentage of community members who are poor in absolute terms may not be the most significant correlate of criminal activity. Instead, rates of criminal activity should vary with the degree of inequality in the distribution of wealth or income.

Empirical studies of the income inequality/crime relationship have also produced mixed results. . . . [S]ome studies have found that both income inequality and poverty are significantly associated with homicide rates (Loftin and Hill, 1974). Others report that economic inequality but not poverty is significantly associated with areal variation in this form of violent criminal activity (Blau, 1977; Blau and Blau, 1982). Still other studies find no significant association between income inequality and homicide (Messner, 1982, 1983; Messner and Tardiff, 1986; Williams 1984).

When consideration is given to other forms of criminal activity, inconsistencies persist. For example, Danzinger (1976) reported that income inequality had a significant, positive relationship with rates of robbery in 222 SMSAs, but Rosenfeld (1986) reported a nonsignificant association between income inequality and robbery rates using a different sample of 125 SMSAs. The few studies that have simultaneously examined the effects of poverty and economic inequality on rates of property offending also yielded divergent findings.

Some studies found a positive effect of both poverty and income inequality on property offending rates (Danzinger, 1976), but others concluded that only economic inequality is significantly related to property offending rates (Jacobs, 1981).

Some research goes beyond the question of whether poverty or income inequality has independent effects on crime rates and focuses on contingencies in the relationship between inequality and crime. Blau and Blau (1982), for example, argue that where *ascribed inequality* is present *violent* behavior will be high. Specifically, they suggest (p. 119) that

> ascriptive socioeconomic inequalities undermines the social integration of a community by creating multiple parallel social differences which widen the separation between social classes, and it creates a situation characterized by much social disorganization and prevalent latent animosities.

Consistent with their hypothesis, Blau and Blau report that areas characterized by extreme racial economic inequality are also areas with high rates of violent crime. However, a subsequent study by Rosenfeld disagrees. According to Rosenfeld (1986:127), "the dollar gap between blacks and whites has no independent influence on crime rates." (See Golden and Messner, 1987, for a discussion of the sources of inconsistency in research examining the racial inequality-violent crime association.)

To summarize, the relationship between aggregate economic conditions and rates of criminal activity remains unclear. Diverse empirical findings have contributed to theoretical ambiguity. The central question persists: Are rates of differing types of criminal activity associated with levels of poverty, economic heterogeneity, or both? Moreover, what are the contingencies of association in the relationship between material well-being and aggregate crime rates? This paper examines these issues with data that include measures of several other theoretically relevant variables. . . .

Crime Rates and Other Attributes of Social Areas

Assessments of the relationship between a neighborhood's economic situation and its rates of criminal activity must also consider a number of other variables that may be associated with the spatial distribution of crime. Among those considered in this study are (1) residential mobility, (2) racial heterogeneity, (3) neighborhood integration, (4) household composition and family disorganization, and (5) population density. Theoretical rationales for how these variables are associated with crime rates vary. However, many of the variables are viewed as important because of their potential association with levels of community social control. For example, rapid population turnover may disrupt primary relationships as well as institutional development. In transient areas, community integration and social control may be weak (Shaw and McKay, 1942), and empirical studies generally show a positive relationship between levels of residential mobility and crime rates (Chilton, 1964; Crutchfield et al., 1982; Sampson, 1985).

The racial heterogeneity of an area may also impede the establishment of common values (Shaw and McKay, 1942). The close proximity of ethnically diverse groups can engender cultural conflict (Sellin, 1938). Each group may have unique institutions and roles, which may impede the development of shared meaning among members of heterogeneous areas. The lack of common interests and shared meaning may undermine the possibility of social integration and increase the potential for delinquency. Lander (1954) and Smith and Jarjoura (1988), for example, found that delinquency rates were highest in racially mixed areas.

Efforts to measure the degree of informal control of youths across communities have used aggregate measures of household composition and family disorganization. The argument for this approach is that areas characterized by high levels of family disorganization and nonfamily households are less able to maintain "scrutiny, supervision and surveillance designed to preclude, deter or detect deviance" (Kornhauser, 1978:24). Thus, communities characterized by high percentages of single-person households (Roncek, 1981) or female-headed households (Sampson, 1985) are more likely to experience high rates of criminal offending than other communities. The extant empirical evidence is consistent with this expectation (e.g., Cohen and Felson, 1979; Smith and Jarjoura, 1988).

Finally, two other community characteristics (urbanization and percentage of nonwhite population) have been examined in the literature on areal variation in rates of criminal activity. Scholars since Wirth (1938) have argued that more densely populated areas are places of greater criminal activity. Specifically, increasing population density makes social experiences impersonal and transitory. Thus, more urbanized areas are less integrated areas, and effective mechanisms of informal social control are less likely to develop. Extant empirical evidence consistently shows that crime rates are higher in more densely populated areas (Blau and Blau, 1982; Danzinger, 1976).

The final control variable considered in this analysis is the percentage of minority population in an area. In earlier studies, the rationale for expecting certain types of crimes to vary with an area's racial composition was the "subculture of violence" thesis and the argument that social values supportive of violence have arisen among blacks from historical circumstances (see, e.g., Curtis, 1974). The proposed positive association between the percentage of minorities and crime rates of communities has received mixed empirical support. Some studies (e.g., Bordua, 1958; Chilton, 1964; Sampson, 1985; Smith and Jarjoura, 1988) found no association between percentage nonwhite and crime rates, but others reported a positive association between these variables (e.g., Carroll and Jackson, 1983; Messner, 1982; Roncek, 1981). The percent nonwhite variable is included in this analysis because of its frequent use in prior studies.

Data and Measures

Data used in this study were originally collected in 1977 as part of a larger study of police behavior.[2] Interviews were conducted in 57 residential areas with members of 11,419 randomly selected households. The 57 areas are within three SMSAs (Rochester, New York; St. Louis, Missouri; and Tampa-St. Petersburg, Florida). Data from the interviews were aggregated within neighborhoods to create neighborhood measures. When a resident did report a victimization, he or she was asked to identify where the victimization occurred. Only those acts that occurred within the boundaries of the study neighborhood were used when calculating neighborhood victimization rates. (See Smith, 1986, and Smith and Jarjoura, 1988, for a more detailed discussion of these data.)

Two victimization-based crime rates are used in this study. Rates of burglary per 1,000 households and serious violent crimes (robberies, rapes, and aggravated assaults) per 1,000 residents were calculated from the victimization data. Across the neighborhoods in the study, burglary rates ranged from 32.7 to 235.1 per 1,000 households and serious violent crime rates ranged from 0 to 21.49 per 1,000 persons. No serious violent victimizations were reported in 15 of the 57 residential areas.

Several measures of neighborhood characteristics were constructed by aggregating information from the/'interviews with residents.... *Residential instability* is measured as the percentage of households that have been in the area for less than three years. *Racial heterogeneity* is the probability that two randomly selected individuals from a neighborhood would be members of different racial groups. *Neighborhood integration* was measured by asking residents how often they or members of their family got together socially with other residents in the area. Higher values on this variable indicate areas of greater social interaction among residents. *Population density* is the number of persons per square mile of land area. *Percent aged 12 to 20* is the percentage of the population in that age group. The variable *percent single parent* is the percentage of single-parent households with children in the age range of 12 to 20 years. *Percent nonwhite* and *percent living alone* are self-explanatory variables.

Two measures of the economic status of social areas are considered in this analysis. The first is the percentage of households with an annual household income of less than $5,000. There is substantial variation in this variable in these data. At the one extreme are neighborhoods that contained no households below this income level, and at the other end of the distribution, 58.4% of the households had annual incomes of less than $5,000. This variable is used to measure the absolute poverty level of neighborhoods. The second measure is the gini coefficient of income concentration. This measure is used because it was used in a number of prior studies that examined the association between income inequality and crime rates. . . .[3]

Findings

... The main concern here is whether an independent statistical association exists between measures of neighborhood economic status and crime rates.... These results show that once the relationship between burglary rates and other neighborhood characteristics is taken into account, measures of a community's economic condition are not significantly associated with rates of burglary. At the same time, both poverty and income inequality are associated with burglary rates in the expected direction. Additional analyses (not reported) that included only one of the economic measures at a time revealed the same results as when both poverty and income inequality were simultaneously added to the model. . . .

[When] attention turns to the relationship between neighborhood characteristics and rates of serious violent crime ... the results show that higher rates of violent crime are associated with residential instability, population density, age composition, and the percentage of nonwhite residents. When economic variables are added to the model ..., crime rates are significantly associated with the percentage of households in an area with annual incomes below $5,000. No evidence emerges of a meaningful association between violent crime rates and economic inequality.

The addition of poverty to the model also specifies the relationship between violent crime rates and other neighborhood attributes. The percentage of nonwhite population and the percentage of the population in the age range of 12 to 20 years, for example, are not significantly associated with rates of violent crime once the percentage of low-income households is added to the model. Conversely, controlling for the proportion of low-income households reveals that violent crime rates are significantly lower in areas that are more socially integrated. Finally, violent crime rates are higher in areas that are more densely populated or characterized by greater residential instability....

To summarize, the relationship between economic conditions of social areas and crime rates varies by type of crime and the measure of economic conditions. Measures of household income inequality have no significant direct or conditional association with burglary or violent crime rates in these data. However, the percentage of low-income households in an area is significantly associated with violent crime rates.

Discussion

This research examined the relative importance of poverty and income inequality in explaining criminal activity across social areas. The results indicate that levels of absolute poverty, measured by the percentage of households with annual incomes below $5,000, are significantly associated with high rates of serious violent crime. Little evidence emerged from this analysis, however, to support the thesis that relative poverty, or income inequality, significantly related to rates of violent criminal activity. These findings lend support to the thesis that severe conditions of material disadvantage (absolute poverty) raise levels of community violence by eroding a community's capacity for social control and self-regulation. Perhaps the sheer lack of adequate resources precludes the development of effective community-based mechanisms of social control. Where social control is weak, restraints on individual behavior are more tentative. But whatever process is at work, the data show that violence is more prevalent in social areas characterized by greater levels of absolute poverty and that this association is independent of several other attributes of the areas.

Neither the level of absolute poverty in an area nor the degree of inequality in the distribution of household income was significantly related to rates of household burglary. These results do not support claims that extreme differences in the distribution of income among individuals lead to rising rates of property crime (Jacobs, 1981), at least at this level of analysis.

Perhaps the strongest evidence to emerge from this analysis is that variation in community crime rates is most strongly associated with several noneconomic attributes of communities. Areas with transient populations were characterized by higher rates of violent crime and burglary. More socially integrated communities had significantly lower rates of both types of crime. Both of these neighborhood characteristics provide a window on a community's capacity to provide and maintain personal networks of common interests. The results of this analysis suggest that where these networks exist, criminal activity is less prevalent. Other findings from this analysis are also consistent with a social control perspective. Burglary rates were significantly higher in areas with larger youthful populations and higher levels of family disorganization. Rates of serious violent crime varied with population density and absolute poverty....

Collectively, findings from this analysis suggest that the meaning and theoretical utility of aggregate measures of social areas may depend on the level of aggregation. For small social areas, such as those considered in this paper, the concept of community social control makes sense, and several empirical relationships are consistent with a social control framework, including the relationship between absolute poverty and violent crime rates. What is less clear is whether the concept of relative poverty (income inequality) is theoretically meaningful for small units of aggregation. Specifically, one element that gives meaning to economic inequality is the notion of a reference group. It may well be that in a mass media society, reference groups that define standards of success or material advantage transcend neighborhood boundaries. It seems more likely that one compares his or her material position in life, not with that of neighbors but instead with generalized images of success in larger frames of reference, such as advertising media. From this viewpoint, the theoretical utility of income inequality seems more appropriate for larger units of aggregation, such as regions of a country or nations themselves. To the extent this is true, further controversy concerning whether absolute poverty or income inequality is more strongly related to rates of criminal activity may miss the point that the two measures may be applicable at different levels of aggregation. In this analysis, which used small units of aggregation, absolute poverty is clearly more relevant to explaining variation in some forms of criminal activity than the degree of inequality in the distribution of income.

Notes

1. The concept *absolute poverty* has been measured in many different ways. The following are several of the most common operationalizations: unemployment/occupational distribution (Bates, 1962; Boggs, 1965; Chilton, 1964; Crutchfield et al., 1982; Decker, 1980; Harries, 1976; Polk, 1957, 1967; Quinney, 1964; Schmid, 1960a, 1960b; Schuessler and Slatin, 1964; Watts and Watts, 1981; Wellford, 1974; Willie, 1967); median income/median family income (Beasley and Antunes, 1974; Bordua, 1958; Chilton, 1964; Decker, 1980; Harries, 1976; Mladenka and Hill, 1976; Schmid, 1960a, 1960b; Schuessler and Slatin, 1964); and education distribution (Bates, 1962; Bordua, 1958; Bursik, 1984; Chilton, 1964; Crutchfield et al., 1982; Harries, 1976; Lander, 1954; Messner, 1983; Mladenka and Hill, 1976; Polk, 1957; Quinney, 1964; Schmid, 1960a, 1960b; Willie, 1967).

2. Because these data were originally collected to study variation in police behavior, the neighborhood boundaries rely heavily on police department definitions of neighborhoods.

3. For reasons given in Atkinson (1970) and Newbery (1970), the gini coefficient is not considered a particularly good measure of income inequality. However, because several prior studies of income inequality and crime rates used this measure, it is used here to maintain comparability with prior research. Computation of gini coefficients follows the method outlined in Shryock and Siegel (1973:178-183). Seven income groupings were used, and Blau and Blau's (1982:121) procedure of incrementing the open-ended highest category by 50%, as described in their footnote 9, was followed.

References

Amemiya, T. 1985. *Advanced Econometrics*. Cambridge. Mass.: Harvard University Press.

Atkinson, A.B. 1970. On the measurement of inequality. *Journal of Economic Theory* 2:244-263.

Bailey, W.C. 1984. Poverty, inequality and city homicide rates: Some not so unexpected findings. *Criminology* 22:531-550.

Bates, W. 1962. Caste, class, and vandalism. *Social Problems* 9:349-358.

Beasley, R.W. and G. Antunes. 1974. The etiology of urban crime: An ecological analysis. *Criminology* 11:439-461.

Beattie, R.H. 1960. Criminal statistics in the United States-1960. *Journal of Criminal Law, Criminology and Police Science* 51:49-65.

Blau, J. and P.M. Blau. 1982. The cost of inequality: Metropolitan structure and violent crime. *American Sociological Review* 47:114-129.

Boggs, S.L. 1965. Urban crime patterns. *American Sociological Review* 30:899-908.

Bonger, W.A. 1916. *Criminality and Economic Conditions*. Boston: Little, Brown.

Bordua, D.J. 1958. Juvenile delinquency and "anomie": An attempt at replication. *Social Problems* 6:230-238.

Brantingham, P.J. and P.L. Brantingham. 1978. A theoretical model of crime site selection. In M.D. Krohn and R.L. Akers (eds.), *Crime, Law and Sanctions*. Newbury Park, Calif.: Sage.

Bursik, R.J. 1984. Urban dynamics and ecological studies of delinquency. *Social Forces* 63:392-413.

Burstein, L. 1975. The use of data from groups for inference about individuals in educational research. Ph.D. dissertation, Stanford University, Calif.

Cantor, D. and K.C. Land. 1985. Unemployment and crime rates in the post-World War II United States: A theoretical and empirical analysis. *American Sociological Review* 50:317-332.

Carroll, L. and P. Jackson. 1983. Inequality, opportunity, and crime rates in central cities. *Criminology* 21:178-194.

Chilton, R.J. 1964. Continuities in delinquency area research: A comparison of studies for Baltimore, Detroit, and Indianapolis. *American Sociological Review* 29:71-83.

Cloward, R.A. and L.E. Ohlin. 1960. *Delinquency and Opportunity: A Theory of Delinquency and Gangs*. New York: Free Press.

Cohen, L.E. and M. Felson. 1979. Social change and crime rate trends: A routine activity approach. *American Sociological Review* 44:588-608.

Cohen, L.E., M. Felson, and K.C. Land. 1980. Property crime rates in the United States: A macrodynamic analysis, 1947-1977; with ex ante forecasts for the mid-1980s. *American Journal of Sociology* 86:90-118.

Crutchfield, R., M. Geerken, and W. Gove. 1982. Crime rates and social integration: the impact of metropolitan mobility. *Criminology* 20:467-478.

Curtis, L.A. 1974. *Criminal Violence*. Lexington, Mass.: D.C. Heath.

Danzinger, S. 1976. Explaining urban crime rates. *Criminology* 14:291-295.

Decker, S.H. 1980. *Criminalization Victimization and Structural Correlates of Twenty Six American Cities*. Saratoga: Century Twenty One Publishing.

Fagan, J., E. Piper, and Y. Cheng. 1987. Contributions of victimization to delinquency in inner cities. *Journal of Criminal Law and Criminology* 78:505-24.

Garofalo, J. 1987. Reassessing the lifestyle model of criminal victimization. In M. Gottfredson and T. Hirschi (eds.), *Positive Criminology*. Newbury Park, Calif.: Sage.

Golden, R.M. and S.F. Messner. 1987. Dimensions of racial inequality and rates of violent crime. *Criminology* 25:525-541.

Guerry, A. 1833. *Essai sur la statistique Morale de la France*. Paris: Crochard.

Harries, K.D. 1976. Cities and crime. *Criminology* 14:369-386.

Jacobs, D. 1981. Inequality and economic crime. *Sociology and Social Research* 66:12-28.

Kornhauser, R.R. 1978. *Social Sources of Delinquency*. Chicago: University of Chicago Press.

Lander, B. 1954. *Toward an Understanding of Juvenile Delinquency*. New York: Columbia University Press.

Loftin, C. and R.H. Hill. 1974. Regional subcultures and homicide. *American Sociological Review* 39:714-24.

Loftin, C. and R.N. Parker. 1985. An error-in-variable model of the effect of poverty on urban homicide rates. *Criminology* 23:269-285.

Maddala, G.S. 1983. *Limited-dependent and qualitative variables in econometrics*. New York: Cambridge University Press.

Maxfield, M.G., D.A. Lewis, and R. Szoc. 1980. Producing official crimes: Verified crime reports as measures of police output. *Social Science Quarterly* 61:221-236.

McCleary, R., B.C. Neinstedt, and J.M. Erven. 1982 Uniform Crime Reports as organizational outcomes: Three time series experiments. *Social Problems* 29:361-372.

Merton, R.K. 1949. *Social Theory and Social Structure*. New York: Free Press.

Messner, S.F. 1982. Poverty, inequality and the urban homicide rate. *Criminology* 20:103-114.

———. 1983. Regional and racial effect on the urban homicide rate: The subculture of violence revisited. *American Journal of Sociology* 88:997-1007.

Messner, S.F. and K. Tardiff. 1986. Economic inequality and levels of homicide: An analysis of urban neighborhoods. *Criminology* 24:297-317.

Mladenka, K.R. and K.Q. Hill. 1976. A re-examination of the etiology of urban crime. *Criminology* 13:491-506.

Nettler, G. 1984. *Explaining Crime*. New York: McGraw-Hill.

Newbery, D. 1970. A theorem on the measurement of inequality. *Journal of Economic Theory* 2:264-266.

O'Brien, R.M. 1983. Metropolitan structure and violent crime: Which measure of crime? *American Sociological Review* 48:434-437.

———. 1985. *Crime and Victimization Data*. Beverly Hills, Calif.: Sage.

Polk, K. 1957. The juvenile delinquent and social areas. *Social Problems* 5:214-217.

———. 1967. Urban social areas and delinquency. *Social Problems* 14:320-325.

Pyle, G. 1974. *The Spatial Dynamics of Crime*. Chicago: University of Chicago Press.

Quetelet, A. 1835. *Research on the Propensity for Crime at Different Ages*, trans, S.F. Sylvester. Cincinnati: Anderson (1984).

Quinney, R. 1964. Crime, delinquency and social areas. *Journal of Research in Crime and Delinquency* 1:149-154.

Roncek, D.W. 1981. Dangerous places: Crime and residential environment. *Social Forces* 60:74-96.

Rosenfeld, R. 1986. Urban crime rates: Effects of inequality, welfare dependency, region, and race. In J.M. Byrne and R.J. Sampson (eds.), *The Social Ecology of Crime*. New York: Springer-Verlag.

Sampson, R.J. 1985. Neighborhood and crime: The structural determinants of personal victimization. *Journal of Research in Crime and Delinquency* 22:7-40.

———. 1986. The effects of urbanization and neighborhood characteristics in criminal victimization. In R.M. Figlio, S. Hakim, and G.F. Rengert (eds.), *Metropolitan Crime Patterns*. Monsey, N.Y.: Criminal Justice Press.

Sampson, R.J. and T.C. Castellano. 1982. Economic inequality and personal victimization. *British Journal of Criminology* 22:363-385.

Schmid, C.F. 1960a. Urban crime areas: Part I. *American Sociological Review* 25:527-443.

———. 1960b. Urban crime areas: Part II. *American Sociological Review* 25:655-678.

Schuessler, K. and G. Slatin. 1964. Sources of variation in U.S. city crime, 1950 and 1960. *Journal of Research in Crime and Delinquency* 1:127-148.

Seidman, D. and M. Couzens. 1974. Getting the crime rate down: Political pressure and crime reporting. *Law and Society Review* 8:457-493.

Sellin, T. 1938. *Culture Conflict and Crime*. New York: Social Science Research Council.

Shaw, C.R. and H. McKay. 1942. *Juvenile Delinquency and Urban Areas*. Chicago: University of Chicago Press.

Shryock, H.S. and J.S. Siegel. 1973. *The Methods and Materials of Demography*. Social and Economic Statistics Administration. Washington, D.C.: U.S. Department of Commerce.

Skogan, W.G. 1976. Crime and crime rates. In W.G. Skogan (ed.), *Sample Surveys of Victims of Crime*. Cambridge, Mass.: Ballinger.

Smith, D.A. 1986. The neighborhood context of police behavior. In A.J. Reiss and M. Tonry, *Communities and Crime*. Chicago: University of Chicago Press.

Smith, D.A. and G.R. Jarjoura. 1988. Social structure and criminal victimization. *Journal of Research in Crime and Delinquency* 25:27-52.

Smith, M.D. and R.N. Parker. 1980. Types of Homicide and Variation in Regional Rates. *Social Forces* 59:137-147.

Social Science Council. 1968. *Research on Poverty*. London: Heinemann.

Taylor, I., P. Walton, and J. Young. 1973. *The new criminology: For a social theory of deviance*. London: Routledge & Kegan Paul.

Vold, G.B. and T.J. Bernard. 1986. *Theoretical Criminology*. New York: Oxford University Press.

Watts, A.D. and T.W. Watts. 1981. Minorities and urban crime. *Urban Affairs Quarterly* 16:423-436.

Wellford, C.F. 1974. Crime and the police. *Criminology* 12:195-213.

White, H. 1980. A heteroscedastic-consistent covariance matrix estimator and a direct test for heteroscodasticity. *Econometrica* 48:817-838.

Williams, K. 1984. Economic sources of homicide: Reestimating the effects of poverty and inequality. *American Sociological Review* 49:283-289.

Willie, C.Y. 1967. The relative contribution of family status and economic status to juvenile delinquency. *Social Problems* 14:326-335.

Wilson, J.Q. 1978. *Varieties of Police Behavior: The Management of Law and Order in Eight Communities*. Cambridge, Mass.: Harvard University Press.

Wirth, L. 1938. Urbanism as a way of life. *American Journal of Sociology* 44:1-24.

Wolfgang, M.E. and F. Ferracuti. 1967. *The Subculture of Violence*. London: Tavistock. ✦

18
Foundation for a General Strain Theory of Crime and Delinquency

Robert Agnew

After dominating deviance research in the 1960s, strain theory came under heavy attack in the 1970s (Bernard, 1984; Cole, 1975), with several prominent researchers suggesting that the theory be abandoned (Hirschi, 1969; Kornhauser, 1978). Strain theory has survived those attacks, but its influence is much diminished (see Agnew, 1985a; Bernard, 1984; Farnworth and Leiber, 1989). In particular, variables derived from strain theory now play a very limited role in explanations of crime/delinquency. Several recent causal models of delinquency, in fact, either entirely exclude strain variables or assign them a small role (e.g., Elliott et al., 1985; Johnson, 1979; Massey and Krohn, 1986; Thornberry, 1987; Tonry et al., 1991). Causal models of crime/delinquency are dominated, instead, by variables derived from differential association/social learning theory and social control theory.

This paper argues that strain theory has a central role to play in explanations of crime/delinquency, but that the theory has to be substantially revised to play this role. Most empirical studies of strain theory continue to rely on the strain models developed by Merton (1938), A. Cohen (1955), and Cloward and Ohlin (1960). In recent years, however, a wealth of research in several fields has questioned certain of the assumptions underlying those theories and pointed to new directions for the development of strain theory. Most notable in this area is the research on stress in medical sociology and psychology, on equity/justice in social psychology, and on aggression in psychology—particularly recent versions of frustration—aggression and social learning theory. Also important is recent research in such areas as the legitimation of stratification, the sociology of emotions, and the urban underclass. Certain researchers have drawn on segments of the above research to suggest new directions for strain theory (Agnew, 1985a; Bernard, 1987; Elliott et al., 1979; Greenberg, 1977), but the revisions suggested have not taken full advantage of this research and, at best, provide only incomplete models of strain and delinquency. (Note that most of the theoretical and empirical work on strain theory has focused on delinquency.) This paper draws on the above literatures, as well as the recent revisions in strain theory, to present the outlines of a general strain theory of crime/delinquency.

The theory is written at the social-psychological level: It focuses on the individual and his or her immediate social environment—although the macro-implications of the theory are explored at various points. The theory is also written with the empirical researcher in mind, and guidelines for testing the theory in adolescent populations are provided. The focus is on adolescents because most currently available data sets capable of testing the theory involve surveys of adolescents. This general theory, it will be argued, is capable of overcoming the theoretical and empirical criticisms of previous strain theories and of complementing the crime/delinquency theories that currently dominate the field. . . .

Strain Theory as Distinguished From Control and Differential Association/Social Learning Theory

Strain, social control, and differential association theory are all sociological theories: They explain delinquency in terms of the individual's social relationships. Strain theory is distinguished from social control and social learning theory in its specification of (1) the type of social relationship that leads to delinquency and (2) the motivation for delinquency. First, strain theory focuses explicitly on *negative relationships with others*: relationships in which the individual is not treated as he or she wants to be treated. Strain theory has typically focused on relationships in which others prevent the individual from achieving positively valued goals. Agnew (1985a), however, broadened the focus of strain theory to include relationships in which others present the individual with noxious or negative stimuli. Social control theory, by contrast, focuses on the *absence of significant relationships with conventional others and institutions*. In particular, delinquency is most likely when (1) the adolescent is not attached to parents, school, or other institutions; (2) parents and others fail to monitor and effectively sanction deviance; (3) the adolescent's actual or anticipated investment in conventional society is minimal; and (4) the adolescent has not internalized conventional beliefs. Social learning theory is distinguished from strain and control theory by its focus on *positive relationships with deviant others*. In particular, delinquency results from association with others who (1) differentially reinforce the adolescent's delinquency, (2) model delinquent behavior, and/or (3) transmit delinquent values.

Second, strain theory argues that adolescents *are pressured into delinquency by the negative affective states—most notably anger and related emotions—that often result from negative relationships* (see Kemper, 1978, and Morgan and Heise, 1988, for typologies of negative affective states). This negative affect creates pressure for corrective action and *may* lead adolescents to (1) make use of illegitimate channels of goal achievement, (2) attack or escape from the source of their adversity, and/or (3) manage their negative affect through the use of illicit drugs. Control theory, by contrast, denies that outside forces pressure the adolescent into delinquency. Rather, the absence of significant relationships with other individuals and groups *frees the adolescent to engage in delinquency*. The freed adolescent either drifts into delinquency or, in some versions of control theory, turns to delinquency in response to inner forces or situational inducements (see Hirschi, 1969:31-34). In differential association/social learning theory, the adolescent commits delinquent acts because group forces lead the adolescent to *view delinquency as a desirable or at least justifiable form of behavior* under certain circumstances.

Strain theory, then, is distinguished by its focus on negative relationships with others and its insistence that such relationships lead to delinquency through the negative affect— especially anger—they sometimes engender. Both dimensions are necessary to differentiate strain theory from control and differential association/social learning theory. In particular, social control and social learning theory sometimes examine negative relationships—although such relationships are not an explicit focus of these theories. Control theory, however, would argue that negative relationships lead to delinquency not because they cause negative affect, but because they lead to a reduction in social control. A control theorist, for example, would argue that physical abuse by parents leads to delinquency because it reduces attachment to parents and the effectiveness of parents as socializing agents. Likewise, differential association/social learning theorists sometimes examine negative relationships—even though theorists in this tradition emphasize that imitation, reinforcement, and the internalization of values are less likely in negative relationships. Social learning theorists, however, would argue that negative relationships—such as those involving physically abusive parents—lead to delinquency by providing models for imitation and implicitly teaching the child that violence and other forms of deviance are acceptable behavior.

Phrased in the above manner, it is easy to see that strain theory complements the other major theories of delinquency in a fundamental way. While these other theories focus on the absence of relationships or on positive relationships, strain theory is the only theory to focus explicitly on negative relationships. And while these other theories view delinquency as the result of drift or of desire, strain theory views it as the result of pressure.

The Major Types of Strain

Negative relationships with others are, quite simply, relationships in which others are not treating the individual as he or she would like to be treated. The classic strain theories of Merton (1938), A. Cohen (1955), and Cloward and Ohlin (1960) focus on only one type of negative relationship: relationships in which others prevent the individual from achieving positively valued goals. In particular, they focus on the goal blockage experienced by lower-class individuals trying to achieve monetary success or middle-class status. More recent versions of strain theory have argued that adolescents are not only concerned about the future goals of monetary success/middle-class status, but are also concerned about the achievement of more immediate goals—such as good grades, popularity with the opposite sex, and doing well in athletics (Agnew, 1984; Elliott and Voss, 1974; Elliott et al., 1985; Empey, 1982; Greenberg, 1977; Quicker, 1974). The focus, however, is still on the achievement of positively valued goals. Most recently, Agnew (1985a) has argued that strain may result not only from the failure to achieve positively valued goals, but also from the inability to escape legally from painful situations. If one draws on the above theories—as well as the stress, equity/justice, and aggression literatures—one can begin to develop a more complete classification of the types of strain.

Three major types of strain are described—each referring to a different type of negative relationship with others. Other individuals may (1) prevent one from achieving positively valued goals, (2) remove or threaten to remove positively valued stimuli that one possesses, or (3) present or threaten to present one with noxious or negatively valued stimuli. These categories of strain are presented as ideal types. There is no expectation, for example, that a factor analysis of strainful events will reproduce these categories. These categories, rather, are presented so as to ensure that the full range of strainful events are considered in empirical research.

Strain as the Failure to Achieve Positively Valued Goals

At least three types of strain fall under this category. The first type encompasses most of the major strain theories in criminology, including the classic strain theories of Merton, A. Cohen, and Cloward and Ohlin, as well as those modern strain theories focusing on the achievement of immediate goals. The other two types of strain in this category are derived from the justice/equity literature and have not been examined in criminology.

Strain as the Disjunction Between Aspirations and Expectations/Actual Achievements. The classic strain theories of Merton, A. Cohen, and Cloward and Ohlin argue that the cultural system encourages everyone to pursue the ideal goals of monetary success and/or middle-class status. Lower-class individuals, however, are often prevented from achieving such goals through legitimate channels. In line with such theories, adolescent strain is typically measured in terms of the disjunction between *aspirations* (or ideal goals) and *expectations* (or expected levels of goal achievement). These theories, however, have been criticized for several reasons (see Agnew, 1986, 1991b; Clinard, 1964; Hirschi, 1969; Kornhauser, 1978; Liska, 1987; also see Bernard, 1984; Farnworth and Leiber, 1989). Among other things, it has been charged that these theories (1) are unable to explain the extensive nature of middle-class delinquency, (2) neglect goals other than monetary success/middle-class status, (3) neglect barriers to goal achievement other than social class, and (4) do not fully specify why only *some* strained individuals turn to delinquency. The most damaging criticism, however, stems from the limited empirical support provided by studies focusing on the disjunction between aspirations and expectations (see Kornhauser, 1978, as well the arguments of Bernard, 1984; Elliott et al., 1985; and Jensen, 1986).

As a consequence of these criticisms, several researchers have revised the above theories. The most popular revision argues that there is a youth subculture that emphasizes a variety of immediate goals. The achievement of these goals is further said to depend on a variety of factors besides social class: factors such as intelligence, physical attractiveness, personality, and athletic ability. As a result, many middle-class individuals find that they lack the traits or skills necessary to achieve their goals through legitimate channels. This version of strain theory, however, continues to argue that strain stems from the inability to achieve certain ideal goals emphasized by the (sub)cultural system. As a consequence, strain continues to be measured in terms of the disjunction between *aspirations* and *actual achievements* (since we are dealing with immediate rather than future goals, actual achievements rather than expected achievements may be examined).

It should be noted that empirical support for this revised version of strain theory is also weak (see Agnew, 1991b, for a summary). At a later point, several possible reasons for the weak empirical support of strain theories focusing on the disjunction between aspirations and expectations/achievements will be discussed. For now, the focus is on classifying the major types of strain.

Strain as the Disjunction Between Expectations and Actual Achievements. As indicated above, strain theories in criminology focus on the inability to achieve *ideal* goals derived from the cultural system. This approach stands in contrast to certain of the research on justice in social psychology. Here the focus is on the disjunction between *expectations* and *actual achievements* (rewards), and it is commonly argued that such expectations are existentially based. In particular, it has been argued that such expectations derive from the individual's past experience and/or from comparisons with referential (or generalized) others who are similar to the individual (see Berger et al., 1972, 1983; Blau, 1964; Homans, 1961; Jasso and Rossi, 1977; Mickelson, 1990; Ross et al., 1971; Thibaut and Kelley, 1959). Much of the research in this area has focused on income expectations, although the above theories apply to expectations regarding all manner of positive stimuli. The justice literature argues that the failure to achieve such expectations may lead to such emotions as anger, resentment, rage, dissatisfaction, disappointment, and unhappiness—that is, all the emotions customarily associated with strain in criminology. Further, it is argued that individuals will be strongly motivated to reduce the gap between expectations and achievements—with deviance being commonly mentioned as one possible option. This literature has not devoted much empirical research to deviance, although limited data suggest that the expectations-achievement gap is related to anger/hostility (Ross et al., 1971).

This alternative conception of strain has been largely neglected in criminology. This is unfortunate because it has the potential to overcome certain of the problems of current strain theories. First, one would expect the disjunction between expectations and actual achievements to be more emotionally distressing than that between aspirations and achievements. Aspirations, by definition, are *ideal* goals. They have something of the utopian in them, and for that reason, the failure to achieve aspirations may not be taken seriously. The failure to achieve expected goals, however, is likely to be taken seriously since such goals are rooted in reality—the individual has previously experienced such goals or has seen similar others experience such goals. Second, this alternative conception of strain assigns a central role to the social comparison process. As A. Cohen (1965) argued in a follow-up to his strain theory, the neglect of social comparison is a major shortcoming of strain theory. The above theories describe one way in which social comparison is important: Social comparison plays a central role in the formation of individual goals (expectations in this case; also see Suls, 1977). Third, the assumption that goals are culturally based has sometimes proved problematic for strain theory (see Kornhauser, 1978). Among other things, it makes it difficult to integrate strain theory with social control and cultural deviance theory (see Hirschi, 1979). These latter theories assume that the individual is weakly tied to the cultural system or tied to alternative/oppositional subcultures. The argument that goals are existentially based, however, paves the way for integrations involving strain theory.¹

Strain as the Disjunction Between Just/Fair Outcomes and Actual Outcomes. The above models of strain assume that individual goals focus on the achievement of specific outcomes. Individual goals, for example, focus on the achievement of a certain amount of money or a certain grade-point average. A third conception of strain, also derived from the justice/equity literature, makes a rather different argument. It claims that individuals do not necessarily enter interactions with specific outcomes in mind. Rather, they enter interactions expecting that certain distributive justice rules will be followed, rules specifying how resources should be allocated. The rule that has received the most attention in the literature is that of equity. An equitable relationship is one in which the outcome/input ratios of the actors involved in an exchange/allocation relationship are equivalent (see Adams, 1963, 1965; Cook and Hegtvedt, 1983; Walster et al., 1978). Outcomes encompass a broad range of positive and negative consequences, while inputs encompass the individual's positive and negative contributions to the exchange. Individuals in a relationship will compare the ratio of their outcomes and inputs to the ratio(s) of specific others in the relationship. If the ratios are equal to one another, they feel that the outcomes are fair or just. This is true, according to equity theorists, even if the outcomes are low. If outcome/input ratios are not equal, actors will feel that the outcomes are unjust and they will experience distress as a result. Such distress is especially likely when individuals feel they have been underrewarded rather than overrewarded (Hegtvedt, 1990).

The equity literature has described the possible reactions to this distress, some of which involve deviance (see Adams, 1963, 1965; Austin, 1977; Walster et al., 1973, 1978; see Stephenson and White, 1968, for an attempt to recast A. Cohen's strain theory in terms of equity theory). In particular, inequity may lead to delinquency for several reasons—all having to do with the restoration of equity. Individuals in inequitable relationships may engage in delinquency in order to (1) increase their outcomes (e.g., by theft); (2) lower their inputs (e.g., truancy from school); (3) lower the outcomes of others (e.g., vandalism, theft, assault); and/or (4) increase the inputs of others (e.g., by being incorrigible or disorderly). In highly inequitable situations, individuals may leave the field (e.g., run away from home) or force others to leave the field.² There has not been any empirical research on the relationship between equity and delinquency, although much data suggest that inequity leads to anger and frustration. A few studies also suggest that insulting and vengeful behaviors may result from inequity (see Cook and Hegtvedt, 1991; Donnerstein and Hatfield, 1982; Hegtvedt, 1990; Mikula, 1986; Sprecher, 1986; Walster et al., 1973, 1978).

It is not difficult to measure equity. Walster et al. (1978:234-242) provide the most complete guide to measurements.³ Sprecher (1986) illustrates how equity may be measured in social surveys; respondents are asked who contributes more to a particular relationship and/or who "gets the best deal" out of a relationship. A still simpler strategy might be to ask respondents how fair or just their interactions with others, such as parents or teachers, are. One would then predict that those involved in unfair relations will be more likely to engage in current and future delinquency.

The literature on equity builds on the strain theory literature in criminology in several ways. First, all of the strain literature assumes that individuals are pursuing some specific outcome, such as a certain amount of money or prestige. The equity literature points out that individuals do not necessarily enter into interactions with specific outcomes in mind, but rather with the expectation that a particular distributive justice rule will be followed. Their goal is that the interaction conform to the justice principle. This perspective, then, points to a new source of strain not considered in the criminology literature. Second, the strain literature in criminology focuses largely on the individual's outcomes. Individuals are assumed to be pursuing a specific goal, and strain is judged in terms of the disjunction between the goal and the actual outcome. The equity literature suggests that this may be an oversimplified conception and that the individual's *inputs* may also have to be considered. In particular, an equity theorist would argue that inputs will condition the individual's evaluation of outcomes. That is, individuals who view their inputs as limited will be more likely to accept limited outcomes as fair. Third, the equity literature also highlights the importance of the social comparison process. In particular, the equity literature stresses that one's evaluation of outcomes is at least partly a function of the outcomes (and inputs) of those with whom one is involved in exchange/allocation relations. A given outcome, then, may be evaluated as fair or unfair depending on the outcomes (and inputs) of others in the exchange/allocation relation.

Summary: Strain as the Failure to Achieve Positively Valued Goals. Three types of strain in this category have been listed: strain as the disjunction between (1) aspirations and expectations/actual achievements, (2) expectations and actual achievements, and (3) just/fair outcomes and actual outcomes. Strain theory in criminology has focused on the first type of strain, arguing that it is most responsible for the delinquency in our society. Major research traditions in the justice/equity field, however, argue that anger and frustration derive primarily from the second two types of strain. To complicate matters further, one can list still additional types of strain in this category. Certain of the literature, for example, has talked of the disjunction between "satisfying outcomes" and reality, between "deserved" outcomes and reality, and between "tolerance levels" or minimally acceptable outcomes and reality. No study has examined all of these types of goals, but taken as a whole the data do suggest that there are often differences among aspirations (ideal outcomes), expectations (expected outcomes), "satisfying" outcomes, "deserved" outcomes, fair or just outcomes, and tolerance levels (Della Fave, 1974; Della Fave and Klobus, 1976; Martin, 1986; Martin and Murray, 1983; Messick and Sentis, 1983; Shepelak and Alwin, 1986). This paper has focused on the three types of strain listed above largely because they dominate the current literature.[4]

Given these multiple sources of strain, one might ask which is the most relevant to the explanation of delinquency. This is a difficult question to answer given current research. The most fruitful strategy at the present time may be to assume that all of the above sources are relevant—that there are several sources of frustration. Alwin (1987), Austin (1977), Crosby and Gonzalez-Intal (1984), Hegtvedt (1991b), Messick and Sentis (1983), and Tornblum (1977) all argue or imply that people often employ a variety of standards to evaluate their situation. Strain theorists, then, might be best advised to employ measures that tap all of the above types of strain. One might, for example, focus on a broad range of positively valued goals and, for each goal, ask adolescents whether they are achieving their ideal outcomes (aspirations), expected outcomes, and just/fair outcomes. One would expect strain to be greatest when several standards were not being met, with perhaps greatest weight being given to expectations and just/fair outcomes.[5]

Strain as the Removal of Positively Valued Stimuli from the Individual

The psychological literature on aggression and the stress literature suggest that strain may involve more than the pursuit of positively valued goals. Certain of the aggression literature, in fact, has come to de-emphasize the pursuit of positively valued goals, pointing out that the blockage of goal-seeking behavior is a relatively weak predictor of aggression, particularly when the goal has never been experienced before (Bandura, 1973; Zillman, 1979). The stress literature has largely neglected the pursuit of positively valued goals as a source of stress. Rather, if one looks at the stressful life events examined in this literature, one finds a focus on (1) events involving the loss of positively valued stimuli and (2) events involving the presentation of noxious or negative stimuli (see Pearlin, 1983, for other typologies of stressful life events/conditions).[6] So, for example, one recent study of adolescent stress employs a life-events list that focuses on such items as the loss of a boyfriend/girlfriend, the death or serious illness of a friend, moving to a new school district, the divorce/separation of one's parents, suspension from school, and the presence of a variety of adverse conditions at work (see Williams and Uchiyama, 1989, for an overview of life-events scales for adolescents; see Compas, 1987, and Compas and Phares, 1991, for overviews of research on adolescent stress).[7] Drawing on the stress literature, then, one may state that a second type of strain or negative relationship involves the actual or anticipated removal (loss) of positively valued stimuli from the individual. As indicated above, numerous examples of such loss can be found in the inventories of stressful life events. The actual or anticipated loss of positively valued stimuli may lead to delinquency as the individual tries to prevent the loss of the positive stimuli, retrieve the lost stimuli or obtain substitute stimuli, seek revenge against those responsible for the loss, or manage the negative affect caused by the loss by taking illicit drugs. While there are no data bearing directly on this type of strain, experimental data indicate that aggression often occurs when positive reinforcement previously administered to an individual is withheld or reduced (Bandura, 1973; Van Houten, 1983). And as discussed below, inventories of stressful life events, which include the loss of positive stimuli, are related to delinquency.

Strain as the Presentation of Negative Stimuli

The literature on stress and the recent psychological literature on aggression also focus on the actual or anticipated presentation of negative or noxious stimuli.[8] Except for the work of Agnew (1985a), however, this category of strain has been neglected in criminology. And even Agnew does not focus on the presentation of noxious stimuli per se, but on the inability of adolescents to escape legally from noxious stimuli. Much data, however, suggest that the presentation of noxious stimuli may lead to aggression and other negative outcomes in certain conditions, even when legal escape from such stimuli is possible (Bandura, 1973; Zillman, 1979). Noxious stimuli may lead to delinquency as the adolescent tries to (1) escape from or avoid the negative stimuli; (2) terminate or alleviate the negative stimuli; (3) seek revenge against the source of the negative stimuli or related targets, although the evidence on displaced aggression is somewhat mixed (see Berkowitz, 1982; Bernard, 1990; Van Houten, 1983; Zillman, 1979); and/or (4) manage the resultant negative affect by taking illicit drugs.

A wide range of noxious stimuli have been examined in the literature, and experimental, survey, and participant observation studies have linked such stimuli to both general and specific measures of delinquency—with the experimental studies focusing on aggression. Delinquency/aggression, in particular, has been linked to such noxious stimuli as child abuse and neglect (Rivera and Widom, 1990), criminal victimization (Lauritsen et al., 1991), physical punishment (Straus, 1991), negative relations with parents (Healy and Bonner, 1969), negative relations with peers (Short and Strodtbeck, 1965), adverse or negative school experiences (Hawkins and Lishner, 1987), a wide range of stressful life events (Gersten et al., 1974; Kaplan et al., 1983; Linsky and Straus, 1986; Mawson, 1987; Novy and Donohue, 1985; Vaux and Ruggiero, 1983), verbal threats and insults, physical pain, unpleasant odors, disgusting scenes, noise, heat, air pollution, personal space violations, and high density (see Anderson and Anderson, 1984; Bandura, 1973, 1983; Berkowitz, 1982, 1986; Mueller, 1983). In one of the few studies in criminology to focus specifically on the presentation of negative stimuli, Agnew (1985a) found that delinquency was related to three scales measuring negative relations at home and school. The effect of the scales on delinquency was partially mediated through a measure of anger, and the effect held when measures of social control and deviant beliefs were controlled. And in a recent study employing longitudinal data, Agnew (1989) found evidence suggesting that the relationship between negative stimuli and delinquency was due to the *causal* effect of the negative stimuli on delinquency (rather than the effect of delinquency on the negative stimuli). Much evidence, then, suggests that the presentation of negative or noxious stimuli constitutes a third major source of strain.

Certain of the negative stimuli listed above, such as physical pain, heat, noise, and pollution, may be experienced as noxious largely for biological reasons (i.e., they may be unconditioned negative stimuli). Others may be conditioned negative stimuli, experienced as noxious largely because of their association with unconditioned negative stimuli (see Berkowitz, 1982). Whatever the case, it is assumed that such stimuli are experienced as noxious regardless of the goals that the individual is pursuing.

The Links Between Strain and Delinquency

Three sources of strain have been presented: strain as the actual or anticipated failure to achieve positively valued goals, strain as the actual or anticipated removal of positively valued stimuli, and strain as the actual or anticipated presentation of negative stimuli. While these types are theoretically distinct from one another, they may sometimes overlap in practice. So, for example, the insults of a teacher may be experienced as adverse because they (1) interfere with the adolescent's aspirations for academic success, (2) result in the violation of a distributive justice rule such as equity, and (3) are conditioned negative stimuli and so are experienced as noxious in and of themselves. Other examples of overlap can be given, and it may sometimes be difficult to disentangle the different types of strain in practice. Once again, however, these categories are ideal types and are presented only to ensure that all events with the potential for creating strain are considered in empirical research.

Each type of strain increases the likelihood that individuals will experience one or more of a range of negative emotions. Those emotions include disappointment, depression, and fear. Anger, however, is the most critical emotional reaction for the purposes of the general strain theory. Anger results when individuals blame their adversity on others, and anger is a key emotion because it increases the individual's level of felt injury, creates a desire for retaliation/revenge, energizes the individual for action, and lowers inhibitions, in part because individuals believe that others will feel their aggression is justified (see Averill, 1982; Berkowitz, 1982; Kemper, 1978; Kluegel and Smith, 1986: Ch. 10; Zillman, 1979). Anger, then, affects the individual in several ways that are conducive to delinquency. Anger is distinct from many of the other types of negative affect in this respect, and this is the reason that anger occupies a special place in the general strain theory.[9] It is important to note, however, that delinquency may still occur in response to other types of negative affect—such as despair, although delinquency is less likely in such cases.[10] The experience of negative affect, especially anger, typically creates a desire to take corrective steps, with delinquency being one possible response. Delinquency may be a method for alleviating strain, that is, for achieving positively valued goals, for protecting or retrieving positive stimuli, or for terminating or escaping from negative stimuli. Delinquency may be used to seek revenge; data suggest that vengeful behavior often occurs even when there is no possibility of eliminating the adversity that stimulated it (Berkowitz, 1982). And delinquency may occur as adolescents try to manage their negative affect through illicit drug use (see Newcomb and Harlow, 1986). The general strain theory, then, has the potential to explain a broad range of delinquency, including theft, aggression, and drug use. . . .

Constraints to Nondelinquent and Delinquent Coping. While there are many adaptations to objective strain, those adaptations are not equally available to everyone. Individuals are constrained in their choice of adaptation(s) by a variety of internal and external factors. The following is a partial list of such factors.

Initial Goals/Values/Identities of the Individual. If the objective strain affects goals/values/identities that are high in absolute and relative importance, and if the individual has few alternative goals/values/identities in which to seek refuge, it will be more difficult to relegate strain to an unimportant area of one's life (see Agnew, 1986; Thoits, 1991a). This is especially the case if the goals/values/identities receive strong social and cultural support (see below). As a result, strain will be more likely to lead to delinquency in such cases.

Individual Coping Resources. A wide range of traits can be listed in this area, including temperament, intelligence, creativity, problem-solving skills, interpersonal skills, self-efficacy, and self-esteem. These traits affect the selection of coping strategies by influencing the individual's sensitivity to objective strains and ability to engage in cognitive, emotional, and behavioral coping (Agnew, 1991a; Averill, 1982; Bernard, 1990; Compas, 1987; Edmunds and Kendrick, 1980; Slaby and Guerra, 1988; Tavris, 1984). Data, for example, suggest that individuals with high self-esteem are more resistant to stress (Averill, 1982; Compas, 1987; Kaplan, 1980; Pearlin and Schooler, 1978; Rosenberg, 1990; Thoits, 1983). Such individuals, therefore, should be less likely to respond to a given objective strain with delinquency. Individuals high in self-efficacy are more likely to feel that their strain can be alleviated by behavioral coping of a nondelinquent nature, and so they too should be less likely to respond to strain with delinquency (see Bandura, 1989, and Wang and Richarde, 1988, on self-efficacy; see Thoits, 1991b, on perceived control).

Conventional Social Support. Vaux (1988) provides an extended discussion of the different types of social support, their measurement, and their effect on outcome variables. Thoits (1984) argues that social support is important because it facilitates the major types of coping. The major types of social support, in fact, correspond to the major types of coping listed above. Thus, there is informational support, instrumental support, and emotional support (House, 1981). Adolescents with conventional social supports, then, should be better able to respond to objective strains in a nondelinquent manner.

Constraints to Delinquent Coping. The crime/delinquency literature has focused on certain variables that constrain delinquent coping. They include (1) the costs and benefits of engaging in delinquency in a particular situation (Clarke and Cornish, 1985), (2) the individual's level of social control (see Hirschi, 1969), and (3) the possession of those "illegitimate means" necessary for many delinquent acts (see Agnew, 1991a, for a full discussion).

Macro-Level Variables. The larger social environment may affect the probability of delinquent versus nondelinquent coping by affecting all of the above factors. First, the social environment may affect coping by influencing the importance attached to selected goals/values/identities. For example, certain ethnographic accounts suggest that there is a strong social and cultural emphasis on the goals of money/status among certain segments of the urban poor. Many poor individuals, in particular, are in a situation in which (1) they face strong economic/status demands, (2) people around them stress the importance of money/status on a regular basis, and (3) few alternative goals are given cultural support (Anderson, 1978; MacLeod, 1987; Sullivan, 1989). As such, these individuals should face more difficulty in cognitively minimizing the importance of money and status.

Second, the larger social environment may affect the individual's sensitivity to particular strains by influencing the individual's beliefs regarding what is and is not adverse. The subculture of violence thesis, for example, is predicated on the assumption that young black males in urban slums are taught that a wide range of provocations and insults are highly adverse. Third, the social environment may influence the individual's ability to minimize cognitively the severity of objective strain. Individuals in some environments are regularly provided with external information about their accomplishments and failings (see Faunce, 1989), and their attempts at cognitively distorting such information are quickly challenged. Such a situation may exist among many adolescents and among those who inhabit the "street-corner world" of the urban poor. Adolescents and those on the street corner live in a very "public world"; one's accomplishments and failings typically occur before a large audience or they quickly become known to such an audience. Further, accounts suggest that this audience regularly reminds individuals of their accomplishments and failings and challenges attempts at cognitive distortion.

Fourth, certain social environments may make it difficult to engage in behavioral coping of a nondelinquent nature. Agnew (1985a) has argued that adolescents often find it difficult to escape legally from negative stimuli, especially negative stimuli encountered in the school, family, and neighborhood. Also, adolescents often lack the resources to negotiate successfully with adults, such as parents and teachers (although see Agnew, 1991a). Similar arguments might be made for the urban underclass. They often lack the resources to negotiate successfully with many others, and they often find it difficult to escape legally from adverse environments—by, for example, quitting their job (if they have a job) or moving to another neighborhood.

The larger social environment, then, may affect individual coping in a variety of ways. And certain groups, such as adolescents and the urban underclass, may face special constraints that make nondelinquent coping more difficult. This may explain the higher rate of deviance among these groups.

Factors Affecting the Disposition to Delinquency. The selection of delinquent versus nondelinquent coping strategies is not only dependent on the constraints to coping, but also on the adolescent's disposition to engage in delinquent versus nondelinquent coping. This disposition is a function of (1) certain temperamental variables (see Tonry et al., 1991), (2) the prior learning history of the adolescent, particularly the extent to which delinquency was reinforced in the past (Bandura, 1973; Berkowitz, 1982), (3) the adolescent's beliefs, particularly the rules defining the appropriate response to provocations (Bernard's, 1990, "regulative rules"), and (4) the adolescent's attributions regarding the causes of his or her adversity. Adolescents who attribute their adversity to others are much more likely to become angry, and as argued earlier, that anger creates a strong predisposition to delinquency. Data and theory from several areas, in fact, suggest that the experience of adversity is most likely to result in deviance when the adversity is blamed on another.[11] The attributions one makes are influenced by a variety of factors, as discussed in recent reviews by Averill (1982), Brewin (1988), R. Cohen (1982), Crittenden (1983, 1989), Kluegel and Smith (1986), and Utne and Kidd (1980). The possibility that there may be demographic and subgroup differences in the rules for assigning blame is of special interest (see Bernard, 1990; Crittenden, 1983, 1989).

A key variable affecting several of the above factors is association with delinquent peers. It has been argued that adolescents who associate with delinquent peers are more likely to be exposed to delinquent models and beliefs and to receive reinforcement for delinquency (see especially, Akers, 1985). It may also be the case that delinquent peers increase the likelihood that adolescents will attribute their adversity to others.

The individual's disposition to delinquency, then, may condition the impact of adversity on delinquency. At the same time, it is important to note that continued experience with adversity may create a disposition for delinquency. This argument has been made by Bernard (1990), Cloward and Ohlin (1960), A. Cohen (1955), Elliott et al. (1979), and others. In particular, it has been argued that under certain conditions the experience of adversity may lead to beliefs favorable to delinquency, lead adolescents to join or form delinquent peer groups, and lead adolescents to blame others for their misfortune.

Virtually all empirical research on strain theory in criminology has neglected the constraints to coping and the adolescent's disposition to delinquency. Researchers, in particular, have failed to examine whether the effect of adversity on delinquency is conditioned by factors such as self-efficacy and association with delinquent peers. This is likely a major reason for the weak empirical support for strain theory.

Conclusion

Much of the recent theoretical work in criminology has focused on the integration of different delinquency theories. This paper has taken an alternative track and, following Hirschi's (1979) advice, has focused on the refinement of a single theory. The general strain theory builds upon traditional strain theory in criminology in several ways. First, the general strain theory points to several new sources of strain. In particular, it focuses on three categories of strain or negative relationships with others: (1) the actual or anticipated failure to achieve positively valued goals, (2) the actual or anticipated removal of positively valued stimuli, and (3) the actual or anticipated presentation of negative stimuli. Most current strain theories in criminology only focus on strain as the failure to achieve positively valued goals, and even then the focus is only on the disjunction between aspirations and expectations/actual achievements. The disjunctions between expectations and achievements and just/fair outcomes and achievements are ignored. The general strain theory, then, significantly expands the focus of strain theory to include all types of negative relations between the individual and others.

Second, the general strain theory more precisely specifies the relationship between strain and delinquency, pointing out that strain is likely to have a cumulative effect on delinquency after a certain threshold level is reached. The theory also points to certain relevant dimensions of strain that should be considered in empirical research, including the magnitude, recency, duration, and clustering of strainful events.

Third, the general strain theory provides a more comprehensive account of the cognitive, behavioral, and emotional adaptations to strain. This account sheds additional light on the reasons why many strained individuals do *not* turn to delinquency, and it may prove useful in devising strategies to prevent and control delinquency. Individuals, in particular, may be taught those nondelinquent coping strategies found to be most effective in preventing delinquency.

Fourth, the general strain theory more fully describes those factors affecting the choice of delinquent versus nondelinquent adaptations. The failure to consider such factors is a fundamental reason for the weak empirical support for strain theory.

Most of the above modifications in strain theory were suggested by research in several areas outside of traditional criminology, most notably the stress research in medical sociology and psychology, the equity/justice research in social psychology, and the aggression research in psychology. With certain exceptions, researchers in criminology have tended to cling to the early strain models of Merton (1938), A. Cohen (1955), and Cloward and Ohlin (1960) and to ignore the developments in related fields. And while these early strain models contain much of value and have had a major influence on the general strain theory in this paper, they do not fully exploit the potential of strain theory. . . .

Notes

1. One need not assume that expectations are existentially based; they may derive from the cultural system as well. Likewise, one need not assume that aspirations derive from the cultural system. The focus in this paper is on *types* of strain rather than *sources of* strain, although a consideration of sources is crucial when the macroimplications of the theory are developed. Additional information on the sources of positively valued goals—including aspirations and expectations—can be found in Alves and Rossi, 1978; Cook and Messick, 1983; Hochschild, 1981; Jasso and Rossi, 1977; Martin and Murray, 1983; Messick and Sentis, 1983; Mickelson, 1990; and Shepelak and Alwin, 1986.
2. Theorists have recently argued that efforts to restore equity need not involve the specific others in the inequitable relationship. If one cannot restore equity with such specific others, there may be an effort to restore "equity with the world" (Austin, 1977; Stephenson and White, 1968; Walster et al., 1978). That is, individuals who feel they have been in-

equitably treated may try to restore equity in the context of a totally different relationship. The adolescent who is inequitably treated by parents, for example, may respond by inequitably treating peers. The concept of "equity with the world" has not been the subject of much empirical research, but it is intriguing because it provides a novel explanation for displayed aggression. It has also been argued that individuals may be distressed not only by their own inequitable treatment, but also by the inequitable treatment of others (see Crosby and Gonzalez-Intal, 1984; Walster et al., 1978.) We may have, then, a sort of vicarious strain, a type little investigated in the literature.

3. The equity literature has been criticized on a number of points, the most prominent being that there are a variety of distribution rules besides equity—such as equality and need (Deutsch, 1975; Folger, 1984; Mikula, 1980; Schwinger, 1980; Utne and Kidd, 1980). Much recent research has focused on the factors that determine the preference for one rule over another (Alves and Rossi, 1978; Cook and Hegtvedt, 1983; Deutsch, 1975; Hegtvedt, 1997, 1991a; Hochschild, 1981; Lerner, 1977; Leventhal, 1976; Leventhal et al., 1980; Schwinger, 1980; Walster et al., 1978). Also, the equity literature argues that individuals compare themselves with similar others with whom they are involved in exchange/allocation relations. However, it has been argued that individuals sometimes compare themselves with dissimilar others, make referential (generalized) rather than local (specific) comparisons, make internal rather than external comparisons, make group-to-group comparisons, or avoid social comparison altogether (see Berger et al., 1972; Hegtvedt, 1991b; Martin and Murray, 1983; see Hegtvedt, 1991b, and Suls and Wills, 1991, for a discussion of the factors affecting the choice of comparison objects). Finally, even if one knows what distribution rule individuals prefer and the types of social comparisons they make, it is still difficult to predict whether they will evaluate their interactions as equitable. Except in unambiguous situations of the type created in experiments, it is hard to predict what inputs and outcomes individuals will define as relevant, how they will weight those inputs and outcomes, and how they will evaluate themselves and others on those inputs and outcomes (Austin, 1977; Hegtvedt, 1991a; Messick and Sentis, 1979, 1983; Walster et al., 1973, 1978). Fortunately, however, the above three problems do not prohibit strain theory from taking advantage of certain of the insights from equity theory. While it is difficult to predict whether individuals will define their relationships as equitable, it is relatively easy to measure equity after the fact.

4. To add a still further complication, it has been suggested that anger may result from the violation of *procedural* as well as distributive justice rules (Folger, 1984, 1986; Lind and Tyler, 1988). Procedural justice does not focus on the fairness of outcomes, but rather on the fairness of the procedures by which individuals decide how to distribute resources. A central issue in procedural justice is whether all individuals have a "voice" in deciding how resources will be distributed. One might, then, ask adolescents about the fairness of the procedures used by parents, teachers, and others to make rules.

5. This strategy assumes that all standards are relevant in a given situation, which may not always be the case. In certain situations, for example, one may make local comparisons but not referential comparisons (see Brickman and Bulman, 1977; Crosby and Gonzales-Intal, 1984). In other situations, social comparison processes may not come into play at all; outcomes may be evaluated in terms of culturally derived standards (see Folger, 1986).

6. The stress literature has also focused on positive events, based on the assumption that such events might lead to stress by overloading the individual. Accumulating evidence, however, suggests that it is only undesirable events that lead to negative outcomes such as depression (e.g., Gersten et al., 1974; Kaplan et al., 1983; Pearlin et al., 1981; Thoits, 1983).

7. Certain individuals have criticized the stress literature for neglecting the failure of individuals to achieve positively valued goals. In particular, it has been charged that the stress literature has neglected "nonevents," or events that are desired or anticipated but do not occur (Dohrenwend and Dohrenwend, 1974; Thoits, 1983). One major distinction between the strain literature in criminology and the stress literature in medical sociology, in fact, is that the former has focused on "nonevents" while the latter has focused on "events."

8. Some researchers have argued that it is often difficult to distinguish the presentation of negative stimuli from the removal of positive stimuli (Michael, 1973; Van Houten, 1983; Zillman, 1979). Suppose, for example, that an adolescent argues with parents. Does this represent the presentation of negative stimuli, (the arguing) or the removal of positive

stimuli (harmonious relations with one's parents)? The point is a valid one, yet the distinction between the two types of strain still seems useful since it helps ensure that all major types of strain are considered by researchers.

9. The focus on blame/anger represents a major distinction between the general strain theory and the strew literature. The stress literature simply focuses on adversity, regardless of whether it is blamed on another. This is perhaps appropriate because the major outcome variables of the stress literature are inner-directed states, like depression and poor health. When the focus shifts to outer-directed behavior, like much delinquency, a concern with blame/anger becomes important.

10. Delinquency may still occur in the absence of blame and anger (see Berkowitz, 1986; Zillman, 1979). Individuals who accept responsibility for their adversity are still subject to negative affect, such as depression, despair, and disappointment (see Kemper, 1978; Kluegel and Smith, 1986). As a result, such individuals will still feel pressure to take corrective action, although the absence of anger places them under less pressure and makes vengeful behavior much less likely. Such individuals, however, may engage in inner-directed delinquency, such as drug use, and if suitably disposed, they may turn to other forms of delinquency as well. Since these individuals lack the strong motivation for revenge and the lowered inhibitions that anger provides, it is assumed that they must have some minimal disposition for deviance before they respond to their adversity with outer-directed delinquency (see the discussion of the disposition to delinquency).

11. This is a major theme in the psychological research on aggression, in much of the recent research on equity, and in the emotions literature, and it is a central theme in Cloward and Ohlin's (1960) strain theory (e.g., Averill, 1982; Berkowitz, 1982; R. Cohen, 1982; Crosby and Gonzales-Intal, 1984; Garrett and Libby, 1973; Kemper, 1978; Leventhal, 1976; Mark and Folger, 1984; Martin and Murray, 1984; Weiner, 1982; Zillman, 1979).

References

Adams, J. Stacy. 1963. Toward an understanding of inequity. *Journal of Abnormal and Social Psychology* 67:422-436.

——. 1965. Inequity in social exchange. In Leonard Berkowitz (ed.), *Advances in Experimental Social Psychology*. New York: Academic Press.

Agnew, Robert. 1983. Social class and success goals: An examination of relative and absolute aspirations. *Sociological Quarterly* 24:435-452.

——. 1984. Goal achievement and delinquency. *Sociology and Social Research* 68:435-451.

——. 1985a. A revised strain theory of delinquency. *Social Forces* 64:151-167.

——. 1985b. Neutralizing the impact of crime. *Criminal Justice and Behavior* 12:221-239.

——. 1986. Challenging strain theory: An examination of goals and goal-blockage. Paper presented at the annual meeting of the American Society of Criminology, Atlanta.

——. 1989. A longitudinal test of the revised strain theory. *Journal of Quantitative Criminology* 5:373-387.

——. 1990. The origins of delinquent events: An examination of offender accounts. *Journal of Research in Crime and Delinquency* 27:267-294.

——. 1991a. Adolescent resources and delinquency. *Criminology* 28:535-566.

——. 1991b. Strain and subcultural crime theory. In Joseph Sheley (ed.), *Criminology: A Contemporary Handbook*. Belmont, Calif.: Wadsworth.

Agnew, Robert and Diane Jones. 1988. Adapting to deprivation: An examination of inflated educational expectations. *Sociological Quarterly* 29:315-337.

Aiken, Leona S. and Stephen G. West. 1991. *Multiple Regression: Testing and Interpreting Interactions*. Newbury Park, Calif.: Sage.

Akers, Ronald L. 1985. *Deviant Behavior: A Social Learning Approach*. Belmont, Calif.: Wadsworth.

Alves, Wayne M. and Peter H. Rossi. 1978. Who should get what? Fairness judgments of the distribution of earnings. *American Journal of Sociology* 84:541-564.

Alwin, Duane F. 1987. Distributive justice and satisfaction with material well-being. *American Sociological Review* 52:83-95.

Anderson, Elijah. 1978. *A Place on the Corner*. Chicago: University of Chicago Press.

Anderson, Craig A. and Dona C. Anderson. 1984. Ambient temperature and violent crime: Tests of the linear and curvilinear hypotheses. *Journal of Personality and Social Psychology* 46:91-97.

Austin, William. 1977. Equity theory and social comparison processes. In Jerry M. Suls and Richard L. Miller (eds.), *Social Comparison Processes*. New York: Hemisphere.

Averill, James R. 1982. *Anger and Aggression*. New York: Springer-Verlag.

Avison, William R. and R. Jay Turner. 1988. Stressful life events and depressive symptoms: Disaggregating the effects of acute stressors

and chronic strains. *Journal of Health and Social Behavior* 29: 253-264.
Bandura, Albert. 1973. *Aggression: A Social Learning Analysis*. Englewood Cliffs, N.J.: Prentice-Hall.
———. 1983. Psychological mechanisms of aggression. In Russell G. Geen and Edward Donnerstein (eds.), *Aggression: Theoretical and Empirical Reviews*. New York: Academic Press.
———. 1989. Human agency and social cognitive theory. *American Psychologist* 44:1175-1184.
Berger, Joseph, Morris Zelditch, Jr., Bo Anderson, and Bernard Cohen. 1972. Structural aspects of distributive justice: A status-value formulation. In Joseph Berger, Morris Zelditch, Jr., and Bo Anderson (eds.), *Sociological Theories in Progress*. New York: Houghton Mifflin.
Berger, Joseph. M. Hamit Fisck, Robert Z. Norman, and David G. Wagner. 1983. The formation of reward expectations in status situations. In David M. Messick and Karen S. Cook (eds.), *Equity Theory: Psychological and Sociological Perspectives*. New York: Praeger.
Berkowitz, Leonard. 1978. Whatever happened to the frustration-aggression hypothesis? *American Behavioral Scientist* 21:691-708.
———. 1982. Aversive conditions as stimuli to aggression. In Leonard Berkowitz (ed.), *Advances in Experimental Social Psychology*. Vol. 15. New York: Academic Press.
———. 1986. *A Survey of Social Psychology*. New York: Holt, Rinehart & Winston.
Bernard, Thomas J. 1984. Control criticisms of strain theories: An assessment of theoretical and empirical adequacy. *Journal of Research in Crime and Delinquency* 21:353-372.
———. 1987. Testing structural strain theories. *Journal of Research in Crime and Delinquency* 24:262-280.
———. 1990. Angry aggression among the "truly disadvantaged." *Criminology* 28:73-96.
Blau, Peter. 1964. *Exchange and Power in Social Life*. New York: John Wiley & Sons.
Brewin, Chris R. 1988. Explanation and adaptation in adversity. In Shirley Fisher and James Reason (eds.), *Handbook of Life Stress, Cognition and Health*. Chichester, England: John Wiley & Sons.
Brickman, Philip and Ronnie Janoff Bulman. 1977. Pleasure and pain in social comparison. In Jerry M. Suls and Richard L. Miller (eds.), *Social Comparison Processes*. New York: Hemisphere.
Clarke, Ronald V. and Derek B. Cornish. 1985. Modeling offenders' decisions: A framework for research and policy. In Michael Tonry and Norval Morris (eds.), *Crime and Justice: An Annual Review of Research*. Vol. 6. Chicago: University of Chicago Press.

Clinard, Marshall B. 1964. *Anomie and Deviant Behavior*. New York: Free Press.
Cloward, Richard A. and Lloyd E. Ohlin. 1960. *Delinquency and Opportunity*. New York: Free Press.
Cohen, Albert K. 1955. *Delinquent Boys*. New York: Free Press.
———. 1965. The sociology of the deviant act: Anomic theory and beyond. *American Sociological Review* 30:5-14.
Cohen, Ronald L. 1982. Perceiving justice: An attributional perspective. In Jerald Greenberg and Ronald L. Cohen (eds.), *Equity and Justice in Social Behavior*. New York: Academic Press.
Cole, Stephen. 1975. The growth of scientific knowledge: Theories of deviance as a case study. In Lewis A. Coser (ed.), *The Idea of Social Structure: Papers in Honor of Robert K. Merton*. New York: Harcourt Brace Jovanovich.
Compas, Bruce E. 1987. Coping with stress during childhood and adolescence. *Psychological Bulletin* 101:393-403.
Compas, Bruce E., Vanessa L. Malcarne, and Karen M. Fondacaro. 1988. Coping with stressful events in older children and young adolescents. *Journal of Consulting and Clinical Psychology* 56:405-411.
Compas, Bruce E. and Vicky Phares. 1991. Stress during childhood and adolescence: Sources of risk and vulnerability. In E. Mark Cummings, Anita L. Greene, and Katherine H. Kaffaker (eds.), *Life-Span Developmental Psychology: Perspectives on Stress and Coping*. Hillsdale, N.J.: Lawrence Erlbaum.
Cook, Karen S., and Karen A. Hegtvedt. 1983. Distributive justice, equity, and equality. *Annual Review of Sociology* 9:217-241.
———. 1991. Empirical evidence of the sense of justice. In Margaret Gruter, Roger D. Masters, Michael T. McGuire (eds.), *The Sense of Justice: An Inquiry into the Biological Foundations of Law*. New York: Greenwood Press.
Cook, Karen S. and David Messick. 1983. Psychological and sociological perspectives on distributive justice: Convergent, divergent, and parallel lines. In David M. Messick and Karen S. Cook (eds.), *Equity Theory: Psychological and Sociological Perspectives*. New York: Praeger.
Cook, Karen S. and Toshio Yamagishi. 1983. Social determinants of equity judgments: The problem of multidimensional input. In David M. Messick and Karen S. Cook (eds.), *Equity Theory: Psychological and Sociological Perspectives*. New York: Praeger.
Crittenden, Kathleen S. 1983. Sociological aspects of attribution. *Annual Review of Sociology* 9:425-446.
———. 1989. Causal attribution in sociocultural context: Toward a self-presentational theory

of attribution processes. *Sociological Quarterly* 30:1-14.

Crosby, Faye and A. Miren Gonzales-Intal. 1984. Relative deprivation and equity theories: Felt injustice and the undeserved benefits of others. In Robert Folger (ed.), *The Sense on Injustice: Social Psychological Perspectives*. New York: Plenum.

Cummings, E. Mark and Mona El-Sheikh. 1991. Children's coping with angry environments: A process-oriented approach. In E. Mark Cummings, Anita L. Greene, and Katherine H. Kaffaker (eds.), *Life-Span Developmental Psychology: Perspectives on Stress and Coping*. Hillsdale, N.J.: Lawrence Erlbaum.

Della Fave, L. Richard. 1974. Success values: Are they universal or class-differentiated? *American Journal of Sociology* 80:153-169.

———. 1980. The meek shall not inherit the earth: Self-evaluations and the legitimacy of stratification. *American Sociological Review* 45:955-971.

Della Fave, L. Richard and Patricia Klobus. 1976. Success values and the value stretch: A biracial comparison. *Sociological Quarterly* 17:491-502.

Deutsch, Morton. 1975. Equity, equality, and need: What determines which value will be used as the basis of distributive justice. *Journal of Social Issues* 31:137-149.

Dohrenwend, Bruce P. 1974. Problems in defining and sampling the relevant population of stressful life events. In Barbara Snell Dohrenwend and Bruce P. Dohrenwend (eds.), *Stressful Life Events: Their Nature and Effects*. New York: John Wiley & Sons.

Dohrenwend, Barbara Snell and Bruce P. Dohrenwend. 1974. Overview and prospects for research on stressful life events. In Barbara Snell Dohrenwend and Bruce P. Dohrenwend (eds.), *Stressful Life Events: Their Nature and Effects*. New York: John Wiley & Sons.

Donnerstein, Edward and Elaine Hatfield. 1982. Aggression and equity. In Jerald Greenberg and Ronald L. Cohen (eds.), *Equity and Justice in Social Behavior*. New York: Academic Press.

Edmunds, G. and D.C. Kendrick. 1980. *The Measurement of Human Aggressiveness*. New York: John Wiley & Sons.

Elliott, Delbert and Harwin Voss. 1974. *Delinquency and Dropout*. Lexington, Mass.: Lexington Books.

Elliott, Delbert, Suzanne Ageton, and Rachel Canter. 1979. An integrated theoretical perspective on delinquent behavior. *Journal of Research in Crime and Delinquency* 16:3-27.

Elliott, Delbert, David Huizinga, and Suzanne Ageton. 1985. *Explaining Delinquency and Drug Use*. Beverly Hills, Calif.: Sage.

Empey, LaMar. 1956. Social class and occupational aspiration: A comparison of absolute and relative measurement. *American Sociological Review* 21:703-709.

———. 1982. *American Delinquency: Its Meaning and Construction*. Homewood, Ill.: Dorsey.

Farnworth, Margaret and Michael J. Leiber. 1989. Strain theory revisited: Economic goals, educational means, and delinquency. *American Sociological Review* 54:263-274.

Faunce, William A. 1989. Occupational status-assignment systems: The effect of status on self-esteem. *American Journal of Sociology* 95:378-400.

Folger, Robert. 1984. Emerging issues in the social psychology of justice. In Robert Folger (ed.), *The Sense of Injustice: Social Psychological Perspectives*. New York: Plenum.

———. 1986. Rethinking equity theory: A referent cognitions model. In Hans Werner Bierhoff, Ronald L. Cohen, and Jerald Greenberg (eds.), *Justice in Social Relations*. New York: Plenum.

Folkman, Susan. 1991. Coping across the life-span: Theoretical issues. In E. Mark Cummings, Anita L. Greene, and Katherine H. Karraker (eds.), *Life-Span Developmental Psychology: Perspectives on Stress and Coping*. Hillsdale, N.J.: Lawrence Erlbaum.

Garrett, James and William L. Libby, Jr. 1973. Role of intentionality in mediating responses to inequity in the dyad. *Journal of Personality and Social Psychology* 28:21-27.

Gersten, Joanne C., Thomas S. Langer, Jeanne G. Eisenberg, and Lida Ozek. 1974. Child behavior and life events: Undesirable change or change per se. In Barbara Snell Dohrenwend and Bruce P. Dohrenwend (eds.), *Stressful Life Events: Their Nature and Effects*. New York: John Wiley & Sons.

Gersten, Joanne C., Thomas S. Langer, Jeanne G. Eisenberg, and Ora Smith-Fagon. 1977. An evaluation of the etiological role of stressful life-change events in psychological disorders. *Journal of Health and Social Behavior* 18:229-244.

Greenberg, David F. 1977. Delinquency and the age structure of society. *Contemporary Crises* 1:189-223.

Gruder, Charles L. 1977. Choice of comparison persons in evaluating oneself. In Jerry M. Suls and Richard L. Miller (eds.), *Social Comparison Processes*. New York: Hemisphere.

Hawkins, J. David and Denise M. Lishner. 1987. Schooling and delinquency. In Elmer H. Johnson (ed.). *Handbook on Crime and Delinquency Prevention*. New York: Greenwood.

Healy, William and Augusta F. Bonner. 1969. *New Light on Delinquency and Its Treatment*. New Haven, Conn.: Yale University Press.

Hegtvedt, Karen A. 1987. When rewards are scarce: Equal or equitable distributions. *Social Forces* 66:183-207.

———. 1990. The effects of relationship structure on emotional responses to inequity. *Social Psychology Quarterly* 53:214-228.

———. 1991a. Justice processes. In Martha Foschi and Edward J. Lawler (eds.), *Group Processes: Sociological Analyses*. Chicago: Nelson-Hall.

———. 1991b. Social comparison processes. In Edgar F. Borgotta and Marie E. Borgotta (eds.), *Encyclopedia of Sociology*. New York: Macmillan.

Hirschi, Travis. 1969. *Causes of Delinquency*. Berkeley: University of California Press.

———. 1979. Separate and unequal is better. *Journal of Research in Crime and Delinquency* 16:34-38.

Hirschi, Travis and Michael Gottfredson. 1986. The distinction between crime and criminality. In Timothy F. Hartnagel and Robert A. Silverman (eds.), *Critique and Explanation*. New Brunswick, N.J.: Transaction Books.

Hochschild, Jennifer L. 1981. *What's Fair: American Beliefs about Distributive Justice*. Cambridge, Mass.: Harvard University Press.

Homans, George C. 1961. *Social Behavior: Its Elementary Forms*. New York: Harcourt, Brace and World.

House, James S. 1981. *Work Stress and Social Support*. Reading, Mass.: Addison-Wesley.

Hyman, Herbert. 1953. The value systems of the different classes: A social-psychological contribution to the analysis of stratification. In Reinhard Bendix and Seymour Martin Lipset (eds.), *Class, Status, and Power*. New York: Free Press.

Jasso, Guillermina. 1980. A new theory of distributive justice. *American Sociological Review* 45:3-32.

Jasso, Guillermina and Peter H. Rossi. 1977. Distributive justice and earned income. *American Sociological Review* 42:639-651.

Jensen, Gary. 1986. Disintegrating integrated theory: A critical analysis of attempts to save strain theory. Paper presented at the annual meeting of the American Society of Criminology, Atlanta.

Johnson, Richard E. 1979. *Juvenile Delinquency and Its Origins*. London: Cambridge University Press.

Kaplan, Howard B. 1980. *Deviant Behavior in Defense of Self*. New York: Academic Press.

Kaplan, Howard B., Cynthia Robbins, and Steven S. Martin. 1983. Toward the testing of a general theory of deviant behavior in longitudinal perspective: Patterns of psychopathology. In James R. Greenley and Roberta G. Simmons (eds.), *Research in Community and Mental Health*. Greenwich, Conn.: Jai Press.

Kemper, Theodore D. 1978. *A Social Interactional Theory of Emotions*. New York: John Wiley & Sons.

Kluegel, James R. and Eliot R. Smith. 1986. *Beliefs about Inequality*. New York: Aldine De Gruyter.

Kornhauser, Ruth Rosner. 1978. *Social Sources of Delinquency*. Chicago: University of Chicago Press.

Labouvie, Erich W. 1986a. Alcohol and marijuana use in relation to adolescent stress. *International Journal of the Addictions* 21:333-345.

———. 1986b. The coping function of adolescent alcohol and drug use. In Rainer K. Silbereisen, Klaus Eyfeth and Georg Rudinger (eds.), *Development as Action in Context*. New York: Springer.

Lauritsen, Janet L., Robert J. Sampson, and John Laub. 1991. The link between offending and victimization among adolescents. *Criminology* 29:265-292.

Lerner, Melvin J. 1977. The justice motive: Some hypotheses as to its origins and forms. *Journal of Personality* 45:1-52.

Leventhal, Gerald S. 1976. The distribution of rewards and resources in groups and organizations. In Leonard Berkowitz and Elaine Walster (eds.), *Advances in Experimental Social Psychology: Equity Theory: Toward a General Theory of Social Interaction*. New York: Academic Press.

Leventhal, Gerald S., Jurgis Karuzajr, and William Rick Fry. 1980. Beyond fairness: A theory of allocation preferences. In Gerald Mikula (ed.), *Justice and Social Interaction*. New York: Springer-Verlag.

Lind, E. Allan and Tom R. Tyler. 1988. *The Social Psychology of Procedural Justice*. New York: Plenum.

Linsky, Arnold S. and Murray A. Straus. 1986. *Social Stress in the United States*. Dover, Mass.: Auburn House.

Liska, Allen E. 1987. *Perspectives on Deviance*. Englewood Cliffs, N.J.: Prentice-Hall.

McClelland, Katherine. 1990. The social management of ambition. *Sociological Quarterly* 31:225-251.

MacLeod, Jay. 1987. *Ain't No Makin' It*. Boulder, Colo.: Westview Press.

Mark, Melvin M. and Robert Folger. 1984. Responses to relative deprivation: A conceptual framework. In Philip Shaver (ed.), *Review of Personality and Social Psychology*. Vol. 5. Beverly Hills, Calif.: Sage.

Martin, Joanne. 1986. When expectations and justice do not coincide: Blue collar visions of a just world. In Hans Werner Bierhoff, Ronald L. Cohen, and Jerald Greenberg (eds.), *Justice in Social Relations*. New York: Plenum.

Martin, Joanne and Alan Murray. 1983. Distributive injustice and unfair exchange. In David M. Messick and Karen S. Cook (eds.), *Equity Theory: Psychological and Social Perspectives*. New York: Praeger.

———. 1984. Catalysts for collective violence: The importance of a psychological approach. In Robert Folger (ed.), *The Sense of Injustice: Social Psychological Perspectives*. New York: Plenum.

Massey, James L. and Marvin Krohn. 1986. A longitudinal examination of an integrated social process model of deviant behavior. *Social Forces* 65:106-134.

Mawson, Anthony R. 1987. *Criminality: A Model of Stress-Induced Crime*. New York: Praeger.

Menaghan, Elizabeth. 1982. Measuring coping effectiveness: A panel analysis of marital problems and coping efforts. *Journal of Health and Social Behavior* 23:220-234.

———. 1983. Individual coping efforts: Moderators of the relationship between life stress and mental health outcomes. In Howard B. Kaplan (ed.), *Psychosocial Stress: Trends in Theory and Research*. New York: Academic Press.

Merton, Robert. 1938. Social structure and anomie. *American Sociological Review* 3:672-682.

Messick, David M. and Keith Sentis. 1979. Fairness and preference. *Journal of Experimental Social Psychology* 15:418-434.

———. 1983. Fairness, preference, and fairness biases. In David M. Messick and Karen S. Cook (eds.), *Equity Theory: Psychological and Sociological Perspectives*. New York: Praeger.

Michael, Jack. 1973. Positive and negative reinforcement, a distinction that is no longer necessary; or a better way to talk about bad things. In Eugene Ramp and George Semb (eds.). *Behavior Analysis: Areas of Research and Application*. Englewood Cliffs, N.J.: Prentice-Hall.

Mickelson, Roslyn Arlin. 1990. The attitude-achievement paradox among black adolescents. *Sociology of Education* 63:44-61.

Mikula, Gerold. 1980. *Justice and Social Interaction*. New York: Springer-Verlag.

———. 1986. The experience of injustice: Toward a better understanding of its phenomenology. In Hans Werner Bierhoff, Ronald L. Cohen, and Jerald Greenberg (eds.), *Justice in Social Relations*. New York: Plenum.

Mirowsky, John and Catherine E. Ross. 1990. The consolation-prize theory of alienation. *American Journal of Sociology* 95:1505-1535.

Morgan, Rick L. and David Heise. 1988. Structure of emotions. *Social Psychology Quarterly* 51:19-31.

Mueller, Charles W. 1983. Environmental stressors and aggressive behavior. In Russell G. Geen and Edward I. Donnerstein (eds.), *Aggression: Theoretical and Empirical Reviews*. Vol. 2. New York: Academic Press.

Newcomb, Michael D. and L.L. Harlow. 1986. Life events and substance use among adolescents: Mediating effects of perceived loss of control and meaninglessness in life. *Journal of Personality and Social Psychology* 51:564-577.

Novy, Diane M. and Stephen Donohue. 1985. The relationship between adolescent life stress events and delinquent conduct including conduct indicating a need for supervision. *Adolescence* 78:313-321.

Pearlin, Leonard I. 1982. The social contexts of stress. In Leo Goldberger and Shlomo Breznitz (eds.), *Handbook of Stress*. New York: Free Press.

———. 1983. Role strains and personal stress. In Howard Kaplan (ed.), *Psychosocial Stress: Trends in Theory and Research*. New York: Academic Press.

Pearlin, Leonard I. and Carmi Schooler. 1978. The structure of coping. *Journal of Health and Social Behavior* 19:2-21.

Pearlin, Leonard I. and Morton A. Lieberman. 1979. Social sources of emotional distress. In Roberta G. Simmons (ed.), *Research in Community and Mental Health*. Vol. 1. Greenwich, Conn.: Jai Press.

Pearlin, Leonard I., Elizabeth G. Menaghan, Morton A. Lieberman, and Joseph T. Mullan. 1981. The stress process. *Journal of Health and Social Behavior* 22:337-356.

Quicker, John. 1974. The effect of goal discrepancy on delinquency. *Social Problems* 22:76-86.

Rivera, Beverly and Cathy Spatz Widom. 1990. Childhood victimization and violent offending. *Violence and Victims* 5:19-35.

Rosenberg, Morris. 1979. *Conceiving the Self*. New York: Basic.

1990. Reflexivity and emotions. *Social Psychology Quarterly* 53:3-12.

Ross, Michael, John Thibaut, and Scott Evenback. 1971. Some determinants of the intensity of social protest. *Journal of Experimental Social Psychology* 7:401-418.

Schwinger, Thomas. 1980. Just allocations of goods: Decisions among three principles. In Gerald Mikula (ed.), *Justice and Social Interaction*. New York: Springer-Verlag.

Shepelak, Norma J. 1987. The role of self-explanations and self-evaluations in legitimating inequality. *American Sociological Review* 52:495-503.

Shepelak, Norma J. and Duane Alwin. 1986. Beliefs about inequality and perceptions of distributive justice. *American Sociological Review* 51:30-46.

Short, James F. and Fred L. Strodtbeck. 1965. *Group Process and Gang Delinquency*. Chicago: University of Chicago Press.

Slaby, Ronald G. and Nancy G. Guerra. 1988. Cognitive mediators of aggression in adolescent offenders: 1. *Developmental Psychology* 24:580-588.

Sprecher, Susan. 1986. The relationship between inequity and emotions in close relationships. *Social Psychology Quarterly* 49:309-321.

Stephenson, G.M. and J.H. White. 1968. An experimental study of some effects of injustice on children's moral behavior. *Journal of Experimental Social Psychology* 4:460-469.

Straus, Murray. 1991. Discipline and deviance: Physical punishment of children and violence and other crimes in adulthood. *Social Problems* 38:133-154.

Sullivan, Mercer L. 1989. *Getting Paid*. Ithaca, N.Y.: Cornell University Press.

Suls, Jerry M. 1977. Social comparison theory and research: An overview from 1954. In Jerry M. Suls and Richard L. Miller (eds.), *Social Comparison Processes*. New York: Hemisphere.

Suls, Jerry M. and Thomas Ashby Wills. 1991. *Social Comparison: Contemporary Theory and Research*. Hillsdale, N.J.: Lawrence Erlbaum.

Tavris, Carol. 1984. On the wisdom of counting to ten. In Philip Shaver (ed.), *Review of Personality and Social Psychology: 5*. Beverly Hills, Calif.: Sage.

Thibaut, John W. and Harold H. Kelley. 1959. *The Social Psychology of Groups*. New York: John Wiley & Sons.

Thoits, Peggy. 1983. Dimensions of life events that influence psychological distress: An evaluation and synthesis of the literature. In Howard B. Kaplan (ed.), *Psychosocial Stress: Trends in Theory and Research*. New York: Academic Press.

———. 1984. Coping, social support, and psychological outcomes: The central role of emotion. In Philip Shaver (ed.), *Review of Personality and Social Psychology: 5*. Beverly Hills, Calif.: Sage.

———. 1989. The sociology of emotions. In W. Richard Scott and Judith Blake (eds.), *Annual Review of Sociology*. Vol. 15. Palo Alto, Calif: Annual Reviews.

———. 1990. Emotional deviance research. In Theodore D. Kemper (ed.), *Research Agendas in the Sociology of Emotions*. Albany: State University of New York Press.

———. 1991a. On merging identity theory and stress research. *Social Psychology Quarterly* 54:101-112.

———. 1991b. Patterns of coping with controllable and uncontrollable events. In E. Mark Cummings, Anita L. Greene, and Katherine H. Karraker (eds.), *Life-Span Developmental Psychology: Perspectives on Stress and Coping*. Hillsdale, N.J.: Lawrence Erlbaum.

Thornberry, Terence P. 1987. Toward an Interactional Theory of Delinquency. *Criminology* 25:863-891.

Tonry, Michael, Lloyd E. Ohlin, and David P. Farrington. 1991. *Human Development and Criminal Behavior*. New York: Springer-Verlag.

Tornblum, Kjell Y. 1977. Distributive justice: Typology and propositions. *Human Relations* 30:1-24.

Utne, Mary Kristine and Robert Kidd. 1980. Equity and attribution. In Gerald Mikula (ed.), *Justice and Social Interaction*. New York: Springer-Verlag.

Van Houten, Ron. 1983. Punishment: From the animal laboratory to the applied setting. In Saul Axelrod and Jack Apsche (eds.), *The Effects of Punishment on Human Behavior*. New York: Academic Press.

Vaux, Alan. 1988. *Social support: Theory, Research, and Intervention*. New York: Praeger.

Vaux, Alan and Mary Ruggiero. 1983. Stressful life change and delinquent behavior. *American Journal of Community Psychology* 11:169-183.

Walster, Elaine, Ellen Berscheid, and G. William Walster. 1973. New directions in equity research. *Journal of Personality and Social Psychology* 25:151-176.

Walster, Elaine, G. William Walster, and Ellen Berscheid. 1978. *Equity: Theory and Research*. Boston: Allyn & Bacon.

Wang, Alvin Y. and R. Stephen Richarde. 1988. Global versus task-specific measures of self-efficacy. *Psychological Record* 38:533-541.

Weiner, Bernard. 1982. The emotional consequences of causal attributions. In Margaret S. Clark and Susan T. Fiske (eds.), *Affect and Cognition: The Seventeenth Annual Carnegie Symposium on Cognition*. Hillsdale, N.J.: Lawrence Erlbaum.

Williams, Carolyn L. and Craige Uchiyama. 1989. Assessment of life events during adolescence: The use of self-report inventories. *Adolescence* 24:95-118.

Wylie, Ruth. 1979. *The Self-Concept*. Vol. 2. Lincoln: University of Nebraska Press.

Zillman, Dolf. 1979. *Hostility and Aggression*. Hillsdale, N.J.: Lawrence Erlbaum. ✦

19
Parents and Drugs: Specifying the Consequences of Attachment

Gary F. Jensen
David Brownfield

One of the most startling and controversial claims in Hirschi's *Causes of Delinquency* (1969:152) was that "we honor those we admire not by imitation, but by adherence to conventional standards." This statement was not limited to admiration of "conventional" or "nondeviant" others, but instead referred specifically to the consequences of attachment to peers *regardless* of their deviant status. In support of this claim, Hirschi (1969:152) noted that "holding delinquency . . . of friends truly constant at any level, the more one respects or admires one's friends, the less likely one is to commit delinquent acts." Thus, the stronger the social bond, the less the delinquency *regardless* of the object of that attachment! This claim reflects a central property of Hirschi's brand of social control theory—a property that has been glossed over in attempts to replicate the study and in attempts to synthesize social control theory and social learning theory (see Conger, 1977).

Hirschi based his theory on the Durkheimian notion that solidarity facilitates conformity to widely shared societal values. He specifically argued that social control theory assumes there is value consensus in the social system under study, in the sense that no distinct strata or differentiated categories of people sharing values that condone or call for crime exist. Thus, those youths who care most about their friends will tend to be those who conform to the law even if their friends are doing otherwise.[1]

Statements by Conger (1976) and Hindelang (1973) to the effect that Hirschi's theory does not take type of friends into account are wrong. Hirschi argues that the deviance of friends makes no difference on the impact of attachment. This is a crucial statement, being one of the few claims that is incontrovertibly inconsistent with cultural deviance, differential association, and social learning theories. In these latter theories attachment to deviant peers constitutes a causal source of involvement in deviance, while in Hirschi's control theory attachment to deviant peers is a barrier to delinquency.

Several people have tried to replicate Hirschi's finding concerning attachment to deviant peers and have obtained different results. Bonds to delinquent others have not been found to inhibit delinquency as Hirschi advocated; however, neither has anyone demonstrated that the strength of bonds to delinquent others significantly enhances the probability of delinquency over and beyond the impact of associating with delinquent peers per se. Hirschi reported a weak but significant negative association between strength of identification with friends and delinquency, while Hindelang reports a weak and statistically insignificant positive association. Another study (Jensen and Erickson, 1978) reports that peer commitment is associated significantly and positively with delinquency only if it is measured using hypothetical choices reflecting the strength of other bonds (e.g., to parents, school, and the law). Measures of absolute commitment to or identification with peers were unrelated to delinquency.

While Hirschi's claim concerning the effect of bonds to peers is in marked contrast to several other theories, his view of the effect of bonds to parents is less controversial. He argues that a "Fagin" pattern of socialization is quite rare and that attachment to parents is justifiably conceived as an attachment to "conventional" others who discourage delinquency. The assumption of value consensus is crucial to this claim, in that at-

From *Criminology*, Volume 21, Number 4 (1983), pp. 543-554. Copyright © 1983 by the American Society of Criminology. Reprinted by permission.

tachment to parents representing a crime-prone *subculture* could facilitate rather than inhibit delinquency. But if consensus on the impropriety of lawbreaking is assumed, or if status-linked subcultures do not exist, then attachment to parents should inhibit delinquency in all socially differentiated categories of youth.

Several other theorists and researchers argue that parental culture emphasizes conventional conduct and disapproves of deviance as well. For example, Johnson (1973:6) attributes drug use to exposure to peer and drug subcultures and argues that parents espouse more traditional attitudes:

> Despite diversity in the adult population, it is probable that the vast majority of middle—and perhaps lower—class adults would agree with the following expectations. The parent culture thinks that high school and college students should try to go on to the next higher educational level; do well in school; attend classes; respect teachers, authorities and laws: abstain from sex before marriage; avoid tobacco, alcohol, and the nonmedical use of drugs; avoid involvement in crime and violent behavior; attend religious services; and respect the property of others.

If parents are conventional, then attachment to parents should be associated with quite conventional commitments, involvements, and beliefs and should act as a general barrier to deviance.

What if parents themselves engage in behavior that is illegal for their children (e.g., alcohol use and smoking) or for children and adults as well (e.g., the use of illicit drugs)? Hirschi's Durkheimian version of social control theory leads to the hypothesis that attachment to parents should act as a barrier to deviance *regardless* of the behavior of parents. While this argument has been challenged with regard to the influence of bonds to deviant peers, its applicability to relationships with parents has not been assessed.

Although contradictory positions about the impact of bonds to deviant peers can be derived from differential association—social learning theory as compared to social control theory, it is not clear whether similarly contrasting hypotheses can be derived when considering categories of parents. From a social learning perspective (Akers et al., 1979:635-655), drug use is a product of differential reinforcement, definitional learning, differential association, and imitation. For youths whose parents are "straight," all of these forces should operate to support law-abiding conduct and inhibit drug use. For drug-using parents, however, social learning theory does not lead to any *single* prediction about either the influence of such parents or the consequences of attachment to such parents.

The theory yields no single prediction for the simple reason that it makes no claims (in advance of analysis) about the relative importance of such processes or about their uniformity. For example, youths may be inclined to imitate or model their parents, but if their parents disapprove of such behavior, then attachment to such parents may inhibit the activity. On the other hand, if parents present conflicting messages, imitation effects may be neutralized by definitional learning or differential reinforcement. Under such circumstances, variable attachment to parents might make no difference to a child's drug use. Finally, if all learning processes consistently facilitate drug use, then the greater the attachment to drug-using parents, the greater the probability of use by their children.

Since Hirschi is specific on the issue, it is possible to specify in advance the findings that would challenge his theory. If attachment to straight or drug-using parents inhibits drug use in children, then his theory is strengthened. If it fails in either or both categories, then something is wrong with the theory. In contrast, social learning theory cannot be falsified in its present form because its advocates advance no claims concerning inconsistency in learning mechanisms. No matter what the findings, social learning theorists can claim to explain them *after the fact*.

Social learning theory does *allow for* possibilities that are not encompassed by Hirschi's brand of control theory, however. Derivation of specific hypotheses that contradict social control theory, though, requires that social learning theorists take positions on some preliminary issues. For example, if (1) drug-using parents tend to reinforce drug use and present definitions favorable to such use and/or (2) imitation effects are more powerful than any conflicting learning processes, then *attachment to drug-using parents should facilitate children's drug use.* If, however, (3) drug-using parents disapprove of children's use and (4) imitation effects are not more powerful than other learning processes, then *attachment to drug-using parents should make no difference for their children's drug use.*

This study attempts a test of these hypotheses for one particular form of illegal activity among American youth—illicit drug use. Specifically, we will test the following hypotheses concerning the effect of attachment to drug-using versus straight parents:

H1: Attachment to both straight and drug-using parents acts as a barrier to their children's drug use (social control theory).

H2: Attachment to straight parents acts as a barrier to their children's drug use, whereas attachment to drug-using parents facilitates their children's drug use (social learning theory with assumptions 1 and/or 2).

H3: Attachment to straight parents acts as a barrier to their children's drug use, whereas attachments to drug-using parents makes no difference for their children's drug use (social learning theory with assumptions 3 and 4).

It is essential at this point to recognize that the issue is not merely the similarity in behavior of parents and children. Ample evidence of a "generational continuity" (Goode, 1972) to drug use exists; that is, parents who use drugs are more likely than parents who abstain to have children who use drugs. This study is concerned with the consequences of the *social bond* between parents and children when the drug activity of parents is taken into account. Hence, the focus is on the further empirical specification of the consequences of attachment.[2]

Study Design

These hypotheses will be examined using survey data collected from students at one high school in Tucson, Arizona in 1977. The metropolitan area of Tucson has a population of about 450,000 and one of the highest crime rates among cities in the United States.

Several influential parents believed that the school studied had a particularly serious drug problem, and the student body was actually under secret surveillance by the police for a period of time. A student organization at the school received permission from the superintendent of the district to conduct a survey under the direction of University of Arizona faculty in order to assess the opinions, perceptions, and reported behavior of the student body regarding drug use.

A questionnaire was administered to students in a stratified random sample of half the classes meeting during a given period. The questionnaires were anonymous and steps were taken to assure students of that fact. Data were obtained from 550 students, or about half the students at the school. The sample consists of both male and female students—primarily white—from families of above-average income. All grades, freshman through senior, are proportionately represented.

High school surveys have been severely restricted in the questions they could present, and only rarely have these included questions about parental deviance. We were allowed to present students with one very limited request for information about parental drug use. They were asked to "circle all of those drugs you think your parents have used," including tobacco (pipe, cigarettes, etc.), alcohol (beer, wine, liquor), marijuana (grass), hard narcotics (like heroin), pep pills, psychedelic drugs such as cocaine ("coke"), tranquilizers, and sleeping pills. The same question was asked about their closest friends. In earlier sections of the questionnaire students were asked how many times in the last twelve months they had used each of these drugs as well.

The students were also presented with statements that have been used in previous research (see Hirschi, 1969; Hindelang, 1973) as measures of attachment to parents, including, "I feel very close to my mother" (CLOSEMA), "I feel very close to my father" (CLOSEPA), "I enjoy doing things with my parents" (ENJOYPAR), "I don't get along with my mother" (ALONGMA), "I don't get along with my father" (ALONGPA).[3]

There are obvious limitations to the measure of parental drug use, in that we could not (1) differentiate between mothers and fathers, (2) ask about extent of use, or (3) identify a specific time period for use. These limitations can affect the interpretation of findings, in that four of the measures of attachment differentiate between mother and father. Moreover, attachment to parents who repeatedly and currently use drugs may not have the same effects as attachment to parents who have tried a drug only once. These limitations will have to be considered in assessing the results and in proposing more extensive, definitive tests.

Findings

We carried out several types of analysis to assess the relationship between attachment and self-reported drug use for children of drug-using and children of abstaining (or straight) parents. In Table 1 we have summarized the correlations between five measures of attachment and the number of types of drugs used by all children. The most striking finding is that every measure of attachment is related significantly and negatively to student drug use among children of straight parents, with correlations ranging between -.25 and -.41. At the other end of the continuum there is not a single significant relationship between attachment and student drug use among children whose parents have used at least five types of drugs. In fact, two of five correlations in that category are positive. There are only four other significant correlations in the entire table, and in every instance the relationship is weaker than among children of straight parents. The strongest associations between attachment and student drug use are found among children of straight parents. The average correlation in that category is -.32 as compared to between -.06 among children of parents with the highest drug use score and -.15 among parents with a score of one.

Table 1
Score by Parental Drug Use Score

Attachment Measures:	Parental Use					
	0	1	2	3	4	5
CLOSEMA	-.25[a]	-.07	-.10	-.04	-.02	-.15
CLOSEPA	-.41[a]	-.16	-.09	-.02	-.20[a]	-.04
ENJOYPAR	-.41[a]	-.14	-.23[a]	-.22[a]	-.22[a]	-.24
ALONGMA	-.26[a]	-.14	-.10	-.10	-.04	+.01
ALONGPA	-.26[a]	-.24	-.06	-.10	-.11	+.11
N	54-56	59-60	188-191	101-104	84-85	48-49

Note: The scores were created by summing perceived parental use and self-reported use of different types of drugs.
a. Significant at the .05 level.

Note that 28 of 30 correlations are negative and that all of the significant correlations are negative. Thus, the direction of the relation ships is consistent with social control theory (Hypothesis 1) in all but two instances. No significant correlations are consistent with Hypothesis 2, and the signs of only two correlations are consistent with that hypothesis. However, the date are quite compatible with Hypothesis 3. Attachment to straight parents is a significant barrier to student drug use *for every measure of attachment*, whereas only 4 of 25 correlations are significant among children whose parents use drugs. Moreover, no significant relationships exist among children of parents with the highest drug use score.[4]

In Table 2 we have summarized the correlations between the five measures of attachment and the two specific forms of drug use—drinking and marijuana use—that were studied by Akers and his colleagues in testing social learning theory. The findings are quite comparable to our results when using a total drug use score. Attachment constitutes a significant barrier to drunkenness among children whose parents abstain from alcohol, but it is not related significantly among children whose parents have used alcohol. Similarly, attachment to parents who have used marijuana (according to their children's reports) is not a significant correlate of children's marijuana use, while attachment to straight parents constitutes a significant barrier in every instance. Four positive relationships exist among children of drug-using parents, but none of them is statistically significant.[5]

Table 2
Simple Correlations Among Measures of Attachment, Marijuana Use, and Drunkenness by Parental Alcohol and Marijuana Use

Parental Use	Alcohol Use		Marijuana Use	
	No	Yes	No	Yes
CLOSEMA	$-.28^a$	$-.04$	$-.12^a$	$-.03$
CLOSEPA	$-.28^a$	$-.06$	$-.16^a$	$+.01$
ENJOYPAR	$-.28^a$	$-.07$	$-.18^a$	$-.09$
ALONGMA	$-.36^a$	$+.05$	$-.09^a$	$+.04$
ALONGPA	$-.24^a$	$-.03$	$-.17^a$	$+.01$
N	80	434	450	63

a. Significant at the .05 level.

Since some of the parents who are categorized as straight for one type of drug may have used others, we also classified parents as "totally straight" (no drug use at all), "conventional users" (drinking, smoking, sleeping pills), and illicit users (marijuana, cocaine, narcotics). In Table 3 we have summarized the relationship between attachment and drunkenness and marijuana use for these three categories of parents. Again, the data suggest that children's perception of parent's behavior is related significantly to children's drug use. Among children of straight parents, *all* relationships are negative and significant. Among children of legal or "conventional" users, six of ten relationships are significant and negative. In contrast, among children of illicit users no single significant relationship exists. Moreover, for children of illicit users the signs are positive in every instance for drunkenness and two of five relationships are positive for marijuana use.

Table 3
Simple Correlations Among Measures of Attachment, Drunkenness, and Marijuana Use by Parental Drug Use Category

Parental Drug Use Category	Straight		Conventional		Illicit	
	Drunk	Marijuana	Drunk	Marijuana	Drunk	Marijuana
CLOSEMA	$-.30^a$	$-.21^a$	$-.06$	$-.12^a$	$+.13$	$-.03$
CLOSEPA	$-.30^a$	$-.37^a$	$-.07$	$-.14^a$	$+.06$	$-.01$
ENJOYPAR	$-.28^a$	$-.35^a$	$-.10^a$	$-.17^a$	$+.16$	$-.11$
ALONGMA	$-.37^a$	$-.24^a$	$+.04$	$-.08^a$	$+.14$	$+.04$
ALONGPA	$-.24^a$	$-.25^a$	$-.04$	$-.16^a$	$+.05$	$+.06$
N	56	56	389	389	69	69

a. Significant at the .05 level.

The pattern of relationships in Table 3 is striking. In all ten instances (two offenses x five measures of attachment) the relationships are ordered from significantly negative among children of straight parents to insignificantly positive or negative among children of illicit users. Although none of the positive relationships is significant, in seven of ten instances the relationships reverse.

In addition to the analysis of self-reported behavior, we also examined the impact of measures of attachment on responses to questions asking if it would be "wrong" to (1) get really drunk, (2) use marijuana, or (3) use a drug like heroin or cocaine. This analysis was carried out controlling for parental alcohol use and parental marijuana use.

The most striking finding was the variation in relationships when comparing children who report parental marijuana use with those who do not think their parents have used marijuana. Among the children of straight parents, attachment was related positively in their evaluations of marijuana use, drunkenness, and the use of more serious drugs as wrong in every instance. Of 15 chi-square statistics, 12 were significant at the .05 level. In contrast, among children of users, the overall direction of the relationships (based on gamma coefficients) was actually negative in 12 of 15 instances; that is, the greater the attachment, the less likely children of users are to define drug use as wrong. However, none of the negative relationships was significant.[6] Comparing children who reported parental alcohol use with children of straight parents did not lead to such consistent reversals, and relationships between attachment and evaluations of drug use were equally likely to be significant in either category.

Summary

This analysis supports several conclusions. First, Hypothesis 1, derived from Hirschi's version of social control theory, can be rejected. The relevance of attachment to children's drug use does depend on the perceived drug use of parents. While attachment to straight parents constitutes a statistically significant barrier to drug use, attachment to drug-using parents rarely enters into significant relationships with children's drug use. However, since only a small proportion of parents are perceived as having used illegal drugs, the relationship between attachment and children's drug use when studying an undifferentiated population is likely to be negative. However, the significance and possibly even the direction of the relationship is affected when parents are differentiated on the basis of perceived use.

If we focus on the statistical significance of individual correlations, then the data are more consistent with Hypothesis 3 than with Hypothesis 2. Attachment to straight parents enters into statistically significant negative relationships with children's drug use, but attachment to drug-using parents is unlikely to enter into statistically significant relationships with children's use. The overall *pattern* of relationships, however, suggests that Hypothesis 2 deserves further consideration. Relationships tend to reverse depending on parental drug use, even though none of the positive correlations is statistically significant. Given the crude measures of the prevalence of parental drug use ("ever" versus "never") and the lack of specific information on mothers' or fathers' use, it may have been difficult for significant reversals to emerge. More precise measures of parental behavior might greatly strengthen any positive relationships.

Theoretical Implications

While these findings have rather obvious implications for Hirschi's brand of social control theory, they are potentially relevant to explaining disparate research findings over time and in different samples. If the activities, values, and beliefs of parents change over time, the consequences of attachment to parents should change over time as well. An interesting hypothesis for future study is that the deviance-inhibiting impact of attachment to parents will be weaker as the rate of past and present deviance by parents increases. It is quite possible that bonds to parents could come to generate behavior that was condemned in previous generations. Similarly, studies of parent-child relationships and delinquency are likely to yield weaker relationships in samples with a large rather than small proportion of deviant parents.

The data also suggest an explanation for the survival and persistence of competing theories of delinquency. Hirschi's hypothesis about the impact of attachment to deviant others can be rejected, but if most parents in a sample are straight, then attachment to parents is likely to act as a barrier to delinquency and drug use in the sample as a whole. However, there may be subcategories within a given sample in which a version of differential association-social learning theory may apply. For example, parents who use marijuana or more serious illicit drugs openly may constitute a small subculture such that positive relationships with them may facilitate rather than inhibit illicit drug use. Johnson (1973:6) may be correct in stating that "the vast majority" of adults feel their children should avoid illegal activity, but such an assertion does not eliminate the possibility of subcultures where normal social learning can lead to behavior in conflict with the law.

Whatever the explanation of the variable consequences of attachment, this study certainly justifies further research on the role of parents in facilitating as well as inhibiting various forms of juvenile delinquency. The behavior and definitions of parents are relevant to specifying the consequences of attachment. Such specification is crucial to identifying the circumstances under which alternative theories of delinquency make sense of complex human behavior.

Notes

1. Hirschi notes that the importance of bonds to different objects is a matter for the *empirical* specification of social control theory. He does not propose in advance of analysis that attachment to deviant peers will be a barrier to deviance but, rather, introduces that argument as a generalization for his findings. However, it is one of the most crucial findings in his study, since it is one of the areas where his version of control theory clearly contradicts cultural deviance as well as so-called commonsense theory.
2. There is some controversy over the importance of imitation as a learning mechanism (see Akers et al., 1979) and on the impact of parental behavior (Kandel, 1974). Using a measure of parental use as reported by parents, Kandel reports that parental drug use has no direct impact on children's drug use. Since children may not be aware of their parents' actual use, *perceived parental use* was used in this study. Kandel argues that this type of measure can be affected by the child's behavior and, hence, could yield misleading correlations. If we were to use actual parental behavior as the measure, however, we could generate misleadingly low correlations as well. We were allowed to gather data on *perceived* parental use. Our analysis indicates that both perceived parental use and perceived friends' use have independent effects on children's drug use.
3. For the sake of consistency we ordered all measures of attachment so that a negative relationship always means the *greater* the attachment, the *less* the drug use. Thus, responses to the two negatively stated items ("I don't get along . . .") were reversed to yield more readily interpreted coefficients.
4. We also carried out a multiple regression analysis in which attachment, parental drug use, and the interaction between the two were examined in relation to student drug use. Measures of attachment were related negatively to drug use and parental use was related positively. There were no instances of significant interaction effects. Although they were not significantly different, the most prominent negative slopes were among children of totally straight parents for four of five measures of attachment.
5. We also carried out an analysis comparing the fit of alternative models to the observed frequencies in multiway contingency tables (see Goodman, 1972a, 1972b, 1973). Parental drug use increased the odds of children's drug use in every instance. Attachment decreased the odds of drunkenness for three of the five measures and attachment decreased the odds of marijuana use in all five instances. It was not necessary to include interaction in the preferred models, although there was a tendency toward more prominent negative associations among children with straight parents.
6. A comparison of hierarchical models supported Hirschi's hypothesis in eleven of fifteen instances. There were two instances where attachment did not affect evaluations (alcohol as wrong by getting along with father and heroin-cocaine as wrong by feeling close to mother). There were two instances of three-way interaction, but analysis of those tables suggests that such apparent interaction was a product of small cell sizes. When collapsed into positive versus negative answers there was no significant interaction. Thus, as has been the case throughout the analysis, the difference in relationships is not of sufficient magnitude to generate significant interaction effects. Nevertheless, such interaction does continue to be suggested by the persistence of variations within categories of parental use.

References

Akers, R. L., M.D. Krohn, L. Lanza-Kaduce, and M. Radosevich. 1979. "Social learning and deviant behavior: a specific test of a general theory." *Amer. Soc. Rev.* 44 (August): 636-655.

Conger, R. D. 1977. "Rejoinder." *Criminology* 15 (May): 117-126.

———. 1976. "Social control and social learning models of delinquent behavior." *Criminology* 14 (May): 17-40.

Goode, E. 1972. *Drugs in American Society*. New York: Knopf.

Goodman, L. A. (1973) "Causal analysis of data from panel studies and other kinds of surveys." *Amer. J. of Sociology* 78 (March): 1135-1191.

———. 1972a. "A modified multiple regression approach to the analysis of dichotomous variables." *Amer. Soc. Rev.* 37 (February): 28-46.

———. 1972b. "A general model for the analysis of surveys." *Amer.J. of Sociology* 77 (May): 1035-1086.

Hindelang, M. J. 1973. "Causes of delinquency: a partial replication and extension." *Social Problems* 20 (Spring): 471-487.

Hirschi, T. 1969. *Causes of Delinquency*. Berkeley: Univ. of California Press.

Jensen, G. F. and M. L. Erickson. 1978. "Peer commitment and delinquent conduct." Unpublished manuscript.

Johnson, B. D. 1973. *Marijuana Users and Drug Subcultures*. New York: John Wiley.

Kandel, D. 1974. "Interpersonal influences on adolescent illegal drug use," pp. 207-240 in E. Josephson and E. E. Carroll (eds.) *Drug Use: Epidemiological and Sociological Approaches*. New York: John Wiley. ✦

20
Structural Position and Violence: Developing a Cultural Explanation

David F. Luckenbill
Daniel P. Doyle

In the United States, as in other nations, members of certain groups engage in a disproportionate amount of criminal violence. Urban and southern residents, for example, have higher rates of violence than rural and northern residents; young adults and males have higher rates of violence than older adults and females; and blacks and lower-income persons have higher rates of violence than whites and middle- and upper-income persons (Curtis, 1974; Nettler, 1982:14-41). These facts raise interesting questions about the relationship between structural position and criminal violence. What is there about residing in an urban or southern area that generates a high rate of violence? What is there about being young or male or black or low-income that generates a high rate of violence?

Cultural and Structural Explanations of Criminal Violence

Sociologists have adopted two generic models in responding to these kinds of questions (Rosenfeld, 1986:116). The cultural model maintains that crime is a product of conformity to a distinctive culture. The basic idea is that crime stems from normative conflict: A complex society contains many groups, some with cultures sanctioning lawful behavior and some with cultures sanctioning unlawful behavior; through intimate contact with groups organized in favor of crime, individuals associate with definitions favorable to unlawful behavior; given extensive association with such definitions, individuals are likely to act in terms of them, committing crime (Kornhauser, 1978:181). A number of scholars have developed theories of violence that embrace this idea (e.g., Brearley, 1970; Curtis, 1975; Gastil, 1971; Silberman, 1978; Wolfgang and Ferracuti, 1967). These theories differ with respect to the source, diffusion, and structural location of a culture of violence, the components of culture that sanction violence, and the degree to which culture shapes behavior. Despite their differences, these theories generally propose that certain structural positions are characterized by high rates of violence because a significant proportion of their occupants subscribe to and act in terms of a culture that sanctions violence. This may be regarded as the core of a cultural explanation of the relationship between structural position and violence.

The structural model maintains that crime is a product of structural discontinuity. The most influential version of this model says that crime stems from inequality, the uneven distribution of resources. Inequality entails the deprivation of some relative to others; the perception of relative deprivation engenders feelings of resentment and hostility; and resentment and hostility stimulate impulses that are ultimately expressed as crimes (Messner and Tardiff, 1986:299). A number of scholars also have developed theories of violence that embrace this idea (e.g., Blau and Blau, 1982; Braithwaite, 1979; Coser, 1963; Danziger and Wheeler, 1975; Hawkins, 1983). These theories differ with respect to the form of inequality that is causally related to violence, the source of inequality, and the conditions under which inequality creates the sense of relative deprivation that leads to violence. Still, they generally propose that certain structural positions are characterized by high rates of violence because a significant proportion of their occupants experience great relative deprivation. This may be regarded as the core of a structural explanation of the relationship between position and violence.

In recent years, a multitude of researchers have assessed the capacity of these explanations to account for the link between structural position and criminal violence. By and large, they have used aggregate data to determine whether cultural or structural variables best explain the distribution of homicide. Their results have been contradictory. Some researchers report that a southern culture of violence effectively explains the higher rates of homicide in southern cities and states (Gastil, 1971; Hackney, 1969; Huff-Corzine et al., 1986), and that a black contraculture of violence effectively explains the higher rates of homicide in cities with large black populations (Curtis, 1975:23-42; Messner, 1983; Rosenfeld, 1986). Others claim that the empirical basis for such accounts is limited. For example, they find a weak association between degrees of southernness and rates of homicide across cities, counties, and states when socioeconomic variables are more rigorously controlled (Bankston and Allen, 1980; Loftin and Hill, 1974; Williams, 1984). They also find few differences between southerners and nonsoutherners, blacks and whites, and other presumably violent and nonviolent members in values and attitudes toward violence (Ball-Rokeach, 1973; Doerner, 1979; Erlanger, 1974; Poland, 1978). Conversely, some researchers report that economic inequality provides an effective explanation of the higher rates of homicide in southern cities and states and in cities with large black populations (Danziger and Wheeler, 1975; Sampson, 1985), and some report that economic inequality associated with race provides an even more effective explanation of high homicide rates (Blau and Blau, 1982; Blau and Golden, 1986; Blau and Schwartz, 1984:173-190). Others claim that such accounts lack support. Using different analytic units or procedures, they find a weak association between degrees of racial and/or economic inequality and rates of homicide across cities, states, and other areas when poverty, southernness, and racial composition are controlled (Bailey, 1984; DeFronzo, 1983; Huff-Corzine et al., 1986; Messner, 1982; Messner and Tardiff, 1986; Rosenfeld, 1986; Williams, 1984).

This body of research suffers from four general weaknesses. First, researchers have not specified fully the linkage between structural position and violence. They make certain assumptions about the way in which position is causally related to violence, but their assumptions often are implicit and lack sufficient grounding (Messner and Tardiff, 1986:299; Nettler, 1984:231). Second, most researchers have used an inappropriate unit of analysis. Violence is performed by individuals in the context of face-to-face interaction and therefore involves a number of psychological and interpersonal processes. Yet most researchers have rejected individual-level data in favor of more convenient aggregate-level data (Nettler, 1984:223). Third, many researchers have used problematic measures of their independent variables. There is doubt, for example, that the southernness or social composition of a city, state, or region is an accurate measure of a violent culture (Allen et al., 1981; Doerner, 1975), and there is doubt that certain value and attitude surveys provide accurate measures of values and attitudes regarding violence (Curtis, 1975:110-14). Fourth, most researchers have used questionable measures of their dependent variable. They have relied on formally recorded violence (typically homicide) to measure criminal violence. Recorded violence merely approximates actual violence, however, and its degree of approximation varies across social space. Whether a violent act is labeled a crime depends on such factors as the status of the participants and the preference of the complainant (Black, 1970; Hawkins, 1983). Whether a violent crime is labeled an assault, an aggravated assault, or a homicide depends on such factors as the availability of medical assistance, and the availability of such assistance varies by class and geographic area (Doerner, 1983; Doerner and Speir, 1986). Moreover, most researchers have used a dependent variable that may not reflect what the cultural and structural explanations try to explain. These theories seem to be designed to explain dispositions toward violence rather than violence per se. These problems are consequential. By neglecting the linkage between position and violence, by using aggregate data, and by using problematic measures of critical variables, researchers have failed to provide a sound assessment of the cultural and structural explanations.

Although the ultimate goal is to understand criminal violence, this article focuses specifically on the relationship between structural position and aggressiveness. We concentrate on aggressiveness because the cultural and structural theories seem more applicable to the explanation of dispositions for violence than violent behavior per se. These theories focus on why certain people are more disposed to violence than others, but they do not specify the situational conditions that channel such dispositions into concrete lines of action (see Cullen, 1984). We concentrate on a cultural explanation because it seems better suited to elaboration at the individual level. Structural treatments commonly assert that an individual's sense of relative deprivation translates a condition of inequality into a disposition for aggression (Messner and Tardiff, 1986:298), but they say little about the circumstances under which that disposition is likely to be manifest. Cultural treatments commonly assert that an individual's extensive association with a culture of violence links a particular structural position with a disposition for aggression, and some comment on the circumstances under which that disposition is likely to be manifest. These comments can be used to specify at the individual level the relationship between position and aggressiveness. Below, we develop a cultural model of that relationship.

Structural Position, Disputatiousness, and Aggressiveness

Researchers have not specified fully the manner in which structural position is related to aggressiveness. Specifically, they have glossed over a significant intervening variable—disputatiousness. The incorporation of disputatiousness provides a more definitive explanation of the relationship.

The literature on dispute development offers a conceptual framework that is helpful in specifying the linkage between structural position and aggressiveness. For analytic purposes, an interpersonal dispute may be seen as the product of three successive events (Felstiner et al., 1981:633-637). First, one must perceive the negative outcome resulting from another's behavior as an injury for which the other is to blame. The transformation of a negative outcome into a grievance is termed "naming."[1] Second, the victim must express the grievance to and demand reparation from the harmdoer. The transformation of a grievance into a demand for reparation is termed "claiming." Third, the harmdoer must reject the victim's claim, in whole or in part. The rejection of a claim transforms interaction into a "dispute," a recognized conflict of interest. The victim may respond to the dispute in any of several ways, ranging from outright capitulation through mobilization of third-party assistance to perseverance and use of force. Adopting the victim's position, disputatiousness is defined as the likelihood of naming and claiming, and aggressiveness is defined as the willingness to persevere and use force to settle the dispute. Aggressiveness may or may not be translated into violence, depending on the circumstances.

Research shows that homicide and assault generally are transactions in which the offender uses force to settle a dispute stemming from a negative outcome (Campbell, 1986; Curtis, 1974:65-79; Felson, 1981; Felson and Steadman, 1983; Hepburn, 1973; Levi, 1980; Luckenbill, 1977). In an analysis of 70 transactions culminating in homicide, for example, Luckenbill (1977) reports that homicide is the product of a "character contest." One begins by attacking another's identity, challenging his or her claim to a valued position in the situation. The other defines the attack as offensive and retaliates, attempting to restore identity either by threatening to injure the challenger if he or she does not withdraw or by using limited force to make the challenger withdraw. Rather than back down and show weakness, the challenger maintains or intensifies the attack. The opponents then battle. Fearing a show of weakness and a loss of face, and recognizing that peaceful or mildly aggressive means have failed to settle the dispute, one or both mobilize available weapons and use massive force, leaving one dead or dying.

Researchers have acknowledged that homicide and assault typically evolve from disputes, but they have ignored a theoretically implicit relationship between structural position, disputatiousness, and aggressiveness. Indeed, they have been satisfied with assessing a cultural explanation by examining the relationship between measures of violent culture (and alternative causal variables) and measures of violent behavior. Moreover, they have increasingly turned their attention from developing this type of explanation to devising different ways of measuring variables and analyzing relationships among them (e.g., Bailey, 1984; Blau and Golden, 1986; Golden and Messner, 1987; Huff-Corzine et al., 1986; Loftin and Parker, 1985; Messner, 1983; Messner and Tardiff, 1986; Parker and Smith, 1979; Sampson, 1985; Simpson, 1985; Smith and Parker, 1980; Williams, 1984). To understand violence, what is needed is the elaboration of a cultural explanation with respect to the relationship among position, disputatiousness, and disposition for violence. Toward this end, we develop a cultural model of disputatiousness and aggressiveness.

A Cultural Model of Differential Disputatiousness and Aggressiveness

According to a cultural explanation, the structural dimensions on which rates of violence vary are the dimensions on which association with a culture of violence varies. For our purposes, a "culture of violence" refers to values favorable to violence. These values need not take the form of a code, and they need not be restricted to a particular collectivity, such as young, black, male, lower-income, urban residents. Instead, they may take various forms, and they may be embraced by various categories of members (see Curtis, 1975:5-13). Structural positions that are characterized by high rates of violence are positions in which a significant proportion of the occupants have had extensive association with such a culture. Cultural treatments imply that a culture of violence fosters naming and claiming as well as aggressing. It follows that positions distributed along these dimensions would differ in the disputatiousness of their occupants. Individuals who occupy positions featuring high rates of violence would be more likely to perceive a negative outcome as injurious, and they would be more willing to express a grievance to and demand reparation from a harmdoer. Thus, in the course of explaining why a homicide typically springs from an altercation, Wolfgang (1958:188-189) argues that

> the significance of a jostle, a slightly derogatory remark, or the appearance of a weapon in the hands of an adversary are stimuli differentially perceived and interpreted by Negroes and whites, males and females. Social expectations of response in particular types of social interaction result in differential "definitions of the situation." A male is usually expected to defend the name and honor of his mother, the virtue of womanhood . . . and to accept no derogation about his race, his age, or his masculinity. . . . The upper-middle and upper social class value system defines and codifies behavioral norms into legal rules that often transcend subcultural mores, and considers many of the social and personnel stimuli that evoke a combative response reaction in the lower classes as "trivial."

Similarly, Horowitz (1983:81-84) suggests that, for residents of one lower-income, inner-city neighborhood, disputatiousness is promoted by a code of personal honor. For men, honor stresses the inviolability of manhood and

> defines breaches of etiquette, violations of a female relative's sexual purity, and accusations of dependency on others, in an adversarial idiom. Honor sensitizes people to violations that are interpersonal as derogations of fundamental properties of the self.

Within a more conventional normative framework these same actions might be appraised and evaluated as mere violations of etiquette that would be ignored or excused, or as violations of the law that would require the police. (p. 80)

Further, positions distributed along these dimensions would differ in the aggressiveness of their occupants. Given a dispute, individuals who occupy positions featuring high rates of violence would be more willing to persevere and use force in settling the dispute. Wolfgang and Ferracuti (1967:267) argue that variation in homicide rates by age, sex, race, and income cannot be explained in terms of variation in the emotional content or intensity of interaction or in the frequency of personal conflict. Rather, such variation can be explained primarily in terms of differences in cultural orientations toward responding to personal conflict. Thus, for many young, male, lower-income persons, "there is a 'lifestyle,' a culturally transmitted and shared willingness to express disdain, disgruntlement, and other hostile feelings in personal interaction by using physical force. The repertoire of response to unpleasant stimuli is delimited for them; it is not simply that more stimuli are displeasing."

Thus, it is proposed that, given variation in association with a culture of violence, occupants of positions distributed along certain structural dimensions differ in their disputatiousness *and* aggressiveness. To be sure, only a fraction of all negative outcomes evolve into disputes and only a fraction of all disputes are settled by force (see Coates and Penrod, 1981; Felson et al., 1986; Felstiner et al., 1981). Nevertheless, with respect to the dimensions of age, sex, race, income, and area of residence, it can be hypothesized that young adults, males, blacks, lower-income persons, and urban and southern residents are more likely than their respective counterparts to name a negative outcome, to claim reparation, and to persevere and use force in resolving a dispute.

Situational Dimensions of Differential Disputatiousness and Aggressiveness

Cultural treatments imply that differential disputatiousness and aggressiveness would be most pronounced in particular situations. In an influential statement, Wolfgang and Ferracuti (1967:158-159) posit that a subculture of violence conflicts with but does not oppose the larger culture; some features are shared with the culture. Nor does the subculture sanction violence in all situations. Rather, it designates that a violent response is expected, if not required, in some situations. Those who advance a cultural explanation commonly identify particular kinds of situations as those for which violence is sanctioned. It would be expected that in those situations differential disputatiousness and aggressiveness would be especially strong.

Cultural treatments often indicate that the situations for which violence is sanctioned are those in which fundamental properties of the self are attacked (Austin, 1980; Bruce, 1979; Campbell, 1986; Curtis, 1975:49-60; Goode, 1969; Gorn, 1985, 1987; Horowitz, 1983:77-92; Miller, 1966). Presumably, a culture of violence emphasizes personal attributes, such as strength, courage, and integrity, and enjoins individuals to be highly sensitive and boldly responsive to affronts. Thus, Gorn (1985:28) reports that in the Old South, where a code of honor thrived, "men were so touchy about their personal reputations that any slight required an apology. This failing, only retribution restored public stature and self-esteem." Along the same lines, Horowitz (1983:81) observes:

> In an honor-bound subculture that emphasizes manhood and defines violations of interpersonal etiquette in an adversarial manner, any action that challenges a person's right to deferential treatment in public—whether derogating a person, offering a favor that may be difficult to return, or demonstrating lack of respect for a female relative's sexual purity—can be interpreted as an insult and a potential threat to manhood. Honor demands that a man be able physically to back his claim to dominance and independence.

Consistently, Wolfgang (1958:188-89) argues that a jostle and a slightly derogatory remark are stimuli differentially perceived by blacks and whites, males and females, and members of other categories, and that "quick resort to physical combat as a measure of daring, courage, or defense of status appears to be a cultural expression, especially for lower socioeconomic class males of both races."

A culture of violence, however, seems less concerned with matters that do not bear purely on the self, such as those involving organizational standing. Indeed, in an analysis of verbal and physical aggression in one neighborhood group, whose code of conduct was likened to that of "the Arthurian knights," Miller et al. (1961) report that members were quite responsive to questions bearing on their strength, skill, and smartness but unresponsive to questions bearing on their church attendance, work experience, and occupational status. In a similar vein, Horowitz (1983:170) observes that in one lower-income, inner-city neighborhood, "most youths experience little difficulty in shifting back and forth between the conduct expected at work and on the street and generally follow the proper rules of comportment specified by each situation. There is no inherent normative conflict."

Some cultural treatments also indicate that the situations for which violence is sanctioned are those in which the harmdoer is an equal (Gorn, 1985; Horowitz, 1983:22-27; Miller et al., 1961; Pitt-Rivers, 1966; Wolfgang and Ferracuti, 1967:258-267). Presumably, a culture of violence regards the personal attacks of equals as significant and encourages individuals to be more sensitive and responsive to them. This inference draws on observations about "honor," which Pitt-Rivers (1966:21) defines as "the value of a person in his own eyes, but also in the eyes of his society. It is his estimation of his own worth, his *claim* to pride, but it is also the acknowledgement of that claim, his excellence recognized by society, his *right* to pride" (italics in original). Honor is dependent on others' evaluations of one's actions, but the power to impugn honor, to induce shame and undermine the self, depends on the relative status of the participants. "An inferior is not deemed to possess sufficient honour to resent the affront of a superior. A superior can ignore the affront of an inferior, since his honour is not committed by it" (Pitt-Rivers, 1966:31). Thus, in the Old South, gentlemen dueled with gentlemen, backwoodsmen fought with backwoodsmen (Gorn, 1985:42; Wyatt-Brown, 1982:355). It is said that people are no longer as concerned with honor as with "dignity," the idea that all persons are intrinsically equal, regardless of their status (see Ayers, 1984:19-33; Berger et al., 1973:83-96). Still, it is conceivable that dignity has not displaced honor entirely, and some investigators suggest that within certain segments of society, including those with high rates of violence, many people continue to act in terms of a code of honor (e.g., Anderson, 1978; Glasgow, 1980; Hannerz, 1969; Hippler, 1974; Horowitz, 1983; Moore, 1978).

Finally, some cultural treatments indicate that the situations for which violence is sanctioned are those that are public (Gorn, 1985; Horowitz, 1983; Pitt-Rivers, 1966). Presumably, a culture of violence enjoins individuals to be especially sensitive and responsive to attacks that occur in public rather than private settings. Honor is an intensely social concept, resting on reputation, community standing, and the esteem of kin and compatriots (Gorn, 1985:39). Accordingly, for those who embrace a code of honor, a public attack is particularly significant, for it brings dishonor. And the response to such an attack must be physical: "violence is triggered by the norms of the code of personal honor" (Horowitz, 1983:82).

It follows that differential disputatiousness and aggressiveness would be most pronounced in particular situations. Individuals who occupy positions featuring high rates of violence would be more disputatious and aggressive than individuals who occupy other positions when a negative outcome involves an equal's attack on the self in a public setting than when it does not. Accordingly, it can be further hypothesized that young adults, males, blacks, lower-income persons, and urban and southern residents are more likely than their respective counterparts to be disputatious and aggressive when a negative outcome bears on a personal attribute, stems from a harmdoer who shares the victim's status, and occurs in public than when it does not.

Prospects for Analysis

How can these hypotheses be empirically tested? It is clear that existing data sources are inadequate. As conceptualized here, naming, claiming, and aggressing are interpersonal in nature and therefore cannot be operationalized using aggregate data. Moreover, disputatiousness and aggressiveness are behavioral dispositions, not behaviors per se. Thus, they cannot be measured by looking at reports of violent behavior. What is needed are individual-level data that adequately measure these dispositions.

Survey research can provide such data, but extant surveys have failed to produce appropriate measures of disputatiousness and aggressiveness. For example, in their test of the subculture of violence thesis, Ball-Rokeach (1973) and Erlanger (1974) measure participation in violence with four survey questions that seem to focus more on the likelihood of having been a *victim* than a *perpetrator* of violence. Ball-Rokeach also uses an index of dispositions toward violence that has been criticized as too abstract and conjectural (Curtis, 1975:111-112). Respondents were asked if they could imagine any situation for which they would approve of a teenage boy punching another boy, a teacher hitting a student, or a judge imposing a death sentence. This seems less a measure of attitudes toward violence than a test of the respondent's ability to imagine a situation horrific enough that violence would clearly be justified.

A more promising approach would entail the use of scenarios. Here, survey respondents would be presented with a set of specific scenarios describing a particular set of circumstances in which a potentially negative outcome that may be attributed to a particular harmdoer is included. The negative outcomes described in the scenarios would range from serious to trivial, and they would vary in terms of the structural position of the participants, the degree to which the negative outcomes represent a potential attack on the individual's self, and the setting of the encounter.

The use of scenarios has several advantages for testing the cultural model. There is a clear recognition that disputatiousness and aggressiveness are individual-level rather than aggregate-level phenomena, and that they are the products of a dynamic process. Moreover, in contrast to the survey design used by Ball-Rokeach, the use of scenarios could make explicit that one is interested in the respondent's willingness to express a grievance, escalate the dispute, and engage in violence. Also, by specifying the nature of the situation, scenarios could provide the respondent with a stronger grounding in reality and thus produce a more realistic measure of dispositions toward violence.

It can be argued that data derived from scenarios are somewhat artificial because respondents are asked to speculate on behavior rather than report on behavior, but that artificiality has possible benefits. For example, the use of scenarios allows experimental manipulations that would not be possible, for ethical reasons, in the real world. Further, the relationship between structural position and disputatiousness and aggressiveness can be readily examined under a variety of circumstances. Respondents also may be more honest since they are not being asked to incriminate themselves for past violent behavior (Jackson et al., 1986:344-345).[2]

How could scenarios be used to measure the key variables? After reading each scenario, respondents would be asked to answer a series of questions regarding how they would respond to the harmdoer if they found themselves in the situation described. These questions would tap the degree to which the respondents would name, claim, and aggress if faced with the particular negative outcome. The first question would ask whether the respondent would be upset and take offense with the harmdoer's action. A positive response would indicate "naming." The second question would be addressed to those who did engage in naming in the situation. Those respondents would be asked whether they would protest to the harmdoer, essentially seeking reparation. A positive response would indicate "claiming." The third question would be addressed to those who did engage in claiming in the situation. Those respondents would be asked if they would use force against the harmdoer if redress was not provided. A positive response would indicate "aggressing."

The responses to the questions could be used to calculate indexes of the tendency to name, claim, and aggress for each respondent. Each index would represent the likelihood that a given respondent will move to another stage in the process that may ultimately lead to violence. The naming index would be the proportion of the scenarios in which the respondent would name (take offense with the harmdoer's action). The claiming index would be the proportion of the scenarios in which the respondent named for which he or she would claim (protest to the harmdoer). The aggressing index would be the proportion of the scenarios in which the respondent claimed for which he or she would be willing to aggress (use force if the demand for redress was unsuccessful). As operationalized here, naming, claiming, and aggressing are not simply measures of the likelihood of being in a particular stage of the process leading to violence. Rather, they are independent measures of the likelihood of moving from one stage to another. Thus, it would be possible for a respondent to have a higher score on the claiming index than on the naming index, for example, if the respondent is a person who does not take offense easily but is likely to demand reparation in those few instances when offense is taken.

Examining the effect of structural position on disputatiousness and aggressiveness under a variety of circumstances would present certain problems in study design. The model's hypotheses necessitate tests of the effect of each structural position for situations in which the negative outcome involves an attack on the self rather than when it does not, the harmdoer is of equal status rather than of another status, and the negative outcome occurs in public rather than in private. In a standard, fully crossed factorial design, respondents would have to be presented with a large number of scenarios in order to examine each of the situational dimensions. That would be especially problematic if one wants to test various conditions (such as different levels of privacy) within each situational dimension. The number of cases needed and the length of the interviews become unmanageable.

A more practical alternative to a standard factorial design would be the use of the "factorial survey" technique developed by Peter H. Rossi and his colleagues (Rossi and Anderson, 1982; Rossi and Nock, 1982). This technique has been used successfully to study the deterrent effect of multiple factors on the decision to drink and drive (Thurman, 1986a), to evade the payment of taxes (Thurman, 1986b), and to engage in a variety of violent and property crimes (Anderson et al., 1983). In a factorial survey, the content of each scenario is generated randomly based on a list of the possible conditions within each situational dimension. The computer selects one of the possible conditions from each of the situational dimensions and inserts it into a skeleton scenario to form a completed scenario (Thurman, 1986b:12). A given scenario might involve a public attack on the self by a harmdoer who is of lower status, the next scenario could be a private attack on the self by a harmdoer of equal status, and so on. Thus, it is possible to examine the relative effect of each condition on the dependent variables within each situational dimension without the need for an enormous number of scenarios.

Conclusion

In this article we have advanced a more fully developed cultural model of the relationship between structural position and criminal violence. The model maintains that, given variation in association with a culture of violence, occupants of positions distributed along certain structural dimensions differ in their disputatiousness and aggressiveness. It also maintains that differential disputatiousness and aggressiveness are most pronounced when a negative outcome involves an equal's attack on the self in a public setting. Assessing these hypotheses requires individual-level data bearing on behavioral dispositions under a variety of circumstances. One methodological procedure for collecting such data would involve presenting respondents with a set of realistic scenarios that vary in theoretically relevant ways. Future research could use this procedure to assess the effects of each of the structural positions separately and in combination with each other under a variety of situational conditions. The findings of such research would enhance our understanding of why certain subgroups of society have higher rates of criminal violence.

Notes

1. The dispute development literature typically distinguishes between "naming," which refers to the perception of a negative outcome as an injury, and "blaming," which refers to the attribution of an injury to a particular harmdoer. This distinction is made on the grounds that identification of a harmdoer often is problematic because the harmdoer often is an organization (see Coates and Penrod, 1981:659-666; Pruitt and Rubin, 1986:100-101). Given our concentration on interpersonal transactions, we combine naming and blaming.
2. Although the proposed model focuses on dispositions toward violence, not violent behavior, there is evidence that expressed intentions are reliable predictors of future behaviors (see Fishbein and Ajzen, 1975; Cialdini et al., 1981; Jackson et al., 1986; Tittle et al., 1986).

References

Allen, H., David, Dennis R. McSeveney, and William B. Bankston. 1981. The influence of southern culture on race-specific homicide rates. *Sociological Spectrum* 1:361-374.
Anderson, Andy B., Anthony R. Harris, and Joann Miller. 1983. Models of deterrence theory. *Social Science Research* 12:236-262.
Anderson, Elijah. 1978. *A Place on the Corner*. Chicago: University of Chicago Press.
Austin, Roy L. 1980. Adolescent subcultures of violence. *Sociological Quarterly* 21:545-561.
Ayers, Edward L. 1984. *Vengeance and Justice*. New York: Oxford University Press.
Bailey, William C. 1984. Poverty, inequality, and city homicide rates: Some not so unexpected findings. *Criminology* 22:531-550.
Ball-Rokeach, Sandra J. 1973. Values and violence: A test of the subculture of violence thesis. *American Sociological Review* 38:736-749.
Bankston, William B. and H. David Allen. 1980. Rural social areas and patterns of homicide: An analysis of lethal violence in Louisiana. *Rural Sociology* 45:223-237.
Berger, Peter, Brigitte Berger, and Hansfried Kellner. 1973. *The Homeless Mind*. New York: Vintage Books.
Black, Donald. 1970. Production of crime rates. *American Sociological Review* 35:733-748.
Blau, Judith R. and Peter M. Blau. 1982. The cost of inequality: Metropolitan structure and violent crime. *American Sociological Review* 47:114-129.
Blau, Peter M. and Reid M. Golden. 1986. Metropolitan structure and criminal violence. *Sociological Quarterly* 27:15-26.
Blau, Peter M. and Joseph E. Schwartz. 1984. *Crosscutting Social Circles*. New York: Academic Press.
Braithwaite, John. 1979. *Inequality, Crime, and Public Policy*. London: Routledge & Kegan Paul.
Brearley, H.C. 1970. The pattern of violence. In W. Couch (ed.), *Culture in the South*. 1935. Westport, Conn.: Negro Universities Press.
Bruce, Dickson D., Jr. 1979. *Violence and Culture in the Antebellum South*. Austin: University of Texas Press.
Campbell, Anne. 1986. The streets and violence. In A. Campbell and J. Gibbs (eds.), *Violent Transactions*. New York: Basil Blackwell.
Cialdini, Robert B., Richard E. Petty, and John T. Cacioppo. 1981. Attitude and attitude change. *Annual Review of Psychology* 32:357-404.
Coates, Dan and Steven Penrod. 1981. Social psychology and the emergence of disputes. *Law and Society Review* 15:655-706.
Coser, Lewis A. 1963. Violence and the social structure. In J. Masserman (ed.), *Science and Psychoanalysis*. Vol. 6. New York: Grune and Stratton.
Cullen, Francis. 1984. *Rethinking Crime and Deviance Theory*. Totowa, N.J.: Rowman and Allanheld.
Curtis, Lynn A. 1974. *Criminal Violence*. Lexington, Mass.: Lexington Books.
———. 1975. *Violence, Race, and Culture*. Lexington, Mass.: D.C. Heath.
Danziger, Sheldon and David Wheeler. 1975. The economics of crime: Punishment or income redistribution. *Review of Social Economy* 33:113-131.

DeFronzo, James. 1983. Economic assistance to impoverished Americans: Relationship to incidence of crime. *Criminology* 21:119-136.

Doerner, William G. 1975. A regional analysis of homicide rates in the United States. *Criminology* 13:90-101.

———. 1979. The violent world of Johnny Reb: An attitudinal analysis of the "regional culture of violence" thesis. *Sociological Forum* 2:61-71.

———. 1983. Why does Johnny Reb die when shot? The impact of medical resources upon lethality. *Sociological Inquiry* 53:1-15.

Doerner, William G. and John C. Speir. 1986. Stitch and sew: The impact of medical resources upon criminally induced lethality. *Criminology* 24:319-330.

Erlanger, Howard S. 1974. The empirical status of the subculture of violence thesis. *Social Problems* 22:280-292.

Felson, Richard R. 1981. An interactionist approach to aggression. In J. Tedeschi (ed.), *Impression Management Theory and Social Psychological Research*. New York: Academic Press.

Felson, Richard B. and Henry J. Steadman. 1983. Situational factors in disputes leading to criminal violence. *Criminology* 21:59-74.

Felson, Richard B., William Baccaglini, and George Gmelch. 1986. Bar-room brawls: Aggression and violence in Irish and American bars. In A. Campbell and J. Gibbs (eds.), *Violent Transactions*. New York: Basil Blackwell.

Felstiner, William L.F., Richard L. Abel, and Austin Sarat. 1981. The emergence and transformation of disputes: Naming, blaming, claiming.... *Law and Society Review* 15:631-654.

Fishbein, Martin and Icek Ajzen. 1975. *Beliefs, Attitudes, Intention and Behavior*. Reading, Mass.: Addison-Wesley.

Gastil, Raymond D. 1971. Homicide and a regional culture of violence. *American Sociological Review* 36:412-427.

Glasgow, Douglas G. 1980. *The Black Underclass*. San Francisco: Jossey-Bass.

Golden, Reid M. and Steven F. Messner. 1987. Dimensions of racial inequality and rates of violent crime. *Criminology* 25:525-541.

Goode, William. 1969. Violence among intimates. In D. Mulvilhill, M. Tumin, and L. Curtis (eds.), *Crimes of Violence*. Vol. 13. Washington, D.C.: Government Printing Office.

Gorn, Elliott J. 1985. "Gouge and bite, pull hair and scratch:" The social significance of fighting in the southern backcountry. *American Historical Review* 90:18-43.

———. 1987. "Good-bye boys, I die a true American:" Homicide, nativism, and working-class culture in antebellum New York City. *Journal of American History* 74:388-410.

Hackney, Sheldon. 1969. Southern violence. In H. Graham and T. Gurr (eds.), *The History of Violence in America*. New York: Bantam.

Hannerz, Ulf. 1969. *Soulside*. New York: Columbia University Press.

Hawkins, Darrell F. 1983. Black and white homicide differentials: Alternatives to an inadequate theory. *Criminal Justice and Behavior* 10:407-440.

Hepburn, John. 1973. Violent behavior in interpersonal relationships. *Sociological Quarterly* 14:419-429.

Hippler, Arthur E. 1974. *Hunter's Point*. New York: Basic Books.

Horowitz, Ruth. 1983. *Honor and the American Dream*. New Brunswick, N.J.: Rutgers University Press.

Huff-Corzine, Lin, Jay Corzine, and David C. Moore. 1986. Southern exposure: Deciphering the South's influence on homicide rates. *Social Forces* 64:906-924.

Jackson, Elton F., Charles R. Tittle, and Mary Jean Burke. 1986. Offense-specific models of the differential association process. *Social Problems* 33:335-356.

Kornhauser, Ruth Rosner. 1978. *Social Sources of Delinquency*. Chicago: University of Chicago Press.

Levi, Ken. 1980. Homicide as conflict resolution. *Deviant Behavior* 1:281-307.

Loftin, Colin and Robert Hill. 1974. Regional subculture and homicide. *American Sociological Review* 39:714-724.

Loftin, Colin and Robert Nash Parker. 1985. An errors-in-variable model of the effect of poverty on urban homicide rates. *Criminology* 23:269-287.

Luckenbill, David F. 1977. Criminal homicide as a situated transaction. *Social Problems* 25:176-186.

Messner, Steven F. 1982. Poverty, inequality, and the urban homicide rate. *Criminology* 20:103-114.

———. 1983. Regional and racial effects on the urban homicide rate: The subculture of violence revisited. *American Journal of Sociology* 88:997-1007.

Messner, Steven F. and Kenneth Tardiff. 1986. Economic inequality and levels of homicide: An analysis of urban neighborhoods. *Criminology* 24:297-317.

Miller, Walter B. 1966. Violent crime in city gangs. *Annals of the American Academy of Political and Social Science* 364:97-112.

Miller, Walter B., Hildred Geertz, and Henry S.G. Cutter. 1961. Aggression in a boys' street-corner group. *Psychiatry* 24:283-298.

Moore, Joan W. 1978. *Homeboys*. Philadelphia: Temple University Press.

Nettler, Gwynn. 1982. *Killing One Another*. Cincinnati: Anderson.

———. 1984. *Explaining Crime*. 3rd ed. New York: McGraw-Hill.

Parker, Robert Nash and M. Dwayne Smith. 1979. Deterrence, poverty, and type of homicide. *American Journal of Sociology* 85:614-624.

Pitt-Rivers, Julian. 1966. Honour and social status. In J. Peristiany (ed.), *Honour and Shame*. Chicago: University of Chicago Press.

Poland, James M. 1978. Subculture of violence: Youth offender value systems. *Criminal Justice and Behavior* 5:159-164.

Pruitt, Dean G. and Jeffrey Z. Rubin. 1986. *Social Conflict*. New York: Random House.

Rosenfeld, Richard. 1986. Urban crime rates: Effects of inequality, welfare dependency, region, and race. In J. Byrne and R. Sampson (eds.), *The Social Ecology of Crime*. New York: Springer-Verlag.

Rossi, Peter H. and Andy B. Anderson. 1982. The factorial survey approach: An introduction. In P. Rossi and S.L. Nock (eds.), *Measuring Social Judgments: The Factorial Survey Approach*. Beverly Hills, Calif.: Sage.

Rossi, Peter H. and S.L. Nock. 1982. *Measuring Social Judgments: The Factorial Survey Approach*. Beverly Hills, Calif.: Sage.

Sampson, Robert J. 1985. Structural sources of variation in race-age-specific rates of offending across major U.S. cities. *Criminology* 23:647-673.

Silberman, Charles E. 1978. *Criminal Violence, Criminal Justice*. New York: Vintage Books.

Simpson, Miles E. 1985. Violent crime, income inequality, and regional culture: Another look. *Sociological Focus* 18:199-208.

Smith, M. Dwayne and Robert Nash Parker. 1980. Type of homicide and variation in regional rates. *Social Forces* 59:136-147.

Thurman, Quint C. 1986a. Estimating social-psychological effects in decisions to drink and drive: A factorial survey approach. *Journal of Studies On Alcohol* 47:447-454.

———. 1986b. Modeling judgments of taxpayer noncompliance. Paper presented at the annual meeting of the American Society of Criminology, Atlanta, Georgia, November.

Tittle, Charles R., Mary Jean Burke, and Elton F. Jackson. 1986. Modeling Sutherland's theory of differential association: Toward an empirical clarification. *Social Forces* 65:404-432.

Williams, Kirk R. 1984. Economic sources of homicide: Reestimating the effects of poverty and inequality. *American Sociological Review* 49:283-289.

Wolfgang, Marvin E. 1958. *Patterns of Criminal Homicide*. Philadelphia: University of Pennsylvania Press.

Wolfgang, Marvin E. and Franco Ferracuti. 1967. *The Subculture of Violence*. London: Tavistock.

Wyatt-Brown, Bertram. 1982. *Southern Honor*. New York: Oxford University Press. ✦

Section VI
The Family, Schools, and Peer Groups

In Sections IV and V, which dealt with various theories of delinquency, emphasis was placed on those social forces that cause or contribute to delinquent behavior. The sociological perspective suggests that the individual adolescent is not solely responsible for his or her predicament but that there are external forces that constrain, shape, and propel youth in certain directions. This means that in searching for ways to eliminate delinquency one cannot look only at individual delinquents but must pay attention to the circumstances of life that influence each individual. In this particular section, three of the preeminent socializing forces that impinge on juveniles will be examined: the family, schools, and peer groups. During adolescence, the individual constantly encounters one or the other of these agents of socialization. As we will see, the family, school, and peer involvement become critical determinants of an adolescent's movement toward law-abiding or law-violating behavior.

The Family and Delinquency

Of all the social institutions that influence the adolescent, none is more critical than the family. It is within the context of the family that the foundation for the rest of life is built. The family is responsible for the first stage of development of values, personality, and self-concept. Early childhood experiences are now seen to be far more critical than was previously thought. Parents become critical role models for their children, and children often begin to see the world through the eyes of their parents. Parents influence children's basic values, initial goals and orientations, and even appreciation for life itself. Children mirror their parents in innumerable ways. For example, parents teach children not only to speak but to use words, phrases, and even tonal inflections that strongly reflect parental speech patterns. Children acquire a taste for foods, a philosophical outlook, a religious and political orientation, and even a pattern of daily events that often are strongly influenced by their families. The starting point for who and what we are begins in the home at a very early age in the home. The research evidence overwhelmingly suggests that families are one of the strongest socializing forces in life and that loving, caring, and nurturing family milieux inhibit delinquency. Social control and social learning theorists see the role of the family as critical; the affective tie that develops between parent and child appears to be one of the most effective insulators against delinquency. But, what if the family is not a warm and loving environment, and the learning that occurs in the home is at odds with the goals of conventional society?

There is a recurring theme in American society that the family as we once knew it is on the verge of collapse. Dramatic changes have occurred in the structure of families, and this had led to a weakening and in some instances virtual obliteration of the American family. Consider the following points:

- The "traditional" image of an American family—working father, a housewife, and two school-age children—

constitutes only 6 percent of U.S. households.
- The United States has the highest divorce rate in the world. For every two marriages there is one divorce. About 55 percent of all divorces in the U.S. involve children. It is estimated that 86 percent of black children and 42 percent of white children will spend some time in a single-parent household.
- About 70 percent of all mothers of school-age children are employed. While the traditional role of a husband has changed little for most males, wives are expected to fill traditional female family roles and work outside the home. Modern women have about half as much time for housework as "traditional" women, and end up working a 40-hour job outside the home and a 40- to 50-hour job inside the home.
- According to the Bureau of the Census, every 32 seconds a 15- to 19-year-old woman in the U.S. becomes pregnant, and every 32 seconds a child is born to an unmarried woman. 19% of white children, 30% of Latino children, and 55% of black children under 18 live with one parent.
- Each year an estimated six million women are beaten by the men they live with, and 30 percent of women who become homicide victims die at the hands of men with whom they had a family relationship.
- It is estimated that 1,261 children were killed in 1992 as a result of child abuse. The U.S. Department of Health reported that 1.5 million children experienced child abuse and neglect.

While many agree that the family is the first line of defense in dealing with the problems of delinquency, it is apparent that the family has been undergoing significant changes. Some forms of family life may now be contributing to delinquency rather than solving it. The first article in this section, by Kevin and Karen Wright, reviews the research on family life and explores how the family may or may not relate to delinquent involvement. Wright and Wright explore the oversimplified conclusion that divorce or single parenting invariably results in adolescent misconduct. The concept of the "broken home" is a complex phenomenon, and just because a mother and father are physically present in the home does not necessarily imply that the home is psychologically "intact." One critical aspect of being a single parent, which generally refers to a female head of household, is that economic stressors become of paramount importance. What may be the critical variable is not simply a female head of household but the relationship of single-parent families with economic hardship. Further, Wright and Wright suggest that a second important consideration is not simply a divorced versus intact family, but whether marital discord occurs within the home.

The more alarming dimension to Wright and Wright's discussion deals with the issue of child abuse and neglect. The authors give a good review of the literature on this subject and show how abuse and delinquency can be related. However, the common observation of a "cycle of violence" where abused children become abusing parents is not clearly supported. Wright and Wright also discuss the developmental processes that occur during adolescence when peers can take on a dominant role and parents' influence of becomes less pronounced. Finally, Wright and Wright review some of the literature on what is a mutual interaction effect between a parent and a delinquent child. One coping strategy for parents of delinquent children is to withdraw from parenting. The bond between parent and child may become increasingly attenuated as delinquent behavior increases. This suggests that the parent–child bond is not a static concept, but one that can undergo constant change.

The School and Delinquency

A second major agent of socialization that impinges on the lives of adolescents is the school. In his classic work, *Schools*

Without Failure, William Glaser states, "I believe that if a child, no matter what his background, can succeed in school, he has an excellent chance for success in life. If he fails at any stage in his educational career—elementary school, junior high school, high school, or college—his chances for success in life are greatly diminished." Schools have become the major gatekeeper for success in American society. For someone not to complete twelve years of education and achieve a high school diploma is tantamount to guaranteed low social status. It is assumed that not only will the typical student complete high school, but that he or she will continue the educational process toward a college degree. Unfortunately, not every student who begins school will graduate with a high school diploma. The overall graduation rate in the U.S. according to the U.S. Department of Education is 72 percent. That is, approximately seven out of 10 students who begin school in the first grade will graduate from high school, and nearly three out of 10 students will drop out. What is even more alarming is that the dropout rate varies greatly by race and ethnicity. While only 24 percent of white males aged 25 years or older have less than a high school diploma, for African-Americans that rate is 42 percent, and for Latinos it is 52 percent. Even more disturbing is that in many inner-city areas this dropout rate is increasing. Some years ago, Jonathan Kozol wrote a book entitled *Death at an Early Age*, in which he describes how the educational institution can effectively destroy the motivation, enthusiasm, and self-esteem of young children. Both Glaser and Kozol see the school as being a critical contributor to delinquency in America. Schools can promote failure, alienation, and resentment. There is a strong association between school failure and delinquency.

Schools, like the family, have been traditionally regarded as safe havens for adolescents, but there is growing evidence that schools are becoming dangerous places. A government report, *Violent Schools—Safe Schools*, documented the increasing problems of property theft and violence in American schools. This report documented more than 100 homicides, 9,000 rapes, 12,000 armed robberies, and $600 million in destroyed property on school grounds. A Bureau of Justice report found that 9 percent of all students were crime victims. Finally, the fear of crime on school grounds has led to the problem of weapons in school. A survey of high-school students by Sheley, McGee, and Wright, in California, Louisiana, New Jersey, and Illinois, found that 9 percent of males and 3 percent of females reported bringing a gun to school "at least now and then."

The second reading in this section, by Cernkovich and Giordano, looks at the issue of schools and delinquency, and whether there are differences between races. They question whether blacks experience school differently than whites and whether the school plays the same role for blacks as for whites in the onset of delinquency. Their findings are quite surprising. While blacks experience a higher dropout rate and appear to be more alienated from schools, Cernkovich and Giordano find that black youth are just as committed to educational success as whites. The school emerges as an important barrier to delinquency for black and white youth despite the fact that blacks experience more failure and more drop out. This study not only confirms the importance of school in preventing delinquent behavior but also demonstrates that even for those who do not achieve high success, the educational institution still emerges as a critical variable.

The Role of Delinquent Peers

Perhaps no area of delinquency research is more complex than that of peers and juvenile gangs. Delinquent behavior as well as nondelinquent behavior tends to be group activity. Normally speaking, adolescents want to belong to or to be part of a social collectivity. Indeed, the adolescent who is a social isolate is often seen as a deviant. Further, most delinquent activity centers around group behavior. For example, auto theft, drinking, vandalism, assaultive behavior, and truancy are behaviors that are typically done in groups. Adolescents acquire friends, and much of their teenage years are spent in the presence of their peers. Innumerable studies of delinquency point out that much of juvenile misbehavior is more akin to social activity than to premeditated acts of deviance. Delinquency often satisfies the juveniles' needs for excitement and togetherness. Even with cases of serious criminal acts, juveniles will report that they acted on the basis of a "dare" or considered the act just "fun and games." Peer pressure or peer influence is often the critical ingredient in explaining why a delinquent act occurred. A juvenile judge once commented that "many juvenile delinquents on their own are perfectly normal but in the context of their peer groups they suddenly can become monsters." The pressure to conform, to belong, and not to be excluded are the principal driving forces in understanding juvenile delinquency. Teaching adolescents the peer-resistant technique of "not going along with their best friends" has proven to be exceedingly difficult.

The third reading in this section, "The Influence of Delinquent Peers: What They Think or What They Do?" by Mark Warr and Mark Stafford, looks at the issue of delinquent friends and delinquent behavior. The issue they specifically wish to address is whether Sutherland's theory that emphasizes peer attitudes or social learning theory's focus on peer behavior is more applicable to the study of delinquency. What they find is that the behavior of friends has a much stronger impact than their attitudes on delinquent behavior. This is not to say that attitudes are unimportant, but simply that "hanging out" with delinquent associates is not as deleterious as participating in delinquent behavior with close associates. The authors suggest that social learning theory, as it relates to delinquent associates, might be a more appropriate method toward understanding delinquency than Sutherland's differential association theory. Warr and Stafford assert that "there can be little doubt that peers are a critical factor in the production of delinquency," but that attitudes are not the critical element.

However, examining the influence of delinquent peers and then considering delinquent gangs brings about a qualitatively different issue. The jump from considering a delinquent peer group to a delinquent gang may seem straightforward, but it is in fact a very complex jump. Gangs are social groupings that have clear organizations, defined leaderships, territorial bases of operation or "turf," membership rules, and a certain continuity of affiliation. There is no standard definition of a gang, but in a general sense a gang is a collectivity of individuals who band together for mutual protection and pursue mutual interests. The difficulty with this general definition is that it includes an exceedingly broad range of adolescent groups, and many of these groups are not necessarily involved in deviant behavior. There is also a misperception that all delinquent activity takes place in the context of gangs, such that the elimination of gangs would be tantamount to the elimination of juvenile delinquency. Gang research began with Frederic Thrasher's 1927 study of delinquent gangs in Chicago. Thrasher theorized that the social, economic, and ecological processes of large urban areas produce *interstitial* areas, or cracks in the normal process of social control. According to Thrasher, groups of adolescents gravitate together as a result of weak family controls, poverty, and social disorganization. These social collectivities thrive on symbols, perceived threat, rituals, and a sense of exclusivity. Thrasher saw the development of gangs as an outgrowth of innocent, everyday behavior. Gangs provided a sense of belonging and togetherness, but were not stable or permanent entities. Membership in a gang was a means for youth in disorganized, inner-city areas to gain acceptance and to exert some control over their situation.

Gang research took on a certain "Hollywood image." The more recent images of the juvenile gang paint a very different picture than the one portrayed by Thrasher. Often the gang is seen as exceedingly violent, well-organized, and controlling large sectors of the inner city. Research in delinquency became synonymous with studying gangs, interviewing gang members, infiltrating gangs, and mobilizing communities to fight the "spreading disease" of juvenile gangs. Gangs do exist and they do inflict havoc in communities, but most delinquent activity does not take place in gangs, nor are all gangs delinquent.

The last reading in this section, by Esbensen and Huizinga, addresses the perceived criminogenic character of gangs. They ask whether gang members become more delinquent because of their membership in a gang, or were delinquent before joining. Is the current situation a case of "birds of a feather flocking together?" The authors show that defining a gang and a gang member is extraordinarily difficult. For some, gangs entailed illegal activity; others considered informal youth groups to be gangs; and a few considered church groups to be gangs. In attempting to define and locate gangs, Esbensen and Huizinga found gang membership to be infrequent, even when they dealt with high-risk adolescents. But their most significant finding is that delinquency precedes gang membership. Gangs do not invent delinquency, and a concerted attempt to eliminate gangs will not solve the delinquency problem. Compare the implications of these findings with the position taken by the International Chiefs of Police who issued the following statement:

> The rise of gangs has fueled much of the increase in violent crime. What were once loosely knit groups of juveniles and young adults involved in petty crimes have become powerful, organized gangs. There appear to be gangs intent on controlling lucrative drug trade through intimidation and murder, and also street gangs simply claiming "turf." Today, as never before, cities and neighborhoods, even though without long histories of youth gang activity, have been literally overrun by both types of gang violence. While gangs are not new, today's level of gang violence, organization, and sophistication is unprecedented.

As can be seen, there still exists enormous conceptual confusion as to what gangs are, what they represent, and where they stand in terms of the overall picture of delinquency.

References

Glaser, William. 1969. *Schools without Failure.* New York: Harper & Row.

Kozol, Jonathan. 1970. *Death at an Early Age: The Destruction of the Hearts and Minds of Negro Children in Boston Public Schools.* Boston: Houghton Mifflin.

International Association of Chiefs of Police. 1993. "Violent Crime in America: Recommendations of the IACP Summit." *Police Chief* (June), 59-60.

National Institute of Education, U.S. Department of Health, Education and Welfare. 1977. *Violent Schools—Safe Schools: The Safe Schools Study Report to the Congress.* Washington, D.C.: Government Printing Office.

Sheley, Joseph, Zina McGee, and James Wright. 1992. "Gun-Related Violence in and around Inner-City Schools." *American Journal of Diseases of Children* 146:677-82.

Thrasher, Frederic M. 1927. *The Gang.* Chicago: University of Chicago Press. ✦

21
Family Life, Delinquency, and Crime: A Policymaker's Guide

Kevin N. Wright
Karen E. Wright

Juvenile Delinquency

... As early as 1915, experts in juvenile delinquency recognized the family's central role in determining delinquency. In *Juvenile Offenders*, Morrison (1915) observed that "among social circumstances which have a hand in determining the future of the individual it is enough for our present purpose to recognize that the family is chief" (p. 121). Seventy years later, Geismar and Wood (1986) drew upon a much expanded literature to reach the same conclusion: "Family functioning variables as a group seem to be inextricably linked to delinquent behavior. Juvenile delinquency appears to occur disproportionately among children in 'unhappy homes'" (p. 30).

Several excellent reviews of this literature have been produced during the last decade. These reviews examine methodological and statistical issues of definition, measurement, control, sampling, and design that are not discussed in this monograph. Readers who wish delve into these topics should consult the original sources as well as the reviews.

Loeber and Dishion (1983) reviewed approximately 70 studies focusing on family characteristics that appear to be associated with subsequent delinquency. They found consistent predictors in relation to age of the child. For example, at age 6, family functioning predicts delinquency. Antisocial behavior and aggressiveness at age 9 indicate delinquent tendencies, while parental criminality at age 10 is a valid predictor. Educational factors predict delinquency at age 15. And finally, at age 16, if the child is involved in delinquency, continued delinquency is predictable....

Snyder and Patterson (1987) found that discipline and positive parenting were modestly related to delinquency. Parental monitoring of the child had a somewhat stronger association, which Snyder and Patterson labeled as moderate. In comparison to these family functioning areas, conflict and problem solving had the weakest relationship with delinquency but still showed evidence of a modest association. The association of family structural characteristics including socioeconomic status, parental absence, parental criminality, and family size was unclear.

Henggeler (1989) reviewed the relationship between family transactions and child psychosocial functioning in 65 studies conducted over a 30-year period and found delinquent behavior to stem from three areas. First, low levels of parental control strategies may be a source of delinquent behavior. Second, if parental controls are present, but are inept or ineffective, youths in these families are at risk for development of delinquency. Finally, the antisocial behavior of parents, including the degree to which deviant methods of meeting goals are acceptable, seems to be a strong predictor of delinquent behavior in young family members (p. 45).

Single-Parent Families

There is an intuitive appeal to the idea that a single parent, particularly when female, will be less able to effectively supervise, guide, and control a child or adolescent to insulate him or her from criminal or delinquent influences.

Research into the idea that single-parent homes may produce more delinquents dates back to the early 19th century. Officials at New York State's Auburn Penitentiary, in an attempt to discern the causes of crime, studied the biographies of incarcerated men. Reports to the legislature in 1829 and 1830 suggested that family disintegration resulting from the death, desertion, or divorce of parents led to undisciplined children who eventually became criminals (Rothman, 1990:65).

Now, well over a century later, researchers continue to examine the family background of unique populations and reach similar conclusions. Like their forerunners, many current investigations lack control groups for comparisons but still offer some insight into what can happen to children in single-parent families. Goetting (1989), for example, found that only 30 percent of children arrested for homicide in Detroit between 1977 and 1984 lived with both parents. In a study of 240 women committed to the California Youth Authority in the 1960s, Rosenbaum (1989) observed that only 7 percent came from intact families.

Two explanations of why single-parent families seem to produce more delinquents are frequently offered. Sociologists Matsueda and Heimer (1987) suggest that single parents can less effectively supervise their children simply because there is only one parent rather than two; consequently their children are more likely to come into contact with delinquent influences. Dornbusch et al. (1985) offer a second explanation, specific to single mothers, suggesting that the mother gives the adolescent a greater say in what he or she can do, thus reducing control over the youth. However, the relationship between single parenthood and delinquency may not be as simple as these commonly held opinions imply.

Teeters and Reinemann (1950) drew the following conclusion about the relationship in their 1950 textbook, *The Challenge of Delinquency*:

> For the student to wend his way through such a welter of conflicting opinion, coming as it does from experts, is indeed a confusing task. What he wants to know is: "Is there a positive relationship between the broken home and delinquency?" Apparently, no definite answer can be made to the question. (p. 153)

Thirty-six years and hundreds of studies later, Wells and Rankin (1986) reached a similar conclusion: "Despite a sizable body of research extending across various academic disciplines, the question of the causal connections between broken homes and delinquency remains unresolved and ambiguous" (p. 68).

The literature reveals conflicting findings and opinions regarding the relationship between family structure and delinquency. The relationship is, indeed, complex. However, from the cumulative body of the research, consistent patterns emerge that provide useful information about the causal relationship.

Many studies examining the singular relationship between single-parent families and delinquency have found a positive relationship (Gibson, 1969; Rutter, 1971; Wilkinson, 1980; Canter, 1982; Rankin, 1983; Matsueda and Heimer, 1987; LeFlore, 1988). Other studies have identified more specific breakdowns. For example, Gove and Crutchfield (1982) found the positive relationship to be true for males but not for females. Rosen (1985) observed a positive association between single-parent households and delinquency for male children in black families. Denno (1985) discovered among black families that the positive association exists for males but not females. Flewelling and Bauman (1990) observed a positive relationship between single-parent families and the use of a controlled substance or engaging in sexual intercourse. Brady et al. (1986), testing in a clinical setting, found that the children of single-parent families exhibited more behavioral problems. Children from single-parent families also appear to be more susceptible to peer pressure (Steinberg, 1987). In an observation study of mother/child interaction, Webster-Stratton (1989) found that single mothers issue more critical statements and that their children exhibit more deviant and noncompliant behaviors.

A major study of 1,517 boys by Loeber et al. (1991) explored the characteristics that linked with changes in offending over time. The researchers found that single parenthood correlated with delinquency across age groups from 7 to 8, 10 to 11, and 13 to 14. Children from single-parent homes were more likely to escalate their delinquency as they passed through adolescence, whereas children raised in two-parent homes were more likely to desist from delinquent behavior as they matured.

The National Incidence Studies on Missing, Abducted, Runaway, and Throwaway Children in America (Finkelhor, Hotaling, and Sedlak, 1990) found that family division played a significant role in determining teenage runaways. "Thrownaway" children were more likely to come from single-parent homes. Furthermore, teenagers run away more often from families with stepparents and live-in boyfriends or girlfriends (Sweet, 1991).

Although the evidence is convincing, other studies contradict those cited. Rosen and Neilson (1982) and Farnworth (1984) found no association between single-parent families and delinquency. White et al. (1987) found a positive relationship to heavy alcohol use but not to delinquency or drug abuse. Gray-Ray and Ray (1990) identified no relationship between family type and delinquency for black children and adolescents. Additional support for this position was found by Parson and Mikawa (1991), who observed no difference between the percentages of incarcerated and nonincarcerated blacks from broken homes.

The association between single-parent families and delinquency is further clouded by a series of studies claiming that negative effects of single-parenthood may be caused by parental practices and family relations. In other words, the problems of single-parent families are explained by how parents relate to their children and how the family as a whole gets along. Several studies also suggest that the effect of single-parent homes is explained by conflict that occurred between the parents before and after the breakup (Herzog and Sudia, 1970; Bane, 1976; Rutter, 1977a and 1977b; Goetting, 1981; Blechman, 1982; Emery, 1982).

Henggeler (1989:48) suggested that greater autonomy for the adolescent (see also Dornbusch et al., 1985; Steinberg and Silverberg, 1986), less parental supervision (see also Steinberg, 1986; Van Voorhis et al., 1988; Laub and Sampson, 1988; Matsueda, 1982), less involvement with parents (see also Van Voorhis et al., 1988; Laub and Sampson, 1988), and, consequently, increased susceptibility to peer pressure determine delinquency. These factors are more likely to be present in single-parent families, although not exclusively so (Siegel and Senna, 1991:243-245). Along these same lines, Bayrakal and Kope (1990) claimed that children in single-parent families tend to grow up too fast (p. 6). These children may have a greater expectation for independence from parental control. For blacks, the presence of a father in the adolescent's life appears to be important (Rosen, 1985; Gray-Ray and Ray, 1990).

Other factors shown to influence this relationship are peer pressure (Steinberg 1987), personality (Widom et al., 1983), social class and criminality on the part of the father (Mednick et al., 1987), and conflict and coping strategies (Kurdek and Sinclair, 1988). Mednick et al. (1990) indicated that divorce followed by a stable family constellation is not associated with increased risk, but divorce followed by additional changes in family configuration significantly increases risk, particularly for adolescent males.

Three recent literature reviews help us to disentangle these disparate research findings. Loeber and Stouthamer-Loeber (1986) reviewed 15 studies, including 40 analyses of structural relationships. The review encompassed information indicating that 33 of the 40 assessments (83 percent) were statistically significant and that the effect of marital separation appeared to be somewhat greater on younger children. Marital discord was shown to be a better predictor of delinquency than family structure. Two studies (Glueck and Glueck, 1950; Zill, 1978) found that the death of a parent did not have the same effect as divorce on the child's behavior, which suggests that it is family relations, not just separation, that affects delinquency. Loeber and Stouthamer-Loeber reviewed two studies of supervision that speak to the single-parent/delinquency question. Stouthamer-Loeber et al. (1984) found that single mothers and unhappily married mothers supervised less diligently and that more of them had negative opinions of their children. Goldstein (1984) found that high supervision in father-absent families reduced the probability of arrest.

A meta-analysis of 50 studies by Wells and Rankin (1991) suggests that the effect of broken homes on delinquency is real and consistent, but of relatively low magnitude. The "prevalence of delinquency in broken homes is 10 to 15 percent higher than in intact homes" (p. 87). The effect is strongest for minor offenses and weakest for serious offenses. The Wells and Rankin review indicates that the type of breakup—death, desertion, or divorce—affects delinquency determination. Further, there appears to be no appreciable or consistent difference in effect on boys versus girls or blacks versus whites, no consistent effect related to the child's age, and, finally, no consistent effect of stepparents presence within the family.

The general patterns observed by Loeber and Stouthamer-Loeber and Wells and Rankin regarding family structure and delinquency are similarly described by McLanahan and Booth (1989:564-565), who discuss more general consequences of growing up in mother-only families. During the 1950s and 1960s, researchers viewed divorce and births to unmarried mothers as pathological, and they expected children in such situations to exhibit undesirable behaviors. In the 1970s, that view began to change. Researchers argued that the differences between mother-only and two-parent families could be explained by other factors such as poverty. Now, studies examining the cumulative findings of the research are recognizing certain negative consequences of growing up in single-parent homes. While these recent studies acknowledge that there may be nothing inherently pathological with single parenthood, such a structure may lead to a set of conditions that contribute to delinquency, for example, greater autonomy for the adolescent, less parental control, and increased susceptibility to peer pressure. Therefore, designing programs that assist the single parent in supervising the child and that free the parent to spend more time with the child may reduce delinquency.

Up until now, this report, like most others, has been somewhat cavalier in its use of language describing different structural arrangements of families, not stopping to precisely define what is being studied. Many researchers use the words "broken" and "intact" to describe family structures. These words are value-laden. The word "broken" possesses a negative connotation and inasmuch as the purpose of this research is to determine the effect of family structure, it seems inappropriate to use a negative label for single-parenthood. Consider at least two examples when the loss of a parent may strengthen family relations: (1) The death of a parent, though tragic for the family, may draw members together, bonding them in a manner that gives the surviving parent considerable influence over the children. (2) The loss of a violent or psychologically abusive parent may remove the source that is pushing children out of the family and creating individual stress. One study found that the outcome of parental absence depended on the competence of the remaining parent. In fact, "separation seemed to have little or no adverse effect when the alternative was an intact family with conflict, low parental esteem, paternal alcoholism, or criminality" (McCord, 1990a:132). A more precise definition of family structure is needed than a simple distinction between one- and two-parent families.

...

McLanahan and Booth (1989:566-569) presented three explanations for the relationship between single-parent or mother-only families and delinquency: (1) economic deprivation, (2) socialization, and (3) neighborhood. In this monograph, a fourth theory is added: the justice system's response.

Looking first at economic deprivation, Denno (1985) and Farrington (1979), in their longitudinal research, showed delinquency to be related to the mother's income at the time of the child's birth and to the father's irregular employment (Morash and Rucker, 1989:83). Other studies indicate that one of two single mothers lives in poverty compared with one in ten two-parent families with children (Garfinkel and McLanahan, 1986). Additionally, studies have found single mothers to have fewer resources (e.g., time and money) to invest in their children.

The second theory, socialization, includes factors that can attenuate the effect of single parenthood, such as autonomy, supervision, affection, and conflict. To this list Morash and Rucker add "low hopes for education" (1989:84). Single parents may be less able to properly supervise, monitor, guide, and support their children to ensure their conformity to societal rules.

The third theory, neighborhood, recognizes that many single-parent families live in social isolation and in economically deprived neighborhoods (Wilson, 1987). This demographic reality results in decreased opportunity for economic mobility and is associated with greater likelihood that children will quit school or become pregnant as teenagers.

Felson (1986) and Felson and Cohen (1980) stated that two-parent households provide increased supervision and surveillance of property, while single parenthood increases likelihood of delinquency and victimization simply by the fact that there is one less person to supervise adolescent behavior. Sampson (1986a, 1986b, 1987) confirmed this second hypothesis and suggested that single-parenthood indirectly decreases formal control because there is evidence of less participation in community and schools by single-parent families. Blau and Blau (1982) argued that marital disruption is a proxy for overall disorganization and alienation in the community.

Fourth, and finally, the criminal justice system may respond differently to the children from single-parent rather than two-parent families. Johnson (1986) argued that family structure is not related to frequency or seriousness of self-reported, illegal behavior but is related to self-reported trouble with police, school, and juvenile court. Johnson concluded that officials may be more likely to respond to the behavior of children from mother-only families. Cogent to this point, Hagan and Palloni (1990) found in their study of the intergenerational transmission of crime within families that after controlling for child-rearing practices, evidence suggested that labeling of family members by crime-control agents tended to reproduce criminal behavior.

In summary, what do we know about single parenthood's contribution to delinquency?

- Economic conditions inherent to single-parent families may place children at greater risk.
- Socialization of children residing in single-parent homes may differ from those residing with two parents.
- "Bad" neighborhoods, where single parents often reside, may contribute to delinquency.

The ways in which the system or officials from formal institutions such as school, police, and courts respond to children from single-parent homes may result in these children being more likely to be identified as delinquent.

What remains unknown or unclear?

- We lack a good understanding of parental practices and differences among the various types of households (McLanahan and Booth, 1989:573).
- We tend to see single-parent families in a monolithic way, neglecting attempts to understand the variations among these families that may produce successes as well as failures. Hartman (1990) indicated that at least 25 percent of all families with children are single-parent households. Most of these families do not produce delinquent children.
- Similarly, we lack knowledge about the variation among two-parent families.

Marital Discord

What effect does observing marital conflict have in determining delinquent behavior? After discussing mother-only family structures, the question that frequently follows asks, "Is a home with a bad marriage better for the children than a home with no marriage?"

In the previous section, we noted that many researchers have attributed the higher rate of delinquency among offspring of single-parent families to the effect of marital discord. Some of the earliest research identified this relationship. Glueck and Glueck (1950) observed that one-third of the delinquent boys in their sample were raised in homes with poor conjugal relations between the parents. Nye's (1958) research indicated like findings, that serious or excessive marital discord predicted delinquency better than divorce or single parenthood. In further support of these findings, Loeber and Stouthamer-Loeber (1986:72) noted that a number of review articles examining the effect of divorce and family conflict (Herzog and Sudia, 1970; Bane, 1976; Rutter, 1977a and 1977b; Goetting, 1981; Blechman, 1982; Emery, 1982) downplayed the relevance of divorce and single parenthood to children's behavioral problems and emphasized marital discord as stronger in predicting delinquency.

Given the general recognition of the importance of marital discord in predicting delinquency, one would expect a considerable body of conclusive research on the topic. However, this is not the case. The overall lack of studies led Koski (1988:33) to conclude that parent-to-parent violence and marital discord has received minimal attention in the research literature.

Still, one does find strong statements within the existing literature regarding the relationship of marital discord and delinquency. Minty (1988) asserts that marital conflict is "strongly associated with juvenile delinquency and conduct disorder" (p. 172). Likewise, Kruttschmitt et al. (1986) found exposure to parental conflict to be one of the most important background experiences affecting violent criminal behavior in young adult males. Additionally, Grych and Fincham (1990) concluded from a literature review that marital conflict is "highly associated" with children's adjustment. In a startling finding, Jaffe et al. (1986) claimed that "boys exposed to violence between parents had a pattern of adjustment problems similar to abused boys" (p. 142) And, finally, Holden and Ritchie (1991) found that children raised in homes where the mother was battered had more behavioral problems and more difficult temperaments and tended to be more aggressive.

A recent study published in *Science* suggested that "the effect of divorce on children can be predicted by conditions that existed well before the separation occurred" (Cherlin et al., 1991:252). Emery (1988) and Long and Forehand (1987) further stated that marital disharmony is the operative factor, not separation or life in a single-parent home....

Literature reviews indicate that marital discord is consistently related to delinquency but that the relationship is of moderate strength among the list of family attributes that contribute to delinquency. Widom (1989b:22) claimed that witnessing violence within the home yields a consistent but modest relationship with delinquency. Similarly, Snyder and Patterson (1987) argued that the relationship between conflict and delinquency is "quite modest and somewhat sketchy" (p. 225). Loeber and Stouthamer-Loeber (1986:77) found in 11 cross-sectional studies and 8 longitudinal studies that marital discord was a medium-strength predictor.

Half of all marriages end in divorce (Wattenberg, 1986:21); consequently, many children witness marital discord preceding divorce. For those who do, the literature and research lacks information about which explicit factors precipitate delinquency. The literature is severely hampered by this lack of adequate attention to the nature and extent of discord, which may vary from occasional verbal confrontations to overt violence. However, although the prevalence of marital discord in this country is extremely high, most of the children involved do not become delinquent.

Grych and Fincham (1990) pointed out that conflict may differ by frequency, intensity, duration, and outcome. Witnesses may vary in age, gender, and ethnicity. Other dimensions such as the resolution and content of the conflict may also influence the effect on the child's development. Grych and Fincham concluded that (1) exposure to frequent incidents of conflict leads to greater problems and cessation of conflict leads to a reduction in problems, (2) the intensity of conflict is related to the level of distress, (3) children as young as age 2 may be influenced by parental conflict, and (4) conflict affects both girls and boys.

What then, do we know about marital discord and delinquency?

- There is consistently a positive relationship.
- Children who witness marital discord are at greater risk of becoming delinquents. Social learning theory argues that aggressive behavior is learned; as parents display aggressive behavior, children learn to imitate it as an acceptable means of achieving goals.
- However, most children who witness arital conflict do not become delinquent.

We do not know much about the specific aspects of conflict that lead to delinquency.

Child Abuse

In the previous section, we discussed the effects of witnessing conflict and violence between parents on children's propensity toward delinquency. What happens when the child is the direct recipient of violence? Does child abuse and neglect lead to subsequent delinquency and criminality?

The relationship between abuse and delinquency has been described as a "cycle of violence" or the "intergenerational transmission of violence" and attributed to the notion that "violence begets violence" (Widom, 1989b:3). Curtis (1963:386) boldly stated that abused and neglected children "become tomorrow's murderers and perpetrators of other crimes of violence" (quoted by Widom, 1989b), and Siegel and Senna (1991) claimed that abuse "encourages [the victims] to use aggression as a means of solving problems, prevents them from feeling empathy for others, and diminishes their ability to cope with stress" (p. 265). Looking directly at juvenile criminals, Lewis et al. (1988) found that of the 37 young people condemned to death in the United States, 12 had been brutally physically abused and 5 had been sodomized by relatives.

One of the strongest positions taken on the relationship of abuse and delinquency comes from Fleisher's (forthcoming) study of the Crips and Bloods, west coast street gangs. Based upon interviews with gang members on the streets and in prison, Fleisher argues that, almost without exception, these boys "grow up in dangerous family environments." Youth may leave home and join gangs to escape the violence or drift away because they are abandoned or neglected by their parents and there is no "comfort, protection, security, or emotional warmth in the home." As a consequence, these young men develop what Fleisher calls a "defensive world view," characterized by six attributes: (1) a feeling of vulnerability and a need to protect oneself, (2) a belief that no one ca be trusted, (3) a need to maintain social distance, (4) a willingness to use violence and intimidation to repel others, (5) an attraction to similarly defensive people, and (6) an expectation that no one will come to their aid. . . .

A review by Howing et al. (1990) indicated that studies based on official records of abuse have found that between 9 and 26 percent of the delinquents have records of abuse (Lewis and Shanok, 1977; Shanok and Lewis, 1981; Kratcoski, 1982), whereas studies based on delinquents' self-reports of abuse indicate the figure to be from 51 to 69 percent (Mouzakitis, 1981; Rhoades and Parker, 1981). Studies of abused children find delinquency rates of 14 to 20 percent (Bolton, Reich, and Guiterres, 1977; Silver, Dublin, and Lourie, 1969). Histories of abuse distinguish violent and nonviolent delinquents, with considerably higher rates of abuse among violent offenders (Alfaro, 1983; Lewis et al., 1985; Lewis et al., 1979;

Shanok and Lewis, 1981; Tarter et al., 1984). The characteristics of the parents also seem to affect whether the abused child will become delinquent (Henggeler, 1989:46).

A 1989b review by Widom concluded that abuse breeds abuse. There appears to be a higher likelihood of abuse among parents who were abused themselves; however, the majority of abusive parents were not themselves abused as children. Based on the research of Kaufman and Zigler (1987), Widom (1989b:8) estimated that about one-third of the individuals who were abused as children will abuse their own children.

In making a connection among abuse, neglect, and delinquency, Widom (1989b) indicated that of those who had been abused or neglected as children, delinquency occurred in fewer than 20 percent of the cases. Various studies found between 8 and 26 percent of the delinquents had been abused.

A review of 12 studies that specifically examined the connections among abuse, neglect, and violent behavior produced contradictory results (Widom, 1989b). Some studies found strong support; others found no difference at all. Of the abused children who became delinquent, the majority were not violent in their delinquency. There was little indication of a lasting effect on violence.

When Widom herself examined the link through developmental/clinical studies, she found, "By and large, these studies indicate with some consistency that abused children manifest more aggressive and problematic behavior even at early ages" (1989b:19). Widom notes that not only do abused children manifest more aggressive and problematic behavior at early ages, but research indicates that these children are not likely to outgrow the aggressive patterns as they mature. Evidence suggests that some victims of abuse become self-abusive and self-destructive.

Overall, the Widom (1989b) review drew several important conclusions. Not all children who grow up in violent homes become violent adults; however, being abused as a child may increase the risk for becoming an abusive parent, a delinquent, or a violent adult criminal. As with the connection between single-parent families, it cannot be said that the road from abuse to delinquent, violent, or criminal behavior is straight or certain (p. 24). Again, the relationships are complex and interrelated.

The empirical research reports specific findings about abuse and its relationship to delinquency. Doerner (1987) found that several types of maltreatment, both physical and emotional, were associated with delinquency. In contrast, Brown (1984) found that only emotional, and not physical, abuse correlated with subsequent delinquency. Burgess et al. (1987) linked sexual abuse with later delinquency. Particularly serious or prolonged abuse was associated with higher rates of deviance.

Widom (1989a and 1989b) said that childhood victimization has a small but strongly indicated long-term consequence on adult criminal records. Twenty-nine percent of abused children compared with 21 percent of the control group were arrested as adults. Widom also points toward findings that abused females did not become violent but had higher rates of status and minor property offenses.

In another study, among abused males parental conflict and family criminality distinguished those who became delinquent from those who did not (Kruttschmitt et al. 1987). Among abused females, Seng (1989) found a two-stage process leading to prostitution: girls first run away, then engage in prostitution to survive. Looking specifically at sexually abused females, Morrow and Sorell (1989) found that the severity of sexual assault (sexual intercourse compared to fondling) was related to lower self-esteem, depression, antisocial behavior, and self-injury. Also the postdisclosure responses by the mother and the perpetrator, when they blamed the victim or demeaned the significance of the victimization, exacerbated the effect.

From the literature, what do we know about the relationship of abuse to delinquency?

- We know there is a link. Being abused increases the risk of delinquency.

- However, most abused children do not become abusive parents, delinquents, or violent adult criminals.

What we do not know is similar to unknown issues concerning parental conflict.
- What are the aspects of the abuse that directly influence delinquency?
- Why do some abused children become delinquent and others do not? Factors such as the frequency, duration, and termination of the abuse must be studied more completely to show how these aspects of abuse influence delinquent behavior.
- Unknown, as well, are important factors for intervention.

Family Effect

Previously, we examined the effect of physical violence inflicted on children by their parents. What about the psychological effects of rejection and the withholding of affection? Do they contribute to delinquency? This section looks at rejection versus affection, involvement, and cohesion within the family unit.

The premise is that children who are raised in supportive, affectionate, and accepting environments tend to become self-aware adults who can formulate their own long-term goals and can successfully pursue socially and economically fulfilling lives. In contrast, children of harsh, unloving, overly critical, and authoritarian parents often become self-absorbed as adults. Their impulsiveness can result in violence and substance abuse (Chollar, 1987:12).

Early research conducted by the Gluecks (1950) found that, indeed, the parents of delinquents were less affectionate. Bandura and Walters (1959) in some early studies concluded that parents, particularly fathers, of delinquents tend to be more rejecting and less affectionate toward their children. Nye (1958) found that parent-child acceptance or, conversely, rejection—mutual and unilateral—was strongly related to delinquency.

It seems probable, then, that rejection of children by their parent(s) may increase the chances for delinquency. Gray-Ray and Ray (1990) found this to be true for black males, and Kroupa's (1988) findings indicate that incarcerated girls perceived their parents as more rejecting than nonincarcerated girls. More generally, Stouthamer-Loeber and Loeber (1986) found lying among young boys to be related to rejection by their mothers and, to a lesser extent, by their fathers. Fighting at home and school was also shown to be related to rejection by parent(s) (Loeber and Dishion, 1984). Even after controlling for other family factors, rejection continued to show moderate relationship with delinquency (Simons, Robertson, and Downs, 1989). Pfouts et al. (1981) stated that children rejected by both parents are more likely to be delinquent than when they are supported and loved by one parent. . . .

Based upon the studies reviewed, parental rejection appears to be among the most powerful predictors of juvenile delinquency. Surprisingly, beyond that we know little about how rejection contributes to delinquency causation. Do parental activities such as monitoring and discipline interact with rejection? What about the developmental aspects of the relationship? Does the age of the child matter? How extensive does the rejection have to be—1 week, 6 months? Much remains to be learned.

The research just discussed examined parents' ties to their children-rejection versus affection, involvement, and cohesion. What about the child's attachment to parents? How does that relate to delinquency?

Hirschi's (1969) social control theory suggests that individuals conform to societal norms when they are "bonded" to society. When ties are weakened or broken, then the individual is free to be criminal. According to Hirschi (1969:16-27), four elements determine the extent to which people bond to society: involvement, commitment, belief, and attachment to society's institutions. Similarly, attachment to conventional parents is considered to be an important link between parent and child. Attachment provides the necessary link that allows parents' ideals and expectations to be expressed and received. When alienated from the parent, the child will not internalize moral rules or develop an adequate conscience (p. 86).

Based upon his own research, Hirschi concluded that "the closer the child's relations with his parents, the more he is attached to and identified with them, the lower his chances of delinquency" (p. 94).

Bonding to parents is viewed as an essential element in the developmental process leading to conformity. Poor child-parent attachment reduces commitment to academic and long-term social and economic goals. Without such commitments, school failure is more likely, thus reducing the chances of conventional success. In this manner, initial absence of child-parent bonding is tied to subsequent bonding with society's conventional institutions.

Several studies support Hirschi's theory about attachment to parents (Linden and Fillmore, 1981; Canter, 1982; Hanson et al., 1984; Agnew, 1985; Figueira-McDonough, 1985; Fagan, Piper, and Moore, 1986; Fagan and Wexler, 1987; Paternoster and Triplett, 1988; Gardner and Shoemaker, 1989; Blaske et al., 1989; Rankin and Wells, 1990; Mak, 1990; Smith, Weiher, and Van Kammen, 1991). However, the research has consistently found that the relationship between attachment to parents and delinquency, although present, is relatively weak and secondary to loyalty and participation in a delinquent peer group (Hanson et al., 1984) or exposure to delinquent influences (Matsueda, 1982; Matsueda and Heimer, 1987). As children mature, their loyalty apparently shifts away from parents toward the peer group.

Four studies (LaGrange and White, 1985; Steinberg and Silverberg, 1986; Smith and Paternoster, 1987; Paternoster, 1988) point to the developmental aspects of attachment. As a child moves into adolescence, a shift in attachment from parents occurs. Paternoster (1988:177) reported that parental influence tends to wane over the 3-year high school period, while friends' influence became slightly stronger.

Based on this research, what do we know about family affect and delinquency?

- A healthy home environment, one in which parents and children share affection, cohesion, and involvement, reduces the risk of delinquency.
- Parental rejection appears to be one of the most significant predictors of delinquency.
- Not only does parental attachment to children influence the likelihood of delinquency, but apparently so does the attachment of the child to the parent. This dual relationship implies an interaction between characteristics of both the parent and the child.

Interaction

Parental rejection appears to influence delinquency. However, delinquent behavior produces considerable stress within the family and may lead to parental rejection. The relationship may be bidirectional or reciprocal in nature. Snyder and Patterson (1987) expressed this idea, noting that "the child is both victim and architect of his own environment" (p. 237).

The components of the reciprocal relationship are complex. Sameroff and Seifer (1983) suggested that "the development of the child appears to be multiply determined by what the child brings to the situation, what [she or he] elicits from the situation, what the environment can offer and what it does offer" (p. 12). Patterson (1982) identified a "coercive cycle" in mother/aggressive-child interactions. Simply stated, the child's antisocial behavior is followed by negative reactions by the parent. This, in turn, escalates the child's antisocial, aggressive behavior, triggering a cycle that is both cause and effect. (See also Bell's 1977 model of reciprocity.)

Widom et al. (1983:287) attempted to explain the personality differences between delinquent and nondelinquent girls, suggesting that the ongoing and reciprocal interaction between harsh, unpredictable environments and individuals with impulsive and stimulation-seeking behavioral styles may initiate a coercive cycle. Gove and Crutchfield (1982:315) found that parents' perceptions or sense of understanding of their child is one of the strongest predictors of juvenile delinquency. They suggested that the tendency not to get along well with the child and dissatisfaction with the child's behavior promotes negative parental behavior—reduced supervision and greater use of physical punishments—which probably further encourages misbehavior on the part of the child. This actuates a vicious cycle that leads to an escalation of the child's misbehavior.

Lytton (1990:683) identified three factors in the reciprocal relationship between parent and child: (1) characteristics of the child, (2) the parental behavior (those elements already discussed, such as supervision, affection, etc.), and (3) reciprocal effects. Before turning to reciprocal effects let us briefly touch on some of the research exploring the role of individual predisposition or background in determining delinquency. In acknowledging the child's role, Loeber and Stouthamer-Loeber (1986) suggested that parents are the child's first really serious victims.

Researchers have found considerable stability in aggressive and antisocial behavior, particularly when that behavior is extensive and initiated at an early age (Olweus, 1979; Loeber, 1982; Huesmann et al., 1984). This evidence has led researchers to postulate a predisposition toward aggression and antisocial behavior that may be transmitted down through generations. Some evidence suggests that the child's tendencies toward antisocial behavior are even stronger than parental influence in determining delinquent outcomes (Lytton, 1990:693; see also Anderson, Lytton, and Romney, 1986.)

A child's predisposition toward impulsive, aggressive, and antisocial behavior has been attributed to genetic (Huesmann et al., 1984) and biological factors. Faretra (1981) identifies several aspects of personal pathology, including genetic determination (Schulsinger, 1980), brain damage and mental retardation (Caputo and Mandell, 1970), low intelligence (Moffitt et al., 1980), neurotic and psychotic disorders, and psychopathic traits, as factors in determining conduct disorder. Henggeler et al. (1986:133) offered a more inclusive explanation implicating many aspects of the child's biopsychosocial makeup, including the child's cognitive strengths and weaknesses, physical appearance, coordination, attitudes, beliefs, and the presence of disabilities or handicaps. The National Health/Education Consortium (1991) expressed a specific biological factor, stating that prenatal health, ingestion of lead and other toxins, and exposure to cocaine and other drugs are all related to brain development and possibly to behavioral problems. . . .

Some researchers have demonstrated that aggressive, antisocial acts in childhood and adolescence predict future delinquent behavior. Faretra (1981) found that among 66 aggressive and disturbed adolescents who had been admitted to an inpatient psychiatric unit, antisocial and criminal behavior persisted into adulthood; however, there was a lessening of the psychiatric involvement.

The most antisocial children in this sample were from homes with histories of antisocial problems, single-parent homes, and/or impoverished homes.

Sanders et al. (1989) examined the interactions among family members and argued that the single best predictor of child deviant behavior is maternal rejection of the child. Interestingly, they found the best predictor of maternal rejection or aversion was the child's deviant behavior. Sanders labeled the problem a "negative reinforcement trap" (p. 80-81). Lytton (1990) and Anderson et al. (1986) have supported this depiction of mother/child relations.

In testing his theory of coercive cycles, Patterson (Patterson, 1986; Patterson and Bank, 1986; Patterson, Dishion, and Bank, 1984) consistently found support for the reciprocal relationship of family relations and conduct disorders. Baldwin and Skinner (1989) replicated the findings.

Recognizing the reciprocal and bidirectional nature of the relationship between child and parents, Henggeler et al. (1986) conducted a treatment experiment using the family-ecological approach for inner-city juvenile offenders and their families. This method addresses the multidimensional nature of behavioral problems, exploring individual deficits such as poor social and problem-solving skills, inappropriate child and family interactions, and problematic transactions with extrafamilial systems such as the peer group and the school. Therapy is individualized and focused on the most important determinants of the child's problem behavior (p. 133). Observation revealed that interactions became warmer and more affectionate with treatment. In turn, parents reported that their children's conduct problems, immature behavior, and relationship with delinquents decreased.

Thornberry (1987:876), speaking from the perspective of social control theory, argued that as the child or adolescent participates or engages in more frequent delinquent behavior while associating increasingly with delinquent peers, his/her bond to conventional society grows weaker. The weakening of the bond to conventional society may be an initial cause of delinquency, as social control theorists have proposed. Continued and increased delinquent acts may become their own indirect cause as they further weaken the youth's bonds to family, school, and conventional beliefs. Results from three longitudinal studies of delinquency and drug use conducted in Pittsburgh, Rochester, and Denver found a modest but significant reciprocal relationship between delinquency and attachment. Prior low levels of family attachment and poor parenting actions (failure to communicate with and monitor children) were related with subsequently higher levels of delinquency and drug use. Conversely, prior high levels of delinquency and drug use were related with subsequently low levels of family attachment and poor parenting. It seems that poor family life makes delinquency worse, and a high level of delinquency makes family life worse (Smith, Weiher, and Van Kammen, 1991; see also Thornberry et al., 1991).

This research on causes of delinquency makes a major contribution to our understanding of the interaction of the family and delinquency.

- A child's predisposition toward impulsive, aggressive, and antisocial behavior may initiate a process within the family that ultimately leads to delinquency.

- Parents of a difficult child may stop parenting to gain peace within the home and may come to reject the child.

- Antisocial patterns established within the family may be exacerbated and reinforced as the child enters school.

- As the child enters adolescence, delinquent acts may further weaken the youth's attachment to family, school, and conventional ties.

The topic of interaction is complex and requires further study as it may lead to new strategies for intervention at a variety of points in the youth's life and his or her family and community. . . .

References

Agnew, Robert. 1985. "Social Control Theory and Delinquency: A Longitudinal Test." *Criminology* 23(1):47-61.

Alfaro, J.D. 1983. "Report on the Relationship Between Child Abuse and Neglect and Later Socially Deviant Behavior." In *Exploring the Relationship Between Child Abuse and Delinquency*, edited by R.J. Hanner and Y.E. Walker. Montclair, NJ: Allanheld, Osmun.

Anderson, Kathleen E., Hugh Lytton, and David R. Romney. 1986. "Mothers' Interactions With Normal and Conduct-Disordered Boys: Who Affects Whom?" *Developmental Psychology* 22(5):604-609.

Baldwin, David V. and Martie L. Skinner. 1989. "Structural Model for Antisocial Behavior: Generalization to Single-Mother Families." *Developmental Psychology* 25(1):45-50.

Bandura, A. and R.H. Walters. 1959. *Adolescent Aggression*. New York: Ronald Press.

Bane, M.J. 1976. "Marital Disruption and the Lives of Children." *Journal of Social Issues* 32:103-117.

Barkley, Russell A. 1990. *Attention-Deficit Hyperactivity Disorder: A Handbook for Diagnosis and Treatment*. New York: Guilford.

Bayrakal, Sadi and Teresa Kope. 1990. "Dysfunction in the Single-Parent and Only-Child Family." *Adolescence* 25:1-7.

Bell, R.Q. 1977. "Socialization Findings Re-examined." In *Child Effects on Adults*, edited by R.Q. Bell and R.V. Harper. Hillsdale, NJ: Erlbaum:53-84.

Blaske, David M., Charles M. Borduin, Scott W. Henggeler, and Barton J. Mann. 1989. "Individual, Family, and Peer Characteristics of Adolescent Sex Offenders and Assaultive Offenders." *Developmental Psychology* 25(5):846-855.

Blau, Judith and Peter Blau. 1982. "The Cost of Inequality: Metropolitan Structure and Violent Crime." *American Sociological Review* 47:114-129.

Blechman, E. 1982. "Are Children With One Parent at Psychological Risk? A Methodological Review." *Journal of Marriage and the Family* 44:179-195.

Bolton, F.G., J.W. Reich, and S.E. Guiterres. 1977. "Delinquency Patterns in Maltreated Children and Siblings." *Victimology* 2:349-357.

Borduin, Charles M., Julie A. Pruitt, and Scott W. Henggeler. 1986. "Family Interactions in Black, Lower-Class Families With Delinquent and Nondelinquent Adolescent Boys." *Journal of Genetic Psychology* 147(3):333-342.

Brady, C. Patrick, James H. Bray, and Linda Zeeb. 1986. "Behavior Problems of Clinic Children: Relation to Parental Marital Status, Age, and Sex of Child." *American Journal of Orthopsychiatry* 56:399-412.

Brown, Stephen E. 1984. "Social Class, Child Maltreatment, and Delinquent Behavior." *Criminology* 22(2) (May):259-278.

Burgess, Ann W., Carol R. Hartman, and Arlene McCormack. 1987. "Abused to Abuser: Antecedents of Socially Deviant Behaviors." *American Journal of Psychiatry* 14 4(11) (November):1431-1436.

Campbell, Anne. 1987. "Self-reported Delinquency and Home Life: Evidence From a Sample of British Girls." *Journal of Youth and Adolescence* 16(2):167-177.

Canter, R.J. 1982. "Family Correlates of Male and Female Delinquency." *Criminology* 20:149-167.

Caputo, D.V. and W. Mandell. 1970. "Consequences of Low Birth Weight." *Developmental Psychology* 3(3):363-383.

Carson, Robert C., James N. Butcher, and James C. Coleman. 1988. *Abnormal Psychology and Modern Life*, 8th ed. New York: Harper Collins.

Cernkovich, Stephen A. and Peggy C. Giordano. 1987. "Family Relationships and Delinquency." *Criminology* 25(2):295-321.

Cherlin, Andrew J., Frank F. Furstenberg, Jr., Lindsey Chase-Lansdale, Kathleen E. Kiernan, Philip K. Robins, Donna Ruane Morrison, and Julien O. Teitler. 1991. "Longitudinal Studies of Effects of Divorce on Children in Great Britain and the United States." *Science* 252 (June):1386-1389.

Chollar, Susan. 1987. "We Reap What We Sow." *Psychology Today* 21:12.

Cochran, Moncrieff, and Inge Bø. 1989. "The Social Networks, Family Involvement, and Pro- and Antisocial Behavior of Adolescent Males in Norway." *Journal of Youth and Adolescence* 18(4):377-398.

Curtis, G.C. 1963. "Violence Breeds Violence—Perhaps?" *American Journal of Psychiatry* 120:386-387.

Denno, Deborah W. 1985. "Sociological and Human Developmental Explanations of Crime: Conflict or Consensus?" *Criminology* 23(4):711-741.

DiLalla, Lisabeth Fisher, Christina M. Mitchell, Michael W. Arthur, and Pauline M. Pagliocca. 1988. "Aggression and Delinquency: Family and Environmental Factors." *Journal of Youth and Adolescence* 17(3):233-246.

Doerner, William G. 1987. "Child Maltreatment Seriousness and Juvenile Delinquency." *Youth and Society* 19(2) (December):197-224.

Dornbusch, Sanford M., J. Merrill Carlsmith, Steven J. Bushwall, Philip L. Ritter, Herbert Leiderman, Albert H. Hastorf, and Ruth T. Gross. 1985. "Single Parents, Extended Households, and the Control of Adolescents." *Child Development* 56:326-341.

Emery, R.E. 1982. "Interpersonal Conflict and the Children of Discord and Divorce." *Psychological Bulletin* 93:310-30.

Fagan, Jeffrey, Elizabeth Piper, and Melinda Moore. 19986. "Violent Delinquents and Urban Youths." *Criminology* 24(3)439-471.

Fagan, Jeffrey and Sandra Wexler. 1987. "Family Origins of Violent Delinquents." *Criminology* 25(3):643-669.

Faretra, G. 1981. "A Profile of Aggression From Adolescence to Adulthood: An 18-year Follow-up of Psychiatrically Disturbed and Violent Adolescents." *American Journal of Orthopsychiatry* 51:439-453.

Farnworth, M. 1984. "Family Structure, Family Attributes, and Delinquency in a Sample of Low-Income, Minority Males and Females." *Journal of Youth and Adolescence* 13:349-364.

Farrington, David P. 1979. "Environmental Stress, Delinquent Behavior, and Convictions." In *Stress and Anxiety*, edited by J.G. Sarason and C.D. Spielberger. Washington, D.C.: Hemisphere.

Felson, Marcus. 1986. "Linking Criminal Choices, Routine Activities, Informal Control, and Criminal Outcomes." In *The Reasoning Criminal: Rational Choice Perspectives on Offending*, edited by Derek B. Cornish and Ronald V. Clarke. New York: Springer-Verlag:119-128.

Felson, Marcus and Lawrence E. Cohen. 1980. "Human Ecology and Crime: A Routine Activity Approach." *Human Ecology* 8(4):389-406.

Figueira-McDonough, Josefina. 1985. "Are Girls Different? Gender Discrepancies Between Delinquent Behavior and Control." *Child Welfare* LXIV(3) (May-June): 273-289.

Finkelhor, David, Gerald Hotaling, and Andrea Sedlak. 1990. *Missing, Abducted, Runaway, and Throwaway Children in America*. First Re-

port. Washington, D.C.: Office of Juvenile Justice and Delinquency Prevention.
Fleisher, Mark. Forthcoming. *Sentenced to Life*.
Flewelling, Robert L., and Karl E. Bauman. 1990. "Family Structure as a Predictor of Initial Substance Abuse and Sexual Intercourse in Early Adolescence." *Journal of Marriage and the Family* 52 (February):171-181.
Fox, Robert, Anthony F. Rotatori, Faye Macklin, Herman Green, and Theresa Fox. 1983. "Socially Maladjusted Adolescents' Perceptions of Their Families." *Psychological Reports* 52:831-834.
Gardner, Le Grande and Donald J. Shoemaker. 1989. "Social Bonding and Delinquency: A Comparative Analysis." *Sociological Quarterly* 30(3):481-500.
Garfinkel, Irwin and Sara S. McLanahan. 1986. *Single Mothers and Their Children: A New American Dilemma*. Washington, D.C.: Urban Institute Press.
Geismar, Ludwig L. and Katherine M. Wood. 1986. *Family and Delinquency: Resocializing the Young Offender*. New York: Human Sciences Press.
Gibson, H.B. 1969. "Early Delinquency in Relation to Broken Homes." *Journal of Child Psychology* 10:195-204.
Glueck, S. and Eleanor Glueck. 1950. *Unraveling Juvenile Delinquency*. Cambridge, MA: Harvard University Press.
Goetting, Ann. 1981. "Divorce Outcome Research." *Journal of Family Issues* 2:350-378.
———. 1989. "Patterns of Homicide Among Children." *Criminal Justice and Behavior* 16(1) (March):63-80.
Goldstein, H.S. 1984. "Parental Composition, Supervision, and Conduct Problems in Youths 12 to 17 Years Old." *Journal of the American Academy of Child Psychiatry* 23:679-684.
Gove, Walter R. and Robert D. Crutchfield. 1982. "The Family and Juvenile Delinquency." *Sociological Quarterly* 23 (Summer):301-319.
Gray-Ray, Phyllis, and Melvin C. Ray. 1990. "Juvenile Delinquency in the Black Community." *Youth and Society* 22(1) (September):67-84.
Grych, John H. and Frank D. Finchman. 1990. "Marital Conflict and Children's Adjustment: A Cognitive-Contextual Framework." *Psychological Bulletin* 108(2):267-290.
Guarino, S. 1985. "Delinquent Youth and Family Violence." Publication No. 14, 020-100-74-4-85-CR, Commonwealth of Massachusetts: Department of Youth Services.
Gully, K.J., H.A. Dengerink, M. Pepping, and D. Bergstrom. 1981. "Research Note: Sibling Contribution to Violent Behavior." *Journal of Marriage and the Family* 43:333-337.
Hagan, John and Alberto Palloni. 1990. "The Social Reproduction of a Criminal Class in Working-Class London, Circa 1950-1980." *American Journal of Sociology* 96 (September):265-299.
Hanson, Cindy L., Scott W. Henggeler, William F. Haefele, and J. Douglas Rodick. 1984. "Demographic, Individual, and Family Relationship Correlates of Serious and Repeated Crime Among Adolescents and Their Siblings." *Journal of Consulting and Clinical Psychology* 52(4):528-538.
Hartman, Ann. 1990. "Family Ties: An Editorial." *Social Work* (May):195-196.
Hartstone, E. and K.V. Hansen. 1984. "The Violent Juvenile Offender: An Empirical Portrait." In *Violent Juvenile Offenders: An Anthology*, edited by R.A. Mathias. San Francisco: National Council on Crime and Delinquency:83-112.
Heatherington, E.M., R. Stowie, and E.H. Ridberg. 1971. "Patterns of Family Interaction and Child Rearing Related to Three Dimensions of Juvenile Delinquency." *Journal of Abnormal Psychology* 77:160-176.
Henggeler, Scott W. 1989. *Delinquency in Adolescence*. Newbury Park: Sage.
Henggeler, Scott W., Cindy L. Henson, Charles M. Borduin, Sylvia M. Watson, and Molly A. Brunk. 1985. "Mother-Son Relationships of Juvenile Felons." *Journal of Consulting and Clinical Psychology* 53(6):942-943.
Henggeler, Scott W., J. Douglas Rodick, Charles M. Borduin, Cindy L. Hanson, Sylvia M. Watson, and Jon R. Urey. 1986. "Multisystemic Treatment of Juvenile Offenders: Effects on Adolescent Behavior and Family Interaction." *Developmental Psychology* 22(1):132-141.
Hershorn, Michael and Alan Rosenbaum. 1985. "Children of Marital Violence: A Closer Look at the Unintended Victims." *American Journal of Orthopsychiatry* 55(2):260-266.
Herzog, E. and C.E. Sudia. 1970. "Boys in Fatherless Families." Washington, D.C.: Office of Child Development.
Hill, John P. and Grayson N. Holmbeck. 1987. "Disagreements About Rules in Families With Seventh-Grade Girls and Boys." *Journal of Youth and Adolescence* 16(3):221-246.
Hirschi, Travis D. 1969. *Causes of Delinquency*. Berkeley, CA: University of California Press.
Holden, George W., and Kathy L. Ritchie. 1991. "Linking Extreme Marital Discord, Child Rearing, and Child Behavior for Problems: Evidence From Battered Women." *Child Development* 62:311-327.
Howing, Phyllis T., John S. Wodarski, P. David Kurtz, James M. Gaudin, Jr., and Emily Neligan Herbst. 1990. "Child Abuse and Delinquency: The Empirical and Theoretical Links." *Social Work* (May):244-249.
Huesmann, L. Rowell, Monroe M. Lefkowitz, Leonard D. Eron, and Leopold O. Walder. 1984. "Stability of Aggression Over Time and

Generations." *Developmental Psychology* 20(6):1120-1134.

Jaffe, Peter, David Wolfe, Susan Wilson, and Lydia Zak. 1986. "Similarities in Behavioral and Social Maladjustment Among Child Victims and Witnesses to Family Violence." *American Journal of Orthopsychiatry* 56(1) (January):142-146.

Johnson, Richard E. 1986. "Family Structure and Delinquency: General Patterns and Gender Differences." *Criminology* 24(1):65-84.

———. 1987. "Mother's Versus Father's Role in Causing Delinquency." *Adolescence* 22(86) (Summer):305-315.

Kaufman, J. and E. Zigler. 1987. "Do Abused Children Become Abusive Parents?" *American Journal of Orthopsychiatry* 57:186-192.

Kolko, David J. and Alan E. Kazdin. 1990. "Matchplay and Firesetting in Children: Relationship to Parent to Parent, Marital, and Family Dysfunction." *Journal of Clinical Child Psychology* 19(3)229-238.

Koski, Patricia R. 1988. "Family Violence and Nonfamily Deviance: Taking Stock of the Literature." *Marriage and Family Review* 12(1-2):23-46.

Kratcoski, Peter C. 1982. "Child Abuse and Violence Against the Family." *Child Welfare* 61(7):435-443.

Kroupa, Steven E. 1988. "Perceived Parental Acceptance and Female Juvenile Delinquency." *Adolescence* 23(89) (Spring):171-185.

Kruttschnitt, Candace, Linda Heath, and David A. Ward. 1986. "Family Violence, Television Viewing Habits, and Other Adolescent Experiences Related to Violent Criminal Behavior." *Criminology* 24(2):235-267.

Kruttschnitt, Candace, David Ward, and Mary Ann Sheble. 1987. "Abuse-Resistant Youth: Some Factors That May Inhibit Violent Criminal Behavior." *Social Forces* 66(2) (December):501-519.

Kurdek, Lawrence A. and Ronald J. Sinclair. 1988. "Adjustment of Young Adolescents in Two-Parent Nuclear, Stepfather, and Mother-Custody Families." *Journal of Consulting and Clinical Psychology* 56(1):91-96.

LaGrange, Randy L., and Helene Raskin White. 1985. "Age Differences in Delinquency: A Test of Theory." *Criminology* 23(1):19-45.

Lane, Theodore W. and Glen E. Davis. 1987. "Child Maltreatment and Juvenile Delinquency: Does a Relationship Exist." In *Prevention of Delinquent Behavior*, edited by John D. Burchard and Sara N. Burchard. Newbury Park: Sage:12-138.

Laub, John H. and Robert J. Sampson. 1988. "Unraveling Families and Delinquency: A Reanalysis of the Gluecks' Data." *Criminology* 26(3):355-379.

LeFlore, Larry. 1988. "Delinquent Youths and Family." *Adolescence* 23(91) (Fall):629-642.

Lewis, D.O., E. Moy, L.D. Jackson, R. Aaronson, N.S. Restifo, S.Serra, and A. Simos. 1985. "Biopsychosocial Characteristics of Children Who Later Murder: A Prospective Study." *American Journal of Psychiatry* 142(10):1161-1167.

Lewis, D.O. and S.S. Shanok. 1977. "Medical Histories of Delinquent and Nondelinquent Children: An Epidemiological Study." *American Journal of Psychiatry* 134(9):1020-1025.

Lewis, D.O., S.S. Shanok, J.H. Pincus, and G.H. Glaser. 1979. "Violent Juvenile Delinquents: Psychiatric, Neurological, Psychological, and Abuse Factors." *Journal of the American Academy of Psychiatry* 18:307-319.

Lewis, Dorothy Otnow, Jonathan H. Pincus, Barbara Bard, Ellis Richardson, Leslie S. Prichep, Marilyn Feldman, and Catherine Yeager. 1988. "Neuropsychiatric, Psychoeducational, and Family Characteristics of 14 Juveniles Condemned to Death in the United States." *American Journal of Psychiatry* 145(5) (May):585-589.

Linden, Rick, and Cathy Fillmore. 1981. "A Comparative Study of Delinquency Involvement." *Canadian Review of Sociology and Anthropology* 18(3):341-361.

Loeber, Rolf. 1982. "The Stability of Antisocial and Delinquent Child Behavior: A Review." *Child Development* 53:1431-1446.

Loeber, Rolf, and Thomas J. Dishion. 1983. "Early Predictors of Male Delinquency: A Review." *Psychological Bulletin* 94(1):68-99.

———. 1984. "Boys Who Fight at Home and School: Conditions Influencing Cross-Setting Consistency." *Journal of Consulting and Clinical Psychology* 52(5):759-768.

Loeber, Rolf and Magda Stouthamer-Loeber. 1986. "Family Factors as Correlates and Predictors of Juvenile Conduct Problems and Delinquency." In *Crime and Justice: An Annual Review of Research*, vol. 7, edited by Michael Tonry and Norval Morris. Chicago: University of Chicago Press:29-149.

Loeber, Rolf, Anne Wylie Weiher, and Carolyn Smith. 1991. "The Relationship Between Family Interaction and Delinquency and Substance Use." In *Urban Delinquency and Substance Abuse: Technical Report*. Vol. 1, edited by David Huizinga, Rolf Loeber, and Terence P. Thornberry. Washington, D.C.: Office of Juvenile Justice and Delinquency.

Long, N. and R. Forehand. 1987. "The Effects of Parental Divorce and Parental Conflict on Children: An Overview." *Developmental and Behavioral Pediatrics* 8:292-296.

Lorion, Raymond P., Patrick H. Tolan, and Robert G. Wahler. 1987. "Prevention." In *Handbook of Juvenile Delinquency*, edited by Herbert C. Quay. New York: John Wiley and Sons:417-450.

Lytton, Hugh. 1990. "Child and Parent Effects in Boys' Conduct Disorder: A Reinterpretation." *Developmental Psychology* 26(5):683-697.

Mak, Anita S. 1990. "Testing a Psychosocial Control Theory of Delinquency." *Criminal Justice and Behavior* 17(2) (June):215-230.

Mann, Barton J., Charles M. Borduin, Scott W. Henggeler, and David Blaske. 1990. "An Investigation of Systemic Conceptualizations of Parent-Child Coalitions and Symptom Change." *Journal of Consulting and Clinical Psychology* 58(3):336-344.

Matsueda, Ross L. 1982. "Testing Control Theory and Differential Association: A Causal Modeling Approach." *American Sociological Review* 47 (August):489-504.

Matsueda, Ross L. and Karen Heimer. 1987. "Race, Family, Structure, and Delinquency: A Test of Differential Association and Social Control Theories." *American Sociological Review* 52 (December):826-840.

McCord, Joan. 1979. "Some Child-Rearing Antecedents of Criminal Behavior in Adult Child-Rearing Men." *Journal of Personality and Social Psychology* 37:1477-1486.

——. 1983. "A Forty-Year Perspective on Effects of Child Abuse and Neglect." *Child Abuse and Neglect* 7:265-270.

——. 1988. "Parental Behavior in the Cycle of Aggression." *Psychiatry* 51 (February):14-23.

——. 1990a. "Long-term Perspectives on Parental Absence." In *Straight and Devious Pathways from Childhood to Adulthood*, edited by Lee N. Robins and Michael Rutter. Cambridge: Cambridge University Press:116-134.

——. 1990b. "Crime in Moral and Social Contexts—The American Society of Criminology, 1989 Presidential Address." *Criminology* 28(1):1-26.

McLanahan, Sara and Karen Booth. 1989. "Mother-Only Families: Problems, Prospects, and Politics." *Journal of Marriage and Family* 51 (August):557-580.

Mednick, Birgitte, Charlotte Reznick, Dennis Hocevar, and Robert Baker. 1987. "Long-Term Effects of Parental Divorce on Young Adult Male Crime." *Journal of Youth and Adolescence* 16(1):31-45.

Mednick, Birgitte, Robert L. Baker, and Linn E. Carothers. 1990. "Patterns of Family Instability and Crime: The Association of Timing of the Family's Disruption with Subsequent Adolescent and Young Adult Criminality." *Journal of Youth and Adolescence* 19(3):201-220.

Minty, Brian. 1988. "Public Care or Distorted Family Relationships: The Antecedents of Violent Crime." *Howard Journal* 27(3) (August):172-187.

Moffitt, E.E., W.F. Gabrielli, S.A. Mednick, and F. Schulsinger. 1980. "Socioeconomic Status, I.Q. and Delinquency." *Journal of Abnormal Psychology* 90(2):152-156.

Morash, Merry and Lila Rucker. 1989. "An Exploratory Study of the Connection of Mother's Age at Childbearing to Her Children's Delinquency in Four Data Sets." *Crime and Delinquency* 35(1) (January):45-93.

Morrison, W. Douglas. 1915. *Juvenile Offenders*. New York: D. Appleton and Company.

Morrow, K. Brent and Gwendolyn T. Sorrell. 1989. "Factors Affecting Self-esteem, Depression, and Negative Behaviors in Sexually Abused Female Adolescents." *Journal of Marriage and Family* 51 (August):677-686.

Mouzakitis, C.M. 1981. "An Inquiry Into the Problem of Child Abuse and Juvenile Delinquency." In *Exploring the Relationship Between Child Abuse and Delinquency*, edited by R.J. Hunner and Y.E. Walker. Montclair, NJ: Allanheld, Osmun:220-231.

National Health/Education Consortium. 1991. "Healthy Brain Development: Precursor to Learning." Washington, D.C.: National Commission to Prevent Infant Mortality, January.

Nye, Ivan F. 1958. *Family Relationships and Delinquent Behavior*. New York: John Wiley and Sons.

Olweus, Dan. 1979. "Stability of Aggressive Reaction Patterns in Males: A Review." *Psychological Bulletin* 86(4):852-875.

Parson, Naida M. and James K. Mikawa. 1991. "Incarceration and Nonincarceration of African-American Men Raised in Black Christian Churches." *Journal of Psychology* 125(2):163-179.

Paternoster, Raymond. 1988. "Examining Three-Wave Deterrence Models: A Question of Temporal Order and Specification." *Journal of Criminal Law and Criminology* 79(1):135-179.

Paternoster, Raymond and Ruth Triplett. 1988. "Disaggregating Self-reported Delinquency and Its Implications for Theory." *Criminology* 26(4):591-647.

Patterson, Gerald R. 1982. *Coercive Family Process*. Eugene, OR: Castalia.

——. 1986. "Performance Models for Antisocial Boys." *American Psychologist* 41(4) (April):432-444.

Patterson, G.R., T.J. Dishion, and L. Bank. 1984. "Family Interaction: A Process Model of Deviancy Training." *Aggressive Behavior* 10:253-267.

Patterson, Gerald R. and Lew Bank. 1986. "Bootstrapping Your Way Into the Nomological Thicket." *Behavior Assessment* 8:49-73.

Pfouts, J.H., J.H. Scholper, and H.C. Henley, Jr. 1981. "Deviant Behaviors of Child Victims and Bystanders in Violent Families." In *Exploring the Relationship Between Child Abuse and Delinquency*, edited by R.J. Hunter and Y.E. Walker. Montclair, NJ: Allanheld, Osmun:79-99.

Rankin, Joseph H. 1983. "The Family Context of Delinquency." *Social Problems* 30(4) (April):466-479.

Rankin, Joseph H., and L. Edward Wells. 1990. "The Effect of Parental Attachments and Direct Controls on Delinquency." *Journal of Research in Crime and Delinquency* 27(2) (May):140-165.

Reich, J.W., and S.E. Guiterres. 1979. "Escape/Aggression Incidence in Sexually Abused Juvenile Delinquents." *Criminal Justice and Behavior* 6:239-243.

Rhoades, P.W. and S.L. Parker. 1981. "The Connection Between Youth Problems and Violence in the Home." Portland, OR: Oregon Coalition Against Domestic and Sexual Violence.

Richards, P., R.A. Berk, and B. Forster. 1979. *Crime as Play: Delinquency in a Middle Class Suburb*. Cambridge, MA: Ballinger.

Rodick, Douglas, Scott W. Henggeler, and Cindy L. Hanson. 1986. "An Evaluation of the Family Adaptability and Cohesion Evaluation Scales and the Circumplex Model." *Journal of Abnormal Child Psychology* 14(1)77-87.

Roff, James D. and Robert D. Wirt. 1985. "The Specifity of Childhood Problem Behavior for Adolescent and Young Adult Maladjustment." *Journal of Clinical Psychology* 41(4) (July):564-571.

Rosen, Lawrence. 1985. "Family and Delinquency: Structure or Function?" *Criminology* 23(3):553-573.

Rosen, Lawrence and Kathleen Neilson. 1982. "Broken Homes and Delinquency." In *Contemporary Criminology*, edited by Leonard Savitz and Norman Johnson. New York: John Wiley and Sons.

Rosenbaum, Jill Leslie. 1989. "Family Dysfunction and Female Delinquency." *Crime and Delinquency* 35(1):31-44.

Rothman, David J. 1990. *The Discovery of the Asylum: Social Order and Disorder in the New Republic*. Boston: Little, Brown, and Co.

Rutter, Michael. 1977a. "The Family Influences." In *Child Psychiatry: Modern Approaches*, edited by M. Rutter and L. Hersov. Oxford: Blackwell.

———. 1977b. "Separation, Loss, and Family Relations." In *Child Psychiatry: Modern Approaches*, edited by M. Rutter and L. Hersov. Oxford: Blackwell.

Sameroff, A. and R. Seifer. 1983. "Sources of Community in Parent-Child Relations." Paper presented at the meetings of the Society for Research in Child Development, Detroit, MI.

Sampson, Robert J. 1986a. "Crime in the Cities: The Effects of Formal and Informal Social Control." In *Crime and Justice Series, Communities and Crime*, vol. 8, edited by Albert J. Reiss, Jr. and Michael Tonry. Chicago: University of Chicago Press:271-311.

———. 1986b. "Neighborhood Family Structure and the Risk of Personal Victimization." In *The Social Ecology of Crime*, edited by James M. Sampson and Robert J. Byrne. New York: Springer Verlag:25-46.

———. 1987. "Does an Intact Family Reduce Burglary Risk for Its Neighbors?" *Social Science Review* 71(3) (April):204-207.

Sanders, Matthew R., Mark R. Dadds, and William Bor. 1989. "Contextual Analysis of Child Oppositional and Maternal Aversive Behaviors in Families of Conduct-Disordered and Nonproblem Children." *Journal of Clinical Child Psychology* 18(1):72-83.

Schulsinger, F. 1980. "Biological Psychopathology." *Annual Review of Psychology* 31:583-606.

Sendi, Ismail B. and Paul G. Blomgren. 1975. "A Comparative Study of Predictive Criteria in the Predisposition of Homicidal Adolescents." *American Journal of Psychiatry* 132:423-427.

Seng, Magnus J. 1989. "Child Sexual Abuse and Adolescent Prostitution: A Comparative Analysis." *Adolescence* 24(95) (Fall):665-675.

Shanok, S.S. and D.O. Lewis. 1981. "Medical Histories of Abused Delinquents." *Child Psychiatry and Human Development* 11:222-231.

Siegel, Larry J. and Joseph J. Senna. 1991. *Juvenile Delinquency*, 4th ed. St. Paul, MN: West Publishing.

Silver, L.B., C.C. Dublin, and R.S. Lourie. 1969. "Does Violence Breed Violence? Contributions from a Study of the Child Abuse Syndrome." *American Journal of Psychiatry* 126:404-407.

Simcha-Fagan, O., T.S. Langer, J.C. Gersten, and J.G. Eisenberg. 1975. "Violent and Antisocial Behavior: A Longitudinal Study of Urban Youth." Unpublished Report. Office of Child Development.

Simons, Ronald L., Joan F. Robertson, and William R. Downs. 1989. "The Nature of the Association Between Parental Rejection and Delinquent Behavior." *Journal of Youth and Adolescence* 18(3):297-310.

Smith, Carolyn, Anne Wylie Weiher, and Welmoet B. Van Kammen. 1991. "Family Attachment and Delinquency." In *Urban Delinquency and Substance Abuse: Technical Report*, vol. 1, edited by David Huizinga, Rolf Loeber, and Terence P. Thornberry, article 8, 1-28. Washington, D.C.: Office of Juvenile Justice and Delinquency Prevention.

Smith, Douglas A. and Raymond Paternoster. 1987. "The Gender Gap in Theories of Deviance: Issues and Evidence." *Journal of Research in Crime And Delinquency* 24(2) (May):140-172.

Smith, Richard M., and James Walters. 1978. "Delinquent and Nondelinquent Males' Perceptions of Their Fathers." *Adolescence* 13(49) (Spring):21-28.

Snyder, James and Gerald Patterson. 1987. "Family Interaction and Delinquent Behavior." In *Handbook of Juvenile Delinquency*, edited by Herbert C. Quay. New York: John Wiley and Sons:216-243.

Sorrels, James M. 1977. "Kids Who Kill." *Crime and Delinquency* 23:312-320.

Steinberg, Laurence. 1986. "Latchkey Children and Susceptibility to Peer Pressure: An Ecological Analysis." *Developmental Psychology* 22(4):433-439.

———. 1987. "Single Parents, Stepparents, and the Susceptibility of Adolescents to Antisocial Peer Pressure." *Child Development* 58:269-275.

Steinberg, Laurence and Susan B. Silverberg. 1986. "The Vicissitudes of Autonomy in early Adolescence." *Child Development* 57:841-851.

Stouthamer-Loeber, M., K.B. Schmaleng, and R. Loeber. 1984. "The Relationship of Single-Parent Family Status and Marital Discord to Antisocial Child Behavior." Unpublished manuscript. Pittsburgh: University of Pittsburgh, Department of Psychiatry.

Straus, Murray A. 1981. "Family Violence and Nonfamily Crime and Violence." Paper presented at the meeting of the American Society of Criminology, Washington, D.C., November.

Straus, Murray A., Richard J. Gelles, and Suzanne K. Steinmetz. 1981. *Behind Closed Doors: Violence in the American Family*. Garden City, NY: Anchor.

Tarter, R., A.M. Hegedus, N.E. Weinstein, and A. Alterman. 1984. "Neuropsychological, Personality, and Familial Characteristics of Physically Abused Delinquents." *Journal of the American Academy of Child Psychiatry* 23:668-674.

Teeters, Negley K., and John Otto Reinemann. 1950. *The Challenge of Delinquency*. New York: Prentice-Hall.

Thornberry, Terence P., Alan J. Lizotte, Marvin D. Krohn, Margaret Farnworth, and Sung Joon Jang. 1991. "Testing Interactional Theory: An Examination of Reciprocal Causal Relationships Among Family, School, and Delinquency." *Journal of Criminal Law and Criminology* 82(1) (spring):3-35.

Tolan, Patrick H. 1987. "Implications of Age of Onset for Delinquency Risk." *Journal of Abnormal Psychology* 15(1):47-65.

———. 1988. "Socioeconomic, Family, and Social Stress Correlates of Adolescent Antisocial and Delinquent Behavior." *Journal of Abnormal Child Psychology* 16(3)317-331.

Tolan, Patrick H. and Raymond P. Lorion. 1988. "Multivariate Approaches to the Identification of Delinquency Proneness in Adolescent Males." *American Journal of Community Psychology* 16(4):547-561.

Van Voorhis, Patricia, Francis T. Cullen, Richard A. Mathers, and Connie Chenoweth Garner. 1988. "The Impact of Family Structure and Quality on Delinquency: A Comparative Assessment of Structural and Functional Factors." *Criminology* 26(2):235-261.

Wattenberg, Esther. 1986. "The Fate of Baby Boomers and Their Children." *Social Work* January-February, 20-28.

Webster-Stratton, Carolyn. 1989. "The Relationship of Marital Support, Conflict, and Divorce to Parent Perceptions, Behaviors, and Childhood Conduct Problems." *Journal of Marriage and Family* 51(May):417-430.

Wells, L. Edward and Joseph H. Rankin. 1986. "The Broken Homes Model of Delinquency: Analytic Issues." *Journal of Research in Crime and Delinquency* 23(1) (February):68-93.

Welsh, R.S. 1976. "Severe Parental Punishment and Delinquency: A Developmental Theory." *Journal of Clinical Child Psychology* 5(1):17-21.

White, Helen Raskin, Robert J. Pandina, and Randy L. LaGrange. 1987. "Longitudinal Predictors of Serious Substance Abuse and Delinquency." *Criminology* 25(3):715-740.

Widom, Cathy Spatz. 1989a. "Child Abuse, Neglect, and Violent Criminal Behavior." *Criminology* 27(2):251-271.

———. 1989b. "Does Violence Beget Violence? A Critical Examination of the Literature." *Psychological Bulletin* 106(1):3-28.

Widom, Cathy Spatz, Faith S. Katkin, Abigail J. Steward, and Mark Fondacaro. 1983. "Multivariate Analysis of Personality and Motivation in Female Delinquents." *Journal of Research in Crime and Delinquency* (July):277-290.

Wilkinson, Karen. 1980. "The Broken Home and Delinquent Behavior: An Alternative Interpretation of Contradictory Findings." In *Understanding Crime: Current Theory and Research*, edited by T. Hirschi and M. Gottfredson. Beverly Hills, CA: Sage:21-42.

Wilson, William Julius. 1987. *The Truly Disadvantaged: The Inner City, the Underclass, and Public Policy*. Chicago: University of Chicago Press.

Zill, N. 1978. "Divorce, Marital Happiness and the Mental Health of Children: Findings for the FCD National Survey of Children." Paper presented to the National Institute of Mental Health Workshop on Divorce and Children, Bethesda, MD. ✦

22
School Bonding, Race, and Delinquency

Stephen A. Cernkovich
Peggy C. Giordano

School and school-related variables assume prominent roles in most major theories of delinquency: disorganized schools (cultural deviance theory), school environments that frustrate students' goals and aspirations (strain theory) a lack of attachment and commitment to the school (control theory), an educational system that provides an inferior education to poor and minority children (conflict theory), and the negative labeling of school failures and "troublemakers" (societal reaction theory)—all increase the likelihood of delinquency (Empey, 1982:289); Siegel and Senna, 1988:300) and/or school dropout (cf. Bachman and O'Malley, 1978; Elliott, 1966; Elliott and Voss, 1974; Hathaway et al., 1969; Polk et al., 1981; Thornberry et al., 1985). Siegel and Senna (1988:302) note the considerable research showing school failure to be a stronger predictor of delinquency than socioeconomic status (also see Kelly and Balch, 1971), race or ethnic background, and peer relations. Further, school failure is predictive of delinquency for middle and upper status youngsters as well as for lower status ones (Braithwaite, 1981; Siegel and Senna, 1988:305), and it is especially common among chronic offenders (cf. Shannon, 1982; West and Farrington, 1977; Wilson and Herrnstein, 1985; Wolfgang et al., 1972). Liska and Reed (1985:548) note that "delinquent youth are less likely to complete assigned work at home or in school, to get good grades, to enjoy school, to aspire to higher education, to get along with their teachers, and even to be in school than are more conventional youth." In his popular textbook, Empey (1982) suggests that difficulties in school may be the single best predictor of delinquent behavior in American society today, although there is some debate as to whether school problems are a cause or an effect of involvement in delinquency (cf. Elliott, 1966; Hargreaves, 1967; Hirschi, 1969; Kelly, 1971, 1974; Kelly and Balch, 1971; Liska and Reed, 1985; Phillips and Kelly, 1979; Polk et al., 1974; Polk and Halferty, 1966; Polk and Schafer, 1972; Rhodes and Reiss, 1969; Schafer and Polk, 1967; Stinchcombe, 1964; Toby, 1957).

The purpose of this research is to describe the manner in which school bonding affects delinquent conduct, focusing in particular on the role of the school in the delinquent involvement of black youths. Paralleling the "gender gap" that characterizes the school-delinquency literature (Rosenbaum and Lasley, 1990:493) is a "racial gap"—a failure to examine racial variation in the impact of school factors on juvenile misconduct. In fact, the research literature is surprisingly silent in general on the issue of racial differences in delinquency. Matsueda and Heimer (1987:826) suggest that three factors are primarily responsible for this lack of attention: the politically sensitive nature of examining racial differences in crime and delinquency; the belief that racial differences in official measures of crime and delinquency do not reflect real differences, but rather are the result of criminal justice system bias; and the difficulty of measuring delinquency and its correlates reliably because of racial differences in the validity of self-report data.

Regardless of the reasons underlying it, this neglect of blacks in delinquency research is challenged both by the more general literature on black adolescence and by a number of empirical realities that suggest that there are important racial differences in schooling—differences that may, in turn, result in differential levels of delinquency involvement: the higher drop-out rate of black compared with white adolescents;[1] charges of racially biased testing, classification, and tracking; negative teacher attitudes toward black students and lower teacher expectations for black than for white students (Ogbu, 1988:177); and the pejorative label of "acting white" by peers of those blacks who are successful in school (Fordham and Ogbu, 1986). Further, research has indicated that race/ethnicity may be an important factor affecting the balancing act between deviant and conventional behavior that is so common during adolescence. Jessor (1982) contends that early involvement in deviant activities may block future participation in educational and occupational pursuits. Clayton and Voss (1981:164) suggest that whites may be better able than blacks to flirt with deviant behavior in adolescence without suffering long-term deleterious effects. There also is evidence from the status-attainment literature that some of the strongest predictors of achievement among whites, such as family status and parental encouragement and influence, are not as powerful in predicting the status attainment of blacks (Burke and Hoelter, 1988; Clark, 1983; Kerckhoff and Campbell, 1977; Porter, 1974; Prom-Jackson et al., 1987).

The considerable ambivalence among blacks regarding the role of education in their lives similarly belies the neglect of race in the school-delinquency equation. While many blacks view the American educational system as the embodiment of the culture's false promise of equality and therefore withhold any serious commitment, there are significant numbers who see it as a means to greater opportunity and an improved social and economic future—as the only means by which they can acquire the skills necessary to compete with whites (cf. Liska and Reed, 1985:557-558). Ogbu (1988:170-181) has noted that while education is valued among blacks, several realities mitigate against their commitment to educational achievement: a "job ceiling" that restricts the employment of blacks, regardless of their level of education; socialization and life experiences that reinforce the reality of this job ceiling and create considerable disillusionment about the merit of expending effort on academic pursuits; and an objectively inferior education which prohibits blacks from competing for more desirable jobs and blocks significant social mobility. Ironically, the response of many blacks to these realities may further increase the likelihood of school failure: disillusionment and alienation; withdrawal of commitment to educational activities that are perceived as having no payoff; the use of "survival strategies" (e.g., nonconventional economic activities) that are incompatible with middle-class classroom behavior; and a general attitude of suspicion, distrust, and hostility toward the school system. To the extent that black youths adopt such a frame of reference early in their lives, they enter school with certain predispositions that inhibit commitment to school and that result in a greater probability of experiencing school difficulties.

Thus, there is considerable evidence suggesting that blacks experience school in a qualitatively different way than whites (also see McAdoo, 1988a, 1988b; McAdoo and McAdoo, 1985). To the extent that school factors are predictive of delinquency involvement—and previous research has shown that they are, at least for white males—such racial variation in school experiences may well be reflected in differential delinquent outcomes. Whether this is the case empirically, however, is largely unknown because of the failure of prior research to examine the role of race in the school-delinquency equation.[2] While quite a bit is known about the role school plays in the lives of white adolescents, very little is known about its role among blacks, unless one is willing to assume that the effects are relatively constant across racial boundaries. As we have noted above, there are several good reasons for guarding against accepting such a characterization in the absence of more direct empirical evidence.

Theoretical Orientation

To a greater degree than the other major delinquency theories, strain and control models see school problems as critical correlates of delinquent involvement. Strain theory (Cloward and Ohlin, 1960; Cohen, 1955; Merton, 1938) suggests that unpleasant school experiences and school failure, especially among lower class and, by implication, minority youths, are important precursors of delinquency involvement. Further, the insensitivity of the educational system to the needs of underprivileged youths is seen as exacerbating the problems they have in adapting to the school environment (Bartol and Bartol, 1989:245-246). Among low-status youths, school is perceived as unrelated to future success; as a result, they see little reason to conform to the demands of the school environment. In this model, school failure leads to the frustration of long-range ambitions, which in turn reduces the student's commitment to conformity, thus increasing the probability of delinquency (Cohen, 1955; Empey, 1982:271-272; Siegel and Senna, 1988:308-309; Stinchcombe, 1964).

Control theory (Hirschi, 1969) also conceptualizes the delinquent as someone who experiences school failure, but it suggests an alternative time ordering of the variables. Lack of attachment to parents and teachers and a weak commitment to educational and occupational goals are prior causally to both school failure and involvement in delinquency (Empey, 1982:271-272; Hirschi, 1969). Adolescents who do not care what their teachers think of them, who do not care about getting good grades, who do not spend much time on homework, who do not have high aspirations for the future, and who generally do not want to be in school—these are the youths who are the most likely candidates for delinquency. From a control theory perspective, lack of school bonding is a critical link in the causal chain leading to delinquency involvement, and this relationship is held to be invariant across class, race, and gender boundaries (Rosenbaum and Lasley, 1990:497).

While control theory arguably has become the dominant perspective for examining the school-delinquency relationship in recent years (Rosenbaum and Lasley, 1990:496), the legacy of strain theory (with its emphasis on the structural sources of crime and delinquency) provides an important framework for any research on blacks. Although not addressed directly by strain theorists, the social context within which schooling takes place is a critical component of the American educational system. Years of attempts to achieve school integration notwithstanding, the American school system continues to be made up of an amalgam of various racial environments along a continuum from complete segregation to complete integration, with considerable variation in school culture, quality, funding, and teacher expertise across types. We believe it is important to understand the effects these different racial environments may have on the behavior and attitudes of the students attending them, particularly black students. Insofar as schools of varying racial composition subject those attending them to differential experiences and cultures, and to strains, frustrations, and failures that vary in both type and magnitude, it is reasonable to believe that individual levels of school bonding will be correspondingly conditioned.

While racial composition of the school setting most probably affects all students to some degree, it may be particularly important for blacks because of the distinct educational experiences they have had in this country and the consequent meaning of education in the black culture. Fordham and Ogbu (1986:177, 181-182) suggest that school achievement historically has been viewed by both blacks and whites as an arena in which only whites can succeed, in which minorities have rarely been given the opportunity to achieve, and in which few minorities were rewarded if they did succeed. That is, many blacks define certain activities and behaviors, among them academic striving and success, as the domain of white Americans. Among the behaviors identified as "acting white" by the students in Fordham and Ogbu's study were "spending a lot of time in the library studying," "working hard to get good grades," and actually "getting good grades." Blacks who engage in such behaviors are labeled by their peers as "acting white" and are negatively sanctioned.

Further, commitment to education is a *subtractive process*: The black student who succeeds in school not only is "acting white" but also is doing so at the cost of "acting black." Academic success places a particularly onerous stigma on the black male: His manhood is questioned by the suspicion that he may be gay. Because it threatens the minority identity on both a cultural and an individual level, academic achievement is opposed socially by the peer group and psychologically by the individual. On a social level the peer group discourages educational striving by negative labeling, exclusion, or even physical assault. On a personal level, individuals resist educational striving out of fear of such responses and to avoid psychological dissonance (Fordham and Ogbu, 1986:182-183, 186, 194).

Given this cultural definition of education, many blacks face a serious dilemma: On the one hand, education clearly is viewed by many as their best avenue to success; on the other hand, success in the school context often is devalued by the peer group. Considerable ambivalence about expending effort and succeeding in school is the result. How do youths finding themselves in this predicament adapt? The best evidence suggests that black students use a variety of strategies to cope with the ambivalence associated with their desire to perform well in school, on the one hand, and the demands of the peer group that they conform in attitude and behavior to the black cultural frame of reference, on the other. Underachievers avoid conflict altogether by limiting academic effort; high achievers minimize negative labeling via such mechanisms as pretending to be someone who does not expend much effort to earn good grades, choosing bullies as friends/protectors in exchange for help with schoolwork, and maintaining a low profile by not joining academic clubs or by cutting classes (Fordham, 1988:60-61; Fordham and Ogbu, 1986:186-187, 194-197). These and other mechanisms allow black students to succeed in school without incurring the wrath of their peers.

School context (i.e., racial composition of the school) is related to this cultural definition of education in that varying racial environments are likely to exert differential pressures on black students toward or away from school commitment and achievement. For example, if Fordham and Ogbu are correct, one would expect blacks attending predominantly black schools to face overwhelming pressure against school success. Highly committed or high-achieving students in this kind of environment would have to possess strong coping mechanisms indeed. On the other hand, black students attending predominantly white schools presumably would find greater levels of support for educational commitment and achievement (or at least lower levels of negative sanctioning from their black peers in the school environment; still, they may be negatively sanctioned for their school success by black peers in other contexts). Those attending racially mixed schools might be the most conflicted of all—receiving mixed messages from their white and black peers. The interaction dynamics in these varying racial contexts are sufficiently complex, however, to make prediction of the pressures, conflicts, and resulting effects on behavior difficult. Nonetheless, there is good reason to believe that school context has something other than a neutral effect on bonding, and as such, it represents an important variable to include in any analysis of school bonding, race, and delinquency.[3]

On the basis of this background, the purpose of this research is to examine the impact of school bonding on the delinquent behavior of black and white youths. Specifically, we are concerned with the relationship between two separate dimensions of school bonding—the *level* of school bonding among black and white youths and the *effect* of school bonding on delinquent conduct. Although there need be no necessary relationship between the level of bonding and the effect of bonding (i.e., differential levels of school bonding do not necessarily result in differential levels of delinquency involvement), there certainly is sufficient theoretical justification for expecting such an association. That is, control theory suggests that the greater the level of school bonding—as evidenced by high degrees of attachment to the school and to teachers, high grades, high aspirations and a commitment to the future, and involvement in such school and school-related activities as homework, athletic teams, school clubs, and school-sponsored events—the lesser the likelihood of involvement in delinquent activities (Hirschi, 1969:16-34, 110-134, 170-182, 191-192). In addition, insofar as school bonding varies by race and according to the racial composition of the school environment, we hypothesize that the school bonding-delinquency relationship will be correspondingly conditioned. . . .

Summary and Discussion

Blacks are surprisingly underrepresented in research on the school and delinquency. This is due in part to the politically sensitive nature of the race issue in American society, to the belief by some researchers that while race is related to official processing it is not an important correlate of self-reported delinquency, and to validity problems associated with the self-reports of blacks (Matsueda and Heimer, 1987:826). The neglect of blacks is due also to the role of race in major delinquency theories. Although control and strain theory have been the dominant theoretical models informing empirical analyses of the school-delinquency relationship historically, neither has spawned a systematic study of the role of race in the causal equation. This is because neither model directly addresses the role of race theoretically: control theory because its key predictors are held to be invariant across racial boundaries, and strain theory because it is a class-based model that deals with race only by implication.[4]

This research introduced race as a key variable in the school bonding-delinquency equation. For some, our findings of no significant differences in the effect of school bonding on delinquency across race-sex subgroups and school racial environments will be interpreted as support for the continued neglect of blacks. That is, our findings appear to vindicate control theory, a model that purports to be constant across racial, sex, and socioeconomic boundaries. We believe such a conclusion would be both premature and mistaken. This is because our research has left unanswered some important questions and has raised additional ones that must be addressed before we can say with any degree of certainty that there are or are not race-specific differentials in the relationship between school bonding and delinquency.

For example, while our final regression analyses suggested that racial context may indeed have an impact on school bonding and delinquency after all, subsample size issues and the potential confounding of school context with several unmeasured variables prohibited asserting this with a great deal of confidence. Similarly, we were unable in this research to examine directly whether our subjects perceived a "job ceiling" regarding their future employability, and whether such a perception conditioned their bonding to the school, or their behavior independent of such bonding. Nor did we investigate whether blacks, especially males, felt pressured by their peers to temper their school achievement out of fear of being labeled as "acting white," and whether this was in any way related to delinquency.

While our earlier research revealed that several dimensions of family and peer relations were differentially related to delinquency involvement among blacks and whites, the most general conclusion from the present data is that there are no important racial differences in the impact of school bonding on delinquency. We believe it is important to understand why this is the case. Perhaps it is because school bonding is qualitatively distinct from family and peer bonding. While family and peer relationships are by definition affective, immediate, and interpersonal, school relationships are more impersonal, future-oriented, and competitive. The school is the major arena for adolescent status competition in American society, an arena where universalistic rules apply, and many blacks, especially those from lower status backgrounds, enter at a competitive disadvantage. As a result, they face a unique set of problems and frustrations (Cohen, 1955). While we have not in this research investigated what it is that minority youths bring to the school that results in their experiencing school in ways that are qualitatively different from white experiences, it is clear that future research needs to examine how cultural and interpersonal relations in the family and among peers influence school bonding and, in turn, delinquency.

An excellent model for the sort of research that is needed is MacLeod's (1987) ethnographic study of lower class teenagers. In marked contrast to the white youths he studied, MacLeod's black respondents believed strongly in the worth and value of education. They viewed the school as a level playing field, an environment in which hard work would pay off to remedy the problems created by racial inequality. Black parents encouraged high aspirations among their children, and the peer group was clearly achievement oriented, valued school success, encouraged high aspirations, and rewarded behavior consistent with these values and goals.[5] Even though the parents of these youths had failed in their quests to succeed, all had renewed hope for the young—an abiding belief that the racial environment had changed substantially to provide more equality of opportunity. The school, in turn, was viewed as the primary mechanism for "making it." Even though they were only moderately successful in school, these black youths did not blame the school or its discriminatory tracking system, its partiality toward higher status youths, or the self-fulfilling consequences of low teacher expectations for minority youths. Rather, they tended to blame themselves for not working hard enough or being smart enough. And despite the objective lack of economic opportunities for those adults around them, these students maintained their commitment to education; for many their aspirations were tempered only after they had finished high school and confronted the harsh realities of the job market (MacLeod, 1987:97-101, 110, 126-130).

Even if we accept this characterization of a strong belief among many blacks in the value and practicality of education (an assumption confirmed by recent empirical studies showing blacks to have higher aspirations than whites from the same socioeconomic backgrounds reversal of the pattern prevailing in the 1960s and early 1970s [MacLeod, 1987:129-130]), our research has highlighted some troubling questions: If blacks are at least as strongly bonded to the school as whites, why does the black drop-out rate continue to outstrip the white rate by a wide margin? Why do blacks continue to be disciplined, suspended, and expelled in greater numbers than whites? Why isn't school bonding more effective in moderating delinquency involvement among blacks? Why is school involvement positively related to delinquency among black males, an association opposite to that found among the other race-sex subgroups?

In framing responses to such questions, we believe our findings on school bonding should be juxtaposed against our earlier research regarding family and peer relationships (Cernkovich and Giordano, 1987; Giordano et al., 1986). Although much research historically has emphasized the dysfunctional features of the black family, our findings point to areas of greater intimacy between black adolescents and their families, in contrast to the lower levels of intimacy and higher levels of conflict we found to characterize white adolescents and their families. Similarly, while their peer relations were quite similar to those of whites in many respects, blacks scored significantly lower on our friendship scale measuring "basic caring and trust," they were less likely to feel pressured by peers into behaving in ways contrary to their wishes, and they were less likely to lie in order to protect their friends. This appears to be due, in part at least, to a somewhat more intimate family base, which results in black adolescents being less likely to seek out peer support or to experience peer pressure with the same degree of intensity as their white counterparts. Such findings clearly challenge the traditional model of black family and peer relationships. We believe our school findings likewise question the accuracy of the dysfunctional model. The black youths in our sample are not isolated and alienated from school; rather they are just as committed and attached as whites, if not more so.

None of these findings means, of course, that black adolescents do not experience peer pressures, are not intimate with their peers, do not have family conflicts, or do not have difficulties in school. But these clearly are matters of degree, and our research suggests that while black adolescent social relations—in the family, with peers, and in school—are quite similar to those of whites in several respects, they also are in many important ways qualitatively different. Such findings reveals the hazards of making generalizations about blacks on the basis of research conducted on whites, and they underscore the necessity for more research directly examining the role of race in the complex processes leading to delinquency involvement.

Notes

1. Contrary to the common belief that the black drop-out problem is enormous and worsening yearly, however, is a recent study reporting that the high school graduation rate of blacks has improved much faster than that of whites and Hispanics over the past two decades. Thus, the critical question may not be why so many black youths drop out of school, but rather, given all the problems of crime, poverty, discrimination, drugs, and pregnancy, why so many stay in school and graduate (DeParle, 1991:1, 14).
2. While Hirschi (1969:120), for example, does examine racial differences in the impact of some school factors on delinquency, such analyses are used to illustrate a point other than the importance of race in his model. He makes it clear that his model applies across racial, gender, and class boundaries.
3. The evidence regarding the influence of the school's racial environment on black children is equivocal, and two conflicting hypotheses have emerged. We note these not with the intention of evaluating their relative efficacy, but because they underscore the importance of the school's racial context. The "contact hypothesis" asserts that school segregation is harmful to the development and self-esteem of black youths. Contact with whites through school integration is seen as bolstering black self-esteem and increasing levels of school achievement. The "insulation hypothesis," however, holds that contact with whites may in fact lower levels of black self-esteem and achievement: Blacks in an integrated school setting may internalize whites' negative image of blacks (Krause, 1985:257-258). Citing Rosenberg (1977), Krause discusses three mechanisms by which this occurs: (1) minority youths in majority group settings are more likely to be exposed to negative communication about themselves or about their group (i.e., racial teasing or putdowns); (2) minority youths in integrated settings come to realize that their norms and values are different from those of the majority group and are considered inferior by the dominant group; (3) minority youths in integrated environments also suffer because of the reference group against which they compare themselves regarding academic performance. Insofar as the academic performance of blacks is below that of whites, blacks in white-dominated schools are comparing themselves to the higher achieving whites, with a consequent lowering of self-esteem when they find their achievement levels lagging. Because the homogeneous environment reduces the magnitude of such discrepancies in academic performance in segregated schools, students making such comparisons to not perceive the lag observed in integrated schools—the reference group is different (Krause, 1985:258-259).
4. To the extent that class differences overlap with and/or are accepted (rightly or wrongly) as proxy measures of race, however, strain theory is less guilty than the control model of failing to incorporate race. Still, race does not assume a prominent role in strain theory.
5. Clearly, not all black youths fit the mold of those studied by MacLeod; he recognizes that many others are pessimistic about their futures and are quite cynical about the equality-of-opportunity ideology symbolized by the educational system (1987:132). Still, the sharp contrast between the positive image of school commitment and achievement within the black peer group portrayed by MacLeod and the negative "acting white" image portrayed by Fordham and Ogbu (1986) further underscores the need for more basic research on black adolescents.

References

Agnew, Robert. 1985. Social control theory and delinquency: A longitudinal test. *Criminology* 23 (February):47-61.

Bachman, Jerald G. and Patrick M. O'Malley. 1978. *Youth in Transition. Vol. VI: Adolescence to Adulthood: Change and Stability in the Lives of Young Men*. Ann Arbor: University of Michigan Press.

Bartol, Curt R. and Anne M. Bartol. 1989. Juvenile *Delinquency: A Systems Approach*. Englewood Cliffs, N.J.: Prentice-Hall.

Bonjean, Charles M., Richard J. Hill, and S. Dale McLemore. 1967. *Sociological Measurement: An Inventory of Scales and Indices*. San Francisco: Chandler Publishing.

Braithwaite, John. 1981. The myth of social class and criminality reconsidered. *American Sociological Review* 46(February):36-57.

Bureau of the Census. 1980. *Alphabetical Index of Industries and Occupations*. 1st ed. 1980 Census of Population. U.S. Department of Commerce. Washington, D.C.: Government Printing Office.

Burke, Peter J. and Jon W. Hoelter. 1988. Identity and sex-race differences in educational and occupational aspirations formation. *Social Science Research* 17:29-47.

Cernkovich, Stephen A. and Peggy C. Giordano. 1987. Family relationships and delinquency. *Criminology* 25(May):401-427.

Cernkovich, Stephen A., Peggy C. Giordano, and M.D. Pugh. 1985. Chronic offenders: The missing cases in self-report delinquency research. *The Journal of Criminal Law and Criminology* 76(Fall):705-732.

Clark, Reginald. 1983. *Family Life and School Achievement*. Chicago: University of Chicago Press.

Clayton, Richard R. and Harwin L. Voss. 1981. *Young Men and Drugs in Manhattan: A Causal Analysis*. NIDA Research Monograph No. 39. Washington, D.C.: Government Printing Office.

Cloward, Richard and Lloyd Ohlin. 1960. *Delinquency and Opportunity*. New York: Free Press.

Cohen, Albert K. 1955. *Delinquent Boys*. New York: Free Press.

DeParle, Jason. 1991. Without fanfare, blacks march to greater high school success. *New York Times*, June 9, 1991:1,14.

Elliott, Delbert J. 1966. Delinquency, school attendance and dropout. *Social Problems* 13:307-314.

Elliott, Delbert and Suzanne Ageton. 1980. Reconciling race and class differences in self-reported and official estimates of delinquency. *American Sociological Review* 45:95-1 10.

Elliott, Delbert and Harwin Voss. 1974. *Delinquency and Dropout*. Lexington, Mass.: Heath.

Empey, LaMar T. 1982. *American Delinquency: Its Meaning and Construction*. Rev. ed. Homewood, Ill.: Dorsey.

Fordham, Signithia. 1988. Racelessness as a factor in black students' school success: Pragmatic strategy or pyrrhic victory? *Harvard Educational Review* 58(February):54-84.

Fordham, Signithia and John U. Ogbu. 1986. Black students' school success: Coping with the "burden of acting white." *The Urban Review* 18(3):176-206.

Giordano, Peggy C., Stephen A. Cernkovich, and M.D. Pugh. 1986. Friendships and delinquency. *American Journal of Sociology* 91(March):1170-1202.

Hargreaves, David H. 1967. *Social Relations in a Secondary School*. London: Routledge and Kegan Paul.

Hathaway, Starke R., Phillis C. Reynolds, and Elio D. Monachesi. 1969. Follow-up of later careers and lives of 1,000 boys who dropped out of high school. *Journal of Consulting and Clinical Psychology* 33:370-380.

Hindelang, Michael J., Travis Hirschi, and Joseph G. Weis. 1981. *Measuring Delinquency*. Beverly Hills, Calif.: Sage.

Hirschi, Travis. 1969. *Causes of Delinquency*. Berkeley: University of California Press.

Hollingshead, August B. and Frederick C. Redlich. 1958. *Social Class and Mental Illness: A Community Study*. New York: John Wiley & Sons.

Jaccard, James, Robert Turrisi, and Choi K. Wan. 1990. *Interaction Effects in Multiple Regression*. Berkeley, Calif.: Sage.

Jessor, Richard. 1982. Problem behavior and developmental transition in adolescence. *The Journal of School Health* (May):295-300.

Johnson, Richard E. 1979. *Juvenile Delinquency and Its Origins*. New York: Cambridge University Press.

Kelly, Delos H. 1971. School failure, academic self-evaluation and school avoidance and deviant behavior. *Youth and Society* 2:489-503.

———. 1974. Track position and delinquent involvement: A preliminary analysis. *Sociology and Social Research* 58:380-386.

Kelly, Delos H. and R.W. Balch. 1971. Social origins and school failure: A reexamination of Cohen's theory of working-class delinquency. *Pacific Sociological Review* 14:413-430.

Kerckhoff, Alan C. and Richard T. Campbell. 1977. Black-white differences in the educational attainment process. *Sociology of Education* 1:15-27.

Krause, Neal. 1985. *Interracial contact in schools and black children's self-esteem. Black Children: Social, Educational, and Parental Environments*. Newbury Park, Calif.: Sage.

Krohn, Marvin and James Massey. 1980. Social control and delinquent behavior: An examination of the elements of the social bond. *The Sociological Quarterly* 21(Autumn):529-543.

LaGrange, Randy and Helene Raskin White. 1985. Age differences in delinquency: A test of theory. *Criminology* 23(February):19-45.

Landis, Judson, Simon Dinitz, and Walter C. Reckless. 1963. Implementing two theories of delinquency: Value orientation and awareness of limited opportunity. *Sociology and Social Research* 47(July):408-416.

Liska, Allen E. and Mark D. Reed. 1985. Ties to conventional institutions and delinquency: Estimating reciprocal effects. *American Sociological Review* 50(August):547-560.

MacLeod, Jay. 1987. *Ain't No Makin' It*. Boulder, Colo.: Westview Press.

McAdoo, Harriette Pipes (ed.). 1988a. *Black Families*. 2d ed. Newbury Park, Calif.: Sage.

———. 1988b. Transgenerational patterns of upward mobility in African-American families. In Harriette Pipes McAdoo (ed.) *Black Families*. 2d ed. Newbury Park, Calif.: Sage.

McAdoo, Harriette Pipes and John L. McAdoo (eds.). 1985. *Black Children: Social, Educational, and Parental Environments*. Newbury Park, Calif.: Sage.

Matsueda, Ross L. and Karen Heimer. 1987. Race, family structure, and delinquency: A test of differential association and social control theories. *American Sociological Review* 52(December):826-840.

Merton, Robert K. 1938. Social structure and anomie. *American Sociological Review* 3:672-682.

Minor, William. N.D. *Maryland Youth Survey*. Institute of Criminal Justice and Criminology. College Park: University of Maryland.

Ogbu, John U. 1988. Black education: A cultural-ecological perspective. In Harriette Pipes McAdoo (ed.), *Black Families*. 2d ed. Newbury Park, Calif.: Sage.

Phillips, John C. and Delos H. Kelly. 1979. School failure and delinquency: Which causes which? *Criminology* 17(August):194-207.

Polk, Kenneth and David Halferty. 1966. School cultures, adolescent commitments, and delinquency. *Journal of Research in Crime and Delinquency* 4(July):82-96.

Polk, Kenneth and Walter E. Schafer. 1972. *Schools and Delinquency*. Englewood Cliffs, N.J.: Prentice-Hall.

Polk, Kenneth, Dean Frease, and F. Lynn Richmond. 1974. Social class, school experience, and delinquency. *Criminology* 12(May):84-96.

Polk, Kenneth, Christine Adler, Gordon Bazemore, Gerald Blake, Sheila Cordray, Garry Coventry, James Galvin, and Mark Temple. 1981. *Becoming Adult: An Analysis of Maturational Development from Age 16 to 30 of a Cohort of Young Men*. Final Report of the Marion County Youth Study. Eugene: University of Oregon.

Porter, James N. 1974. Race, socialization and mobility in educational and early occupational attainment. *American Sociological Review* 39(3):303-316.

Prom-Jackson, Sylvia, T. Johnson, and Michael B. Wallace. 1987. Home environment, talented minority youth, and school achievement. *Journal of Negro Education* 56(1):111-121.

Rhodes, Albert L. and Albert J. Reiss, Jr. 1969. Apathy, truancy and delinquency as an adaptation to school failure. *Social Forces* 48(September):12-22.

Rosenbaum, Jill Leslie and James R. Lasley. 1990. School, community context, and delinquency: Rethinking the gender gap. *Justice Quarterly* 7(September):493-513.

Rosenberg, Morris. 1977. Contextual dissonant effects: Nature and causes. *Psychiatry* 40:205-217.

Schafer, Walter E. and Kenneth Polk. 1967. *Delinquency and the schools*. Appendix M to Task Force Report: Juvenile Delinquency and Youth Crime. President's Commission on Law Enforcement and Administration of Justice. Washington, D.C.: Government Printing Office.

Shannon, Lyle. 1982. *Assessing the Relationship of Adult Criminal Careers to Juvenile Careers: A Summary*. Washington, D.C.: Government Printing Office.

Siegel, Larry J. and Joseph J. Senna. 1988. *Juvenile Delinquency: Theory, Practice, and Law*. 3d ed. St. Paul, Minn.: West.

Stinchcombe, Arthur L. 1964. *Rebellion in a High School*. Chicago: Quadrangle Books.

Thornberry, Terence, Melanie Moore, and R.L. Christenson. 1985. The effect of dropping out of high school on subsequent criminal behavior. *Criminology* 23(February):3-18.

Toby, Jackson. 1957. Social disorganization and stake in conformity. *Journal of Criminal Law, Criminology and Police Science* 48:12-17.

West, David J. and David P. Farrington. 1977. *The Delinquent Way of Life*. London: Heineman.

West, Lloyd and Harvey W. Zingle. 1969. A self-disclosure inventory for adolescents. *Psychological Reports* 23:439-445.

Wilson, James Q. and Richard J. Hermstein. 1985. *Crime and Human Nature*. New York: Simon & Schuster.

Wolfgang, Marvin E., Robert M. Figlio, and Thorsten Sellin. 1972. *Delinquency in a Birth Cohort*. Chicago: University of Chicago Press.

Wolfgang, Marvin E., Robert M. Figlio, Paul E. Tracy, and Simon L. Singer. 1985. *The National Survey of Crime Severity*. U.S. Department of Justice. Washington, D.C.: Bureau of Justice Statistics. ✦

23
The Influence of Delinquent Peers: What They Think or What They Do?

E. Mark Warr
Mark Stafford

Among the most consistent findings of delinquency research is the association between delinquent friends and delinquent behavior. Numerous investigations over several decades have repeatedly found that the more delinquent friends an adolescent has, the more likely he or she is to engage in delinquent behavior (e.g., Akers et al., 1979; Elliott et al., 1985; Erickson and Empey, 1965; Hepburn, 1977; Jensen, 1972; Johnson, 1979; Matsueda and Heimer, 1987; Reiss and Rhodes, 1964; Short, 1957; Tittle et al., 1986; Voss, 1964).

Although the association between delinquent friends and delinquent behavior is well established, the mechanism by which delinquency is socially transmitted remains unclear. The most commonly invoked explanation is Sutherland's theory of differential association, a theory that "has had a massive impact on criminology" (Vold and Bernard, 1986:225). According to this well-known theory, delinquency is learned through intimate social relations among peers, relations in which attitudes, or "definitions," favorable to the violation of law are acquired. In Sutherland's (1947:7) words, "A person becomes delinquent because of an excess of definitions favorable to violation of law over definitions unfavorable to violation of law." To Sutherland, then, the social transmission of delinquency occurs specifically through the dissemination or transference of attitudes about such conduct through peer networks.[1]

Sutherland's theory is appealing because it rightly stresses the importance of peers in adolescent development and culture. Notwithstanding the importance of peers, however, the theory is open to question on at least two grounds. First, the theory assumes that favorable attitudes toward delinquency are a necessary condition for delinquent behavior. Yet the link between attitudes and behavior is notoriously tenuous (e.g., Deutscher, 1973), and it is not difficult to imagine that adolescents commonly engage in delinquent behavior for social or situational reasons without personally condoning or approving of the behavior in which they engage. Moreover, even if prodelinquent attitudes are a necessary condition for delinquency, it does not follow that they are a sufficient condition. For example, criminologists largely agree that delinquent behavior is dependent on both motivation and opportunity (e.g., Cloward and Ohlin, 1960; Cohen and Felson, 1979). Where opportunities for delinquency are scarce or absent, even the most staunch pro-delinquent attitudes will not be readily transformed into actual behavior.

Second, the most commonly cited evidence for differential association—the association between delinquent peers and delinquent behavior—is at best only indirect evidence for the theory. Although such evidence clearly speaks to the relevance of peers, it says nothing about the mechanism through which delinquency is socially transmitted. More specifically, the association cannot be uniquely construed as evidence of attitude transmission from one adolescent to the next.

Attitudes Versus Actions

Whereas Sutherland's theory emphasizes the *attitudes* of peers in the transmission of delinquency, other theories stress the *behavior* of peers. According to social learning theorists (see especially Akers, 1985), delinquent behavior may be adopted through imitating or modeling the behavior of peers or by observing the positive consequences of the model's behavior (vicarious reinforcement).[2] In contrast to Sutherland's theory, neither of these processes requires the transference of attitudes from the model to the observer. The emphasis on peers' behavior is also present, if often only implicitly, in theories that stress collective behavior, situational inducements, or group process in the production of delinquency (cf. Briar and Piliavin, 1965; Gold, 1970; Liska, 1981; Short and Strodtbeck, 1965).

The central distinguishing feature of Sutherland's theory, then, is its insistence on attitude transference as the mechanism by which delinquency is socially transmitted. Accordingly, the contrast between Sutherland's theory and other theories ultimately comes down to this question: Is delinquency a consequence of what peers think, or what they do? The answer is not evident at this time because investigators have largely failed to distinguish or separately measure the attitudes and behavior of peers or have simply accepted one as a proxy for the other.

In this paper, we compare the relative effects of peer attitudes and peer behavior on adolescents' own behavior. We first present some preliminary evidence on the question and then expand the analysis to determine whether peer influences operate directly on adolescents' behavior or whether, as Sutherland argues, they are mediated by adolescents' own attitudes. Finally, we examine the congruence between peers' attitudes and behavior as it affects the delinquent behavior of others.

Data and Measures

Our analysis employs data from the National Youth Survey (NYS). The NYS is a five-year panel study of a national probability sample of 1,726 persons aged 11-17 in 1976 (see Elliot and Ageton, 1980). The NYS is especially well suited for our purpose because it contains a unique set of questions concerning both the attitudes and behavior of peers. Unlike most questions about peers, the NYS questions refer to specific, concrete persons rather than some ill-defined set of friends. That is, respondents were asked to individually name the friends they "ran around with," and were instructed to think of those persons in subsequent questions. The first portion of our analysis employs data from wave III of the NYS, which contains data from interviews conducted in 1979 about events that occurred in 1978.[3]

Respondents' own attitudes toward a variety of delinquent acts were measured using the question, "How wrong is it for someone your age to (act)?" (1—not wrong at all, 2—a little bit wrong, 3—wrong, 4—very wrong). To measure friends' attitudes (as perceived by the respondent), respondents were asked whether their friends would approve or disapprove (1—strongly approve, 2—approve, 3—neither approve nor disapprove, 4—disapprove, 5—strongly disapprove) if they (the respondent) were to commit each of a set of delinquent acts. To simplify the analysis that follows, the direction of these two attitude scales has been reversed so that higher scores indicate approval of the acts in question.

Friends' participation in delinquent behavior was measured by this question, "Think of your friends. During the past year, how many of them (act)?" (1—none of them, 2—very few of them, 3—some of them, 4—most of them, 5—all of them). Respondents' own delinquent behavior was measured by the question, "How many times in the last year have you (act)?" Responses were coded as raw frequencies and as rates (number per day, week, or month). The two measures are highly correlated, and for present purposes we employ raw frequencies with the highest category scored as 5+.

Each of the four questions above asked respondents about a set of offenses, but the set varied from one question to the next. Six offenses, however, were common to all four questions. Of the six, three were felonies with extremely low self-reported frequencies (no more than 3% of respondents committed any of the acts). The three offenses that we analyze here-using marijuana, larceny (stealing something worth less than $5), and cheating on school tests—were each committed by a relatively large proportion (from 15% to 42%) of respondents.[4]

Findings

Regression Analysis

Table 1 reports some initial evidence on the relative effects of peer behavior and peer attitudes. The table shows, for each offense, the regression of respondents' behavior (RB) on friends' attitudes (FA) and friends' behavior (FB). In each case, the standardized coefficients for friends' attitudes and friends' behavior are both highly significant ($p < .001$). However, the relative effects of the two variables are quite different. The effect of friends' behavior is much more pronounced than that of friends' attitudes, on the order of 2.5 to 5.0 times greater. Accordingly, although the attitudes of friends are clearly important in determining the delinquent behavior of adolescents, the behavior of friends appears to be the dominant factor.

Table 1
Regression of Respondent's Behavior on Friends' Attitudes and Friends' Behavior

CHEATING
$RB = .13^{***}FA + .47^{***}FB$ $R = .54$ $N = 1,577$

MARIJUANA
$RB = .22^{***}FA + .58^{***}FB$ $R = .76$ $N = 1,612$

LARCENY
$RB = .09^{***}FA + .44^{***}FB$ $R = .49$ $N = 1,596$

Note: RB = respondent's behavior; FA = friends' attitudes; FB = friends' behavior.
$^{***}p < .001$.

The evidence from Table 1 is simple and straightforward, but it leads to a much larger question. Granted that the attitudes and behavior of friends influence adolescents, how exactly does this process operate? Does the influence of friends operate by altering adolescents' own attitudes and thus, in turn, their behavior? Or do the attitudes and behavior of friends affect adolescents' behavior directly, that is, independently of their own attitudes? As it is conventionally interpreted, Sutherland's theory is quite clear on this matter: The attitudes of friends affect their associates by altering their attitudes. Thus, the theory implies a simple recursive model, that is,

$$FA \longrightarrow RA \longrightarrow RB,$$

where RA is respondent's attitude, and FA and RB are as above.

The issue is more complicated however, when it comes to the behavior of friends. On the one hand, it is entirely possible that the behavior of friends influences adolescents by changing their own attitudes toward delinquency, meaning that the effect of peer behavior, like peer attitudes, is mediated by adolescents' attitudes. Recall, however, that the learning mechanisms stipulated by social learning theory are not dependent on attitude transference, suggesting that the effect of peers' behavior may be direct rather than indirect.

Path Models

To investigate these possibilities, we estimated a path model for each offense incorporating four variables: the attitudes and behavior of friends, and respondents' own attitudes and behavior. The models permit not only a direct test of Sutherland's theory, but also an examination of the effects of peer behavior as well as those of peer attitudes.

Figure 1 shows the fitted model for each offense.[5] In general, the models are strikingly similar, and they point to a number of conclusions. First, the models portray a more complicated process than Sutherland envisioned, but they are nonetheless consistent with his theory. Friends' attitudes do affect adolescents' behavior, and the effect is mediated almost entirely by adolescents' own attitudes. Friends' attitudes do not have a significant direct effect on respondent's behavior in two of the models and they have only a small direct effect for one offense (marijuana). The transference of attitudes about delinquency through peer networks, then, does appear to play an important part in the production of delinquency.

If the models provide support for Sutherland's theory, however, they also reveal its

Figure 1
Path Models of Peer Influence for Three Offenses

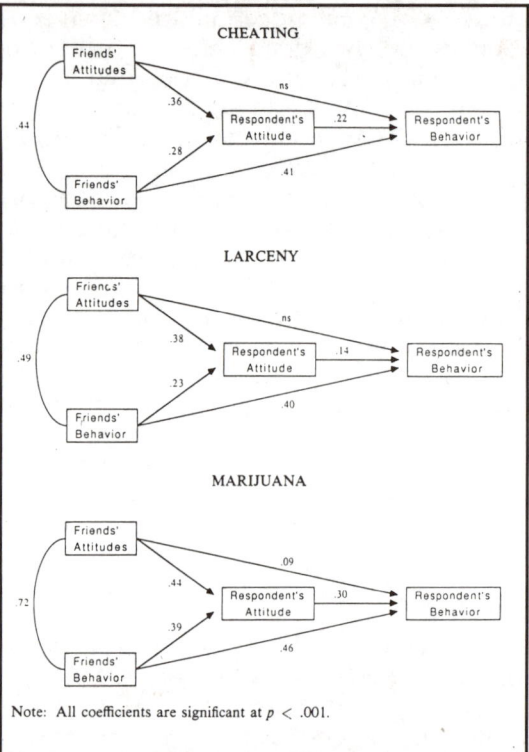

Note: All coefficients are significant at $p < .001$.

limitations. Quite apart from the *attitudes* of friends, the *behavior* of friends exerts a strong influence on respondents' behavior. Part of this influence, as we anticipated, is indirect: The behavior of friends affects adolescents' behavior through their attitudes about delinquency. The effect of peer behavior on respondents' attitude is not as strong as that of peer attitudes, but the effect is nonetheless substantial. Still, the single most striking feature of all three models in Figure 1 is the strong, *direct* effect of peers' behavior on respondent's behavior. No other variable in the models exerts a stronger influence on adolescents' behavior than the behavior of their friends, and the effect of friends' behavior is both direct and substantially greater than that of respondent's attitude or (indirectly) friends' attitudes. Notwithstanding their own attitudes toward delinquency, then, adolescents are strongly influenced by the behavior of their friends.

Longitudinal Models

The preceding findings are clear and persuasive, but they are subject to a general criticism of self-report data. Because self-report measures are normally retrospective in nature (referring to the previous six months or year), self-reported events commonly precede in time other variables measured in social surveys. For example, if a current attitude measured at time t is used to explain self-reported events measured at time t, the events will have occurred prior to their putative cause. Since an effect cannot precede its cause, this feature of self-report data raises questions about the validity of causal models derived from cross-sectional self-report data (e.g., Paternoster, 1987). One way to rectify such problems is to use panel data, with self-report variables

Figure 2
Lagged Models of Peer Influence for Three Offenses

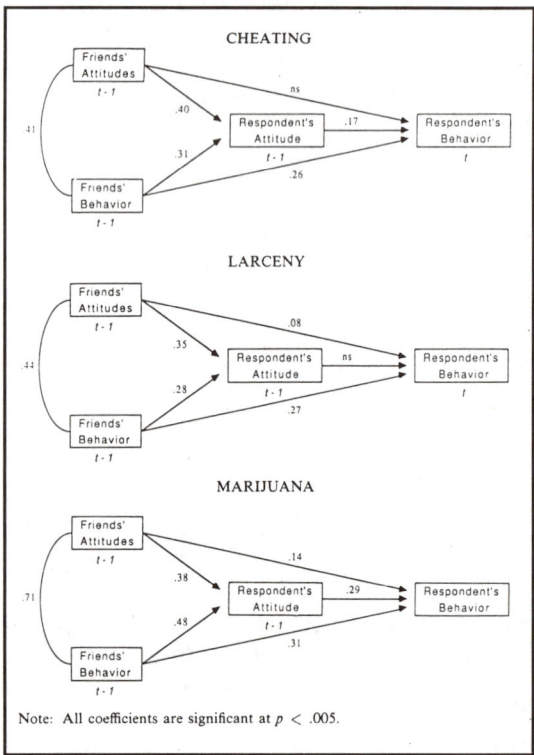

Note: All coefficients are significant at $p < .005$.

measured at, say, time t and exogenous variables measured at time $t - 1$. This approach corrects the temporal ordering of variables, but it does not resolve all temporal questions. For example, in annual panel designs such as that of the NYS, the time between an attitude measured at t and subsequent self-reported behavior measured at $t + 1$ can be as much as a year, and under some circumstances the time lag between exogenous and endogenous variables can become implausibly long (Williams and Hawkins, 1986).

In the present instance, respondent's attitude and friends' attitudes are both current measures (i.e., contemporaneous with the survey), whereas respondent's behavior and friends' behavior are measured retrospectively. To correct the temporal ordering of variables, we reestimated the models from Figure 1 using data from waves II and III of the NYS. As Figure 2 shows, the original wave III (time t) measure of respondent's behavior has been retained, but wave II ($t - 1$) observations have been substituted for friends' attitudes and respondent's attitude. This procedure places both attitude variables temporally prior to respondent's behavior. In addition, the wave III measure of friends' behavior was replaced with the wave II measure. This step is necessary to avoid a logical impossibility (placing an effect—respondent's attitude—before a cause—friends' behavior), and it also has the consequence of lagging friends' behavior and respondent's behavior by one wave. This latter lag is normally defensible, even desirable, but its meaning in this context must be carefully understood. Because respondent's behavior and friends' behavior are both retrospective measures covering the preceding year, and because the two measures are lagged by one year, the time lag between events under these two consecutive time periods can reach as much as two years. Consequently, the models provide a stringent test of the relation between friends' behavior and respondent's behavior.

The fitted lagged model for each offense is presented in Figure 2.[6] Observe first that the relations among the wave II ($t - 1$) variables are quite similar to those from wave III in Figure 1. Indeed, the cross-sectional models in Figure 1 can be replicated rather closely with the wave II data.[7] Our immediate interest, however, is the effect of the time $t - 1$ variables on the time t measure of respondent's behavior. As seen in the figure, the general features of the lagged models parallel those of the cross-sectional models. Friends' attitudes has a weak or statistically insignificant direct effect on respondents' behavior in each case. The effect of respondent's attitude has dropped somewhat for cheating and larceny (below statistical significance, $p = .07$, in the latter case), but remains essentially unchanged for marijuana. The effect of friends' behavior on respondent's behavior has been reduced by approximately one-third in each case, but it nonetheless remains the strongest of any of the lagged effects. Indeed, had we used contemporaneous measures of the two variables, the direct effect of friends' behavior would have exceeded all other effects in the models.

The major features of the longitudinal models, then, are not substantially different from those of the cross-sectional models. Most important, friends' behavior retains a significant, strong, *direct* effect on respondent's behavior, regardless of whether that effect is measured longitudinally or concurrently.

Congruence Between Peer Behavior and Attitudes

Earlier we noted that delinquent behavior and delinquent attitudes are not necessarily congruent, and we presented evidence that the attitudes and behavior of friends have independent or separable effects on the attitudes and behavior of their associates. Still, the issue of congruence gives rise to some interesting questions. First, is the probability of delinquency enhanced when the attitudes and behavior of one's friends are congruent? Put another way, is the influence of peers greatest when those peers do what they say (or think)? Second, when the attitudes and behavior of friends are inconsistent, which of the two exerts a greater influence on adolescents'

Table 2
Congruence Models

CHEATING
$$RB = -1.20 + .31^{***}FA + .59^{***}FB - .03HL + .65^{***}LH + .47^{*}HH$$
$$R = .55 \quad N = 1{,}577$$

MARIJUANA
$$RB = -1.46 + .46^{***}FA + .75^{***}FB + .23HL + .70^{***}LH + .60^{*}HH$$
$$R = .76 \quad N = 1{,}612$$

LARCENY
$$RB = -.60 + .12^{***}FA + .37^{***}FB - .06HL + .81^{***}LH + .71^{*}HH$$
$$R = .50 \quad N = 1{,}596$$

Note: RB = respondent's behavior; FA = friends' attitudes; FB = friends' behavior; HL = high approval, low involvement; LH = low approval, high involvement; HH = high approval, high involvement; and LL (low approval, low involvement) is the omitted category.

* $p < .05$
** $p < .01$
*** $p < .001$

behavior? Or does such incongruence cancel or mitigate the influence of peers?

Answering such questions requires some measure of congruence between friends' attitudes and friends' behavior, but constructing such a measure is not as simple as it might appear. The reason is that congruence and incongruence can take different forms, with quite different consequences. In the present case, congruence occurs when friends both approve of and engage in delinquent behavior *or* when friends disapprove and refrain from such behavior. In the same way, incongruence may take two forms: Friends may approve of delinquent acts but not engage in them, or they may disapprove of such acts but nevertheless commit them.

To capture these distinctions, we first recoded our measures of friends' attitudes and friends' behavior.[8] We collapsed friends' attitudes into two categories—those who approved of the act (scores 4 and 5) and those who disapproved or were indifferent toward the act (scores 1–3). Likewise, friends' behavior was collapsed into two categories—those who said that "most" or "all" of their friends had committed the act during the past year (scores 4 and 5) and those who said that "none," "very few," or "some" of their friends had done so (scores 1–3). Next, dummy variables were constructed to represent the four combinations of these variables—high approval/high involvement (henceforth HH), low approval/low involvement (LL), high approval/low involvement (HL), and low approval/high involvement (LH).

The equations in Table 2 show, for each offense, the regression of respondent's behavior (RB) on the dummy variables, as well as the main effects of friends' attitudes (FA) and friends' behavior (FB). In each case, LL is the omitted (i.e., reference) category. The general features of the models are quite similar across the three offenses, and they paint an intriguing picture. First, congruence between the attitudes and behavior of friends does indeed have an effect above and beyond the main effects of the two variables. The coefficient for HH is positive and statistically significant in each case.

The most striking features of the models, however, are those that pertain to incongruence. The coefficient for HL is not statistically significant in any of the models, meaning that there is no significant difference between the HL and LL groups. In other words, having friends who approve of delinquency has no effect on respondent's behavior when those friends do not also engage in delinquency. On the other hand, the coefficient for LH is significant in each case. That is, friends' involvement in delinquency has a significant effect on respondent's behavior even when those friends do not approve or are indifferent toward those acts.[9]

These findings, then, support two conclusions. First, the effect of friends' attitudes and friends' behavior is in fact enhanced when the two are consistent. Friends who behave as well as think in a delinquent fashion produce the most delinquent associates. However, when the attitudes and behavior of peers are inconsistent, the behavior of peers appears to outweigh or override the attitudes of peers. The actions of peers, it seems, speak louder than their attitudes.

Discussion and Conclusion

The results of our analysis provide both positive and negative evidence for Sutherland's theory of differential association. On the one hand, our findings indicate that attitude transference does indeed play a part in the social transmission of delinquency. The attitudes of adolescents are influenced by the attitudes (and behavior) of their peers, and those attitudes in turn affect delinquency. At the same time, however, our findings suggest that Sutherland's theory is ultimately incomplete. Quite apart from the attitudes of adolescents and those of their friends, the *behavior* of friends has a strong, independent effect on adolescents' behavior.

This finding may appear to be unique, but a careful reading of the literature on differential association over the past several decades shows that we are not the first to come upon this result. In a study of alcohol and marijuana use, Jaquith (1981) found strong effects of both peer use and personal attitudes on adolescents' use of those drugs. However, Jaquith reported the "unexpected" finding that respondent's attitude did *not* mediate the effect of peer behavior: "The major difference between [Sutherland's] model and the trimmed marijuana and alcohol models is the direct path from peer group use to respondent's use that unexpectedly remains in the final models and exceeds in strength the predicted indirect effect" (1981:277). Precisely the same results were reported by Jensen (1972) in a test of differential association theory using data from the Richmond Youth Project. "Association with delinquents and definitions [of delinquency] are independently related to delinquent involvement.... It is clear that the effect of the number of delinquent friends on delinquency is not solely a product of socialization into competing normative standards" (1972:568). More recently, Matsueda and Heimer (1987:831) reported that "The number of delinquent friends ... does have a substantial and statistically significant influence on delinquency," even after controlling for delinquent definitions, attachment to peers and parents, and family structure.[10]

Taken in conjunction with our results, these findings cast serious doubt on the ability of differential association theory to explain fully the influence of delinquent peers. There can be little doubt that peers are a critical factor in the production of delinquency, but the notion of attitude transference on which differential association theory rests does not appear to be a sufficient explanation of peer influence.

Proponents of differential association may object to that conclusion on the grounds that we have failed to identify the appropriate attitudes or definitions that give rise to delinquent behavior. The meaning of Sutherland's "definitions" has been endlessly debated, but surely an adolescent's approval or disapproval of delinquent acts constitutes one element of such definitions. We note in that connection that our measure of delinquent attitudes is in fact related to delinquency, and it does at least partially mediate the effect of peer behavior. Yet we readily concede that there may be other definitions that fully account for peer influence. But until those definitions are identified and assessed, proponents of differential association cannot claim strong support for the theory.

If our analysis underscores the importance of peer behavior, however, it does not explain exactly how delinquent behavior is transferred or transmitted from one adolescent to the next. As we observed earlier, two of the prime suspects are mechanisms stipulated by social learning theory, that is, imitation and vicarious reinforcement.

Measuring these processes in natural settings is likely to prove a difficult task, but several strategies are promising. In addition to questioning adolescents about the delinquent behavior of their friends, investigators should ask questions about the consequences of friends' behavior, both positive (e.g., increases in prestige, friendships, or income) and negative (e.g., social ostracism, arrest) (see Akers et al., 1979, for an example). Such a strategy would not only illuminate the process of vicarious reinforcement, but might also help to integrate differential association and deterrence theory. Although deterrence theorists have scarcely acknowledged the possibility, individuals' perceptions of legal sanctions may be heavily influenced by the perceptions and experiences of their friends. Indeed, the process of general deterrence may be singularly potent within the context of peer networks.

The process of imitation or modeling is more difficult to detect, since there are no external indicia of imitation other than congruence between the model and observer's behavior. The process of modeling might be better understood, however, if investigators were to examine peer influence in domains other than (or in addition to) delinquency, such as school (grades, extracurricular activities), work, and leisure activities. That strategy might help in identifying the most influential models for adolescents and place delinquency within a larger context of social learning.

Finally, investigators should distinguish between adolescents who are merely aware of their friends' behavior and those who have actually witnessed or participated in delinquency with their friends (i.e., as co-offenders). The distinction is critical because it speaks to quite different conceptions of peer influence. To illustrate, whereas differential association emphasizes the learned nature of delinquency, there is nothing in the theory that requires the actual presence of companions in delinquent episodes. By contrast, theories of delinquency that emphasize collective behavior, situational inducements, or group process clearly regard the immediate presence of companions as a necessary stimulus for delinquency. The distinction is no less important for social learning theory, especially if the processes of imitation and vicarious reinforcement are contingent on direct observation of delinquent behavior.

Whatever the mechanism of transmission may ultimately prove to be, our findings suggest that investigators must take care to differentiate the attitudes and behavior of peers in examining the production of delinquency. Sutherland notwithstanding, what peers do appears to be at least as important as what they think.

Notes

1. Differential association is not limited to peer influence; it may be extended to include parents, teachers, and other significant others (see, e.g., Jensen, 1972). Most tests and discussions of the theory, however, have concentrated on peers.
2. Social learning theory contains other mechanisms of learning, including both intrinsic and extrinsic positive and negative reinforcement (Akers, 1985). Imitation and vicarious reinforcement, however, are the two processes that seem to bear most directly on peer influence because they are the most purely *social* mechanisms of learning.
3. Wave III data were the most recent data available at the time this study was undertaken. Waves IV and V have subsequently been released.
4. All of the questions pertaining to marijuana in the NYS refer to both marijuana and hashish. Interviewers were free to use common names ("grass," "pot," "hash") to describe these drugs.
5. All coefficients in the models are significant at $p < .001$. The nonsignificant paths have probabilities $\geq .05$.
6. All coefficients in the models are significant at $p < .005$. The self-report item on cheating was asked of only about half the sample ($N = 814$) in wave II, which means that the effective N for the lagged model is smaller than that for the cross-sectional (wave III) model.
7. None of the coefficients in the cross-sectional wave II and wave III models for cheating and larceny differs by more than .06. The two waves do not contain comparable data on the self-reported frequency of marijuana use, so a comparison of the full models is not possible. Of those coefficients that can be es-

timated for both waves, however, none differs by more than .09.
8. All analyses in this section are based on wave III data.
9. Congruence between friends' behavior and friends' attitudes cannot be modeled with a standard multiplicative interaction term (i.e., $FB \times FA$) because a single term cannot adequately capture the different *types* of congruence. Also, readers will note that although the congruence models in Table 2 contain significant effects, the models provide only a small improvement in fit. This is evidently a consequence of the fairly strong collinearity between the main effects and dummy variables. We believe that the statistical and logical evidence is sufficient in this case to say that the dummy variables are not simply a reconstruction of main effects (particularly when those effects are already in the model). Finally, it is interesting that the largest congruence coefficients are found for the LH, not the HH, groups. This may have some interesting theoretical implications, but the differences between the LH and HH groups are small enough (.10 for marijuana and larceny, and .18 for cheating) that we must resist the temptation to place any substantive interpretation on them.
10. For another example, see Akers et al., 1979.

References

Akers, Ronald L. 1985. *Deviant Behavior: A Social Learning Approach*. Belmont, Calif.: Wadsworth.

Akers, Ronald L., Marvin D. Krohn, Lonn Lanza-Kaduce, and Marcia Radosevich. 1979. Social learning and deviant behavior: A specific test of a general theory. *American Sociological Review* 44:636-655.

Briar, Scott and Irving Piliavin. 1965. Delinquency, situational inducements, and commitment to conformity. *Social Problems* 13:35-45.

Cloward, Richard A. and Lloyd E. Ohlin. 1960. *Delinquency and Opportunity*. Glencoe, Ill.: Free Press.

Cohen, Lawrence E. and Marcus Felson. 1979. Social change and crime rate trends: A routine activity approach. *American Sociological Review* 44:588-608.

Deutscher, Irwin. 1973. *What We Say/What We Do: Sentiments and Acts*. Glencoe, Ill.: Scott, Foresman.

Elliott, Delbert S. and Suzanne S. Ageton. 1980. Reconciling race and class differences in self-reported and official estimates of delinquency. *American Sociological Review* 45:95-110.

Elliott, Delbert S., David Juizinga, and Suzanne S. Ageton. 1985. *Explaining Delinquency and Drug Use*. Beverly Hills, Calif: Sage.

Erickson, Maynard L. and Lamar T. Empey. 1965. Class position, peers, and delinquency. *Sociology and Social Research* 49:268-282.

Gold, Martin. 1970. *Delinquent Behavior in an American City*. Belmont, Calif: Brooks/Cole.

Hepburn, John R. 1977. Testing alternative models of delinquency causation. *Journal of Criminal Law and Criminology* 67:450-460.

Jaquith, Susan M. 1981. Adolescent marijuana and alcohol use: An empirical test of differential association theory. *Criminology* 19:271-280.

Jensen, Gary F. 1972. Parents, peers, and delinquent action: A test of the differential association perspective. *American Journal of Sociology* 78:562-575.

Johnson, Richard E. 1979. *Juvenile Delinquency and Its Origins*. New York: Cambridge University Press.

Liska, Allen E. 1981. *Perspectives on Deviance*. Englewood Cliffs, N.J.: Prentice-Hall.

Matsueda, Ross L. and Karen Heimer. 1987. Race, family structure, and delinquency: A test of differential association and social control theories. *American Sociological Review* 52:826-840.

Paternoster, Raymond. 1987. The deterrent effect of the perceived certainty and severity of punishment: A review of the evidence and issues. *Justice Quarterly* 4:173-217.

Reiss, Albert J., Jr., and A. Lewis Rhodes. 1964. An empirical test of differential association theory. *Journal of Research in Crime and Delinquency* 1:5-18.

Short, James F. 1957. Differential association and delinquency. *Social Problems* 4:233-239.

Short, James F. and Fred L. Strodtbeck. 1965. *Group Process and Gang Delinquency*. Chicago: University of Chicago Press.

Sutherland, Edwin H. 1947. *Criminology*. 4th ed. Philadelphia: Lippincott.

Tittle, Charles R., Mary Jean Burke, and Elton F. Jackson. 1986. Modeling Sutherland's theory of differential association: Toward an empirical clarification. *Social Forces* 65:405-432.

Vold, George B. and Thomas J. Bernard. 1986. *Theoretical Criminology*. 3rd ed. New York: Oxford University Press.

Voss, Harwin L. 1964. Differential association and reported delinquency behavior: A replication. *Social Problems* 12:78-85.

Williams, Kirk R. and Richard Hawkins. 1986. Perceptual research on general deterrence: A critical review. *Law and Society Review* 20(4):545-572. ✦

24
Gangs, Drugs, and Delinquency in a Survey of Urban Youth

Finn-Aage Esbensen
David Huizinga

Gang-related research can be traced back to the early part of this century (e.g., Asbury, 1927; Puffer, 1912; Thrasher, 1927) and has been closely associated with the development of criminological theory. During the 1950s, coinciding with the media coverage of gangs, social science researchers and theorists such as Cohen (1955), Miller (1958), and Cloward and Ohlin (1960) paved the way for subsequent researchers in the scientific study of gangs (e.g., Klein, 1971; Moore, 1978; Short and Strodbeck, 1965; Spergel, 1966). These research efforts were either generally grounded in prior theory or interested in testing new theoretical explanations of gang delinquency. By the 1970s, however, interest in gangs had become passe and some wondered if gangs had met their demise (Bookin-Weiner and Horowitz, 1983).

It was not until the urban gang violence of the early and mid-1980s that academic and media attention once again focused on the gang problem. As with most of the early gang studies, the majority of recent gang research has relied on observational methods and has produced a wealth of information about specific gangs and their members (e.g., Campbell, 1991; Hagedorn, 1988; MacLeod, 1987; Sullivan, 1989; Vigil, 1988). Relatively few gang research projects have used survey methods, however. Notable examples of survey research on gangs include Bowker and Klein (1983), Esbensen et al. (1993), Fagan (1989), Klein (1971), Morash (1983), Thornberry et al. (1993), and Winfree et al. (1991). With the exception of Fagan's (1989) reliance on a snowball sample of gang members, the other studies cited relied on more representative samples of youths.

In addition to observational and survey methods, other gang researchers have relied on law enforcement records to examine gang offenses and to describe gang members. Klein and Maxson (1989) and Spergel (1990) discussed the extent to which official data provide rather subjective assessments of gang behavior.[1]

While research design and methods of data collection have been varied and the generalizability of results has been questioned, concern has also been raised with regard to the applicability of the old gang knowledge to the new gang situation. Hagedorn (1988), for instance, noted the changing nature of the ethnic-racial composition of inner cities and the lack of contemporary research to address the current status of gangs. While being rather critical of prior gang research, he noted that "the theories of the fifties and sixties were rigorously examined by sociologists and for the most part failed to stand the test of empirical verification" (p. 27). A number of other gang commentators have echoed the need for further theoretical and empirical examination of gang formation and behavior. Interestingly, one point of consensus in the voluminous gang literature is the high rate of criminal activity among gang members. Regardless of methodology and design, the consensus is that gang members commit all kinds of crimes at a greater rate than do nongang members.

The call for more empirical analysis of gangs in conjunction with the consistent finding of high rates of offending by gang members provided the impetus for conducting the analyses reported here. Despite almost a century of gang research, an important question (and the one guiding this research) remains: Are gang members more delinquent because of their gang affiliation or were they predisposed to delinquent activity prior to their gang initiation?

That is, is the gang unit a criminogenic peer group, do delinquent youths seek out gangs, or do both processes occur? Using longitudinal data from the first four years (1988-1991) of the ongoing Denver Youth Survey (DYS),[2] we examine the temporal ordering of gang membership and involvement in delinquent activity. . . .

Methods

Definition of Gangs and Gang Membership

Arriving at a definition of the term *gang* is no simple task; considerable debate exists regarding an appropriate definition (see Covey et al., 1992). We have adopted the position espoused by Miller (1974) and Klein and Maxson (1989), that is, in order to be considered a gang, the group must be involved in illegal activity.

Considerable data about gang membership were collected during the survey's 90-minute, in-person interviews. One early finding from this line of questioning was that approximately 5% of youths in the DYS indicated that they were gang members in any given year (39 in wave 1, 37 in wave 2, 41 in wave 3, and 76 in wave 4). Respondents were asked early in the interview if they were "members of a street or youth gang." All those responding affirmatively were later asked a series of questions about their gangs. Examination of this follow-up information indicated that what some of the youths described as gangs could best be defined as informal youth groups, or in some instances, church groups, that did not necessarily include involvement in delinquent behavior. As mentioned above, to be considered a gang member, the youth had to indicate that the gang was involved in illegal activity. An affirmative response to either of two follow-up questions (i.e., perceived gang involvement in fights with other gangs and participation in illegal activities) was used to exclude nondelinquent gangs from the analysis. While the exclusion of respondents who indicated their gang was not involved in these activities reduced the number of potential gang members to 27 in wave 1, 33 in wave 2, 32 in wave 3, and 68 in wave 4, this process permits a more stringent and, arguably, more accurate description of juvenile *delinquent* gang membership and activity. The 32 gang members in wave 3 represent 2.7% of the general sample of youths aged 11 to 17, and the 68 gang members in wave 4 represent 6.7% of the youths when they were 12 to 18 years of age. From this, one might conclude that gang membership is a relatively infrequent phenomenon in Denver, even among this "high-risk" sample of urban youths.

What are these gangs like? Descriptive data provided by respondents paint a picture of what Yablonsky (1959:109) referred to as "near groups"—groups characterized by limited cohesion, impermanence, shifting membership, and diffuse role definition, but at the same time that had some level of identification as a gang, as evidenced by having a gang name and use of gang colors and initiation rites. Year 4 data are representative of the descriptive information provided across the four years of data collection: 97% of the members indicated their gangs had a formal name (37 gangs were identified by the 68 gang members); 86% indicated their gang had initiation rites; and 97% reported that their gang had symbols or colors. With regard to shifting membership and impermanence, when asked what role they would like to have or what role they expect to have in the gang someday, over 60% of year 4 gang members indicated that they would like to *not* be a member and expected *not* to be a member sometime in the future.

Self-reported delinquency data were also collected from all respondents. The measures are improved versions of our earlier work (e.g., Huizinga and Elliott, 1986) and avoid some of the problems of even earlier self-report inventories. The measures exclude traditional trivial offenses, such as defying parental authority, and include serious offenses often excluded from early self-report inventories (e.g., rape, robbery, and aggravated assault). Additionally, follow-up questions were included as integral parts of the measures. These follow-up questions allow for determination of the seriousness and appropriateness of initial responses. If, for example, a respondent indicated that he or she had committed an aggravated assault during the prior year but follow-up information revealed that it was accidental and that the victim truly was not injured, the original response would be changed to zero.

For analysis purposes, our delinquency and drug use measures focus on those behaviors often considered to be of greatest concern. To this end, we developed four levels of delinquency: (1) street offending, (2) other serious offending, (3) minor offending, and (4) nonoffending. We used a subset of the street offenses to create a measure of drug sales[3] in order to address the concern that gangs are disproportionately involved in drug distribution (e.g., Fagan, 1989). One gang expert has even suggested that youth gangs of the 1990s have established a national network of drug distribution similar to the "mafia's" alcohol distribution network during prohibition (Taylor, 1990).

Street offenses focus on serious crimes that occur on the street and are often of concern to citizens and policymakers, alike. *Other serious offenses* includes behaviors that, while not in the street crime category,

Table 1
Demographic Characteristics of the Denver Youth Survey Sample

	Year 1		Year 2		Year 3		Year 4	
	Gang	Nongang	Gang	Nongang	Gang	Nongang	Gang	Nongang
Sex								
Male, N	15	441	27	397	24	555	53	511
Column %	54%	52%	80%	52%	74%	52%	80%	50%
Female, N	12	400	7	390	8	514	13	516
Column %	46%	48%	20%	48%	25%	48%	20%	50%
Total N	27	841	33	801	32	1102	68	1027
Race								
Af.-Am., N	7	320	14	283	15	385	28	371
Column %	26%	38%	42%	37%	48%	36%	42%	36%
Hisp., N	16	374	14	352	14	470	35	443
Column %	60%	45%	43%	46%	42%	44%	52%	43%
White, N	0	71	2	65	0	104	2	103
Column %	—	9%	7%	8%	—	10%	3%	10%
Other, N	4	75	1	67	2	110	2	110
Column %	14%	9%	8%	9%	7%	10%	3%	11%
Total N	27	830	33	801	32	1102	68	1026
Age Birthyear								
1972, N	14	256	11	226	11	228	18	227
Column %	52%	30%	33%	30%	35%	22%	27%	22%
1974, N	10	291	17	268	11	275	20	257
Column %	38%	35%	52%	35%	33%	26%	31%	25%
1976, N	3	294	5	273	10	276	24	257
Column %	10%	35%	16%	36%	32%	26%	36%	25%
1978, N	—	—	—	—	0	291	5	285
Column %						27%	7%	28%
Total N	27	830	33	801	32	1102	68	1027

Note: These data are weighted to represent the stratified sample. As a result, the integral values are approximates and do not always provide the exact percentage.

are nevertheless considered as serious delinquency. *Minor offenses* refers primarily to status offenses and other public nuisance type behaviors. These categories of delinquent behavior generally reflect the seriousness weighting used by Wolfgang et al. (1985). We dichotomized *drug use* into alcohol use and "other drug use," including marijuana and other illicit drugs. For the analyses reported below, all youths were categorized based on their most serious level of involvement in delinquency and drug use. Thus, if an individual reported committing a minor, a serious, and a street offense in a given year, that individual was classified as a street offender. Appendix A provides a listing of the items included in the self-reported delinquency and drug use classifications.

Results

Gang Member Demographics

Gangs have traditionally been thought of as being a predominantly male phenomenon, and relatively few studies have concentrated on female gang members (exceptions include Bowker and Klein, 1983; Campbell, 1990, 1991; Giordano, 1978; Harris, 1988; Morash, 1983; Quicker, 1983). This has resulted in considerable ignorance concerning not only the role of female gang members, but also the number of females involved in gang activity. Campbell (1991) reports a long and rich history of female gangs and female members in male gangs; she suggests that at one point approximately 10% of New York City gang members were female, and that female membership might have been as high as 33% in one gang. Fagan (1990) reported female gang membership to be approximately 33% in his survey.

The demographic characteristics of both gang and nongang members are presented in Table 1. As seen there, the DYS data confirm that a significant proportion of all gang members are female—a fact not generally acknowledged in media presentations of gangs. Cross-sectional analysis of DYS gang data reveals that females constituted from 20% to 46% of gang members during the four-year study period. Thus, while there is evidence that gang members are primarily males, there is reason to believe that females are more involved in gangs than is generally acknowledged. One caveat, however, is that while female gang membership may well be greater than that presented in the popular press, female gang members are less likely to report high levels of involvement in delinquent activity. In wave 3, for example, female gang members reported an average individual offending rate of 14.0 on the general delinquency scale, and male gang members reported an average offending rate of 36.9 offenses on that scale.

As with gender, it is often assumed that gang members are youths from ethnic-racial minority backgrounds (e.g., Fagan, 1989; Spergel, 1990). A 1989 survey of law enforcement officials in 45 cities across the nation found that African-American and Hispanics made up 87% of gang membership (cited in Gurule, 1991). Due to the nature of the DYS sample (78% of the sample is African-American or Hispanic), it is not possible to address the ethnic distribution of gang membership, although it does appear that African-American and Hispanic youths tend to be overrepresented in the DYS gang subsample (ranging from 85% to 94% of gang members in the various years). Given the disproportionate number of minority youths in the sample, however, it should be expected that the majority of gang members would also be African-American or Hispanic.

Gang membership does appear to be somewhat associated with age. In year 4, for example, 27% of gang members were 18 years old, 31% were 16, 36% were 14 years old, and 7% were 12. Given this age distribution, at what age do youths join gangs? Gang members were asked when they joined their gang. Analysis of these responses for year 4 revealed that most did not join until their teenaged years, although a few respondents did indicate that they joined the gang before the age of 12.

Gang Delinquency

Are gang members more involved in delinquency than nongang members? Exami-

Table 2
Year 4 Prevalence and Individual Offending Rates (IOR) of Gang and Nongang Members Controlling for Sex

| | Males | | | | | | Females | | | | | |
| | Gang | | | Nongang | | | Nongang | | | Gang | | |
Offense Type	N	Prev.	IOR	N	Prev.	IOR	N	Prev.	IOR	N	Prev.	IOR
Street	53	.85*	22.3**	511	.18	8.3	13	.76*	5.9	515	.07	2.7
Drug Sales	53	.29*	22.8**	511	.03	30.5	13	.18*	10.5	515	.01	6.8
Serious	53	.83*	31.8**	510	.32	10.0	13	.61*	5.1	516	.18	10.0
Minor	49	.87*	29.0**	500	.56	11.6	13	.93*	18.7	499	.54	10.1
Alcohol Use	53	.71*	48.4**	510	.35	24.1	13	.85*	36.9	516	.32	16.7
Other Drug Use	52	.52*	46.8**	491	.13	20.0	13	.69*	11.9	516	.13	23.6

*$p < .05$ (chi-square).
**$p < .05$ (T test, separate variance estimate of t).

nation of Table 2 results in a firm yes for males and a qualified yes for female gang members.[4] Both prevalence and individual offending rates for gang members and nongang members are reported for four types of delinquent behavior and two types of drug use during year 4. It is important to examine prevalence rates first in that this identifies the number of active offenders involved in each specific behavior.

The prevalence rates for male and female gang members are significantly greater than those for their nongang counterparts. Gang membership is almost synonymous with involvement in all types of delinquency. Male gang members, for example, reported a prevalence rate of .85 for street offenses and .83 for other serious offenses. This is substantially higher than the prevalence rates of .18 and .32, respectively, for nongang males. The difference in prevalence rates is even more pronounced for females; .76 of female gang members reported involvement in street offending compared with .07 for nongang females. For each type of behavior, the prevalence rate for female gang members is consistently greater than that for male nongang members. Gang members during year 4 report being involved in a variety of delinquent activities; with male prevalence rates ranging between .29 for drug sales and .93 for minor offending, these youths clearly do not specialize in any one type of activity.

Nongang members had much lower rates of involvement in all types of delinquent activities and drug use than did the gang members, as evidenced by prevalence rates of .01 and .03 for females and males, respectively, involved in drug sales, and nongang prevalence rates of .07 and .18 for female and male involvement, respectively, in street-level offending (compared with .76 and .85 for female and male gang members).

With respect to the individual offending rates, however, there are no statistically significant differences between female gang and nongang members. Nongang females who were involved in delinquent activity, whether assault, theft, or drug use, reported nearly the same level of activity. Male gang members, however, had individual offending rates, that were two to three times greater than those of nongang males involved in each specific activity, with the exception of drug sales. To illustrate the value of examining both prevalence and individual offending rates, we interpret the street-level offending data for males. While there were only 53 male gang members, 85% of them (45 members) reported involvement in street offenses. Those 45 gang members reported committing an average of 22.3 offenses per person. This translates into 1,003 (45 x 22.3 = 1,003.5) offenses.[5] For the nongang members, only 18% of the 511, or 92 males, reported committing street crimes. And, they reported committing only 8.3 offenses per person, for a total of 764 offenses. Thus, while male gang members accounted for only 33% of street offenders in year 4, they reported committing 57% of street offenses.

Additional analyses were conducted to determine if the level of gang involvement was associated with levels of offending. Gang members were categorized as core or peripheral members based on their responses to the question, How would you describe your position in the gang? All those indicating that they were leaders or one of the top persons were classified as core members. All others were considered as peripheral members. No age or sex differences were found between the core and peripheral members. More important, and perhaps somewhat surprising, introduction of this control did not result in any statistically significant differences between the two levels of gang involvement and self-reported delinquency. That is, the peripheral members reported the same level of delinquent activity as did the core members.

With respect to gang activity, gang members were asked a series of questions about the kinds of activities in which the gang was involved. Given our definition of gangs and desire to describe *delinquent* gangs, the responses listed below confirm that in addition to being delinquent gangs, the *perception* of gang members is that members of their gangs are involved in a wide range of illegal activity. While fights with other gangs is the most frequently mentioned form of illegal activity, approximately three-fourths of the gang members reported that their gang was involved in the following: robberies, joyriding, assaults of other people, thefts of more than $50, and drug sales. Clearly, illegal activities are a prominent part of the *perceived* gang experience, and these descriptions coincide with the self-reported levels of delinquency discussed above. It is interesting, however, that only 30% of male and 18% of female gang members indicated in the self-report inventory that they themselves were involved in drug sales during the preceding year.

Longitudinal Analyses

With four years of longitudinal data available for 85% of the original sample, it becomes possible to examine the stability of gang membership. Consistent with the research literature (e.g., Hagedorn, 1988; Klein, 1971; Short and Strodbeck, 1965; Thornberry et al., 1993; Vigil, 1988; Yablonsky, 1959, 1963), we found gang membership to lack stability.[6] Of the 90 gang youths for whom we have complete data for all four years, 67% were members in only one year, 24% belonged for two years, 6% belonged for three years, and only 3% belonged for all four years.

Table 3
Prevalence of Street Offending Among Gang and Nongang Members Controlling for Year of Membership ($N = 730$)

Year of Gang Membership[a]	N[b]	Prevalence of Street Offending			
		Year 1	Year 2	Year 3	Year 4
Nongang	640	70	72	94	80
		.11	.11	.15	.13
Year 1 Only	10	7	1	2	3
		.72	.09	.20	.28
Year 2 Only	9	2	6	3	3
		.23	.65	.32	.35
Year 3 Only	10	1	2	8	5
		.09	.21	.77	.53
Year 4 Only	31	3	8	12	23
		.10	.25	.39	.74
Years 3 and 4	10	4	7	9	9
		.44	.73	.91	.88
Years 2, 3 and 4[c]	5	3	3	5	5
Years 1, 2, 3 and 4[c]	3	2	3	3	2

Note: These data are weighted to represent the stratified sample. As a result, the integral values are approximates and do not always provide the exact percentage.

[a]These refer to consecutive years of membership. An additional 12 youths reported gang membership during 2 nonconsecutive years.

[b]The N reflects those cases for which four years of complete data are available. For gang members, complete four-year data are available for 90 of 112 (80%) youths. For nongang youths, complete four-year data are available for 640 of 729 (88%) youths.

[c]Samples are too small to allow calculation of reliable prevalence estimates.

A major purpose of this paper is to address the temporal ordering of delinquency and gang membership. That is, are gang members more delinquent prior to becoming gang members or is the heightened level of delinquent activity contemporaneous with gang membership? And, perhaps equally important, what is the delinquency level of gang members in years following their departure from the gang? Answers to these questions help identify gang influences on behavior and address the often-debated theoretical issue of "feathering versus flocking." Table 3 summarizes the relationship between gang membership and street-level offending during the four years examined. This particular analysis is restricted to those youths in the three oldest cohorts for whom complete longitudinal data were available (N = 730).

Annual prevalence data illustrate that, overall, gang members were particularly likely to be involved in street offenses during the year in which they were gang members, with lower levels of involvement both before and after their time in the gang. However, the indication is that regardless of their year of membership, youths who have been gang members at some point in time, have higher prevalence rates for street offending than do youths who have never belonged to a gang. Among year 1 gang members, 72% were classified as street offenders. By years 2, 3, and 4, when these youth were no longer in a gang, the percentage of those youths who were street offenders had decreased substantially and was only slightly higher than the prevalence rate for nongang youths. For year 2 gang members, 23% were classified as street offenders in year 1, 65 in year 2 (when they were gang members), and then 32% and 35%, respectively, in the two subsequent years when they were no longer in the gang. For youths who were gang members during year 3 or year 4, a gradual increase in the number of street offenders can be seen prior to their joining the gang, and then a sharp increase in the prevalence rate over the year immediately preceding gang membership (from 21% to 77% for year 3 gang members and from 39% to 74% for year 4 members). The prevalence rates of street offending for stable gang members, that is, those reporting gang membership for two or more consecutive years, exceed those of the transient, one-year only members.

In Table 3 we controlled for the actual years of gang membership and the prevalence of street offending, which permitted examination of stable and transient members. Due to the low number of stable gang members and interest in other delinquency measures, in Table 4 we report differences in the prevalence rate between gang members and nongang youths for two types of delinquency (street-level offending and other serious offenses) and illicit drug use. In this table, the behavior of gang members in a specific year is tracked for the four-year study period. This means that the stable gang members are included in multiple years, which inflates the overall pattern. However, we thought it inappropriate to exclude stable members from the analysis.

In Table 4, *year of gang membership* refers to all those individuals who reported belonging to a gang that year. *Prevalence of offending* refers to whether these individuals reported engaging in any of the specified behaviors in each year. Consistent with the detailed findings for street offending reported in Table 3, prevalence rates for each type of behavior are highest during the gang member's year of actual gang membership. For example, among the year 3 gang members, 43% committed street offenses in year 1, 55% in year 2, 90% in year 3, and 77% in year 4. Each of these prevalence rates is substantially greater than the comparable annual rate for those youths who were not gang members in year 3, all of which were between .13 and .15. In separate analyses controlling for gang membership status (i.e., transient and stable), similar differences between gang and nongang youths were found, although the differences between transient members and nongang youth were less pronounced.

Examination of these prevalence rates across years permits an assessment of the temporal relationship between gang membership and delinquency. While some people believe that "birds of a feather flock together," others believe in a socialization explanation (e.g., Elliott and Menard, in

Table 4
Prevalence of Street Offending, Serious Offending, and Illegal Drug Use Among Gang and Nongang Members

Year of Gang Membership	Prevalence of Offending							
	Sample Size		Street Offenses		Serious Offenses		Illicit Drug Use	
	Gang	Nongang	Gang	Nongang	Gang	Nongang	Gang	Nongang
Year 1 Membership								
Year 1 Behavior	25	835	.85*	.15	.93*	.36	.42*	.13
Year 2 Behavior	25	766	.41*	.15	.61*	.32	.52*	.15
Year 3 Behavior	21	782	.39*	.20	.51	.36	.36*	.14
Year 4 Behavior	22	779	.40*	.19	.48	.30	.27	.19
Year 2 Membership								
Year 1 Behavior	32	757	.50*	.13	.66*	.37	.29*	.13
Year 2 Behavior	33	764	.69*	.13	.89*	.30	.47*	.13
Year 3 Behavior	30	737	.59*	.18	.68*	.35	.44*	.14
Year 4 Behavior	30	729	.63*	.18	.70*	.28	.39*	.18
Year 3 Membership								
Year 1 Behavior	31	768	.43*	.13	.53	.37	.23	.13
Year 2 Behavior	29	736	.55*	.14	.67*	.32	.42*	.13
Year 3 Behavior	32	1059	.90*	.15	.75*	.32	.60*	.10
Year 4 Behavior	30	1026	.77*	.15	.66*	.27	.42	.15
Year 4 Membership								
Year 1 Behavior	61	733	.33*	1.3	.54*	.35	.13	.13
Year 2 Behavior	60	695	.51*	.12	.73*	.29	.34*	.14
Year 3 Behavior	65	983	.58*	.14	.65*	.31	.37*	.10
Year 4 Behavior	67	1026	.83*	.12	.79*	.25	.56*	.13

*$p < .05$ (chi-square).

press). In Table 4 there is some evidence to support the selection or "birds of a feather" explanation. Gang members have higher prevalence rates of involvement in delinquency in years preceding their gang membership. Year 3 gang members, for example, have a higher rate of participation in street offending (.43 compared with .13), but not other serious offenses or illicit drug use, in year 1 than do nongang members. By year 2, the prevalence rates for year 3 gang members are higher than those of the nongang members for all three behaviors, and in year 3, the largest discrepancy is noted.

While rates of participation are, in fact, higher in years preceding and during gang membership, Table 4 also reveals that these rates of delinquent activity decline in years subsequent to gang membership.[7] By year 4, the year 1 gang members are more similar to those youths who reported never having belonged to a gang, although they still report statistically significant higher rates of participation in street offending (40% compared with 19%).

The preceding discussion focused on the prevalence of street offending and other types of delinquency among gang and nongang members. Of equal importance, and essential to the understanding of the level of delinquent behavior, is examination of individual offending rates, or lambda (i.e., average number of offenses per active offender) for these two groups (Table 5). As with prevalence rates, the individual offending rates of gang members are substantially greater than those of nongang members.[8] As with prevalence rates, gang members clearly have higher offending rates than do nongang members, but this is especially pronounced during the year in which the youths reported being a gang member (e.g., in year 2, gang members categorized as street offenders committed an average of 31.2 street offenses each, compared with 7.6 such offenses for nongang members.

Table 5
Individual Offending Rates of Street Offending, Serious Offending, and Illegal Drug Use Among Gang and Nongang Members

Year of Gang Membership	Individual Offending Rates					
	Street Offenses		Serious Offenses		Illicit Drug Use	
	Gang	Nongang	Gang	Nongang	Gang	Nongang
Year 1 Membership						
Year 1 Behavior	29.2*	6.8	31.4*	8.8	47.4*	15.8
Year 2 Behavior	12.9	6.8	15.0	7.9	34.1	14.9
Year 3 Behavior	7.2	5.9	9.7	5.9	13.1	14.8
Year 4 Behavior	10.7	5.2	17.6*	5.6	26.4	10.9
Year 2 Membership						
Year 1 Behavior	19.7*	4.5	17.3*	7.1	13.0	12.2
Year 2 Behavior	31.2*	7.6	32.2*	11.1	38.2*	17.4
Year 3 Behavior	9.2	8.5	15.3*	6.3	21.0	17.3
Year 4 Behavior	10.8	9.2	11.4	8.1	19.6	14.9
Year 3 Membership						
Year 1 Behavior	13.9*	2.0	12.7*	5.1	10.6	7.1
Year 2 Behavior	20.9*	2.0	24.8*	7.2	22.3*	8.0
Year 4 Behavior	34.5*	5.7	29.8*	8.3	56.8*	23.3
Year 1 Behavior	22.9*	4.2	29.4*	6.6	38.8	20.1
Year 4 Membership						
Year 1 Behavior	8.8*	1.8	9.1*	3.8	3.6	6.2
Year 2 Behavior	13.4*	1.7	22.1*	4.0	11.2	9.2
Year 3 Behavior	14.4*	2.8	13.3*	5.6	27.0*	11.6
Year 4 Behavior	19.7*	6.7	28.1*	10.0	39.5*	21.7

*$p < .05$ (T test, separate variance estimate of t).

Table 5 also reveals that the mean number of street offenses committed by gang members in years preceding their joining the gang is significantly higher than that of nongang members, but that in the years following their departure, there is a dramatic reduction, although they remain more delinquent than their nongang counterparts. By year 2, for example, there were no statistically significant differences between the year 1 gang members and those who were not gang members in year 1. Similarly, by year 3, there were no statistically significant differences for street offending and illicit drug use between the year 2 gang and nongang members.

A popular perception is that gang members are frequent drug users. During their year of membership, gang members reported significantly higher rates of marijuana and other illegal drug use. However, unlike the delinquency measures, drug use prior to and subsequent to gang membership, generally, was not found to be statistically different from the drug use of nongang youths.

In sum, while gang members had higher rates of involvement than nongang members in street offending and other serious offending not only during the year in which they were gang members but also in the years preceding membership, the rate is particularly high and pronounced during the gang years. These higher rates of individual offending, however, decrease substantially once the youths leave the gang. In analyses not presented, this trend is especially pronounced for males in the sample. Illegal drug use fits the same pattern—it is highest during the gang year. However, drug use by gang members is not significantly different from that of nongang members in years when they are not affiliated with a gang.

Summary and Discussion

In the preceding analyses, we addressed three issues: (1) the prevalence and demographic characteristics of gang members in a general survey of urban youths; (2) the relationship between delinquency and drug use among gang youths; and (3) the temporal relationship between offending and gang membership. With regard to the number of urban youths who belong to gangs, two observations should be made. First, even in a sample of high-risk urban youths, gang membership is a statistically infrequent phenomenon. Second, depending on the definition of gang used, different estimates of gang membership are obtained. Prior to controlling for the criminal conduct of gangs, estimates of gang membership were in excess of 5% during each study year. However, when the analysis was restricted to youths who belonged to *delinquent* gangs, slightly less than 3% of the total sample during years 1 through 3 could then be classified as gang members. By year 4, when the cohorts were aged 12 to 18 years, the number of youths reporting to be members of delinquent gangs had increased to almost 7%. Such definitionally induced discrepancies in prevalence of gang membership highlight the need to establish consensus on an operational definition of gangs.

As has been repeatedly argued by Klein and Maxson (1989) and more recently by Spergel and Chance (1991), there is considerable need for a uniform definition of gang and gang behavior. Whether from a research or policy perspective, it is important that a common consensus be reached. While the earlier calls for a uniform definition emphasized jurisdictional differences among law enforcement agencies, our research suggests that a common definition should be employed by survey researchers. A uniform definition of gangs and gang behavior would be a point of departure for a better understanding of a phenomenon that may well be substantially distorted because of a lack of a common means for studying, describing, and regulating gang behavior.

The importance of general surveys is highlighted by examination of the demographic characteristics of gang members. Contrary to much prior research on gangs, females were found to be quite active in gangs (approximately 25% of gang members during the four-year study period were female). While this is higher than the prevailing stereotype, it is consistent with Fagan's (1990) and Campbell's (1991) estimates. Why is it that so many studies fail to report any substantial involvement of females in gangs? It may be, as Campbell (1991:vii) suggests, that writings about gangs, as well as other social science topics, historically have been written by men about men. Thus, female gang membership may well have been systematically underreported in prior research endeavors. A casual examination of early gang research provides some evidence for this argument. Cohen (1955) and Cloward and Ohlin (1960), for example, excluded females from their research and conceptualizations.

A second possibility is that the reliance on official data or purposive samples of gang members has resulted in a biased representation of not only gang membership, but gang behavior as well. Yet another possible explanation may be associated with the sampling or site selection in the DYS and other general surveys. In any localized survey project, it is possible that a particular site or sample is atypical and nonrepresentative of other populations or sites. However, given the similarity of findings between Fagan's (1990) three-city study and the DYS, the high percentage of female gang members may be an accurate accounting of gang membership in the late 1980s. A fourth possibility is that there has been a historical change in female delinquency or in the role of females in gangs. With respect to this issue, Huizinga and Esbensen (1991) reported no change in self-reported levels of offending among two samples of urban females, one from 1978 and the other from 1989.

Another characteristic of gang membership found to be contrary to widely held, media-promoted stereotypes is the notion that youths become gang members for life. While media accounts generally portray gangs as surrogate families for disenfranchised youths, this view is not supported by our research nor by the majority of gang research of the past three decades (e.g., Fagan, 1989; Hagedorn, 1988; Klein, 1971; Short and Strodbeck, 1965; Thornberry et al., 1993; Vigil, 1988; Yablonsky, 1959, 1963). Very few of the youths in the DYS survey reported being in a gang for more than one year. And, many of those youths in a gang indicated that they would like *not* to be a gang member and expected to leave the gang in the future. It appears that the majority of gang members are peripheral or transitory members who drift in and out of the gang.

With regard to involvement in delinquent activity, gang members were found to be considerably more active in all types of delinquency, including drug sales and drug use, than were nongang members. It is important, however, to provide a caveat concerning gang involvement in drug sales. As concluded by Klein et al. (1991), while drug sales/distribution is an activity engaged in by individual gang members, we did not find evidence that drug sales was an organized gang activity involving all gang members. That is, although 80% of the year 4 gang members indicated that the gang was involved in drug sales, only 28% of these very gang members reported that they sold drugs. Further, drug sales is only one of a variety of illegal activities in which the gang is involved. As reported by Fagan (1989), we found that all of the gangs were involved in what Klein (1984) has called "cafeteria-style" delinquency.

The temporal relationship between offending and gang membership is important, and one that can best be examined with longitudinal data of a general population. Participant observation of existing gang members relies on selective retrospective information and generally excludes comparison groups. Cross-sectional surveys cannot examine the developmental sequences that we believe are necessary to explain the process of gang recruitment.

The longitudinal analyses reported here indicate that involvement of gang members in delinquency and drug use is rather strongly patterned. While gang members had higher rates of involvement than nongang members in street crime and other serious forms of offending even before joining the gang, their prevalence and individual offending rates were substantially higher during the actual year of membership. Similar results were also reported in a study of high-risk youths in Rochester, New York (Thornberry et al., 1993). Their findings for "stable" gang members mirrored those reported here. Their "transient" gang members, however, did not appear to have significantly higher rates of offending than nongang members in years prior to or following gang membership. Our findings, in conjunction with those from the Rochester study, lead us to conclude that it is not solely individual characteristics that are associated with higher levels of involvement in street crime. Rather, there may well be factors within the gang milieu that contribute to the criminal behavior of gang members.

Thus, while the high prevalence and individual offending rates prior to gang membership may lead one to espouse the view that they are supportive of a social control perspective, which maintains that people select others of similar values as friends (e.g., Hirschi, 1969), that may be premature. Given that the highest rates of offending occurred during gang years, these data may be more supportive of a learning perspective, which maintains behavior is learned within particular groups and settings (e.g., Burgess and Akers, 1966; Elliott and Menard, in press; Sutherland and Cressey, 1970). A third possibility is what Thornberry et al. (1993:59) have referred to as an "enhancement" model, in which both processes are operative. Without a test of theoretically relevant variables, such conclusions are mere projection. The temporal ordering of such key factors as peer group norms and values and respondent behavior must be examined prior to going beyond the mere speculation stage. Elliott and Menard (in press) have documented with National Youth Survey data that the acquisition of delinquent friends generally precedes the onset of delinquency. The data we have presented suggest that delinquent involvement precedes gang membership. It is here that we do not want to make the tempting juxtaposition and equate gang membership with delinquent friends, for it may well be that gang membership is but a more formalized form of co-offending that was initiated within a delinquent peer group in prior years. Answers to such theoretically important issues should be tested fully, and we hope that our research provides a basis for subsequent work on this issue.

From a policy standpoint, our findings suggest, at least tentatively, that gang intervention strategies should focus not only on decreasing the influence of gangs on individual gang member behavior, but also on the conditions that foster gang development. Although gang members are more highly delinquent than their nongang peers, the trend toward increasing delinquency is prevalent at least two years prior to gang initiation. An important aim should thus be to retard this initial escalation of delinquent activity and disrupt gang effects before peer group behavior becomes formalized within the gang environment.

Notes

1. One common problem, for example, is whether any crime committed by a gang member should be labeled a *gang crime* regardless of the circumstances surrounding the offense. Using law enforcement data from Chicago and Los Angeles, Maxson and Klein (1990) examined gang homicide rates by applying the different definitions of "gang-related" criminal activity used in those two cities. Using the more narrow definition of gang-related homicides employed by the Chicago police (i.e., "a killing is considered gang-related only if it occurs in the course of an explicitly defined collective encounter between two or more gangs"; Maxson and Klein, 1990:77) would reduce the gang homicide rate in Los Angeles by about half. The fact that such discrepancies in prevalence rates can be derived simply by different definitional criteria should cause researchers, theorists, and policymakers substantial discomfort.
2. This research is part of the Program of Research on the Causes and Correlates of Delinquency, with companion projects at the University at Albany-SUNY and the University of Pittsburgh.
3. The drug sale measure consists of two items from the street offending scale. We ran specific analyses to verify that these drug sale items were not "driving" the street offender results.
4. Throughout the analyses reported in this paper, we truncated the self-reported frequency of offending at 99 in order to minimize the effect of "outliers." We also limited the frequency analysis to active offenders and thus use the terms individual offending rates and lambda interchangeably throughout the text to refer to the average offending rate among active offenders. For a discussion of lambda, consult Blumstein et al. (1988).
5. Given what is known about the extent of co-offending among juveniles, it is exceedingly difficult, if not impossible, to make a reasonable transition from offender-specific data to offense data. For example, the fact that 20 youths reported committing an aggravated assault does not necessarily mean that 20 assaults were committed. For discussion of this co-offending issue, consult, for example, Elliott et al. (1985), Fagan (1990), Johnson (1979), and Krohn (1986).
6. In their study of high-risk youth in Rochester, for example, Thornberry et al. (1993) found that 55% of gang members were members for only one year.
7. Analyses in which the sample was disaggregated by gender produced similar results for males. Female gang members, however, only had higher prevalence rates than female nonmembers during the actual year of membership.
8. Once again, analyses disaggregated by gender reveal that these differences are more pronounced for male gang members than female gang members. While males seem to be on a trajectory of increasingly higher rates of offending in years prior to gang initiation, as with prevalence rates, females appear to have higher rates of offending primarily only during their actual year of gang membership.

References

Asbury, Herbert. 1927. *The Gangs of New York.* New York: Capricorn.

Blumstein, Alfred, Jacqueline Cohen, and David Farrington. 1988. Criminal career research: Its value for criminology. *Criminology* 26:1-35.

Bookin-Weiner, Hedy and Ruth Horowitz. 1983. The end of the gang: Fact or fad? *Criminology* 21:585-602.

Bowker, Lee H. and Malcolm W. Klein. 1983. The etiology of female juvenile delinquency and gang membership: A test of psychological and social structural explanations. *Adolescence* 18:740-751.

Burgess, Robert L., and Ronald L. Akers. 1966. A differential association-reinforcement theory of criminal behavior. *Social Problems* 14:128-147.

Campbell, Anne. 1990. Female participation in gangs. In C. Ronald Huff (ed.), *Gangs in America*. Newbury Park, Calif.: Sage.

——. 1991. *The Girls in the Gang*. 2d. ed. Cambridge, Mass.: Basil Blackwell.

Cloward, Richard A. and Lloyd E. Ohlin. 1960. *Delinquency and Opportunity: A Theory of Delinquent Gangs*. New York: Free Press.

Cohen, Albert. 1955. *Delinquent Boys: The Culture of the Gang*. Glencoe, Ill.: Free Press.

Covey, Herbert C., Scott Menard, and Robert J. Franzese. 1992. *Juvenile Gangs*. Springfield, Ill.: Charles C Thomas.

Elliott, Delbert S. and Scott Menard. In press. Delinquent friends and delinquent behavior: Temporal and developmental patterns. In David Hawkins (ed.), *Current Theories of Crime and Deviance*. New York: Springer-Verlag.

Elliott, Delbert S., David Huizinga, and Suzanne S. Ageton. 1985. *Explaining Delinquency and Drug Use*. Beverly Hills, Calif: Sage.

Esbensen, Finn-Aage and David Huizinga. 1990. Community structure and drug use: From a social disorganization perspective. *Justice Quarterly* 7:691-709.

Esbensen, Finn-Aage, David Huizinga, and Anne W. Weiher. 1993. Gang and non-gang youth: Differences in explanatory variables. *Journal of Contemporary Criminal Justice* 9:94-116.

Fagan, Jeffrey. 1989. The social organization of drug use and drug dealing among urban gangs. *Criminology* 27:633-669.

——. 1990. Social processes of delinquency and drug use among urban gangs. In C. Ronald Huff (ed.), *Gangs in America*. Newbury Park, Calif.: Sage.

Giordano, Peggy C. 1978. Girls, guys, and gangs: The changing social context of female delinquency. *Journal of Criminal Law and Criminology* 69:126-132.

Gurule, Jimmy. 1991. The OJP initiative on gangs: Drugs and violence in America. *NIJ Reports* 224:4-5.

Hagedorn, John M. 1988. *People and Folks: Gangs, Crime and the Underclass in a Rustbelt City*. Chicago: Lakeview Press.

Harris, Mary G. 1988. *Cholas: Latino Girls and Gangs*. New York: AMS.

Hirschi, Travis. 1969. *Causes of Delinquency*. Berkeley: University of California Press.

Huizinga, David and Delbert S. Elliott. 1986. Reassessing the reliability and validity of self-report delinquency measures. *Journal of Quantitative Criminology* 2:293-327.

Huizinga, David and Finn-Aage Esbensen. 1991. Are there changes in female delinquency and are there changes in underlying explanatory factors? Paper presented at the Annual Meeting of the American Society of Criminology, San Francisco.

Johnson, Richard E. 1979. *Juvenile Delinquency and Its Origins*. Cambridge: Cambridge University Press.

Klein, Malcolm W. 1971. *Street Gangs and Street Workers*. Englewood Cliffs, N.J.: Prentice-Hall.

——. 1984. Offense specialization and versatility among juveniles. *British Journal of Criminology* 24:185-194.

Klein, Malcolm W. and Cheryl L. Maxson. 1989. Street gang violence. In Neil A. Weiner and Marvin E. Wolfgang (eds.), *Violent Crime, Violent Criminals*. Newbury Park, Calif.: Sage.

Klein, Malcolm W., Cheryl L. Maxson, and Lea C. Cunningham. 1991. "Crack," street gangs, and violence. *Criminology* 29:623-650.

Krohn, Marvin D. 1986. The web of conformity: A network approach of the explanation of delinquent behavior. *Social Problems* 33:s8l-s93.

Lopez, Lou. 1989. *Gangs in Denver*. Denver: Denver Public Schools.

MacLeod, Jay. 1987. *Ain't No Makin' It: Leveled Aspirations in a Low-Income Neighborhood*. Boulder, Colo.: Westview Press.

Maxson, Cheryl L. and Malcolm W. Klein. 1990. Street gang violence: Twice as great or half as great? In C. Ronald Huff (ed.), *Gangs in America*. Newbury Park, Calif.: Sage.

Miller, Walter B. 1958. Lower class culture as a generating milieu for gang delinquency. *Journal of Social Issues* 14:5-19.

——. 1974. American youth gangs: Past and present. In Alfred Blumberg (ed.), *Current Perspectives on Criminal Behavior*. New York: Knopf.

Moore, Joan W. 1978. *Homeboys: Gangs, Drugs, and Prison in the Barrios of Los Angeles*. Philadelphia: Temple University Press.

Morash, Merry. 1983. Gangs, groups, and delinquency. *British Journal of Criminology* 23:309-331.

Puffer, J. Adams. 1912. *The Boy and His Gang*. Boston: Houghton Mifflin.

Quicker, John C. 1983. *Homegirls: Characterizing Chicano Gangs*. San Pedro, Calif.: International University Press.

Short, James F. and Fred L. Strodbeck. 1965. *Group Processes and Gang Delinquency*. Chicago: University of Chicago Press.

Spergel, Irving A. 1966. *Street Gang Work: Theory and Practice*. Reading, Mass.: Addison-Wesley.

——. 1990. Youth gangs: Continuity and change. In Norval Morris and Michael Tonry (eds.), *Crime and Justice: An Annual Review of Research*. Chicago: University of Chicago Press.

Spergel, Irving A. and Ronald L. Chance. 1991. National youth gang suppression and intervention program. *NIJ Reports* 224:21-24.

Sullivan, Mercer L. 1989. *Getting Paid: Youth Crime and Work in the Inner City*. Ithaca, N.Y.: Cornell University Press.

Sutherland, Edwin H. and Donald R. Cressey. 1970. *Criminology*. New York: J.B. Lippincott.

Taylor, Carl S. 1990. Gang imperialism. In C. Ronald Huff (ed.), *Gangs in America*. Newbury Park, Calif.: Sage.

Thornberry, Terence, Marvin D. Krohn, Alan J. Lizotte, and Deborah Chard-Wierschem. 1993. The role of juvenile gangs in facilitating delinquent behavior. *Journal of Research in Crime and Delinquency* 30:55-87.

Thrasher, Frederick M. 1927. *The Gang: A Study of One Thousand Three Hundred Thirteen Gangs in Chicago*. Chicago: University of Chicago Press.

Vigil, James D. 1989. *Barrio Gangs: Street Life and Identity in Southern California*. Austin: University of Texas Press.

Winfree, L. Thomas, Teresa Vigil, and G. Larry Mays. 1991. Social learning theory and youth gangs: A comparison of high school students and adjudicated delinquents. Paper presented at the Annual Meeting of the American Society of Criminology, San Francisco.

Wolfgang, Marvin, Robert M. Figlio, Paul E. Tracy, and Simon I. Singer. 1985. *The National Survey of Crime Severity*. Washington, D.C.: Government Printing Office.

Yablonsky, Lewis. 1959. The delinquent gang as a near group. *Social Problems* 7:108-117.

———. 1963. *The Violent Gang*. New York: Macmillan. ✦

Section VII
Media and Religion

A fundamental premise in sociological criminology has been that everyday, "primary" group relationships involving the family and peers (and to a lesser extent schools) are more crucial for understanding juvenile crime and delinquency than are media of mass communication or institutions involving limited amounts of youths' time, such as religious institutions. In contrast, the general public believes the violent content of popular media to be a major cause of the amount of violence in society (See Figure I). Such a belief is particularly common among older age groups, who see violence on television as a major cause of a perceived breakdown in law and order. Such a belief led to attacks on the content of comic books in the 1950s (Werthman 1954), and was a basis for criticisms of newspapers in the late 1800s (Jensen and Rojek 1992: 318). In contrast, while sociologists acknowledge that young people may imitate what is presented in the media or become "desensitized" to violence as a result of continual exposure, relationships with parents, teachers, and peers are viewed as more consequential in understanding delinquency. The dominant opinion is that media influences are dwarfed by the impact of more consequential variations in social relationships.

While there is experimental research linking televised violence to aggression in play situations immediately following exposure (Eron et al. 1972), a link between criminal and delinquent activity and violence in movies or on television has yet to be established. For example, while researchers have documented large doses of violence on television, including prime-time and children's programs (Comstock et al. 1978; Comstock 1980; Signoreilli et al. 1982), neither trends nor variations in those doses have corresponded with trends and variations in juvenile violence. As summarized in the selection by Milavsky and others, there does appear to be an association between aggression and television viewing when characteristics of youth are studied at one point in time with no controls for background variables that might account for both high rates

FIGURE 1: "DO YOU THINK THERE IS A RELATIONSHIP BETWEEN VIOLENCE ON TELEVISION AND THE CRIME RATE IN THE UNITED STATES, OR NOT?" BY AGE GROUP

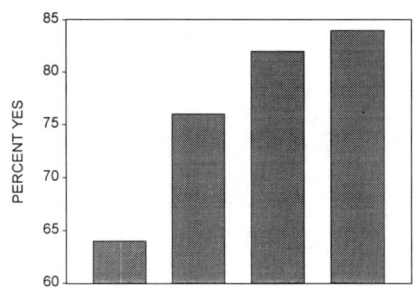

"DO YOU FEEL THAT VIOLENCE ON T.V. AND IN MOVIES IS A MAJOR CAUSE OF THE BREAKDOWN IN LAW AND ORDER, A MINOR CAUSE, OR HARDLY A CAUSE?" BY AGE GROUP

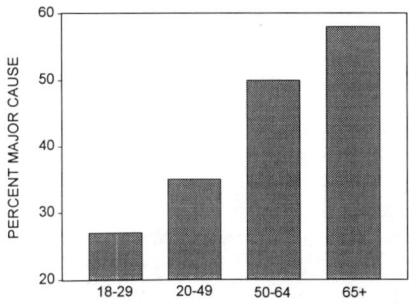

of delinquency and high rates of television viewing. When they studied youth over time they did not find a relationship between television and future violence.

There has not been comparably sophisticated research on the connection between exposure to violence in movies and juvenile violence. Scott Snyder reviews the evidence on "Movies and Juvenile Delinquency" and outlines the theoretical foundations for expecting a relationship. Moreover, he summarizes a considerable number of documented instances where youth have directly imitated behavior seen in movies. There is little doubt that movie violence is imitated occasionally, but the real question is whether that violence would have been avoided without such exposure. Movies might affect the "style" of violence, rather than its occurrence *per se*.

In addition to media influences, most sociological criminologists have been skeptical of the role of religious institutions in the control of delinquent behavior. In contrast to family, school, and peers, relationships within religious institutions have been viewed as secondary to understanding delinquency. Edwin Sutherland, one of the most prominent early theorists, argued that the values or "definitions" of conduct relevant to understanding involvement in juvenile delinquency were not specifically religious values, but were learned widely in interaction with parents, teachers, and other conventional adults (Sutherland and Cressey 1978: 234). He asserted that religiously based definitions and participation in the church were not central to understanding delinquency.

In contemporary debate, advocates of school prayer argue that juvenile crime reflects a "decline" in religiously founded moral beliefs and their replacement by relativistic and "criminogenic" secular values. The implication of such positions is that the specific religious content of certain sacred belief systems can reduce delinquency independent of other constraining forces. Family values are viewed as intimately intertwined with religious values, and the exclusion of religion from public schools is viewed as a sign of moral decay.

The article by Elifson, Petersen, and Hadaway in this section reviews research on the impact of religiosity on delinquency and reports research results on the topic. They report evidence that religiosity is associated with low rates of delinquency, but that such an association reflects the types of family and friends that religious youth are likely to have. Youth who have close, positive relationships with parents and straight friends have low rates of delinquency regardless of religious influences, but religion "may be acting as an antecedent influence."

The general nature of relationships among people in communities or neighborhoods was a central focus of early theories of juvenile delinquency focusing on "social disorganization," but fell out of favor because of critiques of the concept. As noted in Section V, the notion that characteristics of communities that undermine or inhibit communal bonds or network ties has been reintroduced through concepts such as "social integration." Rodney Stark and his colleagues address the relevance of religion and other community characteristics to historical data on crime and delinquency. The link between some measures of delinquency and characteristics of states varies among historical periods. Initially, states with high church membership were most concerned about juvenile delinquency and generated high rates of detention. They argue that with the passage of time, the most "morally" integrated states developed lower rates of delinquency. Together with the research on community characteristics included in Section V, it appears that strong social and communal bonds inhibit delinquency and youth crime.

References

Comstock, G., S. Chafee, N. Katzman, M. McCombs, and O. Roberts. 1978. *Television and Human Behavior*. New York: Columbia University Press.

Comstock, G. 1980. *Television in America*. Beverly Hills, California: Sage Publications.

Eron, L. D., L. R. Huesmann, M. M. Lefkowitz, and L. O. Walder. 1972. "Does Television Violence Cause Aggression?" *American Psychologist* 27:253-63.

Jensen, G. F. and D. G. Rojek. 1992. *Delinquency and Youth Crime*. Prospect Heights, Illinois: Waveland Press, Inc.

Signoreilli, N., L. Gross and M. Morgan. 1982. "Violence in Television Programs: Ten Years Later." Pp. 158-174 in D. Pearl, L. Bouthilet, and J. Lazar. *Television and Behavior*. Volume II. Rockville, Maryland: National Institute of Mental Health.

Sutherland, E. H. and D. R. Cressey. 1978. *Criminology*. 10th Edition. Philadelphia: J. B. Lippincott.

Werthman, F. 1954. *Seduction of the Innocent*. New York: Holt, Rinehart and Winston. ✦

25
Television and Aggression: Results of a Panel Study

J. Ronald Milavsky
Ronald Kessler
Horst Stipp
William S. Rubens

This [article][1] summarizes the results of a research project designed to determine whether continued exposure to violence on television programs causes the development of aggressive behavior patterns among elementary school and high school children. The project, sponsored and carried out by the National Broadcasting Company, surveyed some 3,200 young people over a 3-year period, from 1970 to 1973. A detailed presentation of the complete analysis—which included information obtained not only from the panels of children but also from school teachers, school records, interviews with a sample of mothers, and questionnaires from a sample of fathers—is reported elsewhere (Milavsky et al. 1982).

Background

When the study was designed, the literature on television and violence did not include any longitudinal studies. In 1972, when our data were in the midst of being collected, a two-wave panel study by Lefkowitz, Eron, Walder, and Huesmann was published as part of the Surgeon General's Report on Television and Social Behavior (Comstock and Rubinstein 1972). The Lefkowitz study documented a significant relationship between preference for violent television programs and aggression measured 10 years later. However, the Surgeon General's report regarded its findings "not conclusive" by virtue of several methodological problems with the data collected. In its recommendations for future research the report called for more longitudinal studies on the effects of television on children, emphasizing that "this gap needs to be filled before we can learn something dependable about the long-term effects of repeated exposure to standard television fare" (Surgeon General's Scientific Advisory Committee 1972, p. 114).

Basic Design and Measures

Design

The study was designed as a panel survey, covering a 3-year period (1970 through 1973). Data were obtained from approximately 2,400 elementary school children (second through sixth grades) who were surveyed up to six times and from 800 teenage boys who were surveyed up to five times. Interviews and questionnaires were administered to the respondents and samples of their parents and school teachers.

At the beginning of the study, the younger respondents ranged from 7 through 12 years of age, the older respondents from 12 through 16. Thus, over the 3-year period, our data reflect the behavior of children and adolescents ranging in age from 7 through 19.

The study was conducted in two medium-sized Midwestern cities, Minneapolis, Minnesota, and Ft. Worth, Texas. Both are located in the Central Time Zone, where prime time television programs start 1 hour earlier than in either the East or West. This allows young viewers maximum exposure to programs with violent content. Also, the cities provided many program choices, since each had four commercial and one public television station on the VHF band. Further, the cities were relatively similar in size and in many sociodemographic characteristics, but one (Ft. Worth) had a much higher violent crime rate than the other, allowing an investigation of whether the amount of violent crime actually present in

From *Television and Behavior*, Volume 2 (1982), pp. 138-157. National Institute of Mental Health.

the community affects television's influence.

Pretests indicated that valid and reliable measures of both television exposure and aggression could be obtained from elementary school children as young as second graders with methods we developed. Those methods included a peer-nomination technique for measuring behavior and a self-reported television exposure measure, both geared especially toward the abilities of young respondents. For teenagers, a different methodology, geared toward the characteristics of adolescent boys, was employed. These methods are described later.

Sampling of Respondents. The decision to use a peer-nomination measure of aggression among elementary school children dictated that we sample our young respondents in classroom units. With the cooperation of the local school systems, about 60 classes (30 in each city) were selected. Before selection, the universe of classroom units was stratified by race and socioeconomic status to insure that the sample would include respondents with varied socioeconomic backgrounds. Less than half of all children studied in each city were from schools characterized by the school systems' research departments as "predominantly white middle-class;" the majority were from "predominantly lower-class" schools. About 20 percent of all respondents were black.

Teenagers were sampled differently. Since teens do not spend the entire school day in a single classroom but rotate among different classes with differing compositions, it was not possible to replicate the elementary school design. A probability sample of 200 teen boys was selected from school enrollment lists of the secondary schools that were fed by the elementary schools of our younger sample. This sample was stratified by grade in school and represented the same socioeconomic groups as the elementary school sample. These boys were our core respondents. To allow for the possibility of studying friendship groups, each core respondent was asked to identify his neighborhood friends who were also recruited. These neighborhood friendship groups were brought to interview sessions held at neutral, locations away from home and school. The total set of boys who came to the first interview sessions in the Spring of 1970 formed our core panel sample ($N = 403$). . . .

Aggression Measures

The study focused on purposive aggression, physical or verbal acts intended or known in advance to cause injury to others, rather than on rough play or accidents that might have injury as an unintended or unforeseen consequence. After pretesting a variety of different measures of aggression so defined, it was decided that a peer-nomination measure would be most appropriate for the elementary school sample and a self-report measure for the teenage sample.

Aggression Measures for Children. The measure used for elementary school children was adapted from a peer-nomination technique developed by Eron and Walder (Walder et al. 1961; Eron et al. 1971). Questionnaires contained at least four aggression items in each wave. Two of these concern acts of physical aggression (trying to hurt by pushing and shoving; by hitting and punching) and two, verbal aggression (trying to hurt others by saying mean things; lying to get someone in trouble). Beginning in Wave III, two items tapping more serious antisocial acts were added (stealing and damaging property). . . .

Aggression Measures for Teens. Consistent with prior research on teenage delinquency (Hirschi 1969), our pretests indicated that teenagers' self-reports of aggression are more accurate than informant reports. So, in our teen questionnaire, we asked respondents a battery of questions about their involvement in various types of aggressive activities. On the basis of exploratory factor analyses, four distinct clusters of aggression were uncovered in each of the five waves[2]: (1) *personal aggression,* similar in content to our aggression measure for elementary school children; (2) *aggression against a teacher,* a measure of unruliness or rudeness toward the teacher; (3) *property aggression,* a measure of theft and vandalism; and (4) *delinquency aggres-*

sion. This last measure is of special importance since it measures serious or criminal behaviors, such as involvement in a knife fight, a mugging, car theft, or gang fight. All our teen analyses treated the four dimensions separately.

Scales of personal, teacher, and property aggression were created by adding up scores on the individual items. These measure the frequency with which a respondent engaged in each aggressive act (from 0 to 10 times during the month preceding the data collection). The measure of delinquency used in the analyses is a dichotomy because of the rarity of these kinds of behavior among average teenage boys. . . .

Television Exposure Measures

The measure of television exposure consisted of questions keyed to an extensive program checklist developed on the basis of pretests in which the respondent was asked to indicate the frequency of viewing of a large sample of specific programs. About 45 television programs and movies were selected for children and 55-60 for teens. In Wave I, the samples were drawn randomly to be representative of all kinds of programs from all television stations in the area, but with a high proportion of violent ones. Samples in the two study cities were matched. Thereafter, the program selection was made purposively, to facilitate accurate comparisons across cities and waves. Raw exposure scores were computed by multiplying frequency reports by the length of the program and then summing the viewing-time scores across the programs. The resultant scores were rounded and then divided by 10. These scores represent the "total exposure" measure. A measure of "violent television exposure" was computed by weighting the raw exposure scores with previously published data on adults' perceptions of the amount of violence contained in various programs (Greenberg and Gordon 1972).

Since the recall required of our respondents in reporting television exposure introduced the possibility of unreliable responses, we built in a number of internal checks on the consistency and plausibility of reports. (For example, each checklist contained a "dummy" item, the title of a nonexistent program.) We found a number of younger respondents, but only a few older ones and hardly any teens, who gave viewing reports that were implausible when assessed in this way. All critical analyses of elementary school children data were done twice, once with samples consisting of all respondents and then again with only the more valid reporters. (Teen data are based on total samples.) The replications showed that the inclusion of the "less valid reporters" did not affect the results of the children's over-time data in a significant or systematic way, but it did inflate the size of cross-sectional correlations. . . .

The Analysis Approach

Cross-Sectional Correlations

Since this study was designed, several sample surveys of the relationship between television viewing and aggression have been reported (Comstock 1978). Most of these found positive associations between measures of aggression and exposure to television violence obtained at the same point in time. Our study is no exception. Among elementary school boys, cross-sectional correlations between violent television exposure and aggression range from .08 to .17 and average .11 across the six waves. Correlations for girls are higher, ranging from .15 to .34 with an average of .23. All coefficients for boys and girls are significant at the .05 level.[3] In the teens sample, the average correlations for teacher, property, and delinquency aggression are very small: .06, .03, and .03, respectively. They are higher for the relationship of television exposure to personal aggression, with an average of .13 across the five waves.[4]

It is difficult to make any detailed comparison of these correlations with those reported in previous cross-sectional research, since the measures of television viewing and indicators of aggression used in those studies vary considerably from those used here.[5] The study by McLeod et al. (1972) of high school boys is most directly comparable to our teenage data in that it employed a television exposure score very similar to the one we use here. The correlation between this measure and a scale of "aggressive behavioral delinquency" (consisting of three items: "Been in fights with several people on each side"; "Hurt someone on purpose to get back for something they had done to you"; "Got into a serious fight with another student at school.") was .08 for a sample of Maryland junior high school boys, .23 for senior high boys, and .12 for Wisconsin senior high schoolers. These correlations are roughly similar to those found in the present study between television exposure and personal aggression (the most similar type of aggression we studied to the items contained in their scale).

Showing that two measures are related, however, says very little about causal connections between them. The point-in-time correlations above could result from an effect of earlier television exposure on later aggression, from an effect of aggressiveness on preference for violent television programs, or from third factors influencing both behaviors. In fact, all three of these sorts of influences could be at work simultaneously.

There is some evidence that these correlations are at least partly spurious. When third variables causally antecedent to both television exposure and aggression were controlled, the cross-sectional correlations dropped, often to statistically insignificant levels. For example, among boys when controls for socioeconomic status of the family (as measured by family income, father's/mother's occupation and education) and race were introduced, five of the six coefficients became insignificant and the average of the coefficients dropped from .11 to .06.[6]

Such analyses, however, fail to take advantage of the principal feature of our research design: that it provides observations at multiple points in time. Accordingly, the hypothesized causal influence of television exposure on antisocial behavior was studied with models which are more powerful than cross-sectional models and take advantage of this over-time feature.

The Analysis Model

Our design model is known technically as a "quasiexperiment" (Cook and Campbell 1979). This means our design approximates an experiment in that it uses over-time data to study the relationship between television exposure and later aggression and, at the same time, statistically controls for the initial relationship between television exposure and aggression. . . .

Subgroups

The most persuasive theoretical arguments for a socialization effect of violent television exposure on subsequent aggression postulate that this influence will appear most strongly among children who are predisposed or who are in situations that facilitate television effects. If this is so, we would expect to find consistent and significant relationships between television and aggression only in designated groups of respondents (Klapper 1960; Comstock and Rubinstein 1972, Vol. V, pp. 7, 11, 75; Liebert and Schwartzberg 1977).

Measures were obtained to tap the sorts of factors that might play a role in the television-aggression relationship. Our analysis focused on characteristics that predispose the child to act aggressively (such as a history of aggressiveness, having aggressive friends, use of and support for aggression by mother and father, emotional problems, low school grades, single-parent home, low economic status). We also examined a few characteristics which facilitate aggressive behavior (such as lack of supervision). The sample of boys was divided on the basis of 43 different variables of this sort, one at a time. Most of these were dichotomous, some polytomous, resulting in a total of 95 overlapping subgroups. Fewer data were collected for girls; still, we were able to form 46 groups based on 20 classifications. . . .

An examination of the specific groups where significant television-effect coefficients were found supports the interpretation that chance is the best explanation for the criterion having been reached in a few subgroups. There are a total of five such groups:[7] boys not noted as shy by their teachers; those who help others; those who find movies about real-life violence disgusting; boys who are not good at "make-believe play" (according to teacher, but not according to peer ratings); and those who attend few violent theater movies. These findings for groups are inconsistent with theoretical assumptions about predisposing and facilitating conditions. Indeed, of these five groups, only one could be regarded as "predisposed" (not shy), one is unclear ("make-believe play"),[8] and the remaining three are not predisposed and, in fact, contradict any theoretical expectations. No significant associations were found among virtually all groups who could be considered predisposed, such as boys from one-parent homes and poor students.

Results among elementary school girls were also inconsistent. Significant associations appeared among six subgroups of girls. Some of these could be considered predisposed: those rated by teachers as "not shy" and those high in exposure to violence in comic books and theater movies. Two of these groups are unclear: those not good at make-believe play (according to peers, but not teacher ratings) and those living in Fort Worth. Finally, one group, those extremely low in prior aggression, clearly contradicts theory. . . .

Findings for Teenage Boys

As reported above, four distinct clusters of aggressive behaviors could be detected among the teens. Three of these—personal aggression, aggression against teachers, and property aggression—consist of relatively common behaviors and are discussed first. Subsequently we will discuss delinquency. Since this is a rare kind of behavior in our sample, it was studied separately.

Personal, Teacher, and Property Aggression

. . . The overall pattern of television-effect coefficients . . . is essentially the same as found earlier in the elementary school sample: All coefficients are small, most are positive, and only a few are statistically significant. For personal aggression (part a), six of the eight coefficients are positive and one is significant. The average beta is .023. For teacher aggression (part b), six of the eight coefficients are positive, and two of the positive ones are significant. The average beta is .053. Finally, for property aggression (part c), five coefficients are positive, one of these is significant, and the average beta is .031. . . .

Subgroups. Specifications of the . . . results in subgroups were also estimated. Fifty-two subgroups were examined in all, based on 26 attributes of the respondents, their families, and their environments. Most of these groups were similar to those examined for elementary school boys (such as SES, parental use of punishment and attitudes about aggression, respondent's aggressiveness when younger, performance in school, aggressiveness of friends). Some additional ones were available as well.

As in the case of the elementary school children, overall significance was found in only a few subgroups. Furthermore, the patterns of significance closely resembled a random model. . . .

Delinquency Aggression

Reports of delinquent acts were rare in our sample of teens. . . . 76 percent of the respondents in Wave III, for example, did not report any acts of delinquency, 15 percent reported one, and only 9 percent more than one of the six acts. (These figures compare with about 70 percent who reported personal aggression, 60 percent who reported teacher aggression, and 40 percent who reported property aggression acts during the last 4 weeks in a given wave.) This reduces our ability to assess causal influences and thus makes conclusions about television effects more tentative than they would otherwise be. It also required us to conceptualize involvement in delinquency as a dichotomy (Yes-No) rather than as a frequency continuum. . . .

The t-ratios defining the significance of these relationships [were examined]. Four of these t-ratios are positive, five are negative, and one (a positive one) is significant. As in our earlier analysis, we applied a global test and found that one wave-pair out of the nine could be statistically significant by chance alone. Therefore, we regard this result as statistically insignificant. . . .

Subgroups. We tested the possibility that subgroup differences might be uncovered. But the low incidence of delinquent acts in the sample makes the results of this analysis a good deal less conclusive than those reported for the other samples. These results do replicate those reported above in the other subgroup comparisons, though. The distribution of significant coefficients again agrees with a random model of coefficients. And in only 2 of the 46 groups analyzed are there as many as two significant coefficients out of the nine estimated: among boys whose mothers often use physical punishment and among boys whose mothers get angry frequently. These are groups of "predisposed" boys. However, there is no indication of a significant television effect in related groups, such as those whose fathers use punishment or those who get into serious arguments with their family members. Furthermore, these two significant subgroups are not among those that were significant among children, or among teens with the other aggression measures. . . .

Additional Analyses

Although the analyses reported above failed to document a consistently significant relationship between exposure to television violence and later aggression for either boys, girls, or teens, they showed that more of the coefficients linking television and aggression are positive than negative. This may indicate that television had some very small, but consistent, effect on aggression. Another possibility is that unmeasured common causes of television and aggression led to this pattern of mostly positive signs.

In weighing these possibilities, the pervasiveness and robustness of the positive coefficients are the critical considerations. As we reported, not all the signs were positive. We found that most of the coefficients among elementary school boys and girls were positive. Among teens, most of the coefficients for common types of aggression were positive, but for the delinquency measure the positive and negative signs were about equally divided.

The robustness of the signs can be investigated by introducing controls for possible other causes of the television-aggression relationship into basic model regressions. We assembled a set of control variables—19 for boys and teens, 5 for girls—that we thought might play a part in the sign pattern. These are all characteristics of the respondents or their environments that are causally antecedent to and correlated with both television viewing and aggression. The variables include indicators of the child's socioeconomic background, race, and IQ. These controls were introduced one at a time into two-wave regression models . . . to see if the ratio of positive to negative signs changed. . . .

This analysis shows that the greater number of positive than negative signs is entirely due to common causes of television and aggression among boys and at least partly due to them among girls and teens. The remaining edge for positive signs is so negligible that no assertion about a small, consistent television effect can be made.

Discussion and Conclusions

Our results are in some ways consistent with those found in other research on this topic. In other respects they are different.

Perhaps the clearest contrast between the results reported here and those reported in earlier work is that we found no significant association between violent television exposure and subsequent change in aggression, while the experimental literature has demonstrated that exposure to specific filmed segments influenced several types of aggression. There is nothing necessarily contradictory between such findings and the ones reported here. The experimental literature is concerned with short-term arousal and modeling effects. The existence of the type of long-term socialization effects in a real-life context with which this study deals is not addressed in that literature.

Our results in no way argue that short-term arousal effects do not exist. The results are relevant, though, for understanding the long-term implications of experimentally documented short-term effects. If these short-term effects cumulated and generalized to day-to-day behavior, we would have found clear indications of that in our data. The fact that we did not find evidence of this sort suggests that these short-term effects found experimentally do not lead to stable patterns of aggression.

Like other real-life correlational studies, ours found a significant positive association between television and aggression at a point in time. It is difficult, however, to be very precise in comparing our cross-sectional results with those of the several cross-sectional surveys that have been carried out over the past decade, since our measures of television exposure and aggression differ in some respects from those used by others. But in general terms the sign and size of the correlations found in our samples are similar to those found in previous surveys.

The crucial feature of our study is its longitudinal design. Thus, it is most important to compare our results with the one other major longitudinal survey, by Lefkowitz et al. (1972). This is one instance where our results clearly differ from previous research: Lefkowitz and his associates found a correlation of .31 between their television measure and aggression 10 years later; there is no association of that size in our data.

The design of the Lefkowitz et al. study differs from ours in three important respects: They used a "favorite show" rather than a television exposure measure; the measure of later aggression was based on retrospective nominations rather than on ratings of current behavior; and, finally, their measures were taken 10 years apart instead of our 3-year maximum lag.

Their indicator of television exposure was based on mothers' reports of their children's three favorite programs when the children were in third grade. The use of that measure rather than child self-reports of actual exposure could account for the larger association found in the Lefkowitz study. However, in our own study we used this measure, too, and found that it is a very poor indicator of the child's television exposure. (It is correlated only about .25 with self-reported exposure.) Furthermore, we found that the cross-sectional relationship between the mothers' report of favorite shows (appropriately weighted for the violence content of those shows) and our aggression measures is much less substantial than that between the child's self-reported exposure and these same aggression measures. Indeed, while Lefkowitz et al. found cross-sectional correlations of .21 among third-grade boys between the mothers' report and aggression, we found much smaller cross-sectional correlations ranging from .03 to .09.[9]

The difference between our and their aggression measure could also account for different results. In the Lefkowitz study (1972), nominators in the tenth grade were not asked to rate their peers' aggressiveness at that time, but according to "the way they acted in school" based on "what you last knew of each person from personal observation and contact." The resultant measure is likely to be reputational: The rater has to make an evaluation based on his recollections which are bound to reflect cumulative impressions spread over varying time periods for each rater, as well as for the person being rated. The time reference of the measure is thus vague and the study does not actually measure a 10-year lag. Finally, as pointed out by Chaffee (1972), differences between the early and later aggression and television measures in the Lefkowitz study may have distorted the findings. In our study, television and aggression measures were identical at all time points.

We believe that the results of our study are more compelling than those of Lefkowitz et al. because of the greater validity, consistency, and relevance of the measures we used. We also believe that the richness of the data considered here and the variety of analysis approaches to which we subjected the data increase the confidence in the results we found. In short, we feel that our study was more sensitive to the possibility of detecting an effect of realistic television exposure on actual aggression than any prior research on this subject.

In the present study, criteria for detecting an effect were not met for elementary school boys and girls, or teenage boys. This was true for total samples as well as subgroups considered to be predisposed. In other words, this study did not find evidence that television violence was causally implicated in the development of aggressive behavior patterns among children and adolescents over the time periods studied.

Notes

1. Many technical details of the research project are omitted in this summary.
2. Principal axis solutions were estimated for 13-variable matrices separately at each point in time. Solutions were found to be in four dimensions at each time point, where we arbitrarily used a cutoff of factors that had eigenvalues equal to or greater than 1.0. Solutions were rotated both orthogonally and obliquely. Similar substantive clustering of the individual aggression items was found in both rotation approaches.
3. These correlations are for samples of "valid reporters." When total samples, including "less valid reporters" of their television exposure, are examined, all correlations are higher, averaging .17 for boys, .30 for girls.
4. Personal aggression: range .07 to .16, four significant coefficients; teacher aggression—.06 to .12, four significant; property aggression .03 to .04, none significant; delinquency—.02 to .11, one significant.
5. For example, even though Lefkowitz et al. (1972) used an aggression measure very similar to ours for their third grade sample, their television measure was completely different (not an exposure, but a favorite show measure).
6. McLeod et al. (1972) did not find that controls for SES and race reduced the cross-sectional correlations between television and aggression substantially. The reason could well be that there is little variation in the socioeconomic status of their respondents. Their Wisconsin sample, for example, was all white and the researchers describe their Maryland sample as "atypical in being somewhat higher than average on various measures of socioeconomic status" (1972, 1974). In contrast, our sample was selected in such a way that considerable variation in socioeconomic status was guaranteed. We have both lower class blacks and affluent professional families. For example, 12 percent of our boys have fathers who did not go to school beyond the eighth grade, 19 percent have fathers who graduated from college.
7. A previous paper (Milavsky 1977) reported these findings for boys.
8. J. L. Singer (1971) suggested that children with a poor fantasy life are more predisposed to act aggressively than children who cannot act out their aggressions in their imaginations. However, we found those nominated as engaging in "make-believe play" (by their peers or teachers) to be more aggressive than those who are not.
9. The Lefkowitz et al. study also found that the relationship among boys was much more substantial than that among girls ($r = .02$ for girls). Although we did not collect mother reports from girls, our self-report analysis shows that the cross-sectional television-aggression relationship is higher among girls than boys. This finding of a higher relationship among girls was also reported in McLeod, Atkin, and Chaffee's study of junior high school students.

References

Belson, W. *Television violence and the adolescent boy.* London: Saxon House, 1978.

Bohrnstedt, G. W. Observations on the measurement of change. In Edgar F. Borgatta (Ed.), *Sociological Methodology.* San Francisco: Jossey-Bass, 1969.

Chaffee, S. "Television and adolescent aggressiveness (Overview)" In G. A. Comstock & E. A. Rubinstein (Eds.), *Television and social behavior* (Vol. 3). Television and adolescent aggressiveness. Washington: U.S. Government Printing Office, 1972.

Coffin, T., & S. Tuchman. Rating television programs for violence: A comparison of five surveys. *Journal of Broadcasting* 1972-73, 77, 3-20.

Comstock, G. A., Chaffee, S., Katzman, N., McCombs, M., & Roberts, D. *Television and human behavior.* New York: Columbia University Press, 1978.

Comstock, G. A., & Rubinstein, E. A., (Eds.) Television and social behavior: (Vol. I) *Media content and control.* (Vol. II) Television and social learning. (Vol. III) Television and adolescent aggressiveness. (Vol. IV) Television in day-to-day life: Patterns of use. (Vol. V) Television's effects: Further explorations. Washington: U.S. Government Printing Office 1972.

Cook, T. D., & Campbell, D. T. *Quasi-experimentation: Design and analysis issues for field settings.* Chicago: Rand McNally, 1979.

Donovan, J. *Self-reported deviance in an adolescent sample: Cross-sectional and longitudinal* analyses of personality and social correlates. Unpublished manuscript, Institute for Behavioral Science, University of Colorado, 1974.

Donovan, J. *A typological study of self-reported deviance in a national sample of adolescents.* Unpublished doctoral dissertation, University of Colorado, 1977.

Duncan, O. D. Some linear models for two-wave two-variable panel analysis. *Psychological Bulletin 1969*, 72, 177-182.

———. Unmeasured variables in linear models for panel analysis. In H. L. Costner (Ed.), *Sociological methodology 1972.* San Francisco: Jossey-Bass, 1972.

Eron, L. D., Waider, L., & Lefkowitz, M. *Learning of aggression in children.* Boston: Little, Brown, 1971.

Federal Bureau of Investigation, *U.S. Justice Department Uniform Crime Reports, 1969.* Washington: U.S. Government Printing Office, 1969.

Gerbner, G., Violence in television drama: Trends and symbolic functions, In Comstock, G. A, & E. A. Rubinstein (Eds.), *Television and social behavior (Vol. 1). Media content and control.* Washington: U.S. Government Printing Office, 1972.

Gerbner, G., L. Gross et al., *Violence Profile Number 7: Trends in network television drama and viewer conceptions of social reality, 1967-1975.* Annenberg School of Communications, University of Pennsylvania 1976.

Gerbner, G., & Gross, L. "Living with television: the violence profile." In *Journal of Communication 1976*, 26, 173-199.

Goodman, L. A. Causal analysis of data from panel studies and other kinds of surveys. *American Journal of Sociology 1973*, 78:1135-1191.

Greenberg, B., Ericson, P., & Vlahos, M. Children's television behaviors as perceived by mother and child. In G. A. Comstock & E. A. Rubinstein (Eds.), *Television and social behavior* (Vol. 3). *Television and adolescent aggressiveness.* Washington: U.S. Government Printing Office, 1972.

Greenberg, B. & Gordon, T. Perceptions of violence in television programs: critics and the public. In G. A. Comstock & E. A. Rubinstein (Eds.), *Television and social behavior* (Vol. 1). Media content and control. Washington: U.S. Government Printing Office, 1972.

Heise, D. R. & Bohrnstedt, G. W. Validity, invalidity, and reliability. In E. F. Borgatta and C. M. Bohrnstedt (Eds.), *Sociological methodology 1970.* San Francisco: Jossey-Bass, 1970.

Hirschi, T. *Causes of delinquency.* Berkeley: University of California Press, 1969.

Jöreskog, K. G. A general method for estimating a linear structural equation system. In A. S. Goldberger & O. D. Duncan (Eds.), *Structural equation models in the social sciences.* New York: Academic Press, 1973.

Jöreskog, K. G., & Sörbom, D. *Lisrel IV: Estimation of Linear Structural Relationships by the Method of Maximum Likelihood.* Chicago: International Educational Services, 1977.

Kay, H. Weaknesses in the television-causes-aggression analysis by Eron et al. *American Psychologist 1972*, 27, 970-973.

Kessler, R. C. & Greenberg, D. F. *Linear models of change.* New York: Academic Press, 1981.

Klapper, J. *The effects of mass communication.* New York: Free Press, 1960.

Lekfowitz, M., Eron, L., Walder, L., & Huesmann, L. Television violence and child aggression: A follow-up study. In G. A. Comstock & E. A. Rubinstein (Eds.), *Television and social behavior* (Vol. 3). *Television and adolescent aggressiveness.* Washington: U.S. Government Printing Office, 1972.

Lefkowitz, M. L., Eron, L., Walder, L., & Huesmann, L. R. *Growing up to be violent: A longitudinal study of the development of aggression.* New York: Pergamon Press, 1977.

Liebert, R. M., & Schwartzberg, N. S. Effects of mass media. In M. R. Rosenzweig & L. W. Porter (Eds.), *Annual Review of Psychology 1977*, 29: 141-173.

Lyle, J., & Hoffman, H. Explorations in patterns of television viewing by preschool-age children. In E. A. Rubinstein, G. A. Comstock, & J. P. Murray (Eds.), *Television and social behavior,* (Vol. 4). *Patterns of use.* Washington: U.S. Government Printing Office, 1972.

McLeod, J. M., Atkin, C., & Chaffee, S. Adolescents, parents, and television use: adolescent self-report measures from Maryland and Wisconsin samples. In G. A. Comstock & E. A. Rubinstein (Eds.), *Television and social behavior* (Vol. 3). *Television and adolescent aggressiveness.* Washington: U.S. Government Printing Office, 1972.

Milavsky, J. R. A search for mediators of the effects of TV violence on the aggressive behavior of elementary school boys: Results of a longitudinal panel study. Paper read at the meeting of the American Sociological Association, September 1977.

Milavksy, J. R., Pekowsky, B., & Stipp, H. TV drug advertising and proprietary and illicit drug use among teenage boys. *Public Opinion Quarterly 1975*, 40, 457-481.

Milavsky, J. R., Kessler, R., Stipp, H., & Rubens, W. S. *Television and aggression. Results of a panel study.* Book in preparation, 1982. Nerlove, M., & Press, S. J. Univariate and multivariate log-linear and logistic models. Santa Monica, Calif.: Rand, 1973.

Nielsen, A. C. Co. NTI/NAC Audience Demographics Report, May 1971, Chicago: A. C. Nielsen Co., 1971.

Rogosa, D. A critique of cross-lagged correlation. *Psychological Bulletin 1980*, 88, 245-258.

Singer, J. L. The influence of violence portrayed in television or motion pictures upon overt aggressive behavior. In J. L. Singer (Ed.), *The control of aggression and violence: Cognitive and physiological factors*. New York: Academic Press, 1971.

Stipp, H. H. *Validity in social research: measuring children's television exposure*. Unpublished doctoral dissertation, Columbia University, 1975.

Surgeon General's Scientific Advisory Committee on Television and Social Behavior, *Television and growing up: The impact of televised violence*. Report to the Surgeon General, United States Public Health Service. Washington: U.S. Government Printing Office, 1972.

Walder, L., Abelson, R., Eron, L., et al. Development of a peer-rating measure of aggression. *Psychological Reports 1961*, 9, 497-556.

Weigel, R. H., & Jessor, R. Television and adolescent conventionality. *Public Opinion Quarterly*, 37, 76-90.

Werts, C., & Linn, R. *Study of academic growth using simplex models*. U.S. Department of Health, Education, and Welfare. Washington: National Institute of Education, 1975. ✦

26
Movies and Juvenile Delinquency: An Overview

Scott Snyder

Introduction

Youth between the ages of 12 and 20 comprised 40% of all admissions to American movie theaters in 1981, even though this age group accounted for only 19% of the U.S. resident civilian population (Squire, 1983). These percentages were remarkably similar in surveys taken in 1957 and 1972 (Jowett, 1976). In addition, there were approximately twenty million videocassette recorder (VCR) owners in the U.S. in 1986. Teenagers in homes with VCRs have ready access to them and may be stimulated to attend more movies in theaters as compared to adolescents in homes without VCRs (Ebert, 1990). One example of these emerging demographics is that preteens, ages 11-14, rent violent horror movies in higher numbers than do any other age group in the U.S., according to the editor of *Video Marketing Newsletter*. This group obtains the R-rated movies through older friends, siblings, unsuspecting or desensitized parents, or apathetic video store employees (*National Coalition on Television Violence News*, 1989). Cable TV provides an additional wide array of movies; by 1985, almost 40% of U.S. households had cable (Liebert & Sprafkin, 1988).

As the public is well aware, juvenile delinquency and conduct disorder are quite common (Kazdin, 1987; Farrington, 1987). In 1983, 30% of all persons arrested in the U.S. for index offenses (i.e., murder, forcible rape, aggravated assault, burglary, theft, motor vehicle theft, and arson) were under the age of 18 (Federal Bureau of Investigation, 1984). In a 1972 survey of over 800 juveniles aged 13 to 16, 88% admitted to committing at least one chargeable offense in the preceding three years (Williams & Gold, 1972).

Given the high prevalence of movie-going among the adolescent population and the high rate of juvenile delinquency, it is logical to assume that a large number of both normal and delinquent adolescents are frequent movie viewers. Thus, it is important to know what type of movies different social classes of both delinquent and nondelinquent populations prefer. Although data are sparse, a recent study examined normal adolescent film preferences among three different social classes: suburban middle class, urban middle class, and urban poor. All three groups of adolescents favored movies with themes dealing with physical danger, separation and individuation, self-cohesion and identity, commitment and success, and involving such interests as dance and physical prowess. Students in the urban poor public school preferred movies with action, dancing, violence, and horror, whereas students in the two middle-class schools preferred movies with action and those dealing with adolescence itself (Villela & Markin, 1987).

Identification by the Delinquent with Movies

The delinquent moviegoer may be impressed by the vivid visual presentation characteristic of movies in which images are developed, identified, and easily followed. These images can be understood on an elementary level by the intellectually, educationally, or socially impaired delinquent. The moviemaker often tries to persuade the viewer to experience vicariously the events unfolding on the screen. Identification is one of the principal ways in which adolescents may become vicariously involved with the film. One specific type of identification particularly relevant to the delinquent population is known as *reinforcement of values*. In this form of identification, people approve the values of their

From *Adolescence*, Volume 26, Number 101 (Spring 1991), pp. 121-132. Copyright © 1991 by Libra Publishers, Inc. Reprinted by permission.

own social class and shun those of other social classes (Jarvie, 1978). The delinquent may approve the lifestyle of antisocial film characters and reject more conventional ones.

Film and the Delinquent Peer Group

Films, adolescents, and group dynamics can have a very powerful interrelationship. The audience for movies has been termed "an unstructured group" (Jarvie, 1978). In particular, adolescents in the audience may develop into an informal group which facilitates relationships with other adolescents whose support they actively seek. The adolescent peer group is attracted to the movies because (1) it is removed from the home, (2) other adolescents are likely to be in attendance, and (3) it is a medium which provides a wide variety of examples of human experiences. Movies may serve as a social lubricant when adolescents use the content in group interactions; they provide a common interest which helps adolescents establish rapport with others (Mendelsohn, 1966). The group also is important to the development of identity, status, and self-esteem in the adolescent.

Such effects would be magnified among delinquents, who may intensify their aberrant behavior by identifying with the more violent, aggressive, or emotionally distressing aspects of a movie. Delinquents would tend to view certain movies as a group, either outside the home or in the home when unsupervised.

While Sutherland's influential theory of differential association was developed to account for criminal behavior, its basic principles can be applied to juvenile delinquency as well. Two of its principles are that delinquent behavior is learned in interaction with other persons in a process of communication, and the learning of delinquent behavior principally occurs within intimate personal groups (Sutherland & Cressey, 1978). Numerous studies have explored the relationship between association with delinquent peers and either delinquent behavior or adolescent substance abuse (Gibbons & Krohn, 1986). The findings of these studies have supported Sutherland's theory and led Kandel (1978) to state that the strongest factor in involvement in delinquent behavior is association with delinquent companions.

A recent study found that adolescent subjects accepted the behavior of movie characters as moral even if it was violent or antisocial as long as they could identify with the character. In addition, it was easier for the more aggressive viewer to accept the violence of the film actor. Viemero (1984) found that subjects' acceptance and possible imitation of the characters' behavior was related to the age of the actor. Zuzul (1985) demonstrated that adolescent subjects who viewed innocent victims of filmed aggression tended to identify closely with the victims. They also viewed the concept of aggression significantly more positively than did control groups.

Social Learning Theory, Film, and Juvenile Delinquency

The principles of social learning theory were first presented by Bandura and Walters in 1963. They believed that children develop their personality from exposure to the prevailing culture and experiences with their family and peers. Modeling was felt to play a crucial role in social development.

Bandura and Walters conducted a series of controlled experiments to demonstrate that modeling is one of the most effective ways to teach children new ways of behaving and their consequences. The Bobo doll studies of the early 1960s demonstrated that exposure of young children to films involving aggressive models had the effect of teaching and motivating the subjects to copy novel aggressive acts (Bandura et al., 1963; Bandura, 1965). Exposure to models has also been known to cause disinhibitory effects in which the observation of a particular class of response (for example, an aggressive response) leads to an increased likelihood of displaying other, different responses that are in the same class.

Criticism of these studies centered upon the fact that they measured play as opposed to "real aggression." A number of studies in the sixties addressed this issue by utilizing what came to be referred to as the "aggression machine" (Liebert & Sprafkin, 1988). The method involved measuring how much one person was willing to inflict pain upon another through electric shocks. One early study had hospital attendants, high school boys, and young women view either a film of adolescents engaged in constructive activities or the knife-fight scenes from *Rebel Without a Cause* (Walters & Thomas, 1963). Those who saw the aggressive film in all three groups gave stronger electric shocks to another person compared to those who saw the constructive film.

Similar findings have been found in populations of juvenile delinquents. In one study, delinquent adolescent boys were either treated neutrally or angered. They were then shown one of three films, two of which contained much aggression. Viewing the aggressive films produced increased aggression (as measured by the aggression machine) compared to the neutral film, regardless of whether the delinquents were angered or not. It was also found that delinquents with a previous history of aggressive behavior were more aggressive than nonaggressive delinquents (Hartmann, 1969).

Jeffrey (1965) was the first to suggest that learning theory may account for criminal behavior. Later researchers proposed that adolescents who associated with delinquent peers are more likely to participate in delinquent behavior than those who have not had such interactions. Some evidence suggests that this association may occur prior to the performance of delinquent acts. The most accepted social learning explanation of delinquent behavior proposes that "social bonding" variables, such as imitation of others who engage in deviant acts and positive reinforcement of deviant behavior, increase the likelihood of delinquency (Akers, 1985).

An alternative explanation for the findings in social learning theory experiments came to be known as the instigation theory. This theory proposed that the violent content in social learning theory experiments somehow instigated an immediate aggressive response. The emotional state of the subject would influence the probability that instigation to increased aggression would actually occur (Berkowitz, 1962; Tannenbaum, 1971). The theory proposes that many communication messages can produce varying degrees of emotional arousal and that this could influence any behavior the person is involved in while aroused.

Justification also was found to be a significant factor in modeling cues. It was found that modeled aggression in a movie sequence would make observers act more aggressively if the aggression had appeared justified. Studies by Berkowitz (1965; Berkowitz & Green, 1966) and Hoyt (1970) have confirmed these theoretical propositions. As an example, adolescent boys in Great Britain were noted to have marked increases in aggressive behavior after exposure to violence in a variety of media, including films. In this retrospective study, exposure to violence also led to the creation of a callous attitude toward victims, desensitization toward violence, and stimulation of aggressive acts (Belson, 1978). Investigations of social learning theory and instigation theory have essentially disproved the "symbolic catharsis" doctrine. Originally conceived in the 1950s, this doctrine proposed that the symbolic expression or vicarious enactment of aggression could reduce the likelihood of subsequent aggression when instigated (Feshbach, 1955).

The aforementioned studies were based upon exposure of the audience to an excerpt from a full-length film. Critics proposed that the viewing of such excerpts may not have the same effect as observation of the full-length, unedited version of the film. Parke et al. (1977) addressed this issue by exposing juvenile offenders, incarcerated at a minimum security penal institution, to violent and nonviolent unedited commercial films in four phases of observation and measurement over a 7-week period. They found that such exposure increased aggressive behavior by the viewers. As part of the same study, a similar experiment was conducted using a sample of juvenile delinquents from Belgium. The same results were found, indicating some cross-cultural similarities. Physical aggression was affected most, but the greatest long-term effect was the increase in verbal aggression. The most popular, dominant, and aggressive boys as well as the least popular boys were most influenced by the exposure. The authors proposed a combination of social learning theory and instigation theory to account for their findings. They theorized that delinquents with the greatest prestige and power used aggressive tactics to maintain their position in the hierarchy, while the least popular boys would be victims in aggressive exchanges and exhibited inappropriate aggression to compensate for their low group status.

Similar effects have been found in women. In one study, a group of 81 college females were either angered, treated neutrally, or treated positively. They then viewed a violent, humorous, or neutral film. Afterward they were permitted to be either aggressive toward or reward a fellow student. Women who had been angered increased their aggression after both the aggressive and humorous films (Mueller & Donnerstein, 1983).

A more recent study (Frost & Stauffer, 1987) confirmed earlier findings on the effects of films on violence, while at the same time exploring the issue of social class differences between subjects. A group of affluent undergraduate students was compared to a racially mixed group of residents of an inner-city housing project. Half of each group were males and half were females. Inner-city residents were significantly more aroused than the college sample after viewing filmed violence. Depictions of rape caused the highest response in the inner-city group, but only the fifth highest in the college sample. Both groups were aroused most by viewing a female killing another female. Gender was not found to be a significant factor in arousal to filmed violence. The researchers proposed the concept of "resonance" to explain their findings (Gerbner et al., 1980). This theorizes that when people see things on television which are compatible with their everyday world, the combination may result in a "double dose" of the television theme, which in turn could produce the enhanced physiological arousal noted in the study.

In their review of the literature on the effects of media violence on children, Heath et al. (1989) stated that "a small but genuine association appears to exist between media violence and aggression." They cautioned that bidirectionality existed in many studies, making it difficult to assume a cause-and-effect relationship. Variables such as belief in the reality of the media presentation, predisposition toward violence, an aggressive family environment, identification with aggressive media characters, and how the consequences of aggressive behavior are portrayed may all affect the relationship between media and violence. Some have proposed that even if the effect of media on violent behavior in youth is small, it must be taken seriously because of its grave implications (Rosenthal, 1986). Heath et al. concluded that "many unanswered questions persist, and no interventions are clearly indicated."

Examples of the Effects of Movies on the Juvenile Delinquent

Some of the theoretical and empirical literature on the effects of motion pictures on adolescents has been reviewed. It has been found that films may initiate or at least serve as the final common pathway for a wide array of thoughts, moods, and behaviors of the juvenile delinquent. Thus, a historical look at some specific examples of the effects of movies on adolescent behavior is in order.

One of the earliest illustrations comes from Blumer (1933), who examined the impact of movies on juvenile crime. A 17-year-old male is quoted in the book as saying, "The gang pictures came out and soon had our bunch standing on their heads. They took on the nicknames of characters in the pictures and it wasn't long before we went out on raiding parties of chicken coops and small stores and getting away with ease."

The Warriors was released by Paramount in 1979. The poster used to promote the movie consisted of a picture of armed youths, angry and defiant as they stare back at onlookers. The poster states: "These are the armies of the night. They are 100,000 strong. They outnumber the cops 5 to 1. They could run New York City. Tonight, they're all out to get the Warriors." Within a brief period of time after its release, there were three murders which had been inspired by the film. They occurred in a California farm town, a Palm Springs drive-in, and a Boston street. The film's distributors ended the advertising campaign and offered to pay for additional security at theaters where it was playing (Considine, 1985).

On March 24, 1984, a teenager from Rochester, New York, died after shooting himself with a .38 caliber handgun while playing Russian roulette. The movie *The Deerhunter* recently had been shown in the neighborhood. It was known that the youth had a fascination with films, especially violent ones. On the night of the shooting, he was holding a high school beer-drinking party at his home and had been drinking himself (*National Coalition on Television Violence News*, 1984). At least 43 deaths have been attributed, at least in part, to the movie, with all victims being male and 20 victims under the age of 18.

John Hinckley presumably identified with the protagonist of *Taxi Driver*, Travis Bickle, when he attempted to assassinate President Reagan. Hinckley had developed an obsessive attachment to Jodie Foster (who portrayed a teenage prostitute in the movie) after having viewed the film at least 15 times. In the movie, Travis Bickle first considered assassinating a political candidate at a rally; when that plan failed, he focused his attention on the pimps and other degenerates who controlled Jodie Foster. He became a hero and may have served as an inspirational model for Hinckley. But the prosecutions chief psychiatrist suggested that Hinckley got his ideas about *Taxi Driver* from psychiatric sessions and the media. Theoretically he could have viewed the movie numerous times without fully understanding what the film meant to him. This complication is almost always present in cases of purported movie-inspired violence (Wilson & Hunter, 1983).

Three teenage girls attacked a nine-year-old girl on a California beach four days after seeing the television movie *Born Innocent*. The girls used a bottle to rape their victim, replicating a scene from this 1978 movie. The boyfriend of one of the girls was quoted by her as saying, "Hey, you are doing it just like they did in the picture" (Sharpe, 1978). The victim and her mother filed an $11 million negligence suit against NBC, charging the network with inspiring the rape. However, the U.S. Supreme Court refused to overturn the California court's ruling that networks cannot be held liable for such acts unless they willfully sought to incite such violence.

Wilson and Hunter (1983) reviewed 58 cases of movie-inspired violence which occurred between 1970 and 1982. They concentrated on episodes with a serious outcome. It was found that victims were usually males between the ages of 13 and 24, and that offenders were in their teens or twenties. A handgun was the weapon used in 45 of the cases. Four films, *The Deer Hunter*, *Magnum Force*, *The Warriors*, and *Taxi Driver*, were cited in the majority of the incidents. The authors proposed a three-step process of identification, perseveration of beliefs, and execution of those beliefs to account for the link between pretend violence and real violence.

Prosocial Effects of Movies

Motion pictures may also exert a prosocial effect on adolescents. Positive social learning about adolescent phenomena that are as diverse as peer groups, family systems, and identification may occur as a result of viewing films. However, studies demonstrating positive effects are sparse. In one study, young adolescent boys (ages 12-13) were shown a violent film. It was found that a more negative attitude toward violence resulted if adults disapproved of the violence in the film, whereas adult approval caused an increase in physical and verbal violence in school play and an increased positive attitude toward aggression. Peer approval had less of an effect (Helfgott, 1983). Positive effects of television viewing repeatedly have been found in various studies conducted since the early seventies. Prosocial behavior such as altruism, control of aggressive impulse, delay of gratification, reparation for bad behavior, resistance to temptation, and sympathy have been shown to increase after exposure of youth to certain television programs (Liebert & Sprafkin, 1988). Thus, it can be concluded that films could be utilized in a variety of formats to improve the thinking, mood, and behavior of juvenile delinquents. Social skills training may illustrate such utilization. This technique is used to teach effective ways of dealing with a variety of social scenarios involving interpersonal interaction. For example, the trainer may utilize role playing to demonstrate competent responses to a variety of situations.

Henderson and Hollin (1983) reviewed 15 studies on the use of social skills training with delinquent populations. Although they concluded that research has not demonstrated the durability of the social skills that are acquired, they felt that this training may have value for certain subsets of juvenile delinquents. They strongly encouraged instruction geared to the unique needs of the individual juvenile offender rather than assuming that all adolescents require the same skills. Along with the social skills training, they felt it was necessary to change family and peer group systems.

Films can be readily utilized by providing examples of both appropriate and inappropriate responses to a wide variety of social situations. Chandler (1973), for example, had chronically delinquent boys develop, act out, videotape, and criticize skits involving situations they encountered frequently in their daily lives. He demonstrated that the delinquent offenders could enhance their role-taking abilities through such interventions, and that significant reductions in recidivism occurred at 18-month followup. Such role taking appears to be an important component of social skills training for both delinquent and nondelinquent populations (Urbain & Kendall, 1980).

A danger of such cognitive role-taking instruction is that the delinquent will simply learn more effective ways of performing delinquent acts. The social learning needs to be combined with the development of more prosocial motives and higher levels of moral reasoning. Delinquent adolescents are more likely to demonstrate Stage 1 and 2 (preconventional) moral reasoning. They define right and wrong largely in terms of external consequences, act to avoid punishment, and have little concern for the needs of others. Actions which satisfy their own needs are defined as right. Stage 3 and 4 (conventional) adolescents have internalized family or societal rules and expectations and are at much lower risk of engaging in criminal behavior. Many studies have demonstrated that discussion groups which deal with moral development can produce sociomoral gains in delinquents. These gains in moral reasoning may be associated, in some instances, with long-term changes in the juvenile offenders' behavior in their natural environment (Gordon & Arbuthnot, 1987).

Motion pictures dealing with normal adolescence and with juvenile delinquency can be readily incorporated into such an instructional format (see Appendix). Films provide examples of the different stages of moral development as well as both acceptable and antisocial ways of dealing with moral dilemmas. They could act as a stimulus for discussion on the rights of others. Such discussion could help the delinquent achieve higher levels of moral reasoning and potentially reduce delinquent acts.

The development of cognitive strategies designed to improve self-control and social responsibility, known as problem-solving skills training, has been shown to have promise as a treatment for antisocial and delinquent behavior (Goldstein & Glick, 1987). Combinations of therapies for moral reasoning treatment, social skills training, and problem-solving skills training may have synergistic effects on the juvenile offender (Hengeller, 1989). Films also could be utilized with these treatment techniques to provide examples of desirable versus aberrant problem-solving behavior.

Appendix

Recommended films about juvenile delinquency and conduct disorder: *Are These Our Children*

(1931), *Wild Boys of the Road* (1933), *Mayor of Hell* (1933), *Angels with Dirty Faces* (1934), *Dead End* (1937), *Boys Town* (1938), *Youth Runs Wild* (1944), *City Across the River* (1949), *The Wild One* (1954), *Rebel Without a Cause* (1955), *The Blackboard Jungle* (1955), *The Young Stranger* (1967), *The Young Savages* (1961), *West Side Story* (1961), *To Sir with Love* (1967), *Wild in the Streets* (1968), *Clockwork Orange* (1971), *Badlands* (1974), *Lords of Flatbush* (1974), *The Warriors* (1979), *The Wanderers* (1979), *Over the Edge* (1979), *The Outsiders* (1983), *Rumblefish* (1983), *Bad Boys* (1983), *At Close Range* (1986).

References

Akers, R.L. (1986). *Deviant behavior: A social learning approach* (3rd ed.). Belmont, CA: Wadsworth.

Bandura, A. (1965). Influence of models' reinforcement contingencies on the acquisition of imitative responses. *Journal of Personality and Social Psychology, 1,* 589-595.

Bandura, A., Ross, D., & Ross, S.A. (1963). Imitation of film-mediated aggressive models. *Journal of Abnormal and Social Psychology, 66,* 3-11.

Bandura, A., & Walters, R.H. (1963). *Social learning and personality development*. New York: Holt, Rinehart and Winston.

Belson, W.A. (1978). *Television violence and the adolescent boy*. Westmead, England: Saxon House.

Berkowitz, L. (1962). *Aggression: A social psychological analysis*. New York: McGraw-Hill.

———. (1965). Some aspects of observed aggression. *Journal of Personality and Social Psychology, 2,* 359-369.

Berkowitz, L., & Green, R.G. (1966). Film violence and the cue properties of available targets. *Journal of Personality and Social Psychology, 3,* 525-530.

Blumer, H. (1933). *Movies, delinquency, and crime*. New York: MacMillan.

Chandler, H. (1973). Egocentrism and antisocial behavior: The assessment and training of social perspective-taking skills. *Developmental Psychology, 9,* 326-332.

Considine, D.M. (1985). *The cinema of adolescence*. Jefferson, NC: McFarland.

Ebert, R. (1990). *Roger Ebert's movie home companion*. Kansas City: Universal Press.

Farrington, D.P. (1987). Epidemiology. In H.C. Quay (Ed.), *Handbook of juvenile delinquency* (pp. 33-61). New York: John Wiley.

Federal Bureau of Investigation. (1984). *Uniform crime reports, 1983*. Washington, DC: U.S. Government Printing Office.

Feshbach, S. (1955). The drive-reducing function of fantasy behavior. *Journal of Abnormal Social Psychology, 50,* 3-11.

Frost, R., & Stauffer, J. (1987). The effects of social class, gender, and personality on physiological responses to filmed violence. *Journal of Communication, 37*(2), 29-46.

Gerbner, G., Gross, L., Morgan, M., & Signorelli, N. (1980). The "mainstreaming" of America: Violence profile no. 11. *Journal of Communication, 30*(3), 10-27.

Gibbons, D.C., & Krohn, M.D. (1986). *Delinquent behavior*. Englewood Cliffs, NJ: Prentice-Hall.

Goldstein, A.P., & Glick, B. (1987). *Aggressive replacement training: A comprehensive intervention for aggressive youth*. Champaign, IL: Research Press.

Gordon, D.A., & Arbuthnot, J. (1987). Individual, group, and family interventions. In H.C. Quay (Ed.), *Handbook of juvenile delinquency*. New York: John Wiley.

Hartmann, D.P. (1969). Influence of symbolically modelled instrumental aggression and pain cues on aggressive behavior. *Journal of Personality and Social Psychology, 11,* 280-288.

Heath, L., Bresolin, L.B., & Rinaldi, R.C. (1989). Effects of media violence on children: A review of the literature. *Archives of General Psychiatry, 46,* 376-379.

Helfgott, M.S. (1983). Effects of peer vs. adult approval and disapproval on the aggressive attitudes of male adolescent film viewers. *Dissertation Abstracts Annual, 44,* 115-A.

Henderson, M., & Hollin, C. (1983). A critical review of social skills training with young offenders. *Criminal Justice and Behavior, 10,* 316-341.

Hengeller, S.W. (1989). *Delinquency in adolescence*. Newbury Park, CA: Sage.

Hoyt, J.L. (1970). Effect of media violence "justification" on aggression. *Journal of Broadcasting, 14,* 455-465.

Jarvie, I.C. (1978). *Movies as social criticism*. Metuchen, NJ: Scarecrow Press.

Jeffrey, C.P. (1965). Criminal behavior and learning theory. *Journal of Criminal Law, Criminology, and Police Science, 56* (September), 299-300.

Jowett, G. (1976). *Film: The dramatic art*. Boston: Little, Brown and Co.

Kandel, D. (1978). Convergence in prospective longitudinal surveys of drug use in normal populations. In D.B. Kandel (Ed.), *Longitudinal research on drug use*. New York: Wiley.

Kazdin, A.E. (1987). *Conduct disorders in childhood and adolescence*. Newbury Park: Sage.

Liebert, R.M., & Sprafkin, J. (1988). *The early window: Effects of television on children and youth*. New York: Pergamon Press. Mendelsohn, H. (1966). *Mass entertainment*. New Haven: College and University Press.

Mueller, C.W., & Donnerstein, E. (1983). Film-induced arousal and aggressive behavior. *Journal of Social Psychology, 119,* 61-67.

National Coalition on Television Violence News. (1984). *5*(3-4), March-April.

——. (1989). *10*(1-2), February-March.

Parke, R.D., Berkowitz, L., Leyens, J.P., West, S.G., & Sebastian, R.J. (1977). Some effects of violent and nonviolent movies on the behavior of juvenile delinquents. *Advances in Experimental Social Psychology, 10,* 135-172.

Rosenthal, R. (1986). Media violence, antisocial behavior, and the social consequences of small effects. *Journal of Social Issues, 42,* 141-154.

Sharpe, I. (1978, August 9). "Born Innocent" lawyer is undaunted by suit's dismissal. *San Francisco Examiner.*

Squire, J.E. (1983). *The movie business book.* Englewood Cliffs, NJ: Prentice-Hall.

Sutherland, E.H., & Cressey, D.R. (1978). *Criminology* (10th ed.). Philadelphia: Lippincott.

Tannenbaum, P.H. (1971). Emotional arousal as a mediator of communication effects. *Technical reports of the Commission on Obscenity and Pornography* (Vol. 8). Washington, DC: U.S. Government Printing Office.

Urbain, E.S., & Kendall, P.C. (1980). Review of social-cognitive problem solving interventions with children. *Psycholgical Bulletin, 88,* 109-143.

Viemero, V. (1984). Aggressiviisuss ja film isankareiden kayttaytymisen moralen arviointi [Aggression and moral acceptance of the behavior of film characters]. *Psykologia, 19*(6),420-426.

Villela, L., & Markin, R. (1987). Adolescent film preferences: The world of "Purple Rain"; a psychodynamic interpretation. *Adolescent Psychiatry, 14,* 119-132.

Walters, R.H., & Thomas, E.L. (1963). Enhancement of punitiveness by visual and audiovisual displays. *Canadian Journal of Psychology, 17,* 244-255.

Williams, J.R., & Gold, M. (1972). From delinquent behavior to official delinquency. *Social Problems, 20,* 209-229.

Wilson, W., & Hunter, R. (1983). Movie-inspired violence. *Psychological Reports, 53,* 435-441.

Zuzul, M. (1985). The effects of identification with the "movie victims" on the evaluation of the concept of aggression. *Psychologische Bei Trage, 27*(1), 79-85. ✦

27
Religiosity and Delinquency: A Contextual Analysis

Kirk W. Elifson
David M. Petersen
C. Kirk Hadaway

The relationship between religiosity and delinquency has long been a subject of interest among sociologists, criminologists, and church professionals. At the outset, strong theoretical arguments were developed suggesting that religion promotes social control and encourages the development of moral values and the acceptance of societal norms and values (Davis, 1948: 371-373; Erikson, 1966: 3-19; Fitzpatrick, 1967: 315-330). Despite this orientation, conflicting empirical results have characterized the research in this area. While a number of studies indicated that involvement in formal religious activities was related to not engaging in delinquent activity (Travers and Davis, 1961; Miller, 1965; Rhodes and Reiss, 1970), others, including Kvaraceus (1944) and Hirschi and Stark (1969), reported that religiosity and delinquency are virtually unrelated. More recent studies, however—including those of Burkett and White (1974), Higgins and Albrecht (1977), Albrecht et al. (1977), and Jensen and Erickson (1979)—have incorporated methodological and theoretical refinements that consistently have resulted in a negative relationship between religiosity and delinquency. Nonetheless, in this area of research the large number of studies has often produced more confusion than it has the accumulation of knowledge.

In this article we will consider several issues that were suggested in, or are logical extensions of, previous research. We begin where a number of studies stopped and attempt to examine the relationship between religiosity and delinquency more fully than has been done previously. In order to do so, we focus on the role of religious salience in addition to the usual behavioral measures of religiosity that have been utilized (primarily church attendance). We also use a wide variety of other religious measures and employ denominational controls that allow for contrasting religious ideological differences. Moreover, we include a wide variety of delinquency measures and have incorporated a number of methodological improvements in these indices. Finally, and perhaps most important, we utilize multivariate procedures to examine the relative importance of religious variables when predicting delinquent behavior within the context of demographic and social psychological predictors. While it has been assumed by many researchers that religiosity lessens the likelihood of delinquent acts, an adequate test of religion's importance has not been conducted. Thus, a major contribution of this article is to determine religion's role within a multivariate context.

Previous Research

The review that follows is not meant to be comprehensive, but rather focuses on those specific aspects of previous research that are directly related to this article. A comprehensive survey of the literature is available in Albrecht et al. (1977) and Jensen and Erickson (1979).

Religious Salience

Several researchers have recognized the need to include religious salience, or the importance of religion to an individual, as one of several measures of religiosity, but most failed to include it in their research and employed church attendance instead. An early study by Middleton and Putney (1962) directly incorporates religious salience into their research design, however, and they found that religious salience, as well as re-

From Criminology, Volume 21, Number 4 (1983), pp. 505-527. Copyright © 1983 by the American Society of Criminology. Reprinted by permission.

ligious ideology (belief in God) and religious attendance, were negatively related to "anti-ascetic actions" (victimless crimes).[1] That is, the more religious respondents they studied were less likely to have engaged in such activities as gambling, smoking, petting, and drinking than were the less religious respondents. No significant differences were found between the religious and the nonreligious respondents in terms of "anti-social actions" (victim crimes).

The authors of two more recent investigations independently proposed an interpretation of their findings that hinged on the role of religious salience, but they did not actually include it as a measure. Higgins and Albrecht (1977) found religiosity, as measured by church attendance, to be negatively related to deviant activities in their southern sample. They conjectured that their findings were at variance with Hirschi and Stark's (1969) findings, which were based on a northern California survey, because of greater concern with religion in the South. Albrecht et al. (1977) suggested that their findings, which also differed from those of Hirschi and Stark (1969), were due to the "salience of religion" for their respondents, who were all officially members (active and inactive) of the Mormon Church.

Stark et al. (1980) operationalized what might be termed an ecological measure of religious salience by computing a standardized rate of church membership for Standard Metropolitan Statistical Areas (SMSAs). A variety of crime rates were found to be negatively correlated with church membership rates. Thus, despite various researchers' emphasis on the theoretical importance of religious salience in explaining the relationship between religion and delinquency, it has been nearly 20 years since an effort has been made to employ this important measure of religiosity as a correlate other than when used as an ecological characteristic.

Delinquency Measures

Middleton and Putney (1962) noted that many of the contradictory findings that preceded their research may have stemmed from merging all types of delinquent acts into one composite measure. They were the first scholars to identify the importance of distinguishing between victimless and victim crimes, which they termed "anti-ascetic actions" and "anti-social actions." Later, Burkett and White (1974) also treated delinquency as two separate components to avoid masking the relationship between religion and delinquency when they operationalized victimless and victim crimes independently. Their findings corroborated those of Middleton and Putney (1962), who also reported that church attendance has a much stronger negative relationship to victimless crimes than to victim crimes. Nonetheless, Jensen and Erickson (1979) called for further research on this relationship. Two studies (Higgins and Albrecht, 1977; Jensen and Erickson, 1979) also indicated that the relative seriousness of delinquent acts be considered as it relates to religiosity.

Denominational Controls

Findings have been contradictory with respect to the importance of controlling for ideological religious differences associated with membership in a particular religious group. Hirschi and Stark (1969) and Burkett and White (1974) reported no differences in the relationship between religiosity and delinquency by denomination, while Rhodes and Reiss (1970) and Jensen and Erickson (1979) concluded that denominational differences were crucial to understanding this relationship. Jensen and Erickson reanalyzed the original data used by Hirschi and Stark (1969) and demonstrated that improper denominational controls masked a relatively strong negative relationship between religious attendance and delinquency. A more conclusive test of the influence of denominational controls needs to be conducted due to inadequate sample sizes that were relatively homogeneous with respect to denominational or religious affiliation. Furthermore, while differences have been shown to exist, conclusive patterns associated with denominational differences have not been established.[2]

Relative Importance of Religion

Multivariate inquiries (Middleton and Putney, 1962; Rhodes and Reiss, 1970: Albrecht et al., 1977; and Jensen and Erickson, 1979) have examined the relative importance of religion as a predictor of delinquent activities. Jensen and Erickson (1979) conducted the most thorough investigation, although they did not present their findings in a manner that considers the standarized influence of several demographic and social psychological correlates of delinquency (see also Albrecht et al., 1977). We also are particularly interested in determining the importance of alternative measures of religiosity and their importance relative to nonreligious predictor variables, for we argue, along with Albrecht et al. (1977), that religious variables must be considered in a meaningful context with other predictors of delinquency.

Methods

The Sample

Data for this study were collected during the summer and fall of 1974 from students attending grades 9-12 in 21 public high schools in suburban DeKalb County, which is located in the greater metropolitan Atlanta, Georgia area. A random sample of 600 students and a replacement sample of 600 cases were drawn from a universe of 23,289 white students compiled from official school records.[3] Of the initial sample of 600, 568 respondents were interviewed successfully. Parent and/or student refusals totaled 28, and the remainder of the nonrespondents included persons who could not be located due to incorrect addresses, absence from the area, and so on. The remaining 32 interviews were obtained from the replacement sample. The total sample of adolescents interviewed included 301 males and 299 females. Following parental and respondent permission, one-hour interviews were conducted privately in the adolescents' homes by young white professional interviewers who were matched by sex with the respondents, a procedure that minimizes interviewer effect (Sudman and Bradburn, 1974). The respondents represented the universe from which they were drawn in terms of sex, grade level, and school attended, so we assume that sample bias was minimal.

It is worthy to note, however, that the sample was drawn from a white population of a relatively prosperous metropolitan county. DeKalb County had an 86% white population with a 1970 median family income of $12,824 and educational attainment of 12.5 years. This can be contrasted with the 1973 national median family income of $10,236 and median educational attainment of 12.1 years. The adolescents surveyed are white, male and female, ages 12-18, suburban, and tend to come from families that are well educated and relatively affluent.

Variables

Delinquency Measures. An overall unweighted delinquency scale (Cronbach's coefficient alpha = .73), which was originally validated by Gold (1966) and adapted by Johnston (1973), assesses how often respondents had engaged in 20 delinquent acts in the past year.[4] The five response categories ranged from "never" to "five or more times." The delinquency items were also weighted by seriousness to create an overall weighted delinquency scale (alpha = .74). The weighting procedures are consistent with those devised by Sellin and Wolfgang (1964), Figlio (1975), Gold (1966), and Thomas (1977) for comparable delinquency items. "Serious" offenses were weighted 4, "moderately serious" offenses were weighted 2, and "least serious" offenses were weighted 1. . . .

The multidimensionality of delinquency has been shown to be an important consideration (Scott, 1959; Dentler and Monroe, 1961; Arnold, 1965; Dentler, 1965; Kelly, 1975), and several measures have been incorporated into this research that are based on the assumption of multidimensionality. A factor analysis of the data as reported in Beachy et al. (1979) revealed two salient dimensions. The aggression scale (alpha = .60) included serious fighting, fight with parents, hurt someone badly, hit instructor or supervisor, hit father, gang fighting, hit mother, use knife or gun to get something, set fire to someone else's property, and threaten a person in order to get something. The theft scale (alpha = .64) included theft < $50.00, steal something from a store, steal a car, take expensive part of car, theft > $50.00 and take inexpensive part of car. The items in the two scales were weighted by seriousness of offense in the same manner as were the items in the overall weighted delinquency scale.

Another way of examining seriousness is by contrasting status and nonstatus offenses that were operationalized separately. Status offenses (alpha = .72) included running away from home and arguing or fighting with parents. Nonstatus offenses (alpha = .37) included all the remaining delinquency items, but these did not reach a satisfactory level of reliability (Nunnally, 1967). Items were identified as status versus nonstatus in accordance with the legal statutes of the county in which the data were gathered. Status and nonstatus scale scores were computed by summing the reported frequency of the acts included in each category.

In consonance with previous research (Burkett and White, 1974; Higgins and Albrecht, 1977; Albrecht et al., 1977), our measures of victimless crime include alcohol and marijuana use. Alcohol use and marijuana use were determined by the respondent's frequency of reported use during the prior year. The six possible response categories range from "nearly everyday" to "never." Both are included as separate variables because they have been omitted from standard delinquency scales yet are important indicants of delinquent behavior.[5]

Religious Measures. The respondent's church (or synagogue) attendance and their parents' attendance were assessed by asking the respondents to report both their own and their parents' attendance with respect to eight categories ranging from "more than once a week" to "never."

The respondents who reported a religious affiliation were placed into one of four categories consistent with orthodoxy scales based on a national NORC sample (Stark and Glock, 1968; Hadaway, 1978): (1) liberal, n = 83 (Unitarian, Presbyterian, Episcopalian, United Church of Christ); (2) moderate, n = 126 (Methodist, Lutheran, Christian Church, United Methodist, Wesleyan, Disciples of Christ); (3) conservative, n = 151 (Southern Baptist, Baptist); (4) Catholic, n = 68.[6] Jewish respondents numbered 22 and were excluded from the multivariate analysis when religious affiliation was utilized as a control variable. They were also excluded from all analyses involving religious orthodoxy due to the inappropriateness of the scale for non-christian respondents.

Religious salience was measured by the question, "All in all, how important would you say your religion is in influencing the way you live?" The five possible responses ranged from "extremely important" to "fairly unimportant."

Two items assessed the extent to which the respondent believed that there is "life after death" and that "God answers prayer." These items were considered separately because of their frequent use as independent measures of religiosity. Life after death provides a measure of supernatural belief at an abstract and rather minimal level; the prayer item taps a worldview in which God is seen as continually present and in constant personal contact with the believer through prayer. Both, however, can be considered components of orthodoxy and were therefore included, along with four other items in an orthodoxy scale. An orthodoxy scale (alpha = .88) included the above life after death and personal prayer questions along with four others. Two questions assessed the respondent's belief that God really exists and that Jesus is the divine son of God on a fivepoint scale ranging from "no doubt" to "total doubt." Additionally, the respondents were asked to indicate the likelihood that the "devil actually exists" and that Jesus was born of a virgin. Four responses were possible and ranged from "completely true" to "definitely not true."

A measure of morality was based on the item, "Children should obey all the rules their parents make for them." A six-category Likert response format ranging from "strongly agree" to "strongly disagree" was used to assess the respondent's opinion.

Other Variables. Five other variables were utilized. The respondent's sex and grade point average were included as demographic variables. Respondents were asked to estimate how many of their friends smoke marijuana and were given the choices (1) all, (2) most, (3) some, (4) a few, (5) none.[7] Two social psychological measures were adapted from Kandel et al. (1968). A measure of closeness to mother was developed by combining two items, "How close do you feel to your mother (female guardian)?" with possible responses ranging from "extremely close" to "not very close," and "How much do you want to be like the kind of person your mother (or female guardian) is?" with possible responses ranging from "very much" to "not at all." A final measure, parent's attitudes toward friends, reflected the extent to which the respondents believed their parents approved of their friends.

Results

The data in Table 1 contain the summary bivariate gamma coefficients between selected independent variables and the measures of self-reported delinquency for the sample. The findings provide support for the view that church attendance is related to conventional forms of delinquency; however, the relationship is not strong.[8] Only a weak negative relationship exists between both the respondent's and the parent's attendance at religious services and the general weighted measure of delinquency involvement (gammas of -.17 and -.18, respectively); the relationships are consistent with the most recent studies reviewed earlier. When we examine the two delinquency subscales (aggression and theft) in relationship to religious participation, none of the gamma values approached a weak relationship. We further pursued the relationship between church attendance and delinquent behavior by considering status and nonstatus offenses separately. Again, both respondent's and parent's attendance at church were inversely related to these measures of delinquency. Also consistent with the general pattern of findings in previous research, our data show that a relatively moderate relationship does exist between religious participation and certain "victimless" offenses—that is, the use of alcohol and marijuana. The general pattern of results is quite consistent for the relationships between the use of alcohol and marijuana and church attendance for the respondents and their parents (all gammas are between -.30 and -.35).[9]

In the main, relationships between the measures of religiosity other than church

Table 1
Gamma Coefficients Between Delinquency, Religion, and Morality

	Parent's Church Attendance	Respondent's Church Attendance	Importance of Religion (Salience)	Life After Death	Personal Prayer	Orthodoxy	Obey All Parent's rules (Morality)
Delinquency Measures							
Overall scale (unweighted)	-.14	-.11	-.26	-.07	-.33	-.21	-.37
Overall scale (weighted)	-.18	-.17	-.31	-.18	-.37	-.27	-.37
Aggression dimension (weighted)	-.10	-.09	-.15	-.09	-.15	-.11	-.30
Theft dimension (weighted)	-.08	-.12	-.16	-.15	-.24	-.18	-.23
Miscellaneous dimension (weighted)	-.19	-.19	-.27	-.18	-.27	-.25	-.30
Status offenses	-.21	-.24	-.29	-.22	-.24	-.26	-.40
Nonstatus offenses	-.24	-.25	-.33	-.20	-.39	-.33	-.36
Alcohol use	-.30	-.32	-.32	-.29	-.38	-.36	-.34
Marijuana use	-.35	-.32	-.41	-.32	-.42	-.45	-.44

attendance are also weak to moderate and are related negatively to the commission of conventional as well as victimless delinquent acts. The gamma coefficient between the measure "life after death" and the overall weighted delinquency scale was weak (-.18). Furthermore, the measures of orthodoxy, the importance (salience) of religion, and the use of personal prayer were also related moderately to the weighted composite measure (gammas of -.25, -.31 and -.37). The same general pattern is revealed in Table 1 for these other religiosity measures and the respondents' self-reported use of alcohol and marijuana. Belief in a life after death and the use of alcohol and marijuana are weakly related, but slightly stronger coefficients exist between the other three religiosity measures and the less serious criminal activities of alcohol and marijuana use.

Past research has also revealed a consistent, moderately negative relationship between measures of morality (moral values) and delinquency. Similarly, in the current study those results are affirmed for the general weighted measure of delinquency involvement and the morality item "obey all parent's rules" (gamma of -.37). The use of alcohol and marijuana is also related negatively to an acceptance of moral values (gammas of -.34 and -.44, respectively).

In keeping with previous findings, then, our data reveal that religious participation (church attendance) is related weakly to both the weighted and unweighted measure of delinquency involvement for conventional crimes. On the other hand, a definite relationship exists between several other measures of religiosity, particularly religious salience and personal prayer, and delinquency. Moreover, slightly stronger negative relationships were found to exist between the majority of these religiosity measures and the use of alcohol and marijuana. The value of weighting individual delinquency items by their seriousness is borne out by a direct comparison of the relationships of all overall weighted and unweighted delinquency scales to each of the religion measures. In addition, these data demonstrate that the use of multiple measures of religiosity clarify their relationships to delinquency. It would also seem that religious salience, prayer, and other measures of religiosity are more important than church participation in predicting conventional as well as victimless delinquent behavior. Although not shown in Table 1, we also controlled for sex and found similar relationships for males and females.

... [In] a more detailed examination of the relationship between delinquency as measured by respondent's self-reports with the variables of church attendance, importance of religion, orthodoxy, and a measure of morality, [t]he data show that students who attend church frequently are significantly more likely than infrequent attendees to score low on the weighted composite measure of delinquent behavior. However, the relationship is relatively weak compared to the other three measures of religiosity. ... The weighted measure of delinquency varies in the same predicted pattern according to the respondent's scores on the saliency of religion and orthodoxy. Those students who report that religion is extremely important in their lives are statistically more likely to score low on the overall delinquency measure than are those who report that religion is not a salient factor in their lives. In fact, there is a 31% difference between the extreme categories of religious salience for both the low and high scorers on the delinquency scale (63% versus 32% and 37% versus 68%). Additionally, the data show that highly orthodox respondents are significantly more likely than those with low scores also to have low delinquent behavior scores.

To this point we have examined three measures of religious activity or belief thought by many to be related to delinquency. Another important factor that might preclude delinquent behavior is that of morality: Students who obey all parental rules are more likely than those who do not to be less involved in delinquent behavior. Indeed, as examination of the data ... reveals, this relationship was found to be statistically significant for our sample, and the percentage differences are sizable. ... [A] further examination of the above relationships controlling for sex revealed that the existing patterns remained significant for both males and females.

Although theories that seek to explain the relationship between religion and delinquency generally focus on the role of religion in encouraging the development of moral values, it is assumed that other moral influences also operate in the life of each individual. Parents and peers are two such important influences, and it is conceivable that in many cases they work in an additive fashion with religion to discourage delinquent behavior. . . .

. . . Combining the variables of religious salience, morality, and friends who use marijuana into a composite measure reveals a striking relationship between this new measure and the weighted delinquency scale. The percentage of friends who use marijuana has been included to assess the impact of peer group drug usage on an adolescent's delinquent behavior. While considerable evidence exists that suggests an individual's friends' use of drugs has a major influence on his or her drug usage (Adler and Lotecka, 1973; Kandel, 1973; Tolone and Dermont, 1975) and mixed findings concerning an adolescent's drug usage and propensity to engage in delinquent behavior (Goode, 1970; Johnston, 1973; Beachy et al., 1979), little guidance is available concerning the relationship between an adolescent's peer group drug use and his or her involvement in delinquent behavior. . . . [S]tudents who report that they do not have friends who use marijuana, that they obey all parental rules, and who report that religion is very important in their lives are statistically much more likely than students who report the opposite on these three measures to have low scores on the delinquency scale.

Several potentially important predictors of delinquency, including religious and nonreligious variables, were also examined is a multivariate context to assess the relative value religious measures have vis-à-vis a variety of known nonreligious predictor variables. The role of parental and peer influence, morality, and success in school are all considered important factors by social theorists in creating a social bond and hence inhibiting delinquent acts (Hirschi, 1969). While the sex of the adolescent does not play a major role in accounting for the crime differential between males and females (Jensen and Eve, 1976; Shover et al., 1979), it was included to ensure a more complete model. . . . [R]eligious salience, which had the highest zero-order correlation with the dependent variable, was retained as the sole religion measure.[10]

. . . By examining the beta coefficients and F-ratios for each of the independent variables . . . , it is clear that whether or not one's friends use marijuana is by far the best predictor of delinquency. Three of the next five variables . . . reflect relationships between parents and siblings. What parents think of their child's friends, closeness to one's mother, and whether the respondent thinks he or she should obey parental rules are all fairly important influences in predicting whether a student is delinquent. Also important are sex and grades. Females are less likely to be delinquent than are males, and students who earn good grades are also less likely to be delinquent than are students who earn poor grades. While the primary concern in this article is to assess the relative importance of the predictor variables, it should be noted that 17% of the variance was explained in the dependent variable. Thus, the predictability of delinquency is consistent with other research in the area.

Clearly unimportant as a predictor of delinquency when controls are in effect is religious salience. This finding was surprising given the zero-order gammas . . . between religious salience and several measures of delinquency. Yet it points out the problem of earlier studies that failed to use adequate statistical controls. . . . [W]hen religion is included as a predictor of delinquency in the context of several known predictors, its impact is not statistically significant.[11] Further analysis has shown that religious salience is fairly highly correlated with the non-religious predictors, especially those dealing with parental and peer relationships and morality. It appears that the relationship of religiosity to delinquency is so closely tied to the family and other moral influences that it has little influence that is statistically independent of the other predictor variables....

Discussion

The findings we have presented have important implications for the research that has sought to establish the relationship between religiosity and delinquency. Conflicting results have characterized research in this area from the beginning. Hirschi and Stark (1969) concluded that religion and delinquency were unrelated. Their paper has been a central focus of continuing research for over 10 years. Some of the confusion it created was laid to rest, however, when Jensen and Erickson (1979) reanalyzed the data and showed that methodological problems led Hirschi and Stark (1969) to conclude incorrectly that the variables were unrelated. Other studies (e.g., Burkett and White, 1974; Higgins and Albrecht, 1977; Albrecht et al., 1977) have also reported a negative relationship, a finding confirmed by the present study. By using an extremely wide variety of both religion and delinquency measures, we have shown clearly that a weak to moderate negative zero-order relationship does exist. It is hoped that this finding, along with those of others we have mentioned, should dispel any further doubt about the matter.

In addition to verifying the existence of a relationship between religion and delinquency, the use of many religion and delinquency items has helped specify which measures produce the strongest relationships. Here we followed the suggestion of several earlier authors and incorporated religious salience along with behavioral and belief measures of religiosity. Subsequently, we found salience, belief in the efficacy of personal prayer, and orthodoxy to be generally more substantial correlates of delinquency than the often-used variable, church attendance. This was not surprising, however, given the close conceptual links among salience, orthodox religious belief, and the internalization of religious moral values. The link between religious participation and such values, on the other hand, is not as direct because of the many extrinsic motivations for church attendance.

Previous studies had found that religiosity was related to certain types of delinquent behavior and not to others (Middleton and Putney, 1962; Burkett and White, 1974; Higgins and Albrecht, 1977). In an effort to understand this apparent inconsistency further, we constructed several measures of delinquency that would allow us to replicate and to move beyond previous research. Seriousness of delinquent acts was used to develop a weighted composite delinquency measure that seemed to measure the dependent variable in a more valid manner. This particular scale included a wide variety of delinquent acts, ranging from very minor status offenses such as arguing with parents, to felonies such as armed robbery. Further, delinquent acts were not treated equally but were weighted in two ways by their seriousness and by the number of times the respondent had committed the act. The resulting scale thus has considerable face validity and proves to be more highly related to religiosity than most of our other, less exhaustive indicators. In addition, factor analysis was used to explore the relationship of delinquency as a multidimensional concept with two measures of religiosity. Finally, delinquency was also operationalized as status versus nonstatus offenses, and as victim and victimless offenses. In this latter case, our findings confirmed those of previous studies that suggested that victimless crimes are related more strongly to religiosity than are delinquent acts involving a victim (Albrecht et al., 1977) This special relationship between religion and such activities as drug use, alcohol use, gambling, and unsanctioned sexual behavior (Hoge, 1979) definitely warrants further investigation and may prove to be the key to understanding why religion is related to other forms of delinquent behavior. As others have noted, it may be that in the case of this issue the churches have spoken out and used sanctions while other moral influences in society have been mute. As a result, those influenced by the churches are much less likely to become involved.

Most important, we found that in spite of the relatively strong zero-order relationship between religiosity and delinquency, religion's contribution as a predictor within a multivariate context is insignificant. Why might this be the case? Earlier we suggested that perhaps religion is so intertwined with the family and other moral influences that its direct contribution is almost totally negated. As Hirschi and Stark (1969) noted, there are numerous other moral influences in society other than religion. Irreligious and religious persons generally act within the same legal boundaries. Thus, religion may be but one of the larger set of potential influences that encourage law-abiding behavior. A second possibility is that religion may be acting as an antecedent influence that helps create a family and peer environment not conducive to delinquent behavior. But whatever the answer, we can conclude from this analysis that religious young people are less likely to be delinquent. The apparent source of this tendency seems to be found, however, in the type of families and friends that religious young people have.

Notes

1. Respondents were asked to agree or disagree with the statement, "Religion is one of the most important things in my life."
2. Peek et al. (1979), however, presented evidence that members of fundamental denominations were far more likely to believe that they would be legally sanctioned for drunken driving than did members of nonfundamental denominations.
3. Minority adolescents between the ages of 12 and 19 constituted 16% of Dekalb County's population in 1970 and only 11% of the ninth- through twelfth-grade public high school enrollment in the county during 1974. The decision was made to focus solely on white students in the current study because to include minority adolescents in the analysis would have required oversampling. As a result, the findings cannot be generalized to minority groups.
4. The unreliability of the reporting of events that are distant in time has been documented widely. Memory factors in this study have been minimized due to the age of the respondents and the use of face-to-face interviews (Sudman and Bradburn, 1974). Furthermore, salient activities such as illegal behavior have been shown in past research to lessen recall problems (Cannell and Kahn, 1968).
5. See Gillis and Hagan (1982) for a similar usage of the marijuana question as a single item measure.
6. Several other denominational groups could have been considered conservative; however, their numbers were so small (n = 28) that the resulting conservative category would still have remained overwhelmingly Baptist. For this reason they were excluded from a portion of the analysis, along with other Protestant groups that could not easily be classified.
7. The reporting of illicit drug usage by a friend is most practically assessed using a single-item measure such as that employed in this study. See, for example, Kandel et al. (1973) as one of a number of investigations that have used such a measure.
8. The relationships between church attendance and the delinquency measures included in Table 1 were examined by religious affiliation because church or synagogue attendance has differing meanings for Catholic, Jewish, and Protestant affiliates. Some variation in gamma values was evident when a control was introduced for religious affiliation. The overall gamma, for example, between respondent's church attendance and the weighted delinquency scale as shown in Table 1 was -.17, whereas for Catholic respondents it was -.22, for Jewish respondents it was -.05 (nonsignificant due to a small n), and for Protestant respondents it was -.10. Controls for religious affiliation are discussed later in the article with respect to the multivariate analysis.
9. It can be argued that alcohol usage varies with ethnicity, which is related to religion, and thus ethnicity may act as a confounding variable, particularly for the Catholic respondents. Census data for the Atlanta area suggest that the sample is not likely to be heavily represented by Irish or other ethnic groups whose members are sometimes characterized as heavy drinkers.
10. Separate regression analyses that included personal prayer and attendance rather than religious salience were also conducted. Neither variable was statistically significant, and the regression coefficients associated with the other independent variables were similar to the values [discussed]. . . .
11. . . . Religious salience was also brought into the regression equation prior to the simultaneous inclusion of the remaining variables in

the model. Its contribution remained nonsignificant.

References

Adler, P.T. and L. Lotecka. 1973. "Drug use among high school students." *Int. J. of the Addictions* 8: 537-548.

Albrecht, S.L., B.A. Chadwick, and D.S. Alcorn. 1977. "Religiosity and deviance: application of an attitude-behavior contingent consistency model." *J. for the Scientific Study of Religion* 16: 263-274.

Arnold, W.R. 1965. "Continuities in research: scaling delinquent behavior." *Social Problems* 13: 59-65.

Bardwick J. and E. Douvan. 1972. "Ambivalence: the socialization of women," in J.M. Bardwick (ed.) *Readings in the Psychology of Women*. New York: Harper & Row.

Beachy, G.M., D.M. Petersen and F.S. Pearson. 1979. "Adolescent drug use and delinquency: a research note." *J. of Psychedelic Drugs* 11: 313-316.

Burkett, S.R. and M. White. 1974. "Hellfire and delinquency: another look." *J. for the Scientific Study of Religion* 13: 455-462.

Cannell, C.F. and R.L. Kahn. 1968. "Interviewing," in G. Lindzey and E. Aronson (eds.) *Handbook of Social Psychology*, Vol. 2. Reading, MA: Addison-Wesley.

Davis, K. 1948. *Human Society*. New York: Macmillan.

Dentler, R.A. 1965. Chapter in R.H. Hardt and G.E. Bodine (eds.) *Development of Self-Report Instruments in Delinquency Research*. Syracuse, NY: Syracuse Univ. Press.

Dentler, R.A. and L.J. Monroe. 1961. "Social correlates of early adolescent theft." *Amer. Soc. Rev.* 26: 733-743.

Erikson, K.T. 1966. *Wayward Puritans: A study in the Sociology of Deviance*. New York: John Wiley.

Figlio, R.M. 1975. "The seriousness of offenses: an evaluation by offenders and non-offenders." *J. of Criminal Law and Criminology* 66: 189-200.

Fitzpatrick, J.P. 1967. "The role of religion in programs for the prevention and correction of crime and delinquency," in *Task Force Report: Juvenile Delinquency and Youth Crime*. Washington, DC: Government Printing Office.

Gillis, A.R. and J. Hagan. 1982. "Density, delinquency and design: formal and informal control and the built environment." *Criminology* 19: 514-529.

Gold, M. 1966. "Undetected delinquent behavior." *J. of Research in Crime and Delinquency* 13: 27-47.

Goode, E. 1970. *The Marijuana Smokers*. New York: Basic Books.

Hadaway, C.K. 1978. "Denominational switching and membership growth: in search of relationship." *Soc. Analysis* 39: 321-337.

Higgins, P.C. and G.L. Albrecht. 1977. "Hellfire and delinquency revisited." *Social Forces* 55: 952-958.

Hirschi, T. 1969. *Causes of Delinquency*. Berkeley: Univ. of California Press.

Hirschi, T. and R. Stark. 1969. "Hellfire and delinquency." *Social Problems* 17: 202-213.

Hoge, D.R. 1979. "National contextual factors influencing church trends," in D.R. Hoge and D.A. Roozen (eds.) *Understanding Church Growth and Decline, 1950-1978*. New York: Pilgrim Press.

Jensen, G.F. and R.A. Eve. 1976. "Sex differences in delinquency." *Criminology* 13:427-448.

Jensen, G.F. and M.L. Erickson. 1979. "The religious factor and delinquency: another look at the hellfire hypothesis," in R. Wuthnow (ed.) *The Religious Dimension: New Directions in Quantitative Research*. New York: Academic.

Johnston, L. 1973. *Drugs and American Youth*. Ann Arbor, MI: Institute for Social Research.

Kandel, D.B., G.S. Lesser, G.C. Roberts, and R. Weiss. 1968. *Adolescents in Two Societies: Peers, School, and Family in the United States and Denmark* (2 vols.). Washington, DC: U.S. Department of Health, Education and Welfare.

Kandel, D.B. 1973. "Adolescent marijuana use: role of parents and peers." *Science* 181:1067-1070.

Kelly, D.H. 1975. "Status origins, track position and delinquent involvement: a self-report analysis." *Soc. Q.* 16: 264-271.

Kvaraceus, W.C. 1944. "Delinquent behavior and church attendance." *Sociology and Social Research* 28: 284-289.

Middleton, R. and S. Putney. 1962. "Religion, normative standards, and behavior." *Sociometry* 25: 141-152.

Miller, M. 1965. "The place of religion in the lives of juvenile offenders." *Federal Probation* 29: 50-54.

Nunnally, J.M. 1967. *Psychometric Theory*. New York: McGraw-Hill.

Peek, C.W., H.P. Chalfant, and E.V. Milton. 1979. "Sinners in the hands of an angry God: fundamentalist fears about drunken driving." *J. for the Scientific Study of Religion* 18: 29-39.

Rhodes, A.L. and A.J. Reiss Jr. 1970. "The 'religious factor' and delinquent behavior." *J. of Research in Crime and Delinquency* 7: 83-98.

Scott, J.F. 1959. "Two dimensions of delinquent behavior." *Amer. Soc. Rev.* 24: 240-243.

Sellin, T. and M.E. Wolfgang. 1964. *The Measurement of Delinquency*. New York: John Wiley.

Shover, N., S. Norland, J. James, and W. Thornton. 1979. "Gender roles and delinquency." *Social Forces* 58: 162-175.

Stark, R. and C.Y. Glock. 1968. *American Piety: The Nature of Religious Commitment*. Berkeley: Univ. of California Press.

Stark, R., D.P. Doyle, and L. Kent. 1980. "Rediscovering moral communities: church membership and crime," in T. Hirschi and M. Gottfredson (eds.) *Understanding Crime: Current Theory and Research*. Beverly Hills, CA: Sage.

Sudman, S. and N.M. Bradburn. 1974. *Response Effects in Surveys*. Chicago: AVC.

Thomas, C.W. 1977. "The effect of legal sanctions on juvenile delinquency: a comparison of the labeling and deterrence perspective." Final report submitted to the National Institute of Juvenile Justice and Delinquency Prevention.

Tolone, W.L. and D. Dermott. 1975. "Some correlates of drug use among high school youth in a Midwestern rural community." *Int. J. of the Addictions* 10: 761-777.

Travers, F. and R.G. Davis. 1961. "A study of religious motivation and delinquency." *J. of Educ. Sociology* 34: 205-220. ✦

28
Crime And Delinquency in the Roaring Twenties

Rodney Stark
William Sims Bainbridge
Robert D. Crutchfield
Daniel P. Doyle
Roger Finke

This paper could have and should have been written in the 1920s. The primary theoretical positions it supports were popular then, and the data on which it is based were current, well-known, and available in nearly any university library. Had such a paper been written, much of our own recent research would have been replication studies. Since, to the best of our knowledge, no such paper was ever written, portions of this paper replicate work we have done previously that identified social integration and church membership as potent and independent elements of the moral community. In contemporary data, measures of each element produce robust sociological correlations with many forms of deviance. In this paper we turn the clock back several decades to examine the same fundamental relationships using data for the 1920s. We shall try to replicate three central findings of our earlier work:

1. Social integration of communities is undercut by substantial population turnover. To the degree that a community consists of newcomers and transients, deviance rates will be high (Crutchfield et al., forthcoming; Stark, Doyle, and Rushing, forthcoming; Bainbridge and Stark, 1981).

2. Religion *as such* tends to support conformity. Communities with higher rates of church membership will have lower rates of deviance (Stark, Bainbridge, and Kent, 1981; Stark and Bainbridge, 1980; Stark, Doyle, and Rushing, forthcoming; Bainbridge and Stark, 1981).

3. Elements of social control do not restrain *all* forms of deviance. For example, population turnover and church membership are very highly related to burglary and larceny rates, but they are virtually unrelated to homicide and assault. This has led us to suggest a basic reconceptualization of deviance into two distinct classes (Stark and Crutchfield, forthcoming).

Replication, however, is not our only concern. We are equally concerned with demonstrating the existence and validity of a wealth of neglected data on crime, delinquency, and other forms of deviance for the Roaring Twenties (and even earlier). Indeed, our success in replicating current findings based on high-quality data is a major means for demonstrating the validity of these forgotten historical data sets. This paper devotes considerable space to evaluating and describing these old data sets.

In addition, we shall exploit a unique opportunity presented by these pre-1930 data sets to examine the rise of the juvenile justice system. We attempt to assess the "child-saving" thesis (Platt, 1969) that the juvenile justice system did not primarily arise as a response to juvenile crime. We will try to demonstrate that the juvenile justice system was first instituted in communities with relatively low delinquency rates but with a higher degree of concern for wayward youths. We then try to show that only over time have juvenile commitment rates come to reflect rates of juvenile misbehavior. . . .

Before we turn to our analysis it will be useful to describe these various data sets, examining how they were collected and what they include.

From *Journal of Research in Crime and Delinquency*, Volume 20 (January 1983), pp. 4-23. Copyright © 1983 by Sage Publications, Inc. Reprinted by permission.

Historic Data on Deviance

Like many who do quantitative studies of deviance, we have long bemoaned the lack of older data. The FBI's *Uniform Crime Reports* did not being until 1930. Worse yet, the *UCR* data for early years are deficient because of missing data—many jurisdictions simply did not participate. We know of no data on *reported offenses* nationally before 1930[1] that can be made comparable with the *UCR* statistics; hence, hopes to extend most crime rates backward in time remain unfulfilled. However, while searching the census section of our library for other purposes, we discovered, quite by accident, an amazing array of data on many forms of deviance, especially those forms classified as crime and delinquency. The following data sets are to be found in any moderately complete university library. Taken together these data sources offer a potentially rich resource too long neglected by social scientists. By turning to the past we can gain greater scope for the empirical testing of theories of deviance.

Prisoner Data

Some of the most useful data on crime early in this century are provided by a series of census studies of individuals held in jails and prisons. Beginning in 1850, the United States Bureau of the Census conducted a census of imprisoned offenders every decade. The earliest of these are somewhat spotty in coverage and collected a limited amount of information. However, the census of prisoners conducted in 1910 and the one in 1923 achieved excellent coverage and obtained extremely detailed data. (The Census Bureau continued to provide prison statistics until 1950. After 1950, the responsibility for prison statistics was transferred to the Federal Bureau of Prisons in the Department of Justice.) . . .

Delinquency Data

Much has been written about the "invention" of delinquency (Platt, 1969; Mennel, 1973; Larsen, 1972). But in none of the publications of leading proponents of this view has any use been made of potentially important official statistics. The 1910 and 1923 census enumerations of inmates gathered separate statistics for juveniles in detention. These data permit the computation of two rates: the proportion of the youth population in detention and the annual rate of admission to detention. The latter eliminates variations that might occur if jurisdictions differ in their average length of detention.

The 1910 data were published in 1918 by the United States Bureau of the Census in the volume *Prisoners and Juvenile Delinquents in the United States—1910*. In 1927 came the publication *Children Under Institutional Care—1923*. This later volume not only improves on the 1910 document in thoroughness and detail, it also reports valuable, previously unpublished, data going back as far as 1880. Later in this paper we demonstrate the likelihood that these are valid and valuable data on delinquency by showing how well they support qualitative histories of the juvenile justice system.

Mortality Statistics

While our search of citations in the literature and the questions we directed to leading criminologists suggest that the prison and jail data described above are unknown to criminal justice researchers, data available from the annual volumes of *Mortality Statistics* published by the Census Bureau are known to many researchers, but are widely neglected nonetheless. These data are based on death certificates filed with each county and thus are available for units of analysis smaller than states. Among the most useful of these statistics for social scientists are the annual homicide rates, which go back to the turn of the century. It is well known that homicide is the best reported of all criminal offenses, for the existence of a body is hard to ignore. Undoubtedly some homicides go undetected, as when a poisoned spouse is misdiagnosed as having died of heart failure. Still, such events must be relatively uncommon, and ought to be less common in cities than in rural areas because of the better training of urban coroners. We see no reason to suppose that these data are not of good quality and we have used them in other research (Bainbridge and Stark, 1981)....

The Forgotten Religion Census Reports

All the while criminologists neglected these important sets of historical data, sociologists of religion have lamented because the United States Census has never included data on religion. Such data would make it possible to chart the rise and fall of various denominations, to trace patterns of religious migration, and indeed to include religious variables in a range of demographic and ecological studies. It is quite true that such information is lacking from the regular decennial census. But the astonishing fact is that sociologists of religion have not been aware that the United States Census Bureau conducted massive, exquisitely detailed, national enumerations of church membership in 1890, 1906, 1916, 1926, and 1936. If sociologists noticed these data when they appeared, they were not prompted to use them in research. And there is no evidence that sociologists in recent decades have even known the data existed. But these data too can be found in any moderately complete university library....

Moral Communities and Crime: 1926

The historical data described above are now used to replicate some of our previous research. To the extent that findings for the 1920s resemble those for the 1970s, a strong case can be made that the older data are trustworthy. We begin with an effort to clarify and test control theory in a fashion consistent with Durkheim's notion of the "moral community."

A major element of the moral community is social integration. According to Durkheim deviance results because of weak bonds between the individual and society—when "the bond attaching him to society is slack" (1897:214). The moral community is one in which a high proportion of members have strong bonds to the group. Social integration of a group reflects:

the intensity of the collective life circulating in it. It is more unified and powerful the more active and constant is the intercourse among its members. (Durkheim, 1897:202)

Social integration, then, can be effectively defined in terms of social networks. The greater the density and intensity of interpersonal attachments among members of a group, the more the group is socially integrated. The trouble is that to operationalize this definition one would need good sociometric data for each ecological unit of analysis to be studied. For cities or for states there are no such data and they would be prohibitively expensive to collect.

However, in other work we have developed a wholly satisfactory inferential measure of social integration. Other things being equal, there must be more social integration in communities having primarily a stable population than in communities made up primarily of newcomers and transients. Hence, a measure of population turnover—of the movement of people into and within communities—is a reasonable measure of social integration.

In other work (Crutchfield et al., forthcoming) mobility rates were computed for the sixty-five largest United States metropolitan areas. Measured this way, social integration had a truly strong effect on the crime rate ($r = .63$). For the smaller SMSAs this fine-grained measure was not available. Nonetheless, quite comparable results were gained when change in population size was substituted (Stark et al., 1980).

For the 1920s we have developed a measure more sensitive than simple population change, but perhaps less precise than one based on full data concerning migration. For each city and state it was possible to determine the proportion of the population born out-of-state (excluding the foreign born).[2] Undoubtedly some of these people migrated while very young and had long resided in their current city or state. Still, this measure should serve to distinguish communities with stable populations from those with high proportions of newcomers.

Table 1 shows the strong effect of population turnover on rates of criminal convictions. If incarceration rates for crime reflect the volume of criminal offenses, then the bottom line in the table is an approximation of the overall crime index of the modern *UCR*. It is based on the total number of persons sentenced to prison and jail for each of the forty-four states included in the annual prison census of 1926.

Table 1
Correlations between Population Turnover and Criminal Convictions—1926 (states)

Conviction Offense	Population Turnover	
	r	Significance
Forgery	.73	.001
Larceny	.56	.001
Burglary	.44	.002
Rape	.58	.001
Robbery	.36	.01
Homicide	.18	NS
Assault	.08	NS
Total	.46	.001

The correlation between population turnover (as measured by the proportion of the population born out-of-state) and the incarceration rate is a substantial .46, significant beyond the .001 level. This very closely matches findings for contemporary data based on population change and the *UCR* total crime index. This strongly suggests that one can infer variations in the volume of crimes committed from the volume of persons sentenced to do time. Moreover, internal variations among categories of crime produce the characteristic patterns found in contemporary data (which we discuss conceptually later in this paper). The highest correlation between population turnover and specific offenses is the rate of incarceration for forgery (.73). One supposes that such an offense is unusually likely in places where newcomers and strangers abound. Larceny, burglary, and rape are also highly correlated with population turnover, as they are in modern data. However, homicide and assault are not significantly correlated with population turnover, and this too is consistent with our modern findings. In these data, robbery is weakly, but significantly, correlated with population turnover. This is the one departure from our modern findings, in which robbery is little influenced by population turnover. Yet this difference is wholly plausible. The modern *UCR* robbery category is inundated by trivial offenses. A robbery rate inferred from prison and jail sentences will eliminate much of this trivia. Thus a stronger correlation with population turnover is to be expected.

The important point to be seen from these results is that these differential patterns of correlation between types of offense and population turnover are virtually indistinguishable from those found in contemporary data. The recent data are thought to be of relatively high quality.

They are not based on prisoners, but on the volume of reported offenses. Immense efforts have gone into making the *UCR* more complete and reliable during the past few years. Moreover, the creation of Standard Metropolitan Statistical Areas (SMSAs) provides us with more and better units of analysis than states. Yet, even with states as the units of analysis, the 1926 data sustain precisely the same substantive conclusions as do the modern data. These results inspire faith in the validity of the old data as measures of the underlying crime rates.

A second major element in conceptions of the moral community is the strength of institutions devoted to inculcating moral conformity—the churches. While Durkheim defined religion as that which bound members into a moral community (1915), he regarded religion as such as an epiphenomenon. In *Suicide* (1897) he argued that religion is nothing more than a reflection of social integration and dismissed the possibility that religious belief and participation make an independent contribution to sustaining the moral order.

In earlier work we have rejected Durkheim's claims. We have found strong effects of religion on crime, on delinquency, and on suicide—effects that remain significant when measures of social integration, such as population turnover, are controlled (Stark, Doyle, and Kent, 1980; Stark, Doyle, and Rushing, 1983; Bainbridge and Stark, 1981). Turning to Table 2 we see that our contemporary findings on the relationship between church membership rates and crime rates are replicated fully. Even the magnitudes of the comparable correlations are nearly the same. The only important variation is in robbery, and this for the reasons we have discussed above.

Skeptics might dismiss Table 1 as a stroke of good luck. Table 2 pushes the notion of luck beyond all reasonable probabilities. Using two quite different and theoretically important social control variables, a whole series of subtle relationships are fully replicated using the 1926 data. We submit that this demonstrates the worth of the data.

Table 2
Correlations between Church Membership and Criminal Conviction—1926 (states)

Conviction Offense	Church Membership Rate	
	r	Significance
Forgery	-.56	.001
Larceny	-.50	.001
Burglary	-.42	.001
Rape	-.40	.005
Robbery	-.33	.02
Homicide	-.24	.07
Assault	-.16	NS
Total	.46	.001

Reconceptualizing Deviance

We have noted that not all varieties of crime relate equally strongly to our two elements of the moral community. Indeed, the patterns of weaker and stronger relationships are identical between our two independent variables, both in 1926 and in the early 1970s. Examination of the patterns of the 1970s data led us to suggest that the concept of deviance needed to be reconsidered. Indeed, we have argued that there are two distinct kinds of deviance, only one of which is germane to current sociological theories, while the other seems to have provided the basis for the personality theories of deviance.

A review of sociological theories of deviance reveals a common element. Each regards deviance as a pattern of activities having significant *duration* and based on *conscious motivation*—or at least self-awareness. The portrait of the deviant found in social theory, then, is of a conscious actor who knowingly departs from the dominant moral order and who sustains his deviance for a considerable time.

However, when we closely examine various crimes, some fit this description but others do not. Burglary fits the sociological conception of deviance. The typical burglar is someone fully aware of the illegality of his or her actions, who plans such actions, who has acquired certain basic skills pertinent to entering premises and selecting and selling loot, and who engages in a series of such offenses. But this imagery does not fit the usual homicide. Few murders are premeditated. Typically they occur during a sudden burst of rage followed by deep remorse. Rarely is the offense repeated. Murder, then, often is not prompted by conscious motivation and does not represent a sustained pattern of deviance.

We have divided deviance into two classes based on the differences typical between burglars and murderers. On the one hand are cases of *intentional deviance*, having the character of *calculation* and *duration*. On the other hand are cases of *impulsive deviance*, lacking both calculation and duration. Instead, they represent momentary acts of nonconformity that do not entail conscious exit from the moral order (Stark and Crutchfield, forthcoming).

The utility of this reconceptualization is that it clarifies the pattern of strong and weak correlations between variables tapping social control and various types of offenses. The bulk of offenses in such categories of crime as forgery, burglary, and larceny are acts of intentional deviance. The same is true of rape. Elsewhere we have reported that the majority of rapists are repeaters who go out in search of a victim and who take measures to prevent apprehension. On the other hand, the bulk of offenses categorized as homicide and assault are committed by people who don't "know what they are doing" in the sense of acting on the basis of calculation or continuing their deviance over a sustained period. People usually kill and batter other people because of uncontrolled (possibly uncontrollable) rage. It is true that some people persist in assaultive behavior. But for many of these, the pattern is chronic loss of control, not sustained intention. These are impulsive deviants.

In our work on contemporary data, robbery appeared an anomaly. Our impression of the average robber was of an intentional deviant. Yet robbery, like homicide and assault, was hardly related to such social control variables as population turnover and church membership. That is, the offense fails to respond to social control, which suggests it is impulsive deviance. More careful assessment of what actually goes into the *UCR* robbery category revealed that in fact, a large proportion of robberies are impulsive crimes, often committed by the intoxicated, the deranged, and by people with no prior pattern of offense who simulated a weapon and committed a hold-up on the spur of the moment. As mentioned above, incarcerated robbers are not representative of these impulsive robbers and thus robbery in the 1920s data should in fact correlate with social control—as it does.

Reconceptualizing deviance into impulsive and intentional varieties does more than clear up stable empirical anomalies. Such a reconceptualization specifies the scope of sociological theories of deviance. Thus control theory, for example, only pertains to factors that deter individuals from violating the moral order. People who do not stop to think of the consequences of their actions cannot be deterred. Indeed, we suggest that this explains the failure of many recent attempts to apply subcultural theories of deviance to interpersonal violence (Erlanger, 1974; Ball-Rokeach, 1973). Most such behavior is not conformity to "different" norms. It is unrelated to perceptions of the norms. It is unreflective, impulsive, and episodic.

By recognizing the limits on sociological theories we also can see that they are more empirically potent than has been suggested. Many weak or negative empirical findings are the results of testing sociological theories on measures of deviance to which they do not pertain. Recognizing that our theories deal only with some kinds of deviance also could end the long battle between sociology, on the one hand, and psychology and psychiatry, on the other, over causes of deviant behavior. In our judgment this dispute stems from both sides using a too-global concept of deviance. Sociologists have rightfully resented efforts by psychologists to shrink rational actors deviating in pursuit of calculated gain to people who are "sick." But, sociological theories have little to say about behavior that stems from weak impulse control or from pathologies that arise in intimate interpersonal relations. Impulsive deviance probably is the proper domain of psychologists.

Elsewhere, we pursue these matters at length. Here we must suggest that our successful replication of relationships found in contemporary data indicates that our reconceptualization does not rest on a momentary anomaly. We find equal justification for distinguishing intentional and impulsive deviance in the 1920s. And this, in turn, offers increased confidence in the 1920s data....

Moral Communities and Delinquency

On theoretical grounds we would expect delinquency to respond to elements of social control in the same way as do crime and other forms of deviance. The bulk of serious delinquent offenses, like the total crime rate, is made up of intentional property crimes committed by persons with a pattern of such offenses. This is particularly the case for juveniles sentenced to detention. Thus, rates of serious juvenile offenses, inferred from detention rates, ought to vary in response to church membership and to population turnover.

However, there is reason to suggest that, at least near the turn of the century, juvenile detention rates may not in fact correlate in the expected way with these elements of social control. Suppose that in some parts of the country juvenile offenders were generally ignored and only a few of the most serious offenders were brought before the courts (and then treated mainly as adults). Suppose that in other parts of the country juveniles were brought before special juvenile courts whenever they were detected in unlawful actions, that particular emphasis was give to close surveillance of suspicious juveniles, and that special institutions existed to detain juvenile offenders so they would not be thrown in with an adult convict population. Finally, suppose that juvenile justice systems were instituted first in communities with relatively low rates of crime and delinquency as an expression of the greater moral solidarity of these communities—their heightened concern to save children from a life of crime and punishment. In such circumstances one would expect the highest rates of juvenile detention in those communities where elements of social control were the strongest.

This list of suppositions is in accord with historical accounts of the origins of the juvenile justice system in the United States. The juvenile justice system seems to have been the result of a social movement that began early in the nineteenth century and culminated in the introduction of children's tribunals over the first quarter of the twentieth century (Platt, 1969).

As in the case with many social movements, this one spread via the influence of committed proselytizers, notably judge Benjamin Lindsey and social worker Jane Addams. Lindsey in particular was quite often sought by individuals, organizations, and communities interested in establishing a local court (Larsen, 1972). He became a well known and convincing lobbyist for juvenile court legislation. Parenthetically, it is interesting to note that Lindsey was a judge in Denver, and the 1923 statistics show that Colorado had the third highest rate of admission of juveniles to detention of the forty-five states which published complete reports. Thus, one result of the movement may have been to produce high detention rates in those areas where it was most active.

This movement, like others, could succeed only where there were resources for its mobilization (Oberschall, 1973). It was characterized more by a concern for children than for lowering the incidence of crime, and therefore was more readily accepted by communities who saw it as a plausible way of addressing children's problems (Larsen, 1972; Mennel, 1973). Since one important resource was a socially conscious local population, one would expect this movement to succeed most rapidly in places characterized by high solidarity and by shared moral concerns. Such places, we suggest, would generally be those where religious participation was greater than average. Since strong religion is an expression of strong community, this factor would produce a *positive* correlation between detention of juvenile delinquents and the church membership rate. This works against the underlying tendency for religion to correlate *negatively* with delinquency itself.

Similarly, communities will be more easily mobilized to introduce such innovations as juvenile justice systems to the extent that they have a settled, stable population. That is, we would not expect the first juvenile systems to appear in rapidly growing boom towns or in wild and wide open communities, even if these communities had the highest rates of juvenile offenses. Rather, we would expect the juvenile justice system to appear first in communities with little population turnover.

This line of analysis is consistent with that expressed by those committed to the "child-saver" interpretation of recent history. However, we do not want to confuse the first stages of the spread of the juvenile justice system with its eventual operation after it was universally in operation. Nor need we accept the harsh characterizations of the child-savers as meddlesome class enemies of the less-repressed and boisterous lower-class youths. There also is no reason to suppose that the early juvenile courts committed the innocent and virtuous simply because detention rates might have been higher in communities with lower actual

Table 3
Church Membership, Migration, and Delinquency—1910, 1923, 1971

	Correlation (r) for States			
	Church Membership Rate		Proportion Born in Another State	
Delinquency Rate	r	Significance	r	Significance
1910:				
Juveniles in detention	.22	.09	-.19	.12
Admitted to detention	.31	.02	-.09	NS
1923:				
Juveniles in detention	-.12	NS	.16	NS
Admitted to detention		NS	-.01	NS
1971:				
Juveniles in detention	-.37	.005	.58	.001
Adjudicated delinquent	-.32	.02	..53	.001
Admitted to training schools etc.	-.36	.005	44	.001

Note: The number of states varies from 41 to 48, depending on availability of delinquency data.

rates of offenses. It could as plausibly be the case that detention rates were lower in communities with higher offense rates simply because of the failure of these communities to take needed action.

As it happens, quite good data exist to test various interpretations of the child-saver thesis. The first of these data are for 1910, a time when the juvenile justice system had been instituted in only some parts of the country. Data are available for forty-eight states on the rate of juveniles in detention and the rate at which juveniles were admitted to detention.

Table 3 shows that in fact there is a *positive* correlation between each of these measures of juvenile detention (rate of juveniles in detention and rate of admissions to detention) and the church membership rate (created by interpolating data from the 1906 and 1916 religious censuses). Since we know that church membership was negatively related to adult incarceration rates in 1910, it seems reasonable to infer that church membership also was negatively related to the rate of juvenile offenses. If that is so, then the data do support the idea expressed by the child-saver historians that the juvenile justice system was a response to community concern about wayward young people, not to an unusually severe problem with delinquency. We also see in Table 3 that population turnover is negatively related to juvenile detention rates (albeit the relationships are weak), which also is the reverse of the probable correlation with actual rates of offense. Taken together it seems fair to say that in 1910 it was in states that most closely approximated moral communities that the juvenile justice system was generating the highest rates of detention.

But, as we already have pointed out, this does not mean these communities were the victims of an unfounded ideology of child-saving, nor does it mean that the juvenile justice system, whatever its origins, has continued to reflect primarily community standards rather than actual juvenile behavior. Indeed, when we look at the data for 1923, also shown in Table 3, we see little trace of the correlations found for 1910.[3] In the ensuing thirteen years the juvenile justice system had appeared in many more communities. No longer were only the most solid communities processing juvenile offenders in a special legal system. The juvenile justice system still was not operating everywhere, and thus it still probably does not reflect rates of offense. But neither do the data any longer give good support to a continuation of the child-saver thesis.

Now look at the data for 1971. Once again there are strong correlations. But now the signs are the *reverse* of those for 1910. In 1971, church membership rates were strongly negatively correlated with juvenile incarceration and adjudication rates. And population turnover was very strongly positively correlated with these juvenile rates. Thus, with the passage of time the moral communities have come to have low rates of juvenile detention, while the communities with less solidarity have come to have high rates.

We interpret these trends as evidence about where the juvenile justice system first came into place—in communities with relatively low rates of juvenile offenses. We suggest that it was in fact the very aspects of these communities that deterred deviance that enabled them to be the first to enact juvenile programs. However, with the passage of time, as juvenile programs became universal they functioned in response to real conditions. That is, communities with the most severe rates of juvenile offenses became the ones with the highest rates of juvenile detention.

In our judgment these are interesting, but not surprising, historical trends. We also would not be surprised to learn that the first communities to introduce compulsory education were also the ones with the highest rates for punishing truancy. We fail to see how such patterns would justify elaborate imputations of a false sense of reality or diatribes about imposing middle-class standards on the poor. We would suppose that compulsory education was meant primarily to ensure that poor children got the benefits of schooling. In similar fashion we suggest that the juvenile justice system arose in response to a *real* problem—the existence of juvenile offenders who might benefit from not being ignored and not being thrown into the adult justice system. Surely juvenile offenses were a universal problem. Simply because communities that acted first were not those with the worst problem in no way discredits their action, nor does it warrant praise for those communities that endured high delinquency rates without acting. Perhaps the juvenile justice system has failed to produce the many benefits expected of it by the early reformers who pushed for its adoption. Many reforms do not live up to expectations. But such failures surely are not prima facie evidence that the reformers were either foolish or wicked. And surely there is something to be said in favor of a system that prevented 12-year-olds from being sent off to adult prisons.

Conclusion

Our aims in this paper were both substantive and pedagogical. Substantively, we have used a variety of pre-1930 data to replicate many findings from our contemporary research. We have reconfirmed our findings that population turnover and church membership reflect basic elements of "moral communities." We have also replicated the pattern of strong and weak correlations between these elements of social control and various kinds of crime. This encourages us in our view that deviance needs to be reconceptualized into two varieties, *intentional* and *impulsive* deviance. Sociological theories have much to tell us about the conditions under which intentional deviance occurs. But they have little to say about the causes of impulsive deviance. Failure to note this distinction can lead to inappropriate applications and empirical tests of sociological theories.

Our pedagogical aims were to demonstrate the existence and validity of a variety of data on deviance before 1930. Our ability to replicate closely results based on contemporary data in analyses of these old data sets appears to demonstrate their worth. One can postulate many *possible* sources of error and bias in any data set. But that does not demonstrate that such defects actually exist. We think we have demonstrated that, had social scientists analyzed these data during the 1920s, their empirical results would have stood the test of time. Indeed, our comparisons between the old and the contemporary data did not merely produce "ball park" similarities, but very close, fine-grained correspondence. Data are good enough when they produce good results. Indeed, what other standard can be applied to data?

In closing, we must point out that our use of these data barely scratches their potential. An extraordinary number of good studies can be done using these forgotten data sets. We hope this paper will encourage others to use these valuable materials.

Notes

1. There are such data going back for many decades for some states and for many cities and counties. We suggest that many important questions concerning the rise and fall of offenses could be studied on the basis of data for a variety of local units.
2. Despite the popularity of subcultural theories of deviance among early sociologists and criminologists, the proportion of foreign-born is not related to crime as measured by incarceration rates.
3. Examination of scatter plots alerted us that Rhode Island was an extraordinarily deviant, outlying case that made it appear as if there were correlations in the 1923 data. Rhode Island had a reported juvenile admission rate of 615 per 100,000, four times the national average and twice as high as that for the second highest state. We are unable to determine whether this was a typographical error, a reporting error, or if some special circumstances (such as housing juveniles from elsewhere) were involved. We judged the reasonable solution to be the elimination of Rhode Island from the analysis—especially since Rhode Island is not a deviant case in other years.

References

Bainbridge, W.S., and R. Stark. 1981. "Homicide, Suicide, and Religion." *The Annual Review of the Social Sciences of Religion*, Volume 5. The Hague, The Netherlands: Mouton.

Ball-Rokeach, S.J. 1973. "Values and Violence: A Test of the Subculture of Violence Thesis." *American Sociological Review* 38 (6): 736-749.

Bonacich, E. 1976. "Advanced Capitalism and Black/White Race Relations in the United States: A Split Labor Market Interpretation." *American Sociological Review* 41 (1): 34-51.

Chambliss, W.J., and R.B. Seidman. 1971. *Law, Order, and Power*. Menlo Park, Calif.: Addison-Wesley.

Crutchfield, R.D., M. Geerken, and W. Gove. Forthcoming. "Crime Rates and Social Integration: The Impact of Metropolitan Mobility." *Criminology*.

Douglas, J.D. 1967. *The Social Meaning of Suicide*. Princeton, N.J.: Princeton University Press.

Durkheim, E. 1897. *Suicide: A Study in Sociology*, J.A. Spaulding and G. Simpson, trans. New York: Free Press.

———. 1915. *The Elementary Forms of the Religious Life*. London: Allen and Unwin.

Erlanger, H.S. 1974. "Social Class and Corporal Punishment in Childrearing: A Reassessment." *American Sociological Review* 39 (1): 68-85.

Hechter, M. 1978. "Group Formation and the Cultural Division of Labor." *American Journal of Sociology* 84 (2): 293-318.

Hindenlang, M.J. 1978. "Race and Involvement in Common Law Personal Crimes." *American Sociological Review* 43 (1): 93-109.

Hindenlang, M.J., T. Hirschi, and J.G. Weis. 1979. "Correlates of Delinquency: The Illusion of Discrepancy between Self-Report and Official Measures." *American Sociological Review* 44 (6):995-1014.

Larsen, C.E. 1972. *The Good Fight: The Life and Times of Ben B. Lindsey*. Chicago: Quadrangle Books.

Mennel, R.M. 1973. *Thorns and Thistles: Juvenile Delinquency in the United States, 1825-1940*. Hanover, N.H.: University Press of New England.

National Commission on Law Observance and Enforcement. 1931. *Commission Reports*. Washington, D.C.: Govt. Printing Office.

Oberschall, A. 1973 *Social Conflict and Social Movements*. Englewood Cliffs, N.J.: Prentice-Hall.

Platt, A. M. 1969. *The Child Savers: The Invention of Delinquency*. Chicago: University of Chicago Press.

Stark, R., and W.S. Bainbridge. 1980. "Secularization, Revival, and Cult Formation." *The Annual Review of the Social Sciences of Religion, Volume 4*. The Hague, The Netherlands: Mouton.

Stark, R., W.S. Bainbridge, and L. Kent. 1981. "Cult Membership in the Roaring Twenties." *Sociological Analysis* 42 (2):137-162.

Stark, R., and R. Crutchfield. Forthcoming. "Reconceptualizing Deviance."

Stark, R., D.P. Doyle, and L. Kent. 1980. "Rediscovering Moral Communities: Church Membership and Crime." In *Understanding Crime: Current Theory and Research*, T. Hirschi and M. Gottfredson, eds. Beverly Hills, Calif.: Sage. Pp. 43-52.

Stark, R., D.P. Doyle, and J.L. Rushing. 1983. "Beyond Durkheim: Religion and Suicide." *Journal for the Scientific Study of Religion*.

Stark, R., L. Kent, and D.P. Doyle. 1982. "Religion and Delinquency: The Ecology of a 'Lost' Relationship." *Journal of Research in Crime and Delinquency* 18 (2): 4-24.

U.S. Bureau of the Census. 1918. *Prisoners and Juvenile Delinquents in the United States—1910*. Washington, D.C.: Govt. Printing Office.

———. 1927. *Children under Institutional Care—1923*. Washington, D.C.: Govt. Printing Office. ✦

Section VIII
Deterrence and Labeling

From its inception, the juvenile justice system has been under fire from all sides, often for contradictory reasons. Since juvenile proceedings and records are closed to the public, most people hear about the juvenile court only when a dramatic case involving a serious crime such as murder is covered by the news media. The possibility that a teenager might serve only a few years should the court decide to treat the offender as a juvenile upsets a considerable number of people, who regard such a decision as a potential injustice to the victim and to the community. Such a punishment would not "fit the crime," and even a remote chance of such an occurrence gives rise to criticism of the juvenile justice system in general.

The juvenile justice system is judged harshly for merely carrying out the legal process required by law for making decisions about childhood and adult responsibility. The laws requiring such deliberation have come under attack, and an increasing number of states have lowered the age at which a juvenile is tried as an adult for several kinds of offenses. Indeed, while variations in the use of the death penalty have not been treated as particularly relevant to the study of juvenile delinquency, the fact that an increasing number of juveniles are dealt with by the criminal justice system qualifies it as a relevant topic in contemporary debate.

Periodic outbursts of alarm about juvenile crime and the role of the juvenile court in dealing with the problem focus on situations where the offender could avoid harsher punishment if the case was dealt with in the juvenile system. Of course, such cases account for a minute amount of the activity of the juvenile court. In addition, older juveniles who have committed the most serious crimes are likely to be remanded or waived to the adult system. In the current cycle of public alarm (see Bernard, Section I), it is easy to overlook the fact that the juvenile court and juvenile law have been criticized at other times for being "too tough" and indiscriminate in the punishment of juveniles, as well as for not affording due-process-of-law rights.

Most people are not aware of the fact that many of the rights of due process, including bail, jury trials, transcripts, attorneys at intake and disposition, have not been constitutionally extended to juvenile proceedings. Since the common opinion is that the juvenile justice system is too "soft," people are often surprised to learn that the initial Supreme Court case (*In re Gault,* 1967) extending some modicum of due process to juveniles involved a case in which a youth had been sentenced to several years in a training school for an offense that would have been a misdemeanor, resulting in a fine, for an adult. Observing enough ways in which the juvenile justice system is tougher on juveniles than the adult system is on adults led Ira Schwartz (Director of the Office of Juvenile Justice and Delinquency Prevention under President Jimmy Carter) to write a book, *(In)justice for Juveniles* (1988). In contrast, Alfred Regnery (Director of the same office under President Ronald Reagan) wrote an article critical of the juvenile justice system on the grounds that juveniles were "Getting Away with Murder" (1986), calling for "criminals to be treated as criminals."

Critiques of the juvenile court tend to arise in situations where the punishment may not fit the crime or where offenders may not be incapacitated for a sufficient amount of time to satisfy the public. Hence, *punishment* and *incapacitation* are highlighted as mandates for the juvenile justice system. It is easy to overlook the fact that the vast volume of cases dealt with by the system do not fall in that category and that the nonpunitive orientation of the court may be appropriate for most of the cases it handles. The juvenile court is subject to conflicting expectations and must make thousands of decisions about the appropriate responses to a wide range of different types of cases and individual situations.

The poll data summarized in Section I of this reader indicated that the public generally wants differentiation among juvenile offenders with a tough, punitive response for the most serious offenders and an emphasis on rehabilitation for others. The response to serious offenses should be severe enough to deter other juveniles *(general deterrence)*, discourage future offenses among those punished *(specific deterrence)*, protect society through imprisonment *(incapacitation)*, and reestablish justice for society and victims *(retribution)*. On the other hand, for many (if not most) youth who come into contact with the system, the public is likely to support responses that avoid undue stigma and public attention and work through the youth's parents or guardians to prevent further problems.

Most people agree that responses should be different for different types of offenses. This agreement is one of the reasons for anger about the potential for lax responses to serious offenders. However, the juvenile justice system has been criticized for treating nonserious offenders too severely as well. Until mid-1970s, youths would be punished by the juvenile court both for offenses that would be crimes for adults and for noncriminal problems with the adult world, which labeled the youths as "status offenders," "in need of supervision," or "incorrigible." In fact, reports on juvenile justice in the early 1970s (Lerman 1971) provided evidence that youths committing criminal violations were less likely to be detained or sent to secure confinement than youths who had run away or were charged with other status offenses limited to those under eighteen years of age. Such lack of differentiation violated norms of retributive justice and led critics to challenge the indiscriminate stigmatization of youth.

Not only did indiscriminate intervention violate norms of retributive justice, but juvenile court labeling and processing was also thought to propel youth into careers of more serious crime. A common recommendation for the juvenile justice system was expressed by one of the most prominent labeling theorists, Edwin Shur, as "leave kids alone whenever possible" (1973: 155). While the more radical interpretations of labeling theory called for nonintervention, the actual policy outcome took the form of movements to get status offenders out of institutions (deinstitutionalization) and to "divert" new status offenders into community-based programs (diversion). These ideas were incorporated into national legislation and led to a great reduction in the number of girls held in some form of secure confinement.

The readings in this section illustrate the relevance of deterrence theory and labeling theory to the study of juvenile justice and juvenile delinquency. The first article, by Sharla Rausch, focuses on the diversion movement of the 1970s and 1980s. The movement was based on the view that the indiscriminate processing of status offenders together with delinquent offenders leads to escalating offense careers. From the perspective of deterrence theory, an early, severe intervention for status offenses would have specific deterrent effects for future offending and would lower the odds of future trouble. In contrast, labeling theorists lead us to expect that such intervention would make matters worse in the future. Rausch tests hypotheses derived from the two perspectives, using data on status offenders in Connecticut.

The second reading tests hypotheses involving "general deterrence." If general deterrence processes are at work, then increases in the perceived risk of punishment in the general audience to punishment should lower the odds of future offenses. Nagin and Paternoster couple ideas about the "conditioning" effects of social and moral costs with deterrence hypotheses predicting inverse relations between the risk of legal sanctions and self-reported delinquency. There has been more support for the hypothesis that perceived risk of legal sanctions affects delinquency in the juvenile population (i.e., general deterrence) than for the view that punishment deters those punished from future involvement in delinquency.

The last selection, by Peterson and Bailey, deals with the effect of capital punishment on felony murder. Using monthly homicide statistics and data on executions and the amount of television publicity accorded executions, they test two hypotheses. The traditional deterrence hypothesis suggests that heightened fear of the death penalty in the wake of publicized executions will deter premeditated homicides or homicides occurring in the course of the commitment of other crimes. They also examine the possibility that such executions increase the probability of homicide, an hypothesis based on "brutalization theory." Brutalization theorists argue that legal violence correlates with illegal violence and that surges in executions may lead to *increases* rather than decreases in homicide. As more and more juveniles are liable for execution at younger and younger ages, the deterrent or brutalizing effect of the death penalty is of increasing relevance to juvenile delinquency and youth crime.

References

Lerman, Paul. "Child Convicts." *Trans-Action* 8 (July/August 1971):35–45.

Regnery, Alfred. "Getting Away with Murder: Why the Justice System Needs an Overhaul." *Policy Review* (Fall 1986):65–68.

Schwartz, Ira M. *(In)justice for Juveniles: Rethinking the Best Interests of Children*. Lexington, MA: D.C. Heath and Company, 1989.

Shur, Edwin M. *Radical Nonintervention: Rethinking the Delinquency Problem*. Englewood Cliffs, N.J.: Prentice-Hall, 1973. ✦

29
Court Processing Versus Diversion of Status Offenders: A Test of Deterrence and Labeling Theories

Sharla Rausch

The juvenile justice system remains under attack. Founded on the social and legal philosophy of *parens patriae*, the juvenile court justified its discretionary decision making and relative lack of procedural safeguards by asserting that it was acting in the best interest of the child (Platt, 1977). Criticisms regarding the juvenile court have pertained mainly to the broad use of this discretion and the resulting discrimination in decision making, as well as to the court's failure to meet its rehabilitative goals. In fact, current criticisms levied by proponents of the labeling perspective indicate that the juvenile court may even promote delinquent careers. Thus, instead of being championed as a protector of children, the juvenile justice system is perceived by many as something from which children need protection.

The controversy centers around whether or not contact with the juvenile court results in the propagation of a deviant self-concept and eventually a deviant career. Two divergent theoretical perspectives lie at the heart of this controversy. One, the labeling perspective, contends that juvenile court processing stigmatizes an individual as deviant, and that this labeling, in turn, may result in the development of a deviant self-concept, further law-breaking behavior, and eventually a career in crime. In contrast, the deterrence perspective asserts that juvenile court processing deters further involvement in delinquency.[1]

Status offenses—that is, behavior for which only minors can be referred to court—provide a particularly appropriate context for the comparison of these two theories. Although empirically disputed by Thomas (1976), among others, it is widely believed that status offenders occupy some sort of predelinquent position that leaves them especially vulnerable to societal reaction. Thus, according to this view, the discrepant effects of juvenile court predicted by the labeling and deterrence hypotheses should be particularly strong for status offenders. Therefore, following a brief review of the labeling and deterrence perspectives, this paper will compare the effects on subsequent deviant activities of a program for the diversion of status offenders with the effects of regular juvenile court contact and processing.

Labeling Theory

From the labeling perspective, a deviant career does not emerge directly from an initial act of deviance. It is the imposition of the deviant label by a social audience and the reaction of the individual to this labeling that results in a deviant career. This is particularly the case if the application of the label occurs through a degradation ceremony (e.g., juvenile court processing) and the individual is thus forced to join a deviant group (Matza, 1964) because of newly reduced legitimate opportunities and a now negative self-image (Erikson, 1962).

Studies of the effect of juvenile court labeling on subsequent delinquent behavior have not been overwhelmingly supportive of the labeling perspective. Most have been fraught with methodological weaknesses and have produced, at best, conflicting results (Mahoney, 1974; Klein, 1977). In his critique of the more methodologically sound studies of labeling theory, Tittle (1975a:175) indicates that there is only the

From *Journal of Research in Crime and Delinquency*, Volume 20 (January 1983), pp. 39-54. Copyright © 1983 by Sage Publications, Inc. Reprinted by permission.

weakest support for the labeling perspective: "The most that can be concluded is that social disadvantages may have some effect on labeling and that labeling may have some influence in producing criminal behavior." In his review of the few studies pertaining to early sanctioning effects, Klein (1981) also found slightly greater support for the negative effect of sanctions on future criminal conduct.

Broad reviews indicating a general inability to show treatment effects on criminal or delinquent conduct (Bailey, 1966; Logan, 1972; Martinson, 1974; Blomberg, 1980) also have implications for the labeling perspective. Hirschi (1975) observes that when treatment programs are ranked by the extent to which youths are left alone, it becomes apparent that the inability to show differential treatment effects also implies an inability to show differential labeling effects. Thus Schur's (1973:155) mandate to "leave the kids alone whenever possible" cannot be justified on strictly empirical grounds.

Deterrence Theory

The basic assumption of deterrence theory is that an actor will not participate in deviant behavior if previously experienced punishment or if perceptions regarding the risk of punishment for a particular act suggest that the risks involved outweigh the potential rewards of the act. Despite methodological and interpretative problems associated with recidivism studies (Tittle and Logan, 1973), there appears to be some support for the deterrence argument. With specific regard to delinquency, McEachern et al. (1968) found that there was a decrease in deviant offenses during a one-year follow-up among those delinquents who were under the control of the court. Berg et al. (1978) used a random allocation design to determine the relative effectiveness of two court procedures on truancy. They found that youths who reported regularly to court were substantially less likely to be truant *and* committed fewer criminal offenses than youths who were under the supervision of the social services department. In a follow-up study of the participants of the Cambridge-Somerville youth program, McCord (1980:11) also found that those youths who had been fined for their first conviction were less likely to commit subsequent crimes than were those who had been released without official processing, prompting her to conclude that a "light touch of the law is less effective in deterring crime than is a penalty that clearly shows that an action has been judged to be wrong."

The deterrent effect of a sanction may depend on the individual's history of deviance. A sanction may have more effect on a novice than on a veteran (Thorsell and Klemke, 1972). An individual may become too entrenched in a deviant subculture to care greatly about a label, or may have found that the pleasures associated with the deviant act outweigh the sanctions that are attached to the behavior (Tittle, 1975; Lemert, 1958; Cameron, 1966). If status offenders have relatively little experience with delinquency or with juvenile court, regular court processing might serve to deter them from, rather than to label and commit them to, further delinquency.

In sum, while labeling theory would predict that children processed through the courts will be more recidivistic than those diverted from the courts, deterrence theory would predict the opposite. In the present research, we intend to determine which prediction is better supported by the facts in the case of juveniles referred to detention centers in Connecticut for the commission of status offenses.

Connecticut's Treatment Models

The interpretation of results for the present research is not as straightforward as the above would suggest, however, because the program in question is not merely one of regular court processing versus complete diversion. The program, referred to as the Connecticut Deinstitutionalization of Status Offenders (DSO) project, was designed to compare alternative forms of treatment along two dimensions: (1) court- versus community-based treatment and (2) maximum versus minimum degree of intervention. Thus, the effects of four treatment models, not just two, are being examined. The four treatment groups are: (1) a preprogram comparison group, who received normal court processing and disposition; (2) DSO clients in District 1,[2] implementing the community-based, minimum intervention model, who received crisis intervention counseling aimed at resolving only immediate distress and returning the child quickly to the resources of the family and community, (3) DSO clients in District 2, implementing the court-based, minimum intervention model, who received the same treatment as did clients in District 1, but from probation officers rather than from community agencies, and (4) DSO clients in District 3, implementing the community-based, maximum intervention model, who were supposed to receive all the help that could possibly be provided to them.[3] These four groups (referred to as T0, T1, T2, and T3, respectively) can be seen as covering all possible combinations of the indicated dimensions, as depicted in Figure 1. These two dimensions of nature and degree of response to "problem behavior" are significant to both labeling and deterrence theories. Figure 2 provides a summary of the relative rates of recidivism predicted under labeling and deterrence theories based on these dimensions.

Figure 1
Treatment Models in the Connecticut DSO Project

	Minimum Intervention	Maximum Intervention
Court-based	T2 DSO District 2	T0 Preprogram
Community-based	T1 DSO District 1	T3 DSO District 3

With respect to nature of treatment, the labeling perspective predicts that regular court processing of status offenders will be more stigmatizing than will community-based treatment and therefore will produce

Figure 2
Relative Rates of Recidivism Predicted under Labeling and Deterrence Theories

| | Labeling Theory | | Deterrence Theory | |
	Minimum	Maximum	Minimum	Maximum
Court-based	Medium	Highest	Higher	Medium	Lowest	Lower
Community-based	Lowest	Medium	Lower	Highest	Medium	Higher

higher rates of recidivism. On the other hand, deterrence theory suggests that regular court processing (especially at the initial stage of deviance) is more painful or costly than is community-based treatment and will therefore produce lower rates of recidivism.

With respect to degree of intervention, deterrence theory predicts lower rates of recidivism associated with maximum intervention, while labeling theory predicts lower rates of recidivism with minimum intervention. Again, the rationale is the same. According to labeling theory, the greater the degree of intervention, the greater the stigmatizing effect. According to deterrence theory, the greater the degree of intervention, the greater the deterrent effect.

In making predictions based on the two dimensions in interaction (table cells), labeling theory predicts that the lowest recidivism rates will occur with minimum intervention by a community-based program, and the highest recidivism rates will occur through maximum intervention by the court. Deterrence theory predicts that maximum intervention by the court will result in the least recidivism, while minimum intervention by a community-based program will result in the most recidivism.

For both theoretical perspectives, community-maximum and court-minimum cells represent a conjunction of a high value on one dimension and a low value on the other; therefore, for both perspectives, we can expect medium rates for both of these cells. The model provides no basis for predicting higher rates in one cell than the other on those diagonals.

Methodology

Data Source

Data collected as part of a federally-funded evaluation of the Connecticut DSO project served as the data source for this study. These data were obtained from computerized juvenile court records for both preprogram and DSO program youths, and standardized forms containing additional demographic and legal information for each status offender entering the DSO program.

Because a recommended control group was not incorporated into the Connecticut DSO project design (See Logan et al., 1978, for a discussion of the problems associated with the implementation of the DSO project), a quasi-experimental research design was employed, consisting of a comparison of the four treatment groups on subsequent referrals to court. The preprogram group was chosen in such a way as to make it comparable to the three DSO groups with respect to program eligibility criteria. All status offenders coming to detention were considered eligible except juveniles whose instant offense included charges other than a status offense, juveniles with prior criminal charges still pending, and status offenders who were already under the supervision of the juvenile court at the time of detention.[4]

The total combined sample consisted of 350 status offenders, broken down as follows: preprogram comparison group ($n = 201$), community-based minimum intervention model ($n = 18$), court-based minimum intervention model ($n = 94$), and community-based maximum intervention model ($n = 47$).[5] These numbers varied slightly in the analyses (Tables 1, 2, and 3) because of missing values on some of the variables.

Measurement

Dependent Variable. Recidivism was operationalized as the number of subsequent referrals to the juvenile court during a six-month follow-up period.[6] For the DSO clients, this period was six months from the date of entry into the DSO program. For the preprogram subjects, it was six months from the detentions that would have made them eligible for the DSO program, had it existed at the time. For the purpose of meeting the requirements of multiple classification analysis, the dependent variable was dichotomized (success = no subsequent referrals; failure = one or more subsequent referrals.)[7]

Independent Variable. Treatment was operationalized as the four treatment categories described above (T0, T1, T2, T3).

Control Variables. Several control variables were included in the initial analysis due to their significance in both theoretical perspectives. These control factors include: race (*nonwhite*, which includes blacks, Indians, and Latin Americans; and *white*), sex (*male* and *female*), town size (*small*, indicating a population under 50,000; and *large*, indicating a population of 50,000 or more),[8] prior number of referrals (*none* and *one or more*), offense type (*runaway*, *beyond control*, and *other*, which includes truancy and combination charges), parental occupation (*blue collar* and *white collar*),[9] family status (*not intact*, which includes cases where parents are divorced, separated, dead, or the

Table 1
Percentage of Status Offenders Recidivating by Treament Models and Control Variables

Control Variable	Percentage Recidivating	(n)	Statistical[a] Significance
Treatment models			.87
T0	47	(196)	
T1	44	(18)	
T2	45	(91)	
T3	40	(45)	
Sex			.07
Male	53	(107)	
Female	42	(243)	
Race			.88
Nonwhite	46	(101)	
White	45	(249)	
Town size			.11
Small	41	(167)	
Large	50	(183)	
Family status			.29
Not intact	47	(95)	
Intact	37	(59)	
Parent(s) occupation			.30
Blue collar	42	(50)	
White collar	30	(44)	
Age at first referral			.02
Low-13	54	(125)	
14-16	40	(220)	
Prior referrals			.09
None	41	(177)	
One or more	50	(173)	
Offense type			.05
Runaway	50	(246)	
Beyond control	37	(51)	
Other	34	(53)	

[a] Using Chi Square and F.

Table 2
Comparison of Control Variables for Treatment Groups

	Treatment Model								Significance[a]
	T0		T1		T2		T4		
	%	(n)	%	(n)	%	(n)	%	(n)	
Sex									.23
Male	31	(61)	11	(2)	34	(32)	26	(12)	
Female	69	(138)	89	(16)	66	(62)	74	(35)	
Race									.88
Nonwhite	28	(56)	22	(4)	30	(28)	32	(15)	
White	72	(143)	78	(14)	70	(66)	68	(32)	
Town size									.85
Small	47	(95)	39	(7)	48	(45)	51	(24)	
Large	53	(106)	61	(11)	52	(49)	49	(23)	
Family status									.30
Not intact			56	(10)	57	(54)	70	(33)	
Intact			44	(8)	43	(40)	30	(14)	
Parent(s) occupation									.85
Blue collar			47	(7)	55	(27)	53	(17)	
White collar			53	(8)	45	(22)	47	(15)	
Age at first referral									.15
Low-13	40	(80)	33	(6)	27	(24)	33	(15)	
14-16	60	(118)	67	(12)	73	(66)	67	(30)	
Prior referrals									.001
None	42	(82)	50	(9)	74	(67)	42	(19)	
One or more	58	(114)	50	(9)	26	(24)	58	(26)	
Offense type									.003
Runaway	71	(143)	94	(17)	62	(57)	79	(37)	
Beyond control	16	(33)	6	(1)	12	(11)	17	(8)	
Other	13	(25)	0	(0)	26	(24)	4	(2)	

[a]Using Chi Square and F.

child is living elsewhere than the nuclear family; and *intact*, where the child is living with both parents), and age at first referral (*younger*, including youths through 13; and *older*, including youths ages 14-16). Only those control variables significantly related to either treatment type or recidivism (see Tables 1 and 2)[10] were retained for the multiple classification analysis. These included sex, age at first referral, prior number of referrals, and offense type.

Statistical Technique

Multiple Classification Analysis (MCA) was employed as a means of determining the relative effect of each treatment program on subsequent referrals while controlling for other variables. MCA is particularly useful where independent variables may have no better than nominal measurement and the dependent variable is internally scaled or dichotomous with two approximately equal frequencies. MCA assumes there is no interaction; preliminary analysis of these variables indicated that our data met this criterion. This technique provides an eta coefficient that indicates the proportion of the total sum of squares explained by each independent variable, and a partial beta that is analogous to the standardized regression coefficient (Andrews et al., 1973; Kim and Kohout, 1975).

Results

Initial Findings

Table 1 shows no difference in recidivism between those status offenders handled by the court in the usual manner and those diverted to each of the DSO programs. Although this table presents recidivism as an absolute dichotomy, the results are comparable when measured as a matter of degree. The average number of subsequent referrals is 0.9 for T0, 0.9 for T1, 1.1 for T2, and 1.0 for T3. Thus, our initial findings indicate no differential effects of treatment on recidivism.

It is possible that differences among the program groups on demographic and legal characteristics may have their own effect on recidivism which may mask the effect of treatment. For example, if a better treatment program receives higher risk clients, this may cancel out the effects of that treatment relative to other treatment programs. Table 1 indicates that higher risk candidates consist of younger status offenders and runaways (at $p < .05$) and, to a statistically weaker extent (at $p < .10$), males and those status offenders with one or more prior referrals.[11] Actually, describing these categories as being "high(er) risk" is a little misleading if that is taken to imply that they make very much difference. A better term might be to describe these categories as carrying "marginal risk."

These marginal risk characteristics are not evenly distributed across treatment groups, as shown in Table 2. There is a significant difference across treatment groups in the distribution of runaways and of status offenders with prior referrals. Although not statistically significant at the .05 level, males and younger status offenders are also differentially distributed across treatment groups.

No one treatment group has the largest proportion of marginal risk candidates for all risk categories. However, each group has the largest proportion of marginal risk candidates for at least one risk characteristic, which may or may not be masking the effect of treatment on recidivism. Given this possibility, the next section will present a multivariate analysis, controlling for those demographic and legal characteristics found to be significantly related to either treatment type or recidivism, in an attempt to separate their effects from those of the treatment programs.

Table 3
Effects of Treatment Models, Sex, Age at First Referral, Prior Number of Referrals, and Offense Type on Recidivism

Predictor	(n)	Deviation from Mean Before Adjusting	Deviation from Mean After Adjusting For Other Predictors	Significance of beta
Treatment				
T0	195	.02	.01	
T1	18	−.01	−.02	
T2	89	−.01	.01	
T3	43	−.06	−.06	
		eta = .05	beta = .05	.83
Sex				
Male	104	.08	.07	
Female	241	−.03	−.03	
		eta = .10	beta = .10	.08
Age at first referral				
Low-13	125	.08	.05	
14-16	220	−.05	−.03	
		eta = .13	beta = .08	.17
Prior referrals				
None	175	−.05	−.04	
Some	170	.05	.04	
		eta = .11	beta = .07	.19
Offense type				
Runaway	241	.04	.04	
Beyond control	51	−.08	−.07	
Other	53	−.11	−.11	
		eta = .13	beta = .12	.09

Grand mean = .45 Multiple R = .212 R^2 = .045 (p = .05)

Multivariate Analysis

The results of the four-model comparison are presented in Table 3. The initial finding of no significant difference across all groups is supported by the MCA.[12] This is the case both before and after the collective influence of the control variables is removed (eta = .05, beta = .05), suggesting that there is no effect of treatment type on recidivism being masked by those marginal risk factors identified earlier in the analysis.

The total amount of variance explained by treatment type and demographic and legal characteristics is less than 5 percent (R^2 = .045, p = .048). This runs counter to the labeling theorists' contention that these demographic and legal factors are of prime importance in predicting who will or will not recidivate. However, it is possible that selectivity on these characteristics during the initial screening is such that the importance of these variables becomes minimal. That is, these variables may be predictive only with respect to who is initially referred to detention.

In any case, the primary finding of interest is that when all demographic and legal characteristics are controlled, treatment type has no direct effect on recidivism. Or, at least, it has no *differential* effect on recidivism. "No differential effect" would mean that each treatment type might have some effect, but for one reason or another their effects are the same, perhaps because the four models are not as different in practice as they appear to be in conception. There is some indication that although their designs differed, they were all implemented in the same manner. Further analysis should concentrate on time under control of a DSO contractor or juvenile court personnel or, for the DSO programs, number of counseling sessions, rather than on the actual treatment models.[13]

"No effect," on the other hand, would mean that none of the treatment types achieved any greater success than would have occurred without the intervention of either the court or the DSO project. Therefore, it is not possible to determine if the treatment types employed were effective or ineffective. To have tested the distinction between "no effect" and "no differential effect" would have required the inclusion of a group of status offenders randomly released immediately on referral to court or to the DSO program. Early in the creation of the program, it was decided by the juvenile court that this would not be acceptable because of their belief that "something must be done" with these youths. Thus, given the experimental design, it was not possible to determine the absolute effect of treatment on recidivism, only that the treatment models did not vary with respect to their effects.

Conclusion

The findings of this study provide no support for either labeling or deterrence theory. It makes no difference, with respect to official recidivism, whether status offenders experience juvenile court processing or a diversion treatment program.[14] In short, labeling theory cannot be used to justify a diversion program for status offenders and deterrence theory cannot be used to justify court processing of status offenders. Insofar as the choice is based upon reducing official recidivism, one could justify equally well either giving everyone a diversion program or processing everyone through juvenile court.

However, it is possible that juvenile court processing and diversion programs are superior to radical nonintervention (i.e., doing nothing). It is also possible that doing nothing is superior to either juvenile court processing or diversion. To have examined this possibility, the emphasis of the Connecticut DSO program should not have been on the differential outcome of court processing versus alternative treatment with respect to official recidivism, but on whether the benefits of such intervention (juvenile court *or* alternative programs) justify its use. The necessity of a totally "untreated" control group for such a determination cannot be emphasized enough.

Notes

1. Juvenile court may be either a deterrent relative to some less severe alternative, such as diversion, or a nondeterrent, relative to a more severe alternative, such as adult court and penal sanctions.
2. There are three judicial districts in Connecticut. Each of the three DSO treatment models was implemented in a different judicial district, while the fourth model (regular court processing) was the norm for all three districts before the DSO project.
3. The emphasis of the two minimum intervention programs was on dealing with the immediate crisis, focusing on the family as a whole. Specifically trained counselors (community-based counselors were used in T1 and probation officers were used in T2) provided up to five crisis counseling sessions with the child and family. In contrast to these two minimum intervention models, the maximum intervention model entailed a more in-depth study of the youth, consisting of interviews with family, friends, and school staff; where necessary, perceptual-motor, neurological, and psychological assessments were also administered. The result of this study was a plan of care specifically oriented to the needs of the youth and family. Services were provided by a community-based contractor or the youth was referred by the contractor to other appropriate services within the community. In practice, these services ranged from counseling to dancing lessons. The youth's participation in the program was not to exceed six months.
4. During the program period, those youths eligible for the diversion program had the option of the DSO program or regular court processing. Obviously, this option was not available to preprogram status offenders. This raises the possibility of selectivity bias. For instance, a factor that influenced the decision to participate in the DSO program might also have influenced program effectiveness. Thus, selectivity on the basis of this variable would either mask or simulate a treatment effect. However, care was taken to determine as far as possible any relevant variables on which these groups varied. Where differences occurred, these factors were controlled in all analyses.
5. All these cases involved referral not only to court but to detention as well. The preprogram group consisted of detainees that would have been eligible for the DSO program had one existed at the time, while the three DSO program groups consisted of those detainees eligible for the DSO program who agreed to participate in it.
6. Police arrest data were not available in Connecticut. In practice, however, the official police response to delinquent conduct (particularly status offenses) in Connecticut is referral to court, not arrest (Auerbach Service Bureau, 1977). Therefore, it was felt that subsequent referrals was the best indicator of official recidivism.
7. Initial analysis revealed that the number of subsequent referrals was extremely skewed. An alternative measure of recidivism considered was the change in number of referrals from six months before the instant offense to six months after the instant offense. This measure was only slightly skewed. We decided not to use this measure, however, due

to difficulty in interpretation. This particular measure of recidivism includes the number of prior referrals, which is a control variable, thus complicating the analysis. Further analysis indicated that, in any case, the relationship between the number of subsequent referrals and treatment was similar to that between change in number of referrals and treatment; thus, it seemed justifiable to use the former, more easily interpretable measure. In looking at the distribution of the number of subsequent referrals, it was found that this variable formed an almost equal success/failure dichotomy (54 percent had no subsequent referrals; 46 percent had one or more subsequent referrals). It may be argued that such a dichotomy is too stringent a test of labeling theory. However, initial analyses indicate that the relationship between treatment type and recidivism is the same whether recidivism is measured as a matter of degree or an absolute dichotomy.

8. Town size was included at the suggestion of detention personnel. Detention centers are located in large towns; thus, it takes more time and effort on the part of police to bring a juvenile from a small town to detention. This suggests that only the more serious status offenders are brought to detention centers from small towns. It was also indicated that smaller towns have developed their own diversion resources (i.e., places for runaways, incorrigibles, etc., to seek help).

9. Where both parents work, the more prestigious occupation was used.

10. Given the small and uneven n's for the three DSO models, it was difficult to obtain statistically significant differences across the four treatment groups at the generally accepted .05 level. Thus, we were inclined to consider a more liberal level of statistical significance (i.e., $p < .10$).

11. These characteristics were also related to recidivism (measured as subsequent arrests) in other DSO sites (see Teilmann and Peterson, 1980).

12. The n of only 18 for T1 raises questions regarding the inferences that may be drawn from this program. Ordinarily, a low n creates problems with respect to the reliability and stability of a positive finding. A finding of no difference, especially when duplicated in larger comparison groups, creates less of a problem.

13. It is worth noting that the analysis by the national evaluation team (Teilmann and Peterson, 1980) did include measures of the number and types of services rendered. However, after controlling for various background characteristics, these service factors were found to have little effect on outcome.

14. In a similar evaluation of the Illinois DSO program, Spergel et al. (1981) found that when various demographic and legal characteristics were controlled, there was no difference in recidivism between those status offenders institutionalized and those involved in community-based programs. Unfortunately, like the present study, this study also suffers from the absence of an untreated control group.

References

Andrews, F. M., et al. 1973. *Multiple Classification Analysis*. Ann Arbor, Mich.: Institute for Social Research.

Auerbach Service Bureau. 1977. *The Legal Rights of Children. Children, the Family and the State under Connecticut Law*. Hartford: Auerbach Service Bureau for Connecticut Organizations.

Bailey, W. 1966. "Correctional Outcome: An Evaluation of 100 Reports." *Journal of Criminal Law, Criminology & Police Science* 57 (2): 153-160.

Berg, I., et al. 1978. "The Effect of Two Randomly Allocated Court Procedures on Truancy." *British Journal of Criminology* 18 (3): 232-244.

Blomberg, T. G. 1980. "Widening the Net: An Anomaly in the Evaluation of Diversion Programs." In *Handbook of Criminal Justice Evaluation*, M. W. Klein and K. S. Teilmann, eds. Beverly Hills, Calif.: Sage. Pp. 572-592.

Cameron, M. O. 1964. *The Booster and the Snitch: Department Store Shoplifting*. New York: Free Press of Glencoe.

Erikson, K. 1962. "Notes on the Sociology of Deviance." *Social Problems* 9 (Spring): 307-314.

Hirschi, T. 1975. "Labelling Theory and Juvenile Delinquency: An Assessment of the Evidence." In *The Labelling of Deviance: Evaluating a Perspective*, W. R. Gove, ed. New York: John Wiley. Pp. 181-203.

Kim, J., and F. Kohout. 1975. "Analysis of Variance and Covariance: Subprograms Anova and Oneway." In *SPSS: Statistical Package for the Social Sciences*, 2d ed., Norman H. Nie, et al., eds. New York: McGraw-Hill. Pp. 398-433.

Klein, M. 1981. "A Judicious Slap on the Wrist: Thoughts on Early Sanctions for Juvenile Offenders." In *New Directions in the Rehabilitation of Criminal Offenders*, S. Martin, L. B. Sechrest, and R. Redner, eds. Washington, D.C.: National Academy Press. Pp. 376-393.

Klein, M., et al. 1977. *Diversion as Operationalization of Labeling Theory*. Los Angeles: University of Southern California Social Science Research Institute.

Lemert, E. 1958 "The Behavior of the Systematic Check Forger." *Social Problems* (Fall): 141-149.

Logan, C. 1972. "Evaluation Research in Crime and Delinquency: A Reappraisal." *Journal of Criminal Law, Criminology & Police Science* 63 (3): 378-387.

Logan, C., J. Bacewicz, and S. Rausch. 1978. *An Evaluation of Connecticut's Deinstitutionalization of Status Offenders Program*. Storrs: University of Connecticut.

Mahoney, A. R. 1974. "The Effect of Labeling Upon Youths in the Juvenile Justice System: A Review of the Evidence." *Law & Society Review* 8 (4): 583-614.

Martinson, R. 1974. "What Works?—Questions and Answers about Prison Reform." *The Public Interest* (Spring): 22-54.

Matza, D. 1964. Delinquency and Drift. New York: John Wiley.

McCord, J. 1980. "Myths and Realities about Criminal Sanctions." Paper presented at the American Society of Criminology Convention, San Francisco, November.

McEachern, A., et al. 1968. "The Juvenile Probation System: Simulation for Research and Decision-Making." *American Behavioral Scientist* 11 (3): 1-45.

Platt, A. 1977. *The Child Savers: The Invention of Delinquency*, 2d ed. Chicago: University of Chicago Press.

Schur, E. M. 1973. *Radical Nonintervention: Rethinking the Delinquency Problem*. Englewood Cliffs, N.J.: Prentice-Hall.

Spergel, I. A., F. G. Reamer, and J. P. Lynch. 1981. "Deinstitutionalization of Status Offenders: Individual Outcome and System Effects." *Journal of Research in Crime and Delinquency* 18 (1): 4-33.

Teilmann, K., and J. Peterson. 1980. "What Works for Whom: The Uses of Deinstitutionalization." In National *Evaluation of the Deinstitutionalization of Status Offenders Programs: Executive Summary*, S. Kobrin and M. W. Klein, eds. Los Angeles: University of Southern California Social Science Research Institute. Chapter XVI, pp. 1-85.

Thomas, C. W. 1976. "Are Status Offenders Really So Different? A Comparative and Longitudinal Assessment." *Crime & Delinquency* 22 (4): 438-455.

Thorsell, B., and L. Klemke. 1972. "The Labeling Process: Reinforcement or Deterrent." *Law & Society Review* 6 (February): 393-403.

Tittle, C. R. 1975. "Deterrents or Labeling?" *Social Forces* 53 (3): 399-410.

———. 1975a. "Labelling and Crime: An Empirical Evaluation." *The Labelling of Deviance: Evaluating a Perspective*, W. R. Gove, ed. New York: John Wiley. Pp. 157-179.

Tittle, C. R., and C. H. Logan. 1973. "Sanctions and Deviance: Evidence and Remaining Questions." *Law & Society Review* 7 (3): 371-392. ✦

30
The Preventive Effects of the Perceived Risk of Arrest: Testing an Expanded Conception of Deterrence

Daniel S. Nagin
Raymond Paternoster

The deterrence doctrine postulates an inverse relationship between the perceived certainty and severity of punishment and involvement in delinquent or criminal activity. Empirical tests of this relationship are legion.[1] The earliest of the perceptual deterrence studies relied on cross-sectional survey data. Those studies generally reported evidence that the perceived certainty of punishment, but not perceived severity, deterred criminal involvement (Paternoster, 1987). Cross-sectional perceptual deterrence studies have been largely superseded by studies using panel data (Meier et al., 1984; Paternoster and Iovanni, 1986; Paternoster et al., 1983). The panel studies generally found no evidence of a deterrent effect of either perceived certainty or severity of punishment.

The findings from the perceptual deterrence literature have led some observers to conclude that the perceived certainty and severity of formal sanctions either have no influence or, at best, only a modest influence on delinquency or adult criminality. Those observers interpret the evidence as suggesting instead that conformity is primarily attributable to nonlegal or what is often called "informal" sources of control (Paternoster et al., 1983; Tittle, 1980). Among the informal controls are censure from others in the community, damage to intimate relationships, and loss of employment or other material "stakes."

Reassessing the Deterrence Doctrine: An Expanded Conception of 'Deterrence'

In a reexamination of the perceptual deterrence literature, Williams and Hawkins (1986) have suggested that previous tests of the deterrence doctrine have been guided by too narrow a conception of the deterrence process. Drawing on the theoretical work of Andenaes (1974) and Gibbs (1975), Williams and Hawkins speculate that the formal sanctioning process is augmented by the possibility of informal sanctions. In a nutshell, their argument is this: Community knowledge of an individual's probable involvement in criminal or delinquent acts is a necessary precondition for the operation of informal sanction processes. Such knowledge can be obtained from two distinctly different sources: Either from the arrest (or conviction or sentencing) of the individual or from information networks independent of the formal sanction process. Williams and Hawkins observe that preventive effects may arise from the fear that informal sanctioning processes will be triggered by either of these information sources. They use the term "fear of arrest" to label preventive effects triggered by the formal sanction process and the term "fear of the act" to label preventive effects triggered by information networks separate from the formal sanction process. The crux of their argument is that preventive effects arising from "fear of arrest" should be included in a full accounting of the deterrent effect of formal sanctions. For example, if an individual refrains from committing a criminal act because she fears that an arrest will bring the transgression to the attention of others, and thereby jeopardize valued social relationships, Williams and Hawkins argue (1986:561) that the preventive mecha-

---

From *Criminology*, Volume 29, Number 4 (1991), pp. 561-587. Copyright © 1991 by the American Society of Criminology. Reprinted by permission.

nism is ultimately the result of formal sanctions and, therefore, "part of the general deterrence process." We concur.

Williams and Hawkins' suggestions that formal sanction threats operate as an effective crime inhibitor when the informal costs of punishment are also activated and that such inhibition should be considered as part of the deterrence process are not altogether new ones. Zimring and Hawkins (1973:174) offered an early version of an expanded deterrence theory when they alluded to the possibility that formal punishment may best deter when it "sets off" informal sanctions[2]:

> We must recognize that there are other aspects of the administration of criminal justice which, while forming no part of the formally prescribed punishment, must nevertheless be regarded as part of the threatened consequences. It would be illogical to restrict the definition of threatened consequences in such a way as to exclude such aspects of the enforcement process which are integral parts of the system and may often be as significant as the formally prescribed punishment themselves.... Official *actions* can set off societal *reactions* that may provide potential offenders with more reason to avoid conviction than the officially imposed unpleasantness of punishment (emphasis in original).

In addition, there have been a few attempts in the empirical literature to test this notion. Jensen (1969) found that the perceived certainty of punishment had a deterrent effect that was independent of the level of informal costs. Results similar to Jensen's were reported by Burkett and Jensen (1975), Anderson et al. (1977), Grasmick and Appleton (1977), and Grasmick and McLaughlin (1978).

Previous researchers have not assumed that the deterrence process operates in this manner. In the specification of multivariate perceptual deterrence models, measures of informal sanctions are conventionally entered as additive covariates of self-reported criminal involvement. Thus, by assumption, the model specification treats the influence of informal sanctions as independent of the level of certainty (or severity) of formal sanctions. Williams and Hawkins argue that such a specification conceptually restricts estimates of the deterrent effect of formal sanctions to include only the fear of incurring the cost *directly* attendant to being the target of an enforcement intervention (e.g., incarceration, cost of representation).

In arguing for a more inclusive conception of the deterrence process, Williams and Hawkins identify three kinds of informal sanction costs that may supplement formal sanctions: commitment costs, attachment costs, and the stigma of arrest. *Commitment costs* refer to a person's perception that "past accomplishments" may be jeopardized by an arrest. Such costs arise from an individual's "stakes in conformity" (Becker, 1960). Williams and Hawkins (1986:565) include loss of "future employment chances, educational opportunities, or marriage prospects" among such costs. *Attachment costs* include the loss of valued relationships with intimate others resulting from arrest. *The stigma of arrest* refers to the "reputational damage" of an arrest. They argue (1986:565) that the reason perceptual deterrence research has commonly failed to find any strong evidence of a deterrent effect for perceived certainty is that model specifications, by construction, ignore what may be the most powerful source of deterrence—formal sanctions being augmented by the imposition of informal sanctions.

Empirically Examining the Preventive Mechanisms of Sanction Threats

Much to their credit, Williams and Hawkins (1986:565–566) suggest how one can go about testing for their broadened conception of the preventive effects of sanction threats:

> We would predict that general deterrence is more likely to operate when a person perceives a high probability of arrest *and:* (1) when others disapprove of or generally discredit the potential offender, thus creating a reputational stigma of arrest; (2) when the arrest is perceived as possibly jeopard-

izing relationships with significant others; or (3) when the arrest is seen as possibly destroying past accomplishments and/or future opportunities. If these perceived costs are salient to the individual, deterrence may be achieved even though the person perceives the certainty of arrest as low. If the perceived costs of arrest are minimal, however, we would expect the perceived certainty of arrest to have a weak influence on the deterrence of crime.

Although seemingly straightforward, the above passage might actually suggest three hypotheses: (1) that the effect of the perceived certainty of arrest depends on the level of informal sanction costs, (2) that the effect of informal sanctions depends on the level of formal sanction certainty, and (3) that informal costs and perceived certainty have independent effects. Because Williams and Hawkins repeatedly emphasize that the deterrent effect of formal sanctions should be an increasing function of the level of informal sanctions, in our judgment hypothesis (1) is most faithful to their expanded conceptualization of the deterrence process.

Methods

Data

The data come from a three-wave panel study of high school students in and around a mid-sized city in the southeastern United States. During the 1981 fall semester of the school year, questionnaires were administered in all tenth-grade English classes in nine high schools. The nine schools were selected to be representative of the secondary schools in the area and included a mix of urban, rural, and suburban schools. The gender and racial make-up of the students approximate the gender and racial composition of the standard metropolitan statistical area from which the sample was drawn.

Follow-up questionnaires were administered to the same students during the fall semester of their junior and senior years. At the first administration, approximately 2,700 students completed a questionnaire. The refusal rate was less than 1% of the attending students. In the last administration, during the cohort's senior year, approximately 1,600 members (60%) of the initial cohort completed a questionnaire. The analyses that follow are based on the approximately 1,600 students who completed a questionnaire in their sophomore, junior, and senior years. With a listwise deletion of missing data, the final sample was reduced to 1,123.[3]

Measurement Intervals

Questionnaires were administered at three points in time (T1, T2, T3), each approximately separated by a one-year interval. Measures of all variables were collected at all three times. With the three waves of data, two two-wave panels were constructed for this analysis. The first uses the responses at T1 and T2 and examines the effect of exogenous variables measured at T1 on self-reported delinquency between T1 and T2. This panel captures the period between a student's sophomore and junior year in high school. The second panel examines the effect of exogenous variables measured at T2 on self-reported delinquency that occurred between T2 and T3. This panel focuses on delinquent acts committed between the student's junior and senior year in high school. Figure 1 illustrates the two panel analyses.

Figure 1
Illustration of the Two Panel Designs

T1 Exogenous ⟶ T2 Delinquency
Variables
                T2 Exogenous ⟶ T3 Delinquency
                Variables

First Panel   Second Panel

Measures of Endogenous Variables

At each questionnaire administration, students completed a self-report inventory in which they were asked about their involvement in delinquent acts during the previous 12 months. Although the students were queried about their participation in a variety of delinquent offenses, our focus here is on property delinquency and drug use.

We focus on property delinquency and drug use because they are representative of two distinctly different offense types, each of which may be particularly sensitive to deterrent threats. Property delinquency is the best example of an instrumental crime. Klepper and Nagin (1989a) speculate that for instrumental crimes offenders may be more likely to weigh benefits and costs consciously and therefore to be more sensitive to perceived sanction threats. For a different reason, drug use may also be particularly sensitive to perceived sanction threats. Unlike theft, which is widely condemned as immoral, drug use is a good example of an offense that is *mala prohibita*. Some have speculated (Andenaes, 1974:45) that for such offenses "the law stands alone" and, thus, that the primary bulwark against the commission of such acts is the threat of formal sanctions.

For each of the two types of delinquent acts, two measures of delinquent involvement were constructed. One measures the prevalence of offending and is coded as 1 if the respondent reported committing the particular type of delinquent offense at least once in the prior 12 months and 0 if otherwise. The second indicator of involvement measures the intensity of delinquent offending and equals the number of acts committed during the previous year.

For drug use, the two measures of involvement were constructed from responses to questions concerning the frequency of marijuana use and the frequency of use of any other type of drug. For property delinquency, they were constructed from responses to queries concerning the number of times during the previous year the respondent had committed a petty theft (under $5), a theft of goods valued at between $5 and $50, or had broken into or entered a premises for the purpose of stealing.

The prevalence and incidence measures were constructed so that two types of deterrence could be investigated—absolute and restrictive deterrence. *Absolute deterrence* refers to the circumstance in which a person refrains from committing *any delinquent act* during a given period because of the fear of sanction threats. Examination of absolute deterrence, then, requires a prevalence measure of offending whereby persons are simply categorized as offenders or nonoffenders. *Restrictive deterrence*, on the other hand, refers to the circumstance in which a person does not desist completely from offending because of the risk of punishment, but instead curtails *the frequency of involvement*. Restrictive deterrence, then, is only relevant for the subgroup of persons who are active participants, and it requires a measure of the frequency of their involvement.

Measures of Exogenous Variables

The primary concern of this paper is the illumination of the deterrence process. Since previous research has consistently shown that perceptions of the severity of punishment are unrelated to self-reported delinquency and criminality (Paternoster, 1987; for exceptions, see Grasmick and Bryjak, 1980; Klepper and Nagin, 1989a, 1989b), we focus on perceived certainty. Our measure of certainty is based on the respondents' estimates of the likelihood that they would be arrested if they were to commit each of two delinquent acts, committing a petty theft and using marijuana. This estimate was elicited on a five point Likert-style continuum. The upper end of the scales reflects greater perceived certainty of arrest.

In addition to the perceived certainty of punishment, the model specification includes other factors that prior research suggests are covariates of either participation in or frequency of delinquency. Several are measures of previous delinquent activity. Because the best predictor of current offending has been shown to be previous offending, each model contains a measure of the respondent's previous year's involvement in that particular type of delinquency.[4] Also included are two indicators of the respondent's "delinquent disposition." These are prevalence measures of the respondent's previous involvement in violent acts (carrying a hidden weapon and beating someone up badly) and drug "dealing" (sold drugs).

In addition to previous offending, we hypothesize that participation and frequency will be positively affected by the proportion of one's peers that also engage in the specified type of delinquency. Similarly, we expect involvement to be greater if the respondent perceives that friends will provide positive reinforcement for his or her own involvement. We also expect self-reported delinquency to be both more likely and more frequent for those students not living with both natural parents, for students whose family has received welfare benefits in the past three years, for males, and for nonwhites. Finally, given that delinquency is commonly a group activity, we expect greater delinquency for students who spent more time socializing with their peers.

Previous research has also shown that involvement in delinquency is effectively controlled by strict parental supervision, belief and participation in religious institutions, attachment to conventional figures (e.g., teachers), commitment to conventional goals (e.g., good grades), and a set of conventional beliefs that hold the commission of delinquent acts as morally wrong.

To summarize, we expect both participation and frequency to be associated with the following factors (direction of hypothesized association): (1) prior involvement (+), (2) prior violent delinquency (+), (3) prior drug dealing (+), (4) gender (male +), (5) race (nonwhite +), (6) family not intact (+), (7) receipt of welfare assistance (+), (8) religious commitment (-) (9) grades (-), (10) social activities with peers (+), (11) attachment to teachers (-), (12) parental supervision (-), (13) friends' approval (+), (14) friends' delinquent behavior (+), (15) perceived certainty (-), and (16) moral beliefs (-). Measures of each one of these factors are included in the estimated models. The precise wording of the question used to measure each theoretical concept can be found in the appendix.

Measuring the Preventive Effects of Sanction Threats

Williams and Hawkins describe three types of informal cost that may be incurred as the result of an arrest: the stigma of arrest, attachment costs, and commitment costs. Only the third is of interest here because the data set used in this analysis does not contain adequate measures of the other two.

Commitment costs, as noted, refer to those past accomplishments or anticipated future goals that may be jeopardized or made difficult to achieve as the result of being arrested for committing an offense. As examples, Williams and Hawkins include the risk of endangering future employment chances, educational opportunities, and marriage prospects. They emphasize that fear of incurring commitment costs can only be attributed to deterrence if such costs are perceived to follow from *an arrest for* and not merely the commission of an offense. Appropriate measures of these dimensions of commitment cost, therefore, are indicators of the respondent's perception of the detrimental effect of an arrest on employment prospects, access to educational opportunities, or opportunities on the marriage market. In addition, since the anticipated cost of arrest may depend on what one is arrested for, this measure should be offense specific.

The measures of commitment cost employed here faithfully adhere to the measurement requirements for the concept as described by Williams and Hawkins. Each student was asked to estimate how much his or her chances of (a) getting a good education, (b) having good friends, and (c) getting a good job would be hurt if they were arrested for petty theft and if arrested for marijuana use. The provided response options were, "hurt very little," "hurt a little," and "hurt a lot." If the Williams and Hawkins hypothesis is correct, the deterrent effect of perceived certainty should be greater at higher levels of these different dimensions of commitment cost.

Model Estimation

We suggested earlier that perceptions of sanction risk may have either an absolute or restrictive deterrent effect. To investigate absolute deterrent effects, the outcome variable is dichotomous and equals 1 if the act is committed at least once in the previous year and 0 otherwise. This measures a person's participation in offending, and a probit estimation procedure is used for model estimation. To investigate restrictive deterrent effects, the outcome variable is a frequency count of the number of offenses committed during a one-year period. In this case the dependent variable is censored at zero. Because a sizable proportion of the respondents reported that they did not commit the specified offense during the observation period, ordinary least squares (OLS) regression is not appropriate for estimation. We instead estimated the frequency models with a censored dependent variable procedure, tobit regression.[5] Probit and tobit models were estimated for each offense type (property delinquency and drug use) for each time period (T1–T2 and T2–T3).

Findings

The data analysis proceeds in two steps. We first examine the effect of perceived risk on the prevalence and frequency of involvement in property delinquency and drug use. In this stage the model specification conforms with conventional practice in the literature. . . . [T]he model assumes that the "influence" of perceived certainty is additive and independent of the levels of all other variables. These results are used as a baseline for comparison with the second-stage analysis, in which, per the recommendation of Williams and Hawkins, perceived certainty is interacted with different measures of commitment cost. In the second stage we examine whether the deterrent effect of perceived certainty is an increasing function of commitment cost.[6]

Stage 1—The Effect of Perceived Risk on Property and Drug Delinquency

. . . Focusing first on the coefficient estimates for the variables other than the perceived certainty of arrest, inspection of their signs reveals that most conform with expectations. Of the subset that are significant for both periods, the results suggest that participation in property delinquency is more likely if the student has previously participated, has friends who commit property offenses, or is male. For drug use the patterns are somewhat different. Drug use is more likely if friends use drugs or if the student has previously used drugs. These results mirror the findings for property delinquency. In addition, however, the results also suggest that drug use is more likely if the student's family is not intact and that the probability of drug use is a declining function of grades and an increasing function of time spent socializing. . . .

Turning now to the coefficient estimates for perceived certainty, three of the four estimates are negative. For property delinquency, the estimates for both time periods are negative. For T1—T2, the estimate falls short of statistical significance ($p < .15$), but for T2—T3, the estimate is significant at the .05 level. For drug use the pattern is somewhat problematic. For period T1—T2 the estimate is consistent with expectations—it is negative and highly significant. For period T2—T3, however, the estimate is positive though nonsignificant ($t = .299$). . . .

To summarize the first-stage analysis, we have found fairly consistent evidence of a negative association between the perceived risk of arrest and involvement in property delinquency and drug use. For our students and for the two offenses examined here, the evidence suggests that perceived certainty of arrest is an effective absolute and restrictive deterrent. This finding of a significant deterrent effect for perceived certainty is inconsistent with other panel deterrence studies as well as previously published findings from the data set employed here. We suspect that the null findings of previous panel studies may reflect the manner in which the outcome variable was operationalized and the subsequent model estimation strategy.

Past research has generally measured self-reported delinquency as a continuous variable, counting either individual instances of offending (frequency measures) or the number of offenses committed (variety measures). With a continuous outcome measure, researchers have typically used an ordinary least squares model to estimate structural effects. It has been noted in some recent deterrence research, however, that such continuous measures confound the distinction between absolute and restrictive deterrence (Paternoster, 1989). We have maintained the difference between these two types of deterrence and estimated nonlinear models (probit models for absolute and tobit models for restrictive deterrence), which provided evidence of a significant deterrent effect for the risk of arrest.

What we have not done is include in our models measures of various "informal" costs of sanctions, which have traditionally been included by other researchers in estimating regression-type deterrence models. Earlier, we presented the argument of Williams and Hawkins that the deterrent effect of arrest will be maximized when informal costs are highest. We turn now to a direct test of this hypothesis.

Stage 2—Estimating Other Deterrent Effects of the Fear of Arrest: The Preventive Effects of Commitment Costs

In specifying the form that a test of their hypothesis should take, Williams and Hawkins (1986:566) suggested that the deterrent effect of perceived risk should be greater when the costs are higher: "The greater the perceived costs of arrest . . . the greater should be the negative effect of perceptions of certainty on the incidence of crime." This suggests an interaction effect between the perceived risk of arrest and commitment costs.

Recall that with our data we were able to measure three components of the commitment cost of arrest—educational commitment cost, social commitment cost, and occupational commitment cost. For each of these components of commitment cost, respondents were asked whether an arrest for a specified act would "hurt very little," hurt a little," or "hurt a lot." . . .

We turn now to considering the implication of the results . . . for the Williams and Hawkins hypothesis. Consider first the findings for participation in drug use during T2–T3. Their theory predicts that the null findings of the Stage 1 analysis concerning the deterrent effect of perceived certainty for T2–T3 drug use may be attributable to our failure to interact certainty with the perceived cost of informal sanctions contingent on an arrest. At least for one type of informal cost, commitment cost, the results . . . provide no support for this prediction. Most of the coefficient estimates for the interaction term are positive, all of them are quite small, and none is significant. There is no evidence here that previous null findings were due to the failure to consider the interaction between formal and informal sanctions.

Focusing now on the results pertaining to participation in property delinquency in T1–T2 and T2–T3 and in drug use in T1–T2, the theory predicts that coefficient estimates should become increasingly negative (i.e., monotonically decline) as commitment cost increases. Inspection of the coefficient estimates reveals some limited evidence for such a predicted decline. For property delinquency in T1–T2, the results conform with this prediction for educational commitment cost and for social commitment cost. The deterrent effect of the perceived certainty of arrest is weakest when the informal cost is low and stronger as the perceived informal costs increase (i.e., becomes more negative). For the remaining seven sets of coefficient estimates, however, the results do not conform to the prediction of strictly declining monotonicity. For example, for T2–T3 property delinquency and T1–T2 drug use, the strongest deterrent effect is found at the *lowest* level of perceived educational cost. Similarly, for T1–T2 drug use the deterrent effect is largest at the lowest level of occupational cost. Still another example of a contradictory finding is that for T2–T3 drug use: The largest deterrent effect is found at the midlevel of perceived social cost. . . .

Discussion and Conclusion

In a restatement of the deterrence doctrine, Williams and Hawkins (1986) argue that much prior perceptual deterrence research has been guided by too narrow a conception of the deterrence process. They suggest that previous research has attempted to identify the deterrent effect of sanction threats while "holding constant" factors that may also prevent crime, such as social censure and the material/opportunity costs of sanctions. They point out that such a model specification assumes that informal preventive mechanisms are independent of deterrence. Williams and Hawkins persuasively argue that if such negative consequences are the perceived outcome of an *arrest* (rather than the mere commission of an offense) they should properly be understood as part of the preventive mechanism of deterrence. We agree with their restatement and have attempted in this paper to investigate empirically this expanded theory of the preventive effects of sanction threats.

At least for commitment costs, our results provide little support for the hypothesis that *ceteris paribus* the (absolute) magnitude of the deterrent effect of perceived certainty is an increasing function of perceived informal costs. While we found evidence of a negative and significant association between perceived certainty and delinquent involvement, we found at best only marginal evidence that the magnitude of that association increased with various dimensions of commitment cost. Although contrary to the speculation of Williams and Hawkins, our results are consistent with previous research that has found that sanction threats and perceived informal costs have independent crime-inhibiting effects (Anderson et al., 1977; Burkett and Jensen, 1975; Grasmick and Appleton, 1977; Grasmick and McLaughlin, 1978; Jensen, 1969).

There are a number of possible explanations for our failure to find a stronger interaction effect. One involves statistical power. It may be the case that the loss of statistical power resulting from the estimation of "certainty effects" for separate levels of commitment cost obscured an underlying relationship that is consistent with the Williams and Hawkins theory.[7]

A second explanation involves the student composition of our sample. Williams and Hawkins are rightly critical of the routine reliance on student samples in perceptual deterrence research. Students are a particularly convenient population for survey-based research and particularly so for panel survey research such as this, but they are clearly not representative of the entire population. This deficiency may be particularly important for this study. It may be the case that high school students as a group are not sufficiently mature to have developed clearly distinguishable stakes in conformity. Such stakes form the foundation for the sorts of commitment costs examined in this analysis. It may be that our results would be quite different if our sample had comprised older individuals. The results of a study by Grasmick and Bryjak (1980) that is based on a sample of adults are consistent with this argument.

Alternatively, youths may be quite capable of establishing stakes in conformity, but we have not measured these relevant dimensions. Our measure of commitment costs was restricted to "getting a good education," "having good friends," and "getting a good job." Only for perceived social, costs ("good friends") and only for drug use were these measures of significant import. It may be that there are far more salient commitment cost considerations that youths contemplate when considering the cost of an arrest that we did not measure here. A fruitful line of exploratory work, therefore, would involve ascertaining what kinds of material costs youths perceive would be jeopardized by an arrest and their relative importance.

A third possible reason for our failure to validate the Williams and Hawkins hypotheses may stem from data set limitations that restricted our analysis to an examination of only one type of informal cost—the commitment costs of arrest. Our data had precise measures of commitment costs but no indicators of the other costs discussed in their article—the stigmatic and attachment costs of arrest. It may be that the latter two are more important dimensions of youths' cost considerations than are the type of commitment costs measured here. There is some evidence to support this possibility. In a study of the perceived costs of arrest for spousal assault, Williams and Hawkins (1989) reported that the stigma costs of arrest (personal humiliation) and attachment costs (damaged relationships with others) were more important components of sanction fear than were commitment costs. They also reported that self-stigma was significantly related to participation in wife assault, while the perceived commitment cost of arrest had no effect.

A final explanation of our generally null findings[8] is that there may be a fundamental flaw in the underlying logic of Williams and Hawkins' reconceptualization of deterrence theory. In a study based on the survey responses of a sample of middle-class, midcareer master's degree students, Klepper and Nagin (1989a, 1989b) found evidence that the perception of a nonzero probability of criminal prosecution is an absolute deterrent to tax noncompliance. They reasoned that this finding is consistent with the theory that for this group the combination of commitment, attachment, and stigma costs of criminal prosecution were so enormous that the perception of a nonzero probability of criminal prosecution was an absolute deterrent. The Klepper and Nagin theory is also consistent with their finding that variation in perceived probability of criminal prosecution above the nonzero threshold had no association with willingness to engage in tax noncompliance.

The Klepper and Nagin theory implies that the magnitude of the deterrent effect of perceived certainty is not necessarily an increasing function of the perceived cost of informal sanctions. In the extreme case in which such costs are deemed to be enormous, increases in sanction risk perceptions above a *de minimus* nonzero threshold have no influence on behavior simply because all individuals have already been deterred. This argument implies that the deterrent effect of perceived certainty will not necessarily increase with perceived informal sanction costs.

We cannot distinguish among these interpretations of our results, and thus, we believe it is premature to reject the Williams and Hawkins argument. We do believe, however, that our largely null findings are reason for pause. Notwithstanding, Williams and Hawkins have done a great service to the large community of scholars studying the preventive effects of sanctions. Their article provides a valuable road map for future research. This paper is a first attempt at exploiting that road map. We join them in urging continued research in this area with adult samples and more serious offenses, for only then can researchers begin to construct an empirically faithful theory of criminal deterrence.

Notes

1. For a review of the perceptual deterrence literature, see Paternoster (1987). Prior to the emergence of the perceptual deterrence literature most deterrence studies relied on aggregate data. Such studies typically examined the relationship across geographical areas of the crime rate to aggregate measures of the certainty and severity of punishment. For reviews of this literature, see Zimring and Hawkins (1973), Gibbs (1975), and Nagin (1978).
2. The idea that the effect of formal sanction threats is conditioned by informal sanction costs was also suggested by Tittle and Logan (1973:386) in their early review of the state of deterrence research:

   It may be that some sanction characteristics can become operative only when a certain level has been reached with respect to another characteristic. Thus it could be that formal sanctions can be effective only if reinforced by informal sanctions.

3. There was substantial attrition (approximately 40%) over the three years of the panel design. The drop-out rate in each school was low (less than 5%). There were three other reasons why a student who completed a questionnaire at Time 1 (T1) did not do so at either Time 2 (T2) or Time 3 (T3), absenteeism on the day of the second or third questionnaire administration, students taking a "nontraditional" English class in either their junior or senior year (drama, journalism, or business English), or students moving out of the

school district. Because most students were lost from two high schools that serviced a large military installation, we believe that the primary source of attrition was due to students moving out of their school district. To examine the representativeness of the approximately 1,100 students who completed all three questionnaires, we conducted a logistic regression analysis of the attrition process. The outcome variable was coded 0 for respondents who were there for all three waves of the study and 1 if they completed a questionnaire at T1 but not at either T2 or T3. The exogenous variables included all of the independent variables comprising the substantive models, measures of prior delinquent offending, and a dummy variable coded 1 if the student attended one of the high schools near the military base. The two groups of students did not differ in any substantial way. The best predictor of attrition over time was the dummy school variable.

4. For participation models, prior involvement is measured by a dichotomous variable equal to 1 if the individual had previously participated and 0 otherwise. For frequency models, prior involvement is measured by the frequency of prior offending.

5. In the tobit models estimated here, a lower and upper limit was placed on the data. Since frequency of delinquent involvement is only relevant for those who have committed at least one offense, the lower limit was zero. The self-report data were also skewed at the upper tail because a few respondents reported very high frequencies. An upper limit on the estimated tobit model was placed at the frequency score corresponding to the 90th percentile.

6. All of our models are one-equation models rather than simultaneous equations in a causal or "path" model. We have estimated these one-equation models because Williams and Hawkins's theoretical specification suggested that the effect of the perceived certainty/informal cost interaction term would be a direct one, unmediated by intervening variables. Rather than test a model of the deterrence process of our own contrivance, we wanted a hypothesis test that was most faithful to the ideas of Williams and Hawkins.

7. It is also possible that students' perceptions of commitment costs are not so "fine grained" that they dissect commitment costs into the various components examined in this analysis. To test for this possibility, we constructed several composite measures of perceived commitment cost and entered them into the interactive model outlined in the prior section. . . .

8. It was also possible that our null findings were due to a measurement flaw. Although the indicators of perceived certainty and commitment cost were measured with reference to a single offense, the outcome variables were a composite measure of several related offenses. The analyses were repeated using single-offense measures for self-reported offending that matched the certainty and commitment cost indicators. The results of those analyses were identical to those reported in the body of the text.

References

Amemiya, Takeshi. 1985. *Advanced Econometrics*. Cambridge, Mass. Harvard University Press.

Andenaes, Johannes. 1974. *Punishment and Deterrence*. Ann Arbor: University of Michigan Press.

Anderson, Linda S., Theodore G. Chiricos, and Gordon P. Waldo. 1977. Formal and informal sanctions: A comparison of deterrent effects. *Social Problems* 25:103–114.

Becker, Howard S. 1960. Notes on the concept of commitment. *American Journal of Sociology* 66:32–40.

Burkett, Steven R. and Eric L. Jensen. 1975. Conventional ties, peer influence, and the fear of apprehension: A study of adolescent marijuana use. *Sociological Quarterly* 16:522–533.

Gibbs, Jack P. 1975. *Crime, Punishment and Deterrence*. New York: Elsevier.

Grasmick, Harold G. and Lynn Appleton. 1977. Legal punishment and social stigma: A comparison of two deterrence models. *Social Science Quarterly* 58:15–28.

Grasmick, Harold G. and George J. Bryjak. 1980. The deterrent effect of perceived severity of punishment. *Social Forces* 59:471–491.

Grasmick, Harold G. and Steven D. McLaughlin. 1978. Deterrence and social control: Comment on Silberman. *American Sociological Review* 43:272-277.

Jensen, Gary. 1969. "Crime doesn't pay": Correlates of a shared misunderstanding. *Social Problems* 17:189–201.

Klepper, Steven and Daniel S. Nagin. 1989a. The deterrent effect of the perceived certainty and severity of punishment revisited. *Criminology* 27:721–746.

———. 1989b. Tax compliance and perceptions of the risks of detection and criminal prosecution. *Law and Society Review* 23:209–240.

Maddala, G. S. 1983. *Limited-Dependent and Qualitative Variables in Econometrics*. New York: Cambridge University Press.

Meier, Robert, Steven R. Burkett, and Carol A. Hickman. 1984. Sanction, peers and deviance:

Preliminary models of a social control process. *Sociological Quarterly* 25:67–82.

Nagin, Daniel S. 1978. General deterrence: A review of the empirical evidence. In Alfred Blumstein, Jacqueline Cohen, and Daniel S. Nagin (eds.), *Deterrence and Incapacitation: Estimating the Effects of Criminal Sanctions on Crime Rates*, Washington, D.C.: National Academy of Sciences.

Paternoster, Raymond. 1987. The deterrent effect of the perceived certainty and severity of punishment: A review of the evidence and issues. *Justice Quarterly* 4:173–217.

———. 1989. Absolute and restrictive deterrence in a panel of youth: Explaining the onset, persistence/desistance, and frequency of delinquent offending. *Social Problems* 36:289–309.

Paternoster, Raymond and LeeAnn Iovanni. 1986. The deterrent effect of perceived severity: A reexamination. *Social Forces* 64:751–777.

Paternoster, Raymond, Linda E. Saltzman, Theodore G. Chiricos, and Gordon P. Waldo. 1983. Perceived risk and social control: Do sanctions really deter? *Law and Society Review* 17:457–479.

Tittle, Charles R. 1980. *Sanctions and Deterrence*. New York: Praeger.

Tittle, Charles R. and Charles H. Logan. 1973. Sanctions and deviance: Evidence and remaining questions. *Law and Society Review* 7:371–392.

Williams, Kirk R. and Richard Hawkins. 1986. Perceptual research on general deterrence: A critical review. *Law and Society Review* 20(4):545–572.

Zimring, Franklin E. and Gordon J. Hawkins. 1973. *Deterrence: The Legal Threat in Crime Control*. Chicago: University of Chicago. ✦

31
Felony Murder and Capital Punishment: An Examination of the Deterrence Question

Ruth D. Peterson
William C. Bailey

Introduction

After more than two centuries of study, authorities continue to disagree on empirical grounds about the role of capital punishment in the criminal justice system (see Beccaria, 1963; Bentham, 1962; Ferri, 1917; Garofalo, 1914; Stephen, 1864; Tarde, 1912). Ironically, there is least agreement about the one aspect of the death penalty debate that seems most amenable to scientific inquiry—whether capital punishment is effective in discouraging would-be killers.

Studies in the United States range from the early comparative analyses of homicides in death penalty versus abolitionist jurisdictions (Bedau, 1967; Bye, 1919; Calvert, 1927; Kirkpatrick, 1925; Schuessler, 1952; Sellin, 1955, 1959, 1967; Shipley, 1911; Sutherland, 1925; Vold, 1932) to more recent multivariate analyses of the relationship between execution practices (i.e., certainty) and homicide rates across jurisdictions and over time (Bailey, 1975, 1977, 1980, 1990; Black and Orsagh, 1978; Bowers and Pierce, 1975; Ehrlich, 1975, 1977; Forst, 1977; Kleck, 1979; Layson, 1985; Passell, 1975; Passell and Taylor, 1975; Peterson and Bailey, 1988; Yunker, 1976). In addition, some investigations have examined the effect of execution publicity on homicides (Bailey, 1990; Bailey and Peterson, 1989; Bowers, 1988; Dann, 1935; King, 1978; McFarland, 1983; Phillips, 1980; Savitz, 1958; Stack, 1987).

The vast majority of analyses have reported chance-only associations between homicides and the provision for, and extent of use of, capital punishment. Moreover, some short-term impact studies suggest that the effect of execution publicity is to increase rather than decrease homicides. Such findings have led some to conclude that capital punishment has a "brutalizing" effect, which results in the loss of more, not fewer, innocent lives. For example, Bowers and Pierce (1980:456) contend that instead of deterring homicides, "executions demonstrate that it is correct and appropriate to kill those who have gravely offended us. The fact that such killings are to be performed only by duly appointed officials on duly convicted offenders is a detail that may get obscured by the message that such offenders deserve to die."

The extant research provides a rather consistent lack of support for deterrence hypotheses, but there is disagreement about what this extensive body of literature actually demonstrates. Some scholars are reluctant to regard current findings as definitive due to a serious data quality problem that continues to plague deterrence research—the use of general rather than capital homicides as a dependent measure.

With few exceptions, capital punishment is available in retentionist jurisdictions in the United States only for certain types of homicide.[1] First, there are killings that are commonly referred to as first-degree or premeditated murder.[2] Two elements characterize these types of death-eligible killings: (1) premeditation, which designates intent to violate the law formulated prior to the activity and (2) malice aforethought, which refers to the intent to kill at the time of the act. Criminologists have long agreed that "classic" premeditated murders constitute a small minority of killings—at most 5 to 10% of all homicides (Wolfgang, 1958). In addition to these classic murders, virtually

From *Criminology,* Volume 29, Number 3 (1991), pp. 367-395. Copyright © 1991 by the American Society of Criminology. Reprinted by permission.

all retentionist states have made homicides that result from the commission of certain felonies eligible for the death penalty.[3] Felony murders, as they commonly are termed, and suspected felony killings, constitute 20 to 22% of homicides annually (Federal Bureau of Investigation, 1989) and account for the large majority of capital homicides.[4]

In addition, since the U.S. Supreme Court's ruling in *Gregg vs. Georgia* 1976 (96 Sup. Ct. 2902), executions, to a large degree, have been reserved for felony murderers. To illustrate, for the period under examination in this investigation (1976-1987), there were 93 executions. Of those, 67 (72%) were for murders associated with robbery, rape, burglary and kidnapping. Four involved domestic and family killings, 8 involved police killings, 4 involved classic premeditated murder (contract killings, homicide for insurance benefits, and a killing to silence a witness to a homicide), and the remainder ($n = 10$) involved a variety of other types of circumstances.

Despite the long-term recognition that most homicides are not eligible for capital punishment, the typical practice in deterrence investigations has been to examine rates for all types of homicide combined. Indeed, efforts to examine capital homicides have been confined to two short-term impact studies (Dann, 1935; Savitz, 1958) of a single city (Philadelphia) for a few selected years. Dann (1935) examined probable capital homicides in Philadelphia in the 60 days before and after each of five highly publicized executions in 1927, 1929, 1930, 1931, and 1932. Savitz replicated Dann's study for the period 1944-1947. He examined definite and possible capital homicides in the eight weeks before and after four highly publicized death sentences (not actual executions) were handed down in 1944, 1946 (two), and 1947. Neither study found evidence of deterrence. However, the temporal and geographic generalizability of these findings cannot be assumed.

Beyond these studies, the practice has been to examine total rather than capital Homicides. This procedure is commonplace because most analyses rely on homicide figures published by the Federal Bureau of Investigation (FBI) or the U.S. Department of Health and Human Services. These sources do not differentiate killings by type, and thus, it is not possible to determine from them the number and rate of capital killings.

In short, although scholars on both sides of the death penalty debate agree that a proper test of the deterrent effect of capital punishment must consider capital homicides, the improper operationalization of the dependent variable remains a very serious limitation of deterrence research (Bedau, 1977, 1982; Sellin, 1967, 1980; van den Haag, 1969, 1975; van den Haag and Conrad, 1983; Wilson, 1983). Further advancement of the understanding of this issue requires that this fundamental data problem be addressed. We do so in this investigation.

The Current Investigation

To extend understanding of the deterrence and death penalty issue, we used unpublished FBI homicide data to examine the relationship between capital punishment and felony murder—the most common type of capital homicide. As noted, felony murders and probable felony murders account for about one-fifth of all criminal homicides (Federal Bureau of Investigation, 1989). More important, they represent the vast majority of capital homicides.[5]

To test the effect of capital punishment on capital murder, we conducted national time series analyses of executions and monthly felony murder rates over the 1976-1987 period. If there is merit to the deterrence argument, one would expect a significant inverse relationship between the number of monthly executions and offense rates. Conversely, if executions promote killings due to brutalization, executions and monthly felony murder rates should be positively associated. On the possibility that executions might discourage some types of murder (deterrence), but encourage others (brutalization), we also examined rates for different types of felony murder.

In addition to the importance of the certainty of execution, deterrence theory predicts a significant inverse relationship between the amount of publicity devoted to executions and murder rates. Most recent investigations of the publicity hypothesis have not found evidence of deterrence (or brutalization) when considering the effect of newspaper (Bailey and Peterson, 1989; Stack, 1987)[6] and television (Bailey, 1990) coverage of executions. However, these studies have considered general, and not capital, homicides. In this investigation we explore the publicity hypothesis further by examining the relationship between the amount and type of television coverage devoted to executions and rates for different types of felony murder.

Methods and Procedures

To examine the deterrence hypotheses, we conducted time series analyses of monthly felony murder rates, the frequency of executions, and the amount and type of television coverage devoted to executions over the 144-month period, 1976-1987. The following sociodemographic factors were treated as control variables: (1) percent metropolitan population, (2) percent black population, (3) percent population 16 to 34 years of age, (4) the divorce rate, (5) percent unemployed of the civilian labor force, and (6) percent of the U.S. population receiving Aid to Families with Dependent Children (AFDC) benefits. We also included as control factors (7) annual dummy variables, (8) two seasonal variables that differentiate months with significantly higher/lower than normal felony murder rates,[7] (9) the arrest clearance rate for murder,[8] and (10) the percent of the U.S. population residing in jurisdictions without capital punishment for murder. Previous research has shown a significant inverse relationship between homicide arrest rates and offense rates, presumably due to deterrence (Bailey, 1976, 1990; Bailey and Peterson, 1989; Ehrlich, 1975). In addition, changes over the 1976-1987 period in percent death penalty/abolition population are controlled. It is doubtful that executions have a significant deterrent effect on populations that are not legally subject to capital punishment.

The control variables included in the analysis are not presented as a formal model of felony murder rates. Rather, they are considered to avoid spurious results for the death penalty factors. Because of multicollinearity problems for some of the control variables, the regression results for these factors must be viewed with caution.[9] However, multicollinearity is not a problem for the death penalty variables. The results of collinearity analyses for the capital punishment factors are presented in footnotes when the multivariate results are discussed.

Felony Murder: The Dependent Variable

We operationalized the general rate of felony murder as the total number of monthly felony murder incidents per 100,000 residential populational.[10] In addition to the general rate, we examined the number of incidents per 100,000 population for index felony murders and for each individual type of felony murder reported by the FBI. As noted earlier, some states restrict capital felony murders to killings associated with the FBI's index offenses: rape, robbery, burglary, larceny, vehicle theft, and arson. We label combined rates for these types of killings as "index" felony murders. We also constructed individual rates for killings associated with each of the index offenses and those associated with the other types of felonies reported by the FBI: prostitution and commercialized vice, other felonious sex crimes, narcotics violations, gambling, other felonies, and suspected felony murders. Monthly felony murder data were drawn from unpublished FBI Supplementary Homicide Reports (SHR).[11]

Data from the SHR have certain limitations for this type of investigation. First, compared with the FBI's Uniform Crime Reports (UCR), the SHR are less extensive in scope. Annual homicide victimization counts reported in the UCR are based on data submitted by police departments that serve over 98 percent of the U.S. population. Accordingly, UCR data provide a good estimate of total criminal homicides for the nation. Unfortunately, not all police departments participate in the SHR program. As a result, SHR homicide counts are lower than UCR counts. For example, over the 1976-1987 period, the average number of monthly UCR murders was 1,688, compared with an average of 1,574 SHR criminal homicides.

Nonetheless, the UCR and SHR homicide series are very highly correlated ($r = .89$) for the 1976-1987 period. Also important for this study, there is no indication of a trend over the 144-month period in the number of UCR homicides that do not appear in SHR files. The correlation between a linear time variable (1, 2, ... 144) and the difference between UCR and SHR monthly victim counts is slight: $r = .103$, $R^2 = .011$. Accordingly, SHR data provide a reasonable indicator of monthly homicide patterns over the 1976-1987 period.

A more serious concern is the problem of missing data for cases that do appear in the SHR files. We differentiated felony from other types of killings on the basis of homicide "circumstance" information provided by the police. Unfortunately, circumstance data are not reported for all cases. Over the 1976-1987 period, the percentage of monthly criminal homicides with undetermined circumstances ranged from 9 to 25%.

In a recent paper, Maxfield (1989) examined a major source of the missing data problem for SHR homicides. He argued that often the SHR data submitted by the police reflect only preliminary information about killings. As investigations progress, more information becomes available about homicide circumstances. Unfortunately, because of the SHR reporting schedule (reports are submitted to the FBI monthly), the more complete information often does not appear in SHR records. By comparing homicide circumstance information provided in SHR data (for 1978) with detailed homicide data compiled by Riedel et al. (1985) for Dallas, Memphis, Newark, Oakland, Philadelphia, St. Louis, and San Jose, Maxfield found that "murders initially coded as [circumstances] 'unknown' tend to be 'transformed' into instrumental [rape, robbery, and other sex-related offenses] and property felonies when the investigation is completed" (p. 691).

Based on Maxfield's analysis, for the period examined here, it is likely that the monthly variation in the level of missing circumstance data reflects variation in the undercount of felony murders in the SHR files. This undercount problem could contribute significant bias in a time series analysis of felony murder rates. To compensate for this problem, in the analyses to follow . . . we include as a control variable the percentage of monthly SHR homicide incidents involving missing circumstance information. This variable has the effect of controlling for the likely undercount of felony murders. However, the time series analyses were also conducted without including the "percent missing" control variable. Both analyses produced the same basic pattern of results for the execution and execution publicity variables.

Death Penalty Variables

For the 1976-1987 period, data for the number of monthly executions were drawn from the NAACP Legal Defense and Educational Fund, Inc.'s (1988) *Death Row, U.S.A.* From 1976 through 1987, as noted, there were 93 executions for murder. The number ranged from zero to six per month.

To control for the portion of the population subject to capital punishment for murder, the death penalty status of each jurisdiction in the United States (as of the last day of each year) was determined from the Bureau of Justice Statistic's annual *Capital Punishment* series. Resident population figures were summed for abolitionist jurisdictions, and the sum was divided by the total U.S. population to compute a "percent abolition population" variable (range = 12.0 to 28.3%).

Execution Publicity

This analysis examines the effect of television news coverage of executions for felony murder. Televised execution publicity is examined because in recent decades television has become the most popular and powerful source of news in the United States. Americans rely on television more than all other media sources combined for their daily news (Roper Organization, 1983). Moreover, Americans view television as providing the most "complete," "intelligent," and "unbiased" source of news. Of particular importance, this consensus holds for the populations that are most involved in homicide—young adults, blacks, and low-income and poorly educated persons (Bower, 1985; Comstock et al., 1978; Mediamark Research, 1987).

In a recent paper, Bailey (1990) developed a scheme for examining the amount and types of television news coverage of executions, which we use in our analysis of felony murder. Bailey's scheme relies on data from the Vanderbilt Television News Archive, which began abstracting the ABC, CBS, and NBC evening news programs in 1968. All executions receiving television coverage have been indexed and abstracted since Gary Gilmore was put to death in January 1977. (There were no executions between 1968 and 1976.) Of the 93 executions between 1977 and 1987, 33 (distributed over 25 months) received coverage by one or more of the three television networks.

First, as measures of the amount of television execution publicity, Bailey (1) differentiates (as a dummy variable) between months in which there was none versus some execution publicity, (2) tallies the amount of air time, in minutes, per month devoted to executions,[12] and (3) sums the number of days per month in which there was execution publicity. (The appendix reports for 1977-1987 the names of persons whose executions received television coverage and the amount of coverage provided by the networks.[13])

Second, on the assumption that some types of execution publicity may have a more dramatic effect on homicide than other types, Bailey distinguishes among executions on a qualitative basis. He differentiates, as dummy variables, between months in which (1) artist's drawings were ($n = 6$), or were not, aired illustrating the condemned person's execution; (2) witness accounts were ($n = 11$), or were not, provided of the execution; (3) the executed person's "last words" were ($n = 9$), or were not, presented; offenders were portrayed as (4) "more" ($n = 7$) versus (5) "less" ($n = 7$) deserving of execution; and (6) execution coverage did ($n = 10$) or did not include coverage of anti-execution demonstrations.

Bailey's coding scheme pertains only to execution publicity. Publicity about other aspects of capital cases, such as the handing down of death sentences and appeals of capital convictions are not considered. Nor does he treat as execution publicity news about the activities of abolitionist groups, changes in death penalty legislation, appellate court actions, or coverage of death penalty matters outside the United States.

Following the practice of previous investigators (Bailey, 1990; Bailey and Peterson 1989; Phillips, 1980; Stack, 1987), we coded execution coverage that occurred after the twenty-third of the month as taking place the following month. The assumption here is that execution stories aired at the end of the month will have their greatest impact on homicides the next month.[14]

Alternative Execution Publicity

In our analyses, we did not consider indicators of print media attention to executions. Two primary indicators of the amount of national newspaper coverage of executions, as noted, are the *New York Times Index* and *Facts on File*. (Bailey and Peterson, 1989, and Stack, 1987, consider executions that are noted in both sources as receiving high media publicity.) With the exception of *Facts* for 1987, virtually all executions occurring between 1977 and 1987 (96%) appeared in these sources. Thus, for the period under investigation here, *Times* and *Facts* coverage of executions was essentially not a variable. Nor are there any alternative indicators of the amount of national newspaper coverage devoted to executions.

There are also no systematic figures available on the amount of magazine attention to executions. However, this is not a major concern, because with the exception of a few celebrated cases, a perusal of the tables of content of the major news magazines (*Newsweek, Time, U.S. News and World Report*) shows that they have devoted very little attention to executions. Further, by comparison with television, their circulation is very limited: *Newsweek* = 3,050,000, *Time* = 4,600,000, *U.S. News and World Report* = 2,084,000 (Oxbridge Communications, 1989).

A remaining source of news regarding executions is radio. Unfortunately, no national data are available to measure radio news coverage of executions.

In sum, it would be desirable, but is not possible, to consider additional sources of execution publicity. However, given the importance of television as a source of news, if there is merit to deterrence or brutalization arguments, it should be evident in an analysis of television publicity of executions and felony murders.

Control Variables

Monthly population, unemployment, and AFDC figures were taken from various U.S. government sources, including the *Statistical Abstract of the United States*, *Current Population Reports*, and issues of the *Annual Statistical Supplement* to the *Social Security Bulletin*. The *Statistical Abstracts* provided annual figures for the remaining sociodemographic variables. Homicide arrest data came from the yearly FBI Uniform Crime Reports. When only annual data were available, linear interpolation was employed to estimate monthly figures for the control variables. We do not view using interpolated values for these factors as an important limitation. Precise parameter estimates for the control variables are not of direct concern since they are considered to avoid spurious results for the death penalty factors.

Time Period

The analysis is limited to the period 1976-1987. We consider 1976 as a baseline year in that the first execution since 1967 in the United States took place in January 1977. For the years 1968 through 1976, there were no executions in the United States. However, following the Supreme Court's reaffirmation of capital punishment in *Gregg vs. Georgia* (1976), executions resumed in January 1977. Although it would be desirable to consider the period before the 10-year moratorium on capital punishment (1968-1976), required data are not available for this earlier period. The Vanderbilt Television News Archive (1977-1988) which is the only available source for determining the amount and type of network television news coverage of executions, was not established until 1968. The time series ends with December 1987 because data for a number of the control variables are not yet available for 1988-1990.

Findings

To reiterate, deterrence theory predicts a significant inverse relationship between felony murder rates and the provision for capital punishment, the number of executions, and the amount and type of execution publicity. Conversely, the brutalization argument predicts a significant positive association between felony murder rates and the provision for capital punishment, the number of executions, and the amount and type of media attention devoted to executions. Because previous short-term impact studies of capital punishment and homicide report evidence of both deterrence (Phillips, 1980; Stack, 1987) and brutalization (Bowers, 1988; Bowers and Pierce, 1980; King, 1978), we employed two-tailed tests of statistical significance in considering the findings for the death penalty variables for the analyses to follow.

The first step in the analysis was to examine the autoregressive structure for lag periods through $t-12$ months for the time series for index and total felony murder rates and for each type of felony murder. Here, we are concerned with problems of serial correlation. We used the SAS (Statistical Analysis System) autoregression procedure (SAS Institute, 1984) to identify and, where necessary, to fit autoregressive models. We report Yule-Walker estimates for the autoregressive analyses (Yule, 1927; Walker 1931) and ordinary least squares (OLS) estimates when there is no significant serial correlation.

The left panel of Table 1 reports the results of the analyses in which index felony

Table 1
Regression Analyses of Executions, Amount of Execution Publicity, Index Felony and Total Felony Murder Rates

Predictor Variables	Index Felonies			Total Felonies		
	b (s.e.)	b (s.e.)	b (s.e.)	b (s.e.)	b (s.e.)	b (s.e.)
% Metropolitan Population	-.0084 (.0067)	-.0096 (.0066)	-.0098 (.0067)	-.0141 (.0127)	-.0150 (.0123)	-.0137 (.0124)
% Black Population	.0347 (.0416)	.0370 (.0420)	.0375 (.0408)	-.0918 (.0646)	-.0821 (.0657)	-.0872 (.0644)
% 16-34 Years of Age	.0268*** (.0087)	.0267** (.0088)	.0262** (.0088)	.0272* (.0163)	.0280* (.0163)	.0271* (.0162)
Divorce Rate	-.0143 (.0168)	-.0146 (.0168)	-.0117 (.0169)	.0026 (.0312)	.0004 (.0312)	.0027 (.0311)
Unemployment Rate	-.0015 (.0019)	-.0012 (.0019)	-.0014 (.0018)	-.0030 (.0035)	-.0026 (.0035)	-.0027 (.0035)
% AFDC Population	.0787*** (.0198)	.0776*** (.0198)	.0821*** (.0203)	.1019** (.0370)	.0992** (.0369)	.0996** (.0368)
High Season Variable	.0105*** (.0021)	.0103*** (.0021)	.0103*** (.0022)	—	—	—
Low Season Variable	-.0099*** (.0018)	-.0098*** (.0018)	-.0099*** (.0018)	—	—	—
Homicide Arrest Rate	-.0045*** (.0014)	-.0047*** (.0014)	-.0041** (.0014)	-.0081** (.0025)	-.0083** (.0025)	-.0081** (.0025)
% Abolition Population	.0006 (.0005)	.0007 (.0005)	.0008 (.0005)	.0018 (.0010)	.0017 (.0010)	.0019 (.0010)
Number of Executions	.0005 (.0008)	.0006 (.0008)	.0005 (.0009)	.0001 (.0016)	.0001 (.0015)	-.0002 (.0016)
% Missing SHR Data	.0005 (.0004)	.0005 (.0004)	.0005 (.0004)	-.0007 (.0008)	-.0007 (.0008)	-.0007 (.0008)
Television Dummy (0/1) Variable	.0022 (.0021)	—	—	.0020 (.0040)	—	—
No. of Minutes of Coverage	—	.0002 (.0002)	—	—	.0004 (.0004)	—
No. of Days of Coverage	—	—	.0010 (.0010)	—	—	.0020 (.0020)
Intercept	-.5937 (.8713)	-.5140 (.8588)	-.5560 (.8519)	1.5136 (1.5303)	1.4644 (1.5003)	1.4378 (1.5004)
R^2	.743***	.742***	.778***	.765***	.765***	.764***
Type of Analysis	OLS	OLS	GLS	GLS	GLS	GLS
D.W.	1.95	1.96	—	—	—	—

*$p < .05$ **$p < .01$ ***$p < .001$

murder rates are regressed against the number of monthly executions and indicators of the amount of television attention devoted to executions. The right panel reports results of the analyses for total felony murders.

Table 1 provides no support for the deterrence argument. Over the period, there was a chance-only association between rates for both measures of felony murder and the provision for capital punishment, number of monthly executions, and each indicator of the amount of television coverage devoted to executions: (1) a dummy variable that differentiates months with and without television news coverage, (2) the number of minutes of air time devoted to executions, and (3) the number of days during a month with television coverage of executions.[15]

On the possibility that television coverage of executions provided by the three individual networks may have had a differential effect on killings, the analyses reported in Table 1 were repeated, but with indicators of the amount of execution coverage computed individually for ABC, CBS, and NBC. The appendix shows some variation across networks in television coverage of executions, but the variation proved unrelated to homicides. There was a chance-only association between the percent abolition variable, number of executions, the amount of television attention they received from ABC, CBS, NBC, and index and total felony murder rates. Because these findings parallel so closely those reported in Table 1, they are not presented in tabular form; however, the results are available on request.

The next step in the analysis was to consider each type of felony murder. Again, some types of felony murder may be more responsive to deterrence or brutalization than others.... Robbery murder is the most common type of felony homicide. FBI data show that the annual number of robbery-related killings ranged from 1,605 to 2,162 during the 1976-1987 period. Over the 12 years, robbery murders totaled nearly 22,000.

Again, we see no evidence of either deterrence or brutalization. Robbery murder rates varied independently of the provision for capital. Punishment, the number of monthly executions, and each measure of the amount of television coverage devoted to executions.... [T]he same pattern holds for robbery murder when the analysis is extended to consider individually the amount of coverage provided by the three networks.

The same analyses were conducted for each of the other types of felony murder reported by the FBI (see above).... With the exception of killings associated with vehicle thefts..., the analyses show only chance associations between the execution and media variables and monthly felony murder rates.

As with other types of felony murder, there was only a chance association between rates of vehicle theft murder and the provision for the death penalty and each measure of the amount of execution publicity. However, unlike other types of felony murder, there was a significant positive association between the number of monthly executions and rates for this type of killing. This pattern is puzzling. In the bivariate ($r = .329, p < .001$) and multivariate analyses ($b = .0002, p < .05$), there was a pattern of a higher number of vehicle theft murders for months with a greater number of executions. This is consistent with the brutalization argument, but it is unclear why such a pattern would hold for only one relatively uncommon type of felony murder. Over the 1976-1987 period, auto theft killings numbered only 291 according to SHR files. The number of monthly vehicle theft killings ranged from zero to seven, and rates ranged from zero to .003 ($\bar{x} = .0008$).

Types of Execution Publicity

As noted, it is possible that some types of television coverage of executions may discourage killings (deterrence) and some types may promote murder (brutalization). We explored this question by considering Bailey's six measures of the type of execution coverage provided by the networks (see above)....

Again, the dominant pattern is consistent with the null hypothesis. Total and index felony murder rates vary independently of the number of monthly executions in all cases, and of the "percent abolition population" variable in 11 of the 12 analyses. The exception to the null pattern for the percent abolition variable is for total felony murders ($b = .0020$, s.e. $= .0010, p < .05$) when the "last words" type of media variable is considered.

Also with one exception, the null hypothesis holds for each type of television coverage devoted to executions. The exception again is for the "last words" execution variable. The trade-off is slight ($b = .0068$), but there was a significant positive association between the airing of this type of execution coverage and index felony murder rates. Although this is consistent with "brutalization" predictions, it is not clear why this pattern holds for only one of the six types of execution coverage.

When the analysis of kinds of television coverage is extended to different types of felony murder, we also found no consistent support for the deterrence or brutalization argument. However, we again observed a significant ($p < .05$) positive association ($b = .0002$) between the number of monthly executions and rates of vehicle theft killings. This pattern holds when each type of execution publicity is considered.

The only other departure from the null hypothesis is for killings related to narcotics violations. Here, there was consistently only a chance association between rates and the number of executions ($b = -.0004$ to $.0031$). However, there was a significant negative association between rates and one type of execution publicity. Narcotics murders were significantly lower ($b = -.0031$, $p < .05$) for months when "nondeserving" persons were put to death. . . . For the other qualitative publicity measures, there were slight positive but nonsignificant trade-offs ($b = .0001$ to $.0006$) with rates of narcotics killings.

What is particularly interesting about the relationship between narcotics killings and television coverage of "nondeserving" executions is that in the bivariate analysis, average offense rates are slightly higher for the seven months in which such persons were executed ($\bar{x} = .0170$) than for the other 137 months ($\bar{x} = .0147$) in the time series. Consistent with the bivariate results, one might expect that the execution of "nondeserving" persons would not be terribly effective in discouraging killings because the state may be perceived as acting in a nonlegitimate manner. Or at least, the execution of "deserving" persons might be thought to have a greater deterrent effect. However, this was not the case for narcotics-related killings. One possibility is that the perception of the certainty of execution is increased when the state is willing to put to death even "nondeserving" offenders (youths, the retarded, and homicide accessories). This is of course speculative. It is clear, however, that the pattern for narcotics killings is not a result of problems of multicollinearity. First, the same "other" predictor variables were considered in examining each type of felony murder, but the significant negative results for "nondeserving" executions are unique to narcotics killings. Second, when this indicator of the type of media attention is regressed against the other predictors in the multivariate model, the resulting R^2 value ($.278$) is meager.

In short, we have no adequate explanation for this isolated finding. Nor do we have an explanation for why the number of executions is associated positively (throughout the analysis) with vehicle theft killings, but not with other types of felony murder.

Conclusion

Our results may disappoint proponents of deterrence and proponents of the brutalization argument. We find no consistent evidence that the availability of capital punishment, the number of executions, the amount of television coverage they receive, or the type of television coverage given executions is associated significantly with rates for total and different types of felony murder. These findings are consistent with the vast majority of studies of capital punishment and general homicides.

For reasons that are unclear, however, for the 1976-1987 period, we did observe a pattern of higher rates of vehicle theft killings being associated with a higher number of executions. But in the opposite direction, there were significantly lower rates of *narcotics murder* for months in which "nondeserving" persons were put to death. Although we have no adequate explanation for these two "deviant" patterns, our findings make clear that during the 1976-1987 period most types of felony murder varied independently of the frequency of executions and the amount and type of television publicity that they received.

In conclusion, there is simply no consistent evidence that executions, or their presentation to the national television viewing audience, had anything to do with felony murder during the period of this study. However, caution is warranted in interpreting these null patterns. First, for example, our null findings might be a result of the rather small number of executions during the 1976-1987 period ($n = 93$) and the fact that a minority ($n = 25$) of those executions received television coverage. We urge interested scholars to explore this possibility by extending our analysis for future years.

Second, an analysis such as ours is subject to possible spatial aggregation problems due to the entire nation (the 50 states and the District of Columbia) being the unit of analysis in the time series (Fox and Radelet, 1989). That is, monthly rates for the felony murder and death penalty variables were computed on a national basis. By including the "percent abolition" variable in the analysis, we controlled for the portion of the U.S. population subject to capital punishment. However, over the 1977-1987 period, the vast majority of executions (87/93 = 94%) took place in southern states, although our analysis assumes that residents in all death penalty jurisdictions would be affected equally by executions and execution publicity. This may or may not be the case, but clearly, future investigators should consider replicating our analysis on a regional, and possibly a state, level.

Third, as detailed earlier, SHR data also have certain limitations, including that some homicide incidents are excluded from the SHR and some crime circumstance information is missing for some cases included in the files. Missing SHR cases and data are more or less problematic for different states. Accordingly, an additional argument can be made for replicating our study on a state level.

Perhaps further analyses along the lines suggested will yield support for arguments regarding deterrence or brutalization and felony murder. At present, however, it seems safe to conclude that on a national level, the recent U.S. experience with capital punishment provides little indication that executions either discourage or encourage the most common types of capital homicides—felony murders.

Notes

1. According to a Bureau of Justice Statistics (1987) survey, 37 states provided for capital punishment for one or more types of murder. The list of capital offenses extended to other crimes in six jurisdictions: aircraft piracy (Alabama, Georgia), treason (California, Georgia), train wrecking (California), forcible rape of a child under age 14 years by a person 18 years or older (Mississippi), kidnapping (with a gross permanent physical injury inflicted on the victim) and kidnapping by a state prison inmate with a prior conviction for deliberate homicide or who has been previously declared a persistent felony offender (Montana). The following states had no provision for the death penalty for murder in any form: Alaska, Hawaii, Iowa, Kansas, Maine, Michigan, Minnesota, North Dakota, Rhode Island, West Virginia, and Wisconsin.

2. In some jurisdictions, the distinction between capital and noncapital homicide is the distinction between murder and manslaughter. For those states, *murder* involves planned, intentional killings, and the element of premeditation is absent for *manslaughter*.

3. A sizable majority of states provide for capital punishment for felony murder by (1) statutorily defining felony murder in general, or particular types of felony murder, as capital homicides or (2) providing that the commission of a felony, or a certain type of felony, resulting in a homicide constitutes an aggravating circumstance that is to be considered by a judge/jury in deciding whether to sentence a convicted murderer to death or a term of imprisonment.

4. For some states, the commission of any type of felony homicide qualifies as a capital crime. More typically, however, the types of felony murder that qualify as capital homicides include killings associated with rape, robbery, burglary, arson, and kidnapping (Bureau of Justice Statistics, 1987).

5. To illustrate, in 1987 there were 20,996 criminal homicides in the United States, 20.7% (.207 X 20,096 = 4,160) of which were classified by the FBI (1988:12) as felony or suspected felony murders. By comparison, if

classic premeditated murders constitute 10% of criminal homicides, the number of premeditated crimes ($n = 2,010$) was approximately one-half that level; and one-quarter that number ($n = 1,005$) if they constitute 5% of homicides.

6. Actually, for the 1950-1980 period Stack (1987) reports a significant negative association between monthly homicide rates and executions that received high levels of newspaper coverage—executions that appeared in both the *New York Times Index* and *Facts on File*, a comprehensive national index of major news stories. However, Bailey and Peterson (1989) show that Stack's findings are an artifact due to media coding errors. When corrected, there is a chance—only association between monthly homicide rates and executions receiving high levels of publicity for 1950-1980 and for the more extended period, 1940-1986 (Bailey and Peterson, 1989).

7. Monthly dummy variables are not significantly related to rates of larceny murder, vehicle theft murder, prostitution murder, other sex-offense murder, narcotics murder, "other" felony murder, suspected felony murder, or total felony murder.

8. Unfortunately, there are no national homicide conviction data for the 1976-1987 period. In 1972, the FBI discontinued reporting homicide conviction figures in the annual Uniform Crime Reports due to the small proportion of cases reaching judicial outcome during the reporting year.

9. To illustrate, we regressed each of the sociodemographic and other control variables against the other right-hand variables in the models shown in Tables 1-6. The resulting R^2 values are very high for most of the control factors: percent abolition population (.88), percent unemployment (.92), percent metropolitan population (.92), divorce rate (.95), percent AFDC population (.97), percent 16-34 years of age (.98), percent black population (.99), and homicide arrest rate (.96).

10. For SHR records, criminal homicide incidents may involve multiple victims (and offenders), but most incidents involve a single victim (96.3 to 97.1% for the 1976-1987 period). For this type of investigation, it is of no practical consequence whether one operationalizes offense rates as the number of homicide incidents or victims per 100,000 population. Over the period, the two types of monthly rates are almost perfectly correlated ($r = .992$).

11. Unfortunately, the FBI data do not permit the identification of *premeditated* murders that are not associated with other felonies. Nor does any federal agency collect prosecution and/or judicial data that allow an estimate of the number and rate of premeditated murders. Consequently, it is not possible to examine the effect of capital punishment on classic premeditated murders.

12. Because the size of the viewing audiences for the three evening news programs is not uniform, it would be desirable to compute a weighted execution publicity measure for each network based on audience share. A weighting scheme could also be used in forming a combined execution publicity index for the three networks. Unfortunately, it is not possible to construct weighted measures for the period under consideration. Arbitron television program ratings are available on a quarterly basis during the period, but only for individual markets ($N = 212$), and not for the national viewing audience. Due to market boundaries changing during the 1976-1987 period, and population data being available for most markets only for 1980, accurate national monthly market shares for the ABC, CBS, and NBC evening news programs are not possible. Arbitron does report national quarterly market share figures, but they are simply mean ratings averaged (without weighting) across the 212 individual U.S. market areas. For the above reasons, Arbitron advises against using these "average" figures as estimates of national viewer audiences (S. Cagner, Arbitron Rating Company, personal communication, 1989).

13. The data reported in the appendix reflect the total amount of air time devoted to executions during the months indicated. For some broadcasts, the entire amount of air time was devoted to the execution in question, but in some cases execution stories had mixed content. Often, a broadcast announced an execution but also gave details about the offender and the murder victim, aired statements by officials and other interested parties, and sometimes announced the next scheduled execution. In measuring broadcast time, we recorded the number of minutes for the entire execution story without attempting to differentiate the time devoted to executions per se versus related coverage.

14. As an alternative to considering the effects of monthly (month t) executions and television publicity on homicides, an anonymous reviewer of an earlier version of this paper recommended that we employ a three-month moving average (month $t-2$ + month $t-1$ + month $t/3$) for the death penalty variables in examining homicide rates (for month t). The analysis to follow . . . was replicated using three-month average values for each of the death penalty variables. This alternative

analysis produced no evidence of either deterrence or brutalization. (Results are available in tabular form on request.)

15. To explore possible collinearity problems for the execution variables, we regressed the number of monthly executions and each measure of the amount of execution publicity examined in Table 1 against the other right-hand variables. The resulting multiple R^2 values for the number of executions fall in the .47 to .51 range for the different models. For the measures of the amount of television attention devoted to executions, the R^2 values range from .28 to .34. (The same pattern holds for the execution and media coverage variables when each network is examined individually.) These results give no indication or collinearity problems for any of the execution variables.

References

Bailey, William C. 1975. Murder and capital punishment: Some further evidence. *American Journal of Orthopsychiatry* 45:669-688.

———. 1976. Certainty of arrest and crime rates for major felonies. *Journal of Research in Crime and Delinquency* 13:145-154.

———. 1977. Imprisonment vs. the death penalty as a deterrent to murder. *Law and Human Behavior* 1:239-260.

———. 1980. Deterrence and the celerity of the death penalty: A neglected question in deterrence research. *Social Forces* 58:1308-1333.

———. 1990. Murder and capital punishment: An analysis of television execution publicity. *American Sociological Review* 55:628-633.

Bailey, William C. and Ruth D. Peterson. 1989. Murder and capital punishment: A monthly time series analysis of execution publicity. *American Sociological Review* 54:722-743.

Beccaria, Cesare. 1963. *On Crimes and Punishment*, trans. by H. Paolucci. 1764. Indianapolis: Bobbs-Merrill.

Bedau, Hugo A. 1967. *The Death Penalty in America*. Rev. ed. Garden City, New York: Doubleday.

———. 1977. *The Courts, the Constitution, and Capital Punishment*. Lexington, Mass.: Lexington Books.

———. 1982. *The Death Penalty in America*. 3rd ed. New York: Oxford University Press.

Bentham, Jeremy. 1962. The rationale of punishment. 1843. In John Browning (ed.), *Works of Jeremy Bentham*. New York: Russell & Russell.

Black, Theodore and Thomas Orsagh. 1978. New evidence on the efficacy of sanctions as a deterrent to homicide. *Social Science Quarterly* 58:616-631.

Bower, Robert T. 1985. *The Changing Television Audience in America*. New York: Columbia University Press.

Bowers, William J. 1988. The effect of executions is brutalization, not deterrence. In Kenneth C. Haas and James A. Inciardi (eds.), *Capital Punishment: Legal and Social Science Approaches*. Newbury Park, Calif: Sage.

Bowers, William and Glenn Pierce. 1975. The illusion of deterrence in Isaac Enrlich's research on capital punishment. *Yale Law Journal* 85:187-208.

———. 1980. Deterrence or brutalization: What is the effect of executions? *Crime and Delinquency* 26:453-484.

Bureau of Justice Statistics. 1987. *Capital Punishment, 1986*. Washington, D.C.: Government Printing Office.

Bye, Raymond T. 1919. *Capital Punishment in the United States*. Philadelphia: The Committee on Philanthropic Labor of Philadelphia Yearly Meeting of Friends.

Calvert, E.R. 1927. *Capital Punishment in the Twentieth Century*. Dallas: Taylor Publishing.

Comstock, George A., Steven Chaffee, Nathan Katzman, Maxwell McCombs, and Donald Robert. 1978. *Television and Human Behavior*. New York: Columbia University Press.

Dann, Robert H. 1935. The deterrent effect of capital punishment. *Friends Social Services* 29:1-20.

Enrlich, Isaac. 1975. The deterrent effect of capital punishment: A question of life or death. *The American Economic Review* 65:397-417.

———. 1977. Capital punishment and deterrence: Some further thoughts and additional evidence. *Journal of Political Economy* 85:741-788.

Federal Bureau of Investigation. 1988. *Crime in the United States, 1987*. Uniform Crime Reports. Washington, D.C.: Government Printing Office.

———. 1989. *Crime in the United States, 1988*. Uniform Crime Reports. Washington, D.C.: Government Printing Office.

Ferri, Enrico. 1917. *Criminal Sociology*. English trans. New York: Little, Brown.

Forst, Brian. 1977. The deterrent effect of capital punishment: A cross-state analysis of the 1960s. *Minnesota Law Review* 61:743-767.

Fox, James Alan and Michael L. Radelet. 1989. Persistent flaws in econometric studies of the deterrent effect of the death penalty. *Loyola of Los Angeles Law Review* 23:29-44.

Garolalo, Raffael. 1914. *Criminology*. English trans. Boston: Little, Brown.

King, David R. 1978. The brutalizing effect: Execution publicity and the incidence of homicide in South Carolina. *Social Forces* 57:683-687.

Kirkpatrick, Clifford. 1925. *Capital Punishment*. Philadelphia: Committee of Philanthropic Labor of Philadelphia Yearly Meeting of Friends.

Kleck, Gary. 1979. Capital punishment, gun ownership, and homicide. *American Journal of Sociology* 84:882-910.

Layson, Stephen K. 1985. Homicide and deterrence: A reexamination of the United States time-series evidence. *Southern Economic Journal* 52:68-89.

Maxfield, Michael G. 1989. Circumstances in supplementary homicide reports: Variety and validity. *Criminology* 27:671-695.

McFarland, Sam G. 1983. Is capital punishment a short-term deterrent to homicide? A study of the effects of four recent American executions. *Journal of Criminal Law and Criminology* 74:1014-1030.

Mediamark Research. 1987. *Multimedia Audiences*. New York: Mediamark Research.

NAACP Legal Defense and Educational Fund, Inc. 1988. *Death Row, U.S.A.* New York: NAACP, Legal Defense and Educational Fund.

Oxbridge Communications, Inc. 1989. *The Standard Periodical Directory*. New York: Oxbridge Communications.

Passell, Peter. 1975. The deterrent effect of the death penalty: A statistical test. *Stanford Law Review* 28:61-80.

Passell, Peter and John Taylor. 1975. *The deterrent effect of capital punishment: Another view*. Discussion Paper 74.7509. New York: Columbia University.

Peterson, Ruth D. and William C. Bailey. 1988. Murder and capital punishment in the evolving social context of the post-Furman era. *Social Forces* 66:774-807.

Phillips, David P. 1980. The deterrent effect of capital punishment: New evidence on an old controversy. *American Journal of Sociology* 86:139-148.

Riedel, Marc, Margaret A. Zahn, and Lois Mock. 1985. *The Nature and Patterns of American Homicide*. National Institute of Justice. Washington, D.C.: Government Printing Office.

Roper Organization. 1983. *Trends in Attitudes Towards Television and Other Media: A Twenty Year Review*. New York: Television Information Office.

SAS Institute, Inc. 1984. *SAS/ETS User's Guide*. Version 5. Gary, N.C.: SAS Institute.

Savitz, Leonard. 1958. A study of capital punishment. *Journal of Criminal Law, Criminology and Police Science* 49:338-341.

Schuessler, Karl. 1952. The deterrent effect of the death penalty. *The Annals* 284:54-62.

Sellin, Thorsten. 1955. *In The Royal Commission of Capital Punishment (1949-1953)*. Report Great Britain Parliament (Papers by Command 8932.) London: Her Majesty's Stationery Office.

———. 1959. *The Death Penalty*. Philadelphia: American Law Institute.

———. 1967. *Capital Punishment*. New York: Harper & Row.

———. 1980. *The Penalty of Death*. Beverly Hills, Calif.: Sage.

Shipley, Maynard. 1911. Should capital punishment be abolished? The problem of the hour. *Journal of Criminal Law and Criminology* 2:48-55.

Sutherland, Edwin. 1925. Murder and the death penalty. *Journal of the American Institute of Criminal Law and Criminology* 51:522-529.

Stack, Steven. 1987. Publicized executions and homicide. *American Sociological Review* 52:532-540.

Stephen, James F. 1864. *A History of the Criminal Law in England*. London: Bert Franklin.

Tarde, Gabriel. 1912. *Penal Philosophy*. English Trans. Boston: Little, Brown.

van den Haag, Ernest. 1969. On deterrence and the death penalty. *Journal of Criminal Law, Criminology and Police Science* 60:141-147.

———. 1975. *Punishing Criminals: Concerning a Very Old and Painful Question*. New York: Basic Books.

van den Haag, Ernest and John P. Conrad. 1983. *The Death Penalty: A Debate*. New York: Plenum.

Vanderbilt Television News Archive. 1977. *Vanderbilt Television News Index and Abstracts 1977-1988*. Vanderbilt.

———. 1988. Television News Archive.

Vold, George B. 1932. Can the death penalty prevent crime? *Prison Journal* 12:3-7.

Walker, G. 1931. On periodicity in series of related terms. *Proceedings of the Royal Society*, A131:518.

Wilson, James Q. 1983. *Thinking about Crime*. Rev. ed. New York: Basic Books.

Wolfgang, Marvin E. 1958. *Patterns in Criminal Homicide*. Philadelphia: University of Philadelphia Press.

Yule, George U. 1927. On a method of investigating periodicities in disturbed series, with special reference to Wolfer's sunspot numbers. *Philosophical Transactions*. A226:267.

Yunker, James. 1976. Is the death penalty a deterrent to homicide? Some time series evidence. *Journal of Behavioral Economics* 5:1-32. ✦

Appendix
Executions Receiving Television Publicity, and the Number of Minutes of Coverage, 1977-1987
Minutes of Coverage by Television Network

Yr.	Mo.	Person's Name	ABC	CBS	NBC	Total
77	1	Gary Gilmore	9.17	10.33	7.00	26.50
79	6	John Spenkelink[a]	5.67	5.33	4.33	15.33
79	10	Jesse Bishop	3.50	5.17	2.33	11.00
81	3	Steven Judy	5.17	.67	.00	5.83
82	8	Frank Coppola	.33	.00	.00	.33
82	12	Charlie Brooks	2.17	1.67	.67	4.50
83	4	John Evans[b]	.33	4.50	3.33	8.16
83	5	John Evans[b]	.00	.33	.33	.67
83	9	Jimmy Lee Gray	1.83	2.33	.00	4.17
83	12	Robert Sullivan[a] Robert Wayne Williams John Eldon Smith	9.17	6.50	5.50	21.17
84	2	Anthony Antone[a]	.33	3.17	.17	3.67
84	3	James Autry	.17	.00	.33	.50
84	4	Ronald O'Bryan[a] Arthur Goode Elmo Sonnier	.33	.67	1.83	2.83
84	7	Ivon Stanley	.00	.17	.00	.17
84	11	Thomas Barefoot[a] Ernest Knighton[a] Velma Barfield	3.67	1.00	3.33	8.00
84	12	Alpha Otis Stephens	.17	.00	.00	.17
85	1	Robert Lee Willie[a] Doyle Skillem	8.33	.00	3.17	11.50
85	4	James Briley	.00	1.50	.67	2.17
85	7	Henery Martinez Porter	.00	.83	.00	.83
86	1	James Terry Roach	.33	2.00	.33	2.67
86	4	Daniel Thomas	.00	.00	.33	.33
86	9	Chester Wicker[a]	.00	2.00	.00	2.00
87	6	Jimmy Wingo	.00	2.50	.00	2.50
87	8	John Brogdon[a]	2.67	.00	.00	2.67
87	9	Beauford White[a]	2.50	2.50	.00	5.00

[a]These persons were executed the month prior to the date indicated. Executions occurring after the twenty-third of the month (month t) were coded for the following ($t + 1$) month.

[b]The execution of John Evans took place on April 22, 1983. However, some coverage of the execution was not aired until April 24, 1983. Hence, the publicity for April 24 was coded for May 1983.

321

Section IX
Imprisonment and Alternatives

Of all the dimensions of juvenile delinquency that are under close scrutiny, none is more problematic than the issue of imprisonment. While the original intent of the juvenile court was to keep adolescents out of jail, that "pious wish" has long disappeared and the numbers of juveniles being placed in correctional institutions have steadily increased in the 1980s and 1990s. Every state, as well as the District of Columbia, has at least one juvenile correctional facility. These range in number from one in Maine and Vermont to 92 in New York and 113 in California. Similarly, the number of juveniles in custody ranges from a low of 28 in Vermont to 3,349 in New York and 7,694 in California (*Sourcebook 1993*). Virtually all of these juvenile correctional facilities are filled to capacity and many states report that they are 10 to 15 percent over capacity; some, like California, report being 30 percent over capacity, Ohio was 67 percent over capacity, and South Carolina topped the list at 101 percent over capacity (*Sourcebook 1993*). Even more astounding is the cost of putting an adolescent into one of these juvenile institutions. In 1975 the cost was approximately $10,000 per year for one resident, doubling to $20,000 by 1982, and currently exceeding $35,000 (*Children in Custody*). These figures are restricted to "operating expenditures," which refer to salaries and wages of juvenile correctional personnel, but do not include "capital expenditures," which entail the actual cost of building the facilities. It is estimated that the true cost of institutionalizing a juvenile may be in the vicinity of $50,000 per year when operating and capital expenditures are combined.

After investing some $50,000 per year for each juvenile offender, one would assume that these institutions would have a reasonably good record of success. "Recidivism," or simply "failure rates," reflect juvenile offenders' return to delinquency after institutionalization. Unfortunately, precise recidivism data are difficult to come by, but the data that are available put the relative success at around 50 percent. That is, after spending some $50,000 on a juvenile offender the best guess is that about half of the juveniles will eventually be re-arrested. These juvenile offenders could be sent to the most exclusive schools in the country and states could actually save money!

Although precise data on recidivism are rare, the FBI conducted a noteworthy study of young adult offenders paroled in 1978. The FBI found that six years after these young adult offenders were paroled, 68 percent were re-arrested, more than 50 percent were reconvicted, and nearly 50 percent were reincarcerated. It must be emphasized that these were young adult offenders, but the outcomes clearly suggest that imprisonment fails to prevent future delinquency.

The problems with juvenile imprisonment are numerous and only a few can be discussed in this brief introduction. One major problem is what is called the "custody vs. treatment dilemma." Is the prime objective of correctional personnel simply to take juveniles off the street and hold them in confinement for a period of time or to treat and rehabilitate these offenders? Most correctional personnel consider themselves "guards" charged with seeing that inmates follow the rules and do not escape. Some correctional personnel see their task as treatment oriented and they consider themselves not guards but therapists whose job it is to help rehabilitate offenders. But every correctional institution faces this same dilemma: does the facility exist to be "custodians of inmates," or does it need to be involved in rehabilitating them? Dembo and Dertke (1986) found that the ambivalent role of juvenile correctional personnel contributed to pervasive tension which generated high job burnout and personnel turnover, while those who stayed became cynical, impersonal, and emotionally exhausted.

A second major problem in every correctional setting is what is called the "POW Syndrome." When soldiers are taken as prisoners they are duty-bound not to cooperate with their captors and in some instances even plan disruptions in the prison and contemplate escape. This so-called prisoner-of-war syndrome is also applicable to correctional institutions. Apprehended offenders are "captives" of the state and inmates resist cooperating with their captors. Bartollas, Miller, and Dinitz coined the phrase the "inmate social code" that pervades most correctional institutions. This entails the following: exploit whomever you can; don't play up to staff; don't rat on others; and don't trust anyone. Inmates at most correctional facilities endlessly scheme to manipulate the staff and to take advantage of weaker inmates. This POW honor code then virtually guarantees that little positive rehabilitation will take place in juvenile institutions. It becomes honorable for prisoners to resist their captors.

A third major characteristic of institutions is the "diamond-shaped power structure," which refers to the organization of the status hierarchy in correctional settings. At the top of the hierarchy is a small, powerful clique that dominates institutional life, often referred to as the "heavy" and his "lieutenants." Through intimidation and outright violence, this group establishes itself as the ruling entity in the prison setting. In the middle of the diamond-shaped power structure is the bulk of the inmates or "population" that simply follows the rules set down by the ruling clique. At the bottom of the diamond-shaped power structure is another small group called the "punks," "queers," or "weirdos," who are exploited and manipulated by the ruling clique. Institutions invariably take on this organizational arrangement, and the staff at a correctional facility may even use the ruling clique to help maintain order. The diamond-shaped power structure becomes part of the process of imprisonment in both juvenile and adult facilities, which again suggests that the status hierarchy of a juvenile institution may negate any rehabilitative input from correctional staff.

Because of the increasing frustration with the cost and apparent low success of traditional juvenile institutions, states have been searching for new ways to deal with juvenile offenders. What has emerged is what is called the privatization of corrections, the development of juvenile facilities run by non-profit organizations or by private entrepreneurs who expect to run an institution at a profit. According to the U.S. Department of Justice, some 36,000 youths are housed in 2,032 private juvenile facilities in the United States. While on the surface this might seem to be a positive step in juvenile corrections, there is pervasive uneasiness that by transferring to private organizations the traditional role of the state to punish criminal offenders, private entrepreneurs are eclipsing the legitimate role of government. Public facilities are acquiring more of the "hard-core" delinquent offenders, while private facilities take in status offenders, neglect and abuse cases, and voluntary commitments. As will be seen in the readings, private institutions have the luxury of "skimming off" the least serious category of offenders, while the public facilities end up with the residual category of hard-core offenders.

The first reading in this section is a compendium of national data on youth in public and private correctional facilities in the United States. While it is relatively easy to count the number of juvenile institutions in the country, it is not so simple to compute how many juveniles are confined in these facilities. As is seen in Table 1, one way is to calculate the total number of admissions on an annual basis, which can be a confusing statistic, or to select a particular day (typically February 15th of each year) and report on the number of juveniles confined in one 24-hour day. This report also carefully delineates admissions to public, state-run juvenile institutions, and private, for-profit institutions. Tables 6 and 7 give a complete breakdown by state for the number of juveniles held in public and private facilities. Of the total number of juvenile offenders in public facilities, nearly 95 percent were held for delinquent offenses, 4 percent for status offenses, and 1 percent were "nonoffenders" (dependency, neglect, abuse, etc.). For juveniles found in private facilities, 35 percent were held for delinquent offenses, 18 percent for status offenses, and more than 47 percent were classified as "nonoffenders." That is, nearly two-thirds of the juveniles in private facilities were there for something other than a delinquent offense, while in public facilities nearly all of the offenders were there for a delinquent offense. Private facilities have the option of selecting the particular type of offender they wish to work with, while public facilities must take what is sent to them. Table 9 reports the average length of a stay at public and private facilities. The average stay in public facilities is 200 days, while in private facilities it is 311 days. This means that private facilities, which take in primarily nondelinquent offenders, hold juveniles significantly longer than public facilities.

Another disturbing element in juvenile corrections is that even though youth are held in custody, they are not completely safe. While the numbers are small, it is still distressing to note that juveniles die of suicide, homicide, and illness in correctional facilities. The report ends with some information on juveniles who were sentenced to serve time in adult jails. Despite a concerted effort by the federal government to reduce the jailing of juveniles, nearly 60,000 juvenile jail admissions were made in 1990. There appears to be an increase in the number of youth who are waived or transferred from the juvenile to the adult court, and this might lead to an increase in the number of juveniles found in adult correctional institutions.

The second reading, prepared by Abt Associates, Inc., was commissioned by the Office of Juvenile Justice and Delinquency Prevention. The study examined public and private facilities by using a mail survey and by randomly selecting a sample of 95 public and private facilities for a two-day site visit. The findings highlight problem areas in juvenile correctional facilities and amplify the findings of the previous reading on juveniles in custody. As shown in Table 2, conformance rates for confinement standards by topic areas are nowhere near 100 percent for any topic area. Living space, security, suicidal behavior and health care were seen as having substantial deficiencies. One would assume that of all the topical areas to be examined that these would be the most basic and the easiest to provide. This report also listed several other areas with fewer substantial deficiencies and concluded with a puzzling finding that "conformance to procedural standards had no discernible effect on conditions within facilities." Juvenile institutions may adhere rigidly to written policies and procedures, but this does not ensure that the goals or the outcomes of the institution are positive. The report concludes with a number of cautionary notes regarding the limitations of this study. While the report examined facilities and not necessarily individuals in these correctional facilities, it was the first systematic assessment of conditions of juvenile confinement and dramatizes the need for change in juvenile institutions.

The third reading in this section, entitled "Comprehensive Strategy for Serious, Violent, and Chronic Juvenile Offenders," looks at the problem of violent offenders and the implementation of alternative strategies in addressing this problem. The authors of this report state that admissions to juvenile facilities are at their highest level ever and these facilities are operating over capacity. Juvenile arrests are increasing, particularly for violent offenses; juvenile caseloads are increasing; admissions to juvenile detention and correctional facilities reached an all-time high in 1990; and juvenile court waivers to criminal court and admissions of juveniles to adult prisons have increased dramatically since 1985. The report goes on to argue that some new approaches in intervention models must be developed to deal with the high-risk juvenile offender. The authors suggest comprehensive prevention approaches rather than the traditional rehabilitation model predicated on correctional institutions. In fact, the report seems to completely bypass any discussion of correctional facilities. It looks at the family, school, community organizations, and immediate intervention strategies. In place of traditional institutionalization this report argues for community-based sanctions that include restitution and community service. True prevention calls for strategies that attack the root causes of delinquent behavior. Rather than waiting for delinquency to occur, the prevention approach calls for the assessment of the causes of delinquency and ways to ameliorate those conditions. These could include strategies that address individual characteristics such as personal growth and life skills development, strengthening the family, presenting school opportunities, developing positive peer group influences, and offering a wide array of community-based youth programs.

Fresh, radical, and comprehensive action is called for.

This report suggests the creation of a graduated system of sanctions with quick and decisive response. Following immediate intervention, a broad continuum of intermediate sanctions must be available. This could include day treatment, supervision in the community, drug testing, or boot camps. Secure corrections are far down the sanction ladder and might be needed for chronic juvenile offenders, but the report calls for the creation of small, community-based facilities that offer follow-up care and ensure the successful reintegration of delinquent juveniles back into the community. The tone of the report is optimistic, positive, and progressive, in contrast to the traditional "doom and gloom" accounts of hopelessness and paralysis.

References

Bartollas, Clemons, Stuart J. Miller, and Simon Dinitz. 1976. *Juvenile Victimization: The Institutional Paradox.* New York: Wiley.

Children in Custody. 1991. Juvenile Justice Bulletin. U.S. Department of Justice.

Dembo, R. and M. Dertke. 1986. "Work environment correlates of staff stress in a youth detention facility." *Criminal Justice and Behavior* 13: 328-344.

Maguire, Kathleen and Ann L. Pastore. 1993. *Sourcebook of Criminal Justice Statistics 1993.* Washington, D.C.: U.S. Department of Justice. ✦

32
Juveniles Taken Into Custody: Fiscal Year 1991

Barry Krisberg
Robert DeComo

Most Recent National Data on Juveniles Taken Into Custody

This [article] contains a summary and analysis of the most current national data available on youth in public and private correctional facilities....

This reporting of national data on juvenile correctional facilities relies principally on survey information from the 1989 Census of Public and Private Juvenile Detention, Correctional, and Shelter Facilities, also known as the Children in Custody (CIC) Census. Data on juveniles in adult correctional facilities are from the Bureau of Justice Statistics' 1990 Annual Survey of Jails,[1] the 1990 Census of State and Federal Adult Correctional Facilities, and the results of the 1987 National Correctional Reporting Program....

Juveniles Taken Into Custody: Numbers and Selected Characteristics

No national data currently exist on the numbers and characteristics of youth taken into custody annually. Table 1 presents estimates of the numbers of juvenile admissions and juveniles "in custody" (1-day counts) for the most recent available year. Of the more than 1,000 facilities examined for these estimates, less than one-third were designed to hold juveniles exclusively.

Not included in these counts are data on youth admitted to police lockups. Although there are no reliable national estimates of the number of youth held in the more than 3,940 police and sheriffs' lockups, the 1990 Law Enforcement Management and Administrative Statistics (LEMAS) survey,[2] conducted by the Bureau of Justice Statistics, asked respondents to report on admissions during the 24-hour period ending Friday, June 29, 1990. A total of 747 juveniles were admitted during this period. These youth represented approximately 4 percent of all admissions to police and sheriffs' lockups on that day. Although these data are revealing, these statistics cannot be used to estimate the total number of juveniles taken into custody in lockups during a given year.

Other Federal and private facilities are used for holding juveniles in custody for which data are not currently available. Certain private facilities such as chemical dependency programs and private psychiatric hospitals also hold youth for varying lengths of stay; however, most of these admissions are not the result of court orders, but are voluntary admissions financed through private health care insurance.

The Children in Custody (CIC) Census reported 760,644 juvenile admissions to public and private juvenile facilities in calendar year 1988. In 1990, there were an estimated 59,789 juvenile admissions to adult jails, and during the year ending June 30, 1990, 11,782 persons under age 18 were admitted to State and Federal adult correctional facilities. Admissions reported in this and subsequent tables may reflect multiple counting of youth. For example, if a single youth entered several facilities as part of one legal process or if the youth was taken into custody more than once in a particular admission year, this would result in multiple counting.

The majority of juvenile admissions and 1-day counts were to public juvenile facilities. Most of these admissions occurred in short-term juvenile detention facilities. Table 1 reveals large differences between the admissions data and the 1-day counts. Although the admissions data overestimate the number of youth taken into custody, the 1-day counts underestimate the number of juveniles who enter custody each year.

Most of the current data on the characteristics of youth in juvenile facilities are based on these 1-day counts. While the 1-

---

From *Juveniles Taken Into Custody: Fiscal Year 1991*, September 1993, pp. 11-33. U.S. Department of Justice: Office of Juvenile Justice and Delinquency Prevention.

day censuses provide a snapshot of youth in custody, the data cannot be assumed to represent the characteristics of youth taken into custody during a given annual period. For example, the offense profile of the population on the census date is not representative of youth admitted to the facility on an annual basis. The more serious offenders have a higher probability of being included in any 1-day census because they are more likely to be held for a longer period of time.

What follows are summaries of the latest available data on the characteristics of youth taken into custody, as required by the 1988 Amendments to the JJDP Act.

Regional Custody Patterns

Tables 2 and 3 present the most recent data examined for regional breakdowns of juvenile custody admissions. Table 2 shows that the West had the highest percentage of total youth admissions to public juvenile facilities in 1988, while the Midwest and the South each accounted for approximately 30 percent of admissions to private juvenile facilities that year. The South had the highest percentage of youth admissions to adult jails in 1988. The Northeast had the highest proportion of youth admissions to Federal and State adult correctional facilities during 1989–1990. Table 3 shows the juvenile admission figures as rates per 100,000 eligible youth. The annual admission rate for public juvenile facilities was highest in the West (4,387). Although the Northeast had the highest admissions rate to private juvenile facilities (724) and to adult correctional facilities (114), it had the lowest admissions rate to public juvenile facilities (1,112) and to jails (50). . . .

Admissions and 1-Day Counts by Gender

Table 4 shows a comparison by gender of the distribution of juvenile admissions and 1-day counts in the various facility types. Although females accounted for 18 percent of the admissions to public juvenile facilities, they represented 40 percent of private facility admissions for the most recent census year.

Table 4 also illustrates the impact of using different units of count (admissions versus 1-day counts) on the results. For instance, 62 percent of female juveniles admitted to custody facilities entered public juvenile facilities during 1988, and just over 30 percent of female juvenile admissions were to private facilities, while 6 percent of these admissions were to jails. When 1-day counts are examined, the finding is very different. Based on the 1-day census, 37 percent of the females in custody were in public facilities, whereas 62 percent were in private facilities and less than 1 percent were in jails.

Adjudication Status

Table 5 compares the legal status of males and females admitted to public juvenile facilities. Over three-quarters of juvenile admissions to public facilities for both males and females were for detention. Males were slightly more likely than females to be admitted to public juvenile facilities on commitment status. However, females were more likely than males to be classified as voluntary admissions in these same public facilities.[3]

Reason for Custody by State and Region

Table 6 presents data for each State on the number of juveniles in custody on a given day by whether they were charged as delinquents, status offenders, or nonoffenders. In public and private juvenile facilities combined, 66,132 juveniles (70 percent) were charged with or adjudicated for delinquent offenses, 9,098 (10 percent) were for status offenses, and 18,715 (20 percent) were nonoffenders. Western states held the greatest number of youth for delinquency (24,548 or 37 percent of the Nation's delinquents reported on the 1-day count).

When public and private facilities are considered separately, a different pattern emerges regarding reasons for juveniles in custody. Most private facilities and public shelters; ranches, forestry camps, or farms; and halfway houses or group homes are nonsecure facilities with somewhat different and broader missions that may include holding status offenders and nonoffenders as well as delinquent youth. On the other hand, most public facilities, private detention centers, and training schools are secure facilities for detaining more serious juve-

Table 1
Most Recent Available Data of the Number of Juvenile Admissions and 1-Day Counts

	Number of Facilities	Number of Juvenile Annual Admissions	Number in Custody: 1-Day Counts
Total	11,909	832,215[5]	99,846[5]
Public juvenile facilities[1]	1,100	619,181	56,123
Private juvenile facilities[1]	2,167	141,463	37,822
Adult jails[2]	3,405	59,789	2,301
Adult correctional facilities[3]	1,297	11,782	3,600
Police lockups[4]	3,940	Unknown	Unknown

Note: These data were compiled from a number of seperate statistical sources. The definition of a "Juvenile" differs in each data source. Also, the data on admissions do not represent individual youth taken into custody. However, these are the only data currently available to estimate the number of youth entering custody facilities.

[1] 1989 Census of Public and Private Juvenile Detention, Correctional, and Shelter Facilities: Admissions for Calendar Year 1988; 1-day count census day was 2/15/89. "Juvenile" is defined as a person of an age (usually under 18) specified by State statute who is subject to juvenile court authority at the time of admission regardless of age at the time of the census.

[2] Annual Survey of Jails, 1990: Admissions for the year ending 6/29/90; 1-day count census day was 6/29/90. "Juvenile" is defined as a person subject to juvenile court jurisdiction or a person of juvenile age even though tried as an adult in criminal court.

[3] Census of State and Federal Adult Correctional Facilities, 1990. For the purposes of this report, "juvenile" is defined as a person under 18 years of age. Admissions are reported for the annual period ending 6/29/90; 1-day counts are for 6/29/90.

[4] Law Enforcement Management and Administrative Statistics Survey, 1990. A special analysis provided by the Bureau of Justice Statistics indicates the number of State and local police agencies having responsibility for the administration of at least one lockup.

[5] Totals do not include juveniles admitted to police lockups.

nile offenders. Our results reflect the differential nature of public and private facilities. In public facilities, 53,037 youth (or 95 percent) were held for delinquent offenses, and 2,245 (4 percent) were for status offenses. One percent of youth in public facilities were nonoffenders. However, in private facilities, 13,095 juveniles (35 percent) were held for delinquent acts, 6,853 (18 percent) were status offenders, and the largest percentage (47 percent, or 17,874 youth) was held for reasons (such as abuse and neglect) other than delinquent or status offenses.

The dominance of the Western region in the overall number of youth held for delinquent offenses is largely explained by the population in public juvenile facilities in California. Based on the 1-day counts in 1989, there were 15,774 delinquents in custody in California public facilities. These youth accounted for 24 percent of delinquents in custody nationwide on the census date.

The Northeast region is notable for holding more youth in private facilities than in public facilities (10,185 and 6,504, respectively). Private facilities in New York State reported the highest number of nonoffenders (1,741) and the highest number of status offenders (1,227).

Taking the size of the general juvenile population into account, Table 7 shows national-level custody rates per 100,000 eligible youth by region and State for public and private facilities. Nationally, there were 259 juveniles per 100,000 held for delinquent acts, 36 per 100,000 held for status offenses, and 73 per 100,000 in custody as nonoffenders in both public and private facilities.

For the most part, these custody rates mirror the findings reported in Table 6. The highest rates of custody in public facilities were for delinquent acts. Conversely, the highest rates of custody in private facilities were for nonoffenders.

Striking State-by-State differences occurred in custody rates in public facilities. The highest rate in public facilities for delinquent acts was in the District of Columbia, an entirely urban jurisdiction, where the juvenile custody rate of 665 per 100,000 was more than 3 times the national average of 207 per 100,000. The public custody rates for California and Nevada (second and third highest) were approximately twice the U.S.

Table 2
Number of Juvenile Admissions by Region, 1988

	Total		Public Juvenile Facilities[1]		Private Juvenile Facilities[1]		Jails[2]		State and Federal Adult Correctional Facilities[3]	
	Number	%	Number	%	Number	%	Number	%	Number	%
U.S.	837,689	100%	619,181	100%	141,463	100%	65,263	100%	11,782	100%
Northeast	91,841	11	51,103	8	33,253	23	2,304	3	5,181	44
Midwest	200,401	24	137,296	22	41,899	30	18,774	29	2,432	21
South	260,916	31	188,978	31	39,097	28	29,181	45	3,660	31
West	284,531	34	241,804	39	27,214	19	15,004	23	509	4

Note: These data were compiled from a number of separate statistical series. The definition of a "juvenile" in each data source is different. Also, the data on admissions do not reflect individual youth taken into custody. However, these are the only data currently available to estimate the number of youth entering custody facilities. Comparable data on juveniles in lockups and in State prisons are not available.

States in each region are:
Northeast: Connecticut, Maine, Massachusetts, New Hampshire, New Jersey, New York, Pennsylvania, Rhode Island, and Vermont.
Midwest: Illinois, Indiana, Iowa, Kansas, Michigan, Minnesota, Missouri, North Dakota, Ohio, South Dakota, and Wisconsin.
South: Alabama, Arkansas, Delaware, District of Columbia, Florida, Georgia, Kentucky, Louisiana, Maryland, Mississippi, North Carolina, Oklahoma, South Carolina, Tennessee, Texas, and West Virginia.
West: Alaska, Arizona, California, Colorado, Hawaii, Idaho, Montana, Nevada, New Mexico, Oregon, Utah, Washington, and Wyoming.

[1] 1989 Census of Public and Private Juvenile Detention, Correctional, and Shelter Facilities: Admissions for Calendar Year 1988.
[2] 1988 National Jail Census: Admissions for the year ending 6/29/88. Regional data on jails are only available through the Census of Local Jails because the Annual Survey of Jails generates national estimates only.
[3] Census of State and Federal Adult Correctional Facilities, 1990: Admissions for the year ending 6/29/90.

Table 3
Rates per 100,000 Juvenile Admissions to Custody by Region and Type of Facility, 1988

	Private Juvenile Facilities[1]	Private Juvenile Facilities[1]	Total Juvenile Facilities[1]	Jails[2]	State and Federal Adult Correctional Facilities[3]
U.S.	2,410	551	2,961	254	46
Northeast	1,112	724	1,835	50	114
Mideast	2,097	640	2,737	287	37
South	2,092	433	2,525	323	41
West	4,387	494	4,881	272	9

Note: Rates are calculated per 100,000 youth age 10 to the upper age of original court jurisdiction in each State for 1988 and are rounded to the nearest whole number. Rates for juveniles in State and Federal adult correctional facilities are calculated on the same base for 1989. These data were compiled from a number of separate statistical series. The definition of "juvenile" in each data source is different. Also, the data on admissions do not reflect individual youth taken into custody. However, these are the only data currently available to estimate the number of youth entering custody facilities.

[1] 1989 Census of Public and Private Juvenile Detention, Correctional, and Shelter Facilities: Admissions for Calendar Year 1988.
[2] 1988 National Jail Census: Admissions for the year ending 6/29/88.
[3] Census of State and Federal Adult Correctional Facilities, 1990: Admissions for the year ending 6/29/90.

Table 4
Juvenile Admissions to Custody and 1-Day Counts in Custody by Gender

	Total		Males		Females	
	Number	%	Number	%	Number	%
Admissions, 1988						
Total	825,907	100%	644,647	100%	181,260	100%
Public juvenile facilities[1]	619,181	75	506,309	79	112,872	62
Private juvenile facilities[2]	141,463	17	84,251	13	57,212	32
Adult jails[2]	65,263	8	54,087	8	11,176	6
1-Day Counts, 1989						
Total	96,621	100	77,609	100	18,012	100
Public juvenile facilities[1]	56,123	59	49,443	64	6,680	37
Private juvenile facilities[1]	37,822	39	26,602	34	11,220	62
Adult jails[2]	1,676	2	1,564	2	112	1

Note: These data were compiled from a number of separate statistical series. The definition of a "juvenile" in each data source is different. Also, the data on admissions do not reflect individual youth taken into custody. However, these are the only data currently available to estimate the number of youth entering custody facilities. Comparable data on juveniles in lockups and in State prisons are not available.

[1] 1989 Census of Public and Private Juvenile Detention, Correctional, and Shelter Facilities: Admissions for Calendar Year 1988; 1-day counts for census day 2/15/89.

[2] 1988 National Jail Census: Admissions are for the year ending 6/29/88. 1-Day Counts for Census 6/29/88.

Table 5
Juvenile Admissions to Public Facilities by Adjudication Status and Gender, 1988

Adjudication Status	Total		Males		Females	
	Number	%	Number	%	Number	%
Total	619,181	100%	506,309	100%	112,872	100%
Detention	496,659	80	400,395	79	96,264	85
Commitment	118,219	19	103,690	21	14,529	13
Voluntary*	4,303	1	2,224	**	2,079	2

Note: Comparable data on adjudication status are not available for private facilities, jails, and State correctional facilities.

*A type of admission in which a juvenile voluntarily commits himself or herself to a facility without having been adjudicated by a court. The juvenile may be referred to the facility by parents, court, school or a social agency.

**Denotes less than 0.5 percent.

Source: 1989 Census of Public Juvenile Detention, Correctional, and Shelter Facilities: Admissions for Calendar Year 1988.

average. Nebraska and Alaska stood out for having nonoffenders in their private juvenile facilities at rates over 3 times the national average. These, however, were mostly nonsecure facilities.

Demographic Characteristics

Gender. Figure 1 shows that males are the majority of those held in public and private juvenile correctional facilities. Eighty-one percent of the youth in public and private facilities in 1989 were males. Figure 2 shows that the male in-custody rate per 100,000 age-eligible male youth was 580, while the comparable rate for female youth was 144. The in-custody rate for females was substantially higher in private than in public facilities.

Race/Ethnicity. Comparing youth in custody by race and ethnicity reveals very

Table 6
Juveniles in Custody in Juvenile Facilities by Reason for Custody by Region and State: 1-Day Counts, 1989

	All Facilities			Public Facilities			Private Facilities		
	Delinquent Offenses	Status Offenses	Non-Offenders	Delinquent Offenses	Status Offenses	Non-Offenders	Delinquent Offenses	Status Offenses	Non-Offenders
U.S. Total	66,132	9,098	18,715	53,037	2,245	841	13,095	6,853	17,874
Northeast	10,344	2,299	4,046	6,235	156	113	4,109	2,143	3,933
Connecticut	440	96	359	276	21	0	164	75	359
Maine	290	0	56	262	0	0	28	0	56
Massachusetts	680	81	272	225	0	2	455	81	270
New Hampshire	162	43	34	136	0	0	26	43	34
New Jersey	1,823	125	219	1,794	81	82	29	44	137
New York	3,027	1,232	1,742	2,342	5	1	685	1,227	1,741
Pennsylvania	3,701	654	1,126	1,061	36	28	2,640	618	1,098
Rhode Island	170	65	140	115	13	0	55	52	140
Vermont	51	3	98	24	0	0	27	3	98
Midwest	14,620	3,876	6,016	11,119	1,204	291	3,501	2,672	5,725
Illinois	1,901	102	305	1,800	3	0	101	99	305
Indiana	1,340	595	648	1,035	226	79	305	369	569
Iowa	670	465	494	327	81	39	343	384	455
Kansas	898	158	544	665	28	27	233	130	517
Michigan	2,614	366	800	1,786	120	51	828	246	749
Minnesota	1,042	229	413	624	16	1	418	213	412
Missouri	718	421	588	700	286	22	18	135	566
Nebraska	394	189	412	287	8	4	107	181	408
North Dakota	128	57	75	73	20	0	55	37	75
Ohio	3,379	955	1,059	2,945	376	66	434	579	993
South Dakota	289	101	61	187	31	0	102	70	61
Wisconsin	1,247	238	617	690	9	2	557	229	615
South	16,620	1,700	5,441	14,683	592	327	1,937	1,108	5,114
Alabama	867	176	67	808	83	4	59	93	63
Arkansas	290	16	157	259	3	4	31	13	153
Delaware	161	0	10	146	0	0	15	0	10
D. of Columbia	460	29	13	379	14	3	81	15	10
Florida	2,525	49	747	2,234	16	34	291	33	713
Georgia	1,621	132	444	1,509	73	13	112	59	431
Kentucky	542	196	322	500	97	17	42	99	305
Louisiana	1,112	135	140	1,032	27	15	80	108	125
Maryland	942	80	323	775	7	10	167	73	313

Table 6 (Continued)

	All Facilities			Public Facilities			Private Facilities		
	Delinquent Offenses	Status Offenses	Non-Offenders	Delinquent Offenses	Status Offenses	Non-Offenders	Delinquent Offenses	Status Offenses	Non-Offenders
South	*(Continued)*								
Mississippi	415	39	8	410	35	8	5	4	0
North Carolina	934	154	347	839	25	22	95	129	325
Oklahoma	431	105	372	280	12	30	151	93	342
South Carolina	738	65	87	724	38	5	14	27	82
Tennessee	972	84	268	892	46	34	8-	38	234
Texas	2,826	212	1,358	2,290	38	22	536	174	1,336
Virginia	1,525	173	710	1,435	78	108	90	95	604
West Virginia	259	55	68	171	0	0	88	55	68
West	24,548	1,223	3,212	21,000	293	110	3,548	930	3,102
Alaska	267	32	138	191	0	0	76	32	138
Arizona	1,334	46	214	1,064	20	5	270	26	209
California	17,855	442	1,667	15,774	73	22	2,081	369	1,645
Colorado	850	134	305	546	20	0	304	114	305
Hawaii	85	18	14	80	8	1	5	10	13
Idaho	160	23	34	113	2	0	47	21	34
Montana	205	37	103	177	4	26	28	33	77
Nevada	659	74	43	496	54	16	163	20	27
New Mexico	574	45	91	512	7	5	62	38	86
Oregon	969	80	213	627	1	0	342	79	213
Utah	264	93	81	190	28	6	74	65	75
Washington	1,206	43	221	1,168	1	29	38	42	192

different patterns in public as opposed to private juvenile facilities. Whereas white youth accounted for 40 percent of the 1-day counts in public facilities, they represented 60 percent of the counts in private facilities on the census date (see Figure 3).

Overall, regardless of race, youth are more likely to be held in public than in private facilities (see Figure 4). The most striking differences in custody rates are between racial groups held in the different types of facilities: while white youth were only slightly more likely to be held in a public facility than in a private facility (about 1.3 times), black and Hispanic youth were substantially more likely to be held in public juvenile facilities (2.2 and 2.8 times, respectively).

Age. The vast majority (79 percent) of juveniles in custody in 1989 were between 14 and 17 years old (see Figure 5). In private facilities, a greater proportion of the daily population was under age 14 compared to public facilities (18 percent compared to 6 percent, respectively). The opposite was true for older juveniles: 14 percent of youth in public facilities were 18 and over, whereas only 4 percent of youth in private facilities were over 17.

Offenses and Gender

Table 8 compares the most serious offenses for which male and female juveniles were held in public and private facilities on the 1989 census date. These data are presented separately for public and private fa-

Table 7
1-Day Count Rates of Juveniles in Custody by Reason for Custody by Region and State, 1989

	All Facilities			Public Facilities			Private Facilities*		
	Delinquent Offenses	Status Offenses	Non-Offenders	Delinquent Offenses	Status Offenses	Non-Offenders	Delinquent Offenses	Status Offenses	Non-Offenders
U.S. Total	259	36	73	207	9	3	51	27	70
Northeast	228	51	89	137	3	3	91	47	87
Connecticut	184	40	150	115	9	0	69	31	150
Maine	215	0	41	194	0	0	21	0	41
Massachusetts	142	17	57	47	0	0	95	17	56
New Hampshire	136	36	29	114	0	0	22	36	29
New Jersey	230	16	28	227	10	10	4	6	17
New York	221	90	127	171	0	0	50	89	127
Pennsylvania	297	52	90	85	3	2	212	50	88
Rhode Island	173	66	143	117	13	0	56	53	143
Vermont	84	5	161	39	0	0	44	5	161
Midwest	225	60	93	171	19	5	54	41	88
Illinois	174	9	28	165	0	0	9	9	28
Indiana	204	90	98	157	34	12	46	56	86
Iowa	214	149	158	104	26	12	110	123	145
Kansas	329	58	199	244	10	10	85	48	189
Michigan	241	34	74	165	11	5	76	23	69
Minnesota	221	49	87	132	3	0	89	45	87
Missouri	148	87	121	144	59	5	4	28	116
Nebraska	219	105	229	159	4	2	59	101	227
North Dakota	171	76	100	97	27	0	73	49	100
Ohio	272	77	85	237	30	5	35	47	80
South Dakota	357	125	75	231	38	0	126	86	75
Wisconsin	232	44	115	128	2	0	104	43	114
South	185	19	61	164	7	4	22	12	57
Alabama	173	35	13	161	17	1	12	19	13
Arkansas	99	5	54	88	1	1	11	4	52
Delaware	227	0	14	206	0	0	21	0	14
D. of Columbia	939	59	27	773	29	6	165	31	20
Florida	214	4	63	189	1	3	25	3	60
Georgia	237	19	65	220	11	2	16	9	63
Kentucky	122	44	72	112	22	4	9	22	69
Louisiana	239	29	30	222	6	3	17	23	27
Maryland	197	17	68	162	1	2	35	15	65
Mississippi	121	11	2	119	10	2	1	1	0

Table 7 (Continued)

	All Facilities			Public Facilities			Private Facilities*		
	Delinquent Offenses	Status Offenses	Non-Offenders	Delinquent Offenses	Status Offenses	Non-Offenders	Delinquent Offenses	Status Offenses	Non-Offenders
South (Continued)									
North Carolina	173	29	64	156	5	4	18	24	60
Oklahoma	119	29	102	77	3	8	42	26	94
South Carolina	201	18	24	197	10	1	4	7	22
Tennessee	171	15	47	157	8	6	14	7	41
Texas	160	12	77	129	2	1	30	10	76
Virginia	243	28	113	229	12	17	14	15	96
West Virginia	115	24	30	76	0	0	39	24	30
West	441	22	58	377	5	2	64	17	56
Alaska	453	54	234	324	0	0	129	54	234
Arizona	342	12	55	273	5	1	69	7	54
California	595	15	56	526	2	1	69	12	55
Colorado	246	39	88	158	6	0	88	33	88
Hawaii	75	16	12	71	7	1	4	9	12
Idaho	119	17	25	84	1	0	35	16	25
Montana	220	40	111	190	4	28	30	35	83
Nevada	594	67	39	447	49	14	147	18	24
New Mexico	310	24	49	277	4	3	34	21	46
Oregon	321	26	71	208	0	0	113	26	71
Utah	100	35	31	72	11	2	28	25	29
Washington	238	8	44	230	0	6	7	8	38
Wyoming	190	248	140	98	119	0	92	129	140

Note: Rates are calculated per 100,000 youth age 10 to the upper age of original court jurisdiction in each State for 1989 and are rounded to the nearest whole number.

* May include some out-of-State placements in some jurisdictions.

cilities because reasons for custody in each of these facilities are quite different. About 97 percent of males were held in public facilities for delinquent offenses, whereas just over three-quarters of females in public facilities were in custody for delinquent offenses. Only 2 percent of males in public facilities were held for status offenses, but nearly 17 percent of females were held in public facilities for status offenses.

The offense breakdown for private facilities is vastly different both for juveniles in general and for the experiences of males and females. Only 44 percent of males and

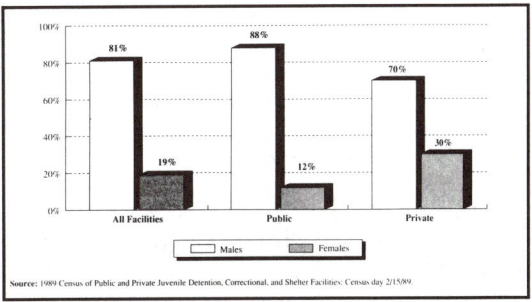

Figure 1
Juveniles in Custody by Gender: 1-Day Counts in Public and Private Facilities, 1989

Source: 1989 Census of Public and Private Juvenile Detention, Correctional, and Shelter Facilities: Census day 2/15/89.

Figure 2
Juveniles in Custody by Gender: 1-Day Count Rates in Public and Private Facilities, 1989

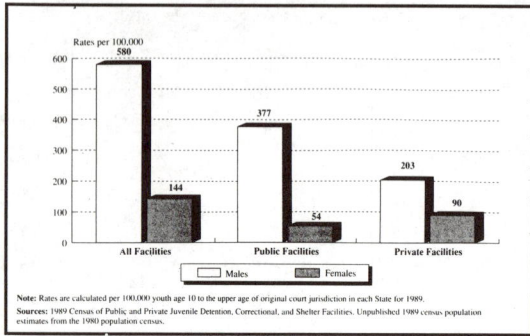

Figure 4
Juveniles in Custody by Race and Ethnicity: 1-Day Count Rates in Public and Private Facilities, 1989

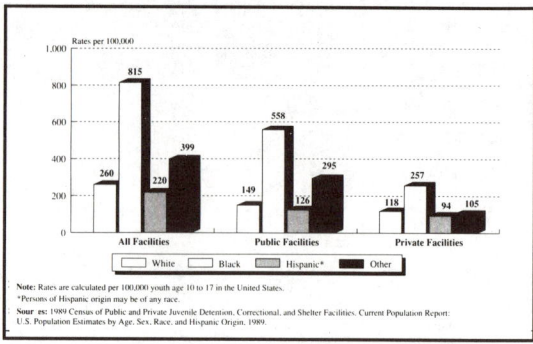

Figure 3
Juveniles in Custody by Race and Ethnicity: 1-Day Count Rates in Public and Private Facilities, 1989

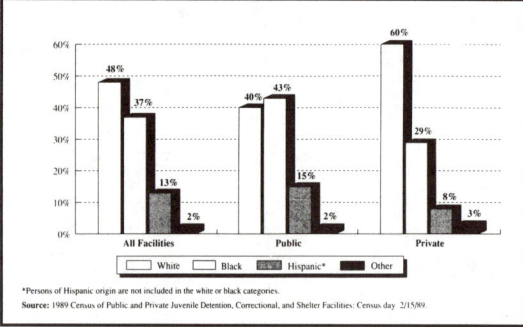

Figure 5
Juveniles in Custody by Age: 1-Day Counts in Public and Private Facilities, 1989

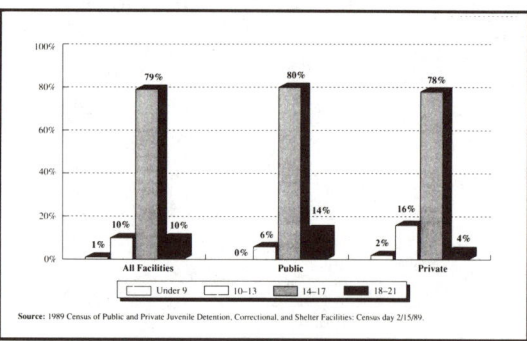

13 percent of females were in custody in private facilities for delinquent offenses. Further, more than one-quarter of the males and more than one-third of the females in custody in private juvenile facilities were nonoffenders (held for reasons of dependency, neglect, abuse, emotional disturbance, or related reasons). Finally, of the males in private facilities, 15 percent were in custody for status offenses and 16 percent for voluntary commitments, while 26 percent of the females were in custody for status offenses and over 24 percent for voluntary commitments.

Length of Stay in Custody

According to the 1989 Children in Custody (CIC) Census, juveniles stayed longer in private juvenile facilities than in public facilities. More detailed breakdowns of facility designations are presented in Table 9 to illustrate this finding on the length of stay. Overall, youth stayed longer in private than in public facilities, even when considering the different types of public and private facilities. For example, a youth sent to a private training school, rather than a public one, on the average remained an additional 4 months.

Deaths in Custody

In the 1989 CIC Census, respondents were asked for the first time about the number of deaths of juveniles in custody during the previous calendar year and the circumstances of those deaths. Tables 10, 11, and 12 present

Table 8
Juveniles in Custody in Public and Private Juvenile Facilities by Reason for Custody and Gender: 1-Day Counts, 1989

	Total	Males	Females
Public Facilities	(N=56,123)	(N=49,443)	(N=6,680)
Delinquent offenses	95%	97%	78%
1. Violent	15	16	9
2. Other personal	10	11	8
3. Serious property	27	29	16
4. Other property	14	14	13
5. Alcohol offenses	1	1	2
6. Drug-related offenses	11	11	6
7. Public order offenses	5	5	6
8. Probation/parole violations	9	8	15
9. Other	3	3	4
Status offenses	4	2	17
Non-offenders	1	1	4
Voluntary commitments	0.5	0	2
Private Facilities	(N=37,822)	(N=26,602)	(N=11,220)
Delinquent offenses	36%	44%	13%
1. Violent	2	3	1
2. Other personal	5	6	1
3. Serious property	9	12	2
4. Other property	10	12	5
5. Alcohol offenses	1	1	1
6. Drug-related offenses	4	5	1
7. Public order offenses	1	1	1
8. Probation/parole violations	1	1	6
9. Other	3	4	1
Status offenses	18	15	26
Non-offenders	29	25	37
Voluntary commitments	18	16	24

Note: Offense categories include the following offenses:

Violent: Murder, nonnegligent manslaughter, forcible rape, robbery, and aggravated assault.
Other personal: Negligent manslaughter, assault, and sexual assault.
Serious property: Burglary, arson, larceny-theft, and motor vehicle theft.
Other property: Vandalism, forgery, counterfeiting, fraud, stolen property, and unauthorized vehicle use.
Public order: Alcohol offenses, drug-related offenses, and public order offenses.
Status: Offenses not considered crimes if committed by adults.
Nonoffenders: Dependency, neglect, abuse, emotional disturbance, retardation, or other.
Source: 1989 Census of Public and Private Juvenile Detention, Correctional, and Shelter Facilities: Census day 2/15/89.

these data for both public and private facilities by region, type of facility, and gender.

From Table 10, 33 deaths were reported in public and 23 in private juvenile facilities in 1988. The majority of fatalities in public facilities occurred in the South and West, whereas the majority of private facility deaths were reported in the Midwest and West. Over half of all deaths in public juvenile facilities (17) were by suicide. The suicide rate (based on annual admissions) for youth admitted to all public and private juvenile facilities was 3.1 per 100,000 admissions. The suicide rate was 10.2 per 100,000 for the general youth population aged 15–19 years in 1986 (Select Committee on Children, Youth, and Families, U.S. Children, Youth, and Their Families: *Current Conditions and Recent Trends,* 1989, p. 189).

Also from Table 10, 8 youth were murdered and 4 died from illnesses. There were no recorded fatalities due to AIDS. Another

20 of the deaths were for other reasons, including accidents.

From Table 11, the majority of deaths in public facilities in 1988 occurred in detention centers and training schools, while the majority of deaths in private facilities occurred in halfway houses and group homes. In public detention centers and training schools, the majority of deaths were by suicide, while the majority of deaths in private halfway houses and group homes were due to accidents and other causes.

From Table 12, over 90 percent of the deaths in both public and private facilities were males. The majority of male deaths in public facilities were by suicide, while the majority of deaths in private facilities were due to other causes such as accidents.

The 1988 National Jail Census reported that 5 juveniles died in jails (4 males and 1 female) in 1988. All but one of these deaths were suicides. Using juvenile admissions to calculate the suicide rate yielded 6 suicides per 100,000 juvenile admissions to jails. This rate is compared with 2 suicides for every 100,000 juvenile admissions to public detention centers.

National Estimates on the Use of Detention

This section gives the most recent data on the use of detention for juveniles, re-

Table 9
Public and Private Dentention and Correctional Facilities: Average Length of Stay (in Days) by Gender, 1988

	Total	Males	Females
Public Facilities			
All short term facilities[1]	16	16	14
Detention Centers	15	15	14
All long-term facilities[2]	167	176	131
Training schools	200	204	169
Private Facilities			
All short-term facilities[1]	23	24	22
Detention centers	24	23	24
All long-term facilities[2]	189	211	150
Training schools	311	314	302

Note: Average length of stay was computed in two steps: (1) the facility-level average length of stay (in days) was multiplied by the number of releases, resulting in "service days" weighted by releases; (2) the resulting weighted "service days" were divided by the total releases on the national level to derive the aggregated U.S. average length of stay.

[1] Short-term facilities refer to those typically holding juveniles awaiting adjudication or other disposition. These generally include detention centers and shelter facilities.

[2] Long-term facilities include those generally holding juveniles who have been adjudicated and committed to custody. These generally include training schools, camps, ranches, and farms.

Source: Census of Public and Private Juvenile Detention, Correctional, and Shelter Facilities: Census day 2/15/89.

Table 10
Deaths in Juvenile Detention and Correctional Facilities by Region, 1988

	Total		Illness		Suicide		Homicide		Other	
	Number	%	Number	%	Number	%	Number	%	Number	%
Public Facilities										
Total	33	100	2	6	17	52	6	18	8	24
Northeast	3	100	0	0	1	33	1	33	1	33
Midwest	4	100	1	25	2	50	0	0	1	25
South	13	100	0	0	7	54	3	23	3	23
West	13	100	1	8	7	54	2	15	3	23
Private Facilities										
Total	23	100	2	9	7	30	2	9	12	52
Northeast	4	100	1	25	1	25	0	0	2	50
Midwest	7	100	0	0	2	29	1	14	4	27
South	4	100	0	0	2	50	0	0	2	50
West	8	100	1	13	2	25	1	13	4	50

Note: Illness may include illnesses or death by natural cause; homicide includes homicide by residents and others. Percentages may not add up due to rounding.

Source: 1989 Census of Public and Private Juvenile Detention, Correctional, and Shelter Facilities: Census day 1/15/89.

Table 11
Deaths in Juvenile Detention and Correctional Facilities by Type of Facility, 1988

	Total		Illness		Suicide		Homicide		Other	
	Number	%	Number	%	Number	%	Number	%	Number	%
Public Facilities										
Total	33	100	2	6	17	52	6	18	8	24
Detention centers	11	100	1	9	7	64	2	18	1	9
Reception/ diagnostic centers	3	100	0	0	3	100	0	0	0	0
Traing schools	16	100	1	6	7	44	2	13	6	38
Ranch/camps or farms	2	100	0	0	0	0	1	50	1	50
Halfway houses/ group homes	1	100	0	0	0	0	1	100	0	0
Private Facilities										
Total	23	100	2	9	7	30	2	9	12	52
Detention centers	4	100	0	0	3	75	0	0	1	25
Reception/ diagnostic centers	1	100	0	0	0	0	0	0	1	100
Training schools	2	100	1	50	1	50	0	0	0	0
Ranch/camps or farms	2	100	0	0	0	0	1	50	1	50
Halfway houses/ group homes	14	100	1	7	3	21	1	7	9	64

Note: Illness may include illness or death by natural cause; homicide includes homicide by residents and others. Percentages may not add up due to rounding.

Source: 1989 Census of Public and Private Juvenile Detention, Correctional, and Shelter facilities: Census day 2/15/89.

ported by the National Center for Juvenile Justice as part of the *Juvenile Court Statistics* series. Since 1929, this series has been the primary source of information on activities of the Nation's juvenile courts. The most recent report describes the number and characteristics of delinquency and status offense cases disposed in 1989 by courts with juvenile jurisdiction. The present report is a product of the National Juvenile Court Data Archive, whose data collection and other activities are funded by OJJDP grants.

The detention data presented below and other data reported in the *Juvenile Court Statistics* series are based on national estimates generated from a large nonprobability sample of courts having jurisdiction over more than 56 percent of the youth population at risk. Therefore, statistical confidence in the estimates cannot be mathematically determined. Although this is a disadvantage, these data provide a more detailed analysis of the characteristics of juveniles taken into this type of custody than do other national data sources such as CIC. For that reason, these national estimates of the use of detention reported through the *Juvenile Court Statistics* series have been included to provide the most complete reporting of the most recent data available on juveniles taken into custody.

A youth may be placed in a detention facility at various points as a case progresses through the juvenile justice system. Detention practices vary by State and by court. Law enforcement agencies may detain juveniles in jails and lockups, court intake officials may order detention, and a judicial decision to detain or continue detention may occur before or after adjudication or disposition. This section presents data only on those detentions that occur in a restrictive facility under court authority while the youth is being processed by the court. Therefore, detentions by law enforcement

Table 12
Deaths in Juvenile Detention and Correctional Facilities by Gender, 1988

	Total		Illness		Suicide		Homicide		Other	
	Number	%	Number	%	Number	%	Number	%	Number	%
Public Facilities										
Total	33	100	2	6	17	52	6	18	8	24
Males	30	100	2	7	16	53	5	15	7	21
Females	3	100	0	0	1	33	1	33	1	33
Private Facilities										
Total	23	100	2	9	7	30	2	9	12	52
Males	22	100	2	9	6	27	2	9	12	55
Females	1	100	0	0	1	100	0	0	0	0

Note: Illness may include illness or death by natural cause; homicide includes homicide by residents and others. Percentages may not add up due to rounding. With the exception of data from the 1988 census, these estimates are based on sample data. Fluctuations in the numbers may be due in part to sampling error.
Source: 1989 Census of Public and Private Juvenile Detention, Correctional, and Shelter Facilities: Census day 2/15/89.

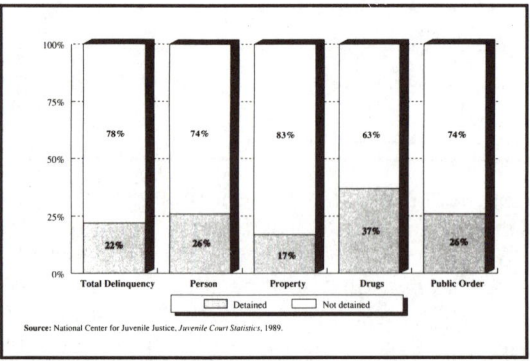

Figure 6
Use of Detention in Delinquency Cases by Offense, 1989

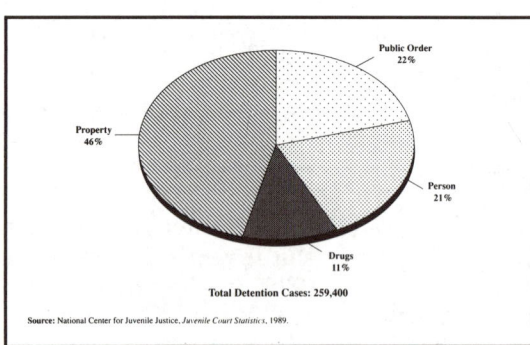

Figure 7
Offence Characteristics of Delinquency Cases Detained, 1989

prior to referral to court intake and those detentions that occur after the disposition of the case are not included in the following discussion.

Detained Delinquency Cases

In 1989, courts with juvenile jurisdiction disposed an estimated 1,189,200 delinquency cases. Youth were held in a detention facility at some point between referral to court intake and case disposition in 259,400 delinquency cases, or 22 percent of all delinquency cases disposed in 1989 (Figure 6). Also in 1989, youth charged with a property offense were least likely to be detained (17 percent), while youth charged with a drug offense were most likely (37 percent). Even though those charged with property offenses were the least likely to be detained, their volume of the courts' caseload accounted for nearly half (46 percent) of the delinquent youth held in detention in 1989 (Figure 7). By comparison, 21 percent of detained youth were charged with a personal offense, 11 percent with a drug offense, and 22 percent with a public order offense.

As Table 13 illustrates, the use of detention has varied depending on gender, race, or age. Delinquency cases involving nonwhite youth were more likely to result in detention (28 percent) than those involving white youth (19 percent). The data also show this variation in the use of detention for white versus nonwhite youth across all offense groups. The greatest racial variation in the use of detention was for youth charged with a drug law violation; 55 percent of nonwhites were detained, compared with 23 percent of white youth. Males were also generally more likely than females to be detained. Only in public order offense cases were females as likely to be detained as males. Finally, older youth (14 years of age and older) were more likely to be detained for all types of delinquent offenses than their younger counterparts.

Detained Status Offense Cases

In 1989, courts with juvenile jurisdiction disposed an estimated 286,300 status offense cases. An estimated 18,300 youth, 6 percent of these status offense cases, were held in a detention facility at some point between referral to court and case disposition (Figure 8). A runaway was the status offender case most likely to be detained (16 percent), while a status offender charged with truancy was the least likely (3 percent). Runaways also accounted for the largest group of detained status offenders (47 percent). See Figure 9.

Table 14 presents data for 1989 on the use of detention for status offenders by gender, race, and age at court referral. White and nonwhite youth were equally likely to be detained for being a runaway and ungovernable.

Table 13
Variation in the Use of Detention in Delinquency Cases by Gender, Race, and Age at Court Referral (Percent of Cases Detained), 1989

	Total Delinquency	Person	Property	Drugs	Public Order
Offense	23%	26%	17%	37%	26%
Gender					
Male	23	27	18	38	27
Female	18	20	13	28	26
Race					
White	19	22	15	23	26
Nonwhite	28	31	23	55	30
Age at Court Referral					
10	6	10	5	*	8
11	10	14	8	31	13
12	13	17	10	29	21
13	18	21	15	33	26
14	22	26	18	35	29
15	25	28	21	38	39
16	25	30	21	37	28
17	25	30	20	37	26

Note: Youth of Hispanic ethnicity were generally included in the white racial category.
* Too few cases to obtain a reliable percentage.
Source: National Center for Juvenile Justice, special analysis of 1989 data from the National Juvenile Court Data Archive.

Nonwhite youth were more likely than white youth to be detained for liquor law violations, while the opposite was true for truancy.

Males and females were almost equally likely to be detained for all types of status offenses; however, males were only slightly more likely to be detained for being a runaway, being ungovernable, and committing a liquor offense. Finally, there was no consistent pattern in the use of detention for status offenses by age groups.

Juveniles in Adult Jails

Data from the Annual Survey of Jails conducted between 1985 and 1990 show some encouraging results for the Federal effort to reduce the jailing of juveniles. Between 1985 and 1990, juveniles admitted to jails

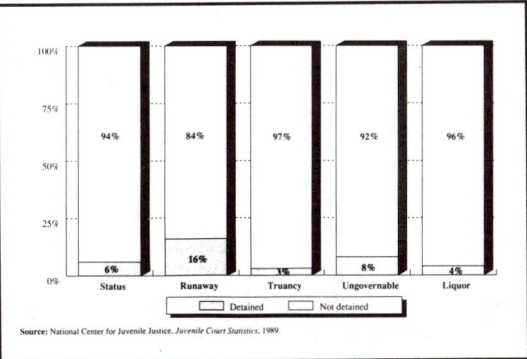

Figure 8
Use of Detention in Status Offense Cases by Offense, 1989

Source: National Center for Juvenile Justice. *Juvenile Court Statistics, 1989.*

Figure 9
Offense Characteristics of Status Offense Cases Detained, 1989

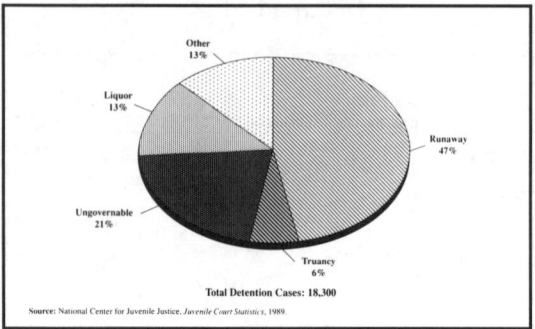

Figure 10
Juvenile Admissions to Jails by Gender, 1985-1990

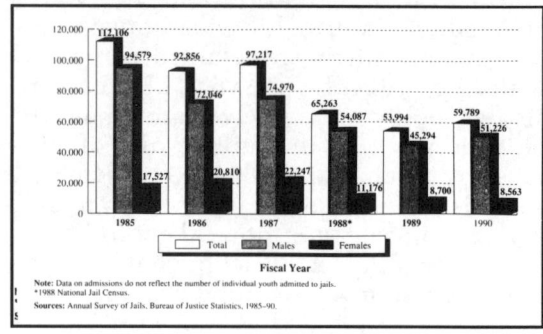

Table 14
Variation in the Use of Detention in Status Offense Cases by Gender, Race, and Age at Court Referral (Percent of Cases Detained), 1989

	Total Status Offense	Runaway	Truancy	Ungovernable	Liquor
Offense	6%	15%	2%	7%	3%
Gender					
Male	6	16	3	8	4
Female	7	14	2	6	2
Race					
White	6	15	3	7	3
Nonwhite	7	16	1	7	7
Age at Court Referral					
10	2	7	0	3	*
11	3	5	3	3	*
12	5	12	1	5	3
13	7	15	3	6	3
14	8	16	3	7	4
15	8	15	2	8	4
16	6	16	2	8	3
17	5	13	2	11	3

Note: Nearly all youth of Hispanic ethnicity were included in the white racial category.
* Too few cases to obtain a reliable percentage.
Source: National Center for Juvenile Justice, Special analysis of 1989 data from the National Juvenile Court Data Archive.

Figure 11
Juvenile Admission Rates to Jails, 1985-1990

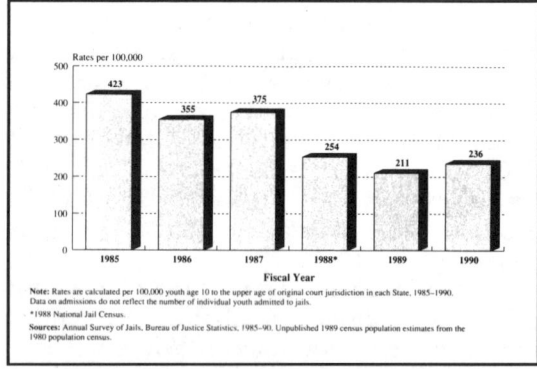

declined from 112,106 to 59,789—a decline of 47 percent (Figure 10).

During this same period, admissions to jail of male and female juveniles declined by 46 and 51 percent, respectively. The jail admissions rate per 100,000 juveniles dropped from 423 to 236 (Figure 11).

Other data from the Annual Survey of Jails reported a 41-percent increase in the number of juveniles in jails based on a 1-day census. The number of juveniles counted in the 1-day jail counts increased from 1,629 to 2,301 between 1985 and 1990 (Figure 12). This finding appears contradictory, given the significant declines in admissions discussed above.

Several possible explanations could account for differences in trends in admissions versus the 1-day counts. Because the Annual Survey of Jails covers about one-third of all local jails, the result is a slight fluctuation in various statistics that stems from sampling error. The reader should recall that juveniles account for a very small fraction of jail admissions and 1-day populations. Thus, any trend data with respect to juveniles might be subject to fairly wide fluctuation from year to year. The trends

Table 15
Youth Under 18 Admitted to State and Federal Correctional Facilities and the Upper Age of Juvenile Court Jurisdiction in Each Reporting State

State	Youth Under 18 Admitted to State and Federal Correctional Facilities[1]	Upper Age of Juvenile Court Jurisdiction[2]
Alabama	66	17
California	14	17
Colorado	11	17
Dist. Columbia	2	17
Georgia	232	16
Illinois	157	16
Iowa	25	17
Kentucky	5	17
Maryland	131	17
Massachusetts	25	16
Michigan	178	16
Minnesota	23	17
Mississippi	48	17
Missouri	86	16
Nebraska	19	17
Nevada	10	17
New Hampshire	1	17
New Jersey	44	17
New York	316	15
North Carolina	538	15
North Dakota	2	17
Ohio	31	17
Oklahoma	53	17
Oregon	14	17
Pennsylvania	25	17
Rhode Island	1	17
South Carolina	224	16
South Dakota	2	17
Tennessee	21	17
Texas	440	16
Utah	2	17
Virginia	75	17
Washington	16	17
Wisconsin	22	17
California Youth Authority	98	
Total	**2,957**	

[1]*National Correctional Reporting Program, 1987.* Data tape provided by the Inter-University Consortium for Political and Social Research (ICPSR 9402), Ann Arbor, Michigan.

[2]*Juvenile Court Statistics,* 1987 (Washington, D.C.: Office of Juvenile Justice and Delinquency Prevention, 1991), pp. 130-131.

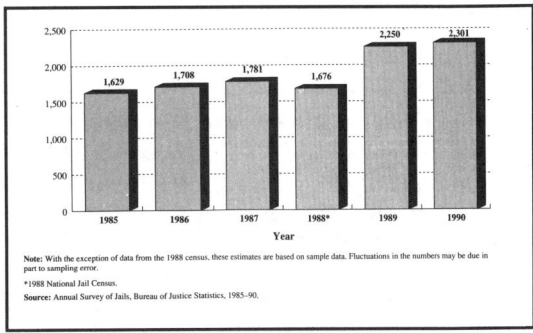

Figure 12
1-Day Counts of Juveniles in Jails, 1985-1990

Note: With the exception of data from the 1988 census, these estimates are based on sample data. Fluctuations in the numbers may be due in part to sampling error.
*1988 National Jail Census.
Source: Annual Survey of Jails, Bureau of Justice Statistics, 1985-90.

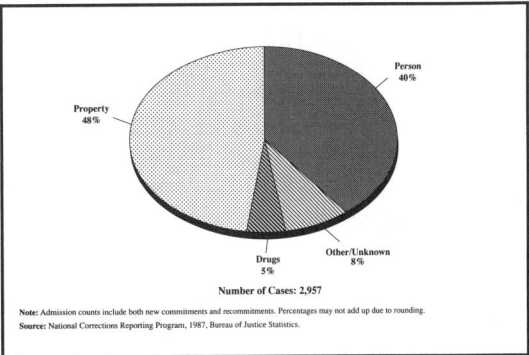

Figure 13
Juveniles Incarcerated by Offense Type: National Corrections Reporting Program, 1987

Number of Cases: 2,957
Note: Admission counts include both new commitments and recommitments. Percentages may not add up due to rounding.
Source: National Corrections Reporting Program, 1987, Bureau of Justice Statistics.

in both juvenile admissions and 1-day counts must be viewed with extreme caution.

A second possible explanation for the discrepancy between admissions and 1-day count data may involve changes in the average length of jail stays. For instance, if States and localities are becoming more successful at diverting juveniles from jails, then the residual number of young who are held in jails may be those charged with the most serious offenses, including those awaiting transfer to adult court. Along the same line, increases in the average length of stay could also account for increases in the 1-day counts of juveniles in jail. Unfortunately, current Federal data collection efforts do not contain sufficient information to determine whether youth entering jails are, indeed, staying longer or what other factors (such as the type of offenses) might be contributing to the higher number of juveniles found in the 1-day counts of national jail populations.

Who Are the Juveniles Entering Adult Correctional Facilities?

Through the National Correctional Reporting Program (NCRP), data are gathered on persons entering State correctional facilities and parole. Data covering calendar year 1987 are available from 33 States, the District of Columbia, the Federal Bureau of Prisons, and the California Youth Authority. Using NCRP data, it is possible to examine the characteristics of persons under age 18 who are taken into custody in State correctional facilities. Although all these individuals have been tried and convicted as adult offenders, it is nonetheless important to examine the attributes of those youth under age 18 who enter adult prisons. The National Correctional Reporting Program contains many of the same variables to be collected by the National Juvenile Corrections System Reporting Program being implemented by NCCD and the Census Bureau. In future reports data from these two data collection systems will be compared.

In 1987, NCRP collected data on 2,957 persons under age 18 entering State and Federal correctional facilities in the participating jurisdictions. Males accounted for the vast majority (97 percent) of under-18 admissions to prisons. The bulk (83 percent) of youth were age 17 at admission. Only 508 were 16 years old or younger, as reported by NCRP.

Of States participating in NCRP, Texas and North Carolina reported the largest number of persons under age 18 entering their prison systems. Texas, which has an upper age of juvenile court jurisdiction of 16, reported 440 such admissions; North Carolina, with an upper age of 15, had 538. Together, these two States accounted for nearly one-third of the reported admissions to NCRP. One should note, though, that certain States such as Florida that had high numbers of "juveniles" reported in the 1990 Census of Adult Correctional Facilities are not represented in the NCRP data. Other States with large numbers of minors admitted to prisons were New York (316), Georgia (232), South Carolina (224), and Michigan (178). South Carolina, Georgia, and Michigan have 16 as the upper age of juvenile court jurisdiction, while New York's upper age is 15 (see Table 15).

Over half (54 percent) of these prison admissions were black youth, and 35 percent were white. Race of the individual was unknown in another 9 percent of cases. Ethnicity data were missing in nearly 40 percent of the cases. For those youth whose ethnicity was determined, about 14 percent were Hispanic.

About one-fifth (21 percent) of youth entering prison had not completed grade school (eighth grade or less). More than half (57 percent) had at least completed the 10th grade. Less than 1 percent had completed high school or possessed a GED.

Figure 13 presents the most serious offenses for which these youngsters were sent to prison. Approximately 8 percent of these youth were convicted of murder or manslaughter. In all, 40 percent were convicted for some personal offense, most typically robbery (18 percent). Forty-eight percent were convicted for some type of property offense. Over half of these—26 percent of all offenders—had burglary as their most serious commitment offense. About 5 percent were sentenced to prison for a drug crime. The average total time served for youth under the age of 18 entering prisons was 20 months.

Notes

1. In the tables that report on juveniles in jails by gender or region, the data were taken from the 1988 National Jail Census. The Annual Survey of Jails does not include data on gender nor can it provide regional estimates.
2. Data are from a special analysis provided by the Bureau of Justice Statistics.
3. Comparable data on adjudication status are not available for private facilities, jails, and State correctional facilities. ✦

33
Conditions of Confinement: Juvenile Detention and Corrections Facilities

ABT Associates, Inc.

In 1988 Congress directed the Office of Juvenile Justice and Delinquency Prevention (OJJDP) to assess conditions of confinement for juveniles, to determine the extent to which those conditions conform to recognized national professional standards, and to report findings to Congress, along with recommendations for improvement.

The congressional mandate must be viewed against the backdrop of changes in juvenile justice. Serious juvenile crime—particularly violent offenses reported to authorities—grew rapidly in recent years. Arrests for violent juvenile offenses and drug offenses rose sharply, even as overall juvenile drug use declined. Policymakers increased the severity of punishments for violent or habitual juvenile offenders. Many States made it easier to sentence serious juvenile offenders as adults.

Admissions to juvenile facilities rose after 1984 and reached an all-time high of nearly 690,000 in 1990. The largest increase was in detention, where admissions rose from just over 400,000 in 1984 to about 570,000 in 1990. The daily population of confined juveniles, based on Children in Custody (CIC) census 1-day counts, increased from about 50,800 in 1979 to about 65,000 in 1991. The populations of all types of facilities increased (except for ranches, where populations declined).

The characteristics of confined juveniles also changed sharply in recent years. Between 1987 and 1991 the proportion of minorities among confined juveniles rose from 53 percent to 63 percent, with the biggest increases among blacks (37 percent to 44 percent) and Hispanics (13 percent to 17 percent). The percentage confined for crimes against persons rose from 22 percent to 28 percent, and those confined for property offenses declined from 40 percent to 34 percent. The percentage confined for drug-related offenses rose between 1987 and 1989, and then declined somewhat in 1991, resulting in an overall increase of 4 percentage points (6 percent to 10 percent).

When Congress mandated the study, it was apparent that crowding was becoming a serious problem in juvenile facilities. By 1987, 36 percent of confined juveniles were held in facilities whose populations exceeded their design capacity. Key problems in adult corrections—crowding, litigation on conditions of confinement, major capacity expansion, and huge increases in costs—were beginning to be evident in juvenile facilities as well. Thus, it was important to learn more about conditions in juvenile confinement facilities, to pinpoint serious problems, and to explore possible remedies.

Study Description

The study was funded in the fall of 1990. The study covered all 984 public (operated by State and local governments) and private juvenile detention centers, reception centers, training schools, and ranches, camps, and farms in the United States. These facilities held about 65,000 juveniles on the date of the 1991 CIC census, or about 69 percent of the juveniles confined on that date in the United States.

Three types of facilities that confine juveniles were excluded: (a) youth halfway houses, shelters, and group homes; (b) police lockups, adult jails, and prisons that

---

From *Conditions of Confinement: Juvenile Detention and Corrections Facilities*, February 1994, pp. 1-13. U.S. Department of Justice: Office of Juvenile Justice and Delinquency Prevention.

and convicted as adults, ... and drug treatment pro... data on conditions of ... facilities.

... justice practitioners ... advisers, consultants, and site ...tors. Key juvenile justice organizations endorsed the study and urged cooperation from the field. . . .

Strategy for Assessing Conditions

We used three approaches, where possible, to assess conditions of confinement.

- First, we measured conformance to 46 assessment criteria that reflected existing national professional standards in 12 areas that represented advisers' perceptions of confined juveniles' most important needs.
- Second, we analyzed data (obtained from the mail survey, the Children in Custody census, and site visits) on other selected aspects of conditions of confinement for which no national standards existed.
- Third, we analyzed data on selected incidents in facilities, including rates of injuries to juveniles and staff, rates of escape and attempted escape, rates of suicidal behavior, and selected security and control practices, such as rates of searches and isolation.

To decide whether serious problems existed, we reviewed data on all three levels, where available. In some cases, conformance rates for a particular assessment criterion were low, but other data on conditions suggested that nonconformance had minimal effects. For example, one assessment criterion required that the interval between an evening meal and the following breakfast be no more than 14 hours. A large proportion of juveniles were confined in facilities that did not conform. However, when we examined facilities' actual practices in more detail, we found most nonconforming facilities missed the deadline by 15 or 20 minutes, and that on all other measures food service appeared generally satisfactory.

In other instances, conformance was moderate or high, but data on conditions or outcomes suggested problems. For example, almost all juveniles were in facilities that conformed to an assessment criterion requiring that facilities pass annual fire inspections. But during site visits we saw a disturbingly high proportion of facilities that had obvious fire safety violations, such as not marking fire exits or posting fire escape routes.

The 46 assessment criteria were organized into 12 topic areas that were, in turn, grouped into 4 broad categories:

Table 1
Assessing Conditions of Confinement

	Number of Assessment Criteria
Basic Needs	
1. Living space	3
2. Health care	6
3. Food, clothing, and hygiene	4
4. Living accommodations	4
Order and Safety	
5. Security	3
6. Controlling suicidal behavior	4
7. Inspections and emergency preparedness	4
Programming	
8. Education	4
9. Recreation	1
10. Treatment services	2
Juveniles' Rights	
11. Access to community	5
12. Limits on staff discretion	6
Total	**46**

In developing measures for the assessment criteria, requirements of nationally recognized standards for juvenile facilities were reviewed. For example, advisers decided that confined juveniles need adequate living space. Several benchmarks of nationally recognized standards were identified. In terms of sleeping space, standards required 70 square feet per juvenile in single rooms and 50 square feet per juvenile in rooms with three or more occupants. Standards also recommended that no more than

25 juveniles be housed in one living unit and that facilities' populations not exceed their design capacity.

We relied mainly on three sets of standards:

- American Correctional Association standards (as amended in 1991), which are used as the basis for accrediting juvenile facilities.
- The National Commission on Correctional Health Care, an affiliate of the American Medical Association, also uses its standards (1984) to accredit health care services in juvenile facilities.
- American Bar Association/Institute for Judicial Administration Standards (1980).

Summary of Findings

The study's findings suggest three major themes:

First, there are several areas in which problems in juvenile facilities are substantial and widespread—most notably living space, health care, security, and control of suicidal behavior. There also are areas where deficiencies, though less serious or widespread, are still important enough to warrant attention.

Second, the findings do not support the premise that high levels of conformance to nationally recognized standards result in improved conditions of confinement. For many important areas of facility operation, practitioners drafting standards did not specify outcomes that should be achieved. Instead, a large proportion of existing standards emphasize procedural regularity, which is, admittedly, an important objective. But we believe that in the future the standards-drafting agencies should emphasize performance-based standards that identify the outcomes facilities should achieve. Performance standards can quickly identify problems and can provide a benchmark against which improvements can be measured. Performance standards are particularly needed in such areas as education, treatment services, and health care—and ultimately, all aspects of facility operation.

Third, we found that deficiencies were distributed widely across facilities. Most had several deficiencies, and the types of deficiencies at these facilities varied considerably. We found few facilities with no deficiencies as well as a few with deficiencies in most areas. If the objective is to substantially improve conditions that confined juveniles experience, then efforts to improve or close a few "bad" facilities, while laudable, will have little overall impact. Rather, substantial improvements will require that a large number of less seriously deficient facilities improve several areas of their operations. . . .

Overview of Conditions

Table 2 displays conformance to assessment criteria from two viewpoints. First, it shows the percentage of confined juveniles held in facilities that conform to all assessment criteria in each of the 12 topic areas (referred to as "juvenile-based" conformance). Second, it shows the percentage of facilities that conform to all assessment criteria (or "facility-based" conformance). The relationship between these two measures tells us whether large or small facilities are more likely to conform. For example, if two-thirds of the juveniles are held in facilities that conform, but only one-third of the facilities conform, that means that bigger facilities are more likely to conform than smaller facilities. Conversely, if two-thirds of the facilities conform, but only one-third of the juveniles are in facilities that conform, then smaller facilities are more likely to conform than bigger ones.

Table 2 should be interpreted cautiously. It is an inherently conservative indicator because a facility must conform to all criteria. Moreover, we emphasize that overall conformance goes beyond conformance standards. Overall conformance must be viewed in light of additional information about the actual conditions and outcomes in facilities.

Table 2 shows that summary conformance rates are seldom high. Only 5 of the 12 topic areas have juvenile-based overall conformance rates of 50 percent or higher, and only 6 have facility-based conformance rates of 50 percent or higher. It also shows that on some topics smaller facilities are more likely to conform, while on others, bigger

Table 2
Summary Performance Rates by Topic Areas

Topic areas in which conditions were assessed	Percentage of confined juveniles in facilities that conform[1]	Percentage of facilities that conform[2]
Basic Needs		
1. Living space (3 criteria)	24%	43%
2. Health care (6 criteria)	26%	35%
3. Food, clothing, and hygiene (4 criteria)	39%	35%
4. Living accommodations (4 criteria)	52%	49%
Order and Security		
5. Security (3 criteria)	20%	27%
6. Controlling suicidal behavior (4 criteria)	25%	51%
7. Inspections and emergency preparedness (4 criteria)	67%	55%
Programming		
8. Education (4 criteria)	55%	57%
9. Recreation (1 criteria)	85%	85%
10. Treatment services (2 criteria)	68%	60%
Juvenile Rights		
11. Access to community (5 criteria)	25%	25%
12. Limits on staff discretion (7 criteria)	49%[3]	76%

[1]This is the percentage of juveniles held in facilities that conform to all assessment criteria in each topic area.
[2]This is the percentage of facilities that conform to all the assessment criteria in each topic area.
[3]This excludes the assessment criteria on search authorization, which required facility administrators to authorize all searches. Only 14 percent of confined juveniles are in facilities that conform to this criterion. With this criterion included, only 6 percent of confined juveniles are in facilities that conform to all criteria.
Source: CIC census and Mail Survey, 1991.

facilities are more likely to conform. For example, on living space, health care, security, controlling suicidal behavior, and limits on staff discretion, smaller facilities are more likely to conform than larger facilities. On inspections and emergency preparedness and treatment services, larger facilities are more likely to conform than smaller facilities.

Table 3 displays data on key incident measures we examined—injuries (juveniles-on-juveniles, juveniles-on-staff, and staff-on-juveniles), escapes (completed, unsuccessful attempts), acts of suicidal behavior (attempted suicides, suicide gestures, self-mutilations), incidents requiring emergency health care, and use of isolation. All these are reported as incident rates per 100 confined juveniles. For injuries, escapes, suicidal behavior, and longer-term isolation, the rates are based on reported incidents during the 30 days before the mail survey. For shorter-term isolation, the rate is based on incidents reported during the 7 days before the mail survey. For emergency health care, rates are based on reported incidents during the 12 months before the mail survey. Table 3 also shows the estimated annual number of incidents, based on these rates.

There was substantial variation in these rates among facilities. A substantial number of juveniles were held in facilities where rates were zero or were very low. A smaller minority were held in facilities where rates were very high.

Areas With Substantial Deficiencies

There are four areas—living space, security, control of suicidal behavior, and health care—in which facilities display substantial and widespread deficiencies.

Table 3
Incident Rates per 100 Juveniles and Annualized Estimates of Incidents in Juvenile Facilities

Type of incident	Rate per 100 juveniles (last 30 days)	Estimated incidents per year
Injuries		
Juvenile-on-juvenile	3.1	24,200
Juvenile-on-staff	1.7	6,900
Staff-on-juvenile	0.2	106
Escapes		
Completed	1.2	9,700
Unsuccessful attempts	1.1	9,800
Acts of suicidal behavior	2.4	17,600
Incidents requiring emergency health care	2.0	18,600
Isolation incidents		
Short-term (1 to 24 hours)	57.0[1]	435,800
Longer-term (more than 24 hours)	11.0	88,900

[1]This does not include very-short-term isolation (up to 1 hour) used to control behavior or instill discipline. Such a practice is common in juvenile facilities and largely not documented, so it is impossible to measure its occurrence with any accuracy.

Source: CIC census and Mail Survey, 1991.

Living Space

A substantial proportion of confined juveniles have inadequate living space. Crowding is a pervasive problem in juvenile facilities. It is evident facilitywide, in living units,[1] and in sleeping rooms.

In 1987, 36 percent of confined juveniles were in facilities whose populations exceeded their reported design capacity. By 1991 that increased to 47 percent. In 1991 one-third of confined juveniles were in living units with 26 or more juveniles, and one-third slept in rooms that were smaller than required by nationally recognized standards. Only about one-fourth of the confined juveniles were in facilities that conformed to all three living space criteria. Hence, almost three-fourths were in facilities that were crowded in some respect. Crowding is more common in larger and less common in smaller facilities.

To eliminate crowded sleeping rooms, slightly over 11,000 juveniles would have to be removed from the confinement facilities or an equal number of new beds would have to be provided in adequately sized sleeping rooms. If that were done, it would still leave about 2,650 juveniles in facilities whose population exceeded design capacity.

Facilities have responded to crowding by restricting intake criteria (particularly in detention), by granting early releases (particularly in training schools), and by refusing to take new admissions when populations reach or exceed capacity (particularly in ranches). As a result, although more facilities have become crowded since 1987, average population levels in crowded facilities have remained at about 120 percent of reported design capacity.

We found that rates of injuries to staff by juveniles were higher in crowded facilities. As the percentage of juveniles who sleep in dormitories with 11 or more residents increased, rates of injuries inflicted by juveniles on juveniles increased. Rates for short-term isolation and searches also were higher in crowded facilities.

We recommend that large dormitories be eliminated from juvenile facilities. No new facilities should be built that contain large dormitories. In existing facilities, large dormitories should be replaced as soon as possible.

Facilities can sometimes adjust intake or durations of confinement to cushion the effects of crowding, but they cannot alter the decisions of police, prosecutors, juvenile judges, and probation and parole officers or the systemic processes that cause crowding.

We recommend that jurisdictions develop policies that regulate the use and duration of juvenile confinement and that guide future development of confinement and nonconfinement placement options. To do this, States and localities should implement a planning process that identifies decisions that affect use of detention and confinement, that identifies characteristics of juveniles processed through the system, and that documents capacities of confinement and nonconfinement placement options.

Security

Security practices are intended to prevent escapes and to provide a safe environment for both juveniles and staff. There are high levels of nonconformance with our security assessment criteria and substantial problems with escapes and injuries in juvenile facilities.

Although 81 percent of confined juveniles are in facilities with three or more facilitywide counts per day, only 62 percent are in facilities that classify juveniles on the basis of risk and use classification results to make housing assignments. Larger facilities are more likely to conform to the counts and classification criteria. Just 36 percent of confined juveniles are in facilities whose supervision staffing ratios conform to assessment criteria. Smaller facilities are more likely to conform to the supervision staff ratio criteria.

Overall, just 20 percent of confined juveniles are in facilities that conform to all three criteria.

In the 30 days before the mail survey, nearly 2,000 juveniles (slightly over 3 percent of the juvenile population) and 650 staff (slightly over 1.7 percent of all staff) were injured by juveniles in these facilities. Injury rates varied greatly. About 10 percent of confined juveniles were in facilities where 8 percent or more of the juveniles were injured by other juveniles in the 30 days before the mail survey, and 1 percent were in facilities where at least one of every four juveniles were injured during that time. A small number of facilities were similarly dangerous for staff. About 10 percent of juveniles were in facilities where 5 percent or more of staff were injured in the 30 days before the mail survey, and 1 percent were in facilities where 17 percent or more of staff were injured during that time.

Juvenile and staff injury rates were higher in crowded facilities, and juvenile-on-juvenile injury rates increased as the percentage of juveniles housed in large dormitories increased. Injury rates for both staff and juveniles were higher in facilities where living units were locked 24 hours a day. In facilities with locked living units we visited, an emphasis on security dominated interactions between staff and juveniles. Of note is that the percentage of juveniles convicted of violent crimes was not related to injury rates.

Classification is supposed to protect juveniles by assessing their propensity to violence and by separating potential predators and victims. However, we found no relationship between conformance to the classification assessment criteria and rates of injury. The reasons are not clear. It is possible that existing classification procedures do not reliably distinguish violence-prone youth or whether crowding diminishes facilities' ability to adequately separate predators and victims or increases the probability that confined youth will encounter violence-prone peers. More study of juvenile classification practices is needed to determine how to improve classification.

During site visits facility administrators and staff frequently said there would be fewer injuries if staffing ratios improved. The study did not support that position. We found no relationship between supervision staffing ratios and rates of injury. However, we found that higher supervision staff turnover rates were associated with increased juvenile-on-staff injury rates. In facilities with high turnover rates, overall levels of staff experience and training are likely to be lower than in facilities with low turnover rates. While we lack data to establish a direct link, during site visits administrators and practitioners frequently stated that inexperienced and less-well-trained staff were more likely to be injured by juveniles.

In the 30 days before the mail survey, slightly over 800 juveniles (about 1.2 percent of the confined population) escaped from confinement facilities, and slightly more than 800 attempted to escape but failed.

We found no relationship between conformance to the classification criteria and escape rates. A growing number of facilities rely on perimeter fences as an obstacle to escape. Since 1987 the percentage of facilities with perimeter fences increased from 38 percent to 47 percent. However, we found no conclusive relationship between perimeter fences and escape rates.

We recommend that juvenile justice agencies conduct detailed comparative studies of facilities with low and high escape and injury rates to identify policies and practices that can materially improve safety and security. These studies should pay special attention to procedures used to classify juveniles and the ways in which classification is used.

Controlling Suicidal Behavior

Suicidal behavior is a serious problem in juvenile confinement facilities. Ten confined juveniles killed themselves in 1990. In the 30 days before the mail survey, 970 juveniles committed 1,487 acts of suicidal behavior (that is, attempted suicide, made suicidal gestures, or engaged in self-mutilation). Thus, about 1.6 percent of confined juveniles engaged in suicidal behavior, and there were 2.4 suicidal behavior incidents for every 100 confined juveniles in the 30 days before the mail survey. On an annualized basis, more than 1,000 juveniles engage in more than 17,000 incidents of suicidal behavior in juvenile facilities.

Just half of the confined juveniles are in facilities that monitor suicidal juveniles at least once every 4 minutes (the length of time after which permanent brain damage can occur in an attempted hanging—the most common method of suicide attempt in juvenile facilities). About three-fourths are in facilities that screen juveniles for indicators of suicide risk at the time of admission, and about three-fourths are in facilities that train staff in suicide prevention. Almost 90 percent are in facilities that have written suicide prevention plans. However, only about one in five confined juveniles are in facilities that conform to all four assessment criteria.

Our analysis showed that facilities that conduct suicide screening at admission and that train staff in suicide prevention have lower rates of suicidal behavior. Other suicide prevention measures—monitoring suicidal juveniles at least once every 4 minutes and written suicide prevention plans—were not associated with suicidal behavior rates. (However, these factors may be vitally important in preventing an attempted suicide from becoming a completed suicide.) Detention centers that conformed to the supervision staffing ratio criteria had lower suicidal behavior rates. We found that as supervision staff turnover rates increased, suicidal behavior rates increased, which underscores the importance of staff training in suicide prevention.

Suicidal behavior rates increased as the percentage of juveniles in single rooms increased. We found, however, that facilities frequently fail to cover housing for suicidal juveniles in their written suicide prevention plans.

We recommend that all juveniles be screened for risk of suicidal behavior immediately upon their admission to confinement facilities.

We recommend that suicidal juveniles be constantly monitored by staff. This means that suicidal youth should not be isolated or placed in a room by themselves. When suicidal juveniles are housed in single rooms, staff should be with them continuously. A mental health professional should assess suicidal youth as quickly as possible and, if they deem it necessary, the youth should be transferred to a medical or mental health facility that is staffed and equipped to deal with suicidal youth.

We also recommend that agencies study the causes of high supervision staff turnover rates, develop strategies to reduce high turnover rates, and soften the effects of turnover by increased training.

Health Care

The most serious problem with health care is that health screenings (at admission) and health appraisals (within 7 days of admission) often are not completed in a timely fashion. Speedy completion of health screenings is needed to ensure that juveniles who are injured, who have acute health problems, or who are intoxicated when presented for admission get immediate medical treatment. Timely health appraisals are required to identify the juveniles' health care needs that require treatment during confinement and to control the spread of communicable diseases.

Over 90 percent of confined juveniles get health screenings at some point, but only 43 percent get them within 1 hour of admission, as required by nationally recognized standards. Smaller facilities are more likely to conform to this health screening criterion. Health screening took more than 3 hours to be completed for almost one-fifth of the population of confined juveniles. Similarly, although 95 percent get health appraisals at some point, only 80 percent get them within a week. Larger facilities are more likely to conform to the health appraisal criteria.

One-third of the juveniles in detention centers have health screenings done by staff who have not been trained by medical personnel to perform health screening. Because the purpose of health screening is to identify juveniles with injuries or conditions that require immediate medical care, using untrained staff to perform the screening is cause for concern.

We recommend that juvenile justice agencies act to ensure that initial health screenings are carried out promptly at admission and to ensure that health appraisals are completed or received within a week after admission. We also recommend that juvenile justice agencies take steps to develop and ensure the use of an adequate training program for nonmedical staff who conduct health screenings.

In addition, there is no data base on individual health needs of confined juveniles, on the health care services provided to them, or on changes in their health status while confined. Without such information, the adequacy of health care in confinement facilities cannot be assessed. Of particular concern is the fact that only 68 percent of confined juveniles are in facilities where tuberculin tests are performed, and only 53 percent are in facilities that test for sexually transmitted diseases.

We recommend that existing public health surveillance systems be expanded to include and separately track confined juveniles. We also recommend a general review of the health needs of confined juveniles and of the health services they receive, based on a review of medical records of a national sample of confined juveniles.

Areas With Less Substantial Deficiencies

Education and Treatment Services

There are two areas—education and treatment services—in which conformance to assessment criteria is generally high but in which we have no foundation for assessing the adequacy of services provided. Although there is extensive anecdotal and experiential evidence on the educational deficiencies and the emotional and mental health problems of juvenile offenders, we have no systematic empirical data on confined youths' educational or treatment needs and problems. Thus, we cannot determine whether facilities provide appropriate programs or whether juveniles make progress during confinement. Major new initiatives are needed to periodically collect such data.

We recommend that Federal agencies support funding of a study to document educational needs and problems of a national sample of confined juveniles and to evaluate the capacity of educational programs in confinement facilities to serve those needs and to address those problems.

We recommend that Federal agencies support funding of a study to document the treatment needs of a national sample of confined juveniles and of the treatment services they receive.

Inspections and Emergency Preparedness

Most juveniles are confined in facilities that have passed recent State or local fire, life safety, and sanitation inspections. Despite that, during site visits we observed a large number of facilities at which fire exits were not marked or fire escape routes were not posted in living units, and a few at which fire exits were blocked with furniture or other objects.

We recommend that State and local fire codes for juvenile facilities be toughened and enforced more vigorously. In particular, we recommend that facilities be inspected more frequently, and that available enforcement authority be exercised more vigorously to correct violations. We also recommend that laws or regulations governing fire and life safety in juvenile facilities be as rigorous as those that apply to schools, hospitals, or other public buildings.

Access to the Community

We estimate that, on average, confined juveniles are held in facilities that are 58 miles from where they live (that distance varies by facility type, so that training schools are, on average, farther from juveniles' homes than are detention centers). Distance and location (e.g., wilderness-based programs) affect juveniles' access to the community. Most confined juveniles have adequate opportunity to visit with families or attorneys, to contact volunteers, and to communicate by mail. However, telephone calls are an exception: almost all juveniles can place a limited number of telephone calls per week, but 45 percent of confined juveniles are in facilities that do not permit them to receive telephone calls.

We recommend that juvenile facilities permit juveniles to receive as well as make telephone calls....

Note

1. A living unit is a self-contained area of a facility where a subgroup of confined juveniles sleep, participate in leisure activities, and attend to hygiene. Generally, juveniles eat, exercise (large muscle activity), and participate in programming outside their living units. ✦

34
Comprehensive Strategy for Serious, Violent, and Chronic Juvenile Offenders

John J. Wilson
James C. Howell

General Principles

The following general principles provide a framework to guide our efforts in the battle to prevent delinquent conduct and reduce juvenile involvement in serious, violent, and chronic delinquency:

- *Strengthen the family* in its primary responsibility to instill moral values and provide guidance and support to children. Where there is no functional family unit, a family surrogate should be established and assisted to guide and nurture the child.
- *Support core social institutions*—schools, religious institutions, and community organizations—in their roles of developing capable, mature, and responsible youth. A goal of each of these societal institutions should be to ensure that children have the opportunity and support to mature into productive law-abiding citizens. A nurturing community environment requires that core social institutions be actively involved in the lives of youth. Community organizations include public and private youth-serving agencies; neighborhood groups; and business and commercial organizations providing employment, training, and other meaningful economic opportunities for youth.
- *Promote delinquency prevention* as the most cost-effective approach to dealing with juvenile delinquency. Families, schools, religious institutions, and community organizations, including citizen volunteers and the private sector, must be enlisted in the Nation's delinquency prevention efforts. These core socializing institutions must be strengthened and assisted in their efforts to ensure that children have the opportunity to become capable and responsible citizens. When children engage in "acting out" behavior, such as status offenses, the family and community, in concert with child welfare agencies, must take primary responsibility for responding with appropriate treatment and support services. Communities must take the lead in designing and building comprehensive prevention approaches that address known risk factors and target other youth at risk of delinquency.
- *Intervene immediately and effectively when delinquent behavior occurs* to successfully prevent delinquent offenders from becoming chronic offenders or progressively committing more serious and violent crimes. Initial intervention efforts, under an umbrella of system authorities (police, intake, and probation), should be centered in the family and other core societal institutions. Juvenile justice system authorities should ensure that an appropriate response occurs and act quickly and firmly if the need for formal system adjudication and sanctions has been demonstrated.
- *Identify and control the small group of serious, violent, and chronic juvenile offenders* who have committed felony offenses or have failed to respond to intervention and nonsecure community-based treatment and rehabilita-

---

From *Comprehensive Strategy for Serious, Violent, and Chronic Juvenile Offenders*, December 1993, pp. 9-24. U.S. Department of Justice: Office of Juvenile Justice and Delinquency Prevention.

tion services offered by the juvenile justice system. Measures to address delinquent offenders who are a threat to community safety may include placements in secure community-based facilities or, when necessary, training schools and other secure juvenile facilities.

Under OJJDP's comprehensive strategy, it is the family and community, supported by our core social institutions, that have *primary* responsibility for meeting the basic socializing needs of our Nation's children. Socially harmful conduct, acting-out behavior, and delinquency may be signs of the family being unable to meet its responsibility. It is at these times that the community must support and assist the family in the socialization process, particularly for youth at the greatest risk of delinquency.

The proposed strategy incorporates two principal components: (1) preventing youth from becoming delinquent by focusing prevention programs on at-risk youth; and (2) improving the juvenile justice system response to delinquent offenders through a system of graduated sanctions and a continuum of treatment alternatives that include immediate intervention, intermediate sanctions, and community-based corrections sanctions, incorporating restitution and community service when appropriate.

Target Populations

The *initial target population* for prevention programs is juveniles at risk of involvement in delinquent activity. While primary delinquency prevention programs provide services to all youth wishing to participate, maximum impact on future delinquent conduct can be achieved by seeking to identify and involve in prevention programs youth at greatest risk of involvement in delinquent activity. This includes youth who exhibit known risk factors for future delinquency; drug and alcohol abuse; and youth who have had contact with the juvenile justice system as nonoffenders (neglected, abused, and dependent), status offenders (runaways, truants, alcohol offenders, and incorrigibles), or minor delinquent offenders.

The *next target population* is youth, both male and female, who have committed delinquent (criminal) acts, including juvenile offenders who evidence a high likelihood of becoming, or who already are, serious, violent, or chronic offenders.

Program Rationale

What can communities and the juvenile justice system do to prevent the development of and interrupt the progression of delinquent and criminal careers? Juvenile justice agencies and programs are one part of a larger picture that involves many other local agencies and programs that are responsible for working with at-risk youth and their families. It is important that juvenile delinquency prevention and intervention programs are integrated with local police, social service, child welfare, school, and family preservation programs and that these programs reflect local community determinations of the most pressing problems and program priorities. Establishing *community planning teams* that include a broad base of participants drawn from local government and the community (e.g., community-based youth development organizations, schools, law enforcement, social service agencies, civic organizations, religious groups, parents, and teens) will help create consensus on priorities and services to be provided as well as build support for a comprehensive program approach that draws on all sectors of the community for participation. Comprehensive approaches to delinquency prevention and intervention will require collaborative efforts between the juvenile justice system and other service provision systems, including mental health, health, child welfare, and education. Developing mechanisms that effectively link these different service providers at the program level will need to be an important component of every community's comprehensive plan.

Evidence suggests that a risk reduction and protective factor enhancement approach to prevention is effective. Risk factors include the family, the school, the peer group, the community, and characteristics of juveniles themselves. The more risk factors present in a community, the greater the likelihood of youth problems in that community as children are exposed to those risk factors. Prevention strategies will need to be comprehensive, addressing each of the risk factors as they relate to the *chronological development* of children being served.

Research and experience in intervention and treatment programming suggest that a highly structured system of graduated sanctions holds significant promise. The goal of graduated sanctions is to increase the effectiveness of the juvenile justice system in responding to juveniles who have committed criminal acts. The system's limited resources have diminished its ability to respond effectively to serious, violent, and chronic juvenile crime. This trend must be reversed by empowering the juvenile justice system to provide accountability and treatment resources to juveniles. This includes gender-specific programs for female offenders, whose rates of delinquency have generally been increasing faster than males in recent years, and who now account for 23 percent of juvenile arrests. It will also require programs for special needs populations such as sex offenders, mentally retarded, emotionally disturbed, and learning disabled delinquents.

The graduated sanctions approach is designed to provide immediate intervention at the first offense to ensure that the juvenile's misbehavior is addressed by the family and community or through formal adjudication and sanctions by the juvenile justice system, as appropriate. Graduated sanctions include a range of intermediate sanctions and secure corrections options to provide intensive treatment that serves the juvenile's needs, provides accountability, and protects the public. They offer an array of referral and dispositional resources for law enforcement, juvenile courts, and juvenile corrections officials. The graduated sanctions component requires that the juvenile justice system's capacity to identify, process, evaluate, refer, and track delinquent offenders be enhanced.

The Juvenile Justice System

The juvenile justice system plays a key role in protecting and guiding juveniles, including responding to juvenile delinquency. Law enforcement plays a key role by conducting investigations, making custody and arrest determinations, or exercising discretionary release authority. Police should be trained in community-based policing techniques and provided with program resources that focus on community youth, such as Police Athletic Leagues and the Drug Abuse Resistance Education (DARE) Program.

The traditional role of the juvenile and family court is to treat and rehabilitate the dependent or wayward minor, using an individualized approach and tailoring its response to the particular needs of the child and family, with goals of: (1) responding to the needs of troubled youth and their families; (2) providing due process while recognizing the rights of the victim; (3) rehabilitating the juvenile offender; and (4) protecting both the juvenile and the public. While juvenile and family courts have been successful in responding to the bulk of youth problems to meet these goals, new ways of organizing and focusing the resources of the juvenile justice system are required to effectively address serious, violent, and chronic juvenile crime. These methods might include the establishment of unified family courts with jurisdiction over all civil and criminal matters affecting the family.

A recent statement by the National Council of Juvenile and Family Court Judges (NCJFCJ) succinctly describes the critical role of the court:

> The Courts must protect children and families when private and other public institutions are unable or fail to meet their obligations. The protection of society by correcting children who break the law, the preservation and reformation of families, and the protection of children from abuse and neglect are missions of the Court. When the family falters, when the basic needs of children go unmet, when the behavior of children is destructive and goes unchecked, juvenile and family courts must

respond. The Court is society's official means of holding itself accountable for the well-being of its children and family unit. . . . (NCJFCJ, "Children and Families First, A Mandate for Change," 1993)

Delinquency Prevention

Most juvenile delinquency efforts have been unsuccessful because of their negative approach—attempting to keep juveniles from misbehaving. Positive approaches that emphasize opportunities for healthy social, physical, and mental development have a much greater likelihood of success. Another weakness of past delinquency prevention efforts is their narrow scope, focusing on only one or two of society's institutions that have responsibility for the social development of children. Most programs have targeted either the school arena or the family. Communities are an often neglected area. Successful delinquency prevention strategies must be positive in their orientation and comprehensive in their scope.

The prevention component of OJJDP's comprehensive strategy is based on a risk-focused delinquency prevention approach (Hawkins and Catalano, 1992). This approach states that to prevent a problem from occurring, the factors contributing to the development of that problem must be identified and then ways must be found (protective factors) to address and ameliorate those factors.

Research conducted over the past half century has clearly documented five categories of causes and correlates of juvenile delinquency: (1) individual characteristics such as alienation, rebelliousness, and lack of bonding to society; (2) family influences such as parental conflict, child abuse, and family history of problem behavior (substance abuse, criminality, teen pregnancy, and school dropouts); (3) school experiences such as early academic failure and lack of commitment to school; (4) peer group influences such as friends who engage in problem behavior (minor criminality, gangs, and violence); and (5) neighborhood and community factors such as economic deprivation, high rates of substance abuse and crime, and low neighborhood attachment. These categories can also be thought of as risk factors.

To counter these causes and risk factors, protective factors must be introduced. Protective factors are qualities or conditions that moderate a juvenile's exposure to risk. Research indicates that protective factors fall into three basic categories: (1) individual characteristics such as a resilient temperament and a positive social orientation; (2) bonding with prosocial family members, teachers, and friends; and (3) healthy beliefs and clear standards for behavior. While individual characteristics are inherent and difficult to change, bonding and clear standards for behavior work together and can be changed. To increase bonding, children must be provided with opportunities to contribute to their families, schools, peer groups, and communities; skills to take advantage of opportunities; and recognition for their efforts to contribute. Simultaneously, parents, teachers, and communities need to set clear standards that endorse prosocial behavior.

Risk Factors
- Individual characteristics.
- Family influences.
- School experiences.
- Peer group influences.
- Neighborhood and community.

The risk-focused delinquency prevention approach calls on communities to identify and understand what risk factors their children are exposed to and to implement programs that counter these risk factors. Communities must enhance protective factors that promote positive behavior, health, well-being, and personal success. Effective delinquency prevention efforts must be comprehensive, covering the five causes or risk factors described below, and correspond to the social development process.

Individual Characteristics

Our children must be taught moral, spiritual, and civic values. The decline in inculcating these values has contributed significantly to increases in delinquent behavior. Therefore, opportunities for teaching positive values must be increased.

Youth Leadership and Service Programs can provide such opportunities and can reinforce and help internalize in children such positive individual traits as discipline, character, self-respect, responsibility, teamwork, healthy lifestyles, and good citizenship. They can also provide opportunities for personal growth, active involvement in education and vocational training, and life skills development.

A Youth Leadership and Service Program could consist of a variety of components targeted to the needs of grade school, junior high, and high school youth. Elementary and junior high school children could be assisted in achieving healthy social development through instillation in them of basic values. High school-aged youth could be supported in the development of leadership skills and community service in preparation for adulthood. The components of a Youth Leadership and Service Program may include the following types of program activities:

- Youth Service Corps.
- Adventure Training (leadership, endurance, and team building).
- Mentoring.
- Recreational.
- Summer camp.
- Literacy and learning disability.
- Law-Related Education.

A variety of prevention programs address individual growth and development, including:

- Head Start.
- Boys and Girls Clubs.
- Scouting.
- 4-H Clubs.
- Recreational activities.
- Leadership and personal development.
- Health and mental health.
- Career youth development.

Family Influences

The family is the most important influence in the lives of children and the first line of defense against delinquency. Programs that strengthen the family and foster healthy growth and development of children from prenatal care through adolescence should be widely available. These programs should encourage the maintenance of a viable family unit and bonding between parent and child, and they should provide support for families in crisis. Such programs should involve other major spheres of influence such as religious institutions, schools, and community-based organizations. By working together, these organizations will have a pronounced impact on preserving the family and preventing delinquency.

To have the greatest impact, assistance must reach families *before* significant problems develop. Therefore, the concept of *earliest point of impact* should guide the development and implementation of prevention programs involving the family. Researchers in the area of juvenile delinquency and the family have found that the following *negative family involvement factors* are predictors of delinquency:

- Inadequate prenatal care.
- Parental rejection.
- Inadequate supervision and inconsistent discipline by parents.
- Family conflict, marital discord, and physical violence.
- Child abuse.

The following programs directly address negative family involvement factors and how to establish protective factors:

- Teen Abstinence and Pregnancy Prevention.
- Parent Effectiveness and Family Skills Training.
- Parent Support Groups.
- Home Instruction Program for Preschool Youngsters.
- Family Crisis Intervention Services.
- Court Appointed Special Advocates.

- Surrogate Families and Respite Care for Families in Crisis.
- Permanency Planning for Foster Children.
- Family Life Education for Teens and Parents.
- Runaway and Homeless Youth Services.

School Experiences

Outside the family, the school has the greatest influence in the lives of children and adolescents. The school profoundly influences the hopes and dreams of youth.

Many of America's children bring one or more of the aforementioned risk factors to school with them, and these factors may hinder the development of their academic and social potential. School prevention programs, including traditional delinquency prevention programs not related to the school's educational mission, can assist the family and the community by identifying at-risk youth, monitoring their progress, and intervening with effective programs at critical times during a youth's development.

School-based prevention programs may include:

- Drug and Alcohol Prevention and Education.
- Bullying Prevention.
- Violence Prevention.
- Alternative Schools.
- Truancy Reduction.
- School Discipline and Safety Improvement.
- Targeted-Literacy Programs in the Primary Grades.
- Law-Related Education.
- Afterschool Programs for Latchkey Children.
- Teen Abstinence and Pregnancy Prevention.
- Values Development.
- Vocational Training.

Providing youth with structured opportunities to develop skills and contribute to the community in nonschool hours is particularly important for at-risk youth who have lower levels of personal and social support. Communities need to develop strategies and programs, such as those recommended by the Carnegie Council on Adolescent Development, to address this need.

Peer Group Influences

Research on the causes and correlates of delinquency confirms that associating with delinquent, drug-using peers is strongly correlated with delinquency and drug use. These relationships are mutually reinforcing. Membership in a gang is strongly related to delinquency and drug use. Those who remain in gangs over long periods of time have high rates of delinquency, particularly during active gang membership.

Peer leadership groups offer an effective means of encouraging leaders of delinquency-prone groups to establish friendships with more conventional peers. These groups have been established in schools, at all levels, across the country. As noted above, school-based afterschool programs for latchkey children also provide the same function for children at high risk for negative influences. Crime prevention programs that educate youth on how to prevent juvenile violence and crime and provide opportunities for youth to actually work on solving specific community delinquency problems are another effective way of encouraging peer leadership.

Promising approaches have been identified for combating juvenile gangs. "Community mobilization" appears to be effective in cities with chronic gang problems and in cities where the gang problem is just beginning. Other promising preventive options include efforts to dissolve associations with delinquent peers and develop alternative behaviors that promote moral development and reject violence as a means of resolving interpersonal disputes. Opportunities to achieve success in conventional, nondelinquent activities are also imperative.

The following programs reflect these principles:
- Gang Prevention and Intervention.
- Conflict Resolution-Peer Mediation.
- Peer Counseling and Tutoring.
- Self-Help Fellowship for Peer Groups.
- Individual Responsibility Training.
- Community Volunteer Service.
- Competitive Athletic Team Participation.
- Teens, Crime, and the Community.

Neighborhood and Community

Children do not choose where they live. Children who live in fear of drug dealers, street violence, and gang shootings cannot enjoy childhood. Children are dependent on parents, neighbors, and police to provide a safe and secure environment in which to play, go to school, and work. Community policing can play an important role in creating a safer environment. Community police officers not only help to reduce criminal activity but also become positive role models and establish caring relationships with the youth and families in a community. On-site neighborhood resource teams, composed of community police officers, social workers, health-care workers, housing experts, and school personnel, can ensure that a wide range of problems are responded to in a timely and coordinated manner. . . .

Graduated Sanctions

An effective juvenile justice system program model for the treatment and rehabilitation of delinquent offenders is one that combines accountability and sanctions with increasingly intensive treatment and rehabilitation services. These graduated sanctions must be wide-ranging to fit the offense and include both intervention and secure corrections components. The intervention component includes the use of immediate intervention and intermediate sanctions, and the secure corrections component includes the use of community confinement and incarceration in training schools, camps, and ranches.

Each of these graduated sanctions components should consist of sublevels, or gradations, that together with appropriate services constitute an integrated approach. The purpose of this approach is to stop the juvenile's further penetration into the system by inducing law-abiding behavior as early as possible through the combination of appropriate intervention and treatment sanctions. The juvenile justice system must work with law enforcement, courts, and corrections to develop reasonable, fair, and humane sanctions.

At each level in the continuum, the family must continue to be integrally involved in treatment and rehabilitation efforts. Aftercare must be a formal component of all residential placements, actively involving the family and the community in supporting and reintegrating the juvenile into the community.

Programs will need to use Risk and Needs Assessments to determine the appropriate placement for the offender. Risk assessments should be based on clearly defined objective criteria that focus on (1) the seriousness of the delinquent act; (2) the potential risk for reoffending, based on the presence of risk factors; and (3) the risk to the public safety. Effective risk assessment at intake, for example, can be used to identify those juveniles who require the use of detention as well as those who can be released to parental custody or diverted to nonsecure community-based programs. Needs assessments will help ensure that (1) different types of problems are taken into account when formulating a case plan; (2) a baseline for monitoring a juvenile's progress is established; (3) periodic reassessments of treatment effectiveness are conducted; and (4) a systemwide data base of treatment needs can be used for the planning and evaluation of programs, policies, and procedures. Together, risk and needs assessments will help to allocate scarce resources more efficiently and effectively. A system of graduated sanctions requires a broad continuum of options.

Intervention

For intervention efforts to be most effective, they must be swift, certain, consistent, and incorporate increasing sanctions, including the possible loss of freedom. As the severity of sanctions increases, so must the intensity of treatment. At each level, offenders must be aware that, should they continue to violate the law, they will be subject to more severe sanctions and could ultimately be confined in a secure setting, ranging from a secure community-based juvenile facility to a training school, camp, or ranch.

The juvenile court plays an important role in the provision of treatment and sanctions. Probation has traditionally been viewed as the court's main vehicle for delivery of treatment services and community supervision. However, traditional probation services and sanctions have not had the resources to effectively target delinquent offenders, particularly serious, violent, and chronic offenders.

The Balanced Approach to juvenile probation is a promising approach that specifies a clear and coherent framework. The Balanced Approach consists of three practical objectives: (1) Accountability; (2) Competency Development; and (3) Community Protection. Accountability refers to the requirement that offenders make amends to the victims and the community for harm caused. Competency Development requires that youth who enter the juvenile justice system should exit the system more capable of being productive and responsible citizens. Community Protection requires that the juvenile justice system ensure public safety.

The following graduated sanctions are proposed within the Intervention component:

Immediate Intervention. First-time delinquent offenders (misdemeanors and nonviolent felonies) and nonserious repeat offenders (generally misdemeanor repeat offenses) must be targeted for system intervention based on their probability of becoming more serious or chronic in their delinquent activities. Nonresidential community-based programs, including prevention programs for at-risk youth, may be appropriate for many of these offenders. Such programs are small and open, located in or near the juvenile's home, and maintain community participation in program planning, operation, and evaluation. Community police officers, working as part of Neighborhood Resource Teams, can help monitor the juvenile's progress. Other offenders may require sanctions tailored to their offense(s) and their needs to deter them from committing additional crimes. The following programs apply to these offenders:

- Neighborhood Resource Teams.
- Diversion.
- Informal Probation.
- School Counselors Serving as Probation Officers.
- Home on Probation.
- Mediation (Victims).
- Community Service.
- Restitution.
- Day-Treatment Programs.
- Alcohol and Drug Abuse Treatment (Outpatient).
- Peer Juries.

Intermediate Sanctions. Offenders who are inappropriate for immediate intervention (first-time serious or violent offenders) or who fail to respond successfully to immediate intervention as evidenced by reoffending (such as repeat property offenders or drug-involved juveniles) would begin with or be subject to intermediate sanctions. These sanctions may be nonresidential or residential.

Many of the serious and violent offenders at this stage may be appropriate for placement in an Intensive Supervision Program as an alternative to secure incarceration. OJJDP's Intensive Supervision of Probationers Program Model is a highly structured, continuously monitored individualized plan that consists of five phases with decreasing levels of restrictiveness: (1) Short-Term Placement in Community Confinement; (2) Day Treatment; (3) Outreach and Tracking;

(4) Routine Supervision; and (5) Discharge and Followup. Other appropriate programs include:

- Drug Testing.
- Weekend Detention.
- Alcohol and Drug Abuse Treatment (Inpatient).
- Challenge Outdoor Programs.
- Community-Based Residential Programs.
- Electronic Monitoring.
- Boot Camp Facilities and Programs.

Secure Corrections

The criminal behavior of many serious, violent, and chronic juvenile offenders requires the application of secure sanctions to hold these offenders accountable for their delinquent acts and to provide a structured treatment environment. Large congregate-care juvenile facilities (training schools, camps, and ranches) have not proven to be particularly effective in rehabilitating juvenile offenders. Although some continued use of these types of facilities will remain a necessary alternative for those juveniles who require enhanced security to protect the public, the establishment of small community-based facilities to provide intensive services in a secure environment offers the best hope for successful treatment of those juveniles who require a structured setting. Secure sanctions are most effective in changing future conduct when they are coupled with comprehensive treatment and rehabilitation services.

Standard parole practices, particularly those that have a primary focus on social control, have not been effective in normalizing the behavior of high-risk juvenile parolees over the long term, and consequently, growing interest has developed in intensive aftercare programs that provide high levels of social control and treatment services. OJJDP's Intensive Community-Based Aftercare for High-Risk Juvenile Parolees Program provides an effective aftercare model:

> The Intensive Aftercare Program incorporates five programmatic principles: (1) preparing youth for progressive responsibility and freedom in the community; (2) facilitating youth-community interaction and involvement; (3) working with both the offender and targeted community support systems (e.g., families, peers, schools, and employers) to facilitate constructive interaction and gradual community adjustment; (4) developing needed resources and community support; and (5) monitoring and ensuring the youth's successful reintegration into the community.

The following graduated sanctions strategies are proposed within the Secure Corrections component:

Community Confinement. Offenders whose presenting offense is sufficiently serious (such as a violent felony) or who fail to respond to intermediate sanctions as evidenced by continued reoffending may be appropriate for community confinement. Offenders at this level represent the more serious (such as repeat felony drug trafficking or property offenders) and violent offenders among the juvenile justice system correctional population.

The concept of community confinement provides secure confinement in small community-based facilities that offer intensive treatment and rehabilitation services. These services include individual and group counseling, educational programs, medical services, and intensive staff supervision. Proximity to the community enables direct and regular family involvement with the treatment process as well as a phased reentry into the community that draws upon community resources and services.

Incarceration in Training Schools, Camps, and Ranches. Juveniles whose confinement in the community would constitute an ongoing threat to community safety or who have failed to respond to community-based corrections may require an extended correctional placement in training schools, camps, ranches, or other secure options that are not community-based. These facilities should offer comprehensive treatment programs for these youth with a focus on education, skills development, and vocational or employment training and experience. These juveniles may include those convicted in the criminal justice system prior to their reaching the age at which they are no longer subject to the original or extended jurisdiction of the juvenile justice system.

Expected Benefits

The proposed strategy provides for a comprehensive approach in responding to delinquent conduct and serious, violent, and chronic criminal behavior, consisting of (1) community protection and public safety, (2) accountability, (3) competency development, (4) individualization, and (5) balanced representation of the interests of the community, victim, and juvenile. By taking these factors into account in each program component, a new direction in the administration of juvenile justice is fostered.

Delinquency Prevention

This major component of the comprehensive strategy involves implementation of delinquency prevention technology that has been demonstrated to be effective. Prevention strategies within the major areas that influence the behavior of youth (individual development, family, school, peer group, and community) parallel the chronological development of children. Because addressing these five areas has been found to be effective in reducing future delinquency among high-risk youth, it should result in fewer children entering the juvenile justice system in demonstration sites. This would, in turn, permit concentration of system resources on fewer delinquents, thereby increasing the effectiveness of the graduated sanctions component and improving the operation of the juvenile justice system.

Graduated Sanctions

This major component of the comprehensive strategy is premised on a firm belief that the juvenile justice system can effectively handle delinquent juvenile behavior through the judicious application of a range of graduated sanctions and a full continuum of treatment and rehabilitation services. Expected benefits of this approach include:

- *Increased juvenile justice system responsiveness.* This program will provide additional referral and dispositional resources for law enforcement, juvenile courts, and juvenile corrections. It will also require these system components to increase their ability to identify, process, evaluate, refer, and track juvenile offenders.

- *Increased juvenile accountability.* Juvenile offenders will be held accountable for their behavior, decreasing the likelihood of their development into serious, violent, or chronic offenders and tomorrow's adult criminals. The juvenile justice system will be held accountable for controlling chronic and serious delinquency while also protecting society. Communities will be held accountable for providing community-based prevention and treatment resources for juveniles.

- *Decreased costs of juvenile corrections.* Applying the appropriate graduated sanctions and developing the required community-based resources should reduce significantly the need for high-cost beds in training schools. Savings from the high costs of operating these facilities could be used to provide treatment in community-based programs and facilities.

- *Increased responsibility of the juvenile justice system.* Many juvenile offenders currently waived or transferred to the criminal justice system could be provided opportunities for intensive services in secure community-based settings or in long-term treatment in juvenile training schools, camps, and ranches.

- *Increased program effectiveness.* As the statistical information presented herein indicates, credible knowledge exists about *who* the chronic, serious, and violent offenders are, that is, their characteristics. Some knowledge also exists about what can effectively be done regarding their treatment and rehabilitation. However, more must be learned about what works best for whom under what circumstances to intervene successfully in the potential criminal careers of serious, violent, and chronic juvenile offenders. Followup research and rigorous evaluation of programs implemented as part of this strategy should produce valuable information.

Crime Reduction

The combined effects of delinquency prevention and increased juvenile justice system effectiveness in intervening immediately and effectively in the lives of delinquent offenders should result in measurable decreases in delinquency in sites where the above concepts are demonstrated. In addition, long-term reduction in crime should result from fewer serious, violent, and chronic delinquents becoming adult criminal offenders.

Reference

National Council of Juvenile and Family Court Judges. 1993. "Children and Families First, A Mandate for Change." ✦

Section X
Diversion, Restitution, and Shock Treatment

There is increasing evidence that "locking kids up and throwing away the key" is not preventing juvenile delinquency. From a deterrence perspective, the notion that juveniles in correctional facilities will cease being delinquent out of fear of future institutionalization is not supported by scientific research. With recidivism rates exceeding 50 percent, arguments based on specific deterrence are not convincing. Juvenile correctional facilities are referred to as "schools for crime," "holding tanks," or "dumping grounds for troubled kids," and there is little evidence that anything positive can come out of a juvenile institution. A second glaring problem is that these facilities are filled to capacity. States are forced to allocate exorbitant sums of money that could be used for more socially meaningful purposes to build new juvenile facilities. In addition to building new juvenile institutions, millions of dollars are allocated annually to maintain those that presently exist. The current practice of "putting bad kids in the slammer" does not have any discernible impact on juvenile crime, and the cost of incarcerating delinquents may be penalizing the taxpayer more than the law violator. For the past two decades there have been some concerted searches for ways to reduce the number of juveniles in institutions, control the escalating cost of the juvenile justice system, and find some practical way to deal with the problem of delinquency.

Juvenile Diversion

One way to deal with the massive numbers being brought into the juvenile justice system is to provide some sort of filtering mechanism whereby minor offenders could bypass the formal juvenile system. The juvenile court was initially legally empowered to deal with all forms of juvenile problems including dependency and neglect, status offenders, and delinquent offenders. In attempting to carry out the original legislation, formulated at the turn of the century, the juvenile court eventually acquired a certain legal ambiguity in trying to be both a social work agency and a court of law. It was theorized that if the juvenile court could be relieved of petty misconduct and turn its attention to matters relating to serious delinquency, it could be more effective. In the mid-1970s, Congress began funding a series of juvenile court initiatives that called for the diversion of status offenders from the juvenile justice system in order to increase attention to serious juvenile misconduct. Ironically, the juvenile court, which was initially created to divert juveniles away from the adult criminal justice system, some seventy-five years later was inspiring new legislation to divert juveniles toward the criminal court.

The basic philosophy of diversion became almost a social movement in the late 1970s and early 1980s. No one could object to the laudable intentions of this second-generation reform movement in the juvenile justice system. Diversion was supported by labeling theorists, differential association theorists, and social learning theorists. It responded to the needs of the "hard-liners" who were talking about getting tough on juvenile delinquents, and diversion enabled the juvenile court to spend more time with serious cases; it was endorsed by humanitarians who were appalled by the sight of adolescents "doing time" in correctional institutions; and it was supported by taxpayer groups who were clamoring for fiscal restraint in government spending. With this overwhelming degree of support, diversion programs were seen as the savior of the juvenile court. Unfortunately, as with so many well-intentioned reform movements, the actual implementation of the approach was not carefully thought out, and many unforeseen stumbling blocks began to appear as diversion programs were created. Perhaps the most prominent problem that arose is the phenomenon of "widening the net." Frazier and Cochran examined diversion programs and found that diverted youthful offenders experienced at least as much involvement with the juvenile justice system as nondiverted offenders. Anderson and Schoen went so far as to call diversion an "unrealistic or harmful fad" that neither rescues juvenile offenders from more serious delinquency nor frees them from juvenile court intrusion in their lives. What occurred was confusion over terms, specifically *diverting youth from* court processing versus *referring youth to* other agencies in the community. This latter approach became known as "alternative encapsulation" in which youth were deflected from the juvenile court and sent to another community-based program. Thus, rather than reducing the number of juveniles in the system, diversion inadvertently brought in more, and the juvenile court became something of a brokerage house, sending adolescents to many different programs as well as processing some in the juvenile court system itself.

The first reading, entitled "Juvenile Diversion and the Potential of Inappropriate Treatment for Offenders," by Rojek, looks at one unintended consequence of diversion: the proliferation of community programs. In the process of deflecting juveniles away from the juvenile court, new quasi-legal programs emerged in the community to supplement the juvenile justice system. In fact, many of these community programs were subcontracted by the juvenile court. Rather than *diverting* adolescents with petty offenses away from the court to their home, with the advent of diversion they were *referred to* community programs. A carnival emerged as various community agencies vied for clients. The result was that an adolescent could end up in a program designed to deal with a problem behavior that did not apply to that particular adolescent. Rojek's research suggests that inappropriate services were not merely a waste of money, but could actually do harm to the individual and make matters worse.

Restitution

A second reform effort, restitution, arose in the late 1970s and also quickly received widespread support. While restitution is one of the oldest forms of court settlement, going back to ancient civilizations and used extensively in medieval England, where "blood money" was required from the offender's family to rectify an injustice to the victim, it had rarely been used in juvenile court. Perhaps the most appealing aspect of restitution is that the victim receives some form of compensation for an injury or a loss caused by an offender. The criminal justice system focuses heavily on the offender, but the victim typically does not "receive his due" aside from knowing that the offender is fined or sent to prison. The process of restitution brings the victim of a crime into focus. The perpetrator is required to account for his or her behavior by rendering justice to the victim. Since sending a person to jail does not restore the damage done to the victim, it may be more equitable to see to it that the offender repays the victim. Like diversion, restitution has intuitive appeal.

While diversion programs were quickly adopted by the juvenile court, restitution programs were introduced more slowly. The tradition in the American court system is to punish the offender; restitution could connote a lack of punishment. Secondly, the criminal justice system had not traditionally been an advocate of the victim, and the concept of victims' rights had not been foremost in the minds of the judiciary. Finally, restitution called for some element of monitoring or follow-up that the juvenile courts were not able to implement readily. For example, if damage was done, the victim would receive compensation, and it would be the court's responsibility to verify that this transfer of funds took place. However, the juvenile courts do not have the personnel to supervise this type of follow-up; restitution becomes in practice a cumbersome procedure, although it has been used in some juvenile courts. Further, it could be argued that restitution could also become a type of treatment or rehabilitation process whereby the juvenile offender repays the victim and sees the potential hardship of committing a crime.

The second reading, by Butts and Snyder, entitled "Restitution and Juvenile Recidivism," looks at the operation of a restitution program in the Utah Juvenile Court. They found that those juvenile offenders who were processed informally but were involved in a restitution program had lower recidivism rates than those not in a restitution program. Similarly, recidivism rates of those ordered by the court to make financial restitution (formal probation) were lower again than those who had probation alone. The authors conclude that the use of restitution is "associated with significant reductions in recidivism." However, the actual percentage difference was around 6 to 7 percent.

The third reading, by Staples, entitled "Restitution as a Sanction in Juvenile Court," examines the issue of restitution from a historical perspective. Two separate systems of justice have arisen: criminal law for offenses against the state and tort law for offenses against a victim who is able to sue for damages. The two legal codes are distinctively different, but restitution forces a merger of the two. Staples raises some intriguing problems with restitution that partially explain why it has not been used extensively in juvenile court. He also raises points about whether restitution is really punishment and how adolescents can be expected to pay victims for the harm committed, given that unemployment rates are traditionally the highest for teenagers. Does restitution then mean that the juvenile court becomes an employment agency? What if the teenager cannot find a job and cannot pay back the victim? Staples raises a number of cautionary notes and ultimately suggests that restitution may not be the savior of the juvenile justice system.

Intensive Supervision Programs

The fourth reading in this section, by Wiebush, entitled "Juvenile Intensive Supervision: The Impact on Felony Offenders Diverted From Institutional Placement," looks at a third way to deal with juvenile offenders. Rather than sentencing them to a correctional facility, intensive supervision allows the adolescent to remain in the community, but under close court supervision. Probation officers involved in intensive supervision conduct frequent spotchecks at home and in school, administer random drug tests, and place restrictions on the adolescent as needed. The object of Wiebush's research was to compare recidivism rates of a group of offenders placed in intensive supervision with those of a "control" group of offenders who were sentenced to a correctional facility and another group of offenders placed on probation. Wiebush is sensitive to the fact that his three groups may not have been exactly identical because adolescents selected for intensive supervision rather than commitment may be somewhat less at-risk youth, and probationers may be even less involved in delinquent behavior. However, after eighteen months, there were discernible differences in recidivism rates among the three groups. Not surprisingly, as shown in Table 4 of the reading, the probation group had the lowest recidivism rate, but this was quite high (68 percent had a new complaint and 62 percent were adjudicated). Both the intensive supervision and committed youth had high recidivism rates (82 percent and 77 percent adjudicated). While this could be interpreted as a failure, it also shows that a group of delinquents that was not committed to a correctional facility fared no worse than a group that was committed. Could one then make the argument that intensive probation represents a financial savings over institutionalization? Staples presents these data in Table 6, and at first it appears that intensive supervision is considerably less expensive than institutionalization. However, Staples shows that cost estimates can be misleading, and intensive supervision is considerably more expensive. The costs of institutionalization remain fairly constant whether the correctional facility is filled or not, but intensive supervision represents "real" money that must be calculated on a per-person basis. In his conclusion, Staples discusses the pros and cons of intensive supervision and suggests that it may be an alternative to incarceration, but not a cost-effective one.

Shock Treatment

"Shock Treatment" is the last plausible alternative to institutionalization, and also the newest approach. While there are various approaches under the generic umbrella of shock treatment, the basic premise is that by having adolescents confront the reality of punishment for deviant behavior, they can be deterred from future criminal acts. The most notable example of this form of aversion therapy is called "scared straight." This program was initiated at Rahway Prison in New Jersey by the inmates themselves. Juveniles who were manifesting delinquent tendencies were brought to the prison and exposed to the realities of the life of a convict. A documentary film entitled *Scared Straight* was produced in 1978 and the film and the program became an instant success. The film depicted 17 problem teenagers who participated in the Scared Straight program and the raw, brutal reality of seeing and hearing what prison life is like. Peter Falk narrated the program and after viewing the intense confrontational session between teenagers and the inmates, Falk asserted that more than 90 percent of teenagers who participated in this program "had crime scared out of them, and 16 out of 17 went straight." Despite the initial excitement of these findings, researchers have gone back and reviewed the program and found it to be far less successful than was touted on the television program (Finckenauer, 1982).

A second and more recent form of shock therapy appeared with the introduction of "boot camps." Whereas programs like Scared Straight are for potential offenders, boot camps are designed for young offenders who have been apprehended and convicted of an offense. However, rather than sentencing them to a traditional correctional facility, they are sent to a boot camp where they are exposed to a form of military training that is designed to rehabilitate young, nonviolent, first-time offenders before they commit major crimes. According to a report written by the General Accounting Office (GAO), boot camps were first introduced in Georgia and Oklahoma in 1983 and 1984 and quickly spread to more than half of the states. Most of the programs are designed to run for 90 days, although some can last as long as 180 days. The programs themselves are composed of military drills, exercise, Spartan living conditions, minimal visitation rights, and intense discipline. The GAO report concluded that "while there is no evidence that boot camps significantly reduce recidivism, they do reduce costs and crowding." However, the GAO report qualified the cost reduction by pointing out that the average daily cost for a boot camp is higher than for traditional correctional institutions, but offenders spend less time in boot camps.

Like Scared Straight programs, boot camps look "flashy" and offer instant appeal. The difficulty with these programs is that they offer little in terms of follow-up care and they adhere to the standard perception of after-the-fact rehabilitation rather than prevention before a deviant act occurs. A school dropout who has low self-esteem, few job skills, and comes from a crime-prone neighborhood does not acquire any radical infusion of skills or abilities in a boot camp. MacKenzie and Piquero, in their article "The Impact of Shock Incarceration Programs on Prison Crowding," review the basic points of boot camps and go on to examine five programs. As was the case with diversion, boot camps represent a case of net widening if they are used as alternatives to probation. Prison crowding will be affected only if boot camps are used for individuals who would ordinarily be sent to a correctional institution. The danger is that boot camps may become co-opted by a pervasive need to "scare the hell out of" offenders who would normally be put on probation, leaving prison crowding unaffected.

The last article in this section, by Morash and Rucker, entitled "A Critical Look at the Idea of Boot Camp as a Correctional Reform," goes a step further and suggests that boot camps may be dehumanizing. The potential for abuse is readily present in boot camps, and the "therapy" of hard physical work for unskilled offenders may not enhance their job skills after they have left the program. The authors question the efficacy of military-style boot camps in producing prosocial behavior. Boot camps are rife with physical and verbal aggression, which are associated with pronounced masculinity. Morash and Rucker question whether these "masculine" traits are the very characteristics that lead to criminal behavior. Again, there has been an enthusiastic acceptance of a new approach to dealing with the problem of delinquency, but it may simply be more of the "same old stuff."

References

Anderson, Dennis and Donald Schoen. 1985. "Diversion Programs: Effect of Stigmatization of Juvenile/Status Offender." *Juvenile and Family Court Journal* 36: 13-25

Frazier, Charles and John Cochran. 1986. "Official Intervention, Diversion from the Juvenile Justice System, and Dynamics of Human Services Work: Effects of a Reform Goal Based on Labeling Theory." *Crime and Delinquency* 32: 157-76.

Finckenauer, James. 1982. *Scared Straight and the Panacea Phenomenon*. Englewood Cliffs, N.J.: Prentice-Hall.

Government Accounting Office. 1993. *Prison Boot Camps: Short-term Prison Costs Reduced, but Long-term Impact Uncertain*. General Accounting Office: Washington: D.C. ✦

35
Juvenile Diversion and the Potential of Inappropriate Treatment for Offenders

Dean G. Rojek

I. Introduction

The literature examining the effectiveness of treatment for juvenile and adult offenders is extremely distressing. In some instances the evaluation of treatment programs might conclude on the note of "slight, inconsistent and of questionable reliability"[1] or "no rehabilitation consequences but some economic utility."[2] However, the most pervasive conclusion is generally reflective of what has been labelled the "nothing-works doctrine."[3] Even the Swedish correctional system, which is often heralded as the world's most progressive, has not succeeded in curbing recidivism. For example, it was found that despite shorter terms of confinement, more open institutions and far more treatment resources than are available in the United States, Swedish correctional institutions seem to produce recidivism rates that are as high as American rates.[4]

Disillusionment with the rehabilitative model has led to the development of new strategies and new approaches in the past decade of the late 1970s and 1980s. Perhaps one of the most strongly acclaimed innovations, at least in the juvenile justice system, is the concept of diversion.

Due to the multi-dimensional quality of diversion and its differing modes of operationalization, it is extremely problematic to arrive at a standard or universal definition of the term.[5] In some instances, diversion refers to turning an offender away from the traditional juvenile justice machinery. In other cases, diversion infers not only a turning away but also a referral to a community alternative. Finally, to confound the concept even more, diversion has also been described as an attempt to "minimize penetration into the juvenile justice system."[6] However, the basic thrust of diversion is to "suspend or terminate juvenile justice processing of youth in favor of release or referral to alternate services."[7]

It has been suggested that the term diversion should refer only to the process of turning juvenile offenders away from the formal juvenile justice system. The term referral would, then, be used to describe not only turning an offender away from the formal system but also directing the offender toward an alternative program.[8] Thus, a juvenile could be *diverted* out of the system and sent home or *referred* to an alternative community-based program.

On the surface it appears that diversion represents a step in the direction of what Lemert[9] has called "judicious nonintervention" but this new process has also introduced a potential danger in the area of procedural safeguards. Specifically, the zeal in adopting the diversion philosophy quickly becomes confounded with the notion that whatever is new is better, and that community-based treatment is more benign and efficacious than treatment in the juvenile justice system. Hence, before adopting a wholehearted endorsement of the diversion ideology, it needs to be demonstrated that this approach is effective, and that it guarantees some degree of procedural due process.

II. Criteria of Effectiveness

A basic consideration in evaluation research is program effectiveness, namely, how well a particular activity achieves its goals or objectives.[10] Any attempt to scientifically demonstrate the effectiveness of a particular program would call for an evaluative design that had an experimental and control group as well as multiple measures of pre-test and post-test behaviors and attitudes. Unfortunately, a cursory review of the evaluations of treatment programs shows that basic research criteria are woefully lacking. For example, most evaluation research techniques use "recidivism-only" criteria. Glaser[11] has pointed out that treatment success or failure cannot be measured simply on the basis of the presence or absence of a re-arrest. A convicted burglar who continues to steal but avoids apprehension is considered rehabilitated, while a convicted burglar who ceases stealing property but is arrested for a drug offense is a recidivist. Hood and Sparks[12] suggested that criteria other than re-arrest or re-conviction may be more meaningful in determining the effectiveness of treatment programs. Social stability, attitudinal changes, involvement in conventional activities, gainful employment and other background characteristics may be more insightful than the presence or absence of an arrest.

A second criterion in considering the success or failure of diversion is what has been termed "counting all outcomes."[13] Typically, evaluation approaches call for a comparison of those who completed a treatment with those who received no treatment. Individuals who did not complete treatment for whatever reasons are normally dropped from the analysis. However, as Lerman[14] pointed out, individuals who were dishonorably discharged from a program or whom he labelled "internal failures," invariably enhanced the success of any program. By screening out untreatable, incorrigible or uncooperative clients, programs can purify their sampling frames and thereby dramatically improve their chances of positive results. On the other hand, comparison or control groups cannot screen out clients, and their success rates can be significantly lower than the experimental program.

In re-examining the apparent success of the Highfield's program for juvenile offenders in New Jersey, Lerman[15] added external failures (recidivists who completed the program) to internal failures (program dropouts) and found that the Highfield's program was no more successful than traditional juvenile offender programs. Similarly, Scarpitti and Stephenson[16] examined the effectiveness of probation as compared to institutionalization. They found that the success rate of probation was artificially inflated. Those who had violated the terms of their probation were sent back to the institution; however, they were not counted as part of the treatment population.

III. Ethical Considerations

While the issue of internal failure or program effectiveness may represent a form of data manipulation, rarely is the question posed whether program dropouts or "untreatables" who are discharged from programs suffer any adverse affects.[17] The inference attributed to internal failure is that individuals assigned to experimental programs but "not amenable to treatment" were simply discharged. However, in the case of juvenile diversion, where there may be a proliferation of alternative services,[18] a subject may be exposed to inappropriate or even harmful treatment. The net result may be that continued deviant behavior is partially the product of the treatment itself.

An examination of the outcome of a juvenile delinquency project entitled Pilot Intensive Counseling Organization (PICO) is a clear case in point.[19] Juvenile offenders were clinically adjudged at intake to be either "amenable" or "nonamenable" to the proposed treatment. The two categories of subjects were then randomly assigned to experimental and control groups. The results from this study indicated that the experimental amenables were significantly more improved on a series of performance criteria than the control amenables, control nonamenables or treated nonamenables. The control nonamenables and control amenables were virtually identical on all outcome performance criteria. However, the treated nonamenables, those deemed not suitable for treatment but were still put in a treatment program, displayed extremely poor community adjustment and high recidivism rates. While the average "lockup" time during the first 33 months after release was 2.1 months for the experimental amenables and 4.8 months for the control amenable and nonamenable groups, the treated nonamenables had an average lockup rate of 5.5 months.

Adams suggested that the reason the treated nonamenables performed so poorly was either too little treatment or the wrong kind of treatment. The insufficient treatment hypothesis suggests that more treatment needed to be given to nonamenables to compensate for their poor socialization, personal disorganization or lack of motivation. The difficulty with this explanation is the wide divergence in social adjustment between the control and treated nonamenables. On the other hand, Adams raised the possibility that the treated nonamenables received the wrong treatment which increased their hostility and contributed to greater deviant behavior. Unfortunately, this issue is not examined in any detail by Adams and the notion of inappropriate treatment continues to be ignored in the evaluation literature.

IV. Data and Methods

Using a sample of juvenile status offenders who were diverted from a large juvenile system in the state of Arizona, the objective of this research will be to evaluate the outcome of three distinct groups of juveniles: (1) a diverted and treated group (Diversion-Referral), (2) a diverted but non-treated group (Pure Diversion), and (3) drop-outs from the diversion-referral group (Internal Failures).[20] The first category, diversion-referral, refers to those status offenders who were not only diverted from the normal processing machinery of the juvenile court but also referred to one of several community-based treatment programs. In theory, community-based programs were funded to specialize in addressing the needs of particular types of offenders. For example, runaways were referred to shelter care facilities, chronic truants to alternative education programs, incorrigibles to counseling programs and alcohol or drug abusers to drug treatment programs.[21] The second category, pure diversion, refers to those status offenders who were apprehended but released to the custody of their parents. In this instance, the arresting officer or court services worker recommended no treatment and no further action was taken. The third category, internal failures,[22] were those subjects who were apprehended, referred to a community-based program but dropped out of the program. These internal failures ranged from "no-shows" (never appeared at the community-based treatment program) to incorrigibles who were dropped by the community-based agency for being "not amenable to treatment."

In order to evaluate the effectiveness of this diversion program, a random sample of subjects was selected for intensive study over a twelve month time span.[23] These subjects were to be interviewed at three points in time (six months apart) but for purposes of this study only the Time 1 and Time 2 findings will be discussed. Each subject was administered a self-reported delinquency questionnaire which listed a series of delinquent behaviors ranging from status offenses to felony acts. A second component of the interview dealt with the respondents' perceptions of seriousness regarding various delinquent acts, rated on a scale ranging from one (extremely serious) to seven (not serious at all). The third part of the interview contained a series of attitudinal and self-esteem items. The attitudinal items had a response range from one (strongly agree) to seven (strongly disagree) and the self-esteem or self-concept measures ranged from one (describes me very well) to four (does not describe me at all).

In addition to the interview information, offense histories were created for each subject using police, juvenile court, sheriff, and state police files. Each subject had by definition one arrest or "police contact" in order to be eligible for this diversion program, thereby constituting a more deviant population than a pure random selection of "normal" adolescents. However, the total number of arrests[24] was not inordinate. While the actual range of arrests varied from one to 27, the average for

Table 1
Means and standard deviations (in parentheses) of performance criteria at Time 1 and Time 2 for three categories of diverted juveniles (N=348)

Performance Criteria	Time 1			Time 2		
	Diverted (N=61)	Referred (N=169)	Dropout (N=118)	Diverted (N=61)	Referred (N=169)	Dropout (N=118)
Family ties	2.08 (.92)	1.99 (.86)	2.00 (.82)	2.03 (.68)	2.00 (.71)	1.91 (.68)
School ties	6.72 (4.34)	6.57 (3.57)	7.32 (4.47)	6.46 (3.34)	6.08 (3.26)	6.84 (3.80)
Legal respect	9.44 (3.46)	10.25 (3.83)	9.97 (3.59)	10.43 (3.14)	10.12 (3.71)	9.17 (3.64)
Peer influence	6.39 (2.74)	7.18 (3.05)	6.76 (2.57)	6.52 (2.09)	7.34 (2.87)	7.26 (2.98)
Positive self-esteem	13.49 (3.74)	14.16 (3.72)	14.42 (3.20)	13.80 (2.80)	13.51 (2.92)	13.42 (3.40)
Negative self-esteem	16.51 (8.53)	15.59 (7.73)	15.18 (7.25)	16.43 (6.58)	15.60 (5.34)	16.39 (6.58)
Seriousness-drugs	8.49 (3.95)	8.09 (4.34)	8.14 (4.32)	9.03 (3.69)	8.88 (4.18)	7.93 (4.32)
Seriousness-property	17.31 (9.31)	19.30 (11.00)	17.57 (9.94)	17.90 (8.92)	18.69 (11.26)	16.56 (11.56)
Seriousness-violence	8.31 (4.93)	8.92 (5.08)	8.22 (4.81)	7.62 (4.04)	8.91 (5.13)	7.89 (5.16)
Arrests	3.29 (3.85)	3.05 (3.56)	2.94 (5.12)	1.00 (1.70)	0.75 (1.67)	1.03 (1.96)
SR-drugs	14.20 (11.87)	12.60 (11.69)	13.32 (12.12)	16.51 (11.81)	13.96 (11.77)	14.66 (11.99)
SR-property	9.74 (8.02)	9.37 (8.78)	9.12 (6.57)	8.70 (9.67)	8.63 (5.51)	9.94 (6.80)
SR-violence	7.51 (7.06)	8.09 (7.92)	7.76 (8.37)	7.31 (8.93)	7.43 (8.46)	8.58 (9.97)

these subjects was 2.9 arrests. The so-called "at-risk" period of juveniles generally covered the age span of 10 to 17, but the vast majority of offenders were between 15 to 17 years of age. Most arrests were for status offenses (52%), followed by property offenses (29%), and serious violent crimes amounting to only 4.7% of the total.[25] In the analysis that is to follow, the subjects will be analyzed in terms of their total number of arrests, and no attempt will be made to categorize specific types of offenses because of the relative infrequency of an arrest and the unevenness of these distributions. . . .

V. Findings

Table 1 shows the means at Time 1 of the thirteen performance measures for those 348 subjects who were diverted, referred, or eventually dropped out.[26] The right-hand portion of Table 1 gives the results recorded at Time 2, six months later. As shown in Table 1, 17.5% (N=61) of the sample were simply diverted and released to the custody of the subject's parents or legal guardians. No treatment of any kind was administered to this group. The second column with the heading of "referred" represents those subjects who were diverted and referred to a community-based program. A total of 169 or 48.6% of the subjects had either completed some type of treatment in a community-based program or were still active participants in a program six months later. The third column entitled "dropout" represents those subjects who were referred to a community-based program but did not complete the treatment.[27] As shown in Table 1, 118 or 33.9% of the subjects were internal failures. Stated another way, of the 287 status offenders who were referred to a community-based program, 59% (N=169) were considered successful and 41% (N=118) were unsuccessful.

In examining the means listed in Table 1, at Time 1, there does not appear to be any demonstrable differences in attitudes, behaviors, self-concept or perceptions of seriousness among the three groups of status offenders. The diverted group was comparable to the referred groups (successful referrals and dropouts), and at the time of their initial arrest it is extremely difficult to ascertain the rationale for referral rather than simple diversion.[28] Examining the differences among the means for each performance criteria at Time 1 with an analysis of variance procedure (results not shown) produced no significant differences. That is, not only is it problematic as to why subjects were referred rather than diverted, but also for those who were referred, there is no clear indication at Time 1 why some would eventually complete treatment and others would drop out.

The second panel on Table 1, showing the outcome measures six months later at Time 2, does not reveal any dramatic change within any of the three treatment categories. An analysis of variance procedure, examining the differences within the three groups at Time 2, did reveal significant differences (results not shown). However, the source of the differences was predominately because the dropout group had poorer outcome results six months later. The differences at Time 2 between the diverted and the referred groups were negligible. These findings are tentative because as will be discussed later, any assessment of change requires a more sophisticated approach than simple differences of means between Time 1 and Time 2.

Before leaving Table 1, it is puzzling how status offenders were originally assigned to diverted or referred categories. As was already indicated, there were no significant differences at Time 1 among the diverted or referred groups on thirteen measures of performance criteria. Using other background characteristics, perhaps some indication can be found to explain this differentiation process. Discriminate analysis is a statistical technique that allows the investigator to create distinct groups and then examine the relative importance of a wide array of variables as to their ability to explain group differences.[29] That is, the question is whether there are significant differences at Time 1 among the three groups of diverted, referred and dropout subjects. In Table 2 the results from discriminate analysis are shown using age, sex, race, instant offense (status offense at Time 1), father's education and welfare status. Age and father's level of education were coded in years, while sex, race and welfare status were dummy coded (Male = 0 and Female = 1, Black = 0 and White = 1, welfare recipient = 0 and no welfare = 1). Finally, the five instant status offenses for which the subject was actually apprehended were also dummy coded (0 = not charged for specific offense and 1 = charged for specific offense).

Table 2 gives the canonical discriminate functions and the structure matrix resulting from discriminate analysis. While two discriminate functions were produced, Wilks' Lambda reveals that only Function 1 has some discriminating power. Similarly, the canonical correlation for Function 1 (.506) indicates a modest relation between the canonical correlates and the discriminate function, while the canonical correlation for Function 2 (.323) is extremely low. The

Table 2
Discriminate analysis of diverted, referred and dropout groups, using social status and sociodemographic variables.

Canonical Discriminate Functions

Functions	% Variance	Canonical Correlation	Wilks' Lambda	Significance Level
1	74.7%	.506	.466	.001
2	25.3%	.323	.896	.05

Structure Matrix

Variables	Function 1	Function 2
Sex	-.592	-
Alcohol	-.296	-
Runaway	-.271	-
Ungovernability	.262	-
Truancy	-.200	-
Curfew	-	.376
Black	-	.293
Age	-	-.217
Father's education	-	.235
Welfare status	-	.155

structure matrix or pooled within group correlations between the canonical discriminate function and the discriminating variables are basically bivariate correlations. The structure coefficients serve as an indicator in understanding the meaning of the canonical discriminant functions. The results in Table 2 indicate that using instant offenses, sociodemographic, and social status variables, there is some degree of discrimination among the three plausible Time 1 classifications of diverted, referred and dropout. While the discriminating power is quite modest, the most important determinant is gender of the subject as seen in Function 1 of Table 2. The results for Function 2 are not meaningful from a statistical or substantive perspective.

The combined findings for Tables One and Two indicate that the decision to divert or refer a status offender was not predicated on any legal or social-psychological need, but predominately the sex of the offender. Re-examining the male-female composition of each of the three groups, it appears that the sex of the status offender is indeed an important determining factor. For female status offenders 12% were diverted and 88% referred, while for males 32% were diverted and 68% referred. Something of a paternalistic attitude appears to be operating in the decision to divert or refer. Females were far more likely than males to be referred to a community-based agency for services. This finding is congruent with other studies suggesting the existence of a double standard in the juvenile justice system.[30]

Referring back to Table 1, it was seen that at Time 1 the three treatment groups did not differ significantly on any of the thirteen performance measures. Similarly, at Time 2 there were some differences among the three groups, but by simply examining the means of the performance measures, the results are not suggestive of dramatic change. However, the methodological and statistical problems associated with the analysis of change over a period of time are complex. A common way of measuring change is to calculate the difference in status between Time 2 and Time 1. However, the difficulty

Table 3
Longitudinal Regression Equations for Treatment Effect, with the Diverted group being the omitted category (standardized regression coefficients).

Independent Variables	Time 2 Positive image	Time 2 Negative image	Time 2 School ties	Time 2 Family ties	Time 2 Legal respect
Time 1	.372***	.147***	.642***	.188**	.255***
Sex	.084	-.037	.059	.058	.097
Age	.017	.051	.016	.050	.089
Race	-.061	.089	-.064	.025	-.020
Referred	.101*	-.098	.053	.145*	.156*
Dropout	-.185**	-.101*	-.165**	-.150*	-.257**
Treatments	.030	.099	.023	.070	-.001
Arrests	.049	-.076	.027	.074	.023
R^2	26.0%	13.6%	32.9%	11.7%	21.7%

*p = .05
**p = .01
***p = .001

with this approach involves the issue of statistical unreliability and the failure to control the effects of Time 1 on Time 2. A more accurate approach is to measure change as a residual of the regression of Time 2 on Time 1. In other words, by regressing Time 2 behaviors and attitudes on the same Time 1 measures, change becomes an expression of the residual of the regression equation.[31]

In Table 3, the thirteen measures of outcome performance are regressed on their respective status at Time 1, controlling for sex (Male = 0 and Female = 1), age, and race (Black = 0 and White = 1). In this type of analysis of covariance technique, one of the three subject groups must be omitted from the regression equation.[32] The diverted group was dropped from the equation, while the referred and dropout groups are included. In essence, this allows a comparison of the means for each included group (referred and dropout) with the omitted group (diverted). In addition to these independent variables, two additional measures were included. The variable labelled "treatments" refers to the total number of different treatment programs that the subject encountered during the six month interval between Time 1 and Time 2. Because seventeen different community programs were funded by the diversion project, many subjects were enrolled in several different treatment programs. It could be argued that the more services being rendered, the more efficacious the treatment. Lastly, the variable "arrests"[33] refers to the number of arrests the subject had at Time 1. This variable is introduced to control for what might be social alienation at Time 1, with the more arrests a subject had at Time 1, the poorer the chances of success.

The analysis of covariance tests given in Tables 3 to 5 show that Time 1 attitudes, self-concepts or behaviors are highly predictive of the same variable at Time 2.[34] Neither sex, age or race has any significant impact on the outcome at Time 2 (with one exception). In comparing the referred subjects and the dropouts with the pure diversion group (the omitted category) there are some dramatic differences. Compared to their status at Time 1, the referred group is significantly better in terms of positive image, family ties, legal respect, self-reported use of drugs (less use) and the number of arrests (fewer arrests). That is, net of the effect of Time 1, the significant regression coefficient associated with the variable "referred" indicates that this group scored higher on certain performance measures than the diverted

Independent Variables	Table 4			
	Time 2 Peer Influence	Time 2 Seriousness-drugs	Time 2 Seriousness-property	Time 2 Seriousness-violence
Time 1	.327***	-.468***	-.409***	-.365***
Sex	.129*	.031	-.060	-.021
Age	.015	.123	-.064	.072
Race	.099	.023	.039	.022
Referred	.081	.084	.018	.099
Dropout	.129**	-.098*	-.227***	-.123*
Treatments	.004	-.015	.004	.009
Arrests	.006	-.020	.005	.056
R^2	21.7%	31.0%	30.6%	24.7%

*$p = .05$
**$p = .01$
***$p = .001$

group. This indicates some positive results for a treatment effect.

On the other hand, the dropout group consistently performed poorer at Time 2, net of Time 1, as compared to the diverted group. In terms of the two self-concept measures, the dropout group declined in positive image and increased in negative self-image. The dropout group recorded significantly lower ties to school and family, and displayed lower respect for the law at Time 2 as compared to the diverted group. Dropouts also revealed stronger peer influence at Time 2 than the diverted group, and viewed the seriousness of drug involvement, property offenses and violent offenses less seriously. Finally, using self-report measures as well as police data, the dropout group was significantly more deviant at Time 2 than the diverted group. Dropouts reported significantly higher means in self-reported drug use and property offenses as well as greater arrests at Time 2 than the diverted group.

The last two independent variables in Tables 3 to 5 are "treatments" (number of services or treatments rendered) and "arrests" (number of arrests at Time 1). In neither

Independent Variables	Table 5			
	Time 2 SR-drugs	Time 2 SR-property	Time 2 SR-violence	Time 2 Arrests
Time 1	.296**	.435***	.261***	.118***
Sex	.051	-.101*	.076	.052
Age	.039	-.076	.040	-.021
Race	.037	-.049	.031	.027
Referred	-.284***	.066	.036	-.126*
Dropout	.268***	.128*	.072	.163**
Treatments	.014	-.040	.031	-.046
Arrests	.018	.031	.050	-
R^2	23.3%	26.6%	14.5%	15.6%

*$p = .05$
**$p = .01$
***$p = .001$

case are any of the coefficients significant for any of the regression models. The final listing in Tables 3 to 5 is R squared or explained variance.[35] It is somewhat surprising that despite knowing a subject's status at Time 1 the predictive power of knowing the same status at Time 2 is relatively modest. The explained variance ranges from a high of 32.9% for school ties to a low of 11.7% for family ties.

VI. Conclusion

Juvenile diversion represents a current attempt to reform a faltering system of justice. The traditional juvenile justice system has been repeatedly criticized for being too punitive, indifferent and ineffective. A generation of reformers has clamored for some form of community-based treatment that would be more benign and more efficacious. Unfortunately, the evidence to date is not totally convincing, showing the old to be that bad or the new to be that good. The irony of the findings in this present research endeavor is that in some ways those subjects who were referred for services in the community did indeed benefit, and an argument might be made for programmed intervention. Yet, what salutory findings did emerge, must be tempered by the harm that might be generated from indiscriminate assignment to treatment programs. While it has not been definitively shown that the dropouts were necessarily alienated by the services themselves, the question of mobilizing a community to provide "treatment" when a patient may not be ill needs careful study. The allegation of sex discrimination and capricious treatment in diversion programs is disconcerting. The findings seem to suggest that social service providers have a responsibility to the community and to their clients to demonstrate beforehand that their programs have a reasonable degree of proven effectiveness. There is evidence which suggests that many clients in this diversion study were lured into treatment programs not because of client needs but in order to fill program slots. Further, there is also a strong possibility that clients were provided services that did not match their initial wants or needs. Reform is often a difficult process to generate but once operational it can be as intolerant and punitive as the system it sought to replace. In this sense, community-based treatment can be as irrational and as vindicatory as traditional systems of justice.

Juveniles who are indiscriminately placed in treatment programs may in fact be exposed to programs that increase the subject's sense of alienation and frustration. Community-based services are often staffed by individuals who are not sufficiently trained in what may be conceived as the legal rights of minors, and in their zeal and enthusiasm to help juveniles, the effort backfires. It may not be inconceivable to suggest that just as pharmaceutical firms are required to demonstrate a drug's efficacy prior to release of the drug, that social service providers also be required to demonstrate that their "medicine" will not kill the patient.

Notes

1. Bailey, "Correctional Outcome: An Evaluation of 100 Reports," 57 *J. Criminology & Police Sci.* 153, 157 (1966).
2. Waldo & Chiricos, "Work Release and Recidivism," 1 *Evaluation Q.* 106 (1977).
3. Martinson, "What Works?—Questions and Answers About Prison Reform," 35 *Pub. Interest* 52 (1974). Martinson concluded:
   > We tried to exclude from our survey those studies which were so poorly done that they simply could not be interpreted. But despite our efforts, a pattern has run through much of this discussion—of studies which "found" effects without making any truly rigorous attempt to exclude competing hypotheses, of extraneous factors permitted to intrude upon the measurements, of recidivism measures which are not all measuring the same thing, of "follow-up" periods which vary enormously and rarely extend beyond the period of legal supervision, of experiments never replicated, of "systems effects" not taken into account, of categories drawn up without any theory to guide the enterprise. It is just possible that some of our treatment programs are working to some extent

but that our research is so bad that it is incapable of telling. *Id.*
4. *See* Bondeson, *Sweden: The Middle Way to Prison Reform in Prisons: Present and Possible* (1979).
5. *See* Rojek & Erikson, "Reforming the Juvenile Justice System: The Diversion of Status Offenders," 16 *L. & Soc'y Rev.* 241 (1981–82).
6. *See* Cressey & McDermott, *Diversion from the Juvenile Justice System* (1973). In this type of diversion, the juvenile offender remains in the formal system, but attempts are made to reduce the exposure of the offender to the juvenile court process.
7. *Office of Juvenile Justice and Delinquency Prevention, Federation Juvenile Delinquency Programs: Social Analysis and Evaluation* (1977).
8. *See* Klein, *Deinstitutionalization and Diversion of Juvenile Offenders: A Litany of Impediments* (M. Morris & M. Tonry, eds. 1979).
9. *See* Lemert, *The Juvenile Court—Quest and Realities,* Task Force Report: Juvenile Delinquency and Youth Crime (1967). Lemert and others from the school of labeling theory argue that the juvenile court ought to be a court of last resort. *Id.* at 96-97. The processing of offenders through the official juvenile or adult criminal justice system creates labels or stigmas that isolate and insulate the offender from society. *Id.* Out of this labeling process emerges the concept of the self-fulfilling prophecy. *Id.*
10. In terms of program evaluation, effectiveness refers to goal attainment, while efficiency refers to the amount of expenditures incurred in achieving a particular goal. Thus, a program can be given a high grade in terms of effectiveness but score very poorly in terms of efficiency.
11. Glaser, *The Effectiveness of Prison and Paroled System* (1985). Glaser also discussed the notion of degrees or success or failure ranging from clear reformation to marginal success or failure, to clear recidivism. Recidivism is not a simple dichotomy but a continuum ranging from clear success to clear failure.
12. *See* Hood & Sparks, *Key Issues in Criminology* (1970).
13. *See* Lerman, "Evaluative Studies of Institutions for Delinquents: Implications for Research and Social Policy," 13 *Soc. Work* 57 (1977).
14. *Id.* at 60.
15. *Id.* at 6.
16. See Scarpitti & Stephenson, "A Study of Probation Effectiveness," 59 *J. Crim. L., Criminology & Police Sci.* (1968).
17. *See supra* note 13.
18. *See supra* note 5.
19. *See* Adams, *Effectiveness of Interview Therapy with Older Youth Authority Wards: An Interim Evaluation of the PICO Project* (California Youth Authority 1961).
20. This research was the result of the Juvenile Justice and Delinquency Act of 1974 which provided federal funds to states who agreed to remove status offenders from detention and correctional facilities. This Act also made available funds to the Office of Juvenile Justice to develop model programs for deinstitutionalization of status offenders. Program proposals were invited nationwide with eleven proposals ultimately funded. *See* Kobrin & Klein, *Community Treatment of Juvenile Offenders* (1983). While the primary emphasis of this legislation was to deinstitutionalize status offenders, the actual implementation of the program generated not only a deinstitutionalization focus but also a diversion and community-based treatment approach towards status offenders. *See supra* note 5.
21. In all, a total of seventeen different community programs were funded. Some were oriented towards specific types of status offenders, for example, runaways and truants, while others were labelled "multi-purpose" service programs. Finally, some programs were essentially recreation programs with no avowed interest in the nature of the offense or a treatment modality. The conceptual confusion between deinstitutionalization and diversion resulted in diverse, disjointed and often contradictory programs within the juvenile court and the community.
22. *See supra* note 13.
23. A monumental problem in any longitudinal study is the issue of sample "mortality." Eligible subjects may refuse to participate in the study or agree initially, and then refuse later on, or cannot be located at a later date. For example, of the 800 status offenders randomly selected for this study, only 523 or 65% agreed to be interviewed at Time 1. Six months later, the sample size shrunk to 348 (66% of the Time 1 subjects) because of refusals or difficulty in locating subjects. Six months after Time 2, the Time 3 sample was even further reduced to 138, which was 40% of the Time 2 sample, 26% of the Time 1 sample and only 17% of the initial sample pool.
24. It is not clear whether juveniles are technically arrested or taken into custody. Because of the noncriminal nature of status offenses, the law of arrest cannot apply fully to juveniles. The Standard Juvenile Court Act, promulgated in 1959, states that taking a juvenile into custody "shall not be deemed an

arrest ... except for the purposes of determining its validity under the Constitution of this State or of the United States." See Uniform Juvenile Court Act, Section 13(b) (1968). For purposes of this discussion, reference to the arrest of juveniles is to be loosely interpreted.

25. See generally Thomas, "Are Status Offenders Really So Different?" 22 Crime & Delinq. 438 (1976). It is interesting to note that while all of the subjects were labeled "status offenders" they were in fact "status-misdemeanor-felony offenders" who happened to be apprehended while committing a status offense. The inappropriateness of the term "status offender" has been repeatedly discussed in the diversion literature.

26. In the context of this discussion, the process of being diverted simply means police contact on the street, with the subject being released to the custody of his or her parents. The referred group were those who were arrested and referred to a community-based agency for further services. See supra note 21. The dropout group refers to those individuals who were arrested and referred for further services but failed to complete the treatment program. The original intent of the enabling legislation simply called for deinstitutionalization. However, in the process of translating the Delinquency Act of 1974, the juvenile courts and the communities that were funded for this demonstration project applied a different interpretation to the legislation. See supra note 20.

27. The tracking instruments used in this project were not sufficiently sensitive to the issue of program dropouts or "internal failures." A supplementary tracking form was used to delineate between "no-shows" and the degree of involvement that dropouts had with a particular treatment before terminating from the program. Unfortunately, the community agencies were not sufficiently trained or sensitized to the needs of accurate data collection. Records were not kept or lost in many instances. Thus, it cannot be determined with precise accuracy how many dropouts simply never appeared at a community-based program versus the number that initially appeared but eventually dropped out. What has been determined is that a vast majority of the dropout groups (perhaps 70% to 75%) did make at least one appearance at the community service agency before dropping out.

28. See supra note 5. There were multiple entry points into the status offender program. A police contact was the most logical entry into the system. However, each of the seventeen community-based programs were also able to bring status offenders into this service network. In theory, status offenders who were experiencing a problem situation could go directly to any component of the program network and seek assistance. For example, a runaway did not have to be arrested to seek shelter care but could be referred to the shelter care facility by another agency, by parents or friends or even by a self-referral. The difficulty with this intake process was that agencies began to seek "self-referrals" simply to fill agency slots. The service provided may have been inappropriate or the adolescent may not even be in need for services, but agencies became involved in a subtle competition for clients. Hence, the police may not have had a vested interest in referring an adolescent to a particular agency, whereas the agencies themselves were obsessed with filling program slots.

29. In a statistical sense, there is great similarity between Factor Analysis and Discriminate Analysis. In Factor Analysis a wide array of variables are inputted to see whether they can be collapsed into meaningful groupings. Discriminate Analysis requires that at least two groups be created initially on the basis of some criteria (e.g. sex, age or race) and then the analysis attempts to determine whether these groups are statistically meaningful in light of the designated discriminating variables.

30. See Chesney-Lind, "Juvenile Delinquency: The Sexualization of Female Crime," Psychology Today, July 1974, at 44.

31. In other words, if there is no change between Time 1 and Time 2, the Time 1 measure should accurately predict the Time 2 score. Regression analysis is a general statistical technique whereby one can analyze the relationship between a dependent variable and a set of independent or predictor variables. If the results from regression analysis are significant for the Time 1 measure but none of the remaining independent variables, then there is no evidence of change. That is, a high proportion of the variance in the dependent variable (Time 2) is explained by the independent variable (Time 1). If the results are significant for some or all independent variables, then the measure of the particular behavior at Time 1 does not fully explain that same behavior at Time 2. That is, the measure of behavior at Time 2 is the product of other forces besides the behavior at Time 1.

32. Analysis of covariance is a special case of regression analysis whereby a difference in the means of certain groups or categories is examined. In order to do this, a technique called "dummy-variable analysis" is utilized which al-

lows a comparison between a group included in a regression equation (given a value of "1") and a "suppressed" group or category (given a value of "0"). If the results are significant, then the two groups differ. On the other hand, non-significant findings indicate the omitted and included groups are similar. That is, their means, interpreted as intercepts on the Y axis, are the same.

33. *See supra* note 24.
34. In every instance, the regression coefficient in Tables 3 to 5 is highly significant for the independent variable listed as "Time 1." Thus, in the first regression model listed in Table 3, the positive image measure at Time 1 was highly predictive of the score at Time 2. The same is true of the second regression equation using negative image as the measure at Time 1, and again at Time 2. In each instance the variable being predicted at Time 2 (positive image, negative image, school ties, etc.) is regressed on its status at Time 1.
35. Explained variance refers to the predictive power of the independent variables to predict the dependent variable. This measure varies from 0% to 100%. The independent variables may be highly significant but the overall predictive power of the regression equation could be quite low. For social science research, an R squared of approximately 20% is seen as a fairly "decent" result. However, 80% of the variable in the dependent variable is unexplained. ✦

36
Restitution and Juvenile Recidivism

Jeffrey A. Butts
Howard N. Snyder

Introduction

Increasingly, juvenile courts require offenders to compensate their victims. Restitution and community service are advocated as steps toward "restorative justice," which attempts to restore the losses of victims and the peace of the community as well as to punish offenders. Restitution programs are designed to hold offenders accountable for their actions, but they may also advance public safety and rehabilitative goals. Although research on this aspect of restitution is scarce, the use of restitution should be assessed, at least in part, by whether it is associated with reduced recidivism.

The National Center for Juvenile Justice reviewed the juvenile court experiences of youth in Utah to explore the relationship between the use of juvenile restitution and recidivism. The Utah Juvenile Court operates a structured restitution program throughout the State (see box). The court encourages victims to claim restitution and orders it in almost every case in which a claim is made. Inasmuch as Utah maintains one of the most comprehensive juvenile court information systems in the Nation, it presents a valuable opportunity to examine the impact of restitution.

The study shows that for cases involving robbery, assault, burglary, theft, auto theft, and vandalism, recidivism is lower when juveniles agree or are ordered to pay restitution to their victims directly or through earnings derived from community service. This difference is apparent for nonpetitioned, informally handled cases as well as adjudicated probation cases.

Study

The study data were obtained from the National Juvenile Court Data Archive, maintained for the Office of Juvenile Justice and Delinquency Prevention by the National Center for Juvenile Justice. Data are provided to the archive by State and local agencies responsible for collecting or reporting information regarding the processing of juvenile court cases.

The study began with archived data on the court careers of 90,702 youth born from 1962 through 1970 and referred to the Utah Juvenile Court between January 1, 1969, and December 31, 1988. These youth were involved in 244,741 juvenile court referrals. Each case in the study represents a separate court referral, but not necessarily a separate individual.

Cases were selected for study if they met the following criteria. First, cases were included in the analysis only if the most serious charge associated with the case was robbery, assault, burglary, theft, auto theft, or vandalism. Previous analyses showed that restitution is a common component in the disposition of such cases. Second, only cases involving youth below the age of 17 at the time of disposition were included. This age restriction ensured that all youth had at least 1 year remaining under juvenile court jurisdiction, so that delinquent offenses occurring within 1 year of disposition would be referred to juvenile court.

Researchers chose two categories of cases to test the association between the use of restitution and recidivism. The first category included 7,233 cases that were handled informally by the probation department (i.e., cases that were not dismissed, but were disposed without filing a petition). The second group consisted of 6,336 adjudicated cases placed on formal probation.

Recidivism was defined as any case in which a youth was returned to court within 1 year of disposition for a new charge of de-

---

From *Juvenile Justice Bulletin*, September 1992. U.S. Department of Justice: Office of Juvenile Justice and Delinquency Prevention.

Table 1
Proportion of nondismissed, informally handled cases in which offenders agreed to pay restitution as part disposition, and prevalence of recidivism within 1 year

	N	Offenders agreeing to pay restitution (percent)	Overall prevalence of recidivism (percent)	Prevalence of recidivism by disposition	
				Informal restitution (n=2,199)	Other informal dispositions (n=5,034)
All nondismissed informal cases	7,233	30%	16%	11%*	18%
Sex					
Male	5,546	33	17	12*	20
Female	1,682	21	11	8	12
Minority status					
White	4,663	34	18	12*	21
Minority	1,057	17	19	16	20
Age at referral					
13 or under	1,789	34	15	11*	17
14	1,383	31	16	11*	19
15	1,929	30	17	10*	19
16	2,132	27	16	13	16
Prior court referrals					
0	4,341	35	9	8*	10
1 or 2	1,613	31	17	16	17
3 or more	1,279	14	37	28*	30
Most serious offense					
Robbery	30	13	23	...	...
Assault	559	10	16	15	16
Burglary	622	28	19	12*	23
Theft	4	625	25	12*	17
Auto theft	244	18	22	...	...
Vandalism	1,153	66	12	11	14

Detail may not add to total due to missing data.
... = Insufficient number of cases to evaluate the difference in recidivism.
* = Difference between recidivism of cases receiving and not receiving restitution is statistically significant: $p(x^2) < .05$

linquency if that charge was disposed by the court either formally or informally. Cases in which new charges were later dismissed did not meet the definition of recidivism. To test the association between the use of restitution and recidivism, researchers compared the recidivism of informally handled youth who agreed to pay restitution with youth who received other types of informal dispositions.[1] The recidivism of adjudicated juveniles placed on formal probation was compared with that of youth placed on formal probation *and* ordered to make restitution.

No data were available on the specific restitution conditions applied to each case, such as the amount of money or the number of hours in the restitution order, nor whether the youth did or did not comply with the restitution order.

Informal Cases

Of the 7,233 nonpetitioned cases in which there was a disposition other than dismissal, 30 percent were disposed informally, with the youth agreeing to pay restitution, while 70 percent received one of several other informal dispositions, including fines, voluntary probation, or referrals to other agencies (Table 1).

Restitution was used more often for nonpetitioned cases in which the youth was male, white, or had few prior court referrals. Restitution was also used slightly more often for younger youth than for older offenders. The offense most frequently disposed with informal restitution was vandalism. Of the 1,153 nondismissed, nonpetitioned vandalism cases, 66 percent resulted in an informal restitution agreement. More than one-fourth of theft and burglary cases were disposed with informal restitution agreements.

In 16 percent of informally handled cases, youth returned to court for new, *nondismissed* delinquency offenses within 12 months of disposition. A larger proportion of males (17 percent) than females (11 percent) recidivated. Recidivism was related to the number of prior referrals; 9 percent of cases without prior referrals recidivated while 37 percent of those with three or more referrals recidivated. Recidivism was unrelated to minority status; 18 percent of white and 19 percent of minority youth recidivated.[2] Youth involved in informally handled vandalism, assault, and theft cases

Restitution in Utah

The statewide Utah Juvenile Court operates a structured juvenile restitution program. In the majority of restitution cases, youth make restitution directly in the form of financial payments. Others may be ordered to participate in community service programs to earn money to make restitution payments. In 1988, financial or community service restitution was used in approximately 30 percent of petitioned cases and 10 percent of nonpetitioned cases.

Under State law, the Utah Juvenile Court may order youth to repair, replace, or make restitution for victims' property and other losses. Probation officers are authorized to develop restitution or community service plans even in cases where youth are not formally brought before the court by petition. In such cases, consent agreements are signed by youth and parents, and restitution is often paid directly to the victim.

An innovative feature of Utah's approach to juvenile restitution, established by State law in 1979, permits the court to withhold a substantial portion of fines paid by juveniles to underwrite a work restitution fund. The fund allows juveniles otherwise unable to pay restitution to work in community service projects in the private or public sector to earn money to compensate their victims. The juveniles' earnings are paid directly from the fund to the victims.

During the past decade, the use of restitution has increased in Utah. In 1980, court-ordered restitution paid by juveniles and returned to victims was just under $250,000. By 1990, that amount had increased to more than $550,000. In recent years, as much as two-thirds of the restitution moneys ordered by the Utah Juvenile Court have been collected and returned to victims.*

---

* The Administrative Office of the Courts (1991). *Utah juvenile court: Restitution and community service program.* Salt Lake City, Utah, Administrative Office of the Courts.

Table 2
Proportion of formal probation cases in which offenders were ordered to pay restitution as part disposition, and prevalence of recidivism within 1 year

	N	Offenders agreeing to pay restitution (percent)	Overall prevalence of recidivism (percent)	Prevalence of recidivism by disposition	
				Restitution with probation (n=3,215)	Probation alone (n=3,121)
All formal probation cases	6,336	51%	35%	32%*	38%
Sex					
Male	5,630	52	36	33*	38%
Female	706	44	28	23*	32
Minority status					
White	4,749	51	35	33*	36
Minority	1,049	46	45	39*	50
Age at referral					
13 or under	1,607	50	35	34	37
14	1,462	51	37	34*	39
15	1,726	51	35	31*	39
16	1,541	51	33	31*	36
Prior court referrals					
0	1,595	58	22	21*	25
1 or 2	2,350	51	34	32*	36
3 or more	2,391	46	45	43	46
Most serious offense					
Robbery	99	46	31	...	...
Assault	408	25	36	34	37
Burglary	2,119	63	33	31*	38
Theft	2,972	44	36	34*	38
Auto theft	288	45	36	31	40
Vandalism	450	68	34	32	39

Detail may not add to total due to missing data.
... = Insufficient number of cases to evaluate the difference in recidivism.
* = Difference between recidivism of cases receiving and not receiving restitution is statistically significant: p (χ2) .05

were slightly less likely to recidivate than those charged with auto theft and robbery.

Restitution and Recidivism

Restitution was associated with significant reductions in the rate of new referrals among nonpetitioned cases. The prevalence of recidivism among cases agreeing to informal restitution was 11 percent, while 18 percent of those receiving other dispositions such as fines and informal probation recidivated (Table 1).

When the analysis was controlled for other case characteristics, the differences in recidivism remained. In cases involving male juveniles, recidivism occurred significantly less often in cases where restitution was paid than in cases involving other informal dispositions (12 percent versus 20 percent). Similarly, among cases involving white youth, 12 percent of informal restitution cases were referred to court for a new delinquency offense within 1 year, compared to 21 percent of cases receiving other informal dispositions.

The use of informal restitution was associated with significantly lower recidivism among cases involving (1) youth under the age of 16, (2) those with no prior court referrals, or (3) those with three or more prior referrals, and (4) youth charged with burglary or theft. In other categories, differences in rates of recidivism were not statistically significant.[3]

Formal Probation Cases

Of the 6,336 formal probation cases studied, 51 percent ordered the youth to pay financial restitution or perform community service to earn money for restitution (Table 2). The likelihood of restitution being included in a formal order of probation varied slightly with the characteristics of the case. Males (52 percent) were somewhat more likely than females (44 percent) to pay restitution. White youth were ordered to make restitution slightly more often than their minority counterparts. Older youth were ordered to pay restitution about as often as younger youth.

Probationers with fewer prior court referrals were more likely to receive restitution as part of a disposition. Cases involving youth with no prior referrals included restitution orders in 58 percent of all formal probation cases; youth with three or more prior court referrals were ordered to make restitution in 46 percent of all cases.

The use of restitution was related to the most serious offense associated with a formal probation case. Of the six offenses targeted for analysis, vandalism (68 percent) and burglary charges (63 percent) were the most likely probation cases to receive restitution orders. Robbery, theft, and auto theft charges received restitution dispositions in just under half of the cases. Restitution was least likely in cases involving charges of assault (25 percent).

Among the formal probation cases meeting the selection criteria for this study, 35 percent were referred to court within 1 year for a new delinquency offense that was not dismissed. Juvenile probationers were more likely to recidivate within 12 months if they were male (36 percent) rather than female (28 percent), minority (45 percent) rather than white (35 percent), or had three or more prior court referrals (45 percent) rather than none (22 percent). The proportion of formal probation cases that recidivated did not appear to be related to the age of the juvenile at the time of court referral or to the most serious offense associated with each case.

Restitution and Recidivism

The relationship between the use of restitution and the prevalence of recidivism was statistically significant in formal probation cases. Of probationers ordered to pay restitution, 32 percent recidivated within the year, while 38 percent of those not paying restitution faced new court referrals within the year. Differences in recidivism were significant for males and females, and white as well as minority youth. Restitution combined with probation was consistently associated with lower recidivism rates than probation alone. Differences in recidivism failed to be significant when youth were under the age of 14 or had three or more prior court referrals. In those cases, however, the direction of the difference still favored the use of restitution.

In cases involving charges of burglary and theft, which represent the majority of all cases in the study, youth who were ordered to pay restitution recidivated significantly less than those placed on probation alone. Formal probation cases in which youth were charged with burglary had a recidivism rate of 31 percent when the disposition included restitution, but 38 percent when probation alone was ordered. Cases involving charges of theft had a recidivism rate of 34 percent if the juvenile was ordered to pay restitution, but 38 percent if restitution was not included in the formal disposition.

Conclusion

The results of this study suggest that the use of restitution is associated with significant reductions in recidivism among certain juvenile offenders. The association is present whether youth are handled informally or placed on formal probation by the court. Juveniles agreeing to pay restitution as an informal disposition, as well as those formally ordered to pay restitution, return to court significantly less often than juveniles who do not pay restitution.

Notes

1. Cases handled without formal court action are described throughout the study as "informal dispositions."
2. Minority youths included blacks, Hispanics, Asians, Pacific Islanders, and Native Americans.
3. All comparisons in this study were tested for statistical significance. Where noted, differences between two numbers were statistically significant at the .05 level according to the x^2 (or chi-square) test of significance. A statistically significant difference at the .05 level indicates that there is less than a 5 percent probability that the difference is due to random error, or chance. Some differences may fail to be significant due to the small number of cases involved in the comparison. ✦

37
Restitution as a Sanction in Juvenile Court

William G. Staples

The use of restitution as a sanction in the juvenile court has become commonplace in the last ten years. Schneider et al. (1977) found that in a survey of 133 randomly selected courts, more than 86% reported the use of restitution. Moreover, since that survey the Office of Juvenile Justice and Delinquency Prevention has spent some $30 million promoting the use of restitution in 85 juvenile courts throughout the United States.

As a sanction imposed by the criminal justice system, restitution requires an offender to make payment, either in the form of money or by performing a service to the crime victim (Hudson and Galaway, 1978). Although unpaid community service resembles restitution, this type of disposition has come to be viewed as a distinctly different type of sanction. Consequently, my arguments here deal primarily with monetary and victim service restitution between offenders and victims.

The wholesale adoption of restitutive justice may be placed within the context of three major trends in criminal justice. These are (1) the individualization of the juvenile court, (2) the growing concern for the victims of crime, and (3) the blurring of traditional distinctions between criminal and tort law. The purpose here is to examine the growth of restitution within the context of these trends and to suggest that restitution is a sociohistorically grounded concept.

Individualized Justice

As traditional anthropological and recent criminological scholarship have noted, notions of justice that were both individualized and criminalized came into being with the development of state societies in the era of industrialization (Pfohl, 1981; Spector, 1981). Prior to this time, in the West, justice had been based primarily on tort law and on the kinship unit rather than on criminal law and the individual offender. The first juvenile courts, however, were an exception. These institutions represented an attempt at limited principles of noncriminalized, non-individualized justice.[1]

As we are all aware, a founding principle of those courts was the decriminalization of youthful misconduct. As Empey (1982: 334) summarizes,

> the court was expected to enforce the modern concept of childhood—the ideas that (1) children go through several stages of development; (2) throughout these stages they are qualitatively different than adults; and (3) until their full emotional, moral, physical and rational skills are cultivated, children should be quarantined from adult vices and responsibilities.

Thus juvenile offenders were to be seen as "delinquents" rather than "criminals" and the court would treat them as such.

Furthermore, the unit of responsibility for juvenile justice was not the individual child alone but the child in the context of the kin group and the community. The parents of the offender were called into court with their offspring; when parents were missing or inadequate, the state acted as parent "in the child's best interest" rather than in the interest of criminal justice.

It has become apparent that the ideal goals of the child-savers never quite materialized. Children never received the due process protection that adults came to have nor did they receive the kind of special care envisioned for them. Critics argue that both abuses of due process and inequality in treatment have produced the need for more formal and adult-like proceedings. Disillusioned with rehabilitative ideology, others have argued for more severe punishment.

Arguments such as these from both sides of the political spectrum have culminated in a trend toward the individualization and hence criminalization of the court. This trend includes the use of determinant sentencing, prosecution of youth in adult courts, removing status offenders from the jurisdiction of the court, lowering the age of accountability, and, finally, the use of monetary restitution.

All these trends have a common underlying principle. That is, they all seek a "parity" of responsibility between adults and juveniles (Zimring, 1979), not only in the formal operating procedures of the court but in the sanctions that are applied as well. Thus, in the case of restitution, juveniles are expected to take responsibility for their actions as are adults in the criminal justice system. As a contract between the offender and the victim, or between the offender and the state acting as victim (not as parent), restitution renders the juvenile, like the adult, an individual moral unit rather than part of a larger familial unit. In this view, the current individualization of juvenile justice was an inevitable occurrence. The original courts only delayed the type of justice most commonly associated with advanced state societies: criminal law and the individual offender.

Growing Concern for Victims

Many observers have noted the increasing attention paid in recent years to the victims of crimes. Hot lines for rape victims, shelters for battered women, victim compensation, witness programs, and the legal right of victims to make formal statements at trials all attest to the growing significance of what had become a neglected part of the justice process. Spector (1981: 132) notes that "victim compensation" is one of the "several new fads in criminal justice" that emphasize that "crimes damage victims as well as 'the social order' or 'society.'"

Whether seen as punishing or rehabilitating the offender, restitution seeks, at a minimum, to give some recognition to the claims of the victim. Proponents of restitution argue that it not only restores the utilitarian balance between offender and victim, it also restores the moral balance by making the offender part of the victimization experience. Schafer (1970: 172) claims that restitution "is something an offender does, not something done for him or to him and as it requires effort on his part it may be especially useful in strengthening his feelings of responsibility."

Criminal and Tort Law

For many centuries criminal and tort law have been divided along several lines. In criminal law the complainant is the state, prosecuting the offender on behalf of the society as a whole rather than the victim. In tort law it is the victim who must make a formal complaint against the offender. Tort law involves the doctrine of strict liability; criminal law is concerned with intent and culpability. To bear full responsibility for a criminal offense is to bear moral responsibility; to bear full responsibility for a tort is merely to face the consequences.

As Spector (1981) also notes, victim compensation as a criminal justice "fad" is "part of a trend to extend civil remedies to offensive behavior." This blurring of the last two centuries' distinction between criminal and tort law has been referred to as "private ordering" in which the state functions as a mediator, as it has traditionally done in civil or tort cases.

Although still not proximate enough for some scholars (Blum-West and Carter, 1983), criminal and civil law have become increasingly close over the past decade. Civil litigation is more and more commonly added to criminal prosecution as in the case, for example, where victims of assailants, or persons negligently treated by organizations, sue individuals within these organizations. Some areas of law such as tax and antipollution statutes involve criminal and civil penalties that are virtually interchangeable. And the state is unceasingly involved in "private ordering" of criminal justice through restitution programs.

The coming together of criminal and tort law and the expansion of restitution have been described as restoring an ancient form of justice—one superseded by the criminal form. The extension of the concept of private ordering from anthropology to the contemporary sociology of law implies the same thing. However, neither ancient nor stateless societies' principles of law can be restored in the present historical context without the coercive power of the state. Today, restitution depends upon the state rather than the kin group or community.

Pfohl (1981) notes that restitution in stateless societies is among the "rituals of reconciliation" that restore the social balance between offending and victimized groups, whereas "rituals of exclusion" are used in state societies to eject individual offenders from the social body. Pfohl (1981: 82) states that "rituals of symbolic satisfaction and restitution ... remove trouble and restore cooperation with a minimum of disruption. These rituals are institutionalized by the troubled parties themselves." However, in state societies restitution represents a criminal sanction rather than a balancing and restorative ritual.

Implications

Currently, restitution has been presented by some as fulfilling virtually all of the classic aims of criminal justice—rehabilitation (Eglash, 1975), punishment (Dagger, 1980; McAnany, 1978; Schafer, 1970), and deterrence (Tittle, 1978), as well as providing satisfaction to victims. Yet, as I have attempted to demonstrate, the utility of restitution as a social control mechanism is historically grounded. The three trends I have sought to identify have so altered the context in which restitution is applied that such changes radically undermine the concept's theoretical base.

The rehabilitative aspect of restitution is said to arise from its restoration of the moral balance between offender and victim. Martin (1981) summarizes the "equity theory" of restitution:

> When all participants in a relationship are receiving equal relative gains, equity exists. When participants find themselves in inequitable situations, both the exploiter and the victim become uncomfortable and react in various ways to reduce both the retaliation distress and the self-concept distress that arises. To reduce distress, the harm-doer may either restore actual equity by compensating the victim or restore psychological equity by rationalizing or justifying his or her behavior.

A key notion in this theory is that the wrongdoer initiates the steps toward reconciliation. Yet restitution as it is applied through the criminal justice system utilizes the coercive power of the state to issue and enforce the contract. In this case, the voluntaristic—thus moralistic—rehabilitative basis is lost. Fulfilling a restitution contract becomes simply settling a tort that severs the matter from moral responsibility. Moreover, the state is the intermediary, the third party in the agreement. Because it is the state that facilitates, enforces, and transfers payments from offender to victim (the system most commonly used), the likelihood of any "moral contract" between victim and offender is further diminished.

As I have argued above, restitution in the context of individualized justice renders the juvenile the sole unit of moral responsibility rather than being the offender within the larger kin group. Restitution under these conditions denotes criminalization. The consequence of this isolation of responsibility is the separation of the juvenile from the family, the very source from which he or she may learn moral responsibility and community respect.

Ideas of punishment and deterrence also become problematic within a contemporary application of restitution. As I have argued, the moral nature of the restitutive act has been muddled by the role of the state and the isolation of responsibility so that it becomes a mere business transaction. Under these conditions it is difficult to attach a sense of "punishment" or deterrence to this process. Indeed, some of those who advocate the use of restitution feel that, by itself, the sanction constitutes insufficient punishment. As Schafer (1970: 126) so aptly put it, restitution by itself

> might weaken the sense of wrongdoing attached to that crime ... [reduce] the terror

which potential wrongdoers might feel of committing a crime . . . expose criminal justice to the danger of criminal escaping punishment and lead to social injustice.

The implication of this view is that rather than a primary sanction, restitution becomes an "add-on" sentence. In fact, this is its most common use today (Schneider et al., 1977; Hudson et al., 1977; Schneider and Schneider, 1980). Rather than a sentencing alternative, restitution becomes an appendage, increasing length of contact with the system and the probability of probation failure.

Finally, although current applications of restitution may not, in reality, support the goals of rehabilitation, punishment, or deterrence, as was hoped, surely it must provide redress for victims? The answer is, very little. If a primary goal is to reimburse victims, official compensation programs are clearly more effective as restitution to victims is dependent not only upon the apprehension of the offender but also on his or her financial capability. In the case of juvenile offenders, this fact is particularly ironic. At a time when unemployment rates for youth are tragically high, the concept of restitution seems almost absurd. So, of course, is subsidizing the employment of offenders. Committing a crime can become, for some, the only means of obtaining a job. Common sense tells us that it would be more productive to provide employment opportunities for youth before they offend rather than subject them to the latest "fad" in criminal justice.

Conclusion

In summary, what I have tried to argue in this article is that methods of social sanction such as restitution are not generalizable to all social settings. Like law itself, they evolve in a particular sociohistorical context. We cannot expect to institute such sanctions in an era when the cultural and institutional settings are radically different, and expect them to satisfy current concerns. As Max Weber argued, "meaning" for social actors arises within the boundaries of historically grounded societal structures. Such "meanings" cannot be rendered intelligible, by the actors involved or by the social scientist, if they are separated from the historical context in which they are organized.

Restitution is yet another example of the way "reforms" are heralded in our society. As Rothman (1971) and others have pointed out, our social control systems are subject to periodic revisions that are heralded as the latest "solution." Restitution may provide an alternative disposition for a small number of juvenile offenders, but it is by no means a panacea.

Note

1. That is, nonindividualized in the sense that the individual's behavior was not interpreted independent of his or her social situation. The court was individual-oriented in that its treatment was said to be tailored to the specific needs of the offender.

References

Blum-West, S. and T. Carter. 1983. "Bringing white-collar crimes back in: an examination of crimes and torts." *Social Problems* 30, 5: 545–554.

Dagger, R. 1980. "Restitution, punishment, and debts to society." Unpublished paper, Department of Political Science, Arizona State University.

Eglash, A. 1975. "Creative restitution: a broader meaning for an old term." *J. of Criminal Law, Criminology, and Police Sci.* 48: 284–290.

Empey, L. 1982. *American Delinquency.* Homewood, IL: Dorsey.

Hudson, J. and B. Galaway. 1978. *Offender Restitution in Theory and Action.* Lexington, MA: Lexington Books.

Hudson, J., B. Galaway, and S. Chesney. 1977. "When criminals repay their victims: a survey of restitution programs." *Judicature* 6, 3: 313–321.

Martin, S. 1981. "Restitution and community service sentences: promising sentencing alternative or passing fad?" in *New Directions in the Rehabilitation of Criminal Offenders.* Washington, DC: National Academy Press.

McAnany, P. 1978. "Restitution as idea and practice: the retributive prospect," in J. Hudson and B. Galaway (eds.) *Offender Restitution in Theory and Action.* Lexington, MA: Lexington Books.

Pfohl, S. 1981. "Labeling criminals," in H. L. Ross (ed.) *Law and Deviance.* Beverly Hills, CA: Sage.

Rothman, D. 1971. *The Discovery of the Asylum: Social Order and Disorder in the New Republic.* Boston: Little, Brown.

Schafer, S. 1970. *Compensation and Restitution to Victims of Crime.* Montclair, NJ: Smith Patterson.

Schneider, P. and A. Schneider. 1980. "An overview of restitution program models in the juvenile justice system." *Juvenile and Family Court J.* 31, 1: 3–22.

Schneider, P., A. Schneider, P. Reiter, and C. Cleary. 1977. "Restitution requirements for juvenile offenders: a survey of practices in American juvenile courts." *Juvenile Justice* 28.

Spector, M. 1981. "Beyond crime: seven methods to control troublesome rascals," in H. L. Ross (ed.) *Law and Deviance.* Beverly Hills, CA: Sage.

Tittle, C. 1978. "Restitution and deterrence: an evaluation of compatibility," in J. Hudson and B. Galaway (eds.) *Offender Restitution in Theory and Action.* Lexington, MA: Lexington Books.

Zimring, F. 1979. "Privilege, maturity, and responsibility: notes on the evolving jurisprudence of adolescence," in L. Empey (ed.) *The Future of Childhood and Juvenile Justice.* Charlottesville: Univ. Press of Virginia. ✦

38
Juvenile Intensive Supervision: The Impact on Felony Offenders Diverted From Institutional Placement

Richard G. Wiebush

In spite of the popularity of the "new" intensive supervision programs (ISPs) in juvenile corrections, very few empirical studies have examined the effectiveness of these interventions. This shortcoming is particularly pronounced in relation to juvenile ISPs designed specifically as alternatives to incarceration. The lack of information is troubling for several reasons. First, the policy debate over the most appropriate response to serious juvenile offenders has not been resolved. We still appear to be in the "watershed period" described by Krisberg and his colleagues (Krisberg, Schwartz, Litsky, and Austin 1986). Whereas some states are embracing the "get tough" strategies of control, incarceration and waiver, others have continued to emphasize rehabilitation and deinstitutionalization (McGarrell 1991). Second, juvenile intensive supervision programs appear to carry a strong intuitive appeal to those on both sides of the debate. They incorporate a new concern for control (e.g., evening and weekend surveillance, strict curfews, random drug testing) and accountability (e.g., strict enforcement of conditions, mandated community service/restitution). Yet they also continue to emphasize service delivery and treatment (Armstrong 1988; Barton and Butts 1990; Wiebush and Hamparian 1991). Moreover, the potential cost savings associated with community-based ISPs are attractive to both liberals and conservatives in times of increasing correctional costs and shrinking budgets (Krisberg, Rodriguez, Bakke, Neuenfeldt, and Steele 1989). The third reason for concern over the lack of empirical information on juvenile ISPs is that the approach has been highly touted, widely adopted, and expanding as if its success had already been demonstrated. At best, this smacks of the "panacea" phenomenon (Finckenauer 1982). At worst, it may be irresponsible in terms of public safety and resource allocations. Given these several concerns, the purpose of the present study is to address the largely unanswered question of whether the new breed of intensive supervision programs can serve as an effective alternative to institutionalization for serious juvenile offenders.

Previous Research

Over the past 5 years, there have been a number of highly publicized evaluations of adult ISPs. The findings have not provided conclusive support for the intensive supervision strategy. Those conducted on ISPs as an alternative to incarceration have shown positive results, particularly in terms of low recidivism rates and cost-effectiveness (Baird and Wagner 1990; Erwin and Bennett 1987; Pearson 1987). Yet some of these studies have been sharply criticized on methodological grounds and the validity of their claims has been questioned (Byrne, Lurigio, and Baird 1989; Petersilia and Turner 1990; Tonry 1990). At the same time, adult studies that have focused on the use of ISPs as an enhancement to probation have consistently found no differences in the outcomes of probationers handled under regular or intensive supervision (Byrne and Kelley 1989; Petersilia and Turner 1990).

The picture with respect to juvenile ISPs is even more problematic. A series of studies from the 1970s and early 1980s has resulted

---

From *Crime and Delinquency*, Volume 39, Number 1 (January 1993) pp. 68-89. Copyright © 1993 by Sage Publications, Inc. Reprinted by permission.

in the widespread view that well-structured alternative programs for juveniles can produce recidivism results comparable to those obtained through incarceration, and do so at a much lower cost (Empey and Lubeck 1971; Empey and Erickson 1972; Grunewald, Laurence, and West 1985; Ohlin, Miller, and Coates 1977; Palmer 1974). However, other research has challenged this assumption (Lerman 1975; Murray and Cox 1979). More germane to the present concern, the alternative approaches cited above were very different programmatically from the form of intensive supervision for juveniles that emerged in the mid- and late 1980s.[1] Consequently, use of these studies to support the use of ISPs may be a tenuous proposition.

What do we know about the effectiveness of the newer version of juvenile ISPs? Three recent national surveys of juvenile intensive programs have concluded that outcome evaluations are virtually nonexistent (Armstrong 1988; Altschuler and Armstrong 1990; Krisberg et al. 1989). The few studies that have been done have focused almost exclusively on ISPs that are enhancement programs in probation (Feinberg 1991; Sametz and Hamparian 1989; Wiebush 1989) or parole (Deschenes 1989; Fagan 1990; Sontheimer, Goodstein, and Kovacevic 1990). These efforts have shown promising but inconclusive results. In particular, many have been hampered by the use of small samples. . . .

This article contributes to the knowledge base on the effectiveness of juvenile intensive supervision programs in general and specifically those designed as alternatives to incarceration. It presents the major findings of a study that compared the 18-month offense-related outcomes of three groups of juvenile felony offenders who were sentenced to alternative forms of intervention. Those interventions were (a) intensive supervision in lieu of incarceration, (b) incarceration followed by parole supervision, or (c) traditional probation supervision. The results show that the recidivism of juvenile felony offenders diverted from an institution and handled in a community-based intensive supervision program was no more extensive or serious than that of the incarcerated youth, nor significantly worse than that of the felony probationers.

The Intensive Supervision Program

Context

The study setting was the Lucas County (Toledo) Ohio Juvenile Court. In the mid-1980s, the Court's felony offender caseload began to expand dramatically, and traditional methods of intervention came under scrutiny. The Court historically had committed a large number of juvenile felons to the state Department of Youth Services (DYS) for institutional placement.[2] Its rate of commitment was the highest among Ohio's six major metropolitan counties. And the number of commitments had increased by 19% (from 210 to 250) between 1984 and 1987.

Several factors led to a search for alternative forms of intervention. First, serious overcrowding in DYS institutions (1,900 youth in facilities designed for 1,350) led state officials to exert pressure on the large counties, and especially Lucas County, to reduce commitments. Second, court staff believed that as a result of the overcrowding, DYS services to committed youth amounted to little more than warehousing. At the same time however, the Court already was placing more than half of all felony offenders on probation. It was reluctant to expand the use of probation for serious offenders, especially those who otherwise would have been committed to DYS. As in many other jurisdictions facing similar problems, the (then) newly emerging intensive supervision models seemed to provide a way out of the dilemma.

The Intensive Supervision Unit

The Lucas County Intensive Supervision Unit (ISU) is designed to serve as an alternative to DYS commitment for nonviolent felony offenders. The program was implemented by the Court's Probation Department in the fall of 1987, with a goal of annually diverting 20% of the youth sentenced to DYS. To control risk among diverted youth, the ISU uses small caseloads, frequent offender contacts, evening and weekend surveillance, a variety of control measures (e.g., house arrest, random drug tests, hourly school monitoring), mandated community service, and offender involvement in a wide range of treatment services.

The ISU incorporates a postsentencing selection mechanism that is designed to ensure that the program serves only those who otherwise would have been incarcerated. The selection process involves an initial screening of all youth sentenced to DYS and, if appropriate, a subsequent in-depth social assessment. For those offenders meeting program selection criteria, ISU staff will ask the presiding judge for a stay of the original commitment order.

The initial screening criteria exclude non-Lucas County residents, youth who have been previously committed to DYS, and those whose instant offense involved either a drug charge, use of a weapon, or victim injury. At the second level of assessment, program staff gauge the youth's (and family's) "amenability" to program intervention using more subjective criteria.

In the period between October 1987 and January 1, 1990, the ISU accepted 119 juveniles, or 30% of those initially screened. This level of intake was lower than expected. As a result, although planned program capacity was 60 youth, the average total ISU caseload during the first 2 years of operation was just 36 juveniles.

The program staff consists of four counselors/case managers, four part-time surveillance staff and a unit supervisor. All program services are delivered in the context of a structured system that consists of four phases. The requirements for each phase are the following:

- Phase 1: minimum of 30 days duration, with house arrest enforced throughout. Minimum of two face-to-face counselor contacts, eight surveillance contacts, one random drug test and one family conference per week. Community service, school attendance, and counseling are mandatory.

- Phase 2: minimum of 60 days duration, with curfew imposed by staff. Minimum of 2 face-to-face counselor and 10 surveillance contacts per week. Drug testing is conducted as needed and family conferences are held twice per month. In addition to ongoing requirements for counseling, community service, and regular school attendance, participation in a 6-week therapeutic group is mandatory.

- Phase 3: minimum of 60 days duration, with continuing curfew. One face-to-face counselor contact and seven surveillance contacts per week. All other Phase 2 requirements remain in place, except that the therapeutic group is replaced by a 6-week life skills group.

- Phase 4: minimum of 30 days duration, with curfew determined by parent. Counselor contact every other week and five surveillance contacts per week. All other requirements remain in place. Successful completion of Phase 4 leads to discharge from court supervision.

The Research

Research Questions

The major focus of this article is on the ISU's impact on recidivism: To what extent was the ISU able to control or reduce the subsequent offending of those felony offenders placed under intensive supervision? If diverted offenders can be handled relatively safely in the community, and at a lower cost, the rationale for the intensive approach is difficult to challenge. Several additional questions are addressed to provide some context for interpreting the outcome results. These include (a) whether the ISU and comparison group samples had similar preprogram characteristics, especially on risk-related measures; (b) whether the services provided to ISU participants were in fact "intensive;" and (c) whether the program was cost-effective.

Table 1
Characteristics of Youth in the Outcome Samples

Characteristics	Probation (N = 87)	ISU[1] (N = 81)	DYS[2] Parole (N = 76)
Demographic			
Mean age**	15.5	15.9	16.2
% White	44.8	56.8	51.3
% male	81.6	88.9	92.1
Offense history			
Mean adjudicated complaints**	2.7	5.4	5.0
Mean adjudicated felonies*,**	1.5	2.6	2.0
Mean offense history score[3],**	12.3	18.9	18.4
Nature of current offense[4]			
% Major felony	8.0	12.3	15.8
% Serious felony	26.4	25.9	17.1
% Other felony	65.5	61.7	67.1
Prior interventions			
% Prior probation**	31.0	65.4	78.9
% Prior placement*	7.4	14.7	31.5
Risk score**			
% Low	30.6	9.0	20.0
% Moderate	41.2	46.2	49.3
% High	28.2	44.9	30.7
Mean**	11.2	13.7	12.4

[1] ISU = Intensive Supervision Unit.
[2] DYS = Department of Youth Services.
[3] The offense history seriousness score is a combined measure of the number of prior offenses and their seriousness.
[4] See appendix for the offense categories and included offenses used in the study.
*Difference between ISU and DYS is significant at .05; **difference between ISU and probation is significant at .05.

Methodology

The evaluation used a quasi-experimental design to assess the program's impact on client outcomes. The experimental group consisted of felony offenders who were originally sentenced to DYS, but who were instead diverted to the ISU. The sample included all ISU youth (N = 81) placed in the program between 10/1/87 and 5/1/89. The primary comparison group was a sample of felony offenders who were sentenced to DYS during the same time period as the ISU cases, and who met all ISU initial-screening eligibility criteria, but who were not accepted into the program. These youth were incarcerated and subsequently released to DYS parole supervision. This sample (N= 76) consisted of all ISU eligibles who were sent to DYS between 10/1/87 and 6/1/88 and who were released to parole by 5/1/89. To provide an additional perspective on ISU outcomes, a second comparison group was used. This group consisted of a 20% sample (N = 87) of felony offenders who were placed on traditional Court probation supervision between 10/1/87 and 5/1/89.

Youth in all three groups were tracked for a standardized 18-month follow-up period. Multiple measures of recidivism were used and all outcome measures included both juvenile and adult offenses. For the DYS cases, the tracking period began on their release to aftercare. This means that the outcome analysis focused on recidivism during the time each group was in the community.[3]

Results

Characteristics of Program Youth

Because the samples in the present study were not randomly selected, it was critical to carefully compare offender preprogram characteristics across the alternative forms of intervention. If the groups were not comparable, any observed differences in outcome could be attributed to the nature of the offenders, rather than program effect. Table 1 compares offender characteristics at the time of program assignment.

When comparing ISU and DYS youth, no significant differences were found in terms of (a) the demographic composition of the groups, (b) the total number of adjudicated complaints, (c) a summary measure of the number and seriousness of prior offenses ("offense history score"), (d) the seriousness of the current felony offense, (e) the proportion previously on probation, or (f) mean risk scores![4]

The only significant differences between these two groups were that the ISU cases had a higher mean number of adjudicated felonies (2.6 vs. 2.0) and that the DYS youth were much more likely to have had a prior out-of-home placement (32% vs. 15%).

The data on the felony probationers suggest that as a group, these youth were generally in a much earlier stage of their court involvement than either the ISU or DYS youth. There were a number of significant differences between the ISU youth and the probationers, especially with respect to offense history measures. In addition to a significant age difference, the ISU youth had a greater number of adjudicated felony complaints and total complaints. The ISU offense history score was also significantly higher than the probation group, as was the mean risk score and the proportion with a previous term of probation.

The risk data are interesting in several respects. First, the difference between ISU and DYS on mean risk score approached significance ($p = .06$). And, although not statistically significant, the proportion of ISU cases in the highest-risk category was considerably larger than that found for DYS (45% vs. 31%). Second, it is unusual in diversion ISPs to find such a large percentage of high-risk people. Typically, such programs attempt to "cream" the institution-bound population and end up with primarily low- or moderate-risk offenders (Byrne et al. 1989; Clear and Hardyman 1990; Pearson 1987). Yet in the ISU almost half the cases (45%) scored as high risk, whereas just 9% scored low.

Based on the above comparisons, it would be reasonable to conclude that the ISU and probation groups were quite different from each other, but that the ISU and DYS youth were highly comparable.[5] However, because the ISU screening process attempts to identify those youth who are most amenable to program intervention, the question of a selection effect arises. There can be little doubt that the selection process resulted in differences between the ISU and DYS groups. Staff of the ISU saw some qualities in the youth they accepted that were not present in the youth they rejected. To the extent that staffs' subjective judgments regarding youth and family amenability are considered valid predictors of risk, selection effects may be a source of bias in the study. However, the similarity of the ISU and DYS samples on objective measures suggests that these two groups in fact were quite comparable. Where differences did exist on objective measures (i.e., the risk scores), the indication is that the ISU cases may have had a greater propensity for failure.

Intensive Supervision?

It is well documented that "intensive" supervision programs frequently are not implemented as planned and may provide a level of service that ends up being not much different from "regular" supervision (Banks, Porter, Rardin, Siler, and Unger 1977; Bennett 1987; Byrne and Kelley 1989; Latessa 1987). This section explores the ex-

Table 2
Mean Monthly Contacts per Case, by Type of Contact

Characteristics	Probation (N = 87)	ISU[1] (N = 81)	DYS[2] Parole (N = 76)
Probation officer and youth, face to face*, **	2.4	5.7	3.1
Probation officer and family, all methods*, **	3.4	7.5	6.3
Surveillance staff, all methods*, **	0	10.3	0

[1] ISU = Intensive Supervision Unit.
[2] DYS = Department of Youth Services.
*Difference between ISU and DYS is significant at .05. **Difference between ISU and probation is significant at .05.

tent to which the ISU was able to provide intensive supervision and the degree to which ISU supervision differed from that given to the DYS and felony probation youth. Measures include frequency of contact and proportion of youth referred for services. In this analysis, the data on supervision and services provided to the DYS youth reflect only the services provided while on parole. However, "services" to these youth also included an average of 7 months of incarceration prior to parole release.

Frequency of Contact. Table 2 shows for each group the average number of monthly contacts, by type of contact, during the supervision period. In each contact category, the ISU youth had a significantly greater number of monthly contacts than did the DYS parolees or the felony probationers.

The average number of face-to-face contacts between the ISU counselors and ISU youth (5.7) was about twice that provided to the youth in the other groups. Moreover, it is the ISU's use of a surveillance component—resulting in an additional 10 contacts per youth each month—that clearly distinguishes it from the other interventions in terms of the intensity of supervision provided.

Referrals for Service. A second dimension to the intensity of service issue is the number and nature of service referrals made on behalf of the youth in each program. As shown in Table 3, the vast majority of ISU youth were referred for services in each of the major service categories examined (cf. "referred any type"), with the exception of employment-related referrals. The high referral rates for counseling (99%) and community service (92%) are particularly striking, and are no doubt linked to the ISU mandate for youth involvement in these services.

The extent to which ISU youth were referred for services was significantly greater than was found among the DYS and probation groups. The only major category in which there was not a significant difference between the ISU and the DYS cases was substance abuse. In all other categories, ISU youth were approximately 2 to 3 times more likely to be referred for services than youth in either of the other groups.

A significantly larger proportion of ISU youth was also referred to several specific types of services within the broad categories. For example, ISU youth were much more likely than the DYS parole cases to be referred for in-patient substance abuse treatment, individual or group counseling, family counseling, life skills programs, special education, and vocational education.

Similar patterns emerged when ISU and felony probation service referrals were compared.

It is obvious from these data that the ISU provided an alternative intervention that must be considered highly intensive. It is also apparent that ISU youth received a level of supervision and services that was very different from that provided to felony probationers and parolees who were handled under traditional forms of supervision.

Recidivism at 18 Months

Several different measures were used to compare the outcomes of the three groups during the 18-month follow-up period. The findings on each are presented below.

Table 3
Referrals for Services

Service Type	Probation (N = 87)	ISU[1] (N = 81)	DYS[2] Parole (N = 76)
Substance abuse			
Referred, any type**	48.1	74.7	62.2
Out-patient treatment**	16.0	44.3	33.8
In-patient treatment*	8.6	20.3	2.7
Urinalysis	41.5	57.0	43.3
Counseling			
Referred, any type*, **	54.3	98.7	58.1
Individual/group*, **	39.5	73.1	48.7
Family*, **	21.0	76.0	10.8
Life skills/other*, **	8.6	56.9	12.2
In-patient	1.2	1.3	2.7
Education			
Referred, any type*, **	24.7	63.3	28.4
Alternative**	22.5	40.5	27.0
Special*, **	1.2	12.7	2.7
Vocational*, **	1.2	13.9	1.4
Employment-related*, **	11.0	27.9	8.2
Community service/restitution*, **	37.0	92.4	21.3

[1] ISU = Intensive Supervision Unit.
[2] DYS = Department of Youth Services.
*Difference between ISU and DYS is significant at .05.
**Difference between ISU and probation is significant at .05.

New Complaints and Adjudications. The data in Table 4 show that about four out of five ISU youth were charged (82%) and adjudicated (77%) for some type of offense during the 18-month follow-up period. About half had new felony complaints (51%) and adjudications (47%). The same proportion had subsequent misdemeanor complaints (47%), but there were relatively few youth with new charges or adjudications for status offenses. Finally, about 60% of the ISU cases were charged and adjudicated for technical violations of probation. (Because many youth were charged with and convicted of multiple offense types, the percentages do not total 100.)

Although these are obviously high rates of reoffending for ISU cases, there were no significant differences between ISU and the comparison groups in the proportion charged or adjudicated for any type of new offense except technical violations. The difference on the latter measure is often found in intensive supervision programs and is associated with the provision of closer monitoring—those who are intensively supervised are more likely to have violations discovered than those who are not (Erwin 1987; Pearson 1987; Wagner 1989). On all other measures, the recidivism of ISU youth was no better and no worse than that found in the DYS population. And, although the proportion of felony probationers with new charges and adjudications of each type tended to be lower than among ISU cases, these differences were not statistically significant (except, again, for probation violations).

An identical pattern occurred when comparing the total and mean number of new adjudications for the groups (data not

Table 4
New Complaints and Adjudications at 18 Months, by Offense Type

	Probation (N = 87)	ISU[1] (N = 81)	DYS[2] Parole (N = 76)
Complaint type			
Any complaint	67.8	81.5	82.9
Felony	37.9	50.6	56.6
Misdemeanor	37.9	46.9	38.2
Status	14.9	13.6	15.8
Probation or parole violations**	42.5	60.5	46.1
Adjudication type			
Any adjudication	61.6	76.5	77.6
Felony	35.6	46.9	53.9
Misdemeanor	27.6	34.6	35.3
Status	13.8	7.4	5.3
Probation or parole violations*, **	35.6	56.8	31.6

[1]ISU = Intensive Supervision Unit.
[2]DYS = Department of Youth Services.
*Difference between ISU and DYS is significant at .05.
**Difference between ISU and probation is significant at .05.

shown in tabular form). During the follow-up period, ISU youth were responsible for a total of 230 separate adjudications, for a group average of just under 3 (2.8) new adjudications per youth. This mean was significantly higher than that found for either DYS (2.1) or probation (1.8). However, this higher number of offenses was driven almost entirely by the significantly greater number of technical violations among the ISU cases. In all other offense categories (felony, misdemeanor, and status), there was no significant difference in the mean number of offenses accounted for by the groups during the follow-up period.

Most Serious Subsequent Offense. Table 5 shows the most serious subsequent offense for which each youth was adjudicated during the 18 months. All specific offenses were grouped into seven categories of seriousness. . . . The data show that there was no significant difference between ISU and the other groups in the seriousness of the new offenses. The similarity between ISU and DYS cases is particularly striking. Less than 10% of each group was subsequently adjudicated for a "major" felony (e.g., rape, armed robbery, felonious assault). About 15% of the youth in each group had a "serious" felony (e.g., burglary, robbery, auto theft) as their most serious subsequent offense. Similarly, 26% of the ISU group and 32% of the DYS cases had an "other" felony as their most serious subsequent offense. Somewhat surprising is the finding that the seriousness of the offenses committed by the felony probationers also closely resembled that of the ISU youth and the parolees. . . .

Time at Risk. To assess the extent to which the groups' recidivism rates may have been affected by their amount of time at risk during the follow-up period, an additional recidivism analysis was conducted controlling for time spent in all types of lockups (including detention, DYS, and prison). The outcome measure used was a new delinquent offense (i.e., either a felony or a misdemeanor). The results (not shown in tabular form) indicate that the amount of time at risk for ISU and DYS cases was nearly identical (15.3 and 15.2 months, respectively), and that the number of delinquent offenses per month at risk (.13) was the same for both groups. In contrast, the

Table 5
Most Serious Subsequent Offense at 10 Months

Type Adjudication	Probation (N = 87)	ISU[1] (N = 81)	DYS[2] Parole (N = 76)
Major felony	2.3	6.2	7.9
Serious felony	9.2	14.8	14.5
Other felony	24.1	25.9	31.6
Misdemeanor-person	2.3	7.4	6.6
Misdemeanor-other	10.3	8.6	9.2
Status	4.6	0	2.6
P/P violation	11.5	13.6	5.3
None	35.6	23.5	22.4
Total	100.0	100.0	100.0
Subtotal			
Felony	35.6	46.9	53.9
Delinquent[3]	48.3	63.0	69.7
Any	64.4	76.5	77.6

[1] ISU = Intensive Supervision Unit.
[2] DYS = Department of Youth Services.
[3] Felony or misdemeanor.

probationers had significantly more time at risk (16.4 months) and had significantly fewer delinquent convictions per month at risk (.07) than the ISU cases.

To summarize these several outcome measures, there was no difference between the ISU and DYS cases in the extent or seriousness of recidivism at 18 months. The sole exception was the disproportionate number of ISU cases charged and adjudicated for probation violations. The picture was somewhat different when ISU and felony probation recidivism was compared. The probationers had significantly fewer offenses per month at risk and were significantly less likely to be incarcerated. On other measures, a trend toward lower recidivism among the probationers was evident. In spite of this pattern, the seriousness of subsequent offenses committed by the probationers was not significantly different from that of the ISU youth.

Costs

Given the finding of "no difference" in outcomes between ISU and DYS youth, a key question is whether ISU represents a cost-effective alternative to DYS. Was the ISU able to deliver the same "product," yet do so at a lower cost?

Cost issues were addressed by comparing the annual cost of an ISU placement with the annual cost of a DYS bed (including parole supervision). This approach involved dividing total annual costs for each program by the average daily population served. Although this does not represent a rigorous or comprehensive cost analysis, it was sufficient for developing preliminary estimates. The data are highlighted in Table 6.

DYS data indicate that the average annualized cost to the state of a committed youth is $32,320. In comparison, the annual cost of one ISU placement is $6,020.[6] This represents savings to the state of just over $26,300 per ISU youth per year. Given an average daily ISU population of 36 youth, the annual savings accounted for by the program would amount to $946,800. Even when the costs associated with ISU net widening (serving youth who otherwise would have been placed on probation) are factored in, the estimated savings still amount to $918,660 per year.[7] Calculating costs in this

Table 6
Comparative Cost Estimates

	ISU[1]	DYS[2]	ISU Savings (Cost)
Full cost basis			
Annualized (in dollars) per youth	6,020	32,320	26,300
Average N youth	36	36	36
Total (in dollars)	216,720	1,163,520	946,800
Marginal cost basis			
Annualized (in dollars) per youth	6,020	1,350	(4,670)
Average N youth	36	36	36
Total (in dollars)	216,720	48,600	(168,120)

[1] ISU = Intensive Supervision Unit.
[2] DYS = Department of Youth Services.

way suggests that the program is quite cost-effective.

However, these figures are misleading. DYS calculates costs by dividing the total institutional operating budget by the average daily population. A portion of all staff time, contractual services (e.g., doctors, psychologists), food, supplies, and so forth is allotted to each committed youth. But, particularly in crowded institutional conditions, the addition or subtraction of a relatively small number of youth has no impact on staffing levels or facility requirements, which are the major cost drivers. In other words, the savings of a single bed does not mean that DYS will spend 32,320 fewer dollars.

Given the small number of beds accounted for by ISU diversion, the only savings would have been those associated with marginal costs such as food and clothing (Baird 1991). DYS annualized costs for these items are approximately $1,350 per youth. Using this figure to calculate program savings produces very different results. If the ISU was responsible for 36 annualized diversions, the program only saved incarceration costs of some $48,600 per year. Unfortunately, this figure represents less than one fourth of the total annual ISU program cost of $216,720. Stated differently, the ISU incurred a net cost of $4,670 per youth and $168,120 per year. Although these are estimates, it appears that given the current level of diversion from DYS, the ISU is costing considerably more than it is saving.

These cost results are partially a function of the relatively low number of youth that were in the ISU at any given time during the evaluation period. However, even if the program had operated at design capacity, it is unlikely that the number of diverted youth would have had the impact necessary to make the ISU cost-effective. The extent of overcrowding in the DYS institutions exacerbates the problem. In facilities that are housing 600–700 youth above capacity, the removal of even 100 youth at any point in time would only ease crowded conditions and produce marginal cost savings. In these circumstances, it was virtually impossible for the Lucas County ISU, regardless of its success on other measures, to be evaluated as cost-effective.

Summary and Discussion

This evaluation focused on a key policy question for juvenile justice: Can intensive supervision programs provide an effective alternative to incarceration for serious juvenile offenders? Based on the Lucas County ISU experience, the answer is "yes, however...." Several major findings inform this conclusion.

First, the ISU handled a group of youth who clearly were serious juvenile offenders. The program youth had an average of almost three felonies each, over five total adjudications, and had been sentenced to DYS for institutional placement. In addition, over 90% of the ISU cases were moderate- or high-risk offenders. Unlike many diversion programs, the ISU was neither widening the net nor simply creaming the institution-bound population in order to work with those who offered the greatest likelihood of success.

Second, the ISU successfully delivered on its promise to provide an "intensive" alternative. Counselors had face-to-face contact with each ISU youth about 6 times per month and had an additional 7 contacts each month with the youth's parents. Surveillance staff provided an additional 10 contacts per youth each month. Moreover, the level at which ISU youth were referred to rehabilitative services was extraordinarily high. And, judging from the high rate of technical violations, the program was serious about holding youth accountable and enforcing the strict conditions of supervision. In each of these areas, the ISU provided a level of supervision and services that was dramatically different from that provided under traditional probation or parole.

Third, the ISU was able to avoid the "human costs" of incarceration for over half the program participants. In spite of increasingly "get tough" policies, most juvenile courts maintain the perspective that incarceration is disruptive to family and community ties, that youth are subjected to intimidation and assault while institutionalized, and that incarceration is itself ultimately a criminogenic influence. These negative impacts on youth are likely exacerbated when facilities are overcrowded to the extent found in DYS.

Fourth, ISU youth had recidivism outcomes that were no worse than those of the youth who were incarcerated in DYS and then released to parole supervision. On all 18-month measures, there were no significant differences between the groups except for the percentage of ISU youth with technical violations. These results demonstrate that an intensive supervision program—if properly implemented—poses no greater threat to public safety than does a traditional incarceration/parole strategy.

Clearly, the ISU served as an effective alternative to DYS commitment. In fact, although the ISU group consisted of more serious and high-risk offenders than was found in the probation group, their outcomes were not substantially worse.

These very positive findings do not mean that intensive supervision programs such as the ISU are a panacea or that there are no concerns about their effectiveness. For example, one might expect, or hope, that the kind of intensive supervision provided by the ISU would result in lower recidivism and increased public safety. Such an outcome was obviously not achieved in Lucas County: Recidivism rates were fairly high (63% with a new delinquent offense, 47% with a new felony); almost half the youth were eventually committed to DYS; and there was no difference in the outcomes of ISU youth and the parolees. One possible explanation for the high recidivism is that the outcome evaluation included those youth who entered the program during what was essentially its start-up phase (i.e., the first 18 months). It may be that recidivism figures will drop with future generations of ISU participants, as the program matures operationally and as staff develop more expertise in working with diverted offenders. However, even if recidivism does not decline in the future, the litmus test for the effectiveness of the ISU will remain whether it produces outcomes that are at least as good as incarceration. The achievement of better outcomes, if that happens, would represent icing on the cake.

A second potential criticism of the ISU and similar programs is that they actually decrease public safety, because program youth commit crimes during the period in which, absent the diversion program, they would have been institutionalized (Tonry 1990). Although this is a valid concern, the argument takes a somewhat narrow and short-term perspective. The recidivism of youth who were locked up (i.e., the DYS parolees) shows that any gains to public safety were short-lived at best. Reoffending was simply delayed, not reduced.[8] Moreover, a logical extension of this public safety argument is that not only should ISU youth not be diverted, but that felony probationers shouldn't be diverted (to probation) either. The felony probationers in our sample also had high rates of recidivism. Should they too have been sent to DYS to better protect the public? Such an approach flies in the face of a juvenile court philosophy that seeks to balance public protection goals with those of rehabilitation and supervision in the least restrictive setting.

There are two final concerns about ISU effectiveness, both of which are related to the limited size of the program and both of which have important implications for ISPs in other jurisdictions. First, the level of ISU enrollment during the evaluation period was not sufficient to make much of an impact on Lucas County commitments to DYS.[9] This lack of impact was largely a function of a precipitous increase in the Court's felony caseload during the first 2 years of the ISU, but it was also a function of a program that operated well below its design capacity of 60 youth. During its first 2 years of operation, the ISU accepted less than one third of all youth screened for the program. Cautious screening and intake criteria may be a necessity for the early stages of a potentially controversial program. However, continuation of a conservative intake policy will likely result in the Court having a small, "model" program that will have an increasingly limited impact on what it set out to accomplish, that is, reduce commitments.

The second "program size" issue is related to cost-effectiveness. In all but the largest county-based ISPs, the ability of a single diversion program to significantly impact state institutional populations is likely limited. Consequently, programs such as the ISU will continue to have difficulty demonstrating cost-effectiveness.

This represents an interesting dilemma. On the one hand, the results of this study indicate that intensive supervision programs can provide an effective alternative to incarceration. On the other hand, county-based ISPs may not be cost-effective. The ability to realize the potential of ISPs then, may rest with the development of statewide ISP implementation strategies in order to assure large-scale diversion. If, for example, just the five other major metropolitan counties in Ohio developed ISU-type diversion programs—similar in size to Lucas County's design capacity—the potential diversions at any point in time would be approximately 350–400 youth. This level of diversion would represent a 20% reduction in the institutional population. It would impact staffing levels at the institutions, possibly affect facility requirements and would translate into substantial savings. Moreover, because these savings would accrue to the state agency, it would be in a position to provide funding—perhaps through a subsidy mechanism—for each of the local ISPs and still realize considerable savings for itself. This potential approach to ISP programming represents an attempt to capitalize on the demonstrated efficacy of intensive supervision as an alternative to incarceration, while increasing the likelihood of achieving cost-effectiveness.

Notes

1. The most important difference is the heavy emphasis on control in the current versions of ISPs. Components such as house arrest, random drug testing, electronic monitoring, surveillance, and 16 hours per day/7 days per week structured coverage were not routine elements of the earlier alternatives to incarceration.
2. In Ohio, only youth who have been adjudicated for felony offenses are eligible for commitment by the county to the state. Once committed to DYS, all youth are placed into one of nine institutional facilities. There are no less restrictive placements.
3. All data on youth's characteristics, program interventions, and outcomes were collected retrospectively from each youth's court file. Although retrospective data collection is sometimes problematic, the Lucas County court files are rich in the range, detail, and consistency of data collected on each youth. The available data were also quite consistent across the three study groups, in spite of the fact that the DYS youth were supervised by a different agency.
4. Differences between the ISU youth and the comparison groups on all measures used in the study were tested for statistical significance using chi-square of two tailed t tests,

as appropriate, with significance set at the .05 level.

5. The issue of group comparability and the seriousness of the ISU cases was also addressed in another part of the evaluation, which is not reported on here. In an examination of program net-widening effects, a two-way (probation vs. DYS) discriminant function analysis was conducted to estimate the sentence ISU youth would have received if the program had not been in place. All ISU youth were processed through the model. The model placed 81% of the ISU cases into the DYS classification and 19% of the ISU youth into the probation classification. This is an additional indicator of the comparability of the ISU and DYS groups. These results also indicate that the program was largely successful in avoiding net widening (see Wiebush 1991).

6. ISU annualized costs were determined by dividing the 1990 program cost ($216,720) by the average daily ISU population ($n = 36$) for 1988 and 1989. Total ISU program costs for 1988 and 1989 were not available. Use of the 1990 cost data will slightly overstate the actual annualized cost for the 1988/1989 ISU youth.

7. Based on the results of the discriminant function analysis (see Note 5), we estimated that 20% ($n = 7$) of the ISU average caseload represented youth who were diverted from probation. If handled on probation, these youth would have cost Lucas County about $2,000 per year or a total of $14,000. Because they were handled in the ISU however, the total annualized cost was $42,140. The difference ($28,140) was subtracted from the initial estimated savings of $946,800.

8. Interestingly, a separate time-to-first complain analysis showed that the first delinquent offense committed by ISU youth did not occur, on average, until almost 7 months after they had entered the program. This elapsed time is about the same as the average length of a DYS institutional stay. Consequently, although ISU youth were free to commit new offenses when they otherwise would have been locked up, they generally did not. Instead, their new offenses did not occur until about the time that they would have been back on the street anyway.

9. Between 1987 and 1989, felony cases increased by 59 (from 486 to 771) and the number of youth sentenced to DYS increased by 71% (from 242 to 413). Even though the ISU diverted 52 cases in 1988 and 55 cases in 1989, the number of youth actually sent to DYS still increased each year. In 1989, the number of youth actually sent to DYS (358) was 48% higher than the number committed in (pre-ISU) 1987 (see Wiebush 1991).

References

Altschuler, David and Troy Armstrong. 1990. *Intensive Community-Based Aftercare Programs: Assessment Report.* Washington, DC: U.S. Office of Juvenile Justice and Delinquency Prevention.

Armstrong, Troy. 1988. "National Survey of Juvenile Intensive Probation Supervision, Parts I and II." *Criminal Justice Abstracts* 2:342–48; 497–523.

——. 1991. "Introduction." Pp. 1–25 in *Intensive Interventions With High-Risk Youth: Promising Approaches in Juvenile Probation and Parole,* edited by T. Armstrong. Monsey, NY: Criminal Justice Press.

Baird, S. Christopher and Dennis Wagner. 1990. *Evaluation of the Florida Community Control Program.* Madison, WI: National Council on Crime and Delinquency.

Banks, J., A. L. Porter, R. L. Rardin, R. R. Siler, and V. E. Unger. 1977. *Summary: Phase I Evaluation of Intensive Special Probation Projects.* Washington, D.C.: U.S. National Institute of Law Enforcement and Criminal Justice.

Barton, William H. and Jeffrey A. Butts. 1990. "Viable Options: Intensive Supervision Programs for Juvenile Delinquents." *Crime & Delinquency* 36:238–56.

Bennett, Lawrence E. 1987. "A Reassessment of Intensive Service Probation." Pp. 113–32 in Intermediate Punishments: Intensive Supervision, Home Confinement and Electronic Surveillance, edited by B. McCarthy. Monsey, NY: Criminal Justice Press.

Byrne, James M. and Linda Kelley. 1989. *Restructuring Probation as an Intermediate Sanction: Evaluation of the Massachusetts Intensive Probation Supervision Program.* Washington, DC: National Institute of Justice.

Byrne, James M, Arthur J. Lurigio, and S. Christopher Baird. 1989. "The Effectiveness of the New Intensive Supervision Programs." *Research in Corrections* 2:1–48.

Clear, Todd R. and Patricia L. Hardyman. 1990. "The New Intensive Supervision Movement." *Crime & Delinquency* 36:42–60.

Deschenes, Elizabeth. 1989. "The Skillman Intensive Aftercare Project." Paper presented at the annual meeting of the American Society of Criminology, Reno, NV, November.

Empey, LaMar T. and Maynard L. Erickson. 1972. *The Provo Experiment: Evaluating Community Control of Delinquency.* Lexington, MA: Lexington Books.

Empey, LaMar T. and Steven G. Lubeck. 1971. *The Silverlake Experiment: Testing Delinquency*

Theory and Community Intervention. Chicago: Aldine.

Erwin, Billie S. 1987. *Evaluation of Intensive Probation Supervision in Georgia.* Atlanta: Department of Corrections.

Erwin, Billie S. and Lawrence E. Bennett. January 1987. "New Dimensions in Probation: Georgia's Experience with Intensive Probation Supervision." *Research in Brief.* Washington, DC: National Institute of Justice, U.S. Department of Justice.

Fagan, Jeffrey A. 1990. "Treatment and Reintegration of Violent Juvenile Offenders: Experimental Results." *Justice Quarterly* 7:233–63.

Feinberg, Norma. 1991. "Juvenile Intensive Supervision: A Longitudinal Evaluation of Program Effectiveness." Pp. 423–47 in *Intensive Interventions with High-Risk Youth: Promising Approaches in Juvenile Probation and Parole*, edited by T. Armstrong. Monsey, NY: Criminal Justice Press.

Finckenauer, James O. 1982. *Scared Straight! and the Panacea Phenomenon.* Englewood Cliffs, NJ: Prentice-Hall.

Grunewald, Paul, S. Laurence, and B. West. 1985. *National Evaluation of the New Pride Replication Program: Executive Summary.* Walnut Creek, CA: Pacific Institute for Research and Evaluation.

Krisberg, Barry, Orlando Rodriguez, Audrey Bakke, Deborah Neuenfeldt, and Patricia Steele. 1989. *Demonstration of Post-Adjudication Non-Residential Intensive Supervision Programs: Assessment Report.* San Francisco: National Council on Crime and Delinquency.

Latessa, Edward. 1987. "The Effectiveness of Intensive Supervision with High Risk Probationers." Pp. 99–112 in *Intermediate Punishments: Intensive Supervision, Home Confinement and Electronic Surveillance*, edited by B. McCarthy. Monsey, NY: Criminal Justice Press.

Lerman, Paul. 1975. *Community Treatment and Social Control: A Critical Analysis of Juvenile Correctional Policy.* Chicago: University of Chicago Press.

McGarrell, Edmund F. 1991. "Differential Effects of Juvenile Justice Reform on the Incarceration Rates of the States." *Crime & Delinquency* 37:262–80.

Murray, Charles A. and Louis A. Cox Jr. 1979. *Beyond Probation.* Beverly Hills, CA: Sage.

Ohlin, Lloyd E., Alden D. Miller, and Robert B. Coates. 1977. *Juvenile Correctional Reform in Massachusetts.* Washington, DC: U.S. Government Printing Office.

Palmer, Ted. 1974. "The Youth Authority's Community Treatment Project." *Federal Probation* 38:3–14.

Pearson, Frank S. 1987. *Research on New Jersey's Intensive Supervision Program.* Washington, DC: National Institute of Justice, U.S. Department of Justice.

Petersilia, Joan and Susan Turner. 1990. "Comparing Intensive and Regular Supervision for High-Risk Probationers: Early Results from an Experiment in California." *Crime & Delinquency* 36:87–111.

Sametz, Lynn and Donna M. Hamparian. 1989. *Innovative Programs in Cuyahoga County Juvenile Court: Intensive Probation Supervision and Probation Classification.* Cleveland, OH: Federation for Community Planning.

Sontheimer, Henry, Lynn Goodstein, and Michael Kovacevic. 1990. *Philadelphia Intensive Aftercare Probation Evaluation Project.* Harrisburg: Pennsylvania Commission on Crime and Delinquency.

Tonry, Michael. 1990. "Stated and Latent Functions of ISP." *Crime & Delinquency* 36:174–91.

Wagner, Dennis. 1989. "Reducing Criminal Risk: An Evaluation of the High Risk Offender Intensive Supervision Project." *Perspectives* 13(3):22–7.

Wiebush, Richard G. 1989. *An Assessment of the Delaware County Intensive Supervision Program.* Columbus: Ohio Governor's Office of Criminal Justice Services.

———. 1991. *Evaluation of the Lucas County Intensive Supervision Unit: Diversionary Impact and Youth Outcomes.* Columbus: Ohio Governor's Office of Criminal Justice Services.

Wiebush, Richard G. and Donna M. Hamparian. 1991. "Variations in 'Doing' Juvenile Intensive Supervision: Programmatic Issues in Four Ohio Jurisdictions." Pp. 153–188 in *Intensive Interventions with High-Risk Youth: Promising Approaches in Juvenile Probation and Parole*, edited by T. Armstrong. Monsey, NY: Criminal Justice Press. ✦

39
The Impact of Shock Incarceration Programs on Prison Crowding

Doris Layton MacKenzie
Alex Piquero

From 1980 to 1990, state and federal prison populations rose 134% to a record 771,243 inmates. By 1990, prisons were operating between 18% and 29% in excess of capacity (Greenfeld 1992). Faced with this crisis in prison crowding, states searched for ways to alleviate the pressure on prisons. Intermediate sanctions were viewed by many as a viable method of addressing the problem. Although originally designed and supported as a method of helping offenders become law-abiding citizens, many intermediate sanctions are currently being promoted and developed with the express purpose of reducing prison crowding (Palumbo and Snyder-Joy 1992). As such, they are expected to provide alternatives to incarceration and lead to a reduction in the number of offenders in prison.

However, in many situations, the goal of reducing prison crowding goes unrealized because intermediate sanctions that were designed as alternatives to incarceration have actually been used for offenders who would otherwise have received a lesser, not a more punitive sentence (Austin and Krisberg 1981; Morris and Tonry 1990). In fact, in a study of community correctional programs, Hylton (1980) found that instead of reducing prison populations, as they were designed to do, the programs actually tripled the proportion of persons under state control. In other words, these programs not only strengthened the net, they also created new nets in the form of community corrections to control more offenders.

In another study, Palumbo and Snyder-Joy (1992) examined the effect of a home arrest program in Arizona. Not only was the program not cost-effective, but there were actually increased rates of technical violations for those in the house arrest program compared to those supervised on regular parole. Furthermore, the house arrest program resulted in placing inmates in house arrest who would have otherwise been on regular probation, thereby widening the net of control. Similar net widening has also been found in juvenile arbitration procedures (Ezell 1989), in the Japanese juvenile justice system (Yokoyama 1986, 1989), and in a study of electronic monitoring in British Columbia, Canada (Mainprize 1992).

Not everyone considers net widening to be a disadvantage of intermediate sanctions; some argue for deterrence, just deserts, and more punishment. In their opinion, the only way we can keep our streets safe is by increasing social control, and this means increasing the number of prison beds. Conservative legislators often support intermediate sanctions in the belief that they will both reduce costs and, at the same time, provide greater control over offenders who might be given probation. From this perspective, any reduction in prison crowding will occur because offenders will be deterred from committing new criminal activities and, therefore, the crime rate will be reduced.

In contrast, those who advocate increased diversion, decriminalization, due process, and decarceration to shrink the net argue that the United States has the highest national incarceration rate and, furthermore, that we can no longer afford to build prisons and keep prisoners locked up for lengthy periods of time. In their opinion, most offenders will eventually be returned to the street and the prison is not the best way to change offenders so that they will not return to criminal activities when they are released. Intermediate sanctions provide a reasonable alternative to incarceration for those who would otherwise be imprisoned....

Boot Camp Prisons

One intermediate sanction, which has become increasingly popular in the past decade, is boot camp prisons. The number and size of these prisons for adult felons have been rapidly escalating. Since boot camps first began in Georgia and Oklahoma in 1983, 29 states and the Federal Bureau of Prisons have opened 46 boot camps. The original camps were small in size, but by 1993 there were over 7,500 prison beds in adult correctional systems devoted to boot camp programs.

There are many reasons for the rapid growth of boot camp prisons. Politicians and policymakers, fearful of a "Willie Horton problem," can appear to be tough on crime by supporting boot camps (MacKenzie and Parent 1991). They, as well as the public, seem to think that boot camps address the lack of discipline and self-control, which they believe are characteristic of young, nonviolent offenders. Correction officials, in contrast, emphasize the importance of these programs in rehabilitating offenders, reducing recidivism, and providing drug education (MacKenzie and Souryal 1991).

Almost everyone expects the boot camps to reduce prison crowding. They differ, however, in how they expect this reduction to occur. Some believe that crowding will be reduced by lowering recidivism rates because fewer offenders will be arrested, convicted, and returned to prison. Thus fewer prisoners will enter prison and the need for prison beds will be reduced.

However, there are different opinions about the mechanisms that initiate these changes in individual offenders. Some argue that recidivism will be reduced because offenders will be deterred from committing new crimes; others argue that the programs will rehabilitate offenders so they will not return to criminal activities once they have been released. In both of these situations, offenders are expected to change as a result of the programs and, therefore, they are expected to have lower rates of recidivism.

Another way boot camp prisons may affect prison crowding is by reducing the time offenders spend in prison. An offender who receives a 5-year sentence to a traditional prison might be eligible for parole after serving one third of the sentence and, with additional time off for good behavior, might be paroled from prison after serving 2 years. In contrast, an offender who completes a boot camp program may be eligible for parole after serving a much shorter time. For instance, an offender with the same 5-year sentence might complete a 3-month boot camp program and be eligible for release after serving only 3 months. In the former case, a prison bed would be needed for 24 months, whereas the boot camp bed would be needed for only 3 months—a difference of 21 months. The boot camp may, in such cases, represent a method for some offenders to earn their way out of prison earlier than they would otherwise be released.

To have an impact on prison crowding, there must be a sufficient number of eligible inmates who successfully complete the program in a shorter time than they would have served in prison. Many shock programs have rigid eligibility criteria that will severely restrict the type of offender who will be considered acceptable for the program. Furthermore, if the program is lengthy or if there is a long wait between entering prison and entry to the program, the net reduction in days served may be minimal. There is evidence from previous studies that offenders with shorter sentences will not volunteer or will drop out of a shock program (MacKenzie, Shaw, and Gowdy 1993). They seem to use a rational decision-making model by weighing the choice of doing "tough time" in the boot camp versus easier but longer time in a traditional prison.

Along with a reduction in recidivism rates and shortening of time in prison, there are other factors that will influence the potential of boot camps to have an impact on prison crowding. One factor that is vitally important is whether offenders are drawn from those who under other circumstances would be incarcerated. If they are not, and the incarceration net is widened by selecting offenders who would otherwise have been on probation or in some other program (e.g., diversion), then the boot camp would increase the number of offenders in prison.

The present study examined five boot camp prisons and explored their potential for reducing prison crowding in the state correctional system. Five states, Florida, Georgia, Louisiana, New York, and South Carolina, participated in an evaluation (MacKenzie 1990). The study had three major components: (a) a process evaluation, (b) a study of offender changes, and (c) an examination of the potential impact of the programs on prison crowding, the focus of this article. The process evaluation included a description of the development and implementation of the boot camp prisons in each site. Interviews were conducted with participants, staff, and administrators, and written reports, policies and procedures, and program documentation were examined. The goals of each program were identified in this process. Consistent with the development of other intermediate sanctions (Morris and Tonry 1990), the two major goals of all five boot camp prisons were (a) changing offenders, and (b) reducing prison crowding (MacKenzie and Souryal 1993). The latter, however, was not a primary goal of many of the individuals interviewed. Many of those working directly with inmates in the shock program emphasized its importance in having an impact on the lives of individual offenders and were not as concerned about reducing prison crowding. However, in almost all of the states, prison crowding had provided a major impetus for developing the boot camp prison.

The Five Boot Camp Programs

Offenders incarcerated in each of the five boot camp prisons were separated from general population inmates in a military-like atmosphere emphasizing strict rules and discipline and were required to participate in drill and physical training. Beyond this common core, there were many differences among programs.[1] Some emphasized treatment, such as education, counseling, or vocational training during the time offenders are incarcerated. For example, inmates in Louisiana and New York boot camp prisons spent 3.5 hours and more than 5 hours per day, respectively, in treatment and education programs. In contrast, inmates in Georgia spent a very short period of time per day in rehabilitative type activities.

Different Program Models

Of particular importance to this study were the differences among sites in entry and exit decision making. To examine differences among programs, we constructed flow charts for each site to describe the process of selection, rejection, dismissal, and completion for each shock program.

A comparison of two flow charts, New York and Georgia, highlights some of the major differences in decision-making processes. In New York, the offenders were sentenced to a term of imprisonment under the supervision of the department of corrections. The department screened the offenders; those who were evaluated as eligible and suitable for the shock incarceration program were given the opportunity to volunteer (Figure 1). If they successfully completed the program, they served 180 days in prison. If they left for any reason, they were required to return to prison and to serve until they were paroled. The only change in this procedure is that there are now some additional restrictions for offenders who are between 26 and 29 years of age.[2]

As can be seen in the flow chart in Figure 2, the decision-making process was very different in Georgia. The chief probation officer determined whether the offender was eligible for the program. A contact was made with the shock staff for verbal confirmation of acceptance to the program and if the answer was "Yes," the probation chief certified to the court that the offender had been accepted into the program. The court could then sentence the offender to the program as a condition of probation. The court retained responsibility over the offender if there were any changes in status (whether

Figure 1

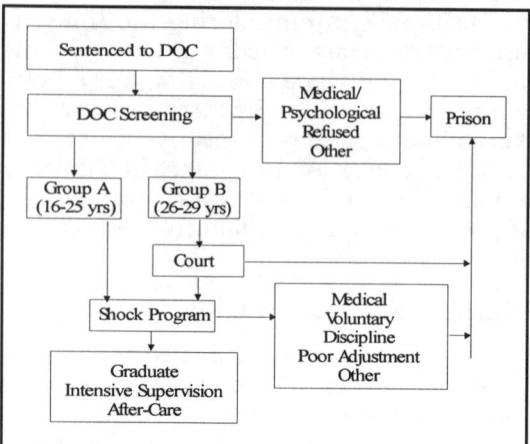

Figure 2

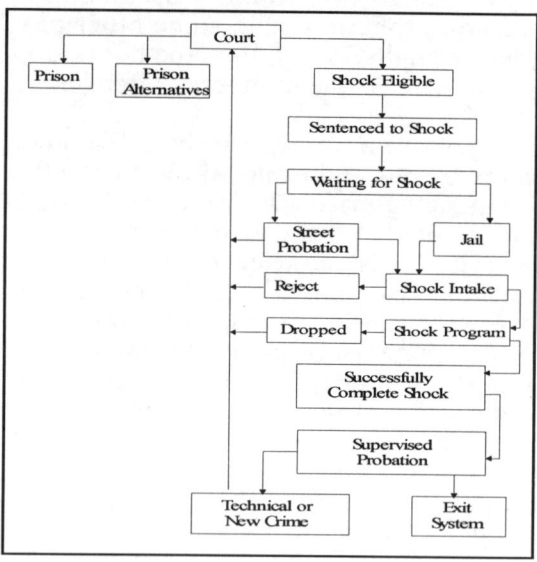

they were rejected by the department of corrections [DOC], dismissed from the program, or their probation was revoked).

When the flow charts from the five shock programs were compared, large differences among programs in the process of entry and exit decision making became evident. There were two basic variants in the selection procedure. In the first, the sentencing judge placed the offender in the program and maintained decision-making authority over him or her until release from the program. At the other extreme, the DOC had complete control over offenders who entered the program. Those who were dismissed before completing the program in this model were sent to prison.

Differences in entry decision-making can easily affect the impact of the shock program on the larger correctional system. As Morris and Tonry (1990) argued: when the court has placement control, the shock program may be more likely to be used as an alternative to probation. If, on the other hand, the DOC has control over who enters the program, there is a higher probability that offenders entering the program would have otherwise spent time in prison.

When we examined the process evaluations of the five sites, we identified at least three variations in placement decision making:

- Judge places in shock and maintains full control over offenders: Georgia, South Carolina.

- DOC selects for shock, judge approves: New York (ages 26–29), Florida.

- DOC has full control over who enters and judge has little or no control: New York (ages 16–25), Louisiana.

Judges had full control over sentencing offenders to shock in both Georgia and South Carolina. In South Carolina, as in Georgia, the judge sentenced offenders to the shock program and offenders remained under the jurisdiction of the court for 90 days. After at least 75 but no more than 90 days, the sentencing judge had the option to either place a shock inmate on probation or convert the offender to the general prison population. Completion of the shock program, therefore, did not ensure release to probation. Offenders who were not placed on probation prior to the 91st day were automatically converted to general population status. Preliminary data from the program indicated that approximately 6% of the offenders who completed the program were converted to the general prison population.

A major issue in South Carolina and Georgia is whether judges used the program as an alternative to probation. If this is the case, they may have sentenced offenders to the program who would have otherwise simply received probation. This is not an unreasonable use of the program because in many cases a judge may believe an offender needs a more restrictive sanction than probation, but something less than a long term of incarceration. At the same time, this practice clashes with the stated goal of reducing crowding. . . .

Characteristics of Offender Participants: Eligibility and Suitability Criteria

To have an impact on crowding, a sufficient number of offenders must enter the shock program. Prior to entry, offenders are evaluated for "appropriateness" for shock. All states have legal mandates that restrict participation to certain classes of offenders. Most states also have additional criteria—which we call suitability criteria—that are consistently used to make decisions regarding qualifications for entry into the shock program. The reasons for the development of suitability criteria vary. For example, in Louisiana, offenders over the age of 39 were considered unsuitable, due to the medical evaluation teams' recommendation that if individuals 40 or older were going to participate in the rigorous physical activity required by the program, additional medical tests would be necessary. Considering the small number of legally eligible offenders over 40, the DOC decided that the cost of such tests would be prohibitive.

Another suitability criterion adopted in Louisiana was a restriction on the entry of offenders with a history of sex offenses. The sex offender prohibition arose early during the operation of the shock program when an offender who had done well in it was denied parole by the board because he had been convicted of a sex offense. The DOC felt strongly that all offenders who successfully completed the program should be released, but the parole board refused to release certain offenders. To avert future problems such as this one, the department in conjunction with the parole board developed a list of "types" of offenders who might be accepted for the program, but not necessarily be paroled; those judged unsuitable were not admitted.

Although the suitability criteria differed among states, all states had some criteria that were consistently used to limit entry to the program. Most programs were designed for youthful offenders. Indeed, Georgia and New York had legislative mandates that limited the age of participants. South Carolina restricted the age further to a maximum of age 24. Florida had no legislative maximum; however, the department set a maximum age of 25 as one of its suitability criteria. Like Florida, Louisiana had no legislative maximum; however, the DOC set a maximum age of 39 as one of its suitability criteria. . . .

The second basic characteristic of offenders entering the shock programs is that, as compared to prison-bound offenders, in general they tended to be lower-risk offenders. This is ensured by various legislative restrictions on sentence length, types of sentence, types of offenses, and criminal histories of offenders. When considering criminal history, Florida and Georgia require that the offender be convicted of a first felony and Florida specifies no previous incarceration; others, such as Louisiana, permit an offender convicted of a second felony to enter if there has been no previous incarceration in a state prison.

Georgia and South Carolina do not statutorily restrict offenders who previously have been incarcerated, but in these states the DOC imposes the condition that the offender have no previous incarcerations as a suitability criterion. In some states, the DOC is even more restrictive regarding criminal history. For example, Louisiana and New York require that offenders have no history of any serious sex offense, and Louisiana and New York will not permit an offender who has a history of assaultive or violent behavior to enter the program. New York requires that offenders have not been convicted of any abscond or escape offense,

Table 1
Program Characteristics and Capacity for Five State Shock Programs Showing Graduation and Dismissal Rates for a 1-Year Period

	Placement Authority				
	Florida: DOC	Georgia: Judge	Louisiana: DOC	New York: DOC	South Carolina: Judge
Voluntary					
Entrance	no	yes	yes	yes	no
Exit	no	no	yes	yes	no
Capacity (beds)	100	250	120	500/1,500	120
Total exits	329.5[1]	932	298	953(1988)	470
(date)		(1989)	(1987)	2,993(1990)	(1989)
Graduated					
n	159.7	849[2]	169	743	395
Percentage	48.5	91.1	56.7	68.7/ 1,907, 63.7	84.0
Time in days	100.5	89	125.7	180	84.2
Dismissed, percentage	51.5	9.0	43.3	31.1/36.3	16.0
Reasons for dismissal, percentage					
Discipline	39.9	3.3	7.4	16.8/7.3	8.3
Medical	8.6	5.7	3.7	1.3/1.3	7.6
Voluntary	-	-	27.5	7.9/12.3	-
Other	3.1	-	4.7	5.1/15.3	-

Note: DOC = Department of Corrections. Values are given for 2 years for New York, 1988 and 1990, when the capacity had greatly increased. If the values did not differ, only one value is given.
[1]This value was calculated as the average from 10/87 to 1/91.
[2]These estimates were based on percentages from actual data for 1984 to 1989.

and the Florida DOC requires that offenders be classified as either medium or minimum security.

In addition to restrictions on criminal history, some states have restrictions on current offense. Most states make the assumption that eligible offenders will be convicted of nonviolent offenses, but New York and South Carolina make this explicit. In contrast, Florida only stipulates that offenders not be convicted of a capital or life felony crime.

A final restriction on offender eligibility is on type and length of sentence. Although there is some variation in the legislative technicalities of these requirements, this is probably due more to variation in sentencing across states rather than to types of offenders eligible. New York requires only that offenders be sentenced to an indeterminate term of imprisonment; however, offenders must be parole eligible within 3 years. More restrictive in its guidelines, South Carolina requires that offenders be convicted of an offense that carries at least a 5-year prison sentence. In Louisiana, offenders must be sentenced to 7 years or less and they must be parole eligible. Similarly, offenders must be sentenced to 6 years or less in Florida and also be parole eligible. As noted above, Florida permits some offenders convicted of violent offenses to enter the program; however, the restriction on sentence length and security classification would limit the seriousness of eligible offenders. At the other extreme, offenders in Georgia must be sentenced to 1 to 5 years of probation, with shock incarceration being a special condition of their probated sentence.

If the program is considered to be an early release from prison (important if the program is expected to reduce crowding), the legal eligibility criteria were most likely developed to limit the severity of the current offense and the past criminal history of offenders who would be eligible for the program and hence early release. The dilemma is that a sufficient pool of offenders who are judged eligible and suitable must be available to enter the program.

Thus, in the majority of states, eligible offenders generally must be young, physically and mentally healthy, and serving short sentences. They cannot have had a very serious past history of crime; in all sites a previous incarceration disqualified an offender from entry. Such severe restrictions on entrants may limit the pool of eligible offenders, and this may be a particular problem in states that select participants from prison-bound offenders. The problem is that there may be too few offenders evaluated as appropriate (eligible and suitable) for entry and, therefore, the number of participants may be insufficient to have an impact on crowding.

Program Characteristics, Capacities, and Completion Rates

As shown in Table 1, these five state programs differ in program capacity, program length, percentage of entrants dismissed prior to graduation, voluntary entry and exit, and the placement authority.[3] In Georgia and South Carolina, the judge has the responsibility for entry decisions, and offenders who are evaluated as unsuitable or who drop out of the program are returned to the court for resentencing. In contrast, in Florida, Louisiana, and New York, offenders are first sentenced to prison and are then selected for program participation by the DOC. If inmates in these states are dismissed from the program or if they voluntarily drop out, they serve the remainder of their sentence in prison. Programs also differ in whether offenders volunteer to participate or whether they can drop out voluntarily. In two states (Florida and South Carolina) offenders do not volunteer to enter and they cannot voluntarily leave. On the other hand, in Louisiana and New York, offenders volunteer to enter and can voluntarily leave. The Georgia program permits voluntary entrance but offenders cannot leave voluntarily.

New York had by far the largest capacity (500), and by 1991 this capacity had been increased to 1,500. Georgia's capacity was much smaller (250); however, approximately the same number of offenders completed the Georgia program in a 1-year period, 932 versus 953 in New York. This shows the influence of both length of time offenders spend in the program and the number of participants who do not complete. Offenders in the Georgia program spend an average of only 89 days in the program and only 9% were dismissed prior to completing the program. In New York these numbers are very different. New York has the largest number of offenders in shock, but the program has the longest duration (180 days). In addition, a substantial number of the entrants do not complete the program (31%).

In the two states (Georgia and South Carolina) where the judge has the most authority over placement in the programs, the largest number of entrants complete shock (8.9% and 16% dismissal rates, respectively). In the other three states, the DOC has control and the noncompletion rates are much higher (ranging from 31.3% to 51.5%).

A relatively high percentage of noncompleters in the two states where judges have authority over offenders are dismissed from shock for medical reasons. In Florida, New York, and Louisiana, the sites where the DOC has authority over decisions after offenders are dismissed from shock, offenders leave either voluntarily or for disciplinary reasons. Offenders in the Florida program cannot leave voluntarily, so the majority of those who leave do so for disciplinary reasons. In New York and Louisiana, offenders can voluntarily exit, but

Table 2
Summary of Variables Used In Bed Space Model for Five State Boot Camp Prisons

	Florida	Georgia	Louisiana	New York[1]	South Carolina
Capacity					
Beds available	100	250	120	500/1,500	120
Total annual capacity (beds/year)	363.6	1,000	360	1,000/3,000	480
Actual yearly completions	329.5	932	298	953/2,993	470
Probability					
Offender would be imprisoned					
Offender would be on probation					
Imprisonment for dropout	0	0	1	1	0
Imprisonment for washout	1	.37	1	1	1
Voluntary dropout	0	0	.28	.08/.12	0
Nonvoluntary removal (washout)	.52	.09	.16	.23/.24	.16
Revocation shock graduate	.16	.27	.17	.16/.09	.24
Revocation probationer	.29	.16	.10	.15/.14	.31
Durations of imprisonment					
Shock duration (months)	3.3	3.0	4.0	6.0	3.0
Shock dropout (months)	0	0	13.7	18.1	0
Shock washout (months)	9.5	2.6	14.5	20.4	12.0
Shock-eligible prisoners (months)	8.5	9.6	20.5	17.9	12.4
Shock graduates revoked (months)	13.4	13.4	10.7	20.6	13.2
Shock-eligible probationer (months)	14.5	22.6	12.0	18.6	10.4

[1]Values for 2 years are given for New York, 1988, followed by 1990 when the capacity had been increased.

surprisingly, the rates of disciplinary dismissals are high in New York, whereas voluntary exit is high in Louisiana.

Thus the biggest differences in dismissal rates are between the sites where the judge has authority over the offender after dismissal and the sites where the DOC has authority. The DOC-authority sites have much higher dismissal rates. Furthermore, in the DOC-authority sites, offenders leave for reasons that are more under their own control (poor behavior or volunteering out) whereas judge-authority dismissals are more often for medical reasons.

Methodology

The model used to estimate bed space needs was based on one developed by MacKenzie and Parent (1991) to estimate the impact of the Louisiana boot camp program on the prison beds needed to accommodate the inmates entering prison. The model estimates the total person-months of confinement saved by determining the difference between the average prison term and the average shock incarceration duration, and multiplying that difference times the program capacity (or the actual number admitted in a year). The initial months saved are then discounted by (a) the probability that the persons would not have been confined (they would have been on probation) and (b) the time served by those who drop out, "wash out," or who are revoked. The model calculates the impact of the program on prison beds and on person-months of confinement.

Table 3
Results of Five Different Models Used to Estimate Beds Saved (+) or Needed (-) by Five State Prison Systems as a Result of the Boot Camp Prison Showing Differences as a Function of the Probability That the Offenders Would Have Been Prison Bound if the Boot Camp Prison Had Not Existed

Models	Probability of Imprisonment				
	0%	25%	50%	75%	100%
Standard model					
Florida	-153	-121	-88	-56	-24
Georgia	-230	-106	18	143	267
Louisiana	-277	-133	12	156	300
New York	-2,807	-1,846	-885	76	1,037
South Carolina	-174	-84	7	97	188
Actual completions					
Florida	-139	-109	-80	-51	-22
Georgia	-214	-99	17	133	249
Louisiana	-229	-110	10	129	249
New York	-2,801	-1,842	-883	75	1,034
South Carolina	-171	-82	7	95	184
Reduced recidivism					
Florida	-137	-105	-73	-40	-8
Georgia	-93	31	156	280	404
Louisiana	-261	-117	28	172	316
New York	-2,653	-1,692	-731	230	1,191
South Carolina	-121	-30	60	151	241
Reduced washouts					
Florida	-95	-63	-31	1	34
Georgia	-240	-116	8	133	257
Louisiana	-257	-112	32	177	321
New York	-2,329	-1,368	-407	554	1,515
South Carolina	-146	-56	35	125	216
Saving prison revocations (parole)					
Florida	-153	-89	-25	39	103
Georgia	-230	-30	169	369	568
Louisiana	-277	-123	30	184	338
New York	-2,807	-1,689	-570	549	1,668
South Carolina	-174	-52	71	194	317

Note: Calculations for New York are based on 1990 data from Table 2.

The variables used in these analyses were program capacity, annual shock capacity, probabilities of washing out and dropping out, probability of imprisonment for washouts, probability of imprisonment for voluntary dropouts, revocation rates for shock graduates, probability of revocation for probationers, average term of imprisonment for shock-eligible offenders, average shock durations duration of imprisonment for shock dropouts, duration of imprisonment for shock washouts, duration of imprisonment for shock graduates who were revoked, duration of imprisonment for shock-eligible offenders who were revoked on probation. . . . Data were obtained from official records and from the results of studies examining each program.[4] Shown in Table 2 are the data for each boot camp program.

Estimating Bed Space Needs

No data were available on the probability that these offenders would be in prison versus probation.[5] Therefore, we employed different models to examine the impact of the shock program on prison crowding if 0%, 25%, 50%, 75%, or 100% of the shock entrants were taken from prison-bound entrants (Table 3). The other variables were the best available estimates of probabilities and durations. By varying the estimates, we could examine the potential these programs had for influencing the need for prison beds.

The bed space model examined the net change in prison beds needed per year as a result of a shock incarceration program.[6] We calculated the person-months of confinement saved by the program and then reduced this by the person-months lost because of the dropouts, the washouts, and the revocations. The resulting estimate of the person-months of confinement was then changed to the number of beds saved (or lost) in a 1-year period as a result of the boot camp program. For example, Florida's boot camp program had an annual capacity of 363.63. If 50% of these offenders would have been prison bound (and, conversely, the remaining 50% would have been probationers), the program would have saved approximately 336 person-months of confinement. However, the program lost 1,396 person-months of confinement due to washouts and revocations (there were no dropouts in Florida) for a net loss in person-months (336 minus 1,396 or -1,067 person-months). This translates to the need for an additional 88 prison beds per year (-1,067 person-months/12months) because of the boot camp prison.

Results

It was clearly evident from the process evaluation of these boot camp prisons that a major goal of all of them was to reduce prison crowding. The bed space analysis examined the effect on need for prison beds depending on whether the entrants to the boot camp prisons were chosen from those who would otherwise be prison-bound offenders or probation bound. Five different variants of the model were examined to inspect how these changed the beds needed. The first model (standard model) examined the changes in bed space when the total annual capacity was used for annual capacity in the model. The second model changed the value for the annual capacity to the number of actual completions in the year (see Table 2). Model 3 examined the effect on bed space by reducing the recidivism rate by 50%. The fourth model reduced the washout rate by 50%, and the fifth model included a term in the calculations to ac-

Figure 3
Estimates of Bed Space Needs and Savings for Four States Showing Changes as a Function of the Probability That Entrants Would Have Been Imprisoned if the Boot Camp Programs Did Not Exist

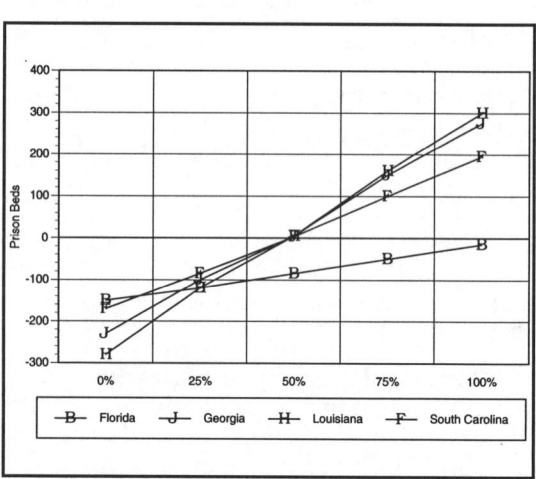

count for additional beds saved due to the parolee return to prison rates.

As expected, as the percentage of prison-bound offenders in the boot camp declined (and conversely probationers increased), the need for prison beds increased. The larger the percentage of the offenders who would otherwise have been in prison, the larger the impact on beds needed, or conversely saved (Table 3). Figure 3 shows the change in estimated bed space savings for four states using the standard model. As the probability that these offenders would have been imprisoned increased to 100%, instead of needing additional beds (indicated by "—" in Table 3) there were beds saved in all systems except in Florida. Even when all of the offenders would have been prison bound, the Florida system would need an additional 24 beds to accommodate the boot camp program.

What is evident from these models is that the predominant factor driving the need for beds is whether the program is used for prisoners or probationers. Widening the net to include a large percentage of probationers means an increased need for prison beds. However, the design and operation of the specific program also had a significant impact on the number of beds needed. A comparatively long program like New York (6 months), which devoted a large number of beds to boot camp offenders, could have had a major impact on prison crowding. Furthermore, changing the parameters in the model also created considerable differences in the estimated need for prison beds in New York (Figure 4). For example, if all entrants are prisoners (e.g., probability of imprisonment = 100%), reducing the washout rate led to an increased savings of 478 beds (1,515 compared to 1,037 at the current washout rate).

The third model we examined for all five states changed the recidivism rates for the shock graduates. This analysis addressed the issue of the short-term impact on prison beds if the recidivism rates of those who successfully completed the shock program were cut in half. Recidivism rates in Georgia (27%), and South Carolina (24%) were high, and reduction of them did increase the bed space savings (or reduced the loss). This was particularly noticeable in Georgia where the estimate was that 404 beds (a difference of 137 beds) would be saved by the program if all of those admitted to the program were prison bound and the recidivism rate was cut in half.

The results from the model reducing the washouts was similar to the results from the recidivism model. When the washout rates were cut in half, the states with the highest washout rates saved the most beds. This made a difference of 478 beds in New York (1,515 compared to 1,037).

As shown in Table 3, adding this savings to the model created a major difference in the estimated bed space. If the programs targeted prison-bound offenders, all of them would result in saving beds. The number of beds saved would be substantial in New York, and in Florida, this model predicted a bed savings if 75% to 100% of the offenders would have been prison bound.

Another important consideration in improving the model is to include the time shock offenders have to wait prior to entering the shock program. Many programs admit participants in platoons or squads. If there are stringent eligibility requirements,

Figure 4
Estimates of Five Different Bed Space Models for New York Showing the Changes That Occur as a Function of Changes in the Probability of Imprisonment and Program Characteristics

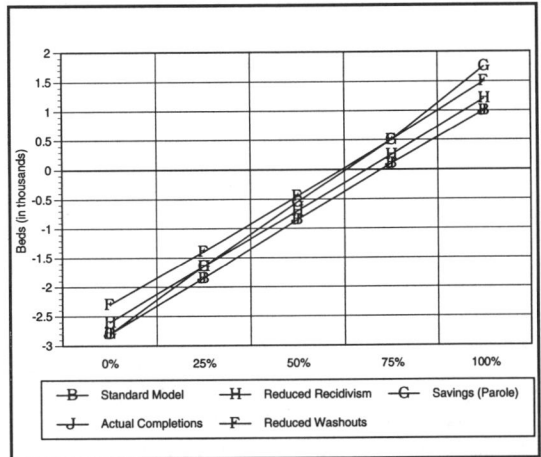

offenders may have to wait several months in prison or jail before being admitted to the boot camp.[7] This time was not included in the early release calculations. To examine the impact of a 2-month waiting period on the demand for bed space, we added 2 months to the shock durations in the model and recalculated the bed space for the different probabilities of imprisonment. At 75% probability of imprisonment, this model estimated that the states would save 21 beds (Florida), 202 beds (Georgia), 124 beds (Louisiana), 49 beds (New York), and 114 beds (South Carolina), a fairly substantial reduction from the original estimates in the model (see Table 3).

Discussion

After reviewing the decision making (see flow charts) and examining the program characteristics, we conclude that there is every reason to believe that the models that most appropriately represented the situation in Florida, Louisiana, and New York were those that are based on 75% to 100% of the shock entrants being prison bound. In all three of these states, the boot camp entrants had been sentenced to prison. Furthermore, those who were judged to be ineligible or unsuitable or who leave the program after entry must complete their sentence in a traditional prison. Although there may have been some who plea bargained or who were sent to prison by the judge because there was a boot camp, in the vast majority of cases we believe that they would have been prison bound had the boot camp not existed. If this assumption is correct, then the most appropriate estimates from the models for these states are the columns representing 75% to 100% probability of imprisonment.

At 100% probability of imprisonment, the different Louisiana models varied from a low of 249 to a high of 338; at 75% probability of imprisonment, these values varied from 129 to 184. If most of the offenders had been in prison and the size of the program stayed the same, changes in the characteristics of the program in the models would not have a major impact on the prison system. Thus, if Louisiana wants to have an impact on prison crowding, it will be important to insure that the participants are selected from those who would otherwise be in prison.

These results are very different for the New York program. First of all, the size of the program means that it could have a significant impact on the prison system. If all of the participants were prison bound, 1,037 to 1,668 beds could be saved by the shock program. However, when only 75% of the participants would be prisoners, only 76 to 549 beds would be saved. Thus even small changes in the percentage of offenders who are prison bound could have a major impact on the prison system. However, the bed savings also depend on other characteristics of the program. If all of the inmates would have been prison bound, as few as 1,037 beds would be saved by the program if the actual completion rates are used to estimate bed space savings. Changes in actual completions or recidivism rates would have a minimal effect on bed space. A much larger impact comes from the model that reduces the number of washouts.

Florida presents a very different picture from the other states. As noted, after examining the program we believe that a large share of these participants would have been prison bound if the program did not exist. Therefore, we focused on the estimates of beds needed or saved if 75% or 100% of the offenders were prisoners. As shown in Table 3, three of the models predict that the program will result in an overall need for prison beds, although the need will be small (ranging from a need for 8 to 56 additional beds). The results seem to be driven by the high washout rate and the small difference between the time served in shock and the time served in prison by those who were shock eligible but did not go to shock.[8] When the washout rate in Florida was reduced, there were bed savings, although this was only 34 beds. However, in the new model adding in the savings due to parolee revocations and their time in prison, 230 beds were saved. It may be reasonable to use this model to estimate bed space savings in Florida because shock-eligible prisoners spent a relatively short period of time in prison. In any case, even if all of the offenders were prison bound, the shock program would have had a minimum effect on prison beds given the overall size of the Florida prison population and therefore, the program has not accomplished the goal of reducing prison crowding. The Florida example demonstrates how important it is to design an intermediate sanction with the program goals clearly recognized. Furthermore, even a program that targets prison-bound offenders may have trouble reducing prison crowding if other aspects of the program are not carefully planned.

After reviewing the decision-making process, we concluded that many of the offenders in boot camps in Georgia and South Carolina would have been given probation if the boot camp had not existed. If this is true, the boot camps in these two states would have increased the demand for prison beds. . . .

Boot camp prisons have attracted the attention of correctional professionals and politicians. Many people believe that one benefit of these programs will be a reduction in prison crowding. Although an intermediate sanction like boot camp may increase the net of correctional control, this is not necessarily always the case. The analyses completed in this article demonstrate how important program design is if the goal of an intermediate sanction is to reduce the prison population. The programs have the potential for reducing prison crowding; however, they also have the potential for substantially increasing the number of offenders in prison. The major factor that will make the difference will be the degree to which the participants would otherwise have been imprisoned. The larger the program, the more important this will be because even if 50% of the offenders were prison bound, the program could result in the need for a considerable number of additional beds. If the goal of a boot camp prison is to reduce prison crowding, a jurisdiction designing a boot camp prison must insure that offender-participants are those who would otherwise be sent to prison.

There are other factors that will influence the number of beds needed by the prison system. Reducing recidivism rates and lowering the dropout and washout rates will also result in bed savings. Even what appears to be a small change in the prison situation, such as increasing the waiting time between entry to prison and admittance to the boot camp, can have a substantial impact on the need for prison beds. However, these will not overcome the influence of net widening. There is no support for the position that boot camp prisons will significantly impact prison crowding by reducing recidivism rates unless they are combined with a program that shortens the prison term of offenders who would otherwise be in prison.

Although many people argue that intermediate sanctions automatically widen the net of control, we argue that widening the net is not an automatic effect of all intermediate sanctions. Determining the impact of such sanctions is an empirical question that can be answered using appropriate data. The model proposed in this article can be used to determine the potential of an intermediate sanction for reducing or increasing the need for prison beds.

Notes

1. For a more complete description of the programs, see MacKenzie and Souryal 1993. The data for this study were collected in 1990, and program descriptions are based on the characteristics of the programs at the time of data collection. Since that time, there have been substantial changes in many of the programs. For instance, Georgia has made substantial changes in all aspects of its program (Flowers, Carr, and Ruback 1991). South Carolina changed from being the responsibility of the department of probation to being the responsibility of the department of corrections. The express purpose of this change was to maximize the shock program's ability to reduce prison crowding by insuring that the offenders participating in the program were prison bound.

2. In 1988 New York permitted offenders up to but not including 26 years of age to enter the program. This was amended in 1989 when inmates age 26 through 29 were admitted to the program with some additional restrictions. By 1992, the age limit was again in-

creased (to 35 years) and the additional requirements for older inmates were eliminated.
3. The capacity of New York's program was greatly increased in 1990 and therefore the values shown in the table include both the 1988 and 1990 values.
4. The numbers and probabilities for Louisiana were taken from the previously published report that was used as a model for this study (see MacKenzie and Parent 1991).
5. In a survey, researchers in New York (New York State Department of Correctional Services 1991) asked judges if they had changed their sentencing practices as a result of the shock program. Only 5% responded that they had sentenced nonviolent felons to prison rather than jail or probation because of the shock program. Another 5% said that they gave longer sentences to insure that offenders would not be eligible for shock, and 14% said that they gave shorter sentences to assure that offenders would be eligible for the shock program. This suggests that only a small percentage of the judges are using the program as an option for offenders who would otherwise be on probation.
6. A detailed description of the formula for calculating bed space estimates is given in MacKenzie and Parent (1991).
7. In examining their early boot camp, New York researchers found that inmates had served an average of 57 days in prison or jail before being admitted to the boot camp. Additionally, during interviews with program officials and inmates in many states, mention was made of a long waiting period between the time of entering prison (or volunteering for the boot camp) and admittance to the program.
8. The amount of time the boot camp participants served was not that much different than the time they would have to spend in a traditional prison. This small difference in time may also account, in part, for the high washout rate in Florida.

References

Austin, James and Barry Krisberg. 1981. "Wider, Stronger and Different Nets." *Journal of Research in Crime and Delinquency* 18:165–96.

Covey, Herbert and Scott Menard. 1984. "Community Corrections Diversions in Colorado." *Journal of Criminal Justice* 12:1–10.

Ezell, Mark. 1989. "Juvenile Arbitration: Net-Widening and Other Unintended Consequences." *Journal of Research in Crime and Delinquency* 26:358–77.

Flowers, G. T., T S. Carr, and R. B. Ruback. 1991. *Special Alternative Incarceration Evaluation*. Atlanta: Georgia Department of Corrections. Unpublished manuscript.

Greenfeld, Larry A. 1992. *Prisons and Prisoners in the United States*. Washington, DC: U.S. Department of Justice, Bureau of Justice Statistics, NCJ-1 37002.

Hylton, J. H. 1980. *Community Corrections and Social Control: A Canadian Perspective*. Regina, Canada: University of Regina.

Jones, Peter. 1990. "Community Corrections in Kansas: Extending Community-Based Corrections or Widening the Net?" *Journal of Research in Crime and Delinquency* 27:79–101.

MacKenzie, Doris L. 1990. "Boot Camp Prisons: Components, Evaluations, and Empirical Issues." *Federal Probation* 54:44–52.

MacKenzie, Doris L. and Dale Parent. 1991. "Shock Incarceration and Prison Crowding in Louisiana." *Journal of Criminal Justice* 19:225–37.

MacKenzie, Doris L, James W. Shaw, and Voncile B. Gowdy. 1993. *An Evaluation of Shock Incarceration in Louisiana*. Washington, DC: U.S. Department of Justice, National Institute of Justice.

MacKenzie, Doris L., and Claire Souryal. 1991. "Boot Camp Survey: Rehabilitation, Recidivism Reduction Out Rank As Main Goals." *Corrections Today*, October, pp. 90–96.

———. 1993, September. *Multi-Site Study of Shock Incarceration: Process Evaluation*. Unpublished report to the National Institute of Justice.

Mainprize, Stephen. 1992. "Electronic Monitoring in Corrections: Assessing Cost Effectiveness and the Potential for Widening the Net of Social Control." *Canadian Journal of Criminology*, April, pp. 161–80.

Morris, Norval and Michael Tonry. 1990. *Between Prison and Probation: Intermediate Punishments in a Rational Sentencing System*. New York: Oxford University Press.

New York State Department of Correctional Services and New York State Division of Parole. 1990. *The Second Annual Report to the Legislature. Shock Incarceration in New York State*. Unpublished report by the Division of Program Planning, Research and Evaluation and the Office of Policy Analysis and Information.

———. 1991. *The Third Annual Report to the Legislature: Shock Incarceration in New York State*. Unpublished report by the Division of Program Planning, Research and Evaluation and the Office of Policy Analysis and Information.

———. 1993. *The Fifth Annual Report to the Legislature: Shock Incarceration in New York State*. Unpublished report by the Division of Program Planning, Research and Evaluation and the Office of Policy Analysis and Information.

Palumbo, D., M. Clifford, and Zoann Snyder-Joy. 1992. "From Net Widening to Intermediate Sanctions: The Transformation of Alternatives to Incarceration from Benevolence to Malevolence." Pp. 229–44 in *Smart Sentencing: The Emergence of Intermediate Sanctions*, edited by J. Byrne, A. Lurigio. and J. Petersilia. Newbury Park, CA: Sage.

Souryal, C. and Doris MacKenzie. 1993. "Shock Incarceration and Recidivism: An Examination of Boot Camp Programs in Four States." In *Intermediate Sanctions: Sentencing in the 90s*, edited by J. O. Smykla and W. L. Selke. Cincinnati, OH: Anderson.

Yokoyama, Minoru. 1986. "The Juvenile Justice System in Japan." In *Youth Crime, Social Control and Prevention*, edited by M. Brusten, J. Graham, N. Herringer, and R Malinowski. Federal Republic of Germany: Centaurus-Verlags-Gesellschaft Pfeffenweiler.

———. 1989. "Net-Widening of the Juvenile Justice System in Japan." *Criminal Justice Review* 14:43–53 ◆

40
A Critical Look at the Idea of Boot Camp as a Correctional Reform

Merry Morash
Lila Rucker

Introduction: The Boot Camp Idea

In several states, correctional boot camps have been used as an alternative to prison in order to deal with the problem of prison overcrowding and public demands for severe treatment (Parent, 1988). Correctional boot camps are styled after the military model for basic training, and, similar to basic training, the participants are primarily young males. However, the "recruits" are offenders, though usually nonviolent and first-time ones (Parent, 1988). Boot camps vary in their purpose, but even when they are instituted primarily to reduce overcrowding, the implicit assumption is that their programs are of equal or greater deterrent or rehabilitative value than a longer prison sentence.

By the end of 1988, boot camps were operating in one county (Orleans Parish, Louisiana) and in eight states (Georgia, Oklahoma, Mississippi, Louisiana, South Carolina, New York, Florida, and Michigan), they were planned in three states (North Carolina, Kansas, and New Hampshire), and they were being considered in at least nine other states (Parent, 1988). The model was also being considered for a large number of youthful Detroit offenders. And in the summer of 1989, the boot camp model was put forth by the House Crime Subcommittee chairman as a potential national strategy for treating drug abusers (Gannett News Service, 1989).

The National Institute of Justice is supporting evaluations of correctional boot camp programs, and other evaluations without federal support are also underway. Such formal evaluations will no doubt provide invaluable evidence of the effect of the programs on participants and, in some cases, on the correctional system (e.g., the resulting diversion of offenders from more restrictive environments). The purpose of this article is to provide another type of assessment, specifically, a critical analysis of the history and assumptions underlying the use of a military model in a correctional setting.

The popular image of military boot camp stresses strict and even cruel discipline, hard work, and authoritarian decision making and control by a drill sergeant. It should be noted that this image does not necessarily conform to either current practices in the U.S. military or to all adaptations of boot camp in correctional settings. However, in a survey of existing correctional boot camp programs, Parent (1988) found commonality in the use of strict discipline, physical training, drill and ceremony, military bearing and courtesy, physical labor, and summary punishment for minor misconduct. Some programs have combined selected elements of the military boot camp model with more traditional forms of rehabilitation. In Oklahoma, for example, the paramilitary structure, including the use of regimentation, has been only one aspect of an otherwise "helping, supportive environment" that is considered by the administration to be a prerequisite if "change is to last or have any carry over" (Kaiser, 1988). In Michigan, the major emphasis has been on developing the "work ethic" by utilizing various motivational tactics (e.g., chants), strong discipline, and rehabilitation (Hengish, 1988). All participants work from 8:00 a.m. to 3:30 p.m. daily; evenings involve educational and therapeutic programs. When more traditional methods of rehabilitation are included, a consideration

From *Crime and Delinquency*, Volume 36, Number 2 (April 1990), pp. 204-222. Copyright © 1990 by Sage Publications, Inc. Reprinted by permission.

of the boot camp idea is more complex, requiring an analysis of both the costs and benefits of mixing the imagery or the reality of a boot camp approach with other measures. ...

The journalistic accounts of boot camps in corrections have celebrated a popular image of a relatively dehumanizing experience that is marked by hard, often meaningless, physical labor. The inmate has been portrayed as deficient, requiring something akin to being beaten over the head in order to become "a man."

The imagery of the people that we send to boot camp as deserving of dehumanizing treatment is in itself troubling, but even more so in light of the fact that the inmates are disproportionately minorities and underclass members. The boot camp idea also raises the disturbing question: Why would a method that has been developed to prepare people to go into war, and as a tool to manage legal violence, be considered as having such potential in deterring or rehabilitating offenders? Wamsley (1972, p. 401) concluded from a review of officers' manuals and prior research that military basic training is designed to promote fundamental values of military subculture, including

(1) acceptance of all-pervasive hierarchy and deference patterns; (2) extreme emphasis on dress, bearing, and grooming; (3) specialized vocabulary; (4) emphasis on honor, integrity, and professional responsibility; (5) emphasis on brotherhood; (6) fighter spirit marked by aggressive enthusiasm; and (7) special reverence for history and traditions. ...

What Has Been Tried and What Works in Corrections?

The correctional boot camp model has been touted as a new idea. However, militarism, the use of hard labor, and efforts to frighten offenders—most recently surfacing in the "Scared Straight" programs—have a long history in prison settings. We will focus first on militarism. In 1821, John Cray, the deputy keeper of the newly constructed Auburn Prison, moved away from the use of solitary confinement when suicides and mental breakdowns increased. As an alternative, he instituted a military regime to maintain order in overcrowded prisons (McKelvey, 1977, p. 14). The regime, which was based in part on his experiences as a Canadian army officer, required downcast eyes, lockstep marching, no talking or other communication among prisoners, and constant activity under close supervision (McKelvey, 1977). The issue for Cray and his contemporaries was the prevention of crime "through fear of punishment; the reformation of offenders being of minor consideration" (Lewis, 1983, p. 26). ...

Some might counter the argument that the militaristic approach opens the door for abusive punishment by pointing out that in contemporary correctional settings, physical punishment and harm are eliminated. However, as Johnson (1987, p. 48; see also Christie, 1981) noted, nonphysical abuse can be viewed as a "civilized" substitute. Also, in some cases physical abuse is a matter of definition, as is seen in the accounts of dropouts from one contemporary boot camp. They reported being treated like "scum," working 18-hour days, being refused permission to use the bathroom, being provoked to aggression by drill instructors, being forced to push a bar of soap along the floor with their noses, and being forced to participate in an exercise called "air raids" in which trainees run and dive face down, landing on their chests with arms stretched out to their sides (Bellew, 1988, p. 10). At least in some settings, the military model has provided a legitimization of severe punishment. It has opened the door for psychological and even physical abuse that would be rejected as cruel and unusual punishment in other correctional settings.

Turning now to work in correctional settings, its persistent use has been supported by its congruence with alternative objectives, including punishment, incapacitation, rehabilitation, and control inside the institution (Lejins, 1970, pp. 309–10). However, the form of work at a particular time has not been influenced just by ideals and objectives, but by basic economic forces (Rusche and Kirchheimer, 1939). For example, in order to protect private enterprise, the treadmill was used to occupy offenders following prohibitions against the use of prison labor (Morse, 1973, p. 33; see also Morash and Anderson, 1978). Also, in the nineteenth century, a major purpose of imprisonment was to teach the regular work habits demanded by employers (Rusche and Kirchheimer, 1939; Melossi and Pavarini, 1981). In contemporary discussions of correctional boot camp programs, work has been justified as both punitive and rehabilitative, as both exemplifying the harsh result of breaking the law and teaching the "work ethic." However, the economic constraints imposed by limited budgeting for rehabilitation efforts and the shrinking number of jobs for unskilled workers have shaped the form of work. Thus, hard physical labor, which has no transfer to the contemporary job market, has been the choice in correctional boot camps.

Further criticism of the form of work used in the boot camp settings rests on empirical research. The literature on work programs in general has not supported the conclusion that they produce a decrease in recidivism (Taggart, 1972; Fogel, 1975, pp. 114-16; Lipton, Martinson, and Wilks, 1975). Especially pertinent to the present analysis, in a recent article Maguire, Flanagan, and Thornberry (1988) showed that labor in a correctional institution was unrelated to recidivism after prisoner differences were taken into account. The exception was work programs that actually provided employment (e.g., Jeffrey and Woolpert, 1974; Rudoff and Esselstyn, 1973). Based on an extensive review of the literature, Gendreau and Ross (1987, p. 380; see also Walter and Mills, 1980) further specified the characteristics of correctional work programs that were related to lower recidivism: "Work programs must enhance practical skills, develop interpersonal skills, minimize prisonization, and ensure that work is not punishment alone." Clearly, the evaluation literature contradicts the idea that hard, often meaningless, labor in the boot camp setting has some positive effect. . . .

Military Boot Camps

The idea of boot camp as applied in correctional settings is often a simplification and exaggeration of an outdated system of military training that has been examined and rejected as unsatisfactory by many experts and scholars and by the military establishment itself. The difficulties that the military has discovered with the traditional boot camp model, and the resulting implications for reforms, could be instructive to people in search of positive correctional measures.

A number of difficulties with what will be referred to as the "traditional" military boot camp approach that is now mimicked in correctional settings were uncovered by a task force appointed in the 1970s (Raupp, 1978; Faris, 1975). The first difficulty with the traditional boot camp approach involved inconsistent philosophies, policies, and procedures. Ten years after the task force report was published, a follow-up study provided further insight into the problem of inconsistency and the related patterns of unreasonable leadership and contrived stressful situations. The study documented the "severe effects" of lack of predictability in such areas as standards for cleanliness and how cadence was called (Marlowe et al., 1988, p. 10). . . .

The second difficulty that the task force identified with traditional boot camp training was a widespread "we-versus-they" attitude and the related view that trainees were deserving of degrading treatment (Raupp, 1978, p. 9). The we-versus-they attitude was manifested by different behavioral and/or dress standards for trainees and for other personnel. Specifically, trainees were given "skin-head" haircuts and were prohibited from swearing and shouting, and physical training was used as punishment.

Aside from the investigative reports sponsored by the military, empirical studies of the effects of military boot camps, the effects of physical training (which is a major component of many correctional boot camp programs), and learning in general have provided relevant findings. Empirical evidence regarding the psychological impact of traditional military basic training on young recruits between the ages of 18 and 22 has demonstrated that "there was no increase in scores on ego-strength, or any other evidence of beneficial psychological effects accruing from basic training" (Ekman, Friesen, and Lutzker, 1962, p. 103). Administration of the MMPI to recruits revealed that "the change in the shape of the [MMPI] profiles suggests that aggressive, impulsive, and energetic features became slightly more prominent" (Ekman et al., 1962, p. 103). The authors concluded that the changes on the subscales imply that

> more callous attitudes, a tendency to ignore the needs of others, and feelings of self-importance increase slightly during basic training. The recruits appear less prone to examine their own responsibility for conflicts, and more ready to react aggressively. (Ekman et al., 1962, p. 104)

The importance of this finding is heightened by the conclusion of Gendreau, Grant, and Leipciger (1979, p. 71) that components of self-esteem that were good predictors of recidivism include the very same characteristics, namely, "self-centered, exploitive of others, easily led, and anxious to please." Sonkin and Walker (1985; see also Walker, 1983; Eisenberg and Micklow, 1979) also speculated that basic training in the military can result in the transfer of violent solutions to family settings. Eisenberg and Micklow (1979, p. 50) therefore proposed that military basic training be modified to include classes on "communication skills, stress reduction, and anger management." Although correctional boot camps do not provide training in the use of weapons or physical assault, they promote an aggressive model of leadership and a conflict-dominated style of interaction that could exacerbate tendencies toward aggression. . . .

Increased aggression and a bond among inmates are not desired outcomes of correctional boot camps, so again the efficacy of using the military boot camp model is in question. Moreover, it is unlikely that the offenders in correctional boot camps are more mentally healthy than Air Force recruits. What is the effect of using such techniques when there is no escape valve through dropping out of the program? And, if only the best-adjusted stay, what is accomplished by the program? The contrast of the Cadet School with the Officer's Training School, which did not use humiliation and severe physical conditions and punishment, provides convincing evidence of the ineffectiveness of such an approach to training people. Wamsley (1972, p. 418) concluded that there was a "lack of a clear utility for Pre-Flight's intense socialization" and that the "socialization process was brutally expensive in human terms and produced exaggerated forms of behavior which were not clearly related to effective task accomplishments."

Additional research has shown that positive improvements in self-esteem result from physical training primarily when the environment is supportive. For example, Hilyer and Mitchell (1979, p. 430) demonstrated that college students with low self-concepts who received physical fitness training in a helpful, facilitative, supportive environment demonstrated an increase in self-concept scores. The improvement was two and one-half times as great as that of low-concept peers who received physical fitness training and no support.

Also contradicting the negatively oriented training strategy that is characteristic of the old-style military boot camp model, virtually no empirically supported criminological theories have suggested that aggressive and unpredictable reactions by authority figures encourage prosocial behavior. The opposite has been promulgated by most learning theorists. For instance, Satir (1973, p. 13) concluded that learning happens only when a person feels valued and is valued, when he or she feels like a connected part of the human race (see also Rogers, 1975, p. 6). Feelings of self-worth can only flourish in an atmosphere in which individual differences are appreciated and mistakes are tolerated; communication is direct, clear, specific, and honest; rules are flexible, human, appropriate, and subject to change; and links to society are open (Satir, 1972, pp. 4–6). Finally, there has been considerable theory and research showing that antisocial behavior is increased when authority figures provide aggressive models for behavior (e.g., Bandura, 1973, pp. 252–53). Research in the sociology of sport has provided further evidence that physical training under the direction of an authoritarian trainer increases aggression (Coakley, 1986).

There is no systematic evidence of the degree to which the problems in traditional-style military boot camps are manifested in correctional settings, but there is evidence that they do occur. The introductory descriptions of the correctional boot camp model clearly reveal a tendency for some of the "drill sergeants" to use negative leadership. Telephone interviews with representatives of nine correctional boot camps show a tendency to focus on "tearing down the individuals and then building them back up." Reflective of this philosophy are negative strategies alluded to earlier, such as the utilization of debasing "welcoming speeches," the "chair position," and "learning experiences" that require men to wear baby bottles around their necks or to carry tree limbs with them all day. . . .

It is true that, as proponents of correctional boot camps claim, many military recruits feel that their survival of basic training is evidence of maturity and a major achievement in their lives (Gottlieb, 1980, pp. 166–67). However, the sense of achievement is linked to the notion that the experience is the first step in preparing them for the unique role of a soldier. Moreover, military boot camp is intended as just a prelude to acquaint the recruits with their new environment, in which they will take more control of their lives (Rabinowitz, 1982, p. 1084). It is not obvious that the boot camp experience alone, including elements of capricious and dehumanizing treatment, would be seen in such a positive light by inmate participants.

Clearly, the view that boot camp is just the first step in a socialization process has not been carried over into the correctional setting. While nearly all programs reported either regular or intensive probation or parole periods following release (Parent, 1988), none of the postrelease programs have had the capability to provide the continuous and multifaceted support network inherent in being a member of the military "family" or process. Postrelease programs are not designed to provide either the tightly knit structure or the guaranteed work that characterize military life.

It could be argued that the purpose of correctional boot camp is not to bind soldiers to their leaders or to develop group solidarity. Thus, the failure of the outmoded military boot camp model to achieve these results may not be a serious concern. Even if we accept this argument, the research on military basic training raises serious questions about the potential for undesirable outcomes, including increased aggression.

Stereotypes of Masculinity and Correctional Measures

The very idea of using physically and verbally aggressive tactics in an effort to "train" people to act in a prosocial manner is fraught with contradiction. The idea rests on the assumption that forceful control is to be valued. The other unstated assumption is that alternative methods for promoting prosocial behavior, such as the development of empathy or a stake in conformity (e.g., through employment), are not equally valued. Feminist theorists (Eichler, 1980; Bernard, 1975) have noted the societywide valuation of the stereotypically masculine characteristics of forcefulness and aggression and of the related devaluation of the stereotypically feminine characteristics of empathy and cooperative group behavior. Heidensohn (1987, p. 25) specifically wrote that programs like boot camp have been "designed to reinforce conventional male behaviour" and that they range from "quasimilitaristic short, sharp shocks to adventure training." . . .

It is not surprising that few have questioned the distorted image of masculinity embodied in the idea of boot camp, for this imagery is implicit in the assumptions of many criminological theories (Naffine, 1987), and it is shared by many offenders. Focusing on criminologists, Naffine (1987) showed how several major theories have presented male offenders' aggression and assertiveness in a positive light while they have devalued characteristics associated with women. To be more specific, major theories have accepted the stereotypical characteristics of men as normal and have presented women as dependent, noncompetitive, and passive. Naffine's (1987, p. 126) analysis revealed the "curious result of extolling the virtues of the male, as a good criminal, and treating conforming women as if they were the socially deviant group." This result has been echoed in the use of a military model that similarly extols the virtues that ate often associated with both masculinity and aggression in our society.

Writing about images of masculinity among economically marginalized men, who are overrepresented in the offender population, Messerschmidt (1986, p. 59) built on the notion that in our society "both masculinity and power are linked with aggression/violence while femininity and powerlessness are linked with nonviolence" (also see Schwendinger and Schwendinger, 1985, p. 161). He went on to note that as a result of the unavailability of jobs that are not degrading, powerless men seek out alternative avenues through which to exercise their masculinity. Other supports of criminality include an orientation toward "exploitative individualism," as opposed to any caring ties to group members, and male bonding, which is the ritual rejection of "weakness" associated with femininity. This rejection is demonstrated through activities like gang fights. Again, there is a parallel with the stereotype of masculinity embodied in the boot camp model. Specifically, Eisenhart (1975) has described military training's emphasis on self-sufficiency and the avoidance of attachment to others.

The irony in emphasizing an aggressive model of masculinity in a correctional setting is that these very characteristics may explain criminality. Theorists working in the area of crime causation have focused on both the identification with male stereotypical traits and roles, which are consistent with illegal behavior (Oakley, 1972, p. 72; see also Tolson, 1977), and the frustration that males feel when they cannot achieve these stereotypes because of low social status (Messerschmidt, 1986, pp. 59-68). The empirical support to link stereotypical masculinity with criminality has been inconsistent (Cullen, Golden, and Cullen, 1979; Norland, James, and Shover, 1978; Thornton and James, 1979; Loy and Norland, 1981). There is some evidence, however, that female stereotypical characteristics predict prosocial behavior (Morash, 1983; Gilligan, 1982; Hoffman, 1975; Eisenberg and Miller, 1987).

An additional irony is found in the inclusion of women in correctional boot camps. Holm (1982, p. 273) observed that in the military, "women . . . suffered from role identification problems when put through military training programs designed traditionally '"to make men out of boys,"' programs that had "more to do with the rites of manhood than the requirements of service jobs." There is serious doubt about the efficacy of placing women in a militaristic environment that emphasizes masculinity and aggressiveness and that in some cases rejects essentially prosocial images and related patterns of interaction associated with the stereotype of femininity.

Alternative Models in Corrections

Correctional policymakers and program staff are not alone in their application of the traditional boot camp model as an approach for training people outside of military settings. Looking again at news reports, we see that the boot camp type of training has been accepted in a variety of organizations as a means to increase the productivity, skill levels, efficiency, and effectiveness of participants. Such enterprises are as diverse as the Electronic Data Systems Corporation (Klausner, 1984, p. 17), the Nick Bollettieri Tennis Academy (Arias, 1986, p. 107), and Japan's Managers' Training School (Bueil, 1983). In keeping with the boot camp model, participants are made to endure humiliation so that a bond can develop with the teacher (Klausner, 1984, p. 17). There appear to be social forces supporting acceptance of the general idea that the boot camp model is appropriate as a method for promoting training and human development. In spite of the societal pressures to use such a model, our assessment has a number of negative implications for the application of boot camps in correctional settings.

The first implication is based on the research on boot camp and the development of human potential in a military setting. At certain times and in certain geographic locations, military personnel have been charged with training and employing populations that are not markedly dissimilar from the economically marginalized young men and women that populate the prisons. They also have been engaged in the imprisonment of people for the violation of criminal laws. A continued examination of their techniques and outcomes could provide further instruction. As a starting point, it might be noted that in the military, the version of boot camp used in correctional settings is not commonly viewed as an effective correctional measure. Furthermore, through *Project 10,000*, the military has been successful in integrating poorly educated recruits into their own workforce, though often in relatively low-skill positions that restricted transfer to the civilian workforce (Sticht et al., 1987). Contrary to critics' anticipation of disciplinary problems with poorly educated recruits, less than 5% of the participants failed to conform to military rules and regulations. The approach to integration involved traditional methods of literacy training coupled with individualized teaching geared to a specific job assignment. This approach is consistent with the findings that we have reviewed on effective work programs in correctional settings.

A second implication of our analysis of the idea of boot camp is that we need to reconsider correctional alternatives. Harris (1983, p. 166) wrote that the "development of a more humane, caring and benevolent society involves a continuing quest for higher standards of decency and good will and an ever decreasing resort to ... degrading sanctions." For her, the continued and fundamental interdependence of self and other is primary, and she thinks in terms of "persuasion, nonviolent action, positive reinforcement, personal example, peer support and the provision of life-sustaining and life-enhancing services and opportunities" (Harris, 1983, p. 166). It is noteworthy that the rehabilitation models of corrections that many experts have publicly rejected reflect a deemphasis on the questionable stereotypes of "how to be a man" that are promoted by the boot camp model.

A third implication has to do with the evaluation of existing and planned boot camp programs. A number of potential, negative outcomes of a boot camp environment have been identified. One of these is increased aggression, including physical and nonphysical punishment, directed against offenders by prison staff. Also included are increased offender aggression, a devaluation of women and so-called "feminine traits" (e.g., sensitivity), and other negative effects of an unpredictable, authoritarian atmosphere. In addition to considering these effects directly, program evaluation should monitor the degree to which the environment is characterized by inconsistent standards and expectations, dysfunctional stress, a we-versus-they attitude, and negative leadership styles. Furthermore, because correctional boot camp programs mix the elements of a military model with less coercive methods of human change, it is important to design research that reveals the actual program elements that produce both desired and undesired program outcomes.

Our review and analysis suggest that even when the elements of the military boot camp model are mixed with traditional rehabilitative approaches, there can be negative outcomes. Thus, the boot camp model is unlikely to provide a panacea for the needs of rehabilitation or for the pressures arising from the problems of both prison overcrowding and public demands for severe punishment. Whether the point is to provide rehabilitation, to deter, or to divert people from prison, alternatives other than boot camp should be given careful consideration.

References

Arias, Ron. 1986. "At Nick Bollettieri's Florida Boot Camp, Tennis Is Played Only One Way, To Win." *People Weekly* October 20:107.

Bandura, Albert. 1973. *Aggression: A Social Learning Analysis*. Englewood Cliffs, NJ: Prentice-Hall.

Bellew, Deena C. 1988. *An Evaluation of IMPACT Using Intensive Interviews: The Inmate Perspective*. Unpublished manuscript. Baton Rouge: Louisiana State University.

Bernard, Jesse. 1975. *Women, Wives, Mothers: Values and Options*. Chicago: Aldine.

Bueil, Barbara. 1983. "Corporate Boot Camp in Japan." *Life* September:40.

Christie, Nils. 1981. *Limits to Pain*. Oxford: Martin Robertson.

Coakley, Jay J. 1986. *Sport in Society: Issues and Controversies*. St. Louis, MO: Mosby.

Cole, George F. 1986. *The American System of Criminal Justice*. Monterey, CA: Brooks/Cole.

Cullen, Francis T., Kathryn M. Golden, and John B. Cullen. 1979. "Sex and Delinquency: A Partial Test of the Masculinity Hypothesis." *Criminology* 17:301–310.

Defense. 1987. "Almanac: People in Active Duty." September/October:32.

Eichler, Margrit. 1980. *The Double Standard: A Feminist Critique of Feminist Social Science*. New York: St. Martin's Press.

Eisenberg, Nancy and Paul A. Miller. 1987. "The Relation of Empathy to Prosocial and Related Behaviors." *Psychological Bulletin* 101:91–119.

Eisenberg, Sue E. and Patricia L. Micklow. 1979. "The Assaulted Wife: 'Catch 22' Revisited." *Women's Rights Law Reporter* 3:138–161.

Eisenhart, R. Wayne. 1975. "You Can't Hack It Little Girl: A Discussion of the Covert Psychological Agenda of Modern Combat Training." *Journal of Social Issues* 31:13–23.

Ekman, Paul, Wallace V. Friesen, and Daniel R. Lutzker. 1962. "Psychological Reactions to Infantry Basic Training." *Journal of Consulting Psychology* 26:103–104.

Enloe, Cynthia. 1983. *Does Khaki Become You? The Militarization of Women's Lives*. Boston: South End.

Faris, John H. 1975. "The Impact of Basic Combat Training: The Role of the Drill Sergeant." Pp. 13–24 in *The Social Psychology of Military Service*, edited by E. Goldman and D. R. Segal. Beverly Hills, CA: Sage.

Finckenauer, James O. 1982. *Scared Straight and the Panacea Phenomenon*. Englewood Cliffs, NJ: Prentice-Hall.

Fogel, David. 1975. *. . .We Are the Living Proof...* Cincinnati: Anderson.

Gannett News Service. 1989. "Boot Camp Prisons." *Lansing State Journal* 135 (June 19): 11.

Gendreau, Paul, Brian A. Grant, and Mary Leipciger. 1979. "Self-Esteem, Incarceration, and Recidivism." *Criminal Justice and Behavior* 6:67–75.

Gendreau, Paul and Robert R. Ross. 1987. "Revivification of Rehabilitation: Evidence from the 1980s." *Justice Quarterly* 4:349–396.

Gilligan, Carol. 1982. *In a Different Voice*. Cambridge, MA: Harvard University Press.

Gottlieb, David. 1980. *Babes in Arms: Youth in the Army*. Beverly Hills, CA: Sage.

Harris, M. Kay. 1983. "Strategies, Values, and the Emerging Generation of Alternatives to Incarceration." *Review of Law and Social Change* 12:141–170.

Heidensohn, Francis. 1987. "Women and Crime: Questions for Criminology." Pp. 16–27 in *Gender, Crime and Justice*, edited by P. Carlen and A. Worrall. Milton Keynes, England: Open University Press.

Hengish, Donald. 1988. Michigan Bureau of Correctional Facilities, Community Alternatives Program. Telephone interview, December 1.

Hilyer, James S. Jr. and William Mitchell. 1979. "Effects of Systematic Physical Fitness Training Combined with Counseling on the Self-Concept of College Students." *Journal of Counseling Psychology* 26:427–436.

Hoffman, Martin L. 1975. "Sex Differences in Moral Internalization and Values." *Journal of Personality and Social Psychology* 32:720–729.

Holm, Jeanne. 1982. *Women in the Military*. Novato, CA: Presidio.

Jeffrey, Ray and Stephen Woolpert. 1974. "Work Furlough as an Alternative to Incarceration: An Assessment of its Effects on Recidivism and Social Cost." *Journal of Criminal Law and Criminology* 65:404–415.

Johnson, Robert. 1987. *Hard Time*. Monterey, CA: Brooks/Cole.

Kaiser, Steven. 1988. Warden, Lexington Assessment and Reception Center. Lexington, Oklahoma. Telephone interview, November 16.

Klausner, Michael. 1984. "Perot's Boot Camp." *Wall Street Journal* (August 3):17.

Larwood, Laurie, Eric Glasser, and Robert McDonald. 1980. "Attitudes of Male and Female Cadets Toward Military Sex Integration." *Sex Roles* 6:381–390.

Lejins, Peter P. 1970. "Ideas Which Have Moved Corrections." *Proceedings of the One Hundredth Annual Congress of Corrections of the American Correctional Association*: 308–322.

Lewis, Roy V. 1983. "Scared Straight—California Style: Evaluation of the San Quentin Squire Program." *Criminal Justice and Behavior* 10:209–226.

Life. 1988. "'Squeeze You Like a Grape': In Georgia, A Prison Boot Camp Sets Kids Straight." July:82.

Lipton, Douglas, Robert Martinson, and Judith Wilks. 1975. *The Effectiveness of Correctional Treatment*. New York: Praeger.

Loy, Pamela and Stephen Norland. 1981. "Gender Convergence and Delinquency." *Sociological Quarterly* 22:275–283.

Maguire, Kathleen E., Timothy J. Flanagan, and Terence P. Thornberry. 1988. "Prison Labor and Recidivism." *Journal of Quantitative Criminology* 4:3–18.

Marlowe, David H., James A. Martin, Robert J. Schneider, Larry Ingraham, Mark A. Vaitkus, and Paul Bartore. 1988. *A Look at Army Training Centers: The Human Dimensions of Leadership and Training*. Washington, DC: Department of Military Psychiatry, Walter Reed Army Institute of Research.

Martin, Douglas. 1988. "New York Tests a Boot Camp for Inmates." *New York Times* March 4:15.

McKelvey, Blake. 1977. *American Prisons: A History of Good Intentions*. Montclair, NJ: Patterson Smith.

Melossi, Dario and Massimo Pavarini. 1981. *The Prison and the Factory: Origins of the Penitentiary System*. London: Macmillan.

Merryfinch, Lesley. 1981. "Militarization/Civilization." Pp. 9–13 in *Loaded Questions: Women in the Military*, edited by W. Chapkis. Washington, DC: Transnational Institute.

Messerschmidt, James W. 1986. *Capitalism, Patriarchy, and Crime: Toward a Socialist Feminist Criminology*. Totowa, NJ: Rowman and Littlefield.

Morash, Merry. 1983. "An Explanation of Juvenile Delinquency: The Integration of Moral-Reasoning Theory and Sociological Knowledge." Pp. 395–410 in *Personality Theory, Moral Development, and Criminal Behavior*, edited by W. S. Laufer and J. M. Day. Lexington, MA: Lexington Books.

Morash, Merry and Etta Anderson. 1978. "Liberal Thinking on Rehabilitation: A Work-Able Solution to Crime?" *Social Problems* 25:556–563.

Morse, Wayne. 1973. "The Attorney General's Survey of Release Procedures." Pp. 23–53 in *Penology: The Evolution of Corrections in America*, edited by G. C. Killinger and P. F. Cromwell, Jr. St. Paul, MN: West.

Naffine, Ngaire. 1987. *Female Crime: The Construction of Women in Criminology*. Sydney: Allen and Unwin.

Norland, Stephen, Jennifer James, and Neal Shover. 1978. "Gender Role Expectations." *Sociology Quarterly* 19:545–554.

Oakley, Ann. 1972. *Sex, Gender and Society*. London: Temple Smith.

O'Brien, Tim. 1979. *If I Die in a Combat Zone, Box Me Up and Ship Me Home*. New York: Dellacorte.

Parent, Dale. 1988. "Shock Incarceration Programs." Paper Presented at the American Correctional Association Winter Conference, Phoenix.

Pisciotta, Alexander W. 1983. "Scientific Reform: The New Penology at Elmira, 1876–1900." *Crime and Delinquency* 29:613–630.

Rabinowitz, Stanley. 1982. "Inauguration for Adulthood: The Military System as an Effective Integrator for Adult Adaptation: An Israel Air Force Base Perspective." *Psychological Reports* 51:1083–1086.

Raspberry, William. 1987. "Boot Camp—In Prison: An Experiment Worth Watching." *Washington Post* March 21: Section H, 21.

Raupp, Edward R. 1978. *Toward Positive Leadership for Initial Entry Training. A Report by the Task Force on Initial Entry Training Leadership*. Fort Monroe, VA: United States Army Training and Doctrine Command.

Rogers, Carl R. 1975. "Empathic: An Unappreciated Way of Being." *Journal of the Counseling Psychologist* 5:2–10.

Ruddick, Sara. 1983. "Drafting Women: Pieces of a Puzzle." Pp. 214–43 in *Conscripts and Volunteers: Military Requirements, Social Justice and the All-Volunteer Force*, edited by R. K. Rullinwindet. Totowa, NJ: Rowman and Allenheld.

Rudoff, Alvin and T. C. Esselstyn. 1973. "Evaluating Work Furlough: A Follow-Up." *Federal Probation* 37:48–53.

Rusche, Georg and Otto Kirchheimer. 1939. *Punishment and Social Structure*. New York: Columbia University Press.

Satir, Virginia. 1972. *Peoplemaking*. Palo Alto, CA: Science and Behavior Books.

Schwendinger, Julia R. and Herman Schwendinger. 1985. *Adolescent Subcultures and Delinquency*. New York: Praeger.

Sitomer, Curtis J. 1987. "Some Young U.S. Offenders Go to 'Boot Camp'—Others are Put in Adult Jails." *Christian Science Monitor* October 27: 1.

Sonkin, Daniel Jay, Del Martin, and Leonard E. Aurbach Walker. 1985. *The Male Batterer: A Treatment Approach*. New York: Springer.

Sticht, Thomas G., William B. Armstrong, Daniel T. Hickey, and John S. Caylor. 1987. *Cast-Off Youth Policy and Training Methods from the Military Experiences*. New York: Praeger.

Stiehm, Judith H. 1981. *Bring Me Men and Women: Mandated Change at the U.S. Air Force Academy*. Berkeley: University of California Press.

——. 1982. "The Protected, the Protector, the Defender." *Women's Studies International Forum* 5:367–376.

——. 1989. *Arms and the Enlisted Woman*. Philadelphia: Temple University Press.

Sullivan, Mercer. 1983. "Youth Crime: New York's Two Varieties." *New York Affairs: Crime and Criminal Justice*. New York: New York University Press.

Taggart, Robert III. 1972. *The Prison of Unemployment*. Baltimore: Johns Hopkins University Press.

Thornton, David, Len Curran, David Grayson, and Vernon Holloway. 1984. *Tougher Regimes in Detention Centres: Report of an Evaluation* by the Young Offender Psychology Unit. London: Her Majesty's Stationery Office.

Thornton, William E. and Jennifer James. 1979. "Masculinity and Delinquency Revisited." *British Journal of Criminology* 19:225–241.

Tolson, Andrew. 1977. *The Limits of Masculinity: Male Identity and the Liberated Woman.* New York: Harper & Row.

Walker, Lenore. 1983. "The Battered Woman Syndrome Study." Pp. 31–48 in *The Dark Side of Families: Current Family Violence Research*, edited by D. Finkelhor, R. J. Gelles, G. Hotaling, and M. Straus. Beverly Hills, CA: Sage.

Walter, Timothy L. and Carolyn M. Mills. 1980. "A Behavioral-Employment Intervention Program for Reducing Juvenile Delinquency." Pp. 185–206 in *Effective Correctional Treatment*, edited by R. R. Ross and P. Gendreau. Toronto: Butterworths.

Wamsley, Gary L. 1972. "Contrasting Institutions of Air Force Socialization: Happenstance or Bellwether?" *American Journal of Sociology* 78:399–417.

Wilson, William Julius. 1987. *The Truly Disadvantaged: Inner City, the Underclass, and Public Policy.* Chicago: University of Chicago Press.

Yudkin, Marcia. 1982. "Reflections on Wolf's *Three Guineas*." *Women's Studies International Forum* 5:263–269.

Yuval-Davis, Nita. 1985. "Front and Rear: The Sexual Division of Labor in the Israeli Army." *Feminist Studies* 11:649–675. ✦

Section XI
The Future of the Juvenile Justice System

The juvenile justice system currently faces an increasingly hopeless task of trying to blend the rhetoric of "compassionate care" and "individualized treatment" with the reality of assembly-line justice, a growing number of hard-core juvenile offenders, and society's increasing intolerance for juvenile crime. In many ways, the juvenile court is a nineteenth-century response to twentieth-century problems. It is predicated on the concept of probation, in which the juvenile court becomes a "kindly parent" and the child is guided through a period of readjustment while in the solicitous care of his or her parents. It was never envisioned that the court would become a hopeless muddle of adolescent offenders who are involved in truancy, robbery, assault, running away from home, teenage pregnancy, drug use, and burglary. At the time of the juvenile court's inception, there was not the pervasive presence of broken homes, single-parent families, teenage pregnancies, dual income families, child abuse or neglect, latchkey children, or children wandering the streets who were "push outs" or "kick outs." In fact, current "demographic, economic, and fiscal forces mean that the juvenile justice system will handle more deeply troubled adolescents in the next several years" (Krisberg and Austin, 1993: 173). It is also becoming increasingly clear that the juvenile crime problem is inextricably interwoven with the country's broader domestic issues. The development of effective delinquency prevention programs depends on "our ability to educate our children, to provide them with adequate housing and health care, to reduce youth unemployment, to prevent and respond effectively to child abuse and neglect, . . . to strengthen families, to prevent drug and alcohol abuse, and to eradicate poverty" (Schwartz, 1989: 178). The legislation that created the juvenile courts some 80 to 90 years ago never envisioned the plethora of problems that would become part of adolescent lifestyles in the late twentieth century.

The first problem that seems to face the juvenile court is an identity crisis. Is the juvenile court a social welfare agency or a court of law? Many feel that the court is asked to do too much. It is not equipped to solve adolescent problems that may be predicated on neglect in the family, school, or local community. The court has jurisdiction over the child, but not over the social milieu in which the child lives. There has been some tinkering with the juvenile justice system to divert noncriminal cases back into the local community, but the juvenile court is still expected to resolve too great a range of adolescent problems. Initially, the juvenile court was created to help adolescents with minor problems, but in recent years the court has been criticized for spending too much time on petty problems and not "getting tough" with hard-core offenders. But do we really want the juvenile court to deal only with serious offenders? With the privatization of juvenile corrections, a high percentage of status offenders and nonoffenders can be shunted out the side door of the juvenile court into the private sector. Having a bifurcated correctional system that may reflect societies' racial and social class divisions may not be a step in the right direction for social justice. The Supreme Court has handed down a few decisions relating to the juvenile justice system, but even the highest court in the land walks a tightrope between due-process-of-law stipulations and the social welfare basis of the juvenile court. While the Supreme Court has mandated some introduction of due process of law into the juvenile court, the social welfare basis of the juvenile system has never changed. Thus, the dilemma remains just what the purpose of the juvenile court is after its first century of existence.

Some states are changing the jurisdictional status of the juvenile court from exclusive to concurrent. That is, originally the juvenile court had exclusive jurisdiction over all juveniles, regardless of their delinquent acts. Juveniles could be transferred or waived to the adult court, but only after a juvenile judge approved the transfer. Concurrent jurisdiction would allow the adult court to share jurisdictions over certain types of serious delinquent acts. However, a bolder step in bypassing the juvenile court altogether is to enact legislation that excludes certain types of delinquent acts from the juvenile court. For example, Georgia code was rewritten as follows:

> The superior court shall have exclusive jurisdiction over any matter concerning any child 13 to 17 years of age who is alleged to have committed any of the following offenses: (i) murder; (ii) voluntary manslaughter; (iii) rape; (iv) aggravated sodomy; (v) aggravated child molestation; (vi) aggravated sexual battery; or (vii) armed robbery if committed with a firearm. (Senate Bill 440, enacted as law May 1, 1994)

Other states have also begun to limit the jurisdiction of the juvenile court. Delaware has excluded cases of first-degree murder, rape, and kidnapping from the juvenile court. Connecticut has made a waiver to adult court mandatory for juveniles charged with serious felony offenses. In Illinois, serious felony offenses, including possession of a deadly weapon in school, are excluded from juvenile court. In Kansas, any child with two prior felony offenses is excluded from the juvenile court. It is becoming increasingly common for state legislatures to revise state statutes relating to the juvenile court and to restrict the exclusive jurisdiction of that court. If this trend continues, juvenile courts could be legislated out of existence, or relegated to playing only a minor role in delinquency matters.

A second way the juvenile court is being threatened is through judicial review. In 1975, the Supreme Court handed down a decision entitled *Donaldson v. O'Connor*. Donaldson had been committed to the Florida state mental hospital in 1957 by his father. For eighteen years, Donaldson petitioned the hospital for his release but it was denied even though there was no evidence that he was dangerous to himself or others. In 1975, the Supreme Court ruled that Donaldson's rights were being denied by his continued confinement without treatment. The Court went further and stated that commitment of an involuntary nature is a deprivation of liberty and the state cannot be a party without due process of law. Mere custodial care in an institution is not sufficient basis for continued confinement.

This right to treatment has been extended to the juvenile justice system. In a series of cases, the federal courts have partially extended the Donaldson ruling to juvenile matters. As of yet, the federal courts have not made sweeping judgments in juvenile custody matters, but there have been many individual cases that relate to the matters of minimal standards or inappropriate disciplinary methods used in juvenile correctional settings. In response to the Donaldson case, there are currently due-process hearings prior to confinement in excess of 24 hours. There are also minimum sanitary, health, educational, and medical resources for juvenile residents. Juxtaposed with the hard-line approach of getting tough on juvenile offenders, the federal courts are introducing a certain degree of right-to-treatment for juvenile offenders that is putting an additional strain on the juvenile system.

For some, the ultimate resolution to the problem of the juvenile court is simply to do away with it. They argue that the juvenile court is a product of another age which has failed to serve the best interests of either delinquent offenders or the community. By abolishing the juvenile court, the criminal court would then assume jurisdiction over *criminal* adolescent behavior. Adolescents would be accorded full protection of due-process-of-law guarantees; if sentenced to a correctional facility, they could be placed in separate quarters, isolated from adult offenders. The myriad categories of status offenses and nonoffenses could be dealt with by the family, school, or local community in a nonlegal fashion. For example, community-based programs could be established to help parents with incorrigibility or running away, and help the school with problems of truancy or unruly behavior in the classroom. The argument claims that these are not criminal matters and do not belong in the courtroom. Further, Musick (1995) suggests that lawyers and judges may not be the best people to deal with juvenile delinquents. He suggests local ministers and successful grandmothers. The essence of this proposal is a radical shift of responsibility from the courtroom back to the local community. While it is doubtful that this drastic proposal would ever be accepted, it is the logical outcome of much of the antijuvenile court rhetoric.

The first reading in this section, entitled "History Overtakes the Juvenile Justice System," by Ferdinand, is a broad historical overview of the juvenile justice system. Ferdinand states that the doctrine of *parens patriae* that began to emerge early in the nineteenth century fit nicely with the need to socialize juveniles into what was seen as the new social order. But there was no special juvenile court, and the needs of juveniles became mangled with torts, contracts, and other court interests. With the advent of the first juvenile code, enacted in Illinois in 1899, the doctrine of *parens patriae* could come to full fruition. The juvenile court seemed to serve a meaningful purpose until after World War II, when criticism of this system of justice began to emerge. Questions arose regarding the effectiveness of treatment in reducing delinquency. Ferdinand argues that it was not so much that the juvenile court failed but that the state never provided solid support for the court to carry out effective treatment.

Ferdinand suggests a more comprehensive approach to delinquency that includes not only a court but a wide array of treatment programs. He suggests that too much attention has been paid to the apprehension, adjudication, and disposition components of the juvenile court, while the treatment phase has been ignored. Ferdinand finds many examples of promising treatment programs, but claims they have not been given sufficient support. He is clearly not ready to abandon the juvenile court; with so many voices calling for the dismantling of the juvenile court, Ferdinand's comments are worth noting.

The second article, entitled "Juvenile (In)Justice and the Criminal Court Alternative," by Feld, picks up where Ferdinand leaves off. According to Feld, the Supreme Court has pushed the juvenile court in a direction that it did not wish to go. The juvenile court took on certain characteristics of the criminal court and became something of a "junior" criminal court. Then, with the introduction of diversion, deinstitutionalization, judicial waivers, and now legislative exclusion of offenses, the juvenile court is in danger of becoming a dangling participle. Feld also sees a movement away from therapeutic, individualized dispositions toward a more punitive court that blurs the distinction between the adult and juvenile courts. He concludes his discussion with what he calls three possible scenarios for the juvenile court. The first scenario suggests that the juvenile court return to its philosophical roots of informal, therapeutic emphasis. The second approach would be to accord juveniles procedural safeguards but keep the juvenile court as a separate entity. The third approach would be to abolish the juvenile court and have juvenile offenders inserted into the adult criminal court.

The third and final reading, entitled "Rethinking the Juvenile Justice System," by Hirschi and Gottfredson, argues that there is no justification for two separate systems and that the distinction between an adult and juvenile offender should be abolished. They argue that the age distribution for criminal offenses follows a similar pattern: rapid increase in the middle teenage years, peaking around 17 or 18, and then a rapid decline in the early 20s. Hirschi and Gottfredson fail to see where juvenile or adult court sanctions have any impact on this age distribution. They question the logic of asserting that juveniles are not responsible for their actions but adults are, as if all adult behavior is rational and premeditated. Another argument for separate justice systems is that juveniles are assumed to be more amenable to treatment; but Hirschi and Gottfredson challenge the notion that age is a predictor of treatment success. They go on to question several other alleged justifications for having a juvenile court and assert that there is no scientific basis for them.

The irony in Hirschi and Gottfredson's proposal is that they suggest a movement of the criminal court toward the juvenile court. The juvenile court tends not to incarcerate but to emphasize less procedural formality and more treatment. This they find to be a positive element which should be retained. They argue that the consolidation of the two systems would "eliminate the possibility of differential treatment due to minuscule differences in age, as when a 217-month-old youth is treated as an adult while a 215-month-old youth, guilty of the same crime, is treated as a juvenile." Their discussion is innovative and refreshing. But could this ever happen?

References

Donaldson v. O'Connor. 422 U.S. 563 (1975).

Krisberg, Barry and James F Austin. 1993. *Reinventing Juvenile Justice.* Sage: Newbury Park, California.

Musick, David. 1995. *An Introduction to the Sociology of Juvenile Delinquency.* State University of New York Press: Albany, N.Y.

Schwartz, Ira M. 1989. *(In)Justice for Juveniles: Rethinking the Best Interests of the Child.* Lexington: Lexington, Massachusetts. ✦

41
History Overtakes the Juvenile Justice System

Theodore N. Ferdinand

Justice systems have a way of shaping their parts to the needs of the whole, and the juvenile justice system is no exception. Many of the juvenile court's problems can be understood in terms of how the court adjusted over the years to the custodial institutions, clientele, and treatment facilities it served. Its deficiencies today stem largely from its roots in the civil courts and the difficulties it encountered in fulfilling *parens patriae* in a system of juvenile institutions already dominated by a custodial if not a punitive viewpoint. The juvenile justice system has acted very much as a loose but dynamic system over the last 165 years, and to understand its difficulties we need to took to the historical contradictions that were built into the juvenile justice system during its early years.

Of particular interest are several questions that have been raised repeatedly over the years. First, what purposes did the juvenile justice system serve when it was introduced in eastern cities during the early 19th century, and what role did the juvenile court play in that system when it was introduced in the early part of the 20th century? Second, why has treatment been such an uneven enterprise in juvenile justice? Is the process of treating delinquents fraught with such obstacles that consistent success is impossible, or are less formidable reasons responsible for this inconsistency? Finally, why has juvenile justice been unable to maintain a *parens patriae* focus within its custodial institutions? Is there an inherent flaw in such institutions that ultimately vetoes any long term effort to improve juveniles in institutions?

Many have addressed these and similar questions, and along these lines Cohen (1985) has identified four distinct approaches to the problems of the justice system. The "conventional" view asserts that flaws in the justice system derive basically from the limitations of its pioneers. If their vision is partly cloudy, or their commitment falters, their reforms ultimately founder on inertia and indifference. But different leaders inject new enthusiasms, and the overall result is gradual progress in the justice system through the cumulated efforts of its visionaries over generations.

The second approach, "we blew it," as represented by David Rothman (1980) in his work, *Conscience and Convenience*, is less optimistic. It sees the sources of ineffectiveness in the justice system in the inevitable triumph of mindless routine and parochial interest over moral purpose. The possibility of lasting progress in the justice system is compromised by custodial inertia and trivial, convenient routine.

Cohen (1985) describes in addition two other approaches: "It's all a con" and, most recently, "destructuring." Foucault (1979) represents the first with his suggestion in *Discipline and Punish* that the justice system before all else buttresses order in civil society by its threat of punishment, however ineffective it may be in rehabilitating offenders. It is indispensable as a reinforcement of responsibility, no matter how dismal its treatment record or brutish its methods. We must forgive its ineffectiveness for the sake of its crucial symbolic value. The "destructuralists," today's visionaries, are less programmatic and more idealistic. They claim that order overwhelms and stultifies humanity, and to reawaken moral ideals in society, order must be sacrificed.

My approach to this issue concedes the importance of juvenile justice as a symbol of responsibility, but I locate the failures of juvenile justice not simply in compromise with routine, nor in the fallibilities of its pio-

---

From *Crime and Delinquency*, Volume 37, Number 2 (April 1991), pp. 202-224. Copyright © 1991 by Sage Publications, Inc. Reprinted by permission.

neers, but in the conflicts that different approaches have built into juvenile justice over the years. We must probe the sources of juvenile justice's ailments in the 19th century, if we ever hope to understand their essential nature and correct them.

The 19th Century Origins of Juvenile Justice

During the Jacksonian era industrialization took firm root in several American cities. As trade with Europe, the Caribbean, and other American cities flourished, as new factories for spinning yam and weaving cloth were built, and as new schools opened, employment grew more plentiful. The slow drift of population to centers of commerce and industry grew very quickly to sizable proportions in the northeast, and several American cities began to encounter adolescent misbehavior and waywardness in a variety of forms (see, for example, Ferdinand 1989, pp. 94-97). Not only were wayward children nuisances on the city's streets, but when convicted of crimes in the criminal courts, they were sometimes sent to adult prisons where they mixed with hardened convicts and became career criminals.

But unless wayward children were criminals, the criminal courts had no jurisdiction over them. A convenient doctrine—*parens patriae*—however, enabled the civil courts to step in and take custody of these wayward or dependent children. The criminal law served for those children who had violated the criminal code, but for those who were merely beyond control, or whose parents were negligent, *parens patriae* sufficed. The child's first responsibility was to obey his or her parents, and the nascent juvenile justice system awaited those few who steadfastly rejected parental authority.

Furthermore, in many eastern cities bold plans for compulsory education were underway (see Schultz 1973). On the eve of the industrial revolution in 1789 Boston authorities established a system of free grammar schools, and in 1821 the city opened its first public high school, Boston English High. By 1826 Boston's school system enrolled a majority of its school-aged children (Kaestle and Vinovskis 1980).

These new schools represented a second arena wherein many children were held accountable. Just as children who were beyond parental control and roamed the city at night could not be ignored, so too children who disrupted school or truanted needed to be held in check. *Parens patriae* was applicable here as well, because the children were in school for their own well being. The schools' problem children became a second concern for the nascent juvenile justice system.

In short as compulsory education and industrialization swept America's cities in the 19th century, they produced a growing troop of wayward, incorrigible children who resisted in one fashion or another the efforts of society to shape them for adulthood. Something like a juvenile justice system was needed to bolster the authority of the family and the school in industrializing America so that both could be more effective in socializing young people. The juvenile justice system, as it emerged, represented the community's attempt to come to grips with a new social status: the juvenile.

At first the effort was limited to the major cities where education and economic development were centered, but soon it spread to entire states as whole regions were developed. The juvenile was expected to be obedient to both parents and teachers, and if he refused, he was held liable by the courts. The juvenile justice system was basically a sociolegal institution for holding juveniles accountable and for strengthening both the family and the school as they adapted to the changing social order.[1]

Recently John Sutton (1988) uncovered evidence that strongly confirms this view of the relationship between emerging school systems and juvenile justice. He investigated the impact of growing school enrollments on the introduction of juvenile reformatories in the latter half of the 19th century and found it more powerful than either industrialization or the growth of government. According to Sutton (1988, p. 114), "from 1850 to 1880, a 1-percent increase in school attendance is associated with a 13-percent increase in adoption rates (of juvenile reformatories)."

As a concept of the juvenile emerged, the juveniles' parents and teachers were responsible for them, and they were expected to obey both. *Parens patriae* was the relevant legal doctrine, because it allowed the state to intervene when either the family or the school was deficient. Because *parens patriae* was available only in the civil courts, juvenile delinquency was lodged in that jurisdiction. It covered all but the major criminal offenses by juveniles, which were still handled in the criminal courts.

Under *parens patriae* the civil courts acted in behalf of the child against ineffective parents or the child himself and provided dispositions that a responsible parent would. If the parents could control the child, the courts accepted them as the proper guardian. For the most part, state appellate courts endorsed this mission for the court, (see, for example, *Ex parte Crouse* 1838; *In re* Ferrier 1882; *Commonwealth v. Fisher* 1905; Garlock 1979, p. 399).

The civil courts still could not deal with juveniles who violated the criminal law, and many communities continued to send serious juvenile offenders to the criminal courts. Although most were sent to juvenile facilities upon conviction, some were still sent to adult institutions (see Garlock 1979, Appendix).

Several facts stand out regarding the juvenile justice system up to 1899. First, it consisted of a very diverse collection of private and public institutions and community programs including probation for minor delinquents and status offenders, all served by the civil court and its doctrine of *parens patriae*. A survey (see Mennel 1973, p. 49) of 30 juvenile reform schools conducted in 1880, for example, found an extraordinary heterogeneity. Six accepted children convicted of crimes punishable by imprisonment, and 14 took children who had committed minor offenses. Thirteen schools specialized in children rebelling against parental authority; seven accepted mainly neglected or deserted children; and five dealt with children committed by their parents for various reasons.[2] Coordination among such a diverse group of custodial institutions and the civil courts must have been difficult, indeed. Second, the civil court with its doctrine of *parens patriae* provided moral leadership within the system. But its authority was at best exhortatory and informal. It had little control over the staffing, budgets, practices, or objectives of the far flung juvenile programs it served.

Third, this system was kept largely separate from the criminal justice system. Juvenile miscreants who warranted a criminal court hearing by virtue of serious offending were handled as adults. The rest were handled by the civil court and sent to juvenile facilities. In the 19th century a bifurcated justice system handled a bifurcated population of juvenile offenders. The early juvenile justice system neatly avoided today's complexity in which serious offenders are handled along with minor offenders in a single, *parens patriae* system.

This system was the result of separate initiatives at several different levels of government over the better part of a century. Even though most juvenile facilities were guided at first by a *parens patriae* philosophy, the system had no central authority that could impose a focus or common mission on the whole. Without a central organizing authority, however, the system was left to respond as local conditions dictated. And it continues today to embrace a growing variety of public and private facilities (Sutton 1990, pp. 1369-70).

Moreover, as the 19th century drew to a close, it was becoming clear that the civil courts could not handle the sheer volume of juvenile cases coming into the system. As early as the Civil War, for example, the mass of juveniles arrested in Boston was already large, and the same was true of other eastern cities as well.

During the 1820s and early 1830s very few juveniles were charged with serious offenses in Boston's felony court—the municipal court. But by 1850 indictments had grown in the municipal court to 220 per 10,000 juveniles (Ferdinand 1989, Figure 2) and were the fastest growing component in Boston's crime problem. Furthermore, between 1849 to 1850 and 1861 to 1862 the arrest rate for juveniles rose 479% from 506 to 2,932 per 10,000 juveniles (Ferdinand 1989, Figure 3).[3] After the Civil War, juvenile arrests in Boston receded somewhat from the high rates of the Civil War period (Ferdinand 1989, Figure 3). Still, from 1870 to 1900 they ranged between 7,900 and 11,200 arrests annually.

This sizable flow of juvenile cases no doubt strengthened the argument that juveniles needed a specialized court—a court that was attuned to their special needs. First, they needed a judge who was familiar with the social psychological nuances of family conflict as well as the legal complexities of family/child problems. They needed a legal doctrine that took into account their social deficits as well as their misbehavior. Juveniles also needed a court whose officers were closely familiar with the range of facilities available for troubled children and could assign each to a program that was geared to his or her own needs....

The New Juvenile Court

In 1899 the Illinois legislature enacted the first juvenile code and established, in Chicago, the first juvenile court. Its jurisdiction extended to virtually all juveniles—serious criminal offenders, status offenders, and neglected and dependent children. It embraced a much wider jurisdiction than the 19th century juvenile justice system ever had. Nevertheless, its mandate was to deal with all of them by means of *parens patriae*.

Several contemporary observers commented on the new court's usefulness. The new court gave custodial institutions "the legal status and powers that they have most stood in need of" and "in large cities juvenile courts are little more than clearing houses to get together the boy or girl that needs help and the agencies that will do the most good" (Sutton 1988, p. 143). It gave authority to social services, it provided intelligent assessments of juveniles, and it assigned them to programs that were closely related to their needs. It offered a specialized knowledge of and commitment to juveniles and their needs that the old civil courts could never provide.

In their enthusiasm, however, the reformers failed to ask whether serious offenders with criminal intent were appropriate subjects for a *parens patriae* court.[4] Furthermore, the new court did little to unify the juvenile justice system. It was still a very loose collection of programs and facilities with no central direction.

Despite these defects the remaining states quickly followed Illinois' example, and 30 states had established juvenile courts by 1920. By 1945 all had. The juvenile justice system was separate from the adult system. *Parens patriae* was the philosophic foundation of the court, and many if not most of its facilities and programs subscribed to that perspective....

Parens Patriae and Fairness

Shortly after World War II the critique of the juvenile court got underway with Paul Tappan's (1946) keen analysis of the court's due process failures. Tappan, a legally trained criminologist, pointed out that many constitutional rights of juveniles were ignored in the *parens patriae* juvenile court.

Others took up the same complaint (see Allen 1964 and Caldwell 1961). They noted that the court's therapeutic measures, even when sincerely applied, often turned out to be worse than routine punishments. It was not unusual in the 1960s to find that status offenders were punished more severely than all but the most serious delinquents (see Creekmore 1976; Cohn 1963; and Terry 1967), and racial discrimination in the juvenile court, though not found in some courts, was all too common (see Thornberry 1973; and Fagan, Slaughter, and Hartstone 1987; but see also Rubin 1985, pp. 203-5; Cohen 1976, pp. 51-54; and Dungworth 1977).[5] Such flagrant violations of equal protection under the law were intolerable especially in the charged atmosphere of the 1960s and 1970s.

A Growing Demand for Reform

In addition to Tappan's early criticism of the court's due process lapses and the discovery of racial and gender biases, steady reports of scandalous conditions in state training schools began to surface (see Rothman 1980, pp. 268-86 and Deutsch 1950). The need for reform in juvenile justice was inescapable, and the response took several forms.

First, the states attempted to cope with difficulties inherent in combining serious and minor offenders in the same system by separating status offenders from delinquents in confinement and later, by removing most of them (status offenders) from the juvenile court's jurisdiction. California differentiated delinquents and status offenders in its original juvenile statute, and in 1962 New York passed a Family Court Act, which among other things distinguished status offenders (renamed PINS) from delinquents. In 1973 the New York Court of Appeals ruled in *In re* Ellery (1973) that the policy of confining PINS with delinquents in an institution was unconstitutional, although in 1974 in *In re* Lavette (1974) the same court ruled that PINS could be confined in facilities organized for PINS.

In the decades that followed many states enacted similar statutes, separating status offenders and delinquents both in definition and treatment, and by the late 1970s many had gone even further by making court-ordered treatment plans for status offenders voluntary. Such children had committed no criminal offense and legally did not deserve custodial confinement.

Juvenile justice in the United States seemed to be following a path charted in Scandinavia in which problem juveniles under 22 years of age are treated voluntarily in social agencies, and serious offenders after 15 years of age are handled in the criminal courts (see Samecki 1988). Such a plan often fails, however, in that it permits status offenders to respond with either a "political" compliance to treatment suggestions or an impulsive rejection of them.

The Failures of Treatment

At the same time ambiguities surrounding the rehabilitative approach spurred the federal government to sponsor a host of delinquency prevention projects. In the mid-1960s under the impetus of President Lyndon Johnson's War on Poverty, a major effort to prevent delinquency and rehabilitate delinquents was undertaken by the Office of Economic Opportunity. As a centerpiece the War on Poverty mounted a massive preventive program on the Lower East Side of Manhattan—Mobilization for Youth. It was modeled after the Chicago Area Projects and addressed the problems of preschool children, juveniles, gangs, schools, and community adults. But it was too broad and complex to evaluate, and we will never know as with the Chicago Area Projects whether this community approach to delinquency prevention was effective.[6]

More specialized programs dealing with distinctive facets of delinquency were also fielded in Boston, Chicago, and elsewhere. Studies of innovative juvenile programs were funded in Michigan, Massachusetts, and Utah, and community-based treatment programs in California were generously supported. The federal government in conjunction with the Ford Foundation and other private groups sought to determine whether juvenile justice could remedy its ills.

Sentiment for reform of the juvenile justice system was strong, but the direction of reform was still hotly debated. Should it focus on predelinquents with the idea of keeping them out of the juvenile justice system, should it reform the court itself, or should it concentrate on juvenile institutions? Much hinged on the outcome of the War on Poverty programs, and millions of dollars were spent to insure that sound methods and skilled researchers were used. But to nearly everyone's dismay, few if any initiatives were effective. In the 1960s the detached worker program investigated by Walter Miller (1962) in Boston and later in Los Angeles by Malcolm Klein (1971) were worse than ineffective. Klein found that in Los Angeles detached workers actually made delinquency worse. Gerald Robin (1969) evaluated the Neighborhood Youth Corps and its attempts to provide counseling, remedial education, and supervised work for juveniles in both Cincinnati and Detroit. He found no positive effect in either program. . . .

The Crisis in Juvenile Justice

The conclusion that treatment does not work seemed to strike a chord in the nation at large, and the advantage swung quickly to those who favored a retributive approach to delinquency. Criminologists had been arguing for decades as to the causes of delinquency and the best methods of treatment. This quarrel was more basic and more serious.

The evidence was by no means unequivocal, but the fact that a retributive response was so widely endorsed suggests that something much deeper was responsible. No doubt a general disillusionment with professionalism and government was a factor as well as the conservative views of the Nixon and Reagan administrations.

If the juvenile court could not provide wholesome treatment for juveniles under its care, it seemed to imply that the *parens patriae* court was discredited. *Parens patriae* was a noble idea, but if the juvenile court could not act effectively as a parent, the least it could do was act effectively as a court by finding guilt justly and by administering punishments fairly. In effect the juvenile court and *parens patriae* were held hostage to the ineffectiveness of community and institutional treatment programs in rehabilitating delinquents!

Why Do Treatment Programs Fail?

As we have seen, the juvenile court has never had much influence over treatment programs, whether in custodial institutions or in the community, because both were almost always organized by independent agencies. The one program the court did control, probation, has been effective in helping delinquents regain their social composure. In effect the juvenile court and *parens patriae* have been evaluated not only in terms of their relevance to the needs of juveniles, but also in terms of their ability to guide the rest of the juvenile justice system along the path of treatment.

The critics of the *parens patriae* court expected it to impose its rehabilitative mission on the rest of juvenile justice despite its very limited ability to shape therapeutic programs whether in the community or in custodial institutions. It was doomed from the start by the contradiction between its mission and its limited authority.

The *parens patriae* court did not fail. The state failed, because it enacted a *parens patriae* court without providing solid support for community and institutional treatment programs. True, state programs, first as individual juvenile institutions and then more recently as systems of state juvenile facilities, have been established, some even predating the juvenile court. But these programs had as their first objective the confinement of juveniles in large institutions where custodial policies and attitudes soon dominated (see Schlossman 1977; Brenzel 1983; Pisciotta 1985). Rehabilitation, though used effectively as a public relations device, was almost always a secondary consideration with these state-based programs. Rarely has a state agency had any responsibility for funding and detecting treatment programs in the community for delinquents. . . .

A Proposal

It would seem that the solution to the problem of effective treatment programs is straightforward. A continuing public authority is needed with responsibility for treatment programs both in the community and in juvenile institutions.[7] Where it should be situated in the hierarchy of state services to juveniles, or the scope and details of its responsibilities to delinquents need not concern us here. Whether it should be an independent department, part of the Department of Social Services, or the Department of Juvenile Corrections and Parole is not at issue at this point. Its mission should be treatment, and it should be in effect the court's rehabilitative arm, just as juvenile corrections is the court's custodial arm.[8]

Treatment programs for juveniles with psychological or social needs are as essential in civil society as unemployment insurance is for adults. Many juveniles need wise, skilled help in making a sound adjustment in adolescence, but unfortunately many cannot get such help from their families or anyone else, and to deny them by abandoning treatment programs is in effect cruel and socially destructive.

Treatment has worked only haphazardly because it has not been championed consistently by experienced agencies with roots in local communities. Where such agencies have emerged, as in Massachusetts during 1972 in the Department of Youth Services and in Utah during 1981 in the Division of Youth Corrections, the results have been generally humane and effective.[9]

Massachusetts under the Department of Youth Services has been using a system of community-based treatment programs for its delinquents since 1972 with solid results (see Loughran 1987). On any given day its youthful clients number about 1,700. Some 1,000 youths live at home and participate in a wide variety of treatment and educational community programs. The remaining children, 700, are divided between foster homes (30), nonsecure residential programs (500), and secure facilities (170). Serious offenders are dealt with via careful screening for violent tendencies, emotional stability, threat to the community, and social needs and are given programming specially designed for their situation.

The results in Massachusetts have been noteworthy (Miller and Ohlin 1985; Krisberg, Austin, and Steele 1989). In the beginning budgetary costs of caring for children via a system of community-based treatment programs were slightly more than for the old network of custodial institutions (Coates, Miller and Ohlin 1976, Chapters 7, 8). However, the two systems were compared as of 1974, after only 2 years experience under the new system. More recently the system has become more effective, and today the annual cost per child in the Department of Youth Services (DYS) is about $23,000 compared with $35,000-40,000 reported by many other states (Krisberg, Austin, and Steele, 1989, pp. 32-37). . . .

The twin goals of rehabilitation and justice can be blended effectively in the juvenile justice system. If dependable diagnostic and treatment programs can be made available to juvenile judges via a state treatment authority, justice in adjudication can be balanced with humane, effective treatment in dispositions.

Bifurcation: A Stumbling Block?

A difficult problem still remains. The history of juvenile justice confirms that secure facilities tend to become more punitive with age. Since the time of the houses of refuge, custodial institutions have shown a clear custodial drift with time (Ferdinand 1989, pp. 87-93).

According to Cohen (1985, pp. 218-35) institutions tend to differentiate themselves into custodial, punitive, exclusionary programs and rehabilitative, community-based, inclusionary programs. Cohen saw this bifurcation as paralleling a bifurcation of the system's clientele. On one hand, we have a small stream of stigmatized, antisocial offenders committed to a criminal way of life. On the other, we have a large stream of tractable but problem-bound offenders who want to become contributing citizens. Punitive, exclusionary programs serve the former and transform them into hardened, predatory criminals who are feared and shunned by the community. Inclusionary programs serve constructive offenders who are still looking for a rewarding life in mainstream society. Many of them, however, become agency-dependent and socially peripheral (see Ferdinand 1989).

According to Cohen (1985, Chapter 7) inclusionary programs themselves become punitive and stigmatizing and are transformed thereby into exclusionary programs by virtue of the fact that newly established programs draw off the best clientele from older programs, leaving them to deal mainly with intractable inmates. As older programs adapt to a deteriorating population mix, they change slowly into punitive centers. Inclusionary programs gradually become exclusionary programs, and a long term pattern of institutional decay is established as the system repeatedly attempts to reform itself by reaching out to more responsive populations and relegating the rest to older, established programs.

Although Cohen was interested primarily in the adult system, he describes almost exactly the century-long development of juvenile justice in the United States (Ferdinand 1989). The houses of refuge were greeted enthusiastically by reform-minded progressives, only to see them transformed into punitive, stigmatizing institutions over the years (Brenzel 1983; Pisciotta 1982). The same was true of the state juvenile reformatories established in the last half of the 19th century (Rothman 1980; Schlossman 1977).

Ultimately, the juvenile correctional system in many states came to resemble a hierarchical system (see Steele and Jacobs 1975, 1977) of punitive, exclusionary institutions at the deep end (the maximum-security level) serving predatory, antisocial inmates, coupled with inclusionary, community-based programs at the shallow end serving a social tractable clientele with more focused problems. As each new program came on stream, it attracted the most promising clientele and the most progressive staff, and the rest were forced to adapt as best they could in the ensuing realignment.

An answer to this repetitive pattern of reform and decay, however, is not difficult to imagine. New programs need not focus on just the more tractable, responsive clientele. They could focus also on the other end—on the more serious, predatory offenders. After all, these are the offenders that spell the most trouble for society in the long run, and any advances in dealing with their problems would certainly be helpful. In this case the older programs would be asked to give up some of their *least* responsive inmates; their inmate mix would improve with each reform at the deep end; and one source of custodial drift, at least, would be arrested. . . .

Conclusion

Few maintain that juvenile justice has lived up to its promise in the United States, and many assert that its future lies basically with a due process/just deserts orientation. If treatment and rehabilitation are abandoned, however, in favor of a just deserts policy whereby serious delinquents are punished in large, custodial institutions, several untoward consequences would probably result.

First, delinquency would deepen in seriousness and expand its sway, laying the foundation for a worsening problem among adult predatory criminals in the years ahead. Second, an important voice for humane programs in the justice system would be stilled with the result that a monolithic retributive system and its programs would prevail not only in delinquency but in criminal justice as a whole.

The difficulties of treating juveniles in residential centers are, however, soluble. Differentiated systems of small, community based treatment facilities in both Massachusetts and Utah have shown themselves as more humane; comparable in cost; and more effective than the traditional network of juvenile custodial institutions. A permanent state agency committed to delinquency treatment programs would be a more responsible manager over the long term than the haphazard collection of private philanthropy, correctional departments, and federal agencies that have spearheaded most treatment reforms in the states up to now.

State departments of treatment services for delinquents also need research arms that can evaluate their programs with an eye to weeding out those programs that are ineffective. They need detailed information on their programs to represent the rehabilitation philosophy to state government and the mass media. The people of a state must ultimately choose the direction that is best for them, but they must be fully informed of the alternatives.

If such departments were available at the state level, it would give an immense lift to the juvenile court. This court has long pursued *parens patriae* in the community but with uncertain success and lately with waning confidence. A department of treatment services could provide both the variety in community programming and political support that the court needs to carry out its mission effectively.

The juvenile court cannot be both classification agent and programs agent for the rehabilitative process. It was never given a mandate to sponsor community-based treatment programs. The court is reasonably effective as a juvenile classification and assignment agency, but it needs an effective right arm to create and evaluate treatment programs throughout the state geared to local needs. Local juvenile courts working hand in glove with a state department of treatment services could finally realize the full potential of *parens patriae*.

To improve the juvenile court it is important to strengthen its links with the rest of the system, especially with those agencies that sponsor treatment programs. Up to now responsibility for these programs has been left mainly to custodial or private initiatives. Without a concept of the system as a whole reform of the court inevitably focuses on inappropriate remedies, and the situation of delinquents only deteriorates. If the failure to rehabilitate juveniles lies with juvenile custodial facilities, reform should focus there and not solely on the *parens patriae* mandate of the court. Historical analysis can pinpoint the sources of the court's difficulties and thereby suggest appropriate lines of reform. Without such analyses our efforts will remain limited by ideological blinders and our reforms will decay as usual into tomorrow's problems.

Notes

1. It is interesting that as the juvenile court's jurisdiction over status offending has eroded in the last 30 years, runaways and school misbehavior have grown dramatically (see Gough 1977, pp. 283-87; Shane 1989). Although other factors have been active in this arena, the court's abandonment of status offenders may have contributed to the reemergence of these problems in the modern era.
2. Overlap among these schools accounts for the fact that their sum is much more than 30.
3. These figures were computed from statistics issued by the Boston Police Department and by the U.S. Bureau of the Census. The population data for 1860 were gathered during an especially turbulent period, and may have missed a substantial portion of the transient population including juveniles. Thus delinquency arrest rates for that period may be overestimated.
4. In this sense the new court was a step back from the old civil court, because it handled both the most hardened, serious offenders in the same way as minor status offenders.
5. There is no room in juvenile justice for racial or gender bias, but most studies of bias have ignored an important fact that throws new light on the problem. Because the community (parents, school officials, and neighbors) enjoys a wide discretion in defining juvenile offending, an officer's decision to make an arrest, or a court's decision to detain a juvenile depends heavily on the biases of the complainant (see Hazard 1976; and Black and Reiss 1970). Where a biased victim demands action against a minority juvenile, chances are good that the police or the court will comply. A dismissal is difficult, if a complainant seeking a punishment is close at hand. Thomas and Cage (1977) found in a study of more than 1,500 juveniles that their sanctioning in court was more severe if someone close to the case was pushing it.
6. Earlier the renowned Chicago Area Projects initiated by Henry Shaw and Clifford McKay in the 1930s probably had been successful, even though a failure to use an experimental design rendered a definitive statement as to their successes impossible (see also Schlossman and Sedlak 1983).
7. We might call this authority the Department of Youth Services. Many states have a Department of Family Services that serves nondelinquent children, and the Department of Youth Services would offer many of the same programs for delinquents and children at risk of delinquency. It would coordinate its efforts with the juvenile courts, just as juvenile corrections does. Three state agencies, therefore, would provide social services to adolescents: Juvenile Corrections, which manages custodial institutions for juveniles; the Department of Youth Services, which manages the treatment effort for juvenile delinquents; and the Department of Family Services, which manages the treatment function for nondelinquent youth. Further consolidation of these three agencies need not be ruled out.
8. Some will say, "The state has already proved its ineptness in programs for youth. It does not deserve a second chance." My response is, if that is true, the *only* alternative is the status quo, that is, a due process court and punitive juvenile institutions. Rehabilitating delinquents is too important to abandon simply because the state has stumbled in its efforts to fulfill *parens patriae*. If we can understand some of the reasons behind the state's ineptness, for example, a primary commitment to security in facilities, we can correct them.

9. Youth Services Bureaus, an offspring of Lyndon Johnson's 1960s campaign against delinquency, represented a similar effort to bring treatment programs together under a single community agency. They were locally financed and suffered budget problems in many small cities, and they often differed with judges as to what delinquents needed.

References

Allen, Francis A. 1964. *The Borderland of Criminal Justice*. Chicago: University of Chicago Press.

Andrews, D.A., Ivan Zinger, Robert D. Hodge, James Bonta, Paul Gendreau, and Francis T. Cullen. 1990. "Does Correctional Treatment Work? A Clinically Relevant and Psychologically Informed Meta-Analysis." *Criminology* 28:369-404.

Black, Donald J. and Albert J. Reiss, Jr. 1970. "Police Control of Juveniles." *American Sociological Review* 15(February):63-77.

Brenzel, Barbara M. 1983. *Daughters of the State*. Cambridge: MIT Press.

Caldwell, R.G. 1961. "The Juvenile Court: Its Development and Some Major Problems." *Journal of Criminal Law, Criminology, and Police Science* 51:493-511.

Coates, Robert B., Alden D. Miller, and Loyd E. Ohlin. 1976. *Diversity on a Youth Correctional System*. Cambridge: Ballinger.

Cohen, Lawrence E. 1976. *Delinquency Dispositions: An Empirical Analysis of Processing Decisions in Three Juvenile Courts*. National Criminal Justice Information and Statistics Service, Law Enforcement Assistance Administration. Washington, DC: U.S. Government Printing Office.

Cohen, Stanley. 1985. *Visions of Social Control*. Cambridge: Polity Press.

Cohn, Yona. 1963. "Criteria for Probation Officers' Recommendations to the Juvenile Court." *Crime and Delinquency* 1:267-75.

Commonwealth v. Fisher 213 Pa. 48, 1905.

Creekmore, Mark. 1976. "Case Processing: Intake, Adjudication, and Disposition." Pp. 119-51 in *Brought to Justice? Juveniles, the Courts, and the Law*, edited by Rosemary Sarri and Yeheskel Hasenfeld. Ann Arbor: University of Michigan.

Deutsch, Albert. 1950. *Our Rejected Children*. Boston: Little, Brown.

Diana, Lewis. 1955. "Is Casework in Probation Necessary?" *Focus* 34(January):1-8.

Dungworth, Terrence. 1977. "Discretion in the Juvenile Justice System: The Impact of Case Characteristics on Prehearing Detention." Pp. 19-43 in *Little Brother Grows Up*, edited by Theodore N. Ferdinand. Beverly Hills, CA: Sage.

Empey, Lamar and Steven G. Lubeck. 1971. *Silverlake Experiment: Testing Delinquency Theory and Community Intervention*. Chicago: Aldine Press.

Empey, Lamar and Maynard Erickson. 1972. *The Provo Experiment: Evaluating Community Control of Delinquency*. Lexington, MA: Lexington Books.

Ex parte Crouse, 4 Whart. 9, Pa. 1838.

Fagan, Jeffery, Ellen Slaughter, and Eliot Hartstone. 1987. "Blind Justice? The Impact of Race on the Juvenile Justice Process." *Crime and Delinquency* 33:224-58.

Ferdinand, Theodore N. 1989. "Juvenile Delinquency or Juvenile Justice: Which Came First?" *Criminology* 27:79-106.

Foucault, Michel. 1979. *Discipline and Punish*. New York: Vintage Books.

Garlock, Peter D. 1979. "'Wayward' Children and the Law, 1820-1900: The Genesis of the Status Offense Jurisdiction of the Juvenile Court." *Georgia Law Review* 13:341-448.

Gough, Aidan R. 1977. "Beyond Control Youth in the Juvenile Court—the Climate for Change." Pp. 271-296 in *Beyond Control: Status Offenders in the Juvenile Court*, edited by Lee F. Teitelbaum and Aidan R. Gough. Cambridge, MA: Ballinger.

Hazard, Geoffrey C., Jr. 1976. "The Jurisprudence of Juvenile Deviance." Pp. 3-19 in *Pursuing Justice for the Child*, edited by Margaret K. Rosenheim. Chicago: University of Chicago Press.

In re Ellery C., 347 N.Y. 2d 51 1973.

In re Ferrier, 103 Ill. 367, 1882.

In re Lavette M., 359 N.Y. 2d 201, 1974.

Kaestle, Carl F. and Maris A. Vinovskis. 1980. *Education and Change*. London: Cambridge University Press.

Klein, Malcolm. 1971. *Street Gangs and Street Workers*. Englewood Cliffs, NJ: Prentice-Hall.

Kobrin, Solomon and Malcolm Klein. 1983. *Community Treatment of Juvenile Offenders*. Beverly Hills, CA: Sage.

Krisberg, Barry, James Austin, and Patricia A. Steele. 1989. *Unlocking Juvenile Corrections: Evaluating the Massachusetts Department of Youth Services*. San Francisco: National Council on Crime and Delinquency.

Lerman, Paul. 1975. *Community Treatment and Control*. Chicago: University of Chicago Press.

Lipsey, Mark W. 1991. "Juvenile Delinquency Treatment: A Meta-Analytic Inquiry into the Variability of Effects." *Meta-Analysis for Explanation: A Casebook*. New York: Russell Sage Foundation.

Loughran, Edward J. 1987. "Juvenile Corrections: The Massachusetts Experience." Pp. 7-18 in *Reinvesting in Youth Corrections Resources: A Tale of Three States*, edited by Lee Eddison. Ann Arbor: School of Social Work, University of Michigan.

Martinson, Robert. 1974. "What Works—Questions and Answers About Prison Reform." *Public Interest* 32:22-54.

Massachusetts Department of Youth Services. 1987. "Annual Report 1986," pp. 1-16. Boston: Author.

Mennel, Robert M. 1973. *Thorns and Thistles*. Hanover, NH: University Press of New England.

Miller, Alden D. and Loyd E. Ohlin. 1985. *Delinquency and Community*. Beverly Hills, CA: Sage.

Miller, Walter. 1962. "The Impact of a 'Total-Community' Delinquency Control Project." *Social Problems* 10:168-91.

Palmer, Ted. 1974. "The Youth Authority Community Treatment Project." *Federal Probation* 38:3-14.

Pisciotta, Alexander W. 1982. "Saving the Children: The Promise and Practice of *Parens Patriae*, 1838-1898." *Crime and Delinquency* 28:410-25.

———. 1985. "Treatment on Trial: The Rhetoric and Reality of the New York House of Refuge, 1857-1935." *American Journal of Legal History* 29:151-81.

Robin, Gerald N. 1969. "Anti-Poverty Programs and Delinquency." *Journal of Criminal Law, Criminology, and Police Science* 60:327.

Rothman, David J. 1980. *Conscience and Convenience*. Boston: Little, Brown.

Rubin, H. Ted. 1985. *Juvenile Justice*, 2nd ed. New York: Random House.

Sarnecki, Jerzy. 1988. *Juvenile Delinquency in Sweden*. Stockholm: National Council for Crime Prevention, Information Division.

Scarpitti, Frank R. and Richard M. Stephenson. 1968. "A Study of Probation Effectiveness." *Journal of Criminal Law, Criminology, and Police Science* 3:361-69.

Schlossman, Steven L. 1977. *Love and the American Delinquent*. Chicago: University of Chicago Press.

Schlossman, Steven L. and Michael Sedlak. 1983. "The Chicago Area Project Revisited." *Crime and Delinquency* 29:398-462.

Schultz, Stanley K. 1973. *The Culture Factory: Boston Public Schools, 1789-1860*. New York: Oxford University Press.

Shane, Paul G. 1989. "Changing Patterns of Homelessness and Runaway Youth." *American Journal of Orthopsychiatry* 59:208-14.

Simon, Cindy and Julie Fagan. 1987. "Youth Corrections in Utah: Remaking a System." *National Conference of State Legislatures* 12:1-12.

Steele, Eric H. and James B. Jacobs. 1975. "A Theory of Prison Systems." *Crime and Delinquency* 21:149-62.

———. 1977. "Untangling Minimum Security: Concepts, Realities, and Implications for Correctional Systems." *Journal of Research in Crime and Delinquency* 14:68-83.

Street, David, Robert D. Vinter, and Charles Perrow. 1966. *Organization for Treatment*. New York: Free Press.

Sutton, John R. 1988. *Stubborn Children*. Berkeley,: University of California Press.

———. 1990. "Bureaucrats and Entrepreneurs: Institutional Responses to Deviant Children, 1890-1920s." *American Journal of Sociology* 95:1367-1400.

Tappan, Paul. 1946. "Treatment Without Trial?" *Social Problems* 24:306-311.

Terry, Robert. 1967. "Discrimination in the Police Handling of Juvenile Offenders by Social Control Agencies." *Journal of Research in Crime and Delinquency* 4:212-20.

Thomas, Charles W. and Robin J. Cage. 1977. "The Effects of Social Characteristics on Juvenile Court Dispositions." *Sociological Quarterly* 18:237-52.

Thornberry, Terence P. 1973. "Race, Socioeconomic Status and Sentencing in the Juvenile Justice System." *Journal of Criminal Law and Criminology* 64:90-98.

Utah State Division of Corrections. 1986. "Planning Task Force Final Report." Salt Lake City, December.

Warren, Marguerite. 1976. "Intervention with Juvenile Delinquents." Pp. 176-204 in *Pursuing Justice for the Child*, edited by Margaret K. Rosenheim. Chicago: University of Chicago Press. ✦

42
Juvenile (In)Justice and the Criminal Court Alternative

Barry C. Feld

The Supreme Court's decision in *In re Gault* (1967) began transforming the juvenile court into a very different institution than the Progressives contemplated. Progressive reformers envisioned an informal court whose dispositions reflected the "best interests" of the child. The Supreme Court engrafted formal procedures at trial onto juvenile courts' individualized treatment sentencing schema. Although the Court's decisions were not intended to alter the juvenile courts' therapeutic mission, legislative, judicial, and administrative responses to *Gault* have modified the courts' jurisdiction, purpose, and procedures (Feld 1984, 1988b). The substantive and procedural convergence between juvenile and criminal courts eliminates most of the conceptual and operational differences between social control strategies for youths and adults. With its transformation from an informal, rehabilitative agency into a scaled-down, second-class criminal court, is there any reason to maintain a separate punitive juvenile court whose only distinction is its persisting procedural deficiencies?

Three types of reforms—jurisdictional, jurisprudential, and procedural—reveal the transformation of the contemporary juvenile court (Feld 1991b). Recognizing that juvenile courts often failed to realize their benevolent purposes has led to two jurisdictional changes. Status offenses are misconduct by juveniles, such as truancy or incorrigibility, that would not be a crime if

committed by an adult. Recent reforms limit the dispositions that noncriminal offenders may receive or even remove status offenses from juvenile court jurisdiction. A second jurisdictional change is the criminalizing of serious juvenile offenders. Increasingly, courts and legislatures transfer some youths from juvenile courts to criminal courts for prosecution as adults (Feld 1987). As jurisdiction contracts with the removal of serious offenders and noncriminal status offenders, the sentences received by delinquents charged with crimes are based on the idea of just deserts rather than their "real needs." Proportional and determinate sentences based on the present offense and prior record, rather than the best interests of the child, dictate the length, location, and intensity of intervention (Feld 1988b). Increased emphasis on formal procedures at trial has accompanied the enhanced role of punishment in sentencing juveniles (Feld 1984). Although, theoretically, juvenile courts' procedures closely resemble those of criminal courts, in reality, the justice routinely afforded juveniles is lower than the minimum insisted upon for adults.

The Progressive Juvenile Court

Prior to the creation of the juvenile court, the only special protections received by youths charged with crimes were those afforded by the common law's infancy *mens rea* defense, which conclusively presumed that children less than 7 years old lacked criminal capacity, those 14 years old or older were responsible, and those between 7 years old and 14 years old were rebuttably irresponsible (Fox 1970b). Changes in the cultural conception of children and in strategies of social control during the 19th century led to the creation of the juvenile court (Fox 1970a; Feld 1991b). By the end of the century, children increasingly were seen as vulnerable, innocent, passive, and dependent beings who needed extended preparation for life (Ainsworth 1991; Sutton 1988). The ideology of crime causation changed, as positivistic criminology, which regarded crime as determined rather than chosen, superseded classical explanations that attributed crime to free-willed actors

(Allen 1981). Attributing criminal behavior to antecedent causes reduced offenders' moral responsibility, focused efforts on reforming rather than punishing them, and fostered the "rehabilitative ideal." At the dawn of the 20th century, Progressive reformers used the new theories of social control and the new ideas about childhood to create a social welfare alternative to criminal courts to treat criminal and noncriminal misconduct by youths.

By redefining social control, Progressive reformers removed children from the adult criminal system and achieved greater flexibility and supervision of children (Platt 1977; Sutton 1988). Progressives envisioned the juvenile court as a welfare agency in which an expert judge, assisted by social workers and probation officers, made individualized dispositions in a child's best interests (Rothman 1980). The inquiry into the "whole" child accorded minor significance to crime because the specific offense indicated little about a child's real needs. They maximized discretion to provide flexibility in diagnosis and treatment and focused on the child's character and lifestyle. Because juvenile courts separated children from adults and provided an alternative to punishment, they rejected procedural safeguards of criminal law such as juries and lawyers. Informal procedures, euphemistic vocabularies, confidential and private hearings, limited access to court records, and findings of "delinquency" eliminated any stigma or implication of a criminal proceeding. Indeterminate, nonproportional dispositions continued for the duration of the minority, because each child's "treatment" needs differed and no limits could be defined in advance. . . .

Transformation of the Juvenile Court: Reformed but not Rehabilitated

Gault (1967), *Winship* (1970), and *McKeiver* (1970) precipitated a procedural and substantive revolution in juvenile justice that unintentionally but inevitably transformed its Progressive conception. By emphasizing criminal procedural regularity in determining delinquency and formalizing the connection between crime and sentence, the Court made explicit a relationship previously implicit and unacknowledged. Legislative and judicial responses to those decisions—decriminalizing status offenders, waiving serious offenders, punitively sentencing delinquents, and formalizing procedures—further the convergence between criminal and juvenile courts.

Noncriminal Status Offenders

The definition and administration of status jurisdiction has been criticized extensively in the post-*Gault* decades. The President's Crime Commission (President's Commission on Law Enforcement and Administration of Justice 1967) recommended narrowing the grounds for juvenile court intervention, and many professional organizations subsequently have advocated reform or elimination of status jurisdiction (American Bar Association [ABA] 1982). Some critics focused on its adverse impact on children because, traditionally, status offenses were a form of delinquency and status offenders were detained and incarcerated in the same institutions as criminal delinquents (Handler and Zatz 1982). Others noted its disabling effects on families and other sources of referral, as parents overloaded juvenile courts with intractable family disputes and schools and social agencies used the court as a "dumping ground" to coercively impose solutions (Andrews and Cohn 1974). Legal critics contended that it was "void for vagueness," denied equal protection and procedural justice, and had a disproportionate impact on poor, minority, and female juveniles (Rubin 1985).

Diversion

Disillusionment with juvenile courts' coercive treatment of noncriminal youths led to efforts to divert, deinstitutionalize, and decriminalize them. The Federal Juvenile Justice and Delinquency Prevention Act (1974) required states to begin a process of removing noncriminal offenders from secure detention and correctional facilities and provided an impetus to divert status offenders from juvenile court and decarcerate those remaining in the system (Handler and Zatz 1982).

Progressives created the juvenile court to divert youths from criminal courts and deliver services; now diversion exists to shift otherwise eligible youths away from juvenile court to provide services on an informal basis. Many question whether diversion programs have been implemented coherently or effectively (Klein 1979). Rather than reducing the court's client population, diversion may have had a "net widening" effect, as juveniles who previously would have been released now are subject to informal intervention (Klein 1979).

Deinstitutionalization

Although the numbers of status offenders in secure facilities declined by the mid-1980s, those efforts were frustrated by amendments to the Federal Juvenile Justice Act (1974) in 1980, which weakened the restrictions on secure confinement and allowed youths who ran away from nonsecure placements or violated court orders to be charged with contempt of court and incarcerated (Schwartz 1989). Although subsequent probation violations may result in confinement, juveniles adjudicated for status offenses often receive fewer procedural fights than do youths charged with delinquency (Smith 1992).

Decriminalization

Almost every state "decriminalized" conduct that is illegal only for children by creating nondelinquency classifications such as Persons or Children in Need of Supervision (PINS or CHINS) (Rubin 1985). Such label changes simply shift youths from one jurisdictional category to another without significantly limiting courts' dispositional authority. Using labels of convenience, officials may relabel former status offenders downward as dependent or neglected youths, upward as delinquent offenders, or laterally into a "hidden system" of control in chemical dependency facilities and mental hospitals (Weithorn 1988).

Sentencing Juveniles

Historically, juvenile courts imposed indeterminate and nonproportional sentences to achieve the delinquent offender's best interests In the post-Gault era, a fundamental change in the jurisprudence of sentencing occurred as the offense rather than the offender began to dominate the decision (Von Hirsch 1976). A shift in sentencing philosophy from rehabilitation to retribution is evident in the response to serious juvenile offenders and in routine sentencing of delinquent offenders. . . .

Judicial Waiver

Judicial waiver embodies the juvenile court's approach to individual sentencing. In *Kent v. United States* (1966), the Court mandated procedural due process at a waiver hearing where a judge assesses a youth's amenability to treatment or dangerousness. But, if there are no effective treatment programs for serious juvenile offenders, no valid or reliable clinical tests with which to diagnose youths' treatment potential, and no scientific bases by which accurately to predict future dangerousness, then judicial waiver statutes are simply broad grants of standardless discretion (Feld 1978, 1987; Zimring 1991). The inherent subjectivity of discretionary waiver results in racial disparities (Fagan, Forst, and Vivona 1987), and "justice by geography" as different courts within a single state interpret and apply the law inconsistently (Feld 1990a).

Treatment as a juvenile or punishment as an adult is based on an arbitrary line that has no criminological significance other than its legal consequences. There is a relationship between age and crime, and crime rates for many offenses peak in mid- to late adolescence. Rational sentencing requires a coordinated response to active young offenders on both sides of the juvenile/adult line because offenders are not irresponsible children one day and responsible adults the next, except as a matter of law, juvenile and criminal courts may work at cross-purposes when juveniles make the transition to criminal courts. Most juveniles judicially waived are charged with property crimes like burglary rather than with serious offenses against the person; when they appear in criminal courts as adult first offenders, typically they are not imprisoned (Feld 1987; Hamparian et al. 1982). . . .

Juvenile Court Sentencing Practices

Juvenile court judges enjoy great discretion because of paternalistic assumptions about children and the need to look beyond the offense to their best interests. The exercise of judicial discretion raises concerns about its discriminatory impact, however, because poor and minority youths are disproportionately overrepresented in juvenile correctional institutions (Pope and Feyerherm 1990a, 1990b; Krisberg et al. 1987).

Although evaluations of juvenile court sentencing practices are contradictory, two general findings emerge. First, present offense and prior record account for most of the variance in sentencing that can be explained (McCarthy and Smith 1986; Fagan, Slaughter, and Hartstone 1987; Feld 1989). Second, after controlling for present offense and prior record, individualized discretion is often synonymous with racial disparities in sentencing juveniles (Pope and Feyerherm 1990a, 1990b; Krisberg et al. 1987; Fagan, Slaughter, and Hartstone 1987). A comprehensive review of the influence of race on juvenile sentencing concluded that "race effects may occur at various decision points, they may be direct or indirect, and they may accumulate as youths are processed through the system" (Pope and Feyerherm 1990a, p. 331). Although offense variables exhibit a stronger relationship with dispositions than do social variables, most of the variance in sentencing juveniles remains unexplained. The recent changes in juvenile court sentencing statutes may reflect disquiet with individualized justice, idiosyncratic exercises of discretion, and the inequalities that result (Feld 1988b).

Conditions of Juvenile Confinement

Gault (1967) belatedly recognized the longstanding contradictions between rehabilitative rhetoric and punitive reality; conditions of confinement motivated the Court to insist upon minimal procedural safeguards for juveniles. Contemporary evaluations of juvenile institutions reveal a continuing gap between rehabilitative rhetoric and punitive reality (Feld 1977, 1981). Simultaneously, lawsuits challenged conditions of confinement, alleged that they violated inmates' "right to treatment," inflicted "cruel and unusual punishment," and provided another outside view of juvenile corrections. A number of courts found inmates beaten by staff, injected with drugs for social control purposes, deprived of minimally adequate care and individualized treatment, routinely locked in solitary confinement, forced to do repetitive and degrading make-work, and provided minimal clinical services (Feld 1990b). The reality for juveniles confined in many treatment facilities is one of violence and punishment.

Effectiveness of Treatment

Evaluations of juvenile treatment programs provide scant support for their effectiveness (Whitehead and Lab 1989; Lab and Whitehead 1998). Empirical evaluations question both the efficacy of treatment programs and the scientific underpinnings of those who administer the enterprise. Although the general conclusion that "nothing works" in juvenile corrections has not been persuasively refuted (Melton 1989), it has been strenuously resisted by those who contend that some types of programs may have positive effects on selected clients under certain conditions (Palmer 1991).

The critique of the juvenile court does not rest on the premise that nothing works or ever can work. Even if some demonstration model programs produce positive changes for some youths under some conditions, after a century of unfulfilled promises, a continuing societal unwillingness to commit scare resources to rehabilitative endeavors, and treatment strategies of dubious efficacy, the possibility of effective treatment is inadequate to justify an entire separate justice system.

Procedural Convergence Between Juvenile and Criminal Courts

A strong nationwide movement, both in theory and in practice, away from therapeutic, individualized dispositions and toward punitive, offense-based sentences eliminates many of the differences between juvenile and adult sentencing practices (Feld 1988b, 1990b). These changes repudiate juvenile courts' original assumptions that youths should be treated differently than adults, that they operate in a youth's best interest, and that rehabilitation is indeterminate and cannot be limited by fixed-time punishment....

Jury Trials in Juvenile Court

Procedural safeguards are critical when sentences are punitive/rather than therapeutic. In denying juries to juveniles, *McKeiver* (1970) posited virtual parity between the accuracy of judges and juries when finding facts. But juries provide special protections to assure factual accuracy, use a higher evidentiary threshold when they apply *Winship*'s (1970) "proof beyond a reasonable doubt" standard, and acquit more readily than do judges (Feld 1984; Ainsworth 1991).

Moreover, *McKeiver* (1970) simply ignored that juries prevent governmental oppression by protecting against weak or biased judges, injecting the community's values into law, and increasing the visibility and accountability of justice administration (Feld 1984; *Duncan v. Louisiana* 1968). Such protections are even more crucial in juvenile courts, which labor behind closed doors immune from public scrutiny.

The Right to Counsel in Juvenile Court

Gault (1967) established a constitutional right to an attorney in delinquency proceedings. Despite formal legal changes, the actual delivery of legal services in juvenile courts lags behind; it appears that in many states, half or less of all juveniles receive the assistance of counsel (Feld 1988a, 1989). One study (Feld 1988a) reported that in three of the six states surveyed, only 37.5%, 47.7%, and 52.7% of juveniles charged with delinquency and status offenses were represented. Research in Minnesota (Feld 1989, 1991a) indicates that most juveniles are unrepresented and that many youths removed from their homes or confined in correctional institutions lacked counsel.

The most common explanation for why so many juveniles are unrepresented is that they waive their right to counsel. Courts use the adult standard—"knowing, intelligent, and voluntary" under the "totality of the circumstances"—to assess the validity of juveniles' waivers of constitutional rights (*Fare v. Michael C.* 1979). The crucial issue for juveniles, as for adults, is whether waiver of counsel can be knowing, intelligent, and voluntary when it is made by a child alone without consulting with an attorney. Because juveniles are not as competent as adults, commentators criticize the "totality" approach to waivers as an instance of treating juveniles like adults when equality puts them at a disadvantage (Grisso 1980, 1981).

The Future of the Juvenile Court: Three Scenarios

For several decades, juvenile courts have deflected, co-opted, ignored, or accommodated constitutional and legislative reforms with minimal institutional change. The juvenile court remains essentially unreformed despite its transformation from a welfare agency into a scaled-down, second-class criminal court. Public and political concerns about drugs and youth crime encourage repressing rather than rehabilitating young offenders. Fiscal constraints, budget deficits, and competition from other interest groups reduce the likelihood that treatment services for delinquents will expand. Coupling these punitive policies with societal unwillingness to provide for the welfare of children in general, much less those who commit crimes, is there any reason to believe the juvenile court can be rehabilitated?

What is the justification for maintaining a separate court system whose only distinction is that it uses procedures under which no adult would consent to be tried (Feld 1988b; Ainsworth 1991)? Whereas most commentators acknowledge the emergence of a punitive juvenile court, they recoil at the prospect of its outright abolition, emphasize that children are different, and strive to maintain separation between delinquents and criminals (Melton 1989; Rosenberg 1993). Most conclude, however, that juvenile courts need a new rationale that melds punishment with reduced culpability and procedural justice. . . .

Return to Informal, Rehabilitative Juvenile Justice

Proponents of informal, therapeutic juvenile courts contend that the experiment should not be declared a failure because it has never been implemented effectively (Ferdinand 1989, 1991). From its inception, juvenile courts and correctional facilities have had more in common with penal facilities than welfare agencies (Rothman 1980). Despite its long-standing and readily apparent failures of implementation, proposals persist to reinvigorate the juvenile court as an informal, welfare agency (Edwards 1992).

Even if a flood of resources and a coterie of clinicians suddenly inundated a juvenile court, it would be a dubious policy to recreate it as originally conceived. Despite formal statutes and procedural rules, the "individualized justice" of juvenile courts is substantively and procedurally lawless. To the extent that judges individualize decisions in offenders' best interests, judicial discretion is formally unrestricted. But without practical scientific or clinical bases by which to classify or treat, the exercise of sound discretion is simply a euphemism for judicial subjectivity. Individualization treats similarly situated offenders differently on the basis of personal characteristics and imposes unequal sanctions on invidious bases.

Procedural informality is the concomitant of substantive discretion. If clinical decision making is unconstrained substantively, then it cannot be limited procedurally either, because every case is unique. Although lawyers manipulate legal rules for their clients' advantage, a court without objective laws or formal procedures is unfavorable terrain. But without lawyers to invoke laws, no mechanisms exist to make juvenile courts conform to legal mandates. Closed, informal, confidential proceedings reduce visibility and accountability and preclude external checks on coercive intervention. . . .

Juvenile Courts' Penal Emphasis

When social services and social control are combined in one setting, as in juvenile court, custodial considerations quickly subordinate social welfare concerns. Historically, juvenile courts purported to resolve the tension between social welfare and social control by asserting that dispositions in a child's best interests achieved individual and public welfare simultaneously. In reality, some youths who commit crimes do not need social services, whereas others cannot be meaningfully rehabilitated. And, many more children with social service needs do not commit crimes.

Juvenile courts' subordination of individual welfare to custody and control stems from its fundamentally penal focus. Delinquency jurisdiction is not based on characteristics of children for which they are not responsible and for whom intervention could mean an improvement in their lives—their lack of decent education, their lack of adequate housing, their unmet medical needs, or their family or social circumstances (National Commission on Children 1991). Rather, delinquency jurisdiction is based on criminal law violations that are the youths' fault and for which the youths are responsible (Fox 1970b). As long as juvenile courts emphasize criminal characteristics of children least likely to elicit sympathy and ignore social conditions most likely to engender a desire to nurture and help, they reinforce punitive rather than rehabilitative impulses. Operating in a societal context that does not provide adequately for children in general, intervention in the lives of those who commit crimes inevitably serves purposes of penal social control, regardless of the court's ability to deliver social welfare.

Due Process and Punishment in Juvenile Court

Acknowledging that juvenile courts punish imposes an obligation to provide all criminal procedural safeguards because "the condition of being a boy does not justify a kangaroo court" (*Gault* 1967, p. 28). Although procedural parity with adults may end the juvenile court experiment, to fail to do so perpetuates injustice. Punishing juveniles in the name of treatment and denying them basic safeguards fosters injustice that thwarts any reform efforts.

Developing rationales to respond to young offenders requires reconciling contradictory impulses engendered when the child is a criminal and the criminal is a child. If juvenile courts provide neither therapy nor justice, then the alternatives are either (a) to make juvenile courts more like criminal courts, or (b) to make criminal courts more like juvenile courts. Whether young offenders ultimately are tried in a separate juvenile court or in a criminal court raises basic issues of substance and procedure. Issues of substantive justice include developing and implementing a doctrinal rationale to sentence young offenders differently, and more leniently, than older defendants (Feld 1988b). Issues of procedural justice include providing youths with all of the procedural safeguards adults receive and additional protections that recognize their immaturity (Rosenberg 1980; Feld 1984).

Most commentators who recoil from abolishing juvenile court instead propose to transform it into an explicitly penal one, albeit one that limits punishment based on reduced culpability and provides enhanced procedural justice (Melton 1989; ABA 1980a). The paradigm of the "new juvenile court" is the American Bar Association's Juvenile Justice Standards. The Juvenile Justice Standards recommend repeal of jurisdiction over status offenders, use of proportional and determinate sentences to sanction delinquent offenders, use of offense criteria to regularize pretrial detention and judicial transfer decisions, and provision of all criminal procedural safeguards, including nonwaivable counsel and jury trials (Flicker 1983; Wizner and Keller 1977). Although the ABA's "criminal juvenile court" combines reduced culpability sentencing and greater procedural justice, it fails to explain why these principles should be implemented in a separate juvenile court rather than in a criminal court (Melton 1989; Gardner 1989). The ABA's Juvenile Justice Standards assert that "removal of the treatment rationale does not destroy the rationale for a separate system or for utilization of an ameliorative approach; it does, however, require a different rationale" (ABA 1980b, p. 19, note 5). Unfortunately, although the ABA standards virtually replicate the adult criminal process, they provide no rationale for a separate juvenile system. . . .

The only real difference between the ABA's criminal juvenile court and adult criminal courts is that the former would impose shorter sentences (ABA 1980c; Wizner and Keller 1977). Particularly for serious young offenders, the sanctions imposed in juvenile court are less than those of criminal courts, and a separate court might be the only way to achieve those shorter sentences and insulate youths from criminal courts.

But, recent research suggests that there might be a relationship between increased procedural formality and sentencing severity in juvenile courts. Despite statutes and rules of statewide applicability, juvenile courts are highly variable. Urban courts, which typically are the most formal, also detain and sentence more severely than do their more traditional, rural counterparts (Feld 1991a). If procedural formality increases substantive severity, could a separate criminal juvenile court continue to afford leniency? Will juvenile courts' procedural convergence with criminal courts increase repressiveness and erode present sentencing differences? Can juvenile courts only be lenient because discretion is hidden behind closed doors? Would imposing the rule of law prevent them from affording leniency to most youths? The ABA Standards do not even recognize, much less answer, these questions.

Young Offenders in Criminal Court

If the primary reason a child is in court is because he or she committed a crime, then the child could be tried in criminal courts alongside adult counterparts. Before returning young offenders to criminal courts, however, a legislature must address issues of substance and procedure in order to create a juvenile criminal court. Substantively, a legislature must develop a rationale to sentence young offenders differently and more leniently than older defendants. Procedurally, it must afford youths full parity with adults and additional safeguards.

Substantive Justice—Juveniles' Criminal Responsibility

The primary virtue of the contemporary juvenile court is that young serious offenders typically receive shorter sentences than do adults convicted of comparable crimes. One premise of juvenile justice is that youths should survive the mistakes of adolescence with their life chances intact, and this goal would be threatened by the draconian sentences frequently inflicted on 19-year-old "adults." However, even juvenile courts' seeming virtue of shorter sentences for serious offenders is offset by the far more numerous minor offenders who receive longer sentences as juveniles than they would as adults.

Shorter sentences for young people do not require that they be tried in separate juvenile courts. Criminal law doctrines and policies provide rationales to sentence youths less severely than adults in criminal courts (Feld 1988b; Melton 1989). Juvenile courts simply extended upward by a few years the common law's infancy presumptions that immature young people lack criminal capacity (Fox 1970b). "Diminished responsibility" doctrines provide additional rationale for shorter sentences for youths, because within a framework of "deserved" punishments, it would be unjust to sentence youths and adults alike (ABA 1980c). Although an offender's age is of little relevance when assessing harm, youthfulness is highly pertinent when assessing culpability. . . .

'Youth Discount'

Shorter sentences for reduced culpability is a more modest rationale to treat young people differently from adults than the juvenile court's rehabilitative claims. Criminal courts can provide shorter sentences for reduced culpability with fractional reductions of adult sentences in the form of an explicit "youth discount." For example, a 14-year-old might receive 33% of the adult penalty, a 16-year-old 66%, and an 18-year-old the adult penalty, as is presently the case (Feld 1988b). Of course, explicit fractional youth discount sentence reductions can only be calculated against a backdrop of realistic, humane, and determinate adult sentencing practices. For youths younger than 14 years old, the common-law mens rea infancy defense acquires a new vitality for shorter sentences or even noncriminal alternative dispositions (Fox 1970b).

A graduated age-culpability sentencing scheme avoids the inconsistency and injustice played out in binary either/or juvenile versus adult judicial waiver determinations (Feld 1987). Sentences that young people receive might differ by orders of magnitude, depending upon whether or not transfer is ordered. Because of the profound consequences, waiver hearings consume a disproportionate amount of juvenile court time and resources. Abolishing juvenile court eliminates waiver hearings, saves resources that are ultimately expended to no purpose, reduces the "punishment gap" when youths cross from one system to the other, and assures similar consequences for similar offenders. . . .

Punishing youths does not require incarcerating them with adults in jails and prisons. Departments of corrections already classify inmates, and existing juvenile detention facilities and institutions provide options for age-segregated dispositional facilities. Insisting explicitly on humane conditions of confinement could do as much to improve the lives of incarcerated youths as has the "right to treatment" or the "rehabilitative ideal" (Feld 1977, 1991). Recognizing that most young offenders return to society imposes an obligation to provide resources for self-improvement on a voluntary basis.

Procedural Justice for Youth

Since *Gault*, most of the procedures of criminal courts are supposed to be routine aspects of juvenile courts as well. Generally, both courts apply the same laws of arrest, search, identification, and interrogation to adults and juveniles, and increasingly subject juveniles charged with felony offenses to similar fingerprinting and booking processes as adults (Feld 1984; Dawson 1990). The more formal and adversarial nature of juvenile court procedures reflects the attenuation between the court's therapeutic mission and its social control functions. The many instances in which states treat juvenile offenders procedurally like adult criminal defendants is one aspect of this process (Feld 1984). Despite the procedural convergence, it remains nearly as true today as 2 decades ago that "the child receives the worst of both worlds" (*Kent* 1966, p. 556). Most states provide neither special safeguards to protect juveniles from the consequences of their immaturity nor the full panoply of adult procedural safeguards to protect them from punitive state intervention.

Youths' differences in age and competence require them to receive more protections than adults, rather than less. The rationales to sentence youths differently and more leniently than adults also justify providing them with all of the procedural safeguards adults receive and additional protections that recognize their immaturity. This dual-maximal strategy explicitly provides enhanced protection for children because of their vulnerability and immaturity (Feld 1984; Rosenberg 1980; Melton 1989). As contrasted with current practices, for example, a dual-maximal procedural strategy produces different results with respect to waivers of constitutional rights. Although counsel is the prerequisite to procedural justice for juveniles, many youths do not receive the assistance of counsel because courts use the adult standard and find they waived the right in a "knowing, intelligent, and voluntary" manner under the "totality of the circumstances." The Juvenile Justice Standards recognize youths' limitations in dealing with the law and provide that the right to counsel attaches when a youth is taken into custody, that it is self-invoking and does not require an affirmative request as is the case for adults, and that youths must consult with counsel prior to waiving counsel or at interrogation (ABA 1980a).

Providing youths with full procedural parity in criminal courts and additional substantive and procedural safeguards could afford more protection than does the juvenile court. A youth concerned about adverse publicity could waive the right to public trial. If a youth successfully completes a sentence without recidivating, then expunging criminal records and eliminating collateral disabilities could avoid criminal labels and afford as much relief from an isolated act of folly as does the juvenile court's confidentiality.

The conceptual problems of creating a juvenile criminal court are soluble. The difficulty is political. Even though juvenile courts currently provide uneven leniency, could legislators who want to get tough on crime vote for a youth-discount sentencing provision that explicitly recognizes youthfulness as a mitigating factor in sentencing? Even though young people presently possess some constitutional rights, would politicians be willing to provide a justice system that assures those rights would be realistically and routinely exercised? Or, would they rather maintain a juvenile system that provides neither therapy nor justice, that elevates social control over social welfare, and that abuses children while claiming to protect them?

Abolishing juvenile court forces a long overdue and critical reassessment of the meaning of "childhood" (Ainsworth 1991). A society that regards young people as fundamentally different from adults easily justifies an inferior justice system and conveniently rationalizes it on the grounds that children are entitled only to custody, not liberty (*Schall v. Martin* 1984). The ideology of therapeutic justice and its discretionary apparatus persist because the social control is directed at children. Despite humanitarian claims of being a child-centered nation, cultural and legal conceptions of children support institutional arrangements that deny the personhood of young people. Rethinking the juvenile court requires critically reassessing the meaning of childhood and creating social institutions to assure the welfare of the next generation.

References

Ainsworth, Janet. 1991. "Re-imagining Childhood and Reconstructing the Legal Order: The Case for Abolishing the Juvenile Court." *North Carolina Law Review* 69:1093-1133.

Allen, Francis A. 1981. *The Decline of the Rehabilitative Ideal: Penal Policy and Social Purpose.* New Haven, CT: Yale University Press.

American Bar Association—Institute of Judicial Administration. 1980a. *Juvenile Justice Standards Relating to Counsel for Private Parties.* Cambridge, MA: Ballinger.

———. 1980b. *Juvenile Justice Standards Relating to Dispositions.* Cambridge, MA: Ballinger.

———. 1980c. *Juvenile Justice Standards Relating to Juvenile Delinquency and Sanctions.* Cambridge, MA: Ballinger.

———. 1982. *Juvenile Justice Standards Relating to Noncriminal Misbehavior.* Cambridge, MA: Ballinger.

Andrews, R. Hale and Andrew H. Cohn. 1974. "Ungovernability: The Unjustifiable Jurisdiction," *Yale Law Journal* 83:1393-1409.

Dawson, Robert. 1990. "The Future of Juvenile Justice: Is It Time to Abolish the System?" *Journal of Criminal Law & Criminology* 81:136-55.

Edwards, Leonard P. 1992. "The Juvenile Court and the Role of the Juvenile Court Judge." *Juvenile and Family Court Journal* 43:1-45.

Fagan, Jeffrey, Marlin Forst, and Scott Vivona. 1987. "Racial Determinants of the Judicial Transfer Decision: Prosecuting Violent Youth in Criminal Court." *Crime & Delinquency* 33:259-86.

Fagan, Jeffrey, Ellen Slaughter, and Eliot Hartstone. 1987. "Blind Justice? The Impact of Race on the Juvenile Justice Process." *Crime & Delinquency* 33: 224-58.

Feld, Harry C. 1977. *Neutralizing Inmate Violence: Juvenile Offenders in Institutions.* Cambridge, MA: Ballinger.

———. 1978. "Reference of for Adult Prosecution: The Legislative Alternative to Asking Unanswerable Questions." *Minnesota Law Review* 62:515-618.

———. 1981. "A Comparative Analysis of Organizational Structure and Inmate Subcultures in Institutions for Juvenile Offenders." *Crime & Delinquency* 27:336-63.

———. 1984. "Criminalizing Juvenile Justice: Rules of Procedure for Juvenile Court." *Minnesota Law Review* 69:141-276.

———. 1987. "Juvenile Court Meets the Principle of Offense: Legislative Changes in Juvenile Waiver Statutes." *Journal of Criminal Law and Criminology* 78:471-533.

———. 1988a. "*In re Gault* Revisited: A Cross-State Comparison of the Right to Counsel in Juvenile Court." *Crime & Delinquency* 34:393-424.

———. 1988b. "Juvenile Court Meets the Principle of Offense: Punishment, Treatment, and the Difference it Makes." *Boston University Law Review* 68:821-915.

———. 1989. " The Right to Counsel in Juvenile Court: An Empirical Study of When Lawyers Appear and the Difference They Make." *Journal of Criminal Law and Criminology* 79:1185-1.46.

———. 1990a. "Bad Law Makes Hard Cases: Reflections on Teen-Aged Axe-Murderers, Judicial Activism, and Legislative Default." *Journal of Law and Inequality* 8:1-101.

———. 1990b. "The Punitive Juvenile Court and the Quality of Procedural Justice: Disjunctions Between Rhetoric and Reality." *Crime & Delinquency* 36:443-66.

———. 1991a. "Justice by Geography: Urban, Suburban, and Rural Variations in Juvenile Justice Administration." *Journal of Criminal Law and Criminology* 82:156-2 10.

———. 1991b. "The Transformation of the Juvenile Court." *Minnesota Law Review* 75:691-725.

Ferdinand, Theodore N. 1989. "Juvenile Delinquency or Juvenile Justice: Which Came First?" *Criminology* 27:79-106.

———. 1991. "History Overtakes the Juvenile Justice System." *Crime & Delinquency* 37:204-24.

Flicker. Barbara. 1983. *Standards for Juvenile Justice. A Summary and Analysis,* 2nd ed. Cambridge. MA: Ballinger.

Fox, Sanford J. 1970a. "Juvenile Justice Reform: An Historical Perspective." *Stanford Law Review* 22:1187-1239.

———. 1970b. "Responsibility in the Juvenile Court." *William & Mary Law Review* 11:659-84.

Gardner, Martin. 1989. "The Right of Juvenile Offenders to Be Punished: Some Implications of Treating Kids as Persons." *Nebraska Law Review* 68:182-215.

Grisso, Thomas. 1980. "Juveniles' Capacities to Waive Miranda Rights: An Empirical Analysis." *California Law Review* 68:1134-66.

———. 1991. *Juveniles' Waiver of Rights.* New York: Plenum.

Hamparian, Donna, Linda Estep, Susan Muntean, Ramon Priestino, Robert Swisher, Paul Wallace, and Joseph White. 1982. *Youth in Adult Courts: Between Two Worlds.* Washington, DC: Office of Juvenile Justice and Delinquency Prevention.

Handler, Joel F. and Julie Zatz, eds. 1982. *Neither Angels Nor Thieves: Studies in Deinstitutionali-*

zation of *Status Offenders*. Washington, DC: National Academy Press.

Klein, Malcolm W. 1979. "Deinstitutionalization and Diversion of Juvenile Offenders: A Litany of Impediments." Pp. 145-201 in *Crime and Justice: An Annual Review*, edited by M. Tonry and N. Morris. Chicago: University of Chicago Press.

Krisberg, Barry, Ira Schwartz, Gideon Fishman, Zvi Eisikovits, Edna Guttman, and Karen Joe. 1987. "The Incarceration of Minority Youth." *Crime & Delinquency* 33:173-205.

Lab, Steven P. and John T. Whitehead. 1988. "An Analysis of Juvenile Correctional Treatment." *Crime & Delinquency* 34:60-83.

Maiza, David. 1964. *Delinquency and Drift*. New York: Wiley.

McCarthy, Belinda and Brent L. Smith. 1986, "The Conceptualization of Discrimination in the Juvenile Justice Process: The Impact of Administrative Factors and Screening Decisions on Juvenile Court Dispositions." *Criminology* 24:41-64.

Melton, Gary B. 1989. "Taking *Gault* Seriously Toward a New Juvenile Court." *Nebraska Law Review* 68:146-81.

National Commission on Children. 1991. *Beyond Rhetoric: A New American Agenda for Children and Families*. Washington. DC: U.S. Government Printing Office.

Palmer, Ted. 1991. "The Effectiveness of Intervention: Recent Trends and Current Issues." *Crime & Delinquency* 37:330-46.

Platt, Anthony. 1977. *The Child Savers*. 2nd ed. Chicago: University of Chicago Press.

Pope, Carl E. and William H. Feyerherm. 1990a. "Minority Status and Juvenile Justice Processing: An Assessment of the Research Literature (Part I). *Criminal Justice Abstracts* 22:327-35.

——. 1990b. "Minority Status and Juvenile Justice Processing: An Assessment of the Research Literature (Part II)." *Criminal Justice Abstracts* 22:527-42.

President's Commission on Law Enforcement and Administration of Justice. 1967. *The Challenge of Crime in a Free Society*. Washington, DC: U.S. Government Printing Office.

Rosenberg, Irene M. 1980. "The Constitutional Rights of Children Charged with Crime: Proposal for a Return to the Not So Distant Past." *University of California Los Angeles Law Review* 27:656-721.

——. 1993. Leaving Bad Enough Alone: A Response to the Juvenile Court Abolitionists." *Wisconsin Law Review* 1993:163-85.

Rothman. David J. 1990. *Conscience and Convenience: The Asylum and Its Alternative in Progressive America*. Boston: Little, Brown.

Rubin, H. Ted. 1979. "Retain the Juvenile Court? Legislative Developments, Reform Directions and the Call for Abolition." *Crime & Delinquency* 25:281-98.

——. 1985. *Juvenile Justice: Policy, Practice, and Law*. 2nd ed. New York: Random House.

Schwartz, Ira M. 1989. *(In)Justice for Juveniles: Rethinking the Best Interests of the Child*. Lexington, MA: Lexington Books.

Smith, Erin. 1992. "In a Child's Best Interest: Juvenile Status Offenders Deserve Procedural Due Process." *Journal of Law & Inequality* 10:253-303.

Sutton, John R. 1988. *Stubborn Children: Controlling Delinquency in the United States*. Berkeley: University of California Press.

Twentieth Century Fund Task Force on Sentencing Policy Toward Young Offenders. 1978. *Confronting Youth Crime*. New York: Holmes & Meier.

Von Hirsch, Andrew. 1976. *Doing Justice*. New York: Hill and Wang.

Walkover, Andrew. 1984. "The Infancy Defense in the New Juvenile Court." *University of California Los Angeles Law Review* 31:503-62.

Weithorn, Lois A. 1988. "Mental Hospitalization of Troublesome Youth: An Analysis of Skyrocketing Admission Rates." *Stanford Law Review* 40:773-838.

Whitehead, John T. and Steven P. Lab. 1989. "A Meta-Analysis of Juvenile Correctional Treatment." *Journal of Research in Crime and Delinquency* 26:267-95.

Wizner, Steven and Mary F. Keller. 1977. "The Penal Model of Juvenile Justice: Is Juvenile Court Delinquency Jurisdiction Obsolete?" *New York University Law Review* 52:1120-35.

Zimring, Franklin. 1982. *The Changing Legal World of Adolescence*. New York: Free Press.

——. 1991. "The Treatment of Hard Cases in American Juvenile Justice: In Defense of Discretionary Waiver." *Notre Dame Journal of Law, Ethics and Public Polity* 5:267-80.

Cases

Breed v. Jones, 421 U.S. 519 (1975).
Duncan v. Louisiana, 391 U S. 145 (1968).
Fare v. Michael C., 442 U.S, 707 (1979).
In re Gault, 387 U.S. 1 (1967).
Kent v. United States, 383 U.S. 541 (1966).
McKeiver v. Pennsylvania, 403 U.S. 528 (1970).
Schall v. Martin, 467 U.S. 260 (1984).
Stanford v. Kentucky, 109 S.Ct. 2974 (1989).
Thompson v. Oklahoma, 487 U.S. 815 (1988).
In re Winship, 397 U.S. 358 (1970).

Statutes

Federal Juvenile Justice and Delinquency Prevention Act of 1974. 42 U.S.C. §§ 5601 et seq. ✦

43
Rethinking the Juvenile Justice System

Travis Hirschi
Michael R. Gottfredson

Ten or so years ago we became concerned about the connection between juvenile delinquency and adult crime. At that time, it was widely believed that most "delinquents" stopped offending as adults and became "nondelinquents." The existence of large numbers of adult offenders thus required an explanation distinct from the explanation of juvenile delinquency. Or, at least, theories were required to account in some complex way for the delinquents who did and those who did not become adult criminals. However handled, the usual stance was that the connection between delinquency and crime was complex, and contingent on the effectiveness of the juvenile justice system.

All this was of course consistent with the assumptions of the juvenile justice system: This system from the beginning has assumed differences in the causes of crime associated with stages of development over the life course, that, as one moves from childhood, to adolescence, to adulthood, the meaning of offenses differs such that they reflect different causes and require different modes of "treatment" by the state.

Many of the questions now facing the justice system may be traced to the assumption of developmental stages: Should we consider the juvenile records of adult offenders; what are the proper conditions for waiver to adult court; what is the appropriate age of automatic adult jurisdiction; how should we deal with status offenses; what are the benefits of diversion from the juvenile justice system; and what should we do with juveniles who commit very serious offenses? All of these questions reflect the influence of the idea that the meaning of acts is contingent on identifiable stages of the life course. In this article, we try to approach such questions from a different point of view—from the point of view of a theory that sees the causes of all crimes as identical, whatever the age of the offender. This view is based in part on the well-established connection between age and crime, in which crime is found to follow a predictable path over the life course, reaching its high point in the late teen years. By the way, our perspective is also influenced by research showing that the general public does not see differences in the seriousness of crimes based on the age of the offender (Sellin and Wolfgang 1964).

The Theory

Our theory (Gottfredson and Hirschi 1990) asserts that following childhood the population can be meaningfully ranked in terms of self-control, the tendency to consider or ignore the long-term consequences of one's acts. Acts that have long-term negative consequences for the actor are more frequently engaged in by those low on self-control. Such acts include crime, delinquency, recklessness, school misconduct, and drug use. The theory posits that the continuum of self-control is created by early childhood socialization practices. Once created, self-control is a stable individual difference responsible for considerable continuity in the tendency to deviant behavior over the life course, a tendency that manifests itself in a wide variety of misconduct.

Because criminal and deviant acts satisfy ordinary motives and desires, and are defined by lack of concern for long-term consequences, it follows that they are available to everyone throughout life. They require little cognitive complexity, little learning, planning, or skill. They are available to everyone not constrained by fear of the long term. Opportunities for such acts of course vary by age: School truancy is available to

From *Crime and Delinquency*, Volume 39, Number 2 (April 1993), pp. 262-271. Copyright © 1993 by Sage Publications, Inc. Reprinted by permission.

children, but auto theft is not available until adolescence, and embezzlement is usually available only to adults. Guardianship also varies by age. Given that only minimal intervention is required to deter most crime, the presence of an adult is usually sufficient to prevent crime among children. In fact, at some ages, the commission of criminal acts is prima facie evidence that adult supervision is inadequate.

What does the theory say about the issues that have traditionally plagued the juvenile justice system? Let us begin with the basic question, the age that property marks the boundary between juveniles and adults for purposes of penal treatment.

Age, Crime, and Court Jurisdiction

Figure 1 depicts the distribution of robbery in the United States by age. Robbery is an important, serious crime. It is the offense of record for one fourth of adults in prison and about one eighth of juveniles in penal institutions. As is obvious from the figure, robbery peaks at about age 17, and declines sharply thereafter. As is also obvious, the rate of decline between 29 and 34 is about as steep as the rate of decline between 19 and 24. Put another way, there is no apparent impact of justice system sanctioning (or of life course events) on the distribution of robbery. The rate would decline from its peak without intervention. Changing from juvenile to adult sanctions has no apparent impact on the rate (which begins to decline before juveniles legally become adults). As we and others have shown, we could substitute virtually any offense for robbery and achieve the same result. The decline in crime with age is continuous or monotonic throughout life, for all groups, whether or not they possess a distinct juvenile justice system. The age distribution was the same before the invention of the juvenile court. It would presumably be the same were the juvenile court abolished. (The current age distribution in the United States is for all intents and purposes identical to the distributions in England and Wales for 1842-44 and 1908—see Hirschi and Gottfredson 1983).

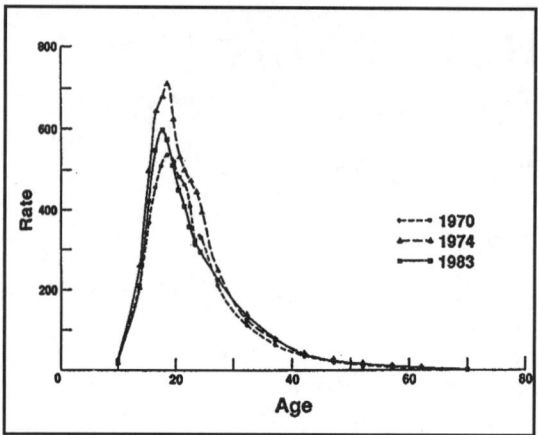

Figure 1
Robbery Rates by Age

These distributions apply regardless of the activity level of offenders. The distinction between prevalence and incidence is not helpful in accounting for the distribution. Credible evidence disputes the belief that the crime rate declines with age because some offenders drop out, while others remain active at a high rate. In fact, crime declines with age whatever the intervention by the state and whatever the prior activity level of the offender (see, e.g., Haapanen 1990).

Justifications for Separate Systems

So how do we justify treating children differently from adults? Let us examine some possibilities. One is that the criminal behavior of children is less *serious*. One way to think about seriousness is in terms of harm or damage; another is to think about the implications of the act for the future behavior of the offender. It is common to think of adult crimes as more serious than juvenile delinquencies on both counts. However, the evidence says otherwise. Seriousness does not vary by age—offenders do not escalate their offenses as they get older (see, e.g., Wolfgang, Figlio, and Sellin 1972). Another justification for treating offenders differentially by age is that adults but not young people are *responsible* for their acts. This is another way of saying that young people do not or cannot anticipate the consequences of their acts, particularly their effects on other people. This is what we refer to as low self-control, and we have no quarrel with the idea that it is central to an understanding of criminal behavior. But if people can be excused from the penalties of the law because they have low self-control, and if self-control is a stable individual trait, we would be forced by the same logic to excuse adult offenders as well. Daniel Glaser (1972) has indeed advanced the idea that some adult offenders are simply people who have not grown up, referring to them as "adolescent recapitulators."

Still a third reason for differential response by the justice system is the idea that young people are more malleable then adults, more receptive to treatment, and more capable of being rehabilitated. Actually, the evidence suggests that individual differences are established before the age of intervention by the juvenile court (apparently by ages 8-10, see Glueck and Glueck 1950; West and Farrington 1973), and that these differences remain remarkably stable over long periods of time. No one appears to have shown that age is a predictor of treatment success, a finding that would seem to be required by the juvenile court hypothesis. A definite theoretical advantage to early treatment is that its benefits would be enjoyed for a longer period of time. If we accept this argument, however, it seems to us that treatment would take place very early, so early that it could in no manner be sponsored by the justice system, or justified by the behavior of the child.

A fourth reason for separate treatment of juveniles is the existence of a distinct class of behaviors that are rightly considered deviant for children but which cannot reasonably be considered deviant for adults—these are of course the so-called *status offenses*.

But there are conceptual and empirical problems with the distinction between delinquent acts and status offenses. It is easily shown that behaviors analogous to status offenses among adults are also punished by the justice system or have negative consequences for those involved in them. In fact, in the United States, offenses involving alcohol and drugs are the most frequent cause of arrest *among adults*. A serious and not that uncommon offense in the United States is resisting arrest, the adult equivalent of incorrigibility. Among adults, truancy and tardiness for work can have as serious long-term consequences as the equivalent behaviors among children with respect to school. On the empirical level, it turns out that status offenses predict delinquent acts as well as delinquent acts predict delinquent acts. Put another way, juvenile offenses do not form delinquent or status clusters, but are generally highly intercorrelated. Delinquents do not specialize in one type of offense any more than adults.

The lack of clustering among offenses suggests another point too often misrepresented in the literature. Consistent with the idea of self-control, the data do not reveal specialization in particular acts or sequences of acts from one class to another. Offenders do not progress from status offenses to serious or violent acts, just as they do not progress from thievery to murder. All that we can say is that the person committing one act is more likely to commit all other acts; we cannot specify the nature or type of subsequent acts the offender is likely to commit.

Within the general theory of crime, all acts are in one sense similar (as indicators of the underlying state of the individual), and in consequence do not provide justification for differential treatment. If the number of deviant acts in a limited period of time is relevant to system response, this suggests focusing greater attention on children and adolescents and less on adults, and once again takes us outside the justice system.

Still another justification for a separate juvenile justice system is that it allows for the treatment of problem behavior without jeopardizing the life chances of the child. Currently in the United States, this question is surrounded in controversy. Some argue that juvenile records should be made available to adult courts. Others argue for the traditional sanctity of the juvenile record. On a practical level, separate record systems compound the problem of developing an accurate account of the offender's history (something a researcher would worry about!). But the real issue is the value of the record for criminal justice decision making vis-à-vis its negative impact on the individual's chances of success in life.

It is difficult to establish the prejudicial effect of a juvenile court record over and above the persistent effect on behavior of low self-control. This effect works in two ways to reduce the significance of information on the prior record of the offender. For one thing, it reduces the likelihood that the offender will rise to a position that would be jeopardized by information about his or her prior criminal conduct. For another, it increases the likelihood of conduct that would make knowledge of prior conduct redundant. If the offender avoids further contact with the system over a reasonable period of time, there should be no point in maintaining a file on him or her. But this is true regardless of age.

Another possible justification for a dividing line is the *dependency* of youth, that there is a point before which people require the care and attention of responsible adults and after which they should be free to take care of themselves. The juvenile court thus intervenes to insure the health and safety of pins, jins, chins, or mins, or simply dependent and neglected or abused children. We would not deny that the state has a responsibility to care for people who cannot care adequately for themselves. However, this welfare rationale differs so radically from the criminal rationale for intervention that it need not be discussed further here. Incidentally, the welfare justification does not really justify an adult/juvenile distinction, because many people in need of state assistance are not juveniles.

A historic justification for the distinction is that it provides separate facilities, where children can be isolated from the *corrupting influence* of hardened offenders. This rationale stems from the belief embodied in the saying that prisons are schools for crime. The failure to find differences in recidivism among offenders based on the amount of time served, or, for that matter, between probation and prison, casts doubt on this theory (Empey and Erickson 1972; Murray and Cox 1979) as, of course, does the age distribution of crime, which shows younger offenders being *more* criminal than adult offenders.

Perhaps the most popular justification for the distinction between juvenile delinquency and adult crime is that it provides justification for "treating" juveniles rather than punishing them, as an excuse for *leniency* toward children. This justification draws support from the recurrent tendency to demand that adult sanctions be applied to adolescents guilty of heinous acts—i.e., from the assumption that if the distinction were abandoned, the full force of the criminal law would come down on the heads of children, that the adult system would be applied to juveniles, rather than vice versa.

Which System Should Prevail?

There is good historical reason to believe that fears of excessive punitiveness toward children are unjustified. But to the extent we have a choice in these matters it seems to us that the evidence suggests that the drift of public policy should be in the other direction—i.e., that we should as far as possible attempt to replace the current system with a system modeled more on the juvenile than on the criminal justice system. Evidence in favor of this direction of change is amply provided by experience in the United States.

Statistics from the United States show that as of 1987 there were on any given day something like 41,000 juveniles detained for serious crimes; the same count for adults in the same year shows something like 600,000 incarcerated in state and federal prisons. This in spite of the fact that in any given year juveniles (those 18 or younger) account for about a third of arrests for serious crimes.

If we were applying the system to adults we now apply to children, there would be a crisis in prison construction in the United States of unheard of proportions—but the problem would not be *insufficient* cell space. Looked at from the other direction, if we applied the adult incarceration rate to the juvenile arrest rate, we would experience a seven-fold increase in the number of juveniles behind bars.

No one would support the latter proposal. Yet the fact of the matter is—as we have shown—incarceration of juveniles should have greater impact on the crime rate than incarceration of adults. If our societies can survive a situation in which relatively high rate offenders are left on the streets, they could surely survive a situation in which relatively low rate offenders are released.

But of course the juvenile system is not fully described by the fact that it makes relatively little use of incarceration. It is also described by greater emphasis on treatment, by less procedural formality, and by less concern for the nature of specific offenses (i.e., the state of being delinquent or in need of supervision is more important than precise legal definitions of the offender's acts—e.g., second-degree burglary). All of these features of the juvenile justice system are of course now under attack. In the eyes of some, they make it inferior to the adult system, with its emphasis on deterrence and incapacitation, its insistence on legal formality, and its attendant concern for the nature of the specific offense rather than the character of the offender.

Given the current popularity of the due process-adult model, on what grounds can one argue for extension of the traditional delinquency model to adult offenders? Recall the various justifications for the current separation of the two systems discussed above. On inspection, it seems to us, all seem to point to change in the direction suggested:

1. The crimes of adults are *not* more serious than those of juveniles.
2. Adult offenders are not different from juvenile offenders in terms of self-control—i.e., neither appears to consider the long-term consequences of their acts. However, if there is a difference in likelihood of subsequent offending, it would appear to favor adults, whose overall rate of offending is declining.
3. The idea that young people are more malleable than adults with respect to criminality has not been shown, and, again, evidence suggests that adults have a declining crime rate regardless of treatment.
4. There is no class of acts that can reasonably be considered deviant for children but not for adults. Indicators of criminality among children are also indicators of criminality among adults. Therefore, for purely crime control purposes, there is no reason to treat acts differentially according to age.
5. If benefits accrue to children from limiting the stigma attached to criminal justice proceedings (through expunging of records and the like), it is hard to see why a similar rationale would not apply to adults.
6. The welfare interest of the juvenile court would not be affected by its extension to adults who for whatever reason (i.e., mental incapacitation, temporary homelessness, spousal abuse) are unable to care for themselves.
7. As mentioned above, the corruption argument for separate facilities for juveniles and adults can be turned on its head, because there are reasons to think that juvenile offenders are as corrupt as adults. The "physical danger" argument is also usually misguided, because classification by security (or assault) risk is already widely practiced.

So, if there are no obvious costs, what would be the benefits of such a system?

One, already mentioned, would be marked reduction in the number of persons incarcerated, without corresponding increases in the crime rate. Given the extremely high costs of incarceration, the savings to taxpayers could be substantial.

Deemphasis on deterrence and incapacitation would undermine the criminal justice system more generally, leading to reduction in demand for law enforcement and court personnel, and perhaps directing attention toward prevention of criminal acts and the development of self-control.

Consolidation of the two systems would eliminate the possibility of differential treatment due to minuscule differences in age, as when a 217-month-old youth is treated as an adult while a 215-month-old youth, guilty of the same crime, is treated as a juvenile. It would eliminate the tendency of officials in the juvenile justice system to incarcerate or otherwise deal harshly with juveniles in the last year of their eligibility in order to "teach them a lesson" before they are lost forever to the adult system. It would remove the impossible task of deciding when it is appropriate to begin to treat sexually active or drug-using youngsters as adults responsible for their own behavior. All of this suggests that advantage naturally accrues to being defined as a juvenile. In fact, that is not always the case. In New York City it is said that youths overstate their age in anticipation of more lenient treatment in the adult system, and sporadic research indicates that youth waived to the adult system in anticipation of more punitive dispositions actually serve less time than their counterparts in the juvenile justice system.

Elimination of separate systems would eliminate the duplication in research, personnel, records, and facilities required by current arrangements.

Yes, but what are the costs of abolishing the distinction between adult and juvenile systems? Let us attack this question by focusing on cases that more or less define the extremes of the two systems as they now operate. For the adult system, the extreme case is the serial killer with a lengthy prior record who expresses no remorse for his or her violent acts against helpless strangers. We see no reason for complicating the issue with such cases. They should be handled with dispatch by a system of retributive justice *that makes no pretense about crime control or rehabilitation.*

At the other extreme is the 10-year-old child whose only "crime" is that she has been neglected by her family. Here too we see no reason for complicating the issue with such cases. Absent a crime control purpose, this case too can be handled easily by a system set up solely with the welfare of the client in mind—with no false pretense to a crime-prevention function.

For the run-of-the-mill case, involving theft or alcohol, effort should be devoted as now to restitution and whatever restriction or punishment the offense suggests. The assumption throughout should be that the function of the criminal justice system is to manage offenders, not to build a case against them that can be used only after they have passed beyond the age of maximal criminality.

Although our theory suggests to many that we have a profoundly pessimistic view of human nature and a profoundly cynical view of the ability of the state to change the behavior of its citizens for the better, the fact is that we see no evidence of darkly sinister motives operating behind most criminal acts, and we are actually impressed by the relatively fleeting nature of the years of high criminal activity. Given that the cause of crime is low self-control, all that is required to reduce the crime problem to manageable proportions is to teach people early in life that they will be better off in the long run if they pay attention to the eventual consequences of their current behavior.

References

Empey, LaMar and Maynard Erickson. 1972. *The Provo Experiment* Lexington, MA: D.C. Heath.

Glaser, Daniel. 1972. *Adult Crime and Social Policy.* Englewood Cliffs, NJ: Prentice-Hall.

Glueck, Sheldon and Eleanor Glueck. 1950. *Unraveling Juvenile Delinquency*. Cambridge, MA: Harvard University Press.

Gottfredson, Michael and Travis Hirschi. 1990. *A General Theory of Crime*. Stanford, CA: Stanford University Press.

Haapanen, Rudy. 1990. *Selective Incapacitation and the Serious Offender*. New York: Springer Verlag.

Hirschi, Travis and Michael Gottfredson. 1983. "Age and the Explanation of Crime." *American Journal of Sociology* 89:552-84.

Murray, Charles and Louis Cox. 1979. *Beyond Probation*. Beverly Hills, CA: Sage.

Sellin, Thorsten and Marvin Wolfgang. 1964. *Measurement of Delinquency*. New York: Wiley.

West, Donald and David Farrington. 1973. *Who Becomes Delinquent?* London: Heinemann.

Wolfgang, Marvin, Robert Figlio, and Thorsten Sellin. 1972. *Delinquency in a Birth Cohort*. Chicago:University of Chicago Press. ✦